English Spelling

A Reference Guide

English Spelling

A Reference Guide

Revised Edition

Trevor Schindeler

Rock's Mills Press
Rock's Mills, Ontario • Oakville, Ontario
2024

Published by
Rock's Mills Press
www.rocksmillspress.com

Copyright © 2024, 2019 by Trevor Schindeler.
All rights reserved. All rights reserved. No part of this publication may be reproduced, stored in a retrieval system or transmitted in any form or by any means—electronic, mechanical, photocopying, and recording or otherwise—without prior written permission from the author, with the exception of brief passages quoted in reviews.

Library and Archives Canada Cataloguing in Publication Data has been applied for.

For information, including permissions requests and bulk, trade, and library orders, contact us at: customer.service@rocksmillspress.com

For my wife Lloy, with love

Table of Contents

Introduction

    Our Alphabetic System of Writing 1

    Why is English Spelling so Difficult? 3

    A Guide to Reading This Book 5

Part A: The Structure of English Spelling

    A1 Introduction 7

    A2 Semantics: The Meaning of Words 8

    A3 Phonetics: The Sound of Words 11

    A4 Vowel Sounds 14

    A5 Consonant Sounds 16

    A6 Voiced and Unvoiced Phonemes 18

    A7 Syllables 19

    A8 The Doubling Principle 24

    A9 The Three Letter Rule 34

    A10 Silent Letters 35

    A11 Diacritical Letters 37

    A12 The "i" Before "e" Rule 42

Part B Spelling Long Vowel Sounds

    B1 Long Vowel Spelling Patterns 49

    B2 Spelling the Long "A" Vowel Sound 56

    B3 Spelling the Long "E" Vowel Sound 65

    B4 Spelling the Long "I" Vowel Sound 77

    B5 Spelling the Long "O" Vowel Sound 87

    B6 Spelling the Long "U" Vowel Sound Heard in "True" 95

    B7 Spelling the Long "U" Vowel Sound Heard in "Music" 104

Part C Spelling Short Vowel Sounds

- C1 Short Vowel Spelling Patterns ... 111
- C2 Spelling the Short "A" Vowel Sound ... 117
- C3 Spelling the Broad "A" Vowel Sound ... 122
- C4 Spelling the Short "E" Vowel Sound ... 129
- C5 Spelling the Short "I" Vowel Sound ... 136
- C6 Spelling the Short "O" Vowel Sound ... 147
- C7 Spelling the Short "U" Vowel Sound Heard in "Up", "But", and "Run" ... 157
- C8 Spelling the Short "U" Vowel Sound Heard in "Put", "Bush", and "Sugar" ... 161
- C9 Spelling the Short "U" Vowel Sound Heard in "Cure", "Pure", and "Curious" ... 163

Part D Spelling Other Vowel Sounds

- D1 Spelling the Vowel Diphthong Heard in "Coin" and "Toy" ... 167
- D2 Spelling the Vowel Diphthong Heard in "Loud" and "Cow" ... 169
- D3 Spelling the Schwa Vowel Sound ... 173
- D4 Spelling L-Influenced Vowel Sounds ... 192
- D5 Spelling R-Influenced Vowel Sounds ... 194

Part E Spelling Consonant Sounds

- E1 Introduction ... 205
- E2 Spelling the Consonant "B" Sound ... 212
- E3 Spelling the Soft "C/S" Consonant Sound ... 215
- E4 Spelling the Hard "C/K" Consonant Sound ... 226
- E5 Spelling the Consonant "KW" Sound ... 239
- E6 Spelling the Consonant "D" Sound ... 239
- E7 Spelling the Consonant "F" Sound ... 243
- E8 Spelling the Soft "G/J" Consonant Sound ... 248
- E9 Spelling the Hard "G" Consonant Sound ... 254
- E10 Spelling the Consonant "H" Sound ... 259
- E11 Spelling the Consonant "L" Sound ... 262
- E12 Spelling the Consonant "M" Sound ... 266
- E13 Spelling the Consonant "N" Sound Heard in "Nice" ... 270
- E14 Spelling the Consonant "NG" Sound ... 278
- E15 Spelling the Consonant "P" Sound ... 283
- E16 Spelling the Consonant "Q" Sound ... 286
- E17 Spelling the Consonant "R" Sound ... 287

E18 Spelling the Consonant "S" Sound 292

E19 Spelling the Consonant "T" Sound 292

E20 Spelling the Consonant "V" Sound 300

E21 Spelling the Consonant "W" Sound 303

E22 Spelling the Consonant "X" Sound 307

E23 Spelling the Consonant "Y" Sound 310

E24 Spelling the Consonant "Z" Sound 312

E25 Spelling the Consonant "CH" Sound 318

E26 Spelling the Consonant "SH" Sound 322

E27 Spelling the Consonant "TH" Sound 331

E28 Spelling the Consonant "ZH" Sound 334

Part F Consonant Blends

F1 Introduction 339

F2 Common Consonant Blends 340

Part G Prefixes

G1 Introduction 365

G2 Simple Prefixes 366

G3 Allomorphs of "ad-": "a-", "ac-", "af-", "ag-", "al-", "an-", "ap-", "ar-", "as-", and "at-" 385

G4 Allomorphs of "com-": "co-", "col-", "con-", and "cor-" 387

G5 Allomorphs of "in-" Meaning "Not": "ig-", "il-", "im-", and "ir-" 388

G6 Allomorphs of "in-" Meaning "In" or "On": "il-", "im-", and "ir-" 390

G7 Allomorphs of "ob-": "o-", "oc-", "of-", and "op-" 391

G8 Allomorphs of "sub-": "suc-", "suf-", "sug-", "sum-", "sup-", "sur-", and "sus-" 392

G9 Allomorphs of "syn-": "sy-", "syl-", and "sym-" 393

Part H Root Words

H1 Introduction 395

H2 Common Root Words 396

Part I Suffixes

I1 Introduction 417

I2 Word Ends with Final Silent Letter "e" Following a Consonant as in "Bake" 418

I3 Word Ends with Final Silent Letter "e" Following a Vowel as in "Tie" 425

I4 Word Ends with "y" Following a Consonant as in "Beauty" 428

I5 Word Ends with "y" Following a Vowel as in "Employ" 431

I6 Word Ends with a Vowel Other Than "y" or Silent "e" 433

I7 Word Ends with a Single Vowel Followed by a Final Pronounced Consonant as in "Plan" 434

I8 Word Ends with Two Vowels Followed by a Single, Final, Consonant as in "Boat" 443

I9 Word Ends with a Single Vowel Followed by Two Consonants as in "Child" 445

I10 Word Ends with One or More Silent Consonants as in "Glow" 447

I11 Word Ends with Two Vowels Followed by Two Consonants 449

I12 Suffix Word Families 449

Part J Grammatical Considerations

J1 Parts of Speech 461

J2 Use of Suffixes to Indicate Grammatical Function 462

J3 Verbs 465

J4 Regular Verbs 467

J5 Irregular Verbs 470

J6 Past Tense Spelled with Suffix "-ed" and "t" 473

J7 Adjectives 476

J8 Adverbs 479

J9 Nouns 482

J10 Pronouns 482

Part K Plurals

K1 Introduction 487

K2 The General Rule 488

K3 Plural Nouns That Do Not Change Form 490

K4 Plurals That Change the Spelling of the Base Word 491

K5 Words That End With the Letters "-ch" 491

K6 Words That End With the Letters "-f", "-ff", and "-fe" 492

K7 Words That End With the Letter "-o" 493

K8 Words That End With the Letters "-s" or "-ss" 494

K9 Words That End with the Letters "-sh" 495

K10 Words That End With the Letter "-x" 495

K11 Words That End With the Letter "-y" 496

K12 Words That End With the Letter "-z" 498

K13 Compound and Hyphenated Words 498

K14 Foreign Plurals 498

K15 Other Plurals 500

Part L Possessives

L1 Introduction 501
L2 Singular Nouns 501
L3 Plural Nouns 503
L4 Compound Nouns 503
L5 Pronouns 504
L6 Common and Separate Possession 507
L7 Inanimate Objects and Abstract Concepts 508

Part M Onsets and Rimes

M1 Introduction 509
M2 Common Rimes 510

Part N Compound and Hyphenated Words

N1 Introduction 537
N2 No Hyphen Required 537
N3 Hyphens Required 540
N4 Plural Compound Words 543
N5 Portmanteau Words 544

Part O Contractions

O1 Introduction 545
O2 Common Contractions 545

Part P Acronyms

P1 Acronyms 549

Introduction

In this age of smartphones and AI-powered spell-checking, some people question the need to understand the mechanics of English spelling. There are, however, important benefits to understanding spelling that go beyond getting words typed out correctly. Knowing how spelling works remains essential because it forms the foundation for both reading comprehension and good writing. A knowledge of our English spelling system is required to read accurately and to write proficiently. Spelling skills are fundamental to good communication, and open the door to vast stores of human knowledge.

This book sets out, in a systematic and comprehensive manner, all of the spelling patterns found in written English. Becoming aware of a spelling pattern will help you to notice it when reading and, eventually, to apply it when writing. In time, reading and writing skills will improve, and a deeper appreciation of our spelling system will be acquired.

This book also describes the structures and conventions that govern the spelling of words. While dictionaries tell us how to spell a word, this book explains why! However, in spelling, as in life, there is not always a good reason for everything. The reason for the spelling of many words is often grounded in history, not principle; and, to that extent, we simply have to accept spelling as it is.

Our Alphabetic System of Writing

English has an alphabetic system of writing.[1] That simply means that the letters of the alphabet are used to represent in writing the sounds we pronounce when speaking. Spoken English consists of a small number of speech sounds called "phonemes". The word "cat", for example, is pronounced using three phonemes that correspond to each letter in the word "c - a - t". Phonemes allow us to distinguish between different spoken words. A single phoneme, for example, distinguishes the word "cat" from the word "hat".

Our alphabetic system of writing developed over thousands of years. The earliest form of recorded communication consisted of pictures called "pictographs". Over time, a system of writing developed in which different pictographs were used symbolically to represent specific words. However, it is difficult to express complex ideas using pictographs as not all words can easily be represented by a picture.

This led to the practice of representing words using "sounds-like" pictures called phonograms. This caused a fundamental shift in emphasis. The visual importance of pictographs gave way to the auditory emphasis of phonograms. Slowly, a system developed in which phonograms came to represent all of the syllables spoken in a language. Any word could be written down using phonograms to represent each of the syllables heard in the word.

While this was a step forward, it was not entirely satisfactory because spoken languages typically contain thousands of different syllables. It is estimated that the English language contains 5,000 different syllables.[2] As it is very difficult to learn so many different phonograms, only the educated elite could learn to read and write. Eventually, people began to use a form of shorthand in which a symbol came to represent not a whole syllable, but only the individual phonemes that made up the syllable. As just a small number of phonemes combine together to make up thousands of syllables, far fewer symbols (which we call "letters") were required.

The Phoenicians developed a system of writing that consisted of only nineteen letters. Only consonant sounds were represented. This was possible because consonant sounds cannot be pronounced without also pronouncing a vowel sound. The Greeks adopted the Phoenician system of writing. However, as they did not need some of the Phoenician consonant sounds, the Greeks used some of the letters to represent vowel sounds. The Romans adapted the Greek alphabet to represent all of the phonemes heard in Latin. In turn, the English adopted the Roman alphabet. While the Roman alphabet was well suited for representing spoken Latin, it was less suitable for representing spoken English, which contains phonemes that are not heard in Latin. New letters, such as "w", were added, and existing letters were combined in novel ways to represent the English phonemes. In this way, an alphabetic system of writing was created in which each phoneme came to be represented by symbols that we know of today as the letters of the alphabet. The final collection of twenty-six letters found in the English alphabet was set during the Middle Ages.

The alphabetic system of writing proved to be a great improvement over the earlier systems of writing. Just twenty-six letters can be combined to represent thousands of syllables and hundreds of thousands of words. With only twenty-six letters in the English alphabet, most people can master learning it. If English spelling was perfectly alphabetic, any person who learns the alphabet would be able to read and write any English word. Some languages, such as Finnish, are highly alphabetic so that spelling closely reflects phonetics. English spelling is far less alphabetic. It contains very few phonemes that are consistently represented by a single letter or spelling pattern. Nevertheless, written English is alphabetic in principle, and mastering the alphabetic code remains essential to learning how to read and write.

Why is English Spelling so Difficult?

There is no doubt that English spelling is difficult. There are many strange spelling patterns. For example, the consonant "r" sound heard in "run" may be spelled with the letters "lo" as in the word "colonel"; the long "i" vowel sound heard in "kite" may be spelled with the letters "oy" as in the word "coyote"; and the long "o" vowel sound heard in "boat" may be spelled with the letters "ew" as in the word "sew". There are a number of reasons why English spelling is particularly difficult.

To begin with, the English alphabet has only twenty-six letters with which to represent over forty phonemes that are heard in spoken English. The shortage of letters for representing speech sounds adds complexity to English spelling. However, this alone would not make English spelling particularly difficult. A greater problem is that there is seldom a single letter or spelling pattern that is always used to spell a particular phoneme. There are, for instance, at least twenty ways in which to spell the long "a" vowel sound heard in "bake".

Why are there multiple spelling patterns for most phonemes? The reasons are primarily historical. During ancient times the inhabitants of the British Isles spoke a variety of Celtic languages which developed into Welsh, Irish, and Scottish. Latin was introduced when Britain established diplomatic and trading links with the Roman Empire in 55 BC following an expedition to the island by Julius Caesar. In 43 AD, almost a hundred years later, Roman legions began their conquest of Britain under Emperor Claudius. The Romans, who spoke Latin, continued to rule much of Britain until 410 AD when, besieged by Germanic tribes, Rome could no longer spare soldiers to defend such a remote territory. After the Romans departed, waves of Germanic settlers known as Anglo-Saxons began invading southern Britain, known today as England. However, despite this influx of Anglo-Saxons, Latin continued to be spoken by the upper classes and remained the official language of government until the 6th century.

The Anglo-Saxons adopted the Roman alphabet and over time developed a unique language that came to be called "English".[3] Beginning in 789 AD, Vikings from Denmark, Norway, and Sweden began to raid and settle in England introducing many Scandinavian words into the English language. Then, in the year 1066 AD, Normans from northern France conquered England. For hundreds of years, French was spoken by the British upper classes and was the official language of government in England. Everything came full circle during the Renaissance which began around 1300 AD. During the Renaissance scholars rediscovered the Greek and Latin languages, and hundreds of Greek and Latin words entered into the English language.

While German, Latin, Greek, French, and Scandinavian languages all made significant contributions to the development of English, numerous other languages have made smaller contributions. For example, Celtic contributed the word "whiskey", Spanish contributed the word "chocolate", and Arabic contributed the word "sugar". English scholars often retained the original spelling of foreign words. As each contributing language had its own spelling system, a wide variety of spelling patterns have been incorporated into written English. As a result, there are usually many different ways to spell each phoneme heard in spoken English.

Another factor that has made English spelling difficult is that prior to the introduction of dictionaries there was no such thing as standard spelling. Thousands of people over hundreds of years have had a hand in determining the spelling of different words. Spelling varied widely from place to place as people spelled words phonetically according to how they individually heard and pronounced words. Religious institutions, particularly monasteries, played an important role in the development of spelling. Monks would transcribe copies of the bible and other religious documents by hand according to local tradition. Officials of the King would write out letters and legal documents according to local practice. Even the introduction of the printing press in England in 1476 did not result in standardized English spelling. Printers used whatever spelling their local readers would best understand.

Standard spelling only became possible with the advent of dictionaries. However, English dictionaries did not attempt to impose a consistent system of spelling. Rather, dictionary writers simply recorded how different words were actually spelled at the time. Dr. Samuel Johnson's *A Dictionary of the English Language*, written in 1755, contributed enormously to the standardization of English spelling. However, Johnson decided to emphasize the historical origin and meaning of words, rather than phonics, when determining which spelling to adopt.[4] His dictionary, therefore, preserved and perpetuated the wide variety of patterns found in English spelling. While this has made it easier for modern-day readers to enjoy the works of Shakespeare, it makes learning to read and write a challenge.

Another factor that has made English spelling difficult is that, while spelling remains relatively constant over time, pronunciation has changed continuously. When the spelling of a word was first determined, there was often a close relationship between how the word was spelled and how it was pronounced. For example, at one time the letter "b" in the word "tomb" and the letter "w" in the word "tow" were pronounced.[5] The pronunciation of words has not only changed over time, it has also changed from place to place. There are many different regional dialects of spoken English so that pronunciation varies widely around the world. No spelling system can accommodate such wide variations in pronunciation.

Given the history of English spelling, it is perhaps surprising that there is any logic to English spelling at all. In France, the *Académie Française* was established in 1634 to guide the development of the French language.[6] No such institution has ever assumed responsibility for ensuring that English spelling developed in a logical fashion. However, for all of its complexity and perhaps because of it, English is a useful and versatile language. The *Oxford English Dictionary* lists over 500,000 regular words and as many more technical and scientific terms. In comparison, German has about

185,000 words and French less than 100,000 words.[7] The number of words found in the English vocabulary reflects both the willingness of the language to adopt foreign words and its versatility in coining new words.

A Guide to Reading This Book

When reading this book, please note the following:

1. Thousands of high-frequency words and hundreds of other words were carefully analyzed to produce this book. The number of words listed for a particular spelling pattern provides a rough indication of how often it is used.

2. Spelling patterns are usually divided into major, minor, and rare spelling patterns.

3. A distinction is made between vowel letters and vowel sounds. For example, vowel letters "ai" represent the short "e" vowel sound as in the word "said".

4. A distinction is made between consonant letters and consonant sounds. For example, consonant letters "gh" represent the consonant "f" sound as in the word "laugh".

5. In the word lists, the letter or letter combination being illustrated is usually printed in bold font. Other letters that play a role in the spelling pattern may be underlined or italicized.

6. Letters placed within brackets as in "c(i)", are pronounced in their own right and also have an influence over the sound being illustrated.

7. An underscore as in "u_e" represents a consonant letter that may vary from word to word.

8. A dash as in "cor-" indicates that the spelling pattern occurs at the beginning of a word or syllable. A dash as in "-ove" indicates that the spelling pattern occurs at the end of a word or syllable.

9. It can be difficult to determine which spelling pattern silent letters attach to. For this reason, silent letters are sometimes identified with more than one spelling pattern. For example, the silent letters "ch" found in the word "yacht" are identified as being part of the short "o" vowel sound in C6.3 and also as being part of the consonant "t" sound in E19.3.

10. Many words have multiple pronunciations, and it is not practical to list each possible pronunciation. Instead, this book attempts to identify the pronunciation that best reflects general spelling conventions. However, a

number of sample words are listed more than once in order to illustrate different pronunciations of the same spelling pattern. Such words are printed in *italics*.

11. With some words, American, Canadian, and British spelling and/or pronunciation differs. Such differences are noted with the abbreviations (USA), (CAN), and (UK) respectively. Alternative spellings are sometimes provided in brackets.

12. When words are broken down into syllables, the syllabic breaks shown are not always the same as those found in dictionaries. Rather, words are broken down into syllables in keeping with the general spelling convention being discussed. While the dictionary may reflect how people usually pronounce such words, for spelling purposes it is helpful to emphasize the application of general spelling conventions.

Part A: The Structure of English Spelling

The structures or building blocks of English spelling make it possible for us to learn to read and write the thousands of words found in our vocabularies. Part A explores the underlying structures that govern the spelling of English words and introduces terminology that is useful for describing aspects of our spelling system.

A1   Introduction

English spelling provides a way to represent in writing all of the words we use in our spoken language. There are two underlying structures, semantic and phonetic, that govern the formation and spelling of words.

The semantic structure relates to the meaning of words. Written words are made up of smaller parts called "morphemes". A morpheme is the smallest part of a word that conveys meaning. There are three kinds of morphemes: "prefixes", "root words", and "suffixes". Each morpheme has a specific meaning and each morpheme adds to the meaning of the word as a whole.

The phonetic structure relates to the sound of words, and provides guidance about how to pronounce them. Words are made up of one or more syllables. Syllables, as explained below, are made up of "onsets" and "rimes". Individual word sounds are called "phonemes". Phonemes consist of vowel sounds and consonant sounds. Vowels and consonants perform different functions in the pronunciation of words.

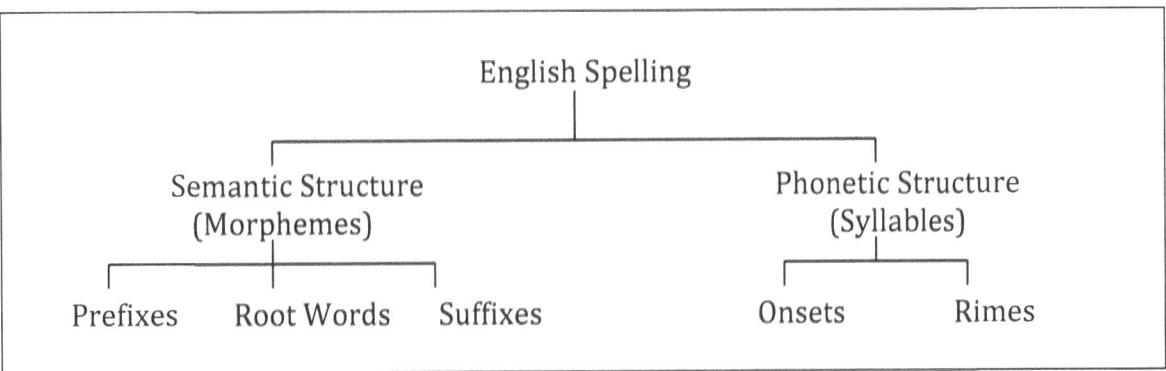

English spelling attempts to provide both semantic information and phonetic information so as to convey both the meaning and the pronunciation of words.

While meaning and pronunciation usually meld together seamlessly, at times they veer apart. When semantics and phonetics conflict, semantics usually trumps phonetics, which may cause spelling difficulties. For example, it is semantics not phonetics that dictates the spelling of the words "to", "too", and "two".

As written English evolved, a number of spelling conventions were adopted that govern how the letters of the alphabet are to be used to represent the phonemes heard in speech. It is a convention of English spelling, for example, that the letter "b" is used to represent the consonant "b" sound heard in "best". English spelling conventions can be both subtle and complex.

A2   Semantics: The Meaning of Words

Semantics refers to the meaning of words as opposed to the sound of words. In English spelling semantics trumps phonetics. People make up new words to express ideas that other words do not adequately express. People do not string together a bunch of sounds and then go looking for a meaning to attach to their new "word".

There is a semantic structure to the spelling of words that is based upon morphemes.

A2.1 Morphemes: Prefixes, Root Words, and Suffixes

As mentioned above, words are made up of smaller component parts called "morphemes". A morpheme is the smallest part of a word that conveys meaning. A morpheme cannot be broken down into yet smaller components and still convey meaning. There are three kinds of morphemes: "prefixes", "root words", and "suffixes".

At the core of every word is a root which gives the word its essential meaning. Some words consist of only a root. Additional letters, called "affixes", may be added to the beginning or to the end of a root. An affix added to the beginning of a root is called a "prefix". An affix added to the end of a root word is called a "suffix". Many words have both a prefix and a suffix, and it is possible to attach more than one prefix or suffix. Prefixes and suffixes create new words by adding to the meaning of the root.

The syllable "dict", for example, is a root word that means "to speak" in Latin. Adding the prefix "contra-" (meaning "against") to "dict" creates the word "contradict". Adding the suffix "-ate" (which forms verbs) to "dict" creates the word "dictate". Each morpheme adds to the meaning of the word as a whole.

Morphemes may be divided into "lexical morphemes" and "relational morphemes". A lexical morpheme conveys a particular meaning in and of itself. A relational morpheme only conveys grammatical meaning in relation to the word to which it is attached. Morphemes may also be divided into "free morphemes" and "bound morphemes". Free morphemes can function as free-standing words. Bound morphemes cannot function as free-standing words and are only used attached to other morphemes.

The word "dogs", which contains two morphemes, illustrates these distinctions. The root word "dog" is a lexical morpheme because it conveys a particular meaning. It is also a free morpheme because it can function as a free-standing word. The suffix "-s" is a relational morpheme because it only conveys grammatical meaning in relation to words to which it is attached by creating the plural form. The suffix "-s" is also a bound morpheme because it cannot function as a free-standing word.

A base word is any word to which a prefix or suffix may be added. Some base words are also root words. However, most base words are not root words because they already have a prefix or suffix attached.

A2.2 The Grammatical Function of Words

An important aspect of semantics is grammar. A number of spelling patterns are determined by the grammatical functions that words perform.

Spelling often determines, for instance, whether a word can be used as a noun, a verb, or an adjective; whether a noun is singular or plural; the tense of verbs, and the like. Suffixes are particularly important in signalling the grammatical role of words. The verb "sing", for example, can be made into a noun by adding the suffix "-er" to create "singer". The noun "child" can be made into the adjective by adding the suffix "-ish" to create "childish".

Sometimes, spelling patterns reflect grammatical functions better than phonetics. Consider, for example, how to spell the past tense of the words "fix", "divide", and "sail". A phonetic approach would suggest spelling the past tense of these words as "fixt", dividid", and "saild", rather than "fixed", "divided", and "sailed". Knowing that the past tense of regular verbs is always spelled by adding the suffix "-ed" helps us to avoid such mistakes. This is a good example of morphemic spelling which is discussed below.

A2.3 Morphemic Spelling

When modern English spelling was first being standardized, both semantics and phonetics were taken into consideration.[8] It is a semantic principle that words with related meanings should share similar spellings. Closely related to semantics is the etymology (historical origin) of words. It is an etymological principle that the spelling of a word should reflect its historical origins. For example, the words "sign", "signal", and "signature" are all based on the Latin word *signum* meaning "mark" and share related meanings.

Preserving the spelling of a morpheme between words that are pronounced differently is referred to as "morphemic spelling". English spelling often preserves morphemic spelling at the expense of phonetics. In the morphemic root word "sign", for example, the letter "g" is silent, while in "signal" and "signature" it is pronounced. Keeping the silent letter "g" in "sign" allows a reader to quickly recognize related meanings in "signal" and "signature". Prefixes, root words, and suffixes all form morphemic word families.

It is helpful to think of English spelling as being just as concerned about revealing the origin and meaning of a word as it is with showing how to pronounce it. If English spelling was strictly phonetic, there would be a significant reduction in the amount of meaning conveyed to readers. Morphemic spelling provides a number of advantages[9]:

1) The preservation of silent letters helps to identify morphemic word families:

- The letter "b" in "bomb" and "bombard"
- The letter "c" in "muscle" and "muscular"
- The letter "d" in "handkerchief" and "hand"
- The letter "g" in "sign", "signal", and "signature"
- The letter "k" in "knowledge" and "acknowledge"
- The letter "n" in "column" and "columnist"
- The letter "t" in "soften" and "soft"
- The letter "w" in "two", "twice", and "twenty"

2) The preservation of spelling patterns between words that are pronounced differently helps to identify morphemic word families. For example, the letters "ea" in "meaning" are pronounced with the long "e" vowel sound while the letters "ea" in "meant" are pronounced with the short "e" vowel sound. Keeping the same spelling pattern allows a reader to quickly recognize related meanings in both words:

- The letter "a" in "nation" and "national"
- The letter "c" in "critic" and "criticize"
- The letter "c" in "medicine" and "medicate"
- The letter "e" in "extreme" and "extremity"
- The letters "ea" in "meaning" and "meant"
- The letter "i" in "child" and "children"
- The letter "o" in "one" and "only"
- The letter "s" in "revise" and "revision"

3) The preservation of spelling patterns of word endings that are pronounced differently helps to indicate the common meaning:

i) The suffix "-ed" creates the past tense of regular verbs:
- "-ed" is pronounced "d" in "sailed", "closed", and "dreamed"
- "-ed" is pronounced "t" in "fixed", "ducked", and "passed"
- "-ed" is pronounced "id" in "divided", "arrested", and "sacred"

ii) The suffix "-s" creates plurals:
- "-s" is pronounced "s" in "cups", "units", and "packs"
- "-s" is pronounced "z" in "friends", "lions", and "times"
- "-s" is pronounced "iz" in "horses", "judges", "wages"

A3 Phonetics: The Sound of Words

Phonetics refers to the sounds of words as opposed to the meaning of words. English is both a spoken language and a written language. As between our spoken language and our written language, our spoken language is primary. People generally pronounce words with little regard for how they are spelled. We learn to speak before we learn to read. The pronunciation of words varies from place to place and has changed significantly over time. On the other hand, spelling has remained relatively consistent, at least since dictionaries were first created. That said, English spelling does endeavour to indicate how words are pronounced.

There is a phonetic structure to the pronunciation of words that is based upon syllables and the representation of word sounds with the letters of the alphabet. Spelling conventions govern how the letters of the alphabet are used to represent the different phonemes. Spelling conventions are reflected in a significant number of particular spelling patterns.

A3.1 Representing Vowel Sounds and Consonant Sounds

It is important to distinguish between letters, which are symbols, and the phonemes that the letters represent. Generally speaking, letters "a", "e", "i", "o", "u", and "y" are used to represent vowel sounds and are, therefore, called vowel letters. The remain letters "b", "c", "d", "f", "g", "h", "j", "k", "l", "m", "n", "p", "q", "r", "s", "t", "v", "w", "x", "y", and "z" are used to represent consonant sounds and are, therefore, called consonant letters.

You may note that the letter "y" is listed both as a vowel letter and as a consonant letter. While the letter "y" does not represent its own unique vowel sound, it is commonly used to represent the long "e", long "i", and short "i" vowel sounds. As well, the letter "y" is used to represent the consonant "y" sound heard in the word "yes".

The letter "y" only represents the consonant "y" sound at the beginning of a word or syllable as in "**y**ear" and "law-**y**er". In any other position, the letter "y" represents a vowel sound. At the end of a root word, as in "cr**y**" and "fl**y**", it usually represents the long "i" vowel sound. As a suffix, as in "happ**y**" or "motherl**y**", it usually represents the long "e" vowel sound. Within a word or syllable, it is used to represent both the long "i" vowel sound as in "st**y**le" and "t**y**rant" and the short "i" vowel sound as in "m**y**th" and "s**y**mbol".

A number of consonant letters, particularly "g", "gh", "h", "l", "p", "t", "s", and "w", are occasionally used to help represent vowel sounds. Likewise, a number of vowel letters are occasionally used to help represent consonant sounds, particularly the letters "i", "e", and "u". Such cross-over letters are considered to be silent.

Not all phonemes are as easy to name as the long "a" vowel sound heard in "cake" or the consonant "y" sound heard in "yes". This is why linguists prefer to use symbols to represent each of the different phonemes. However, that makes it difficult to discuss them. This book avoids the use of obscure symbols by naming phonemes as simply as possible.

A3.2 Reading Right to Left

As children, we are taught to read words from left to right. What many people are not aware of is that, at the same time, we are also reading individual words from right to left. This is because the pronunciation of a particular letter is often determined by the letters that follow it. That is, we are not only reading the letters of a word from left to right, but we are also reading the letters from right to left.[10]

The pronunciation of a particular letter is often determined by the letters that follow it. Long vowel sounds, for instance, are often identified by a final silent letter "e". In the word "write", for example, the final silent letter "e" signals that the letter "i" is pronounced with the long "i" vowel sound. Similarly, a short vowel sound is often identified by the double consonant letters that follow it. In the word "happy", for example, the double "pp" spelling pattern signals that the letter "a" is pronounced with the short "a" vowel sound.

Consider, for example, how the letter "o" is pronounced in: "hot", "hoot", "hook", "hour", "hope", and "hoist". The initial letter "h" does not provide any phonetic cues as to the pronunciation of the following letter "o". Rather, the phonetic cues are all provided by the letters that follow the letter "o". "Hot" rhymes with "got" and "not". "Hoot" rhymes with "boot" and "shoot". "Hook" rhymes with "book" and "look". "Hour" rhymes with "our" and "sour". "Hope" rhymes with "cope" and "rope". "Hoist" rhymes with "joist" and "moist". These examples also illustrate the important role played by rimes in English spelling. See A7.1 for a discussion about rimes.

English spelling is also characterized by sequential redundancy; if certain letters are found in certain positions within a word, then a predictable range of other letters will follow.[11] A well known example is the letter "q". In any position, the letter "q" is almost always followed by the letter "u". Other instances of sequential redundancy are less well known. If the letter "t" is the first letter of a word, for example, it is almost always followed by a vowel letter or by consonant letters "h", "r" and "w" as in "throw", "track" and "twin". An initial letter "t" is rarely followed by other consonant letters such as "d" or "p". Readers come to rely upon sequential redundancy subconsciously. Some letters go together and others do not.

A3.3 Vowel Digraphs

A vowel digraph is a string of two or more letters that join together to represent a single vowel sound. The letters "ea" in the word "meat" is an example of a vowel digraph. Likewise, the letters "-igh" in the word "high" is a vowel digraph.

Vowel digraphs may be distinguished from vowel diphthongs. A vowel diphthong is a string of two or more letters that represent a phoneme that changes from one vowel sound to another during speech without a syllabic break. The vowel sounds heard in the words "coin" and "loud" are vowel diphthongs.

Vowel digraphs may also be distinguished from "link letter" spelling patterns as heard in the words "fluid" and "cruel". With a "link letter" spelling pattern, two vowel letters also represent two vowel sounds, but the two vowel sounds are separated by a syllabic break.

A3.4 Consonant Digraphs

A consonant digraph is a string of two or more letters that join together to represent a single consonant sound. The letters "sh" in "show" and the letters "ck" in "sack" are two examples of consonant digraphs. Syllables may begin and/or end with a consonant digraph.

There are several consonant sounds that are not represented by a specific consonant letter that are usually associated with a particular consonant digraph. These include the consonant "ch" sound heard twice in the word "church"; the consonant "sh" sound heard in the word "shell"; and the consonant "th" sounds heard in the words "this" and "that". Unfortunately, the consonant "zh" sound heard in the words "beige" and "vision" is not even associated with a particular consonant digraph.

Consonant digraphs may be distinguished from consonant blends in which two or three consonant sounds blend together, but each individual consonant sound is still pronounced.

A3.5 Consonant Blends

A consonant blend occurs when two or three consonant sounds flow together without a syllabic break and each consonant sound is still pronounced. The letters "bl-" in "black" and the letters "-mpt" in "prompt" are two examples of consonant blends. Consonant blends often form onsets and help to form rimes. That is, a syllable may begin with a consonant blend and/or end with a consonant blend.

Consonant blends may be distinguished from consonant digraphs. A consonant digraph is a string of two or more letters that join together to represent a single consonant sound.

A4 Vowel Sounds

Vowel sounds are produced by expelling air through our mouth without the air being stopped or restricted by our lips or tongue. That is why we can pronounce vowel sounds "a - e -i - o - u" all at once without closing our mouth. The kind of vowel sound produced is largely determined by the shape of our lips and the position of our tongue.

Vowel sounds are "voiced". That is, our vocal cords vibrate when pronouncing vowel sounds. Some consonant sounds are voiced and some are unvoiced.

Every syllable contains a vowel sound and a syllable may consist of just a single vowel sound. A syllable does not require a consonant sound. The vowel is usually the most prominent sound heard in a syllable.

Six kinds of vowel sounds may be identified:
1) Long vowel sounds
2) Short vowel sounds
3) Diphthongal vowel sounds
4) The schwa vowel sound
5) L-controlled vowel sounds
6) R-controlled vowel sounds

A4.1 Long Vowel Sounds

A long vowel sound names itself. There are six long vowel sounds:

- The long "**a**" vowel sound heard in "**a**gent", "c**a**ke", and "m**a**jor"
- The long "**e**" vowel sound heard in "m**e**", "**e**vil", and "s**ee**d"
- The long "**i**" vowel sound heard in "l**i**ke", "p**ie**", and "ch**i**ld"
- The long "**o**" vowel sound heard in "st**o**ne", "hell**o**", and "**o**ver"
- The long "**u**" vowel sound heard in "fl**u**", "tr**u**e", and "tr**u**th"
- The long "**u**" vowel sound heard in "**u**nit", "m**u**sic", and "f**u**ture"

The term "long vowel sound" is somewhat misleading. The long "a" vowel sound heard in "cake" is not a stretched out version of the short "a" vowel sound heard in "cat". Long vowel spelling patterns are explored in Part B.

A4.2 Short Vowel Sounds

A short vowel sound does not name itself. There are eight short vowel sounds:

- The short "**a**" vowel sound heard in "**a**dd", "c**a**t", and "fl**a**sh"
- The broad "**a**" vowel sound heard as in "**a**rt", "b**a**rn", and "sh**a**rk"
- The short "**e**" vowel sound heard in "**e**nd", "p**e**t", and "th**e**n"
- The short "**i**" vowel sound heard in "**i**t", "t**i**p", and "k**i**ng"

- The short "**o**" vowel sound heard in "**o**ff", "l**o**ng", and "r**o**ck"
- The short "**u**" vowel sound heard in "**u**p", "b**u**t", and "r**u**n"
- The short "**u**" vowel sound heard in "p**u**ll", "b**u**sh", and "s**u**gar"
- The short "**u**" vowel sound heard in "c**u**re", "p**u**re", and "c**u**rious"

The term "short vowel sound" is somewhat misleading. The short "a" vowel sound heard in "cat" is not a shortened version of the long "a" vowel sound heard in "cake". Short vowel spelling patterns are explored in Part C.

A4.3 Diphthongal Vowel Sounds

A diphthong is a complex vowel sound that changes in pronunciation during speech. Unfortunately, diphthongs are not associated with a particular letter or spelling pattern and for this reason are not easily named.

There are two vowel diphthongs. One diphthong is heard in the word "coin". If pronounced slowly, you may note that the "oi" sound in "coin" begins with the long "o" vowel sound and ends with the long "e" vowel sound without a break in the flow of air through the mouth. A second diphthong is heard in the word "loud". If pronounced slowly, you may note that the "ou" sound in "loud" begins with a short "a" vowel sound and ends with the consonant "w" sound without a break in the flow of air through the mouth.

Vowel diphthongs may be distinguished from "link letter" spelling patterns. With a link letter spelling pattern, one vowel sound is also immediately followed by another vowel sound as heard in the word "fluid". However, with a link letter spelling pattern there is a syllabic break or pause between the two vowel sounds as in "flu-id". With vowel diphthongs, as heard in "coin" and "loud", there is no syllabic break or pause between the two vowel sounds.

Vowel diphthongs are explored in sections D1 and D2.

A4.4 The Schwa Vowel Sound

"Schwa" is the name given to the weak or neutral vowel sound heard in the second syllable of the words "circ**u**s" and "fam**ou**s". When pronouncing polysyllabic words, words with two or more syllables, one syllable will be stressed more than the others. Vowels in stressed syllables are articulated clearly. You can hear a distinctive long, short, or diphthongal vowel sound. Vowel sounds in unstressed syllables are not articulated clearly, and, as a result, lose their distinctive sound. Instead, the schwa vowel sound is heard.

Schwa is a very common vowel sound. It causes spelling problems because, unfortunately, it is not associated with a particular letter or spelling pattern.

The schwa vowel sound is explored in D3.

A4.5 L-controlled Vowel Sounds

The pronunciation of vowels that are followed by a single pronounced letter "l" is often modified.

For example, pronounce the word "seal" carefully. Three sounds may heard: a soft "c/s" consonant sound, a long "e" vowel sound, and a final "-ull" sound. Compare the "-ull" sound in "seal" to the consonant "l" sound heard in "like" or "lucky". The "-ull" sound is made up of the schwa vowel sound followed by the consonant "l" sound. This is one example of an "l-influenced" vowel sound.

"L-influenced" vowel sounds are explored in D4.

A4.6 R-controlled Vowel Sounds

The pronunciation of vowels that are followed by a single pronounced letter "r" is often modified.

For example, pronounce the word "bird" carefully. The letter "i" is not pronounced with either the long "i" vowel sound heard in "like" or the short "i" vowel sound heard in "pit". The same vowel sound is heard in the words "earn", "germ", and "word". It is best described as being a stressed schwa vowel sound. This is one example of an "r-influenced" vowel sound.

"R-influenced" vowel sounds are explored in D5.

A5 Consonant Sounds

Consonant sounds are produced by closing our mouth in different ways. Air is momentarily restricted or blocked by our tongue or our lips from being expelled from our mouth. Our tongue or lips briefly close to block or restrict the flow of air. This is why it is not possible to pronounce consonant sounds such as "b - c - d - f - g" all at once without closing our lips or touching the top of our mouth with our tongue.

While a syllable does not require a consonant sound, consonant sounds often mark the beginning and/or the end of a syllable. Consonant sounds form the backbone of speech because they help us to recognize the words being spoken.

Most consonant sounds are easily named. For example, the letter "f" is used to name the consonant "f" sound. However, the actual consonant sound is not the same as the letter name. Consonant sounds are heard best when full words are pronounced.

A5.1 Regular Consonant Sounds

There are twenty regular consonant sounds that are commonly associated with a corresponding consonant letter.

1) The consonant "b" sound is heard twice in the word "**b**a**b**y".

2) The first sound heard in the words "**c**ity" and "**c**ivil" is the same as the first sound heard in the words "**s**alt" and "**s**illy". In this book it is called the soft "c/s" consonant sound.

3) The first sound heard in the words "**c**at" and "**c**ook" is the same as the first sound heard in the words "**k**ey" and "**k**ind". In this book it is called the hard "c/k" consonant sound. The letter "q" also represents the hard "c/k" consonant sound.

4) The consonant "d" sound is heard twice in the word "**d**ivi**d**e".

5) The consonant "f" sound is the first sound heard in the word "**f**ather".

6) The first sound heard in the words "**g**entle" and "**g**ym" is the same as the first sound heard in the words "**j**am" and "**j**elly". In this book it is called the soft "g/j" consonant sound.

7) The hard "g" consonant sound is the first sound heard in the word "**g**oat".

8) The consonant "h" sound is the first sound heard in the word "**h**appy".

9) The consonant "l" sound is the first sound heard in the word "**l**and".

10) The consonant "m" sound is the first sound heard in the word "**m**other".

11) The consonant "n" sound is the first sound heard in the word "**n**ice".

12) There is a second consonant "n" sound which is heard in the words "i**n**k" and "si**ng**". In this book it is called the consonant "ng" sound.

13) The consonant "p" sound is the first sound heard in the word "**p**et".

14) The consonant "r" sound is the first sound heard in the word "**r**ice".

15) The consonant "t" sound is the first sound heard in the word "**t**all".

16) The consonant "v" sound is the first sound heard in the word "**v**an".

17) The consonant "w" sound is the first sound heard in the word "**w**in".

18) The letter "x" does not represent a unique consonant sound. Rather, the consonant "x" sound is made up of the hard "c/k" consonant sound

followed by the soft "c/s" consonant sound as heard in the words "a**x**e" and "fo**x**".

19) The consonant "y" sound is the first sound heard in the word "**y**es".

20) The consonant "z" sound is the first sound heard in the word "**z**oo".

A5.2 Other Consonant Sounds

There are four consonant sounds that are not associated with a particular consonant letter. In this book these sounds are named using the consonant digraph that is most closely associated with the sound.

1) The consonant "ch" sound is heard twice in the word "**ch**ur**ch**".

2) The consonant "sh" sound is the first sound heard in the word "**sh**ell".

3) The consonant "th" sound is the first sound heard in the words "**th**is" and "**th**ink". Actually, there are two different consonant "th" sounds. If you listen carefully, you may note that the "th" sound heard in "**th**is" and "**th**at" sounds different than the "th" sound heard in "**th**ink" and "**th**in".

4) The consonant "zh" sound is heard in the words "bei**ge**" and "vi**si**on".

A6 Voiced and Unvoiced Phonemes

Our vocal cords vibrate when pronouncing certain sounds but not others. If our vocal cords vibrate, the phoneme is said to be "voiced". If our vocal cords do not vibrate, the phoneme is "unvoiced".

Our vocal cords vibrate when pronouncing vowels, so all vowel sounds are voiced.[12] Some consonant sounds are voiced, and some are unvoiced as set out below.[13] The difference between voiced and unvoiced consonant sounds can be heard in the words "zoo" and "sue". The consonant "z" sound heard in "zoo" is voiced and the soft "c/s" consonant sound heard in "sue" is unvoiced.

Unvoiced Consonant Sounds	Voiced Consonant Sounds
The soft "c/s" consonant sound	The consonant "b" sound
The hard "c/k" consonant sound	The consonant "d" sound
The consonant "f" sound	The soft "g/j" consonant sound
The consonant "h" sound	The hard "g" consonant sound
The consonant "p" sound	The consonant "l" sound
The consonant "t" sound	The consonant "r" sound
The consonant "ch" sound	The consonant "v" sound

The consonant "sh" sound	The consonant "w" sound
The consonant "th" sound in "thing"	The consonant "y" sound
	The consonant "z" sound
	The consonant "th" sound in "this"
	The consonant "zh" sound

A7 Syllables

Words are made up of syllables. A syllable is an uninterrupted flow of speech sounds. When speaking, words are pronounced syllable by syllable with a short pause or "syllabic break" between syllables. Some words are composed of only one syllable. Other words are composed of two, three, or more syllables. For example:

- The word "cat" has one syllable.
- The word "kitten" has two-syllables.
- The word "animal" has three syllables.

Pronounce the words "cat", "kitten", and "animal" carefully. As there is no pause when saying the word "cat", it is a single-syllable word. There is one pause when saying the word "kit-ten", so it is a two-syllable word. There are two pauses when saying the word "an-i-mal", so it is a three-syllable word.

Spelling conventions are applied syllable by syllable, so it is helpful to analyze words syllable by syllable. By listening carefully for syllables, and by accounting for each syllable with letters, spelling can become more accurate.

Fluent readers are able to break words into syllables quickly and automatically. Strings of letters that represent syllables tend to be more common than other strings. The letters in a syllable reinforce each other to form a recognizable spelling unit. For example, many syllables begin with the letters "fl", including "flip, "flop", and "fly", but not with the letters "lf". While the letters "fl" support each other and are quickly recognized as part of a syllable, the letters "l" and "f" repel each other. Where the letters "lf" are found in words, there will be a syllabic break between them. The word "fulfill", for example, is pronounced "ful-fill". Readers are able, therefore, to identify both syllables and syllabic breaks with little conscious effort.

A7.1 Onsets and Rimes

Words are made up of syllables. Syllables, in turn, are made up of onsets and rimes. The word "rime" is a variation on the spelling of the word "rhyme". A rime, unlike other rhymes, is always spelled the same way.

An onset consists of all of the consonant sounds, if any, that are pronounced before the vowel sound in a syllable. A rime consists of all of the sounds that follow the onset. Every rime begins with a vowel sound and may end with one or more consonant sounds. Consider, for example, the single-syllable words "day", "dog", "log", and "lay". The words "day" and "dog" share the same onset being the letter "d-", and the words "dog" and "log" share the same rime being the letters "-og". Likewise, the words "log" and "lay" share the same onset being the letter "l-", and the words "day" and "lay" share the same rime being the letters "-ay".

While every syllable has a rime, not all syllables have an onset. The single-syllable word "act", for example, does not have an onset. The whole of the word "act" is a rime. A rime may consist of just a vowel sound. The single-letter word "a" consists of only a rime. Likewise, in the words "per-i-od" and "an-i-mal", the single-letter syllable "-i-" forms a rime by itself without any consonant sounds.

Onsets and rimes help to mark the beginning and the end of a syllable. An onset may consist of a single consonant letter as in "**k**ind", a consonant blend as in "**cl**ock", or a consonant digraph as in "**sh**ow". Similarly, a rime may end with a vowel sound as in the word "go", with a single consonant letter as in "se**t**", with a consonant blend as in "be**st**", or with a consonant digraph as in "do**ck**".

A7.2 Open and Closed Syllables

There are two kinds of syllables: open syllables and closed syllables.

An open syllable ends with a vowel sound. Open syllables usually end with one or two vowel letters as in the first syllables of "m**u**-sic" and "s**ea**-son". Sometimes open syllables end with silent consonant letters as in the words "h**igh**-er" and "arr-**ow**". Also, a single vowel letter may form an open syllable. The letter "i" in the word "fur-**i**-ous", for example, forms an open syllable by itself.

A closed syllable ends with a consonant sound. A closed syllable may end with a single consonant letter as in the first syllable of "pro**b**-lem", with a consonant blend as in the word "wo**rld**-ly", or with a consonant digraph as in the first syllable of the word "ri**ch**-er".

A7.3 Stressed and Unstressed Syllables

As discussed inA4.4, when pronouncing words composed of two or more syllables, one syllable will be emphasized or stressed more than the other syllables. In stressed syllables, vowels tend to be articulated clearly. We can hear a distinct long, short, or diphthongal vowel sound. In unstressed syllables, vowels are not articulated clearly, and the schwa vowel sound is heard as in the second syllable of "circ**u**s" and "fam**ou**s".

Unfortunately, while dictionaries indicate the amount of stress placed on each syllable, our spelling system does not have a way of showing where stress falls. However, while there are exceptions, the following generalizations hold true for most words.

1. Single-syllable words such as "ate", "peace", "kind", "doe", and "do" are almost always stressed. For this reason, many spelling programs begin with single-syllable words as the spelling-to-sound correspondence is more predictable.

2. With two-syllable words, such as "instant" and "silent", the first syllable is usually stressed and the second syllable is unstressed. However, with compound words such as "airplane" and "flashlight", both of the single-syllable root words are usually stressed.

3. With polysyllabic words, such as "calculus" and "eloquent", the amount of stress placed on each syllable varies. Usually, one syllable is given the most stress (primary accent), and the other syllables are given weaker (secondary accent) or no stress. Often, the first syllable is stressed and the final syllable is unstressed. There may be more than one unstressed syllable.

Spelling would be much easier if all syllables were stressed or if there was a spelling pattern to represent the schwa vowel sound. For spelling purposes, it is helpful to place stress on each syllable to clarify the correct spelling of words. With the word "instant", for example, one could pronounce the letter "a" with the short "a" vowel sound rather than with the unstressed schwa vowel sound.

A7.4 The Division of Words into Syllables

Words that contain two or more vowel sounds will be pronounced with two or more syllables. Words are generally divided into syllables as follows:

1. Every syllable has at least one vowel letter.

2. While a syllable may have more than one vowel letter, every syllable has one and only one vowel sound. For spelling purposes, a vowel diphthong is treated as a single vowel sound.

3. A syllable that consists of just a vowel sound may be represented by a single vowel letter. The letter "i" in "per-**i**-od", for example, forms a syllable by itself.

4. In addition to the one vowel sound, a syllable may begin with one or more consonant sounds and may also end with one or more consonant sounds. However, a syllable does not require a consonant sound, and a syllable never consists of just consonant sounds. Syllabic "l" and syllabic "n" sounds are exceptions to this rule. However, even these sounds are pronounced with the assistance of a faint schwa vowel sound.

5. Compound words divide between the words that make up the compound. The compound word "sunset", for example, is pronounced "sun-set".

6. Words often divide into syllables between consonant sounds. The word "danger", for example, is pronounced "da**n**-**g**er". However, a consonant digraph that represents a single consonant sound will stay together. The word "descend", for example, is pronounced "de-**sc**end". The consonant digraph "sc" represents a single consonant sound.

7. If three or four consonant letters run together, a syllabic break will divide one consonant sound from a remaining consonant blend or consonant digraph. The words "umbrella" and "parchment", for example, are pronounced "u**m**-**br**ella" and "pa**rch**-**m**ent" respectively.

8. If a word contains a prefix, there is generally a syllabic break between the prefix and the base word. The word "reflect", for example, is pronounced "**re**-flect".

9. As discussed further below, long vowel sounds are usually pronounced in open syllables. There is a syllabic break following long vowel sounds forming open syllables as heard in "**fi**-nal" and "**rea**-son".

10. As discussed further below, short vowel sounds are usually pronounced in closed syllables. A short vowel syllable will break following a consonant sound forming a closed syllable as heard in "pe**n**-cil" and "fi**sh**-ing". Short vowel letters are often followed by double consonants. For spelling purposes, when double consonants lie between two syllables, it is helpful to pronounce both consonants as in "su**m**-**m**er" and "zi**p**-**p**er". Words such as "sla**mm**ed" and "tri**pp**ed" are single-syllable words, so only one consonant sound can be pronounced. If a short vowel letter is followed by a single consonant, the syllabic break will still fall after the consonant forming a closed syllable as heard in "wa**g**-on".

11. When two vowel letters sit side-by-side and each vowel is pronounced, a syllabic break may fall between them. The word "poet", for example, is pronounced "po-et". In this book, this is referred to as a "link letter" spelling pattern. This does not occur with vowel diphthongs as heard in "joint" and "shout".

12. Words that end with the "-le" spelling pattern following a consonant letter are divided before the consonant letter. The word "tur**tle**", for example, is pronounced "tur-**tle**".

It is a characteristic of English speech that most syllables begin with a consonant sound.[14] A syllable beginning with a vowel sounds incomplete. This might come as a surprise because many common words begin with a vowel sound. Upon close examination, however, many of the words that begin with a vowel are structure words, not content words. Content words, such as nouns and verbs, are used to express ideas. Structure words, such as conjunctives and prepositions, perform the grammatical function of binding content words together into sentences. On their own, structure words express very little meaning.

A relatively small number of single-syllable structure words that begin with a vowel are used over and over again including pronouns such as "I", "us", and "our"; conjunctions such as "and", "if", and "or"; exclamations such as "ah" and "oh"; and prepositions. A preposition is a word such as "after", "in", and "out" that is used with a noun or pronoun to show direction, location, or time, or to introduce an object. As well, there are a number of compound content words such as "<u>af</u>ternoon", "<u>in</u>doors", and "<u>out</u>side" that are composed of a preposition attached to a content word. Further, there are many content words such as "<u>a</u>sleep", "<u>ex</u>hale", and "<u>inter</u>view" that begin with a Latin preposition. All of the above disguises the fact that the majority of syllables do, in fact, begin with a consonant sound.

The tendency in English speech to begin syllables with a consonant sound becomes more apparent when adding a suffix that begins with a vowel to a root word that ends with a consonant. Lacking an initial consonant, a suffix that begins with a vowel is not a complete syllable in itself. The suffix becomes a complete syllable only by capturing the final consonant of the root word to which it is attached. Adding the suffix "-ing" to the word "bake" creates "baking" which is pronounced "ba-**k**ing". Likewise, adding the suffix "-ing" to the word "jump" creates "jumping" which is pronounced "ju**m**-**p**ing".

Consider the effect of adding the suffix "-or" to the word "prospect". While the word "prospect" ends with the consonant blend "-ct", the word "prospector" is pronounced "pros-pe**c**-**t**or". The letter "c" closes the preceding syllable "pec-", and the letter "t" attaches as an onset to the suffix "-or" forming the final syllable "-tor".

The ability of a suffix to capture a preceding final consonant can be heard by considering the word "hand". The final consonant "d" sound in the word "hand" is barely pronounced by careful speakers and not at all by many. However, the addition of a suffix that begins with a vowel letter such as "-ed", "-ing", and "-y" emphasizes the consonant "d" sound which is clearly heard in "han-**d**ed", "han-**d**ing", and "han-**d**y".

An interesting effect occurs when adding a suffix that begins with the letter "i", such as "-ion" and "-ial", to a base word that end with the letter "t". For example, adding the suffix "-ion" to the base word "product" creates "production" which is pronounced "pro-du**c**-**t**ion". The letter "t" attaches to the suffix to form the syllable "-tion" and, in the process, comes to represent the consonant "sh" sound. Likewise, adding the suffix "-ial" to base word "part" produces "partial" which is pronounced "par-**t**ial". Again, the letter "t" attaches to the suffix to form the syllable "-tial" and, in the process, comes to represent the consonant "sh" sound.

A8 The Doubling Principle

A8.1 The Doubling Principle

Early in the history of English spelling, scholars searched for a way to distinguish between long and short vowel sounds using the limited number of vowel letters found in the Latin alphabet. One solution that they devised is for long vowel letters to be followed by one consonant letter and for short vowel letters to be followed by two consonant letters. This convention, referred to below as the doubling principle, is integral to native English spelling. If there is only one consonant between two vowel letters, it signals that the first vowel is pronounced with a long vowel sound. Two consonants between two vowel letters signals that the first vowel is pronounced with a short vowel sound.

As discussed in A7.4, the doubling principle reflects the tendency in English speech for syllables to begin with a consonant sound. This tendency has important ramifications. If there is only one consonant letter between syllables, it will usually attach as an onset to the following syllable. The result is that the first syllable will be left open and, consequently, pronounced with a long vowel sound. The words "writing", "paper", and "begin", for example, are pronounced "wry-ting", "pay-per", and "bee-gin". If there are two consonant letters between syllables, one will usually remain attached to the preceding syllable and the second will attach as an onset to the following syllable. The result is that the first syllable will be closed and, consequently, pronounced with a short vowel sound. The words "lasting", "empire", and "window", for example, are pronounced "las-ting", "em-pire", and "win-dow".

The application of the doubling principle is most dramatic when adding a suffix that begins with a vowel letter, including "-able", "-ed", "-en", "-er", "-es", "-est", "-et", "-ing", "-ish", "-ow", and "-y", to a short vowel syllable that ends with a single final consonant letter. The single final consonant letter is doubled, hence the "doubling principle" of English spelling. For example, adding the suffix "-ing" to "mop" produces "mopping". Likewise, adding the suffix "-en" to "forgot" produces "forgotten".

The ability of suffixes to capture a preceding final consonant helps to explain the doubling of consonants in English spelling. Consider the word "snip". The short "i" vowel sound heard in "snip" is found in a closed syllable that ends with a single consonant letter. Adding a suffix that begins with a vowel letter without doubling the letter "p" will cause the "i" to be pronounced with a long vowel sound. For example, adding the suffix "-er" to "snip" produces "sni-per". The suffix "-er" captures the "p". As a result, the remaining syllable "sni-" is left open and consequently pronounced with the long "i" vowel sound. Doubling the letter "p" produces "snip-per" which preserves the short closed syllable "snip-".

Two consonant letters function to protect a short vowel syllable from the lengthening effect of a following vowel letter. Long vowel sounds are usually represented by two vowel letters and are most often found in open syllables. The second vowel letter signals that first vowel letter is pronounced with a long vowel sound. The two vowel letters may sit side-by-side forming a vowel digraph as in the first syllable of the word "p**ea**-nut". Often, however, the two vowel letters representing the long vowel sound are separated by a single consonant letter. In the word "fi-**na**l", for example, the letter "i" is lengthened by the following letter "a". This is the same function that is often performed by a final silent letter "e". With the word "li**ke**", for example, the letter "i" is lengthened by the final silent letter "e".

Conversely, a vowel followed by two consonant letters is protected from being lengthened by a following vowel letter. The word "dinner", for example, is pronounced with the short "i" vowel sound while the word "diner" is pronounced with the long "i" vowel sound. In the word "di**nn**er", the double "nn" protects the short "i" vowel sound from the lengthening effect of the following letter "e". Without the protection of two consonant letters, as in the word "di**ne**r", the letter "i" is lengthened by the following vowel letter "e".

The doubling principle results in many words with double consonants including "ribbon", "address", "coffee", "suggest", "fellow", "hammer", "funny", "zipper", "berry", and "butter". The question arises, should double consonants be pronounced as one phoneme or two? Should "ribbon", for example, be pronounced as "ri**b**-on" or as "ri**b**-**b**on"? Most dictionaries indicate that double consonants only represent a single consonant sound. However, Margaret M. Bishop makes a convincing argument in her book *The ABC's and All Their Tricks* that both consonants are pronounced because of our tendency to begin syllables with a consonant sound.[15] For spelling purposes, it is helpful to pronounce both consonants if possible. With words such as "hopped" and "snipped" it is not possible to pronounce both consonants because they are found in single-syllable words. The following letter "e" is not pronounced.

With short vowel syllables that already end with two consonant letters, there is no need to double the final consonant when adding a suffix that begins with a vowel letter. Adding the suffix "-er" to the word "farm", for example, produces "fa**rm**er" which is pronounced "far-**m**er". The letter "a" is pronounced with a short vowel sound in a closed syllable. Likewise, adding the suffix "-**i**ng" to the word "du**mp**" produces "du**mp**ing" which is pronounced "dum-**p**ing". The letter "u" is pronounced with a short vowel sound in a closed syllable.

The ability of suffixes that begin with a vowel sound to capture a preceding consonant is also found with the suffix "-le". This is because the suffix "-le" is pronounced "-ul". A faint schwa vowel sound is pronounced just before the consonant "l" sound. The "-ul" sound, in turn, captures the preceding consonant. As a result, words such as "turtle" and "candle" are pronounced "tur-**t**ul" and "can-**d**ul" respectively.

The doubling principle helps readers distinguish between many pairs of words that differ only in the long and short vowel sounds heard in the root word. Compare the long "a" vowel sound in "l**a**-**d**y" to the short "a" vowel sound in "l**ad**-**d**er". Likewise, compare the long "i" vowel sound in "d**i**-**n**er" to the short "i" vowel sound in "d**in**-**n**er".

Root Pronounced with a Long Vowel Sound	Root Pronounced with a Short Vowel Sound
• cutest	• cutting
• diner	• dinner
• griped	• gripped
• hoping	• hopping
• lady	• ladder
• mated	• matted
• moping	• mopping
• pining	• pinning
• riding	• ridding
• sloping	• slopping
• sniping	• snipping
• super	• supper
• waging	• wagging

It must be noted, however, that two consonants between two vowel letters are not always divided between syllables. Sometimes two consonants will stay together and attach to either the preceding or the following syllable. While a consonant blend will often divide when a suffix is added to a base word, the blend may remain intact if it can form an onset to the following syllable. The word "fragrance", for example, is pronounced "fra-grance". The consonant blend "gr" is able to form an onset to the syllable "-grance". This leaves the preceding syllable "fra-" open, allowing the letter "a" to be pronounced with the long "a" vowel sound.

As well, consonant digraphs such as "ch", "ck", "ph", "sh", and "th" function as single consonants and so remain undivided. The words "butcher" and "coaching", for example, are pronounced "butch-er" and "coa-ching" respectively. Likewise, the word "packet" is pronounced "pack-et". The words "nephew" and "cipher" are pronounced "neph-ew" and "ci-pher". The words "fishing" and "crochet" are pronounced "fish-ing" and "cro-chet". And, the words "gather" and "clothing" are pronounced "gath-er" and "clo-thing". As a rule, open syllables are long and closed syllables are short.

A8.2 Exceptions to the Doubling Principle

The doubling principle is central to native English spelling. Unfortunately, however, there are many words that do not conform to the doubling principle.

1.	The doubling principle does not apply to single-syllable short vowel words such as "cat", "bed", and "hit" or to final short vowel syllables as found in "basket", "forbid", and "commit". The final consonant is not followed by vowel letter, so there is no need to protect the short vowel sound from the lengthening effect of a following vowel. That said, many single-syllable short vowel words such as "add", "mend", and "odd" and final short vowel syllables such as "abs__en__t", "att__a__ck", and "dent__is__t" end with two consonant letters.

2. The doubling principle does not apply when a short vowel sound is represented by a vowel digraph. So, for example, the doubling principle does not apply to words such as "__au__dio", "__aw__ful", "c__oo__kie", "d__aw__ning", "__Eu__rope", "h__ei__ress", "h__o__nest", "l__eo__pard", "l__ieu__tenant", or "m__ea__dow". These spelling patterns are not particularly common as vowel digraphs usually represent long vowel sounds.

3. The doubling principle does not apply to consonant letter "v". So, for example, the letter "v" is not doubled following short vowel sounds in words such as "c__i__vil", "cl__e__ver", "g__i__ven", and "s__e__veral". It is a convention that the letter "v" is not doubled because it would become confused with the letter "w" which has a different sound and function. Two rare exceptions to this rule are the words "s__a__vvy" and "r__e__vved".

4. The doubling principle does not apply to consonant letter "x". So, for example, the letter "x" is not doubled following short vowel sounds in words such as "__e__xit", "__e__xact", "m__a__ximum", "M__e__xico", and "s__a__xophone". The letter "x" already represents two consonant sounds, most often the hard "c/k" consonant sound followed by the soft "c/s" consonant sound.

5. The doubling principle does not apply to the unstressed schwa vowel sound.

The doubling principle protects short vowel syllables from the lengthening affect of a following vowel letter. As only stressed syllables are pronounced with a distinct vowel sound, it follows that doubling would not apply to unstressed schwa syllables as heard in "c__a__nal", "env__e__lope", "gen__e__ral", and "tail__o__red". On the other hand, unstressed schwa vowels may be followed by two consonant letters as in "lib__er__ty", "p__er__mit", and "wild__er__ness" because there is no need to create a long sounding open syllable.

Many words end with a closed unstressed schwa vowel syllable as heard in "moth__er__". As unstressed syllables do not have a distinct vowel sound to protect, a suffix beginning with a vowel letter is added without doubling the final consonant. Adding the suffix "-ing" to "moth__er__", for example, produces "moth__er__**ing**".

If you pronounce the following words carefully, it is possible to hear the difference between stressed and unstressed syllables. Stressed short vowel sounds are followed by double consonants. Unstressed schwa vowel sounds are not. See D3.

Stressed Vowel Sound	Unstressed Vowel Sound
confe__rr__ed, confe__rr__ing	confe__r__ence
defe__rr__ed, defe__rr__ing	defe__r__ence
infe__rr__ed infe__rr__ing	infe__r__ence
prefe__rr__ed, prefe__rr__ing	prefe__r__ence

ref**e**_rr_al, ref**e**_rr_ed, ref**e**_rr_ing	ref**e**_r_ee, ref**e**_r_ence, ref**e**_r_endum
transf**e**_rr_ed, transf**e**_rr_ing, transf**e**_rr_able	transf**e**_r_ability
beg**i**_nn_er, beg**i**_nn_ing	diff**e**_r_ence, diff**e**_r_ent, diff**e**_r_ing
adm**i**_tt_ance, adm**i**_tt_ed, adm**i**_tt_ing	equ**a**_l_ed, equ**a**_l_ing
comm**i**_tt_able, comm**i**_tt_ed, comm**i**_tt_ing	lab**e**_l_ed, lab**e**_l_ing
comp**e**_ll_ed, comp**e**_ll_ing	reas**o**_n_able, reas**o**_n_ed, reas**o**_n_ing
occ**u**_rr_ed, occ**u**_rr_ing, occ**u**_rr_ence	foc**u**_s_ed, foc**u**_s_ing
forb**i**_dd_en, forb**i**_dd_ing	op**e**_n_ed, op**e**_n_ing, op**e**_n_er
perm**i**_tt_ed, perm**i**_tt_ing	prohib**i**_t_ed, prohib**i**_t_ing

6. The doubling principle does not apply to words that follow Latin spelling conventions. The following discussion is adapted from Margaret M. Bishop's book *The ABC's and All Their Tricks*.[16]

While many languages have contributed to English spelling, the primary roots are found in Old English and Latin. Old English evolved within the geographic boundaries of the British Isles. Latin was imported into English through various channels. At the time that Standard English spelling was being established in the 1700's, scholars all read, wrote, and spoke Latin. English and Latin were able to merge into one written language because Old English scholars had long ago adopted the Latin alphabet with relatively minor changes. While this merger has made English a versatile language, it means that there are two spelling systems: a native English spelling system that applies to words that are Old English in origin and a Latin spelling system that applies to words that are Latin in origin.

In Latin spelling, short vowel sounds are usually heard in stressed syllables while long vowel sounds are heard in unstressed syllables. An unstressed long vowel syllable will generally go short if stress shifts onto it. For example, the unstressed long "o" vowel sound heard in "produce" becomes short when stressed as heard in "product". Note that the short "o" vowel letter in "pr**o**duce" is not followed by two consonant letters.

This highlights an important difference between native English and Latin spelling. While English spelling follows the doubling principle, Latin spelling does not. In Latin spelling, a single vowel letter in a stressed syllable is usually pronounced with a short vowel sound even when separated from a following vowel letter by a single consonant. This can be heard in words such as "c**a**bin", "cl**i**nic", "**i**magine", "s**u**burban", and "tr**e**mendous".

The difficulty lies in distinguishing between native English and Latin words. Very generally, shorter words follow native English spelling principles and longer words follow Latin spelling principles. This reflects the relatively humble origins of native English words and the more exalted origins of Latin words. More particularly:

a) Single-syllable words generally follow native English spelling principles regardless of origin.

b) Longer words with four or more syllables usually follow Latin spelling principles. Double consonants sometimes occur, but not because of the doubling principle. Rather, double consonants usually result from adding Latin prefixes.

c) If a two and three syllable word begins with a native English prefix or ends with a native English suffix, then English spelling conventions generally apply.

Native English Prefixes

Most native English prefixes are lexical morphemes. They can stand alone as independent words in their own right although they do not always retain the same meaning. Native English prefixes include "a-", "be-", "for-", "to-", and "with-" as found in "**a**fford", "**be**hind", "**for**give", "**to**day", and "**with**hold". Directional prefixes such as "in-", "out-", "up-", "down-", and "after-" as found in "**in**side", "**out**doors", "**up**beat", "**down**cast", and "**after**glow" function like compound words. Prefixes such "fore-", "mis-", and "un-" as heard in "**fore**arm", "**mis**take", and "**un**willing" do not stand as free-standing words.

Native English Suffixes

There are a number of native English suffixes that begin with a consonant letter including "-dom", "-ful", "-hood", "-less", "-ly", "-s", and "-ward" as found in "free**dom**", "joy**ful**", "child**hood**", "thought**less**", "saf<u>e</u>**ly**", "car<u>e</u>**s**", and "back**ward**". On the other hand, there is only one Latin suffix, the suffix "-ment", that begins with a consonant letter as found in "base**ment**" and "state**ment**".

There are a number of native English suffixes that begin with a vowel letter including "-able", "-ed", "-en", "-er", "-es", "-est", "-et", "-ing", "-ish", "-le", "-ow', and "-y" as found in "accept**able**", "clean**ed**", "damp**en**", "fast**er**", "teach**es**", "fast**est**", "crump**et**", "runn**ing**", "child**ish**", "stab**le**", "fell**ow**', and "funn**y**". If a word ends with any other suffix, then Latin spelling principles apply.

d) If a two and three syllable word begins with a Latin prefix or ends with a Latin suffix, then Latin spelling conventions generally apply.

Latin Prefixes

Latin prefixes are bound morphemes. Most cannot stand alone as English words, although they may have stood alone as Latin words. There are four kinds of Latin prefixes.

i)   Single-syllable prefixes that end with a vowel letter such as "de-", "pre-", "pro-", "re-", and "se-" as found in "**de**bate", "**pre**amble", "**pro**blem", "**re**search", and "**se**clude". These prefixes are added to the root word without spelling changes.

ii)   Single-syllable prefixes that end with a consonant letter such as "ab-", "ad-", "con-", "dis-", "ex-", "in-", "ob-", "per-", "sub-", and "trans-" as heard in "**ab**dicate", "**ad**apt", "**con**ceal", "**dis**agree", "**ex**amine", "**in**cite", "**ob**ject", "**per**suade", "**sub**ject", and "**trans**form". These prefixes are usually pronounced with a short vowel sound.

When the root word begins with a vowel letter, these prefixes can be added without spelling changes as in "**ab**use", "**ad**opt", "**ob**ey", "**per**use", and "**sub**urb". This results in only one consonant letter between the vowel of the prefix and the first vowel of the root word. As heard in "**di**sagree", "**ex**amine", and "**in**ert", this often results in a short vowel being followed by a single consonant contrary to the doubling principle.

Sometimes when the root word begins with a consonant letter, the prefix can be added without spelling changes if it is easy to pronounce. This is the case with words such as "**ab**dicate", "**con**ceal", "**in**cite", "**ob**ject", "**per**suade", "**sub**ject", and "**trans**form".

Often, however, it is difficult to pronounce a prefix that ends with a consonant letter when attached to a root word that also begins with a consonant letter. In this case, the prefix may "assimilate". The final consonant of the prefix is dropped, and the first consonant of the root word is doubled. For example, when the prefix "ab-" is added to the root word "fect" it is spelled "a**ff**ect". The letter "b" is dropped and the letter "f" is doubled. These spelling patterns are called "allomorphs". Allomorphs are the primary source of double consonants in Latin spelling. As well, double consonants may occur incidentally when a prefix ends and the root word begins with the same consonant letter. This is the case with "a**d-d**iction", "co**n-n**ive", "di**s-s**ect", and "i**n-n**ate".

Also, due to difficult pronunciation, the last consonant of the prefix is sometimes dropped altogether when added to a root word that begins with a consonant letter. This is the case with "**a**vert", "**di**gest", "**di**late", "**e**dict", "**e**lect", "**e**mit", and "**o**mit".

iii)   There are a number of two-syllable Latin prefixes including "circum-", "contra-", "extra-", "inter-", "intra-", "para-", "peri-", "super-", and "tele-" as heard in "**circum**vent", "**contra**band", "**extra**ct", "**inter**cede", "**intra**dermal", "**para**dox", "**peri**meter", "**super**lative", and "**tele**scope". The prefixes "extra-" and "super-" are able, of course, to stand alone as English words.

iv)   There are a number of numerical Latin prefixes including "bi-" meaning "two", "cent-" meaning "hundred", "deca-" meaning "ten", "hemi-" meaning "half", "milli-" meaning "thousand", "mono-" meaning "one", "omni-" meaning "all", "poly-" meaning "many", "quadr-" meaning "four", "quint-" meaning "five", "semi-" meaning "half", and "tri-" meaning "three".

Latin Suffixes

While a number of native English suffixes begin with a consonant letter, only one Latin suffix does: the suffix "-ment". The suffix "-ment" may be added to long vowel root words that end with a final silent letter "e" as in "bas**e**ment" and "stat**e**ment". The letter "e" remains silent in the derived word.

There are numerous Latin suffixes that begin with a vowel letter that can be divided into different groups. Each group has different characteristics.

i)   One group of suffixes begin with vowel letters "a", "e", "o", or "u", (but not vowel letter "i"), including "-a", "-age", "-al", "-an", "-ant", "-ance", "-ar", "-ate", "-ent", "-ency", "-o", "-on", "-or", "-ous", "-um", "-ure", and "-us". These are found in words such as "camer**a**". "vanill**a**", "advant**age**", "dam**age**", "origin**al**", "extern**al**", "Spart**an**", "urb**an**", "extravag**ant**", "extravag**ance**", "particul**ar**", "popul**ar**", "amput**ate**", "demonstr**ate**", "depend**ent**", "depend**ency**", "domin**o**", "innuend**o**", "aband**on**", "ars**on**", "credit**or**", "jur**or**", "monoton**ous**", "tremend**ous**", "maxim**um**", "minim**um**", "advent**ure**", "agricult**ure**", "cact**us**" and "circ**us**".

The second syllable of many two-syllable words ends with one of these suffixes. The stress usually falls on the root which is the first syllable. Being stressed, the first vowel is often pronounced with a short sound in a closed syllable as in "ju**r**-or", "me**t**-al" and "pe**d**-al". Note that there is only one consonant letter between vowel sounds contrary to the doubling principle. This is a feature of Latin spelling; vowel letters are often pronounced with a short vowel sound without being separated from a following vowel letter by two consonant letters. Sometimes, however, the first vowel is pronounced with a long sound in an open syllable as in "d<u>o</u>-**n**ate", "f<u>a</u>-**t**al", "tr<u>i</u>-**d**ent" and "t<u>o</u>-**t**al".

ii)   A second group of suffixes begin with vowel letter "i" which is followed by a second vowel letter. This includes suffixes "-ia", "-ial", "-ian", "-iance", "-iant", "-iar", "-iate", "-ience", "-ient", "-io", "-ion", "-ior", "-iot", "-ious", "-ium", and "-ius" as found in words such as "pneumon**ia**", "ser**ial**", "spec**ial**", "politic**ian**", "magic**ian**", "rad**iance**", "rad**iant**", "pecul**iar**", "infur**iate**", "conven**ience**", "conven**ient**", "len**ient**", "portfol**io**", "rad**io**", "fract**ion**", "nat**ion**", "behav**ior**/behav**iour**", "sav**ior**/sav**iour**", "id**iot**", "patr**iot**", "cur**ious**", "fur**ious**", "prem**ium**", "ted**ium**", and "rad**ius**".

Sometimes, the letter "i" results from changing a letter "y" into an "i" upon adding a second suffix. For example, adding the suffix "-est" to "happ**y**" produces "happ**i**est".

These are often two-syllable suffixes. Both the letter "i" and the following vowel are pronounced forming a link letter spelling pattern. In the word "ser**ial**", for example, the letter "i" is pronounced with the long "e" vowel sound and the letter "a" is pronounced with the schwa vowel sound. Sometimes the letter "i" is pronounced with consonant "y" sound as heard in "mill**i**on", "jun**i**or", and "behav**i**our".

A preceding vowel letter "a", "e", "o", or "u" will be long if there is only one consonant letter between it and the suffix. In "ra-dio", "pre-vious", "pho-bia", and "stu-dious", for example, the vowel letter preceding the suffix is pronounced with a long sound in an open syllable. On the other hand, a preceding vowel letter "i" will be short if there is only one consonant letter between it and the suffix. In "id-iot", for example, the first letter "i" is pronounced with a short vowel sound in a closed syllable. This spelling is contrary to the doubling principle.

While the word endings such as "-cial, "-sion", and "-tion" appear to be suffixes, they result from the final consonant of a root word attaching to a suffix to form a consonant digraph sound. Adding the suffix "-ial" to "race", for example, produces "racial". The letters "ci" represent the consonant "sh" sound. Likewise, adding the suffix "-ion" to "erode" produces "erosion". The letters "si" represent the consonant "zh" sound. Adding the suffix "-ion" to "product" produces "production". The letters "ti" represent the consonant "sh" sound.

iii) A third group of suffixes is spelled with a single vowel letter "i" including "-ic", "-ice", "-id", "-il", "-ile", "-in", "-ine", "-it", "-ite", "-ive", and "-ize". These are found in words such as "critic", "panic", "novice", "frigid", "rigid", "civil", "peril", "docile", "sterile", "cabin", "robin", "examine", "famine", "credit", "habit", "despite", "respite", "survive", and "baptize"

The syllable preceding the suffix "-ic" is often pronounced with a short vowel sound even if there is only one consonant letter between vowel sounds. This can be heard in words such as "panic", "epic", "critic", and "comic". The preceding syllable will be pronounced with a short vowel sound even when long in the base word. Compare, for example, the long vowel sounds heard in "athlete" and "paralyze" to the short vowel sounds heard in "athletic" and "paralytic".

iv) The two-syllable suffix "-ity" is similar to the suffix "-ic". The syllable preceding "-ity" is usually pronounced with a short vowel sound even if there is only one consonant letter between vowel sounds. This can be heard in words such as "capacity", "serenity", "timidity", and "commodity". The preceding syllable will be pronounced with a short vowel sound even when long in the base word. Compare, for example, the long vowel sounds heard in "serene" and "divine" to the short vowel sounds heard in "serenity" and "divinity".

v) A number of suffixes begin with the letter "u" vowel sound including "-ual", "-ue", "-ule", "-une", "-uous", and "-ure" as found in "continue", "continuous", "failure", "figure", "fortune", "measure", "nature", "picture", "pressure", "schedule", and "usual".

With some of these words the letter "u" is pronounced with the long "u" vowel sound heard in "cure" and "pure". That is, a consonant "y" sound is pronounced at the beginning of the "u" vowel sound. This can be heard in "continue", "continuous", "failure", "figure", and "tenure".

In other words, however, the final consonant of the root word attaches to the consonant "y" sound to produce other consonant sounds. In "gradual", "individual", "procedure", and "schedule", for example, the letters "du" represent the soft "g/j" consonant sound. In "adventure", "nature", "picture", "signature", and "temperature" the letters "tu" represent the consonant "ch" sound. In "censure", "insure", "fissure", and "pressure", the letters "su" and "ssu" represent the consonant "sh" sound. In "disclosure", "measure", "pressure", and "usual", the letters "su" represent the consonant "zh" sound.

vi)   A number of suffixes are both native English and Latin. These include "-able", "-er", "-et", "ible", "-ish", "-le", and "-y".

- While the suffix "-able" is Latin in origin, it is often added as a suffix to English words as in "laughable" and "understandable". However, "-able" is also found in Latin words such as "comparable", "preferable", "probable", and "vulnerable" that do not follow the doubling principle.

- The suffix "-er" was introduced into English through both German and Latin. German words such as "batter" and "hammer" follow the doubling principle. In Latin words such as "proper" short vowels are not followed by two consonants.

- While the suffix "-et" is French in origin, it was incorporated into some English words early on so that English spelling conventions were applied. Words such as "bonnet" and "pocket" follow the doubling principle. French words that were adopted into English more recently such as "cabinet", "comet", "facet", "omelet", and "tenet" follow Latin spelling so short vowels are not followed by two consonant letters.

- The suffix "-ible" is Latin in origin. Words that end with the suffix "ible" such as "divisible", "legible", and "visible" do not follow the doubling principle.

- The syllable preceding "-ish" is often pronounced with a short vowel sound even if there is only one consonant letter between vowel sounds. This can be heard in words such as "finish", "polish", "punish", "relish", and "vanish". When attached to stand alone English root words the suffix "-ish" produces adjectives meaning "like a __". Adding the suffix "-ish" to "fool", for example, produces "foolish" meaning "like a fool".

- While the suffix "-le" is Latin in origin, it was incorporated into some English words so early on that English spelling conventions were applied. Words such as "battle" and "middle" follow the doubling principle. French words that were adopted into English more recently such as "tr<u>e</u>ble" and "tr<u>i</u>ple" follow Latin spelling, so short vowels are not followed by two consonant letters.

- The suffix "-y" was introduced into English through both German and Latin. Words that are German in origin such as "f<u>u</u>nny" and "h<u>a</u>ppy" follow the doubling principle. In Latin words such as "c<u>i</u>ty", "c<u>o</u>py", "st<u>u</u>dy", "v<u>a</u>ry", and "v<u>e</u>ry" short vowels are not followed by two consonants.

A9 The Three Letter Rule

One of the more charming conventions of English spelling is referred to as the "three letter rule". The three letter rule helps readers to distinguish between content words and structure words. Content words are words, such as nouns and verbs, which are used to express ideas. Structure words are words, such as prepositions and conjunctives, which perform the grammatical function of binding content words together into coherent sentences. On their own, structure words express very little meaning.

While there are exceptions, it is a convention of English spelling that content words are to be composed of three or more letters. Structure words, on the other hand, are often spelled with only two letters. The following content and structure words are homophones: words that sound the same but are spelled differently. Many content words are only distinguished by the addition of a third letter.

Structure Words	Content Words
oh (interjection)	owe
by (preposition)	buy, bye
to (preposition)	too, two
or (conjunctive)	oar, ore
an (preposition)	Ann
in (preposition)	inn
no (interjection)	know
so (conjunctive)	sew, sow
be (auxiliary verb)	bee
hi (interjection)	high

There are only a few content words that are spelled with fewer than three letters. The word "axe" is spelled both with and without the final silent letter "e".

Short Content Words	Longer Homophones
ax (noun)	axe
I (pronoun)	aye, eye
we (pronoun)	wee
pi (numerical term)	pie

go (verb) ox (noun) it (pronoun)	Gogh

Often, a final silent letter "e" is used to create a three letter content word. All of the following words, except for "awe", are pronounced with a long vowel sound. The final silent letter "e" is not strictly required because a final long vowel sound may be represented by a single vowel letter.

aw<u>e</u>	ew<u>e</u>	ly<u>e</u>	te<u>e</u>
ay<u>e</u>	**ey<u>e</u>**	or<u>e</u>	ti<u>e</u>
be<u>e</u>	fe<u>e</u>	ow<u>e</u>	to<u>e</u>
by<u>e</u>	fo<u>e</u>	pi<u>e</u>	vi<u>e</u>
cu<u>e</u>	ho<u>e</u>	ro<u>e</u>	we<u>e</u>
di<u>e</u>	hu<u>e</u>	ru<u>e</u>	wo<u>e</u>
do<u>e</u>	Jo<u>e</u>	ry<u>e</u>	
du<u>e</u>	le<u>e</u>	se<u>e</u>	
dy<u>e</u>	li<u>e</u>	su<u>e</u>	

In the following words the final consonant is doubled for the purpose of creating three letter content words. These spelling patterns also conform to the doubling principle. All of the following words are pronounced with a short vowel sound.

| a**dd** | o**dd** | err | i**nn** |
| e**gg** | e**bb** | i**ll** | |

There are a few other three letter content words of note.

bow	key	pew	sew
buy	low	row	tea
guy	mow	sea	tow

There are, of course, hundreds of thousands of content words that are spelled with more than three letters.

A10 Silent Letters

A10.1   Silent Vowel Letters

Silent vowel letters are found in words for a number of reasons.

Silent vowel letters are often found in vowel digraphs, such as the letters "ai" in the word "train" which represent the long "a" vowel sound. While it may be argued that the two letters combine to represent the vowel sound, the second vowel letter is usually considered to be silent.

Many words end with a final silent letter "e". A final silent letter "e" performs a number of functions. The most common function is to signal that the preceding vowel letter is pronounced with a long vowel sound. For example, a final silent letter "e" signals that the letter "o" in "hope" is pronounced with the long "o" vowel sound. Without a final silent letter "e", the word "hop" is pronounced with a short vowel sound.

Silent vowel letters are also found in many consonant digraphs. In the word "antique", for example, the hard "c/k" consonant sound is spelled "que". Likewise, in the word "guitar" the hard "g" consonant sound is spelled "gu". In the word "prince" the final silent letter "e" signals that the adjacent letter "c" is pronounced with the soft "c/s" consonant sound.

A10.2   Silent Consonant Letters

Silent consonant letters are found in words for a number of reasons. Letters "j", "v", and "y" are the only consonant letters that are never, or very rarely, silent.

As discussed in A2.3, silent consonant letters sometimes result from morphemic spelling in words such as "si**g**n" and "si**g**nal", "colum**n**" and "colum**n**ist". The preservation of silent letters shows the common meaning and origin of related words.

Occasionally, silent consonant letters help readers distinguish between two unrelated words. The addition of the letter "w", for example, helps readers distinguish between the words "**w**hole" and "hole". Likewise, the letter "b" helps readers distinguish between the words "plum**b**" and "plum".

Silent consonant letters are found in consonant digraphs such as "ch", "ck", "sh", and "th" as heard in words such as "church", "sack", "shell", and "that". While it may be argued that the two letters combine to represent the consonant sound, the second consonant letter may be considered silent. A few consonant digraphs contain three letters. In the word "catch", for example, the consonant "ch" sound is represented by the letters "tch". The letter "t" and the letter "h" may both be considered silent.

With double consonants, as in "bubble" and "terrace", the second consonant letter is often considered to be silent. Most dictionaries indicate that double consonants represent only a single consonant sound. However, Margaret M. Bishop makes a convincing argument in her book *The ABC's and All Their Tricks* that both consonants are usually pronounced because of our tendency to begin syllables with a consonant sound.[17] For spelling purposes, it is helpful to pronounce both consonants if possible. With some words, such as "hopped" and "snipped", it is not possible to pronounce both consonants because they are found in single-syllable words. The following letter "e" is silent.

A surprising number of vowel digraphs contain one or more silent consonant letters. In the word "sleigh", for example, the long "a" vowel sound is spelled "eigh". The letters "igh" are considered silent. Likewise, in the word "crawl" the short "o" vowel sound is spelled with the letters "aw". The letter "w" is considered silent.

A11 Diacritical Letters

As discussed in the Introduction, the English alphabet has only twenty-six letters with which to represent over forty different phonemes. As a solution to this problem, early scholars combined letters together to represent the extra phonemes and to resolve other spelling dilemmas. While many letters join together to represent various word sounds, letters "e", "h", "i", and "u" in particular are called upon to perform this function. These are called diacritical letters because they are used the same way diacritical marks are used in dictionaries to indicate word sounds. A diacritical letter is usually silent.

A11.1   Final Silent Letter "e"

Many words such as "invade", "prince", "dodge", "bathe", "horse", "plague", "have", "dare", "more", "where", "fire", "feature", "measure", "seizure", "cure", "sure" and "blaze" end with a final silent letter "e".

A final letter "e" is, in fact, only very rarely pronounced. Exceptions include the words "adobe", apostrophe", "be", "he", "me", "recipe", "she", "ukulele", "we", and "ye" where the final letter "e" represents the long "e" vowel sound. With the word "coyote" the letter "e" is pronounced with the long "e" vowel sound by some people and is silent when pronounced by other people. The final letter "e" in the word "the" is most often pronounced with the schwa vowel sound. With words such as "café", "exposé", and "soufflé" the final letter "é" is pronounced with the long "a" vowel sound. In most other words, a final letter "e" is silent.

A final silent letter "e" has many different functions in spelling including:

1. The most common function of a final silent letter "e" is to signal that the preceding vowel letter is pronounced with a long vowel sound. With the word "wine", for example, the final silent letter "e" signals that the preceding letter "i" is pronounced with the long "i" vowel sound. Likewise, with the word "invade" the final silent letter "e" signals that the preceding letter "a" is pronounced with the long "a" vowel sound.

    With words that end with two vowel letters, such as "sundae", "see", "tie", "toe", and "blue", a final silent letter "e" also signals that the adjacent vowel letter is pronounced with a long vowel sound.

Many short vowel words become long vowel words with the addition of a final silent letter "e". With the addition of a final silent letter "e", for example, the word "fat" becomes "fate", "pet" becomes "Pete", "hid" becomes "hide", "hop" becomes "hope", and "cut" become "cute".

2. A final silent letter "e" is added to many words, such as "hou**se**" and "hor**se**", which would otherwise end with the letter "s". It is a convention of English spelling that root words do not end with the letter "s". This is because the suffix "-s" is often added to create the plural, possessive, and third-person-singular forms of words. To indicate that a root word is not plural, possessive, or third-person-singular, a final silent letter "e" is often added following the letter "s".

3. A final silent letter "e" following the letter "c", as in "prin**ce**" and "dan**ce**", signals that the adjacent letter "c" is pronounced with the soft "c/s" consonant sound.

4. A final silent letter "e" following the letter "g", as in "dod**ge**" and "coura**ge**", signals that the adjacent letter "g" is pronounced with the soft "g/j" consonant sound.

5. A final silent letter "e" following the letters "ng", as in "lu**nge**" and "ra**nge**", signals that the letter "n" is pronounced with the consonant "n" sound and the letter "g" is pronounced with the soft "g/j" consonant sound. Without the final letter "e", as in "lung" and "rang", the letter "n" is pronounced with the consonant "ng" sound heard in "sing" and the letter "g" is silent.

6. A final silent letter "e" following the letters "th", as in "ba**the**" and "brea**the**", signals that the letters "th" are pronounced with the voiced consonant "th" sound heard in "this" and "that". With voiced phonemes the vocal cords vibrate during pronunciation. Without a final silent letter "e", as in "bath" and "breath", the unvoiced consonant "th" sound is heard.

7. A final "-le" spelling pattern following a consonant letter, as in "mar**ble**" and "ta**ble**", signals that a schwa vowel sound is pronounced just before the consonant "l" sound. The words "marble" and "table", for example, are pronounced "mar-bull" and "tay-bull".

8. A final "-re" spelling pattern following a consonant letter, as in "a**cre**" and "thea**tre**", signals that a schwa vowel sound is pronounced just before the consonant "r" sound. The words "acre" and "theatre", for example, are pronounced "aye-cur" and "thee-a-tur".

9. A final "-re" spelling pattern following a vowel letter, as in "d**are**", "wh**ere**", "m**ore**", "f**ire**", "feat**ure**", "meas**ure**", "seiz**ure**", "c**ure**", and "s**ure**" represents a number of different word endings:

- With word endings "-are", "-ere", and "-ore", as in "d<u>are</u>", "wh<u>ere</u>", and "m<u>ore</u>", the first vowel is usually pronounced with a short vowel sound and not the r-influenced schwa vowel sound. "Dare" and "where" are pronounced with the short "e" vowel sound heard in the word "pet". "More" is pronounced with the short "o" vowel sound heard in the word "born".

- With word ending "-ire", as in "f<u>ire</u>", a schwa vowel sound is pronounced between the long "i" vowel sound and the consonant "r" sound. The word "fire", for example, is pronounced "fi-ur".

- With word endings "-ture", "-sure", and "-zure", as in "fea**tu**r<u>e</u>", "mea**su**r<u>e</u>", and "sei**zu**r<u>e</u>", a schwa vowel sound is pronounced just before the consonant "r" sound. The word "feature", for example, is pronounced "fee-chur". The letters "tu" usually represent the "ch" consonant sound. The letters "su" and "zu" usually represent the "zh" consonant sound.

10. A final silent letter "e" is found following the letter "u" at the end of words, such as "gl**u**<u>e</u>", "plag**u**<u>e</u>", and "contin**u**<u>e</u>", because it is a convention of English spelling that words do not end with the letter "u". This convention applies whether or not the letter "u" is pronounced. The words "flu", "gnu", and "menu" are exceptions to this rule.

11. A final silent letter "e" is found following the letter "v" at the end of words, such as "gi**v**<u>e</u>" and "ha**v**<u>e</u>", because it is a convention of English spelling that words do not end with the letter "v". Abbreviations such as "rev" and "Slav" are exceptions to this rule.

12. A final silent letter "e" is found following a single letter "z" at the end of words, such as "bree**z**<u>e</u>" and "squee**z**<u>e</u>", because it is a convention of English spelling that words do not end with a single letter "z". Abbreviations such as "quiz" and "wiz" and foreign words such as "fez" are exceptions to this rule.

13. A final silent letter "e" following the letters "ch", as in "crè**ch**<u>e</u>" and "mousta**ch**<u>e</u>", indicates that the "ch" spelling pattern is pronounced with the "sh" consonant sound. This spelling is French in origin.

14. A final silent letter "e" following a consonant letter "t", as in "eli**te**", "peti**te**", "rou**te**", and "sui**te**", indicates that the letter "t" is pronounced. In French spelling a final letter "t" is silent as (not) heard in "ballet" and "depot". Adding a final silent letter "e" causes the letter "t" to be pronounced.

15. A final silent letter "e" is added to a number French words that end with double consonants including "bague**tte**", "casse**tte**", "cigare**tte**", "ga**ffe**", "rose**tte**", and "ushere**tte**".

16. A final silent letter "e" is sometimes used to create three letter words as in "be**e**", "dy**e**", and "hu**e**". It is a convention of English spelling that content words are spelled with three or more letters.

17. A final silent letter "e" is sometimes used to distinguish surnames from ordinary words. This spelling is found in names such as "Cook**e**", "Crew**e**", "Brown**e**", "Good**e**", "How**e**", "Moor**e**", "Pain**e**", and "Wolf**e**".

18. A final silent letter "e" is added to some words to distinguish them from other similar words. This is seen with the words "bell**e**" and "bell", and "born**e**" and "born".

Given all of the above functions, it is important to remember that a final silent letter "e" does not always signal that the preceding vowel letter is pronounced with a long vowel sound. In "prince", "courage", and "have", for example, the final silent letter "e" does not signal a long vowel sound.

It is also possible for a final silent letter "e" to perform two functions. It can both signal that that the preceding vowel letter is pronounced with a long vowel sound and perform another of the above functions. For example, with the word "cage" the final silent letter "e" helps to signal that the preceding letter "a" is pronounced with the long "a" vowel sound, and it also signals that the adjacent letter "g" is pronounced with the soft "g/j" consonant sound.

A11.2 The Letter "h"

The letter "h" performs diacritical functions by helping to represent a variety of consonant and vowel sounds.

The letter "h" combines with other consonants to form consonant digraphs "ch", "gh", "kh", "ph", "rh", "sh", "th", and "wh". The letter "h" is usually silent. The letter "h" also combines with several vowel letters to form vowel digraphs "ah", "eh", and "oh". The letter "h" is always silent.

1. The "ah" spelling pattern represents the broad "a" vowel sound heard in "hurr**ah**" and "sh**ah**".

2. The "ch" spelling pattern, unfortunately, represents three different consonant sounds including the hard "c/k" consonant sound heard in "**Ch**ristmas", the consonant "ch" sound heard twice in the word "**ch**ur**ch**", and the consonant "sh" sound heard in "ma**ch**ine". There is no general rule that governs which sound is represented when. However, the consonant "ch" sound is the most

common of the three. Words in which the "ch" spelling pattern represents the hard "c/k" consonant sound are Greek in origin. Words in which the "ch" spelling pattern represents the consonant "sh" sound are French in origin.

3. The "eh" spelling pattern represents the long "a" vowel sound heard in the word "**eh**". This may be the only instance of this spelling pattern.

4. The "gh" spelling pattern helps to represent both consonant and vowel sounds. In words such as "lau**gh**" and "cou**gh**", for example, the "gh" spelling pattern represents the consonant "f" sound. In a few words, such as "**gh**ost" and "**gh**etto", the "gh" spelling pattern represents the hard "g" consonant sound. The majority of the time, however, as heard in the words "hi**gh**" and "thou**gh**", the "gh" spelling pattern helps to represent a variety of vowel sounds. The letters "gh" are silent.

5. The "kh" spelling pattern represents the hard "c/k" consonant sound heard in "**kh**aki" and "**kh**an".

6. The "oh" spelling pattern represents the long "o" vowel sound heard in "**oh**" and "**oh**m".

7. The "ph" spelling pattern represents the consonant "f" sound heard in the words "**ph**onics" and "tele**ph**one". This spelling pattern is in Greek origin and is very consistent.

8. The "rh" and "rrh" spelling patterns represent the consonant "r" sound heard in "**rh**ino" and "my**rrh**".

9. The "sh" spelling pattern represents the consonant "sh" sound heard in the words "**sh**ell", "fa**sh**ion" and "ra**sh**". While this spelling pattern is consistent there are, unfortunately, many other spelling patterns that also represent the consonant "sh" sound.

10. The "th" spelling pattern represents both the voiced consonant "th" sound, as heard in "**th**is" and "**th**at", and the unvoiced consonant "th" sound as heard in "**th**in" and "**th**ank". This spelling pattern is very consistent.

11. The "wh" spelling pattern is unusual. When the "wh" spelling pattern is followed by the letter "o", as in "**wh**o", "**wh**om" and "**wh**ose", the letter "w" is silent and only the letter "h" is pronounced. When the "wh" spelling pattern is followed by a different vowel letter as in "**wh**ale, "**wh**eat", and "**wh**iff, the letter "w" is pronounced and the letter "h" is silent. With such words some speakers pronounce a consonant "h" sound before pronouncing the consonant "w" sound.

A11.3　　The Letter "i"

The letter "i" performs diacritical functions by helping to represent a number of consonant sounds.

The letter "i" performs a diacritical function by helping to signal the consonant "sh" sound following consonant letters "c", "s", "sc", "ss", "t", and "x". This may be heard in the words "fa**ci**al", "con**sci**ous", "pen**si**on", "admi**ssi**on", "pa**ti**ent", "no**ti**on", and "comple**xi**on". In most words, the letter "i" itself is silent. In a few words, such as "appre**ci**ate" and "par**ti**ality", the letter "i" is pronounced in its own right.

The use of "ci", "si", "sci", "ssi", "ti", and "xi" spelling patterns to represent the consonant "sh" sound is a common spelling pattern. However, there are exceptions. In "Chris**ti**an", "con**sci**ous", and "**ce**llo", for instance, the "ti", "sci", and "c(e)" spelling patterns represent the consonant "ch" sound. In "an**ci**ent" the "ci" spelling pattern is pronounced with either the consonant "ch" sound or the consonant "sh" sound. In "A**si**an", "divi**si**on", and "equa**ti**on" the "si" and "ti" spelling patterns represent the consonant "zh" sound. Another exception is the word "jui**ci**er" in which the letter "c" is pronounced with the soft "c/s" consonant sound.

A11.4　　The Letter "u"

The letter "u" performs a diacritical function by helping to represent the hard "g" consonant sound.

To understand why, one must appreciate that the letter "g" is usually pronounced with the soft "g/j" consonant sound when followed by vowel letters "e", "i" and "y". Conversely, the letter "g" is usually pronounced with a hard "g" consonant sound when followed by vowel letters "a", "o" and "u". A dilemma for early scholars was how to indicate that the letter "g" is to be pronounced with a hard "g" consonant sound when it is followed by vowel letters "e", "i", or "y" for other reasons. Their solution was to insert the letter "u" following the letter "g" to indicate that the "g" is pronounced with a hard "g" consonant sound and not the soft "g/j" consonant sound.

When the letters "gu" are followed by "e" or "i" the letter "u" is usually silent as (not) heard in words such as "**gu**ide", "**gu**ess", "ro**gu**e", and "lea**gu**e". However, there are exceptions. In words such as "an**gu**ish" and "**Gu**elph" the letter "u" is pronounced with the consonant "w" sound. In "disgust" the letter "u" is pronounced with a short "u" vowel sound. In words such as "**gu**ard", "**gu**arantee", and "**gu**ardian", the silent letter "u" is not required to signal the hard "g" sound.

A12 The "i" Before "e" Rule

A popular spelling rule is to put "i" before "e" except after "c". A popular schoolroom poem reads:

> Put *i* before *e*,
> Except after *c*,
> Or when sounded like *a*,
> As in *neighbour* and *weigh*;
> And except *seize* and *seizure*,
> And also *leisure*,
> *Weird*, *height*, and *either*,
> *Forfeit* and *neither*.[18]

The spelling rule set out in this poem never constituted a true spelling convention. Rather, it reflects the poet's observation that many words are spelled with the "ie" spelling pattern except following the letter "c" or when pronounced with the long "a" vowel sound. Unfortunately, there are many exceptions to this rule.

A12.1 Applying the Rule: "i" before "e"

The "i" before "e" spelling pattern is found in many words.

The "ie" spelling pattern represents the long "e" vowel sound in many words:

ach**ie**ve	f**ie**nd	n**ie**ce	shr**ie**k
ap**ie**ce	fr**ie**ze	p**ie**ce	s**ie**ge
bel**ie**f	gr**ie**f	pr**ie**st	th**ie**f
bel**ie**ve	gr**ie**ve	rel**ie**f	w**ie**ld
br**ie**f	hyg**ie**ne	rel**ie**ve	y**ie**ld
ch**ie**f	l**ie**n	repr**ie**ve	
f**ie**ld	med**ie**val	sh**ie**ld	

In the following words "ie" represents a final long "e" vowel sound:

bean**ie**	cadd**ie**	dog**ie** (calf)	mov**ie**
bird**ie**	calor**ie**	gen**ie**	prair**ie**
boog**ie**	coll**ie**	goal**ie**	sort**ie**
boog**ie**-woog**ie**	cook**ie**	hipp**ie**	spec**ie**
brown**ie**	dogg**ie**	lass**ie**	

The "ie" spelling pattern represents the short "i" vowel sound in a few words:

f**ie**rce	misch**ie**vous	s**ie**ve
misch**ie**f	p**ie**rce	

In the following words "ie" represents a final long "i" vowel sound:

d**ie**	l**ie**	p**ie**	v**ie**
f**ie**	magp**ie**	t**ie**	
hog-t**ie**	neckt**ie**	unt**ie**	

The "ie" spelling pattern often results from adding a suffix that begins with the letter "e", such as "-ed", "-er", "-es", and "-est", to a base word that ends with a letter "y" following a consonant letter. The word "baby", for example, becomes "babies".

In the following words "ie" represents the long "e" vowel sound:

accompanied	carries	heavier	puppies
accompanies	copied	heaviest	rabies
armies	copier	holies	salaried
authorities	copies	hurried	salaries
babied	countries	hurries	series
babies	duties	ladies	species
beauties	families	livelier	steadies
bunnies	fluffier	lonelier	stories
buried	fluffiest	married	studied
buries	fortieth	marries	studies
campanies	friendlier	necessaries	worried
candied	friendliest	partier	
candies	happier	parties	
carrier	happiest	pitied	

In the follow words, "ie" represents the long "i" vowel sound:

applied	dried	fried	spied
applies	drier	identified	tied
cried	dries	identifies	
cries	driest	relies	

An "ie" link letter spelling pattern is found in a number of words. In the following words the letter "i" is pronounced with the long "e" vowel sound:

alien	audience	clothier	transient

In the following link letter words, the letter "i" is pronounced with the long "i" vowel sound:

anxiety	hierarchy	quiet	variety
fiery	notoriety	sobriety	

The short "e" vowel sound is spelled with the "ie" spelling pattern in the word "friend". The mnemonic phrase "a fri**end** to the **end**" may be helpful in remembering this unique spelling pattern.

friend

The long "u" vowel sound is represented by the "ieu" and "iew" spelling patterns in the following words:

adieu	*lieutenant*	**view**

In the following words the "ie" spelling pattern is incidental. The letters "ti" represent the consonant "sh" sound.

pat**ie**nce pat**ie**nt quot**ie**nt

A12.2   Applying the Rule: Except after "c"

The following words follow the "i" before "e" except after "c" spelling rule.

Following the letter "c", the "ei" spelling pattern usually represents the long "e" vowel sound. While the list of words is not long, many are commonly used.

ceiling	conceive	deceive	receipt
conceit	deceit	perceive	receive

A12.3   Applying the Rule: Or when sounded like "a" as in "neighbour" and "weigh"

The following words follow the "'i' before 'e' except when sounded like 'a' as in 'neighbour' and 'weigh'" spelling rule.

The long "a" vowel sound is represented by the "-ei", "eig" and "eigh" spelling pattern in the following words. The letters "g" and "gh" are silent.

b**ei**ge	fr**eigh**t	n**eigh**bour (UK, CAN)	s**ei**ne
chow m**ei**n	h**ei**nous	n**eigh**bourhood (UK, CAN)	*sh**ei**k(h)*
d**eig**n	inv**eigh**		sk**ei**n
eight	inv**ei**gle	n**eigh**bourly (UK, CAN)	sl**eigh**
eighteen	n**eigh**		v**ei**l
eighth	n**eigh**bor (USA)	r**eig**n	v**ei**n
eighty	n**eigh**borhood (USA)	r**ei**n	w**eigh**
f**ei**nt	n**eigh**borly (USA)	r**ein**deer	w**eigh**t

A12.4   Exceptions: "e" before "i" <u>not</u> after "c"

The following words do not follow the "i" before "e" except after "c" spelling rule. That is, the "ei" spelling pattern does not follow the letter "c".

The long "e" vowel sound is represented by the "ei" spelling pattern in the following words. It may be noted that several proper names, such as "Keith" and "Sheila", follow this spelling pattern.

| caff**ei**ne | cod**ei**ne | *either* | K**ei**th |

Leigh	*neither*	Reid	*sheik(h)*
leisure	O'Neil	seize	Sheila
Neil	protein	seizure	

Also, in the word "deity" a link letter "e" is pronounced with the long "e" vowel sound.

deity

The short "e" vowel sound is represented by the "ei" spelling pattern in the following words:

heifer	heiress	leisure
heir	heirloom	their

The long "i" vowel sound is represented by the "ei" and "eigh" spelling patterns in the following words. The letters "gh" are silent.

eider	feisty	kaleidoscope	sleight
eiderdown	geiger counter	*neither*	stein
either	height	seismic	
Fahrenheit	heist	seismograph	

The short "i" vowel sound is represented by the "ei" spelling pattern in the following words:

counterfeit	forfeit	surfeit	weird
foreign	sovereign	weir	

A12.5 Exceptions: "i" before "e" <u>after</u> "c"

The following words do not follow the "i" before "e" except after "c" spelling rule. The "ie" spelling pattern is found following the letter "c".

In the following words the "ie" spelling pattern represents the long "e" vowel sound following the letter "c":

currencies	policies	species
mercies	specie	

In the following word, the "ie" spelling pattern represents the short "i" vowel sound:

financier

In the following words, a link letter "i" is pronounced with the long "e" vowel sound:

fancier				glacier				omniscient

In the following words, a link letter "i" is pronounced with the long "i" vowel sound:

science			scientific			scientist			society

A12.6   Exceptions: "ci" pronounced "ch" or "sh"

In the following words the "ie" spelling pattern appears incidentally. The letters "ci" spelling represent the consonant "ch" and "sh" sounds. The letter "e" usually represents the schwa vowel sound.

ancient	deficient	prescience	sufficient
conscience	efficiency	proficient	
deficiency	efficient	sufficiency	

Part B: Spelling Long Vowel Sounds

B1 Long Vowel Spelling Patterns

B1.1 Introduction

As discussed in Part A, a long vowel sound names itself. There are six long vowel sounds including two long "u" vowel sounds:

- The long "**a**" vowel sound heard in "**a**gent", "c**a**ke", and "m**a**jor"
- The long "**e**" vowel sound heard in "m**e**", "**e**vil", and "s**ee**d"
- The long "**i**" vowel sound heard in "l**i**ke", "p**ie**", and "ch**i**ld"
- The long "**o**" vowel sound heard in "st**o**ne", "hell**o**", and "**o**ver"
- The long "**u**" vowel sound heard in "fl**u**", "tr**u**e", and "tr**u**th"
- The long "**u**" vowel sound heard in "**u**nit", "m**u**sic", and "f**u**ture"

The term "long vowel sound" is somewhat misleading. The long "a" vowel sound heard in "cake" is not a stretched-out version of the short "a" vowel sound heard in "cat". Rather, long vowel sounds require two mouth movements to produce.[19] The mouth opens wide to begin the sound and then glides closed to end the sound.

Long vowel sounds are also referred to as "free vowels" because they may be pronounced in "open syllables" that end with a vowel sound as heard in "day", "see", and "fly". There is a tendency in English speech to end syllables with our mouth closed.[20] Because long vowel sounds end with the mouth gliding towards closed, there is no need to bring a long vowel sound to an end with a consonant sound.

As a general rule, long vowel sounds are represented by two vowel letters. The function of the second vowel is to signal that the first is pronounced with a long vowel sound. While long vowel sounds are usually heard in open syllables, there are exceptions to this rule. The majority of long vowel sounds are represented by one of the following spelling patterns.

B1.2 Final Silent Letter "E"

As discussed in A11, a final silent letter "e" performs many functions in English spelling. The most important function is to indicate that a preceding vowel letter is pronounced with a long vowel sound. This spelling pattern follows the general rule that long vowel sounds are represented by two vowel letters.

A final silent letter "e" often signals a long vowel sound in a closed syllable. The long vowel sound is represented by a single vowel letter followed by a consonant and a final silent letter "e". In the word "mistake", for example, the final silent letter "e" signals that the preceding letter "a" is pronounced with the long "a" vowel sound. Because the "e" is silent, "mistake" ends with the hard "c/k" consonant sound in a closed syllable.

awake	complete	gratitude	mistake
awoke	confuse	lemonade	survive
centipede	decide	magazine	
compete	explode	memorize	

This spelling pattern is also found in single-syllable long vowel words.

age	eve	June	scene
bathe	face	like	tube
bike	fame	note	type
crime	fuse	prove	use
cube	hike	rope	wage
cute	hope	role	
dove	huge	rule	

Many single-syllable long vowel words are distinguished from similar looking short vowel words by a final silent letter "e".

can → cane	hop → hope	quit → quite
cap → cape	lob → lobe	rid → ride
cut → cute	man → mane	rob → robe
din → dine	mat → mate	sit → site
glad → glade	mop → mope	slop → slope
grip → gripe	pin → pine	snip → snipe
hat → hate	plan → plane	wag → wage

B1.3 Single Vowel Followed by a Consonant Onset

This spelling pattern is consistent with the doubling principle discussed in Part A. A single consonant between two vowel letters signals that the first vowel is pronounced with a long vowel sound. Two consonants between two vowel letters signals that the first vowel is pronounced with a short vowel sound.

Long vowel sounds are usually represented by two vowel letters. Often, as discussed below, the two letters form a vowel digraph as in the words "season" and "clue". Sometimes, however, the two vowel letters are separated by a consonant. In the word "lake", for example, a final silent letter "e" signals that the preceding vowel letter "a" is pronounced with the long "a" vowel sound. The letters "a" and "e" are separated by consonant letter "k".

Similarly, within words, the two vowels representing a long vowel sound may be separated by a consonant onset. The long vowel sound is heard in an open syllable. The word "bacon", for example, is pronounced "ba-con". The letter "a" is pronounced with the long "a" vowel sound in an open syllable. Following the onset "c", the letter "o" is still able to lengthen the sound of the preceding letter "a". This is a common spelling pattern as found in words such as "be-fore", "fi-nal", and "mo-tel".

While the onset separating the two vowel letters is usually a single consonant letter as in "ba-con", occasionally it is a consonant digraph such as the letters "th" in "bathing" ("ba-thing") or a consonant blend such as the letters "pr" in "apron" ("a-pron").

In contrast, short vowel sounds are most often represented by a single vowel letter and are heard in closed syllables that end with a consonant sound. The short vowel sound will usually be followed by two consonant letters, often double consonants. Two consonant letters function to protect the short vowel letter from the lengthening affect of the following vowel. The word "tennis", for example, is pronounced "ten-nis". The letter "e" is pronounced with the short "e" vowel sound in a closed syllable. The double "nn" protects the "e" from the lengthening affect of the following letter "i".

Compare the words "super" and "supper". In "super", the letter "u" is pronounced with a long "u" vowel sound in an open syllable: "su-per". The single letter "p" allows the "u" to be lengthened by the following letter "e". In "supper", on the other hand, the letter "u" is pronounced with a short "u" vowel sound in a closed syllable: "sup-per". The double "pp" protects the letter "u" from the lengthening effect of the following letter "e".

These spelling patterns work because, as discussed in Part A, it is a characteristic of English speech that syllables begin with a consonant sound. When there is only one consonant letter between vowels, as in "whi-ten" and "ta-king", the consonant usually attaches to the following syllable. This leaves the first vowel letter in an open syllable making it long. With two consonant letters between vowels, as in "han-dy" and "glad-den", one consonant is able to remain attached to the first syllable keeping the vowel short in a closed syllable. The second consonant is free to attach to the following vowel completing the syllable.

These spelling patterns are used to identify vowel sounds in many words. Compare the long "a" vowel sound in "waging" (pronounced "way-ging") to the short "a" vowel sound in "wagging" (pronounced "wag-ging"). Likewise, compare the long "i" vowel sound in "diner" (pronounced "die-ner") to the short "i" vowel sound in "dinner" (pronounced "din-ner").

Dictionaries sometimes show long vowel sounds in closed syllables when they could easily be pronounced in open syllables. For example, dictionaries divide the words "diner" and "later" into syllables as "din-er" and "lat-er". However, such words may easily be pronounced as "di-ner" and "la-ter" in keeping with the general rule. While the dictionary may reflect how many people pronounce such words, for spelling purposes it is helpful to pronounce long vowel sounds in open syllables whenever possible.

apron (**a**-pr**o**n)
bacon (b**a**-c**o**n)
basic (b**a**-s**i**c)
bathing (b**a**-th**i**ng)
before (b**e**-f**o**re)

diner (d**i**-n**e**r)
final (f**i**-n**a**l)
frozen (fr**o**-z**e**n)
later (l**a**-ter)
legal (l**e**-g**a**l)

motel (m**o**-t**e**l)
open (**o**-p**e**n)
super (s**u**-p**e**r)

<u>Exceptions to Above Spelling Pattern</u>

Long vowel sounds are occasionally heard in closed syllables followed by two consonants. "Danger" and "ranger", for example, are pronounced "dai**n**-**g**er" and "rai**n**-**g**er". The long "a" vowel sound is heard in a closed syllable. This is because the letters "ng" cannot form the onset of the second syllable.

In a number of words, such as "senior" and "union" (pronounced "see**n**-**y**ur" and "yuo**n**-**y**un"), a closed long vowel syllable is followed by a consonant "y" sound that is not clearly represented in the spelling of the words.

ancient (**an**-chent)
conv**e**nience (conv**en**-yence)
conv**e**nient (conv**en**-yent)
d**a**nger (d**an**-ger)
j**u**nior (j**un**-yur)
only (**on**-ly)

pec**u**liar (pec**ul**-yur)
r**a**nger (r**an**-ger)
s**e**nior (s**en**-yur)
T**u**esday (T**ues**-day)
union (**un**-yun)

B1.4 Vowel Digraphs

Long vowel sounds are usually represented by two vowel letters. Often, the two vowel letters sit side-by-side representing a single long vowel sound as in the first syllable of the word "s**ea**son". This is a vowel digraph, a string of two or more letters that join together to represent a single vowel sound. The second silent vowel letter signals that the first is pronounced with a long vowel sound. In the word "s**ea**son", for example, the letter "a" indicates that the preceding letter "e" is pronounced with the long "e" vowel sound.

Silent consonant letters sometimes function as vowels to help form vowel digraphs as in the words "s**ew**age", "ball**et**", and "s**igh**".

Unfortunately, the first vowel letter of a vowel digraph does not always represent the expected long vowel sound. In the word "h**ei**nous", for example, the letters "ei" represent the long "a" vowel sound, not the long "e" vowel sound. Likewise, in the word "cougar" the letters "ou" represent a long "u" vowel sound, not the long "o" vowel sound.

Within words, long vowel digraphs are usually found in open syllables that break following the long vowel sound as in "s**ea**-son".

Dictionaries sometimes show long vowel sounds in closed syllables when they could easily be pronounced in open syllables. For example, dictionaries divide the words "beauty" and "Easter" into syllables as "b**eau**t-y" and "**Ea**st-er". However, such words may easily be pronounced as "b**eau**-ty" and "**Ea**-ster" in keeping with the general rule. While the dictionary may reflect how many people pronounce such words, for spelling purposes it is helpful to pronounce long vowel sounds in open syllables whenever possible.

beauty (b**eau**-ty)	freedom (fr**ee**-dom)	reason (r**ea**-son)
cougar (c**ou**-gar)	heinous (h**ei**-nous)	routine (r**ou**-tine)
daily (d**ai**-ly)	neighbour (UK, CAN)	season (s**ea**-son)
Easter (**Ea**-ster)	(n**eigh**-bour)	sewage (s**ew**-age)

Many words end with a final long vowel digraph. Note that some words end with a final silent letter "e". It may also be noted that English words rarely end with a short vowel sound.

agr**ee**	ball**et**	ob**ey**	revu**e**
alth**ough**	chimn**ey**	obo**e**	shamp**oo**
arr**ow**	continu**e**	prairi**e**	tomorr**ow**
aw**ay**	hock**ey**	pursu**e**	

This spelling pattern is also found in single-syllable words.

b**ay**	cr**ew**	h**igh**	sn**ow**
bl**ew**	d**ay**	kn**ew**	su**e**
bl**ow**	do**e**	n**ew**	th**ey**
b**ow**	du**e**	s**ee**	ti**e**
b**uy**	f**ew**	sho**e**	to**e**
by**e**	gl**ow**	sh**ow**	t**oo**
ch**ew**	gr**ew**	s**igh**	vi**ew**
clu**e**	gr**ow**	sl**ow**	y**ou**

At the end of words, long vowel digraphs are also found in final closed syllables.

aftern**oo**n (after-n**oo**n)	asl**ee**p (a-sl**ee**p)
appl**ie**d (a-ppl**ie**d)	ballr**oo**m (ball-r**oo**m)

beneath (be-neath)
between (be-tween)
complain (com-plain)
conceit (con-ceit)
explain (ex-plain)
fifteen (fif-teen)
identified (i-dent-if-ied)

mushroom (mush-room)
pursuit (pur-suit)
recruit (re-cruit)
relief (re-lief)
remain (re-main)
succeed (suc-ceed)

In single-syllable words, long vowel digraphs are also found in closed single-syllable words.

aid	**eigh**t	gr**ea**t	r**eig**n
aim	f**ee**t	l**ie**n	r**oo**m
b**oa**t	f**eu**d	m**ai**d	s**ai**l
d**ee**p	f**ol**k	m**ea**t	s**ou**l
dr**ea**m	fr**ie**d	m**igh**t	s**ou**p
eat	fr**ui**t	m**oo**n	v**ei**n

<u>Exceptions to Above Spelling Pattern</u>

With words such as "b**ou**lder", "p**ou**ltry", and "sh**ou**lder" the long "o" vowel sound is pronounced in a closed syllable as in "b**ou**l-der", "p**ou**l-try", and "sh**ou**l-der". This is because the letters "ld" and "lt" cannot form the onset of the second syllable.

b**ou**lder (b**ou**l-der)   sh**ou**lder (sh**ou**l-der)
p**ou**ltry (p**ou**l-try)   s**ol**dier (s**ol**-dier)

B1.5 The Link Letter Spelling Pattern

With the link letter spelling pattern, one vowel sound is followed by a second vowel sound with a syllabic break or pause between the two vowel sounds. The first vowel is pronounced with a long vowel sound in an open syllable.

Examples of the link letter spelling pattern are found in the words "fl**u**id" and "court**e**ous". The word "fl**u**id" is pronounced "flu-id". The letter "u" is pronounced with a long "u" vowel sound in an open syllable. Often, the long vowel sound may form an open syllable by itself as with the long "e" vowel sound in "court**e**ous" (pronounced "court-**e**-ous").

The first vowel letter is long because it is pronounced in an open syllable. The second vowel letter, although pronounced, still functions to lengthen the sound of the first vowel. In "fl**u**id" the letter "u" is lengthened by the following letter "i". Likewise, in "court**e**ous" the letter "e" is lengthened by the following letter "o".

This is called a "link letter" spelling pattern because the first vowel letter often functions to link a root word to a suffix that begins with a vowel letter.

The "link letter" spelling pattern may be distinguished from vowel diphthongs because the two vowel sounds are divided by a syllabic break. With vowel diphthongs two vowel sounds are pronounced one following the other without a syllabic break as heard in the words "toy" and "loud". Vowel diphthongs are explored in sections D1 and D2.

bionic (bi-**o**nic)	doing (d**o**-**i**ng)	hyena (h**y**-**e**na)
cereal (cer-**e**-**a**l)	fluid (fl**u**-**i**d)	period (per-**i**-**o**d)
courteous (court-**e**-**ou**s)	fuel (f**u**-**e**l)	poet (p**o**-**e**t)
cruel (cr**u**-**e**l)	hideous (hid-**e**-**ou**s)	

B1.6 Single Final Vowel Letter

In final syllables, a long vowel sound may be represented by a single final vowel letter. The long vowel sound is heard, of course, in an open syllable. This spelling pattern is contrary to the general rule that long vowel sounds are represented by two vowel letters.

It may be noted that English words rarely end with a short vowel sound.

alib**i**	int**o**	potat**o**	volcan**o**
appl**y**	men**u**	spaghett**i**	
bab**y**	multipl**y**	tomat**o**	
happ**y**	ont**o**	ukulel**e**	

This spelling pattern is also found in single-syllable long vowel words.

b**e**	fl**y**	m**e**	s**o**
b**y**	gn**u**	n**o**	t**o**
cr**y**	g**o**	p**i**	tr**y**
d**o**	h**e**	sh**e**	w**e**
fl**u**	h**i**	sk**i**	wh**o**

B1.7 Single Vowel Followed by Two Final Consonants

Contrary to the doubling principle and contrary to the general rule that long vowel sounds are represented by two vowel letters, single-syllable long vowel words are often spelled with a single vowel followed by two final consonant letters as in "m**os**t", "hi**nd**", and "tro**ll**". Unfortunately, many single-syllable short vowel words also follow this spelling pattern.

bind	blind	bold	both

child	h**o**ld	m**o**st	r**o**ll
c**o**ld	k**i**nd	**o**ld	s**o**ld
c**o**mb	m**i**ld	p**i**nt	tr**u**th
g**o**ld	m**i**nd	p**o**st	w**i**ld

It may be noted that closed single-syllable long vowel words are rarely, if ever, spelled with a single vowel letter followed by a single pronounced final consonant. This spelling pattern is reserved for single-syllable short vowel words. Many single-syllable short vowel words such as "bed", "hug", and "men" are spelled with a single vowel letter followed by a single pronounced final consonant.

It may also be noted that very few polysyllabic words end with a closed long vowel syllable spelled with a single vowel letter. Only the following examples were found. On the other hand, this is a very common spelling pattern for final short vowel syllables.

alm**o**st	contr**o**l	patr**o**l	rem**i**nd
beh**i**nd	enr**o**l (Also enroll)	reb**i**nd	unk**i**nd

It is interesting to note that the doubling principle is applied when adding a suffix that begins with a vowel letter.

- contr**o**l → contro**ll**ed, contro**ll**ing
- enr**o**l (Also enroll) → enro**ll**ed, enro**ll**ing
- patr**o**l → patro**ll**ed, patro**ll**ing

B2 Spelling the Long "A" Vowel Sound

There are many spelling patterns for the long "a" vowel sound heard in "cake". They have been divided into major, minor, and rare spelling patterns.

B2.1 Major Spelling Patterns

There are four major spelling patterns for the long "a" vowel sound heard in "cake".

a) Final "-a_e"

The long "a" vowel sound heard in "cake" may be represented by the "-a_e" spelling pattern. It is found in:

- Closed final syllables ("de-bat<u>e</u>")
- Closed single-syllable words ("bak<u>e</u>")
- Closed syllables ("bas<u>e</u>-ment", "stat<u>e</u>-ment")

The final silent letter "e" signals that the preceding letter "a" is pronounced with a long vowel sound. Usually, only one consonant letter separates the letter "a" from the letter "e". Occasionally, a consonant digraph ("ba**th**e") or a consonant blend ("ha**st**e") may separate the two vowel letters.

In some words, the final silent letter "e" performs a second function. With words such as "place", the "e" signals that the adjacent letter "c" is pronounced with the soft "c/s" consonant sound. With words such as "change", the "e" signals that the adjacent letter "g" is pronounced with the soft "g" or "j" consonant sound. With words such as "chase", the "e" satisfies the convention that base words do not end with the letter "s". With words such as "cave", the "e" satisfies the convention that words do not end with the letter "v".

When the words "alternate", "associate", "certificate", "legitimate", "moderate", and "predicate" are being used as verbs, "-ate" is pronounced with the long "a" vowel sound. When these words are being used as nouns or adjectives, "-ate" is usually pronounced with the short "i" vowel sound. The word "legitimate" is pronounced with the schwa vowel sound when being used as an adjective.

ache	cave	female	legitimate (Verb)
age	*certificate* (verb)	flame	lemonade
ale	change	foretaste	made
alternate (verb)	changeless	frame	make
ape	changeling	frustrate	male
arrange	chase	gale	maple
arrangement	chaste	game	mate
associate (verb)	chasten	gate	mistake
ate	complicate	gave	*moderate* (verb)
awake	congratulate	gaze	name
bake	create	glade	operate
base	cultivate	grace	overate
baste	date	grade	page
bathe	debate	grange	palisade
became	demonstrate	grateful	parade
behave	disgrace	grave	paste
blade	disgraceful	haste	pavement
blame	distaste	hasten	persuade
blockade	distasteful	hate	phase
bracelet	educate	hesitate	phrase
brake	engage	hurricane	place
brave	engaged	imitate	plane
cage	escape	insane	plate
cake	estrange	interchange	*predicate* (verb)
calculate	exchange	interchangeable	race
came	face	invade	rage
cane	fade	lake	range
cape	fame	lane	rate
case	fate	late	rearrange

relate	separate	state	taste
replace	shake	statement	tasted
replacement	shame	strafe	trade
safe	shave	strange	translate
safety	skate	stranger	unable
sake	slave	strangest	vane
sale	snake	table	wage
salesman	space	take	wake
same	spade	tale	waste
save	stage	tame	wasteful
scale	stake	tape	wave

b) "a" Followed by a Consonant Onset

The long "a" vowel sound heard in "cake" may be represented by a single letter "a" followed by a consonant onset and a second vowel letter. It is found in:

- Open syllables ("ba-sic", "na-tion", "vol-ca-no")

The consonant onset separating the two vowel letters will consist of a single consonant letter ("ba-sic"), a consonant digraph ("ba-thing"), or a consonant blend ("A-pril").

Words such as "able" and "table" are pronounced "a-bull" and "ta-bull". The letters "-le" signal that a schwa vowel sound is pronounced before the consonant "l" sound. The preceding consonant letter attaches to the "-ull" sound to complete the final syllable. This leaves the letter "a" in an open, long sounding syllable. In contrast, words such as "startle" and "battle" are pronounced "star-tull" and "bat-tull". Having two consonants between vowel sounds allows one consonant to keep the letter "a" in a closed, short sounding syllable.

With words marked by an asterisk, such as "ancient" and "ranger", the long "a" vowel sound cannot be readily pronounced as an open syllable. With the word "hasten", the consonant digraph "st" represents the soft "c/s" consonant sound, and the letter "t" is silent.

able	association	behaviour (UK, CAN)	corporation
acreage	baby	bravery	crazy
Adin	bacon	cable	creative
agency	bagel	Canadian	danger*
agent	baker	classification	discrimination
alien	basic	complacency	education
ancient*	basin	complication	elevator
application	basis	congratulation	equation
April	bathing	conversation	erasure
apron	behavior (USA)		famous

fav*o*r (USA)	lat*er*	pap*e*r	reputat*io*n
fav*ou*r (UK, CAN)	laz*y*	pastr*y*	sacr*e*d
flav*o*r (USA)	legislat*io*n	pat*i*ence	scathing
flav*ou*r (UK, CAN)	mangy*	pat*i*ent	shak*e*n
generat*io*n	maj*o*r	persua*si*on	situat*io*n
grav*y*	matrix	plan*e*d	slav*e*ry
hal*o*	moderation	pollinat*io*n	stam*e*n
hast*e*n	multiplicat*io*n	populat*io*n	stat*io*n
hatr*e*d	named	potat*o*	table
hesitat*io*n	nat*io*n	pronunciation	taking
imaginat*io*n	nat*i*ve	qualificat*io*n	tasty
inflat*io*n	nat*u*re	quotation	tomat*o*
informat*io*n	nav*y*	races	transportat*io*n
lab*o*r (USA)	oasis	rad*ar*	vac*a*nt
lab*ou*r (UK, CAN)	occa*si*on	rad*io*	vacat*io*n
lad*ie*s	operat*io*n	ranger*	vagrant
lad*y*	operat*o*r	raz*o*r	volcan*o*
las*e*r	organizat*io*n	relat*io*n	

c) "ai"

The long "a" vowel sound heard in "cake" may be represented by the "ai" vowel digraph. It is found in:

- Open syllables ("d**ai**-ly", d**ai**-sy)
- Closed syllables ("**ai**l-ment", "com-pl**ai**n")
- Closed single-syllable words ("**ai**m")

English spelling does not favour ending words with the letter "i". For this reason, the "ai" spelling pattern is found within words as in "l**ai**d" and "procl**ai**m" and not as a word ending. As a word ending, the "i" becomes a "y", resulting in the "-ay" spelling pattern. Compare, for example, the words "p**ai**n" and "p**ay**".

With words such as "praise", "traipse", and "waive", the final silent letter "e" is not required to represent the long "a" vowel sound. Rather, it performs other functions. With the word "praise", for example, the final silent "e" is added because English spelling avoids having singular nouns and verbs end with the letter "s".

afraid	braise	daisy	faint
again	chain	detail	faith
ailment	claim	Elaine	gaiety
aim	complain	entertain	gain
available	contain	exclaim	grain
bail	container	explain	jail
bait	curtail	fail	laid
brain	daily	failure	maid

mail	praise	remain	trail
maim	prevail	sail	train
main	proclaim	sailor	traipse
mermaid	raid	slain	vain
paid	rail	Spain	waif
pail	railroad	stain	wail
pain	rain	straight	waist
paint	raise	tail	wait
plain	raisin	tailor	waive

d)   "-ay"

The long "a" vowel sound heard in "cake" may be represented by the "-ay" vowel digraph. It is found in:

- Open syllables ("p**ay**-ment", "holi-d**ay**")
- Open single-syllable words ("b**ay**")

The "-ay" spelling pattern is used as a word ending. For this reason, it is usually found in open syllables as in "p**ay**-ment" and "aw**ay**". Within closed syllables, the "y" often becomes an "i", resulting in the "ai" spelling pattern. Compare, for example, the words "p**ay**" and "p**ai**n". It is a convention of English spelling that words do not end with the letter "i".

always	gay	nay	spray
astray	gray	noonday	stay
away	hay	Norway	stayed
bay	hearsay	okay	stowaway
birthday	highway	pay	stray
causeway	holiday	payable	Sunday
clay	jay	payment	sway
crayon	Jayme	photoplay	Taylor
day	lay	play	Thursday
daybreak	layman	playing	today
daylight	mainstay	portray	tramway
decay	may	pray	tray
dismay	May	railway	Tuesday
driveway	mayhem	ray	way
flay	mayor	runway	wayfarer
Friday	*Monday*	Saturday	wayward
gangway	nay	say	Wednesday

B2.2 Minor Spelling Patterns

There are six minor spelling patterns for the long "a" vowel sound heard in "cake".

a) "aigh"

The long "a" vowel sound heard in "cake" may be represented by the "aigh" vowel digraph. The letters "igh" are silent. This is a variation on the "ai" spelling pattern. It is found in:

- Closed syllables ("str**aigh**t", "str**aigh**t-en")

The word "straight" is a closed single-syllable word. The other words listed below are derived from the word "straight". While this spelling pattern is found in only a small number of words, some of the words are frequently used.

| straight | straighter | straighten | straightjacket |

b) "ea"

The long "a" vowel sound heard in "cake" may be represented by the "ea" vowel digraph. It is found in:

- Closed syllables ("br**ea**k", "gr**ea**t-er")

While this spelling pattern is found in only a small number of words, the words are frequently used.

| break | breaking | greater | steak |
| breaker | great | greatest | Yeats |

c) "ei"

The long "a" vowel sound heard in "cake" may be represented by the "ei" vowel digraph. It is found in:

- Open syllables ("h**ei**-nous", "sur-v**ei**-llance")
- Closed syllables ("v**ei**n", "r**ei**n-deer")

English spelling does not favour ending words with the letter "i". For this reason, the "ei" spelling pattern is found within words as in "v**ei**n" and not as a word ending. As a word ending, the "i" becomes a "y", resulting in the "-ey" spelling pattern. Compare, for example, the words "r**ei**n" and "pr**ey**".

This is an application of the "i" before "e" except when sounded like "a" as in "neighbour" and "weigh" rule.

beige	heinous	reindeer	surveillance
chow mein	inveigle	seine	veil
feint	rein	*sheik* (Also sheikh)	vein

d) "eig" and "eigh"

The long "a" vowel sound heard in "cake" may be represented by the "eig" and "eigh" vowel digraphs. The letters "g" and "gh" are silent. It is found in:

- Open syllables ("w**eigh**", "**eigh**-teen")
- Closed single-syllable words ("**eigh**t", "w**eigh**t")

This is an application of the "i" before "e" except when sounded like "a" as in "neighbour" and "weigh" rule.

d**eig**n	fr**eigh**ter	n**eigh**borly (USA)	r**eig**n
eight	inv**eigh**	n**eigh**bour (UK, CAN)	sl**eigh**
eighteen	n**eigh**	n**eigh**bourhood (UK, CAN)	surv**ei**llance
eighth	n**eigh**bor (USA)	n**eigh**bourly (UK, CAN)	v**ei**n
eighty	n**eigh**borhood (USA)		w**eigh**
fr**eigh**t			w**eigh**t

e) "-et"

The long "a" vowel sound heard in "cake" may be represented by the "-et" vowel digraph. The letter "t" is silent. This spelling pattern is French in origin. It is found in:

- Open final syllables ("ball-**et**")

In French spelling a final consonant letter "t" is silent. Adding a final silent letter "e" causes the letter "t" to be pronounced as heard in "route" and "suite".

ber**et**	gourm**et**	bouqu**et**
buff**et**	sobriqu**et**	croch**et**
croqu**et**	ball**et**	ricoch**et**

f) "-ey"

The long "a" vowel sound heard in "cake" may be represented by the "-ey" vowel digraph. It is found in:

- Open syllables ("ob**ey**", "sur v**ey**-or")

The "-ey" spelling pattern is used as a word ending. For this reason, it is usually found in open syllables as in "th**ey**" and "surv**ey**". Within closed syllables, the "y" often becomes an "i", resulting in the "ei" spelling pattern. Compare, for example, the words "pr**ey**" and "r**ei**n". It is a convention of English spelling that words do not end with the letter "i".

As heard in "key" and "hockey", the "-ey" spelling pattern usually represents the long "e" vowel sound.

ab**ey**ance	disob**ey**	ob**ey**	surv**ey**
conv**ey**	gr**ey** (UK, CAN)	pr**ey**	surv**ey**or
conv**ey**ance	gr**ey**hound	purv**ey**	th**ey**
conv**ey**er	h**ey**	purv**ey**or	wh**ey**

B2.3 Rare Spelling Patterns

There are at least ten rare spelling patterns for the long "a" vowel sound heard in "cake".

a) "a"

The long "a" vowel sound heard in "cake" may be represented by the letter "a" as a single letter word.

While this is a rare spelling, it is a very common word. Grammatically speaking, the word "a" is one of two indefinite articles used in English as in "that is *a* cat". The other indefinite article is the word "an" as in "that is *an* old cat". The only definite article in English is the word "the" as in "that is *the* cat we adopted".

a

b) "ae"

The long "a" vowel sound heard in "cake" may be represented by the "ae" vowel digraph. It is found in:

- Open syllables ("G**ae**-lic", "sun-d**ae**")
- Compound words ("m**ae**l-strom")

G**ae**lic   m**ae**lstrom   sund**ae**

c) Linking "a-"

The long "a" vowel sound heard in "cake" may be represented by a linking letter "a-" followed by another vowel letter that is also pronounced. It is found in:

- Open syllables ("mo-sa-ic")

mos**a**ic

d) "ao"

The long "a" vowel sound heard in "cake" may be represented by the "ao" vowel digraph. It is found in:

- Closed single-syllable words. ("ga**o**l")

ga**o**l (UK)

e) "au"

The long "a" vowel sound heard in "cake" may be represented by the "au" vowel digraph. It is found in:

- Closed single-syllable words ("g**au**ge")

With the word "gauge", the final silent letter "e" indicates that the adjacent letter "g" is pronounced with the soft "g" consonant sound.

g**au**ge

f) "-é" and "-ée"

The long "a" vowel sound heard in "cake" may be represented by the letter "-é" and the vowel digraph "ée". These spelling patterns are French in origin. It is found in:

- Open syllables ("caf-**é**", "pr**é**-cis")

caf**é**	fianc**é**	pr**é**cis
expos**é**	fianc**ée**	souffl**é**

g) "-ee"

The long "a" vowel sound heard in "cake" may be represented by the "-ee" vowel digraph. This spelling pattern is French in origin. It is found in:

- Open final syllables ("mat-in-**ee**")

matin**ee**

h) "-e_e"

The long "a" vowel sound heard in "cake" may be represented by the "-e_e" spelling pattern. The final letter "e" is silent. This spelling pattern is French in origin. It is found in:

- Closed single-syllable words ("cr**e**p**e**", "su**e**d**e**")

The final silent letter "e" signals that the preceding letter "e" is pronounced with a long vowel sound. With the word "suede", the letter "u" represents the consonant "w" sound.

cr**ep**e   su**ed**e

i)   "eh"

The long "a" vowel sound heard in "cake" may be represented by the "eh" vowel digraph. The letter "h" is silent. The word "eh" may be the only instance of this spelling pattern.

eh

j)   "ez"

The long "a" vowel sound heard in "cake" may be represented by the "ez" vowel digraph. The letter "z" is silent. This spelling pattern is French in origin. It is found in:

- Open syllables ("rend-**ez**-vous")
- Open single-syllable words ("ch**ez**")

ch**ez**   rend**ez**vous   laiss**ez**-faire

B3   Spelling the Long "E" Vowel Sound

There are many spelling patterns for the long "e" vowel sound heard in "m**e**". They have been divided into major, minor, and rare spelling patterns.

B3.1 Major Spelling Patterns

There are ten major spelling patterns for the long "e" vowel sound heard in "m**e**".

a)   Final "-e_e"

The long "e" vowel sound heard in "me" may be represented by the "-e_e" spelling pattern. It is found in:

- Closed final syllables ("ath-l**et**e")
- Closed single-syllable words ("**ev**e")

The final silent letter "e" signals that the preceding letter "e" is pronounced with a long vowel sound. Usually, only one consonant letter separates the first letter "e" from the final letter "e". Occasionally, a consonant digraph or a consonant blend may separate the two vowel letters.

In some words, the final silent letter "e" performs a second function. With the word "Japanese", the "e" satisfies the convention that base words do not end with the letter "s". With the word "eve", the "e" satisfies the convention that words do not end with the letter "v". With the word "eve", the final silent letter "e" also helps to satisfy the "three letter rule".

athlete	eve	intervene	scheme
centipede	extreme	Japanese	serene
Chinese	gene	obsolete	stampede
compete	*here*	Pete	supreme
complete	impede	recede	theme
concrete	incomplete	scene	these

b) "e" Followed by a Consonant Onset

The long "e" vowel sound heard in "me" may be represented by a single letter "e" followed by a consonant onset and a second vowel letter. It is found in:

- Open syllables ("le-gal", "com-ple-tion")

The consonant onset separating the two vowel letters will consist of a single consonant letter ("le-**g**al"), a consonant digraph ("de-**sc**end"), or a consonant blend ("se-**cr**et").

Many words contain a long sounding letter "e" that results from adding the prefixes "pre-" and "re-" to base words. Only a few sample words are listed here.

With words marked by an asterisk, such as "convenience" and "convenient", the long "e" vowel sound cannot be readily pronounced as an open syllable.

arena	beside	*decision*	determine
became	between	*decisive*	Egypt
because	beyond	*declare*	elastic
become	centimeter (USA)	*decrease*	elect
before	centimetre (UK, CAN)	deduct	electric
began	completion	defeat	eleven
begin	convenience*	defence (UK, CAN)	emergency
behave	convenient*	defend	enormous
behavior (USA)	*decay*	defense (USA)	enough
behaviour (UK, CAN)	*deceit*	depart	equal
behind	*deceive*	depend	equation
belief	December	descend	equipment
belong	decent	descent	erase
beneath	decide	*detail*	Ethan
		detect	evade

even	meter	pretense (USA)	reproduction
evening	metre (UK, CAN)	prevent	research
event	obedience	prevention	resource
evil	obedient	previous	*review*
female	Peter	recent	scenery
frequent	prepare	recess	secret
genie	present	rehash	secretion
hero	preserve	relapse	senior*
illegal	pretend	remake	*series*
immediate	pretence (UK, CAN)	*repeat*	vehicle
legal		reproduce	*zebra* (USA)

c) "ea"

The long "e" vowel sound heard in "me" may be represented by the "ea" vowel digraph. It is found in:

- Open syllables ("cr**ea**-ture", "p**ea**-nut")
- Closed syllables ("be-n**ea**th")
- Open and closed single-syllable words ("t**ea**", "b**ea**st", "s**ea**t")

The "ea" spelling pattern is used both as a word ending as in "t**ea**" and within closed syllables as in "b**ea**k".

The letters "ea" also represent the short "e" vowel sound. There are pairs of long "e"/short "e" words that share the "ea" spelling pattern including "clean"/"cleanser", "deal"/"dealt", "heal"/"health", "heave"/"heavy", "leap"/"leapt", "mean"/"meant", and "please"/"pleasure". This is an example of morphemic spelling.

With words such as "breathe", "leave", "peace", and "please", the final silent letter "e" is not required to represent the long "e" vowel sound. Rather, it performs other functions. With the word "peace", for example, the final silent "e" indicates that the adjacent letter "c" is pronounced with the soft "c/s" consonant sound. The final silent letter "e" in the word "breathe" helps to distinguish it from the word "breath".

beach	cheat	eagle	grease
bead	clean	ear	heal
beak	cream	ease	heap
beam	creature	easel	*hear*
bean	deal	easily	heat
beast	decrease	east	increase
beat	defeat	Easter	lead (verb)
beaver	disease	eastern	leader
beneath	dream	easy	leaf
breathe	each	eat	league
cheap	eager	feast	lean

leap	peaceful	scream	stream
least	peach	sea	tea
Leata	peak	season	teach
leave	peal	seat	team
leave	peanut	sheaf	treat
meal	please	sneaky	weak
mean	preach	speak	weave
meat	reach	squeak	wheat
neat	read (present tense)	steal	wreath
pea	reason	stealing	
peace	repeat	steam	

d) "ee"

The long "e" vowel sound heard in "me" may be represented by the "ee" vowel digraph. It is found in:

- Open syllables ("fr**ee**-dom", "coff-**ee**")
- Closed final syllables ("a-sl**eep**")
- Open and closed single-syllable words ("fr**ee**", "b**eef**")

The "ee" spelling pattern is used both as a word ending as in "free" and within closed syllables as in "beef".

As with other vowel digraphs, the second letter "e" functions to lengthen the first letter "e".

agree	deep	geese	peel
absentee	degree	glee	queen
asleep	disagree	greed	reed
bee	eel	green	reef
beech	eighteen	greet	reel
beef	emcee	Halloween	reeve
been	employee	indeed	referee
beet	fee	keep	screen
between	feed	knee	see
bleed	feel	lee	seed
breeze	feet	Lee	seem
cheep	fifteen	leek	seen
cheese	flee	meet	seventeen
coffee	fourteen	need	sheep
committee	free	needle	sheet
creed	freed	nineteen	sixteen
creek	freedom	parakeet	skeet
creep	freeze	pee	sleep
deed	gee	peek	sleet

sneeze	steely	sweep	three
speech	steep	sweet	tree
speed	steeply	tee	wee
spree	steer	teepee	weed
squeeze	street	teeth	week
steel	succeed	thirteen	wheel

e) "ei"

The long "e" vowel sound heard in "me" may be represented by the "ei" vowel digraph. It is found in:

- Open syllables ("**ei**-ther", "s**ei**-zure")
- Closed final syllables ("pro-t**ei**n", "re-c**ei**pt")
- Closed single-syllable words ("N**ei**l")

English spelling does not favour ending words with the letter "i". For this reason, the "ei" spelling pattern is found within words as in "s**ei**ze" and "cod**ei**ne" and not as a word ending. As a word ending, the "i" becomes a "y", resulting in the "-ey" spelling pattern. Compare, for example, the words "c**ei**ling" and "hock**ey**".

Many of the following words are exceptions to the "i" before "e" except after "c" rule. In particular, with proper names such as "Neil" and "Sheila", the long "e" vowel sound is usually represented by the "ei" spelling pattern and not the "ie" spelling pattern. Words such as "ceiling" and "receipt" conform to the rule because the letters "ei" follow the letter "c".

caff**ei**ne	dec**ei**ve	*n**ei**ther* (USA)	R**ei**d
c**ei**ling	*ei**ther* (USA)	O'N**ei**l	s**ei**ze
cod**ei**ne	K**ei**th	perc**ei**ve	s**ei**zure
conc**ei**t	L**ei**gh	prot**ei**n	*sh**ei**k(h)*
conc**ei**ve	*l**ei**sure* (USA)	rec**ei**pt	Sh**ei**la
dec**ei**t	N**ei**l	rec**ei**ve	

f) "-ey"

The long "e" vowel sound heard in "me" may be represented by the "-ey" vowel digraph. It is found in:

- Open syllables ("k**ey**-hole", "hock-**ey**")
- Open single-syllable words ("k**ey**")

The "-ey" spelling pattern is used as a word ending. For this reason, it is usually found in open syllables as in "k**ey**hole" and "hon**ey**". Within closed syllables, the "y" often becomes an "i", resulting in the "ei" spelling pattern. Compare, for example, the words "hock**ey**" and "conc**ei**t". It is a convention of English spelling that words do not end with the letter "i".

abb**ey**	hock**ey**	k**ey**	pull**ey**
all**ey**	hon**ey**	k**ey**hole	troll**ey**
barl**ey**	jers**ey**	kidn**ey**	turk**ey**
chimn**ey**	Jers**ey**	mon**ey**	Turk**ey**
donk**ey**	jock**ey**	monk**ey**	vall**ey**
Guernsey	journ**ey**	parsl**ey**	

g)   "ie"

The long "e" vowel sound heard in "me" may be represented by the "ie" vowel digraph. It is found in:

- Open syllables ("med-**ie**-val", "mov-**ie**")
- Closed final syllables ("bel-**ie**f", "hurr-**ie**d")
- Closed single-syllable words. ("f**ie**ld")

The "ie" spelling pattern often results from adding a suffix that begins with the letter "e" such as "-ed", "-er", "-es", and "-est" to a base word that ends with a letter "y" following a consonant. The letter "y" is changed to an "i" before adding the suffix. For example, the word "baby" becomes "babies". Sometimes, this results in the letter "i" serving as a "link letter", as in "cop-**i**-er" and "happ-**i**-er", linking the root word to a suffix that begins with a vowel. The single letter "i" is pronounced as an open syllable.

The final open "-ie" spelling pattern is found in two-syllable words such as "birdie" and "hippie". It is often used to form diminutive words expressing smallness in size, endearment, and occasionally condescension. The final silent letter "e" signals that the preceding letter "i" is pronounced with a long vowel sound, albeit a long "e" and not a long "i" vowel sound. In single-syllable words, such as "die" and "tie", the final "-ie" spelling pattern represents the short "i" vowel sound.

This is an application of the "i" before "e" except after "c" rule.

With words such as "achieve" and "niece", the final silent letter "e" is not required to represent the long "e" vowel sound. Rather, it performs other functions. With the word "achieve", the final silent letter "e" satisfies the convention that words do not end with the letter "v". With the word "niece", the final silent "e" indicates that the adjacent letter "c" is pronounced with the soft "c/s" consonant sound.

accompan**ie**d	authorit**ie**s	bel**ie**f	bourgeois**ie**
accompan**ie**s	bab**ie**d	bel**ie**ve	br**ie**f
ach**ie**ve	bab**ie**s	birdie	browni**e**
ap**ie**ce	beani**e**	boog**ie**	bunn**ie**s
arm**ie**s	beaut**ie**s	boog**ie**-woog**ie**	bur**ie**d

bur**ies**	fi**e**nd	lad**ies**	rel**ie**f
cadd**ie**	fi**e**rce	lass**ie**	rel**ie**ve
calor**ie**	fluff**ier**	l**ie**n	repr**ie**ve
cand**ied**	fluff**iest**	livel**ier**	rever**ie**
cand**ies**	fort**ieth**	lonel**ier**	salar**ied**
carr**ier**	friendl**ier**	marr**ied**	salar**ies**
carr**ies**	friendl**iest**	marr**ies**	ser**ies**
ch**ie**f	fr**ie**ze	med**ie**val	sh**ie**ld
coll**ie**	gen**ie**	menager**ie**	shr**ie**k
compan**ies**	goal**ie**	merc**ies**	s**ie**ge
cook**ie**	gr**ie**f	mov**ie**	sort**ie**
cop**ied**	gr**ie**ve	necessar**ies**	spec**ie**
cop**ier**	happ**ier**	n**ie**ce	spec**ies**
cop**ies**	happ**iest**	part**ier**	stead**ies**
coter**ie**	heav**ier**	part**ies**	stor**ies**
countr**ies**	heav**iest**	p**ie**ce	stud**ied**
dog**ie** (calf)	hipp**ie**	pit**ied**	stud**ies**
dut**ies**	hol**ies**	prair**ie**	th**ie**f
eer**ie**	hurr**ied**	pr**ie**st	w**ie**ld
famil**ies**	hurr**ies**	pupp**ies**	worr**ied**
f**ie**ld	hyg**ie**ne	rab**ies**	y**ie**ld

h) Linking "e-"

The long "e" vowel sound heard in "me" may be represented by a linking letter "e-" followed by another vowel letter that is also pronounced. It is found in:

- Open syllables ("cr**e**-ate", "hid-**e**-ous")

Andr**e**a	d**e**ity	instantan**e**ous	simultan**e**ous
ar**e**a	erron**e**ous	lin**e**ar	spontan**e**ous
b**e**ing	ether**e**al	miscellan**e**ous	th**e**ater (USA)
cer**e**al	gall**e**on	miscr**e**ant	th**e**atre (UK, CAN)
cham**e**leon	hid**e**ous	Montr**e**al	th**e**atrical
court**e**ous	homogen**e**ous	mus**e**um	
cr**e**ate	id**e**a	nucl**e**ar	

i) Linking "i-"

The long "e" vowel sound heard in "me" may be represented by a linking letter "i-" followed by another vowel letter that is also pronounced. It is found in:

- Open syllables ("fur-**i**-ous", "me-d**i**-an")

aer**i**al	ammon**i**a	assoc**i**ation	bacter**i**a
al**i**en	appropr**i**ate	aud**i**ence	barr**i**er

Canadian	glacier	material	radio
carriage	gladiator	median	retaliate
carrier	glorious	medium	scorpion
champion	gradient	mysterious	secretarial
chariot	guardian	notorious	serial
clothier	happier	obedience	serious
cordial	idiot	obedient	studious
curious	immediate	obvious	superior
devious	Indian	omniscience	tedious
dubious	industrious	patriot	transient
experience	inferior	patriotism	trivial
exterior	ingredient	period	various
fancier	insignia	precarious	victorious
fluffier	interior	pronunciation	
furious	librarian	radiant	
genial	malaria	radiator	

j) Single Final "-y"

The long "e" vowel sound heard in "me" may be represented by a single final letter "-y". It is found in:

- Open final syllables ("berr-**y**", "lib-er-t**y**")

This spelling pattern is only found in words that have two or more syllables. With single-syllable words, such as "fly" and "try", a single final letter "y" is pronounced with the long "i" vowel sound.

In a few words, such as "baby" and "lady", the letter "y" lengthens the sound of the preceding vowel letter. However, this is not a reliable spelling pattern. A final "y" does not always lengthen the sound of the preceding vowel letter as heard in "city" and "pity".

abilit**y**	baker**y**	carr**y**	countr**y**
absolutel**y**	beaut**y**	centur**y**	crann**y**
activit**y**	berr**y**	ceremon**y**	craz**y**
agenc**y**	bod**y**	certainl**y**	customar**y**
alread**y**	boundar**y**	certaint**y**	dadd**y**
angr**y**	braver**y**	cherr**y**	dail**y**
anxiet**y**	briber**y**	cit**y**	dair**y**
an**y**	bunn**y**	classif**y**	deliver**y**
apolog**y**	bur**y**	cloud**y**	democrac**y**
arm**y**	bus**y**	colon**y**	dictionar**y**
bab**y**	Calgar**y**	communit**y**	difficult**y**
badl**y**	cand**y**	compan**y**	dirt**y**
bagg**y**	carefull**y**	cop**y**	discover**y**

duty	Harry	mostly	sassy
early	heavenly	motherly	satisfactory
easily	heavy	muddy	scary
easy	history	mystery	scenery
economy	hobby	naughty	seventy
efficiency	holy	navy	shiny
eighty	honesty	nearly	silly
elderly	hourly	necessary	simplicity
emergency	hungry	ninety	simply
empty	hurry	noisy	sincerely
enemy	immediately	nursery	sixty
energy	industry	only	skinny
envy	inquiry	opportunity	slavery
especially	Italy	ordinary	slowly
every	January	particularly	smelly
exactly	jealousy	party	sneaky
facility	jewellery (UK, CAN)	pastry	snowy
factory	jewelry (USA)	penalty	society
fairy	jolly	penny	softly
family	juicy	photography	sorry
February	laboratory	pity	spooky
fifty	lady	plenty	steady
finally	lately	policy	story
fluffy	lazy	pony	story
forty	liberty	possibly	study
foxy	library	poverty	stuffy
frequency	likely	pretty	suddenly
friendly	literary	property	sunny
funny	lonely	puppy	supply
fussy	lovely	qualify	swiftly
gaiety	loyalty	quality	sympathy
generally	lucky	quantity	tacky
geology	lumpy	quickly	thirsty
geography	machinery	quietly	thirty
Germany	mainly	rainy	tidy
ghostly	majority	ready	tiny
glory	many	really	treasury
granny	marry	remedy	trophy
grizzly	memory	responsibility	truly
grocery	mercy	rivalry	tummy
grungy	merry	robbery	twenty
guilty	misery	rocky	ugly
hairy	modesty	royalty	uncanny
handy	momentary	safety	unfortunately
happy	mommy	salary	unity
hardly		sandy	university

usual**y**	victor**y**	wind**y**
variet**y**	wav**y**	witt**y**
ver**y**	wealth**y**	worr**y**

B3.2 Minor Spelling Patterns

There are four minor spelling patterns for the long "e" vowel sound heard in "me".

a) Single Final "-e"

The long "e" vowel sound heard in "me" may be represented by a single final letter "-e". It is found in:

- Open final syllables ("rec-i-p**e**")
- Open single-syllable words ("sh**e**")

A single final letter "e" is only very rarely pronounced. This is because a single final letter "e" usually performs other functions. With words such as "be" and "she", which have only one vowel letter, the letter "e" must be pronounced as every word and syllable requires a vowel sound.

adob**e**	*coyote*	recip**e**	ukulel**e**
apostroph**e**	h**e**	sh**e**	w**e**
b**e**	m**e**	*the* (Stressed)	

b) "i" Followed by a Consonant Onset

The long "e" vowel sound heard in "me" may be represented by a single letter "i" followed by a consonant onset and a second vowel letter. It is found in:

- Open syllables ("k**i**-w**i**", "mo-squ**i**-t**o**")

The consonant onset separating the two vowel letters will consist of a single consonant letter ("ki-**w**i"), a consonant digraph, or a consonant blend ("li-**tr**e").

beautiful	liter (USA)	mosqu**i**to
k**i**wi	litre (UK, CAN)	

c) Final "-i"

The long "e" vowel sound heard in "me" may be represented by a single final letter "-i". It is found in:

- Open final syllables ("ki-w**i**")
- Open single-syllable words ("sk**i**")

English spelling does not favour words ending with the letter "i". All of the following words are foreign in origin or abbreviations of longer words.

Hawaii
kiwi
maxi (abbreviation of "maximum")
mini (abbreviation of "minimum")
ravioli
ski
spaghetti
taxi (abbreviation of "taxicab")

d) Final "-i_e"

The long "e" vowel sound heard in "me" may be represented by the "-i_e" spelling pattern. It is found in:

- Closed final syllables. ("sar-dine")

The final silent letter "e" signals that the preceding letter "i" is pronounced with a long vowel sound. Usually, only one consonant letter separates the letter "i" from the letter "e". This is an unexpected spelling pattern. Usually, the "-e_e" spelling pattern represents a long "e" vowel sound.

automobile
machine
magazine
police
prestige
ravine
routine
sardine

B3.3 Rare Spelling Patterns

There are at least eight rare spelling patterns for the long "e" vowel sound heard in "me".

a) "ae"

The long "e" vowel sound heard in "me" may be represented by the "ae" vowel digraph. It is found in:

- Open syllables ("Cae-sar", "al-gae")

aegis
aeon
Aesop
algae
alumnae
archaeology
(Also "archeology")
Caesar
encyclopaedia
(Also encyclopedia)
paean

b) "-ay"

The long "e" vowel sound heard in "me" may be represented by the "-ay" vowel digraph. It is found in:

- Open single-syllable words ("quay")

quay

c) "eo"

The long "e" vowel sound heard in "me" may be represented by the "eo" vowel digraph. It is found in:

- Open syllables ("p**eo**-ple")

The letters "eo" often appear incidentally. In words such as "pig**eo**n" and "gorg**eo**us", a silent letter "e" helps to represent the soft "g/j" consonant sound. In words such as "g**e**-**o**graphy" and "court**e**-**o**us" the letters "eo" form a link letter spelling pattern.

p**eo**ple   townsp**eo**ple

d) "i"

The long "e" vowel sound heard in "me" may be represented by the letter "i". It is found in:

- Open syllables ("concert**i**-na")
- Closed final syllables ("an-t**i**que")

ant**i**que   concert**i**na

e) "-is"

The long "e" vowel sound heard in "me" may be represented by the "-is" vowel digraph. This spelling pattern is French in origin. It is found in:

- Open final syllables ("chass-**is**", "de-br**is**")
- Closed final syllables ("verdi-gr**is**")

The letter "s" is silent in "chassis" and "debris" and is pronounced in "verdigris".

chass**is**   debr**is**   verdigr**is**

f) "-it"

The long "e" vowel sound heard in "me" may be represented by the "-it" vowel digraph. This spelling pattern is French in origin. The letter "t" is silent. It is found in:

- Open final syllables ("pet-**it**")

In French spelling a final consonant letter "t" is silent. Adding a final silent letter "e" causes the letter "t" to be pronounced as heard in "route" and "suite".

pet**it**

g)   "oe"

The long "e" vowel sound heard in "me" may be represented by the "oe" vowel digraph. It is found in:

- Open syllables ("a-m**oe**-ba", "Ph**oe**-nix")

Sometimes, the letters "oe" appear incidentally. In the word "po-et", for example, the letters "oe" form a link letter spelling pattern.

am**oe**ba	ph**oe**be	Ph**oe**nix
onomatop**oe**ia	Ph**oe**be	subp**oe**na

h)   Linking "y-"

The long "e" vowel sound heard in "me" may be represented by a linking letter "y-" followed by another vowel letter that is also pronounced. It is found in:

- Open syllables ("em-br**y**-o", "hal-**cy**-on")

em br**y** o   hal**cy**on

B4   Spelling the Long "I" Vowel Sound

There are many spelling patterns for the long "i" vowel sound heard in "like". They have been divided into major, minor, and rare spelling patterns.

It may be noted that English spelling does not favour words ending with the letter "i".

B4.1 Major Spelling Patterns

There are eight major spelling patterns for the long "i" vowel sound heard in "like".

a)   Final "-i_e"

The long "i" vowel sound heard in "like" may be represented by the "-i_e" spelling pattern. It is found in:

- Closed syllables. ("lik_e_-able", "de-cid_e_")
- Closed single-syllable words. ("lik_e_")

The final silent letter "e" signals that the preceding letter "i" is pronounced with a long vowel sound. Usually, only one consonant letter separates the letter "i" from the final letter "e". Occasionally, a consonant digraph ("lith<u>e</u>") or a consonant blend may separate the two vowel letters.

In some words, the final silent letter "e" performs a second function. With words that end with the "-ire" spelling pattern, such as "fire", the "e" signals that a schwa vowel sound is pronounced just before the consonant "r" sound as in "fi-ur". With words such as "price", the "e" signals that the adjacent letter "c" is pronounced with the soft "c/s" consonant sound. With words such as "oblige", the "e" signals that the adjacent letter "g" is pronounced with the soft "g" or "j" consonant sound. With words such as "guise", the "e" satisfies the convention that base words do not end with the letter "s". With words such as "arrive" and "organize", the "e" satisfies the convention that words do not end with the letters "v" or "z".

admire	empire	line	ride
advertise	energize	lithe	ripe
advice	entire	live (Adj.)	rise
advise	excite	memorize	sacrifice
alike	exercise	mice	satellite
alive	*fertile*	mile	shine
arise	file	mine	side
arrive	fine	*missile*	site
aside	finite	nice	size
awhile	fire	nine	slide
beside	five	nineteen	slime
bike	*fragile*	ninety	smile
bite	gibe	oblige	snipe
bribe	grime	organize	spine
civilize	gripe	pine	spite
combine	guide	pipe	stile
confine	guise	polite	strike
crime	hide	prescribe	stripe
decide	hike	price	surprise
decline	hire	pride	survive
describe	hive	prize	tide
desire	ice	provide	time
despise	ignite	realise (UK, CAN)	tine
despite	improvise	realize (USA, CAN)	tire (USA, CAN)
dine	inquire	recite	tribe
dire	inside	recognize	twice
dislike	invite	require	unite
dive	kite	respite	vice (UK, CAN)
divide	knife	retire	vine
divine	life	revive	vise (USA)
drive	like	rice	white

wid**e**	win**e**	wir**e**	writ**e**
wif**e**	wip**e**	wis**e**	

b) "i" Followed by a Consonant Onset

The long "i" vowel sound heard in "like" may be represented by a single letter "i" followed by a consonant onset and a second vowel letter. It is found in:

- Open syllables ("fi-n**a**l", "envi-r**o**nment", "ti-tle")

Words such as "idle" and "title" are pronounced "i-d**u**ll" and "ti-t**u**ll". The letters "-le" signal that a schwa vowel sound is pronounced before the consonant "l" sound. The preceding consonant letter attaches to the "-ull" sound to complete the final syllable. This leaves the letter "i" in an open, long sounding syllable. Conversely, words such as "little" and "middle" are pronounced "l**i**t-**t**ull" and "m**i**d-**d**le". In keeping with the doubling principle, having two consonants between vowel sounds allows one consonant to keep the letter "i" in a closed, short sounding syllable.

The consonant onset separating the two vowel letters will consist of a single consonant letter ("fi-**n**al"), a consonant digraph, or a consonant blend ("li-**br**ary").

Bibl**e**	ibis	license	rival
bicycle	idea	liken	shining
bilingual	ideal	mica	shiny
Chinese	idl**e**	*minute* (Time)	silence
decisive	idol	organization	silent
diner	inquiry	pilot	spicy
dining	iris	pirate	tidy
dinosaur	iron	private	tiger
environment	item	Regina	tiny
final	ivy	rifl**e**	titl**e**
Friday	librarian	ripen	unidentified
gigantic	library	rising	writing

c) "y" Followed by a Consonant Onset

The long "i" vowel sound heard in "like" may be represented by a single letter "y" followed by a consonant onset and a second vowel letter. This spelling pattern is Greek in origin. It is found in:

- Open syllables ("n**y**-l**o**n", "d**y**-n**a**m-ic")

The consonant onset separating the two vowel letters will consist of a single consonant letter ("ny-**l**on"), a consonant digraph ("psy-**ch**ology"), or a consonant blend ("hy-**dr**ant").

The word "cycle" is pronounced "cy-cull". The letters "-le" signal that a schwa vowel sound is pronounced before the consonant "l" sound. The preceding consonant letter attaches to the "-ull" sound to complete the final syllable.

It may be noted that the letter "y" represents the same vowel sound as the letter "i" in the same position. Compare the long "i" vowel sounds in "ti-**g**er" and "ty-**r**ant" and the short "i" vowel sounds in "chi**m**-**n**ey" and "cry**s**-**t**al".

bygone	dynamic	nylon	python
byway	hyacinth	phylum	stylish
cyanide	hybrid	psychologist	typhoon
cycle	hydrant	psychology	tyrant
cyclone	hydro	psychopath	
cypress	hyphen	pylon	

d)   "ie"

The long "i" vowel sound heard in "like" may be represented by the "ie" vowel digraph. It is found in:

- Open final syllables ("neck-tie", "magpie")
- Closed final syllables ("i-dent-i-fied")
- Open and closed single-syllable words. ("pie", "cried")

The "ie" spelling pattern is found in number of three letter words such as "lie", "pie", and "tie". While the final silent letter "e" is not strictly required to represent the long "i" sound, because long vowel sounds may be represented by a single final vowel letter, this spelling helps to satisfy the three letter rule for content words.

The "ie" spelling pattern often results from adding a suffix that begins with the letter "e", such as "-ed", "-er", "-es", and "-est", to a base word that ends with a letter "y" following a consonant. The "y" is changed to an "i" before adding the suffix. For example, the word "cry" becomes "cried".

With some words, such as "driest", the letter "i" serves as a "link letter" linking the root word to a suffix that begins with a vowel. The single letter "i" is pronounced in open syllables as in "dri-est".

This is an application of the "i" before "e" except after "c" rule.

applied	die	hog-tie	pie
applies	dried	identified	relied
cried	drier	identifies	relies
cries	dries	lie	replied
denied	flies	magpie	replies
denies	fried	necktie	satisfied

spied	tied	vie
tie	unidentified	

e) "igh"

The long "i" vowel sound heard in "like" may be represented by the "igh" vowel digraph. The letters "gh" are silent. This spelling pattern is Old German in origin. It is found in:

- Open single-syllable words ("h**igh**", "s**igh**")
- Closed single-syllable words that end with the letter "t" ("f**igh**t", "l**igh**t")
- Words derived from the above words ("h**igh**-ly", "l**igh**t-ning")

The "igh" spelling pattern is used both within words as in "n**igh**t" and as a word ending as in "s**igh**".

While this spelling pattern is found in only a limited number of words, some of the words are frequently used.

blight	high	might	sight
bright	highly	nigh	slight
delight	knight	night	thigh
fight	light	right	tight
flight	lighting	sigh	
fright	lightning	sighing	

f) Linking "i-"

The long "i" vowel sound heard in "like" may be represented by a linking "i-" followed by another vowel letter that is also pronounced. It is found in:

- Open syllables ("sci-ence", "var-**i**-ety")

The words "science", "scientific", "scientist", and "society" are exceptions to the "i" before "e" except after "c" rule.

anxiety	hiatus	psychiatrist	sobriety
appliance	hierarchy	quiet	societal
biology	Iowa	reliable	society
bionic	liar	riot	trial
driest	lion	science	variety
fiery	notoriety	scientific	violence
giant	pioneer	scientist	violent

g)   Single Final "-y"

The long "i" vowel sound heard in "like" may be represented by a single final letter "-y". In English spelling, the letter "y" is found at the end of words, not "i". It is found in:

- Open final syllables ("Jul-**y**")
- Open single-syllable words ("cr**y**")

This spelling pattern is most often found in single-syllable words such as "cr**y**" and "fl**y**". In longer words a single final letter "-y" is usually pronounced with the long "e" vowel sound as heard in "bab**y**" and "happ**y**". As listed below, there are exceptions to this rule including the words "appl**y**" and "repl**y**".

appl**y**	fr**y**	pl**y**	spr**y**
b**y**	gu**y**	pr**y**	sp**y**
cr**y**	Jul**y**	repl**y**	st**y**
def**y**	modif**y**	satisf**y**	tr**y**
den**y**	multipl**y**	sh**y**	wh**y**
dr**y**	m**y**	sk**y**	wr**y**
fl**y**	occup**y**	sl**y**	

h)   "i" Followed by Two Final Consonants

In single-syllable words the long "i" vowel sound heard in "like" may be represented by a single letter "i" followed by two consonant letters. It is found in:

- Closed single-syllable words ("chi<u>ld</u>", "mi<u>nd</u>")

This spelling pattern is contrary to the general rule that long vowel sounds are represented by two vowel letters. All of the following are closed single-syllable words.

bind	find	mild	sign
blind	grind	mind	wild
child	hind	ninth	wind (Verb)
climb	kind	pint	

This spelling pattern is seldom found in longer words except for those derived from single-syllable words. The word "align" is a rare exception.

<u>a</u>lign	child<u>ish</u>	grind<u>ing</u>	<u>re</u>mind
<u>be</u>hind	climb<u>ing</u>	kind<u>ly</u>	<u>re</u>sign
blind<u>ly</u>	<u>de</u>sign	mind<u>ful</u>	sign<u>ing</u>

It may be noted that derived words are often pronounced with the short "i" vowel sound when a suffix is added. This is an example of morphemic spelling.

children	kindred	signal	winded
hindrance	malignant	wilderness	

B4.2 Minor Spelling Patterns

There are five minor spelling patterns for the long "i" vowel sound heard in "like".

a) "ei"

The long "i" vowel sound heard in "like" may be represented by the "ei" vowel digraph. It is found in:

- Open syllables ("**ei**-derdown", "kal**ei**-doscope")
- Closed final syllables ("Fahren-h**ei**t")
- Closed single-syllable words ("h**ei**st", "st**ei**n")

English spelling does not favour ending words with the letter "i". For this reason, the "ei" spelling pattern is found within words as in "**ei**der" and "h**ei**st" and not as a word ending. As a word ending, the "i" may become a "y", resulting in the "-ey" spelling pattern. However, no sample words could be found for the long "i" vowel sound.

This spelling pattern is contrary to the "i" before "e" except after "c" rule.

eider	Fahrenh**ei**t	kal**ei**doscope	st**ei**n
eiderdown	H**ei**di	*n**ei**ther* (UK)	
*e**i**ther* (UK)	h**ei**st	s**ei**smic	

b) Single Final "-i"

The long "i" vowel sound heard in "like" may be represented by a single final letter "-i". It is found in:

- Open final syllables. ("al-i-b**i**")
- Open single-syllable words. ("h**i**")

This is not a common spelling pattern because English spelling does not favour words ending with the letter "i".

It may be noted that the letter "y" represents the same vowel sound as the letter "i" in the same position. Compare the long "i" vowel sound heard in "fung**i**" and "den**y**". A final long "i" vowel sound is usually spelled with the letter "-y" as heard in "cry" and "reply".

ali**bi**	fun**gi**	**I**	Rab**bi**
alum**ni**	**hi**	**pi**	

c) "-uy"

The long "i" vowel sound heard in "like" may be represented by the "-uy" vowel digraph. It is found in:

- Open syllables ("b**uy**-er")
- Open single-syllable words ("b**uy**", "g**uy**")

While this spelling pattern is found in only a limited number of words, some of the words are frequently used.

b**uy**	b**uy**er	g**uy**

d) Final "-y_e"

The long "i" vowel sound heard in "like" may be represented by the "-y_e" spelling pattern. It is found in:

- Closed final syllables. ("an-al-**yse**")
- Closed single-syllable words. ("st**yle**")

The final silent letter "e" signals that the preceding letter "y" is pronounced with a long vowel sound. Usually, only one consonant letter separates the letter "y" from the letter "e". Occasionally, a consonant digraph ("sc**y****the**") or a consonant blend may separate the two vowel letters.

It may be noted that the letter "y" represents the same vowel sound as the letter "i" in the same position. Compare the long "i" vowel sound heard in "t**i**me" and "t**y**pe".

anal**yse** (UK, CAN)	paral**yse** (UK, CAN)	sc**ythe**	t**yre** (UK)
anal**yze** (USA, CAN)	paral**yze** (USA, CAN)	st**yle**	
electrol**yte**	rh**yme**	th**yme**	
l**yre**		t**ype**	

e) "-ye"

The long "i" vowel sound heard in "like" may be represented by the "-ye" vowel digraph. It is found in:

- Open single-syllable words. ("b**ye**", "d**ye**")

While the final silent letter "e" is not strictly required to represent the long "i" sound, because long vowel sounds may be represented by a single final vowel letter, this spelling pattern helps to satisfy the three letter rule for content words.

b**ye**	**eye**	r**ye**
d**ye**	l**ye**	

B4.3 Rare Spelling Patterns

There are at least nine rare spelling patterns for the long "i" vowel sound heard in "like".

a) "ai" and "ais"

The long "i" vowel sound heard in "like" may be represented by vowel digraphs "ai" and "ais". The letter "s" is silent. It is found in:

- Open syllables ("Th**ai**-land", "Ha-w**ai**-ee", "Shang-h**ai**")
- Closed single-syllable words ("**ais**le")

aisle	*Hawaii*	*Shanghai*	*Thailand*

b) "ay"

The long "i" vowel sound heard in "like" may be represented by the "ay" vowel digraph. It is found in:

- Open syllables ("b**ay**-ou", "pap-**ay**-a")

b**ay**ou	c**ay**enne	pap**ay**a

c) "eigh"

The long "i" vowel sound heard in "like" may be represented by the "eigh" vowel digraph. The letters "gh" are silent. It is found in:

- Closed single-syllable words ("h**eigh**t", "sl**eigh**t")

This spelling pattern is contrary to the "i" before "e" except after "c" rule.

h**eigh**t	sl**eigh**t

d) "ey"

The long "i" vowel sound heard in "like" may be represented by the "ey" vowel digraph. It is found in:

- Open syllables ("g**ey**-ser")

g**ey**ser

e) "ia"

The long "i" vowel sound heard in "like" may be represented by the "ia" vowel digraph. It is found in:

- Open syllables ("d**ia**-mond")

d**ia**mond

f) "is"

The long "i" vowel sound heard in "like" may be represented by the "is" vowel digraph. The letter "s" is silent. It is found in:

- Open syllables ("**is**-land", "v**is**-count")
- Closed single-syllable words ("**is**l_e_")

island   **is**le   v**is**count

g) "oy"

The long "i" vowel sound heard in "like" may be represented by the "oy" vowel digraph. It is found in:

- Open syllables ("c**oy**-ote")

c**oy**ote

h) "ui"

The long "i" vowel sound heard in "like" appears to be represented by the vowel digraph "ui".

This spelling pattern is incidental. The silent letter "u" protects the hard "g" consonant sound from being softened by the following letter "i". The long "i" vowel sound is actually represented by the "-i_e" spelling pattern.

gui_d_e   gui_s_e

i) Linking "y-"

The long "i" vowel sound heard in "like" may be represented by a linking letter "y-" followed by another vowel letter that is also pronounced. It is found in:

- Open syllables ("h**y**-e-na", "l**y**-ing")

c**y**anide   h**y**ena   l**y**ing   R**y**an

B5   Spelling the Long "O" Vowel Sound

There are many spelling patterns for the long "o" vowel sound heard in "st**o**ne". They have been divided into major, minor, and rare spelling patterns.

B5.1 Major Spelling Patterns

There are six major spelling patterns for the long "o" vowel sound heard in "st**o**ne".

a)   Final "-o_e"

The long "o" vowel sound heard in "stone" may be represented by the "-o_e" spelling pattern. It is found in:

- Closed final syllables. ("com-p**o**s**e**", "ex-pl**o**d**e**")
- Closed single-syllable words. ("h**o**p**e**", "z**o**n**e**")

The final silent letter "e" signals that the preceding letter "o" is pronounced with a long vowel sound. Usually, only one consonant letter separates the letter "o" from the final letter "e". Occasionally, a consonant digraph ("clo**th**e") or a consonant blend may separate the two vowel letters.

The letter "r" often affects the quality of the preceding vowel sound. For some speakers, the vowel sound heard in words such as "chore" and "sore" falls somewhere between the long "o" vowel sound heard in "stone" and the short "o" vowel sound heard in "law".

In some words, the final silent letter "e" performs a second function. With words such as "force", the "e" signals that the adjacent letter "c" is pronounced with the soft "c/s" consonant sound. With words such as "enclose", the "e" satisfies the convention that base words do not end with the letter "s". With words such as "dove" and "doze", the "e" satisfies the convention that words do not end with the letters "v" or "z".

al**o**n**e**	ch**o**k**e**	c**o**d**e**	c**o**v**e**
aw**o**k**e**	*ch**o**r**e***	c**o**k**e**	dem**o**t**e**
b**o**n**e**	cl**o**s**e**	comp**o**s**e**	den**o**t**e**
br**o**k**e**	cl**o**th**e**	c**o**n**e**	dev**o**t**e**
*b**o**r**e***	cl**o**th**es**	c**o**p**e**	discl**o**s**e**

dove	lobe	remote	store
doze	lone	rode	stove
drove	mole	role	stroke
enclose	*more*	rope	suppose
envelope	nose	rose	tadpole
explode	note	rote	telephone
explore	ode	scope	those
expose	oppose	*score*	throne
exposé	*ore*	shore	token
force	owe	slope	tone
froze	phone	slope	vote
grove	poke	smoke	whole
home	pole	*snore*	woke
hope	port	sole	*wore*
hose	postpone	*sore*	wove
ignore	promote	spoke	wrote
impose	propose	stole	zone
joke	provoke	stone	

b) "o" Followed by a Consonant Onset

The long "o" vowel sound heard in "stone" may be represented by a single letter "o" followed by a consonant onset and a second vowel letter. It is found in:

- Open syllables ("fr**o**-z<u>e</u>n", "expl**o**-s<u>i</u>ve")

The consonant onset separating the two vowel letters will consist of a single consonant letter ("fro-**z**en"), a consonant digraph ("clo-**th**ing"), or a consonant blend ("pro-**gr**am").

Words such as "ogle" and "noble" are pronounced "**o**-**g**ull" and "n**o**-**b**ull". The letters "-le" signal that a schwa vowel sound is pronounced before the consonant "l" sound. The preceding consonant letter attaches to the "-ull" sound to complete the final syllable. This leaves the letter "o" in an open, long sounding syllable. Conversely, words such as "bottle" are pronounced "b**ot**-**t**ull". In keeping with the doubling principle, having two consonants between vowel sounds allows one consonant to keep the letter "o" in a closed, short sounding syllable.

With words marked by an asterisk, such as "only" and "soldier", the long "o" vowel sound cannot be readily pronounced as an open syllable.

ass**o**ciation	cerem**o**ny	expl**o**sive	h**o**tel
aut**o**mobile	cl**o**thing	fr**o**zen	l**o**cal
b**o**nus	c**o**zy	gr**o**cery	m**o**dem
b**o**ny	def**o**liate	h**o**ly	m**o**ment
br**o**ken	expl**o**sion	h**o**ping	m**o**tel

motion	okra	potential	proposal
motor	Olympic	process	protect
noble	omission	procession	provide
noted	omit	produce	robot
notice	only*	production	rogue
obedience	open	profession	social
obedient	*opinion*	professor	solar
obey	over	program (USA, CAN)	soldier*
obituary	Owen	programme (UK)	stolen
oboe	ozone	progress	total
ocean	photograph	project	trophy
October	polar	pronounce	
ogle	pony	pronunciation	
okay	potato		

There are very few words in which a single letter "o" represents the long "o" vowel sound in a final closed syllable. It is interesting to note that the doubling principle is applied when adding a suffix that begins with a vowel letter.

- control → controlled, controlling,
- enrol (Also enroll) → enrolled, enrolling
- patrol → patrolled, patrolling

c) "oa"

The long "o" vowel sound heard in "stone" may be represented by the "oa" vowel digraph. It is found in:

- Closed single-syllable words ("goal", roast)
- Words to which a suffix has been added ("roast-ing")

The "oa" spelling pattern is used within words and so is often found in closed single-syllable words such as "boat". It is not used to form word endings.

boast	float	load	roan
boasting	foal	loaf	roast
boat	foam	loan	roasting
coach	goal	loaves	soap
coaching	goalie	moat	throat
coal	goat	oak	toad
coast	groan	roach	toast
coat	hoax	road	toasted

d) "-ow"

The long "o" vowel sound heard in "stone" may be represented by the "-ow" vowel digraph. The letter "w" is silent. It is found in:

- Open syllables. ("**ow**-ner", "yell-**ow**")
- Closed final syllables. ("un-kn**ow**n")
- Open and closed single-syllable words ("sn**ow**", "gr**ow**n")

The "-ow" spelling pattern is used as a word ending. For this reason, it is usually found in open syllables as in "bl**ow**" and "wind**ow**". Within closed syllables, the "w" often becomes a "u" resulting in the "ou" spelling pattern. Compare, for example, the words "will**ow**" and "b**ou**lder". It is a convention of English spelling that words do not end with the letter "u".

The "ow" spelling pattern also represents the vowel diphthong sound heard in the words "cow" and "loud". Depending on the meaning with which they are used, the words "bow" and "row" are pronounced both ways.

arr**ow**	gl**ow**	narr**ow**	thr**ow**
bel**ow**	gr**ow**	**ow**n	thr**ow**n
bl**ow**	gr**ow**n	**ow**ner	tomorr**ow**
bl**ow**n	gr**ow**th	*r**ow***	t**ow**
borr**ow**	holl**ow**	shad**ow**	unkn**ow**n
*b**ow***	kn**ow**	sh**ow**	wid**ow**
b**ow**l	kn**ow**n	sl**ow**	will**ow**
bungal**ow**	l**ow**	sn**ow**	wind**ow**
fell**ow**	mead**ow**	s**ow**	yell**ow**
foll**ow**	m**ow**	swall**ow**	

e) Linking "o-"

The long "o" vowel sound heard in "stone" may be represented by a linking letter "o-" followed by another vowel letter that is also pronounced. It is found in:

- Open syllables ("g**o**-ing", "p**o**-em")

g**o**ing	k**o**ala	p**o**em	p**o**et

f) "o" Followed by Two Consonants

In single-syllable words, the long "o" vowel sound heard in "stone" may be represented by a single letter "o" followed by two or more consonant letters. It is found in:

- Closed single-syllable words ("j**o**lt", "tr**o**ll")

This spelling pattern is contrary to the general rule that long vowel sounds are represented by two vowel letters. The following are all closed single-syllable words.

With words that end with "-lk", as in "f<u>ol</u>k", the "l" is silent. With some speakers the "o(r)" spelling pattern, as in "fort" and "scorn", is pronounced somewhere between the long "o" sound heard in "stone" and the short "o" sound heard in "law".

bold	*forth*	most	*sort*
both	ghost	old	*sport*
cold	gold	post	*thorn*
colt	gross	roll	told
comb	hold	scold	troll
fold	host	*scorn*	volt
folk	jolt	*short*	
fort	molt (USA)	sold	

This spelling pattern is rarely found in longer words. The following are mostly derived from single-syllable words.

almost	holster	*report*	soldier
behold	postpone	revolt	*support*

B5.2 Minor Spelling Patterns

There are four minor spelling patterns for the long "a" vowel sound heard in "stone".

a)   Single Final "-o"

The long "o" vowel sound heard in "stone" may be represented by a single final letter "-o". It is found in:

- Open final syllables. ("hell-o")
- Open single-syllable words ("go")

ago	hello	portfolio	studio
also	hero	potato	Toronto
cameo	ho	radio	video
Chicago	Mexico	ratio	volcano
duo	mosquito	rodeo	zero
folio	no	scenario	
go	patio	so	
halo	Pluto	stereo	

b) "-oe"

The long "o" vowel sound heard in "stone" may be represented by the "-oe" vowel digraph. It is found in:

- Open final syllables ("o-b**oe**")
- Open single-syllable words ("t**oe**")

While the final silent letter "e" is not strictly required to represent the long "o" sound, because a long vowel sound may be represented by a single final vowel letter, this spelling pattern helps to satisfy the three letter rule for content words.

al**oe**s	h**oe**	r**oe**	t**oe**
d**oe**	J**oe**	r**oe**buck	t**oe**s
f**oe**	mistlet**oe**	thr**oe**s	w**oe**
g**oe**s	ob**oe**	tipt**oe**	w**oe**ful

c) "ou"

The long "o" vowel sound heard in "stone" may be represented by the "ou" vowel digraph. It is found in:

- Open syllables ("*b**ou**-quet*")
- Closed syllables that end with the letter "l" ("b**ou**l-der", "sh**ou**l-der")
- Closed single-syllable words ("f**ou**r", "f**ou**rth", "m**ou**ld")

English spelling does not favour ending words with the letter "u". For this reason, the "ou" spelling pattern is found within words as in "s**ou**l" and not as a word ending. As a word ending, the "u" becomes a "w", resulting in the "-ow" spelling pattern. Compare, for example, the words "b**ou**lder" and "will**ow**".

With words marked by an asterisk, such as "boulder" and "poultry", the long "o" vowel sound cannot be readily pronounced in an open syllable.

b**ou**lder*	*f**ou**rth*	p**ou**ltice*	s**ou**l
*b**ou**quet*	m**ou**ld	p**ou**ltry*	
*f**ou**r*	m**ou**lt (UK, CAN)	sh**ou**lder*	

d) "-ough"

The long "o" vowel sound heard in "stone" may be represented by the "-ough" vowel digraph. The letters "gh" are silent. It is found in:

- Open final syllables ("al-th**ough**", "fur-l**ough**")
- Open single-syllable words ("d**ough**", "th**ough**")

While this spelling pattern is found in only a limited number of words, some of the words are frequently used.

alth**ough**	d**ough**	thor**ough**
bor**ough**	fur**lough**	th**ough**

B5.3 Rare Spelling Patterns

There are at least ten rare spelling patterns for the long "o" vowel sound heard in "stone".

a)   "-aoh"

The long "o" vowel sound heard in "stone" may be represented by the "-aoh" vowel digraph. The letter "h" is silent. It is found in:

- Open syllables ("Phar-**aoh**")

Phar**aoh**

b)   "au"

The long "o" vowel sound heard in "stone" may be represented by the "au" vowel digraph. It is found in:

- Open syllables ("ch**au**-ffeur")
- Closed single-syllable words ("m**au**<u>ve</u>")

ch**au**ffeur	ch**au**vinism	m**au**ve

c)   "-eau"

The long "o" vowel sound heard in "stone" may be represented by the "-eau" vowel digraph. This spelling pattern is French in origin. It is found in:

- Open syllables ("bur**eau**")
- Open single-syllable words ("b**eau**")

b**eau**	bur**eau**	plat**eau**

d)   "eo"

The long "o" vowel sound heard in "stone" may be represented by the "eo" vowel digraph. It is found in:

- Open syllables ("y**eo**-man")

The letters "eo" often appear incidentally. In words such as "pi**ge**on" and "gor**ge**ous", a silent letter "e" helps to represent the soft "g/j" consonant sound. In words such as "**ge**-**o**graphy" and "court**e**-**o**us", the letters "eo" form a link letter spelling pattern.

y**eo**man   y**eo**manry

e)   "eou"

The long "o" vowel sound heard in "stone" may be represented by the "eou" vowel digraph. It is found in:

- Closed single-syllable words ("S**eou**l")

S**eo**ul

f)   "-ew"

The long "o" vowel sound heard in "stone" may be represented by the "-ew" vowel digraph. The letter "w" is silent. It is found in:

- Open syllables ("s**ew**", "s**ew**-ing")

s**ew**   s**ew**ing

g)   "oh"

The long "o" vowel sound heard in "stone" may be represented by the "oh" vowel digraph. The letter "h" is silent. It is found in:

- Open single-syllable words ("**oh**")
- Closed single-syllable words ("**oh**m")

d**oh** (musical note "C")   **oh**m
oh   s**oh** (musical note "G")

h)   "ol"

The long "o" vowel sound heard in "stone" may be represented by the "ol" vowel digraph. The letter "l" is silent. It is found in:

- Closed single-syllable words. ("f**ol**k")

f**ol**k   m**ol**t (USA)   y**ol**k

i) "oo"

The long "o" vowel sound heard in "stone" may be represented by the "oo" vowel digraph. It is found in:

- Open syllables ("R**oo**-se-velt")
- Closed single-syllable words ("br**oo**ch")

br**oo**ch   R**oo**sevelt

j) "-ot"

The long "o" vowel sound heard in "stone" may be represented by the "-ot" vowel digraph. The letter "t" is silent. This spelling pattern is French in origin. It is found in:

- Open syllables ("de-p**ot**")

In French spelling a final consonant letter "t" is silent. Adding a final silent letter "e" causes the letter "t" to be pronounced as heard in "route" and "suite".

dep**ot**

B6 Spelling the Long "U" Vowel Sound Heard in "True"

As heard in the words "true" and "music", there are two different pronunciations of the long "u" vowel sound. Both "true" and "music" are pronounced with a long "u" vowel sound. However, in the word "music" a consonant "y" sound, as heard in "yes", is pronounced before the long "u" vowel sound. A consonant "y" sound is not pronounced in the word "true". Only spelling patterns used to represent the long "u" sound heard in "true" are discussed in this section.

There are many spelling patterns for the long "u" vowel sound heard in "true". They have been divided into major, minor, and rare spelling patterns.

B6.1 Major Spelling Patterns

There are seven major spelling patterns for the long "u" vowel sound heard in "true".

a) Final "-u_e"

The long "u" vowel sound heard in "true" may be represented by the "-u_e" spelling pattern. It is found in:

- Closed final syllables ("in-cl**u**d**e**")
- Closed single-syllable words ("fl**u**t**e**", "r**u**l**e**")

The final silent letter "e" signals that the preceding letter "u" is pronounced with a long vowel sound. Usually, only one consonant letter separates the letter "u" from the letter "e". Occasionally, a consonant digraph or a consonant blend may separate the two vowel letters.

In some words, the final silent letter "e" performs a second function. With words such as "produce", the "e" signals that the adjacent letter "c" is pronounced with the soft "c/s" consonant sound.

absolute	*dupe*	*minute*	rude
assume	exclude	plume	rule
astute	flute	*produce*	spruce
brute	gratitude	protrude	*statute*
conclude	include	prude	*tube*
costume	introduce	*prune*	*tune*
crude	intrude	*reduce*	
deduce	June	reproduce	
dilute	lute	resume	

b) "u" Followed by a Consonant Onset

The long "u" vowel sound heard in "true" may be represented by a single letter "u" followed by a consonant onset and a second vowel letter. It is found in:

- Open syllables ("**u**-n**i**t", "cr**u**-s**a**de", "opport**u**-n**i**ty")

The consonant onset separating the two vowel letters will consist of a single consonant letter ("su-**p**er"), a consonant digraph, or a consonant blend ("nu-**cl**ear").

With words marked by an asterisk, such as "junior", the long "u" vowel sound cannot be readily pronounced as an open syllable.

brutish	humor (USA)	numerous	*stupid*
consumer	humour (UK, CAN)	opportunity	super
crucial	inclusive	plumage	*truly*
crusade	intrusion	Pluto	*tulip*
duty	July	pollution	tuna
educate	junior*	ruby	tuning
education	Jupiter	rumor	*tunic*
flu	lubricate	solution	unit
hula	nuclear	*student*	

c) "-ew"

The long "u" vowel sound heard in "true" may be represented by the "-ew" vowel digraph. The letter "w" is silent. It is found in:

- Open syllables ("s**ew**-age", "st**ew**-ardess")
- Open and closed single-syllable words ("n**ew**", "shr**ew**d")

The "-ew" spelling pattern is used as a word ending. For this reason, it is usually found in open syllables as in "st**ew**-ard" and "curf**ew**". Within closed syllables, the "w" often becomes a "u" resulting in the "eu" spelling pattern. Compare, for example, the words "neph**ew**" and "n**eu**tral". It is a convention of English spelling that words do not end with the letter "u".

bl**ew**	h**ew**	l**ew**d	shr**ew**d
ch**ew**	h**ew**n	*mild**ew***	*st**ew***
cr**ew**	J**ew**	neph**ew**	st**ew**ard
curf**ew**	j**ew**el	*n**ew***	st**ew**ardess
d**ew**	j**ew**ellery (UK, CAN)	n**ew**s	str**ew**n
dr**ew**	*j**ew**elry* (USA)	n**ew**t	thr**ew**
fl**ew**	*kn**ew***	scr**ew**	y**ew**
gr**ew**		s**ew**age	

d) "oo"

The long "u" vowel sound heard in "true" may be represented by the "oo" vowel digraph. It is found in:

- Open and closed final syllables. ("sham-p**oo**", "ma-r**oo**n")
- Open and closed single-syllable words. ("z**oo**", "f**oo**d")

The "oo" spelling pattern is used both within words as in "b**oo**t" and as a word ending as in "t**oo**".

aftern**oo**n	firepr**oo**f	**oo**ze	s**oo**n
ball**oo**n	f**oo**d	pap**oo**se	sp**oo**ky
ballr**oo**m	f**oo**l	p**oo**l	sp**oo**n
bl**oo**m	gl**oo**m	pr**oo**f	st**oo**l
b**oo**	g**oo**se	racc**oo**n	tab**oo**
b**oo**m	h**oo**ves	redw**oo**d	tatt**oo**
b**oo**t	l**oo**p	r**oo**f	toadst**oo**l
b**oo**th	l**oo**se	r**oo**m	t**oo**
br**oo**d	l**oo**sen	r**oo**st	t**oo**l
br**oo**m	mar**oo**n	r**oo**ster	t**oo**th
ch**oo**se	m**oo**d	r**oo**t	w**oo**
c**oo**	m**oo**n	sch**oo**l	z**oo**
c**oo**l	m**oo**se	shamp**oo**	z**oo**m
cuck**oo**	mushr**oo**m	sh**oo**t	
d**oo**m	n**oo**n	sm**oo**th	

e) "ou"

The long "u" vowel sound heard in "true" may be represented by the "ou" vowel digraph. This spelling pattern is French in origin. It is found in:

- Open syllables ("c**ou**-gar", "r**ou**-tine", "car-i-b**ou**")
- Open and closed single-syllable words ("y**ou**", "s**ou**p")

The words "bayou", "caribou", and "you" are exceptions to the convention that words do not end with the letter "u". The words "bayou" and "caribou" are both French in origin.

In French spelling a final consonant letter "t" is silent. Adding a final silent letter "e" causes the letter "t" to be pronounced as heard in "route" and "suite".

bay**ou**	c**ou**sc**ou**s	r**ou**ge	w**ou**nd (Injury)
*b**ou**quet*	cr**ou**p	r**ou**te	y**ou**
carib**ou**	gh**ou**l	r**ou**tine	y**ou**th
c**ou**gar	gr**ou**p	s**ou**p	
c**ou**pon	Khart**ou**m	t**ou**can	

f) "-ue"

The long "u" vowel sound heard in "true" may be represented by the "-ue" vowel digraph. It is found in:

- Open final syllables ("av-en-**ue**")
- Open single-syllable words ("gl**ue**")
- Closed syllables very rarely ("T**ue**s-day")

The "-ue" spelling pattern is used as a word ending. For this reason, it is usually found in open syllables as in "d**ue**" and "purs**ue**". Within closed syllables, the "e" often becomes an "i" resulting in the "ei" spelling pattern. Compare, for example, the words "gl**ue**" and "j**ui**ce". It is a convention of English spelling that words do not end with the letter "i".

A final silent letter "e" is not required to help represent the long "u" sound because a long vowel sound may be represented by a single final vowel letter. However, it is a convention of English spelling that words do not end with the letter "u". As well, the final silent letter "e" helps to satisfy the three letter rule in words such as "due" and "sue".

With the word "Tuesday", the long "u" vowel sound cannot be readily pronounced as an open syllable.

aven**ue**	bl**ue**	cl**ue**	constr**ue**

due	pursue	subdue	true
flue	residue	sue	*Tuesday**
glue	*revenue*	Sue	untrue
issue	statue	tissue	virtue

g) Linking "u-"

The long "u" vowel sound heard in "true" may be represented by a linking letter "u-" followed by another vowel letter that is also pronounced. It is found in:

- Open syllables ("cr**u**-el", "sit-**u**-ation")

cruel	gradual	influential	situation
February	individual	punctual	truant
fluent	influence	ruin	

B6.2 Minor Spelling Patterns

There are five minor spelling patterns for the long "u" vowel sound heard in "tr**ue**".

a) "eu"

The long "u" vowel sound heard in "true" may be represented by the "eu" vowel digraph. It is found in:

- Open syllables ("rh**eu**-matism")
- Closed single-syllable words ("sl**eu**th")

English spelling does not favour ending words with the letter "u". For this reason, the "eu" spelling pattern is found within words as in "sl**eu**th" and not as a word ending. As a word ending, the "u" becomes a "w", resulting in the "-ew" spelling pattern. Compare, for example, the words "n**eu**tral" and "neph**ew**".

maneuver (USA)	*neutron*	rheumatism
neutral	*pneumonia*	sleuth

b) "o" Followed by a Consonant Onset

The long "u" vowel sound heard in "true" may be represented by a single letter "o" followed by a consonant onset and a second vowel letter. It is found in:

- Open syllables ("l**o**-s**e**r", "appr**o**-v**a**l")

The consonant onset separating the two vowel letters will consist of a single consonant letter ("mo-**v**ie"), a consonant digraph, or a consonant blend.

altogether   loser   *today*
appr**o**val m**o**vie

c) Single Final "-o"

The long "u" vowel sound heard in "true" may be represented by a single final letter "-o". It is found in:

- Open final syllables ("in-t**o**")
- Open single-syllable words ("wh**o**")

While this spelling pattern is found in only a small number of words, all of the words are frequently used.

d**o**   ont**o**   wh**o**
int**o**   t**o**

d) Final "-o_e"

The long "u" vowel sound heard in "true" may be represented by the "-o_e" spelling pattern. It is found in:

- Closed final syllables. ("a-ppr**ove**")
- Closed single-syllable words. ("m**ove**", "pr**ove**")

The final silent letter "e" signals that the preceding letter "o" is pronounced with a long vowel sound. Usually, only one consonant letter separates the letter "o" from the letter "e". Occasionally, a consonant digraph or a consonant blend may separate the two vowel letters.

In some words, the final silent letter "e" performs a second function. With words such as "lose", the "e" satisfies the convention that base words do not end with the letter "s". With words such as "prove", the "e" satisfies the convention that words do not end with the letter "v".

appr**ove**   lo**se**   pr**ove**
disappr**ove**   m**ove**   wh**ose**

e) "ui"

The long "u" vowel sound heard in "true" may be represented by the "ui" vowel digraph. It is found in:

- Open syllables ("n**ui**-sance")
- Closed final syllables ("re-cr**uit**")
- Closed single-syllable words ("s**uit**")

English spelling does not favour ending words with the letter "i". For this reason, the "ui" spelling pattern is found within words as in "fr**ui**t" and "recr**ui**t" and not as a word ending. As a word ending, the "i" becomes an "e", resulting in the "-ue" spelling pattern. Compare, for example, the words "j**ui**ce" and "gl**ue**".

br**ui**se	j**ui**ce	recr**ui**t	s**ui**tor
cr**ui**se	j**ui**cy	sl**ui**ce	uns**ui**table
cr**ui**ser	laws**ui**t	s**ui**t	
fr**ui**t	*n**ui**sance*	s**ui**table	
fr**ui**tful	*purs**ui**t*	s**ui**tcase	

B6.3 Rare Spelling Patterns

There are at least ten rare spelling patterns for the long "u" vowel sound heard in "tr**ue**".

a) "-ieu"

The long "u" vowel sound heard in "true" may be represented by the "ieu" vowel digraph. This spelling pattern is French in origin. It is found in:

- Open syllables ("l**ieu**-tenant")
- Open single-syllable words ("ad**ieu**","l**ieu**")

This is an application of the "i" before "e" except after "c" rule.

In the United States the word "lieutenant" is pronounced "loo–tenunt" with the long "u" vowel sound heard in true. In Britain and Canada the word "lieutenant" is pronounced "lef-tenunt", with a short "e" vowel sound followed by a consonant "f" sound.

*ad**ieu***   *l**ieu**tenant*   **l**ieu**

b) Linking "o-"

The long "u" vowel sound heard in "true" may be represented by a linking letter "o-" followed by another vowel letter that is also pronounced. It is found in:

- Open syllables ("d**o**-ing")

d**o**ing

c) "o" Followed by One or Two Final Consonants

In single-syllable words the long "u" vowel sound heard in "true" may be represented by a single letter "o" followed by one or two consonant letters. It is found in:

- Closed single-syllable words ("t**o**mb", "wh**o**m")

This spelling pattern is contrary to the general rule that long vowel sounds are represented by two vowel letters. All of the following are closed single-syllable words.

The word "whom" is unique. Long vowel sounds represented by a single vowel letter in single-syllable words are usually followed by two consonant letters as in "mind" and "bold".

t**o**mb   wh**o**m   w**o**mb

d) "-oe"

The long "u" vowel sound heard in "true" may be represented by the "-oe" vowel digraph. It is found in:

- Open final syllables ("can-**oe**")
- Open single-syllable words ("sh**oe**")

The final silent letter "e" helps to distinguish words that end with the long "u" sound from words that end with the long "o" vowel sound as in "hello" and "Toronto".

can**oe**   sh**oe**

e) "oeu"

The long "u" vowel sound heard in "true" may be represented by the "oeu" vowel digraph. This spelling pattern is French in origin. It is found in:

- Open syllables ("man**oeu**-vre ")

man**oeu**vre (UK, CAN)

f) "ough"

The long "u" vowel sound heard in "true" may be represented by the "ough" vowel digraph. The letters "gh" are silent. It is found in:

- Open single-syllable words ("thr**ough**")
- Compound words ("thr**ough**-out")

thr**ough**   thr**ough**out

g) "-oup"

The long "u" vowel sound heard in "true" may be represented by the "oup" vowel digraph. The letter "p" is silent. It is found in:

- Open single-syllable words ("c**oup**")

c**oup**

h) "u" Followed by Two Final Consonants

In single-syllable words, the long "u" vowel sound heard in "true" may be represented by a single letter "u" followed by two consonant letters. It is found in:

- Closed single-syllable words ("tr**u**th")

tr**u**th

i) Single Final "-u"

The long "u" vowel sound heard in "true" may be represented by a single final letter "-u". It is found in:

- Open single-syllable words. ("fl**u**", "gn**u**")

This spelling pattern is contrary to the convention that words do not end with the letter "u".

fl**u**   *gn**u***

j) "-wo"

The long "u" vowel sound heard in "true" may be represented by the "-wo" vowel digraph. The letter "w" is silent. It is found in:

- Open single-syllable words ("t**wo**")

This is an example of morphemic spelling. The letter "w" is pronounced in related words such as "twenty", "twentieth", "twelve", twelfth", and "twice".

t**wo**

B7 Spelling the Long "U" Vowel Sound Heard in "Music"

As heard in the words "true" and "music", there are two different pronunciations of the long "u" vowel sound. Both "true" and "music" are pronounced with a long "u" vowel sound. However, in the word "music" a consonant "y" sound, as heard in "yes", is pronounced before the long "u" vowel sound. A consonant "y" sound is not pronounced in the word "true". Only spelling patterns used to represent the long "u" sound heard in "music" are discussed in this section.

There are many spelling patterns for the long "u" vowel sound heard in "m**u**sic". They have been divided into major, minor, and rare spelling patterns.

B7.1 Major Spelling Patterns

There are three major spelling patterns for the long "u" vowel sound heard in "music".

a) Final "-u_e"

The long "u" vowel sound heard in "music" may be represented by the "-u_e" spelling pattern. It is found in:

- Closed final syllables ("con-fu**se**")
- Closed single-syllable words ("cut**e**", "hug**e**")

The final silent letter "e" signals that the preceding letter "u" is pronounced with a long vowel sound. Usually, only one consonant letter separates the letter "u" from the letter "e". Occasionally, a consonant digraph or a consonant blend may separate the two vowel letters.

In some words, the final silent letter "e" performs a second function. With words such as "reduce", the "e" signals that the adjacent letter "c" is pronounced with the soft "c/s" consonant sound. With words such as "huge", the "e" signals that the adjacent letter "g" is pronounced with the soft "g" or "j" consonant sound. With words such as "amuse", the "e" satisfies the convention that base words do not end with the letter "s". With the word "use", the final silent letter "e" also helps to satisfy the "three letter rule".

abuse	*costume*	execute	refuge
accuse	cube	fume	refuse
acute	cute	huge	*statute*
amuse	*deduce*	*minute* (Small)	tribute
astute	deluge	mule	*tube*
compute	dispute	*produce*	tune
confuse	*dupe*	rebuke	use
contribute	excuse	*reduce*	volume

b) "u" Followed by a Consonant Onset

The long "u" vowel sound heard in "music" may be represented by a single letter "u" followed by a consonant onset and a second vowel letter. It is found in:

- Open syllables ("fu-ture", "cal-cu-late")

The consonant onset separating the two vowel letters will consist of a single consonant letter ("hu-man"), a consonant digraph, or a consonant blend.

The word "bugle" is pronounced "bu-gull". The letters "-le" signal that a schwa vowel sound is pronounced before the consonant "l" sound. The preceding consonant letter attaches to the "-ull" sound to complete the final syllable. This leaves the letter "u" in an open, long sounding syllable. Conversely, words such as "struggle" are pronounced "strug-gull". In keeping with the doubling principle, having two consonants between vowel sounds allows one consonant to keep the letter "u" in a closed, short sounding syllable.

With words marked by an asterisk, such as "peculiar" and "union", the long "u" vowel sound cannot be readily pronounced as an open syllable.

ambulance	formula	particular	union*
bugle	funeral	peculiar*	unit
calculate	future	population	unite
community	human	pupil	unity
computer	humid	regulate	universal
confusion	insoluble	reputation	universe
contribution	monument	*student*	university
Cuba	museum	*stupid*	unusual
cubic	music	*tulip*	usual
Cupid	musician	*tunic*	
duty	occupy	ukulele	

c) "-ue"

The long "u" vowel sound heard in "music" may be represented by the "-ue" vowel digraph. It is found in:

- Open final syllables ("bar-be-cue")
- Open single-syllable words ("cue")
- Closed syllables very rarely ("Tues-day")

The "-ue" spelling pattern is used as a word ending. For this reason, it is often found in open syllables as in "cue" and "argue". Within closed syllables, the "e" often becomes an "i" resulting in the "ui" spelling pattern. Compare, for example, the words "rescue" and "nuisance". It is a convention of English spelling that words do not end with the letter "i".

A final silent letter "e" is not required to help represent the long "u" sound because a long vowel sound may be represented by a single final vowel letter. However, it is a convention of English spelling that words do not end with the letter "u". As well, the final silent letter "e" helps to satisfy the three letter rule in words such as "cue" and "due".

The word "queue" is unique in that the vowel letters "ue" are repeated. The first "ue" spelling pattern helps to represent the hard "c/k" consonant sound. The second "ue" spelling pattern represents the long "u" vowel sound.

With the word "Tuesday", the long "u" vowel sound cannot be readily pronounced as an open syllable.

arg**ue**	c**ue**	que**ue**	T**ue**sday*
*aven**ue***	*d**ue***	resc**ue**	val**ue**
barbec**ue**	h**ue**	*reven**ue***	ven**ue**
contin**ue**	*iss**ue***	rev**ue**	

B7.2 Minor Spelling Patterns

There are five minor spelling patterns for the long "u" vowel sound heard in "m**u**sic".

a) "eau"

The long "u" vowel sound heard in "music" may be represented by the "eau" vowel digraph. This spelling pattern is French in origin. It is found in:

- Open syllables (""b**eau**-ty", "b**eau**-ti-ful"")

Dictionaries show the "eau" spelling pattern as being pronounced in closed syllables as in "b**eau**t-y" and "b**eau**t-iful". For spelling purposes, however, it is helpful to pronounce the long "u" vowel sound within an open syllable as in "b**eau**-ty" and "b**eau**-tiful".

While this spelling pattern is found in only a small number of words, the following words are frequently used.

b**eau**tiful   b**eau**ty

b) "eu"

The long "u" vowel sound heard in "music" may be represented by the "eu" vowel digraph. It is found in:

- Open syllables ("**eu**-logy")

- Closed single-syllable words ("fe**u**d")

English spelling does not favour ending words with the letter "u". For this reason, the "eu" spelling pattern is found within words as in "feud" and not as a word ending. As a word ending, the "u" becomes a "w", resulting in the "-ew" spelling pattern. Compare, for example, the words "n**eu**tral" and "curf**ew**".

Eugene	**Eu**rope	feud	*neutral*
eulogy	**Eu**stachian	feudal	*neutron*
eunuch	d**eu**ce	*maneuver* (USA)	*pneumonia*

c) "-ew"

The long "u" vowel sound heard in "music" may be represented by the "-ew" vowel digraph. The letter "w" is silent. It is found in:

- Open syllables ("p**ew**-ter", "sk**ew**-er", "neph-**ew**")
- Open and closed single-syllable words ("f**ew**", "n**ew**t")

The "-ew" spelling pattern is used as a word ending. For this reason, it is usually found in open syllables as in "p**ew**-ter" and "curf**ew**". Within closed syllables, the "w" often becomes a "u" resulting in the "eu" spelling pattern. Compare, for example, the words "curf**ew**" and "n**eu**tral". It is a convention of English spelling that words do not end with the letter "u".

curf**ew**	*mild**ew***	pew	*stew*
few	nephew	pewter	
knew	*new*	skew	
mew	*newt*	skewer	

d) "-iew"

The long "u" vowel sound heard in "music" may be represented by the "-iew" vowel digraph. The letter "w" is silent. It is found in:

- Open syllables ("v**iew**-er", "re-v**iew**")
- Open single-syllable words ("v**iew**")

While this spelling pattern is found in only a small number of words, some of the words are frequently used.

rev**iew**	v**iew**	v**iew**er

e) Linking "u-"

The long "u" vowel sound heard in "music" may be represented by a linking letter "u-" followed by another vowel letter that is also pronounced. It is found in:

- Open syllables ("f**u**-el", "man-**u**-al")

contin**uu**m	Jan**u**ary	stren**uo**us
f**u**el	man**u**al	val**u**able

B7.3 Rare Spelling Patterns

There are at least six rare spelling patterns for the long "u" vowel sound heard in "music".

a) "ewe"

The long "u" vowel sound heard in "music" may be represented by the "ewe" vowel digraph. The final silent letter "e" helps to satisfy the three letter rule. It is found in:

- Open single-syllable words ("**ewe**")

ewe

b) "-ieu"

The long "u" vowel sound heard in "music" may be represented by the "-ieu" vowel digraph. This spelling pattern is French in origin. It is found in:

- Open single-syllable words ("ad**ieu**")

*ad**ieu***

c) Single Final "-u"

The long "u" vowel sound heard in "music" may be represented by a single final letter "-u". This spelling pattern is contrary to the convention that words do not end with the letter "u". It is found in:

- Open final syllables ("men-**u**")
- Open single-syllable words ("gn**u**")

*gn**u***   men**u**

d)   "ui"

The long "u" vowel sound heard in "music" may be represented by the "ui" vowel digraph. It is found in:

- Open syllables ("n**ui**-sance")
- Closed final syllables ("pur-s**ui**t")

English spelling does not favour ending words with the letter "i". For this reason, the "ui" spelling pattern is found within words as in "purs**ui**t" and not as a word ending. As a word ending, the "i" becomes an "e", resulting in the "-ue" spelling pattern. Compare, for example, the words "n**ui**sance" and "resc**ue**".

*n**ui**sance*   *purs**ui**t*

e)   "-ut"

The long "u" vowel sound heard in "music" may be represented by the "-ut" vowel digraph. This spelling pattern is French in origin. The letter "t" is silent. It is found in:

- Open final syllables ("de-b**ut**")

In French spelling a final consonant letter "t" is silent. Adding a final silent letter "e" causes the letter "t" to be pronounced as heard in "route" and "suite".

deb**ut**

f)   "uu"

The long "u" vowel sound heard in "music" may be represented by the "uu" vowel digraph. It is found in:

- Closed final syllables ("vac-**uu**m")

vac**uu**m

Part C: Spelling Short Vowel Sounds

C1 Short Vowel Spelling Patterns

C1.1 Introduction

As discussed in A4.2, a short vowel sound does not name itself. There are eight short vowel sounds including two short "a" vowel sounds and three short "u" vowel sounds:

- The short "**a**" vowel sound heard in "**a**dd", "c**a**t", and "fl**a**sh"
- The broad "**a**" vowel sound heard as in "**a**rt", "b**a**rn", and "sh**a**rk"
- The short "**e**" vowel sound heard in "**e**nd", "p**e**t", and "th**e**n"
- The short "**i**" vowel sound heard in "**i**t", "t**i**p", and "k**i**ng"
- The short "**o**" vowel sound heard in "**o**ff", "l**o**ng", and "r**o**ck"
- The short "**u**" vowel sound heard in "**u**p", "b**u**t", and "r**u**n"
- The short "**u**" vowel sound heard in "p**u**ll", "b**u**sh", and "s**u**gar"
- The short "**u**" vowel sound heard in "c**u**re", "p**u**re", and "c**u**rious"

The term "short vowel sound" is somewhat misleading. The short "a" vowel sound heard in "cat" is not a shortened version the long "a" vowel sound heard in "cake". Short vowel sounds are called "short" because, unlike long vowel sounds, they only require one mouth movement. Our mouth opens to produce the sound and remains open.

Short vowel sounds are sometimes referred to as "checked vowels" because they are usually pronounced in closed syllables that end with a consonant sound as heard in "cat", "pet", and "tip". As discussed in B1.1, there is a tendency in English speech to end syllables with our mouth closed. As our mouth remains open when pronouncing short vowel sounds, there is an urge to end the syllable with a consonant sound in order to close our mouth. As a result, relatively few English words or syllables end with a short vowel sound.

There are exceptions to the rule that short vowel sounds are pronounced in closed syllables including the short "o" vowel sound spelled "-aw", as in "jaw" and "law", and words that end with the unstressed schwa vowel sound spelled "-a" as in "soda" and "tuna". Our mouth does not open very wide when pronouncing the schwa vowel sound so perhaps that is why it makes an acceptable word ending.

Most often, short vowel sounds are represented by a single vowel letter and are found in closed syllables that end with a consonant sound. However, short vowel sounds are also represented by a wide variety of vowel digraphs found in closed syllables.

C1.2 Single Vowel Letter

C1.2 a)   Single Vowel Followed by Two Consonant Letters

A short vowel sound represented by a single vowel letter is usually followed by two consonant letters if there is another vowel letter after the short vowel sound.

This is in keeping with the doubling principle discussed in A8.1. One consonant between two vowel letters signals that the first vowel is pronounced with a long vowel sound. Two consonants between two vowel letters signals that the first vowel is pronounced with a short vowel sound. The short vowel sound is pronounced in a closed syllable.

This spelling pattern reflects our tendency to begin syllables with a consonant sound. If there is only one consonant letter between syllables, it will usually attach as an onset to the following syllable. The result is that the first syllable will be left open and, consequently, pronounced with a long vowel sound as heard in "wri-**t**ing", "pa-**p**er", and "be-**g**in". If there are two consonant letters between syllables, one will usually remain attached to the preceding syllable, and the second will attach as an onset to the following syllable. The result is that the first syllable will be closed and, consequently, pronounced with a short vowel sound as heard in "la**s**-**t**ing", "e**m**-**p**ire", and "wi**n**-**d**ow".

As discussed in Part B, long vowel sounds are usually represented by two vowel letters. The second vowel letter signals that first vowel is pronounced with a long sound. The two vowel letters may sit side-by-side forming a vowel digraph as in the first syllable of the word "p**ea**-nut". Often, however, the two vowel letters representing the long vowel sound are separated by a single consonant. This occurs in long vowel words that end with a final silent letter "e". In "**a**p**e**", for example, the final silent letter "e" lengthens the sound of the preceding letter "a". This also occurs within words. In "f**i**n**a**l", for example, the letter "a" lengthens the sound of the preceding letter "i".

On the other hand, two consonant letters between vowels protect the first vowel from the lengthening effect of the following vowel letter. The word "plaster", for example, is pronounced "pl**as**-ter". The letter "a" is pronounced with the short "a" vowel sound in a closed syllable. Two consonant letters protect the letter "a" from the lengthening effect of the following vowel letter "e". Likewise, the word "dentist" is pronounced "d**en**-tist". The letter "e" is pronounced with the short "e" vowel sound in a closed syllable. Two consonant letters protect the letter "e" from the lengthening effect of the following vowel letter "i".

Sometimes, two consonant letters form a consonant digraph as in "pa**ck**age" and "fi**sh**ing". For spelling purposes, the word "package" may be pronounced "p**ac**-**k**age". The first letter "a" is pronounced with the short "a" vowel sound in a closed syllable. The word "fishing" is pronounced "fi**sh**-ing". The first letter "i" is pronounced with the short "i" vowel sound in a closed syllable. It is not helpful to pronounce the consonant "sh" sound twice.

When a short vowel sound is followed by three pronounced consonant letters, two of the letters will form a consonant blend. The word will be divided into syllables keeping the consonant blend together. In the word "hamster", for example, the letters "st" form a consonant blend so that the word is divided into syllables as "h**a**m-**st**er". Likewise, in the word "enclosed" the letters "cl" form a consonant blend so that the word is divided into syllables as "**e**n-**cl**osed".

The doubling principle applies even when the following vowel sound is not actually represented by a vowel letter. This occurs in words that end with "-le" following two consonant letters. The word "turtle", for example, is pronounced "t**ur**-tull". Two consonant letters protect the short vowel sound from being lengthened by a following schwa vowel sound that is not represented in the spelling.

bargain (b**ar**-gain) enclosed (**e**n-**cl**osed) plaster (pl**a**s-**t**er)
blacken (bl**a**c-**k**en) fishing (fi**sh**-ing) problem (pr**o**b-**l**em)
buckle (b**u**c-**k**ull) hamster (h**a**m-**st**er) sister (s**i**s-**t**er)
dentist (d**e**n-**t**ist) lasting (l**a**s-**t**ing) turtle (t**ur**-tull
empire (e**m**-**p**ire) package (p**a**c-**k**age) window (w**i**n-**d**ow)

C1.2 b) Single Vowel Followed by Double Consonants

The doubling principle discussed in A8.1 is most dramatically illustrated when a single short vowel letter is followed by double consonants as in "h**a**ppy", "d**i**nner", "k**i**tten", and "t**e**nnis". Two consonant letters following a single vowel protect it from the lengthening effect of a following vowel letter. The short vowel sound is heard in a closed syllable.

The word "dinner", for example, is pronounced "d**i**n-**n**er". The first "n" remains attached to the preceding syllable and the second "n" is free to attach as an onset to the following syllable. The letter "i" remains in a closed syllable and is, consequently, pronounced with the short "i" vowel sound. The double "nn" spelling pattern protects the "i" from the lengthening effect of the following letter "e". On the other hand, the word "diner" is pronounced "d**i**-**n**er". The single letter "n" attaches as an onset to the following syllable. The letter "i" is left in an open syllable and is, consequently, pronounced with the long "i" vowel sound. Without the protection of two consonant letters, the letter "i" is lengthened by the following letter "e".

Likewise, in "sup-per", the double "pp" protects the short "u" vowel sound from the lengthening effect of the following letter "e". Without the protection of two consonant letters, as in "su-per", the letter "u" is pronounced with a long "u" vowel sound.

Dictionaries usually indicate that double consonants represent only one consonant sound. Margaret M. Bishop, however, makes a convincing argument in her book *The ABC's and All Their Tricks* that both consonant letters are pronounced because of our tendency to begin syllables with a consonant sound.[21] For spelling purposes, it is helpful to pronounce both consonants if possible as in "hap-py", "kit-ten", and "ten-nis". With some words, such as "hopped" and "snipped", it is not possible to pronounce both consonants because they are found in single-syllable words.

Following a single short vowel letter, most consonants may be doubled. This results in "bb", "cc", "dd", "ff", "gg", "ll", "mm", "nn", "pp", "rr", "ss", "tt", and "zz" spelling patterns. It may be noted that consonant letters "h", "j", "k", "q", "v", "w", and "x" are never or, in the case of the letters "j" and "v", very rarely doubled.

When a single short vowel letter is followed by the consonant "ch" sound, the doubling principle produces the "-tch" spelling pattern as in the words "catcher" and "watching". For spelling purposes, "catcher" and "watching" may be pronounced "cat-cher" and "wat-ching".

When a single short vowel letter is followed by a soft "g/j" consonant sound, the doubling principle produces the "-dge" spelling pattern as in the words "judge" and "bludgeon". The final silent letter "e" may be dropped as in the word "judgment". However, keeping the silent letter "e", as in "judgement", helps to signal the preceding soft "g/j" consonant sound.

When a word begins with a short or schwa vowel sound, dictionaries often show the vowel sound being pronounced in an open syllable. For example, dictionaries indicate that the word "apply" is pronounced "a-pply". However, initial short and schwa vowel sounds can usually be pronounced within a closed syllable, as in "ap-ply", in keeping with the general rule. For spelling purposes, it is helpful to pronounce short and schwa vowel sounds within closed syllables whenever possible.

The doubling principle applies even when the following vowel sound is not actually represented by a vowel letter. This occurs in words that end with "-le" following two consonant letters. The word "battle", for example, is pronounced "bat-tull". Double consonants protect the short vowel sound from being lengthened by a following schwa vowel sound that is not represented in the spelling.

applied (ap-plied) dinner (din-ner) mitten (mit-ten
apply (ap-ply) happy (hap-py) rabbit (rab-bit)
battle (bat-tull) judgment (judg-ment) struggle (strug-gull)
bitten (bit-ten) kitten (kit-ten) tennis (ten-nis)
catcher (cat-cher) middle (mid-dull) watching (wat-ching)

C1.2 c) Short Vowel Single-syllable Words and Final Syllables

The doubling principle does not apply to single-syllable short vowel words or to final short vowel syllables.

As discussed in C1.2 a), a short vowel sound represented by a single vowel letter is usually followed by two consonant letters if there is another vowel letter after the short vowel sound. If the short vowel sound is not followed by another vowel letter, there is no need for the protection provided by two consonant letters.

As single-syllable short vowel words and final short vowel syllables are not followed by another vowel letter, they may end with a single consonant letter. For example, the single-syllable short vowel word "drag" ends with a single consonant letter "g". Likewise, in the word "admit" the final short vowel syllable "-mit" ends with a single consonant letter "t".

Many single-syllable short vowel words are spelled with a single vowel letter followed by a single final consonant letter.

bad	get	is	sat
bat	has	mad	sit
bed	his	mat	this
bus	hit	men	thus
drag	hug	rat	twit
gas	hut	sad	vet

This spelling pattern is reserved for single-syllable short vowel words. Single-syllable long vowel words rarely end with a single consonant letter.

As well, many longer words end with a short vowel syllable that is represented by a single vowel letter followed by a single consonant letter.

admit	cabin	forbid	planet
allot	commit	forget	regret
basket	compel	impel	relax
begin	credit	jacket	remit
begun	dispel	omit	submit
bullet	excel	permit	women

It should be noted, however, that when a suffix that begins with a vowel letter is added to such words the short vowel sound will now be followed by another vowel letter. The protection provided by two consonants is again required. For this reason, the final consonant of the base word is doubled. The word "drag" becomes "dragged" with the addition of the suffix "-ed". Likewise, the word "admit", for example, becomes "admitting" with the addition of the suffix "-ing". Double consonants now protect the short vowel sound from lengthening effect of the following vowel letter.

While single-syllable short vowel words may end with a single consonant letter, many end with two or three consonant letters.

a̲dd	du̲mp	li̲st	ri̲ch
ba̲ck	fi̲ll	ma̲sk	sa̲ck
be̲nd	fu̲ss	me̲nd	si̲ng
bla̲ck	gra̲ss	mu̲ch	te̲nt
bo̲ss	ju̲dge	o̲dd	wa̲tch
ca̲mp	la̲mp	pa̲th	wi̲tch

Unfortunately, and contrary to the doubling principle, many single-syllable long vowel words such as "bind" and "most" follow the same spelling pattern.

Likewise, many longer words end with a short vowel syllable that is spelled with a single vowel letter followed by two or three consonant letters. Such short vowel syllable endings help to signal the short vowel sound.

abse̲nt	atta̲ck	denti̲st	greate̲st
acce̲pt	bewi̲tch	discu̲ss	hone̲st
acro̲ss	constru̲ct	getti̲ng	lovi̲ng

C1.3 Short Vowel Digraphs

Short vowel sounds are also represented by vowel digraphs. Consonant letters are often used to form short vowel digraphs.

The doubling principle does not apply when a short vowel sound is represented by a vowel digraph. However, the short vowel sound is still most often found in closed syllables as heard in "m**ea**d-ow" and "**ho**n-est". When found in open syllables, as in "**aw**-ful" and "hur**rah**", the vowel digraph often ends with a consonant letter.

Although short vowel digraphs tend to be minor or rare spelling patterns, there are, unfortunately, many of them.

app**ear**	ch**eer**	h**ear**	m**ea**dow
audio	cl**ear**	h**eir**	pl**ai**d
awful	c**oo**kie	**ho**nest	st**al**k
b**ear**	engin**eer**	hur**rah**	w**oul**d
c**al**f	**Eu**rope	kn**ow**ledge	
c**augh**t	forf**ei**t	l**eo**pard	

C1.4 Exceptions to the Doubling Principle

Unfortunately, many words do not comply with the doubling principle. See Part A for further discussion.

C2 Spelling the Short "A" Vowel Sound

There are many spelling patterns for the short "a" vowel sound heard in "cat". They have been divided into major and rare spelling patterns.

C2.1 Major Spelling Patterns

Thankfully, there is only one major spelling pattern for the short "a" vowel sound heard in "cat".

a) **"a"**

The short "a" vowel sound heard in "cat" may be represented by a single letter "a":

- Followed by two consonants ("establish", "tractor", "packet")
- Followed by double consonants ("carrot", "happen")
- In closed single-syllable words and final syllables ("bad", "program")

The short "a" vowel sound is heard in a closed syllable.

It may be noted that the "a(l)" and "a(ll)" spelling patterns often represent the short "o" vowel sound as heard in "almost" and "stall".

Also note that when the "a(r)" spelling pattern is followed by a consonant letter other than "r", it usually represents the broad "a" vowel sound as heard in "carpet" and "large". In keeping with the doubling principle, however, the "a(rr)" spelling pattern usually represents the short "a" vowel sound as heard in "arrow" and "barren".

Further, it may be noted that when the "a(r)" spelling pattern is followed by a vowel, the "a" is usually pronounced with the short "e" vowel sound as heard in "parent" and "various". In "character" and "paragraph", however, the "a(r)" spelling pattern is pronounced with the short "a" vowel sound.

The word "prepare" is unusual. The word ending "-are" is usually pronounced with the short "e" vowel sound as in "care", "dare", and "scare". Words marked by an asterisk do not follow the doubling principle.

absence	ac*id**	actor	admire
absent	act	actress	admission
absolute	action	actual	admit
access	active	add	adult*
accident	activity	address	*advance*

advantage	attack	can	dazzle
adventure	attic	Canada*	defendant
advertise	attract	canal	demand
advice	avalanche*	cancer	disaster
advise	avenue*	candle	dissatisfy*
Africa	average*	candy	drag
aft	avoid*	cannon	dragon*
after	axle	cannot	drank
aghast	back	canyon	elastic
agriculture	bad	cap	embarrassment
Al	badge	capital*	establish
albino	badger	captain	exact
album	bag	carriage	examine*
alcohol	baggage	carrot	example
algebra	balance*	carry	expand
allegation	ballad	cash	expanse
alley	ban	*cast*	extract
alligator	band	*caste*	fact
alphabet	bang	castle	factory
altitude	ban*ish**	cat	familiarity
am	bank	catch	family*
ambition	banquet	cattle	fan
ambitious	*barrel*	champion	fantastic
ambulance	barren	chance	fashion
an	basket	channel	fast
analysis	bat	chapter	fasten
and	*bath*	character*	fat
Andrew	battle	charity	fatality
anger	began	clam	fatten
angle	black	class	fatter
angry	blanket	classification	flag
animal*	blast	command	flange
answer	bracket	companion*	flash
ant	branch	comparison	flat
anxiety	brand	comrade	flatten
anxious	brass	congratulate*	flax
application	broadcast	contract	fragment
arrow	cab	corral	France
as	cabin*	crack	frantic
ash	calcium	craft	gadget
ask	calculate	crash	gal
astronaut	*calf*	dad	gallant
at	Calgary	daddy	gallon
athlete	callous	damage*	gallop
Atlantic	camera*	damp	gander
atmosphere	camp	*dance*	gang

gap	inhab*it**	matter	program (USA, CAN)
ga**rr**ison	international*	mechanic*	programme (UK)
ga**th**er	Italian*	metallic	quacked
gigantic	italics	morale	rabbit
giraffe	jacket	mortality*	raccoon
giraffe	January*	nap	radish*
glad	Japan	narrate	raft
glass	laboratory*	narrow	rally
gnat	lack	national*	ran
grab	ladder	natural*	ranch
grad	lamp	pack	rang
gradual*	land	packet	rank
gram	language	pad	rapid*
grammar	lap	pal	rat
grammatical	lapsc	palace*	rather
grammatical*	Larry	pan	reality*
grand	last	pan*ic**	relapse
grant	lasting	pansy	relax
grass	latter	pants	sacrifice
gratitude*	locale	paragraph*	sad
gra*v*el*	mad	paramount*	sadden
habit*	madden	parent*	saddle
habitat*	magazine*	parity*	salad*
had	magic*	pa**rr**ot	salary*
Hal	malfunction	pass	Sally
Halloween	malnutrition	passenger	*salve*
halve	malpractice	past	sample
ham	man	pasture	sand
hamburger	manage*	pat	sandal
hammer	manager*	patch	sandwich
hamster	manner	*path*	sandy
hand	manse	patriotism	sang
handle	mansion	pattern	sapling
handy	manual*	peculiarity*	sat
hang	map	performance	satchel
happen	marathon	perhaps	satellite*
happy	marriage	photograph	satisfaction*
Harry	married	plan	satisfy*
has	marry	planet*	Saturday*
hat	mask	planned	Saturn*
have	mass	plant	scatter
hilarious	mast	plaster	scratch
honor**ary**	*master*	plastic	shack
hospitality	mat	practical	shadow*
imagination*	match	practice	shall
imagine*	mathematics	prepare	

shallow	swam	thank	valley
slam	tact	that	valuable*
smash	tadpole	theatrical	value*
Spanish*	tag	track	valve
spank	talc	tractor	van
splash	tallow	traffic	vanish*
staff	Tamara	*trance*	vanquish
stag	tan	transatlantic	vat
stallion	tank	transfer	visio**nary**
stamp	tap	translate	volcanic*
stand	tarry	transportation	wagon*
standing	task	trap	wax
strap	tax	trapper	wrap
subsi**diary***	telegraph	travel*	wrath
subtract	than	valentine*	

C2.2 Rare Spelling Patterns

There are at least eight rare spelling patterns for the short "a" vowel sound heard in "cat".

a) "ae"

The short "a" vowel sound heard in "cat" may be represented by the "ae" vowel digraph. The doubling principle does not apply to short vowel sounds represented by a vowel digraph. It is found in:

- Closed syllables ("aer-ial")

*ae*rial

b) "ai"

The short "a" vowel sound heard in "cat" may be represented by the "ai" vowel digraph. The doubling principle does not apply to short vowel sounds represented by a vowel digraph. It is found in:

- Closed syllables ("hair", "plaid")

air   *hair*   *plaid*

c) "al"

The short "a" vowel sound heard in "cat" may be represented by the "al" vowel digraph. The doubling principle does not apply to short vowel sounds represented by a vowel digraph. The letter "l" is silent. It is found in:

- Closed syllables that end with the letter "f" ("ca**lf**", "ha**lf**")

calf   *half*

d)   "au"

The short "a" vowel sound heard in "cat" may be represented by the "au" vowel digraph. The doubling principle does not apply to short vowel sounds represented by a vowel digraph. It is found in:

- Closed syllables ("<u>au</u>nt", "l<u>au</u>gh-ter")

aunt   *draught* (UK, CAN)   *laugh*   *laughter*

e)   "aye"

The short "a" vowel sound heard in "cat" may be represented by the "aye" vowel digraph. The doubling principle does not apply to short vowel sounds represented by a vowel digraph. It is found in:

- Closed syllables ("pr<u>aye</u>r")

prayer

f)   "ea"

The short "a" vowel sound heard in "cat" may be represented by the "ea" vowel digraph. The doubling principle does not apply to short vowel sounds represented by a vowel digraph. It is found in:

- Closed single-syllables words ("b<u>ea</u>r")

bear

g)   "ei"

The short "a" vowel sound heard in "cat" may be represented by the "ei" vowel digraph. The doubling principle does not apply to short vowel sounds represented by a vowel digraph. It is found in:

- Closed syllables ("th<u>ei</u>r")

This spelling pattern is contrary to the "i" before "e" except after "c" rule.

their

h)   "i"

The short "a" vowel sound heard in "cat" may be represented by a single letter "i":

- Followed by two consonants ("mer**i**ngue")

mer**i**ngue

C3   Spelling the Broad "A" Vowel Sound

The broad "a" vowel sound heard in "**a**rt", "b**a**rn", and "sh**a**rk" and the short "o" vowel sound heard in "**o**ff", "l**o**ng", and "r**o**ck" are very similar. Dictionaries indicate that many words may be pronounced with either vowel sound. The pronunciation given to particular words changes from place to place and not everyone distinguishes between the two sounds.

In particular, not everyone pronounces the broad "a" vowel sound. For example, some people pronounce the words "ant" and "aunt" the same way. Other people, however, pronounce the word "ant" with the short "a" vowel sound and pronounce the word "aunt" with the broad "a" vowel sound. If a person pronounces the word "aunt" with the broad "a" vowel sound, he or she will likely pronounce the following words with the same vowel sound.

There are many different spelling patterns for the broad "a" vowel sound heard in "**a**rt". They have been divided into major, minor, and rare spelling patterns.

C3.1 Major Spelling Patterns

There are three major spelling patterns for the broad "a" vowel sound heard in "**a**rt".

a)   "a"

The broad "a" vowel sound heard in "art" may be represented by a single letter "a":

- Followed by two consonants ("**a**fter", "m**a**ster")
- Followed by double consonants ("gir**a**ffe")
- In closed single-syllable words and final syllables ("**a**ft", "**a**ll", "gar**a**ge", "restaur**a**nt")
- In open final syllables ("h**a**", "llam**a**")
- Following the consonant "w" sound ("squ**a**d", "su**a**ve", "w**a**sh", "schw**a**")

A single final letter "a" is often pronounced with the broad "a" vowel sound as heard in "br**a**", "h**a**", "m**a**", "llam**a**", "Omah**a**", and "schw**a**".

This spelling of the broad "a" vowel sound is often found following a consonant "w" sound as heard in "squad", "squat", "suave", "swab", and "wash". Note, however, that the pronunciation changes to short "o" when followed by consonant letter "r" as heard in "quart", "war", "warden", "warm", and "warn".

With words such as "garage", "massage" and "sabotage", the final silent letter "e" signals that the adjacent letter "g" is pronounced with the soft "g/j" consonant sound.

In a number of the following words, including "father", "Chicago", "Hawaii", "llama", the broad "a" vowel sound is usually pronounced in an open syllable.

Words marked by an asterisk do not follow the doubling principle.

aft	father	Omaha	squander
after	garage	*path*	squat
aghast	*giraffe*	quaff	suave
aha	ha	*qualification**	swab
all	*halve*	quantity	swallow
ask	Hawaii	restaurant	swat
bath	llama*	sabotage	*trance*
bra	ma	*salve*	wander
cast	massage	schwa	was
caste	*master*	squab	wash
Chicago	mirage	squabble	*what*
*dance**	montage	squad	

b)   "a(r)"

The broad "a" vowel sound heard in "art" may be represented by the "a(r)" spelling pattern. The letter "r" is pronounced. It is found in:

- Closed syllables when followed by different consonant letter ("art", "barber")
- Closed final syllables that end with the letter "r" ("car", "cougar")

This spelling of the broad "a" vowel sound is an r-influenced vowel sound.

Note that when the "a(r)" spelling pattern is followed by a vowel, and not a consonant, it is often pronounced with the short "a" vowel sound as in "character" and "paragraph" or with the short "e" vowel sound as in "dare" and "various". The broad "a" vowel sound is heard when the letters "a(r)" are followed by a different consonant letter as in "farmer" or when "a(r)" forms a word ending as in "radar".

In keeping with the doubling principle, the "rr" spelling pattern usually follows a regular short vowel sound, as heard in "carry" and "barrel", not the broad "a" vowel sound. The word "starry" is an exception.

Some speakers do not pronounce the consonant "r" sound before another consonant or a pause. This is referred to as "r-dropping". With such speakers, however, words such "card" and "cart" do not simply rhyme with "cad" or "cat". Rather, such words are pronounced with the broad "a" vowel sound.

With the word "are", the final silent letter "e" helps to satisfy the three letter rule.

ap**ar**t	**car**	guit**ar**	**par**ties
arbor (USA)	**car**bohydrate	h**ar**bor (USA)	**par**tner
arbour (UK, CAN)	**car**d	h**ar**bour (UK, CAN)	**par**ty
arc	**car**nival	h**ar**d	ph**ar**macy
arch	**car**nivore	h**ar**m	rad**ar**
architect	**car**pet	h**ar**mony	reg**ar**d
ardent	**car**t	h**ar**vest	rem**ar**k
ardor (USA)	**car**ve	j**ar**	s**ar**dine
ardour (UK, CAN)	**char**ge	l**ar**d	sc**ar**let
are	**char**latan	l**ar**ge	sh**ar**k
argue	**char**m	l**ar**ger	sh**ar**p
arm	coug**ar**	M**ar**ch	sm**ar**t
armor (USA)	d**ar**k	m**ar**ch	sp**ar**k
armour (UK, CAN)	dep**ar**t	m**ar**k	sp**ar**se
army	dep**ar**tment	m**ar**ket	st**ar**
arsenal	dep**ar**ture	m**ar**lin	st**ar**ry
art	dis**ar**m	M**ar**s	st**ar**t
article	disreg**ar**d	M**ar**tian	st**ar**tle
artificial	f**ar**	m**ar**velous	st**ar**ve
b**ar**	f**ar**ce	p**ar**cel	t**ar**
b**ar**b	f**ar**m	p**ar**don	t**ar**paulin
b**ar**ber	f**ar**mer	p**ar**k	v**ar**nish
b**ar**gain	f**ar**ther	p**ar**liament	y**ar**d
b**ar**ge	foolh**ar**dy	p**ar**sley	y**ar**n
b**ar**k	g**ar**bage	p**ar**t	
b**ar**ley	g**ar**den	p**ar**ticle	
b**ar**n	gu**ar**d	p**ar**ticular	

c) "o"

The broad "a" vowel sound heard in "art" may be represented by a single letter "o":

- Followed by two consonants ("h<u>o</u>ckey", "c<u>o</u>nquer")
- Followed by double consonants ("c<u>o</u>mmon", "c<u>o</u>ttage")
- In closed single-syllable words and final syllables ("p<u>o</u>t", "Amaz<u>o</u>n")

The broad "a" vowel sound is heard in a closed syllable.

With the word "gone", the final silent letter "e" does not appear to perform a useful function. The "-o(ne)" spelling pattern, as heard in "done" and "none", also represents the short "u" vowel sound.

Words marked by an asterisk do not follow the doubling principle.

ab*o*lish*	c*o*mplicate	g*o*lf	m*o*nster
acc*o*mplish	c*o*mposition	g*o*ne	M*o*ntreal
acr*o*ss	c*o*ncert	g*o*t	n*o*t
ad*o*pt	c*o*nduct (noun)	h*o*bby	*o*bjection
Amaz*o*n	c*o*nfidence	h*o*ckey	*o*bstacle
ap*o*logy*	c*o*nfident	h*o*liday*	*o*bvious
archae*o*logist*	c*o*nquer	H*o*lland	*O*ctober
ast*o*nish*	c*o*nquest	h*o*llow	*o*ctopus
auth*o*rities*	c*o*nscious	h*o*lly	*o*dd
bi*o*logist*	c*o*nstant	h*o*mily*	*o*ff
bi*o*nic	c*o*ntribution	h*o*p	*o*ffer
bl*o*nd	c*o*nversation	h*o*pped	*o*ffice
bl*o*ssom	c*o*pper	h*o*pping	*o*ften
b*o*dy*	c*o*py*	horiz*o*ntal	*o*live*
b*o*mb	cor*o*llary	h*o*spital	*o*n
b*o*ss	c*o*st	h*o*t	*o*nto
b*o*ther	c*o*t	h*o*vel*	*o*perate*
b*o*ttle	c*o*ttage	ide*o*logy*	*o*peration*
b*o*ttom	c*o*tton	imp*o*ssible	*o*perator*
b*o*x	cr*o*p	inv*o*lve	*o*pportunity
br*o*ccoli	cr*o*ss	inv*o*lve	*o*pposite
cann*o*t	d*o*ck	ir*o*nic*	*o*pposition
ch*o*colate*	d*o*ctor	j*o*b	*o*ption
ch*o*p	d*o*g	j*o*g	*o*ptional
cl*o*ck	d*o*ll	j*o*lly	*o*x
cl*o*g	d*o*llar	kn*o*b	*o*xen*
cl*o*set*	d*o*lly	kn*o*ck	*O*z
cl*o*t	d*o*lphin	l*o*bster	ph*o*tography
cl*o*th	d*o*nkey	l*o*ck	p*o*cket
c*o*b	d*o*t	l*o*dger	p*o*licy*
c*o*cky	dr*o*p	l*o*ft	p*o*lish*
c*o*d	ec*o*nomy*	l*o*g	p*o*litician*
c*o*ffee	ex*o*tic*	l*o*llipop	p*o*litics*
c*o*ffin	f*o*g	l*o*ss	p*o*llen
c*o*llar	f*o*llow	l*o*st	p*o*llination
c*o*llege	f*o*lly	l*o*t	p*o*lygon*
c*o*lony*	f*o*nd	m*o*del*	p*o*nd
c*o*lumn*	f*o*reign*	m*o*derate*	p*o*p
c*o*mbine	f*o*rest*	m*o*dern*	p*o*pular*
c*o*mic*	forg*o*t	m*o*dest*	p*o*pulation*
c*o*mmerce	fr*o*g	m*o*lecule*	p*o*sitive*
c*o*mmon	fr*o*st	m*o*m	p*o*ssible
c*o*mpetition	G*o*d	m*o*mmy	p*o*t

p*o*verty*	r*o*bin*	s*o*ften	t*o*nic*
pr*o*bable*	r*o*bot*	sol*e*mn*	top
pr*o*blem	r*o*ck	s*o*lid*	top
pr*o*duct*	r*o*cket	s*o*luble*	t*o*pic*
pr*o*fit*	r*o*d	s*o*lve*	tr*o*d
pr*o*mise*	r*o*t	s*o*rry	tr*o*lley
pr*o*mpt	r*o*tten	s*o*vereign*	unc*o*nscious
pr*o*per*	sh*o*ck	sp*o*t	up*o*n
pr*o*perty*	sh*o*p	st*o*ck	v*o*lcano
pr*o*vince*	sh*o*t	st*o*lid*	v*o*lume*
resp*o*nd	s*o*ccer	st*o*p	v*o*lunteer*
resp*o*nsible	s*o*ck	the*o*logy*	z*o*ology*
rev*o*lver	s*o*cket	t*o*lerant*	
r*o*b	s*o*cks	t*o*lerate	
r*o*bber	s*o*ft	t*o*morrow	

C3.2 Minor Spelling Patterns

There is only one minor spelling pattern for the broad "a" vowel sound heard in "art".

b)   "ea(r)"

The broad "a" vowel sound heard in "art" may be represented by the "ea(r)" vowel digraph. The doubling principle does not apply to short vowel sounds represented by a vowel digraph. The letter "r" is pronounced. It is found in:

- Closed syllables ("h*ea*rth", "h*ea*rt")

This spelling of the broad "a" vowel sound is an r-influenced vowel sound.

h*ea*rt	h*ea*rtbeat	h*ea*rtbroken	h*ea*rtily
h*ea*rtache	h*ea*rtbreak	h*ea*rth	h*ea*rty

C3.3 Rare Spelling Patterns

There are at least ten rare spelling patterns for the broad "a" vowel sound heard in "art".

a)   "aa(r)"

The broad "a" vowel sound heard in "art" may be represented by the "aa(r)" vowel digraph. The doubling principle does not apply to short vowel sounds represented by a vowel digraph. The letter "r" is pronounced. It is found in:

- Closed syllables ("baz-*aa*r")

baz**aar**

b) "ah"

The broad "a" vowel sound heard in "art" may be represented by the "ah" vowel digraph. The letter "h" is silent. Unlike most short vowel digraphs, it is found in:

- Open syllables ("Br<u>ah</u>-man", "hu-rr<u>ah</u>")

ah	Br**ah**man	*hurr**ah***	*sh**ah***
b**ah**	d**ah**lia	*pari**ah***	*Ut**ah***

c) "al"

The broad "a" vowel sound heard in "art" may be represented by the "al" vowel digraph. The letter "l" is silent. While silent, the letter "l" affects the pronunciation of the letter "a". It is found in:

- Closed syllables ("c**al**m", "h**al**f")
- Open syllables ("**al**-mond")

The words "calf" and "half" are also pronounced with the short "a" vowel sound.

almond	c**al**m	p**al**m
*c**al**f*	*h**al**f*	ps**al**m

d) "au"

The broad "a" vowel sound heard in "art" may be represented by the "au" vowel digraph. It is found in:

- Closed syllables ("*<u>au</u>nt*", "*l<u>au</u>gh*")

aunt	*draught* (UK, CAN)	*laugh*

e) "e"

The broad "a" vowel sound heard in "art" may be represented by a single letter "e":

- Followed by two consonants ("*<u>e</u>ntrée*", "*s<u>e</u>rgeant*")

This spelling pattern is French in origin.

entrée	*sergeant*

f) "eau"

The broad "a" vowel sound heard in "art" may be represented by the "eau" vowel digraph. This spelling pattern is French in origin. Unlike most short vowel digraphs, It is found in:

- Open syllables ("bu-r**eau**-cra-cy")

bureaucracy

g) "ho(n)-"

The broad "a" vowel sound heard in "art" may be represented by the "ho(n)-" vowel digraph. The doubling principle does not apply to short vowel sounds represented by a vowel digraph. The letter "h" is silent. The letter "n" is pronounced. It is found in:

- Closed syllables ("**ho**n-est", "**ho**n-our")

| **ho**nest | **ho**nor (USA) | **ho**nour (UK, CAN) | **ho**nourable (UK, CAN) |
| **ho**nesty | **ho**norable (USA) | | |

h) "i"

The broad "a" vowel sound heard in "art" may be represented by a single letter "i":

- Followed by two consonants ("l**i**ngerie")

lingerie

This spelling pattern is French in origin.

i) "ou"

The broad "a" vowel sound heard in "art" may be represented by the "ou" vowel digraph. It is found in:

- Closed syllables ("tr**ou**gh")

trough

j) "ow"

The broad "a" vowel sound heard in "art" may be represented by the "ow" vowel digraph. The letter "w" is silent. Unlike most short vowel digraphs, it is found in:

- Open syllables ("kn**ow**-ledge")

knowledge

C4 Spelling the Short "E" Vowel Sound

There are many spelling patterns for the short "e" vowel sound heard in "p**e**t". They have been divided into major, minor, and rare spelling patterns.

C4.1 Major Spelling Patterns

There are only two major spelling patterns for the short "e" vowel sound heard in "p**e**t".

a) **"e"**

The short "e" vowel sound heard in "pet" may be represented by a single letter "e":

- Followed by two consonants ("d**e**ntist", "")
- Followed by double consonants ("f**e**llow", "b**e**rry")
- In closed single-syllable words and final syllables ("b**e**d", "forg**e**t")

The short "e" vowel sound is heard in a closed syllable.

Some words follow the doubling principle in a roundabout way. With the word "**equ**ine", the vowel letter "u" functions as a consonant letter "w". With words such as "**ex**act" and "**ex**it", the letter "x" represents a hard "c/k" consonant sound followed by the soft "c/s" consonant sound.

When a syllable that ends with a single letter "r" is followed by a vowel, the syllable is usually pronounced with the r-influenced schwa vowel sound heard in "diff**e**rence". In "c**e**remony" and "p**e**rish", however, the "e(r)" spelling pattern is pronounced with the short "e" vowel sound contrary to the doubling principle. In keeping with the doubling principle, words such as "b**e**rry" and "t**e**rrible" are pronounced with the short "e" vowel sound.

It may be noted that none of the following words are spelled with the letters "e(r)" followed by a different consonant letter. When the letters "e(r)" are followed by a different consonant, the "e" is often pronounced with the stressed r-influenced vowel sound heard in "bird".

The words "there" and "where" are pronounced with the short "e" vowel sound and not the r-influenced schwa vowel sound. When the "-re" word ending follows vowel letters "a", "e", and "o", as in "dare", "where", and "more", the vowel is usually pronounced with a short vowel sound.

Words marked by an asterisk do not follow the doubling principle.

absent	correct	else	exhaust
accept	credit*	else	exhibit
address	debt	empire	exhibition
adventure	December	employ	exist*
aesthetic*	defence (UK, CAN)	employee	exit*
altogether	defend	empty	expect
arrest	defense (USA)	enclose	expend
attempt	definite*	encourage	expense
attend	delicate*	end	expensive
attention	delve	enemy*	experience
attentive	democrat*	energy*	experiment
bed	den	enforce	expert
beg	dense	engine	explain
bell	dentist	enjoy	explode
belt	depend	enter	explore
bench	depth	entertain	explosion
bend	descend	entire	explosive
berry	descent	entitle	express
best	desk	entrance	extend
bet	detect*	envelope	extent
better	detest*	environment	extra
bless	develop*	envy	extreme
buried*	devil*	equine*	February
cement	direct	erect	fed
cent	direction	err	federal*
center (USA, CAN)	director	error	fell
centimeter (USA)	discontent	escape	fellow
centimetre (UK, CAN)	disrespect	especially*	felt
centre (UK, CAN)	distress	essence	fence
century	dress	establish	flesh
ceremony*	edge	estimate	*forest*
check	educate*	event	forget
cherry	education*	ever*	French
chest	effect	evidence*	fresh
clever*	efficiency	exact*	general*
collect	efficient	examine*	generation*
commence	effort	example*	generous*
compel	egg	excel	gentle
confess	elder	excellent	get
confession	elderly	except	harvest
connect	elect	excess	held
conquest	electric	exchange	helicopter*
consent	elephant*	excite	hell
content	elevator*	exclaim	hello
contest	eleven*	excuse	helmet
	elf	exercise*	help

helpful	merry	prejudice	request
hen	mess	presence	rescue
hence	message	*present**	respect
herself	messenger	*president**	rest
hesitate*	met	press	restaurant
himself	metal*	pressure	scent
hotel	method	pretence (UK, CAN)	second*
immense	metric	pretend	self
index	Mexican*	pretense (USA)	selfish
influential	Mexico*	prevent	sell
inquest	modem	prevention	send
insect	motel	princess	sense
inspect	necessary*	process	sent
intelligence	neck	procession	sentence
intend	negative*	profession	separate*
intention	neglect	professor	September
interest	nephew	progress	set
invent	nest	project	settle
invention	net	prospect	seven*
itself	never*	protect	several*
jet	next	question	sex
kept	nonsense	recess	shelf
led	November	recognition*	shell
left	object	recognize*	shelter
leg	objection	recommend*	shelve
legislation*	offence (UK, CAN)	record*	shepherd
lend	offend	red	sheriff*
length	offense (USA)	redden	skeleton*
less	ourselves	referee*	slept
lesson	pen	reference*	smell
lest	penalty*	reflect	special*
let	pencil	reflection	spell
letter	penny	refresh	spelt
letting	pension	refreshing	spend
lettuce	percent	register*	spent
level*	perfect	regret	splendid
mechanism	perish*	regular*	stem
medal*	pet	relative*	step
medical*	pledge	remedy*	strength
medicine*	plenty	remember	stretch
medium*	possess	rent	stretching
melt	possession	repetition*	subject
member	potential	represent*	suggest
memory*	precious	reputation*	suggestion
men	preference		suspect
mention	pregnant		swell

sympathetic*	tenth	umbrella	west
telegraph*	terrible	unidentified	wet
telephone*	terror	unless	when
television*	Terry	upset	whence
tell	test	vegetable*	where
temper	them	velvet	whether
temperature	then	very	wreck
temple	there	vessel	wrecking
tempt	together	vet	yell
ten	trek	wedding	yellow
tend	tremble	Wednesday	yes
tender	twelfth	welcome	yet
tense	twelve	well	*zebra* (UK, CAN)
tent	twenty	went	

b)   "ea"

The short "e" vowel sound heard in "pet" may be represented by the "ea" vowel digraph. The doubling principle does not apply to short vowel sounds represented by a vowel digraph. It is found in:

- Closed syllables ("br**ea**d", "sw**ea**t-er", "a-h**ea**d")

While numerous vowel digraphs represent a variety of short vowel sounds, this is the only vowel digraph that warrants inclusion as a major short vowel spelling pattern.

A few of the following words, including "pear" and "tear", are spelled with the letters "ea(r)". However, the "ea(r)" spelling pattern usually represents the stressed r-influenced vowel sound heard in "bird".

The letters "ea" also represent the long "e" vowel sound. There are pairs of long "e"/short "e" words that share the "ea" spelling pattern including "clean"/"cleanser", "deal"/"dealt", "heal"/"health", "heave"/"heavy", "leap"/"leapt", "mean"/"meant", and "please"/"pleasure". This is an example of morphemic spelling.

ahead	death	leapt	realm
already	dread	leather	spread
bear	feather	meadow	steady
bread	head	meant	stealth
breadth	health	measure	swear
breakfast	heather	pear	sweat
breast	heaven	peasant	sweater
breath	heavy	pleasant	tear
cleanser	instead	pleasure	thread
dead	jealous	read (past tense)	threat
deaf	lead (the metal)	ready	tread

treasure   weapon   weather
wealth   wear

C4.2 Minor Spelling Patterns

There are two minor spelling patterns for the short "e" vowel sound heard in "pet".

a)   "a(r)"

The short "e" vowel sound heard in "pet" may be represented by the "a(r)" spelling pattern. The letter "r" is pronounced. It is found in:

- Closed syllables followed by a vowel letter ("bare", "librar-ian", "scar-y")

This spelling of the short "e" vowel sound is an r-influenced vowel sound.

It may be noted that in the following words, the letter "r" is followed by a vowel letter. When the "a(r)" spelling pattern is followed by a consonant letter, it is usually pronounced with the broad "a" vowel sound as heard in "army" and "partner".

With words such as "care" and "spare" the final silent letter "e" signals that the preceding letter "a" is pronounced with a short vowel sound and not the r-influenced schwa vowel sound.

Words marked by an asterisk do not follow the doubling principle.

apparent*	dictionary*	momentary*	spare
area*	fare	necessary*	square
bare	February*	ordinary*	stare
care	January*	parent*	various*
compare	librarian*	rare	vary*
customary*	library*	scare	ware
dare	literary*	scary*	wary*
declare	mare	share	

b)   "ai" and "ai(r)"

The short "e" vowel sound heard in "pet" may be represented by the "ai" vowel digraph. The doubling principle does not apply to short vowel sounds represented by a vowel digraph. It is found in:

- Closed syllables ("again", "hair", "prair-ie")

The "ai" spelling pattern is usually followed by a pronounced letter "r". The words "again" and "said" are exceptions to this rule.

affair	despair	pair	stair
again	fair	prairie	upstairs
air	*hair*	repair	
chair	hairy	said	

C4.3 Rare Spelling Patterns

There are at least ten rare spelling patterns for the short "e" vowel sound heard in "pet".

a)   "a"

The short "e" vowel sound heard in "pet" may be represented by a single letter "a":

- In closed syllables ("**a**n-y", "m**a**n-y")

Words marked by an asterisk do not follow the doubling principle.

any*   many*

b)   "ae"

The short "e" vowel sound heard in "pet" may be represented by the "ae" vowel digraph. The doubling principle does not apply to short vowel sounds represented by a vowel digraph. It is found in:

- Closed syllables ("**ae**s-thetic", "**ae**r-ial")

aesthetic   *aerial*

c)   "ay" and "aye"

The short "e" vowel sound heard in "pet" may be represented by the "ay" and "aye" vowel digraphs in closed syllables. The doubling principle does not apply to short vowel sounds represented by a vowel digraph. It is found in:

- Closed syllables ("pr**ay**er", "s**ay**s")

pr**ay**er   s**ay**s

d)   "ei" and "hei"

The short "e" vowel sound heard in "pet" may be represented by the "ei" and "hei" vowel digraphs. The doubling principle does not apply to short vowel sounds represented by a vowel digraph. It is found in:

- Closed syllables ("h**ei**ress", "th**ei**r")

The letter "h" is silent in the words "heir", "heiress", and "heirloom and is pronounced in the word "heifer". This spelling pattern is contrary to the "i" before "e" except after "c" rule.

h**ei**fer	**hei**ress	l**ei**sure
heir	**hei**rloom	*th**ei**r*

e)   "eo"

The short "e" vowel sound heard in "pet" may be represented by the "eo" vowel digraph. The doubling principle does not apply to short vowel sounds represented by a vowel digraph. It is found in:

- Closed syllables ("j**eo**p-ar-dy", "l**eo**p-ard")

j**eo**pardize	j**eo**pardy	L**eo**nard	l**eo**pard

f)   "i"

The short "e" vowel sound heard in "pet" may be represented by a single letter "i":

- Followed by double consonants ("van**i**lla")

*van**i**lla*

g)   "ie"

The short "e" vowel sound heard in "pet" may be represented by the "ie" vowel digraph. It is found in:

- Closed syllables ("fr**ie**nd")

This spelling pattern is contrary to the "i" before "e" except after "c" rule. The mnemonic phrase "a fri**end** to the **end**" may be helpful in remembering this unique spelling pattern.

fr**ie**nd

h)   "ieu"

The short "e" vowel sound heard in "pet" may be represented by the "ieu" vowel digraph. Unlike most short vowel digraphs, it is found in:

- Open syllables ("l**ieu**-ten-ant")

In Britain and Canada, the word "lieutenant" is pronounced "l**ef**-t**e**nunt" with a short "e" vowel sound followed by a consonant "f" sound. In the United States the word "lieutenant" is pronounced "l**oo**-tenunt" with a long "u" vowel sound.

*l**ieu**tenant*

i)   "u(r)"

The short "e" vowel sound heard in "pet" may be represented by the "u(r)" spelling pattern. The letter "r" is pronounced. It is found in:

- Closed syllables ("b**ur**-i-al", "b**ur**-y")

Words marked by an asterisk do not follow the doubling principle.

*b**ur**ial**   *b**ur**y**

j)   "ue"

The short "e" vowel sound heard in "pet" appears to be represented by the "ue" vowel digraph.

This spelling is incidental. The letter "g" is followed by a silent letter "u" when the hard "g" consonant sound would otherwise be followed by vowel letters "e", "i" or "y" as in "guest", "guide", and "guy". The silent letter "u" protects the letter "g" from being pronounced with the soft "g/j" consonant sound.

guess   **gue**st

C5   Spelling the Short "I" Vowel Sound

There are many spelling patterns for the short "i" vowel sound heard in "**i**t", "t**i**p", and "k**i**ng". They have been divided into major, minor, and rare spelling patterns.

In English spelling, the letter "i" is generally not found at the end of words.

C5.1 Major Spelling Patterns

There are five major spelling patterns for the short "i" vowel sound heard in "**i**t".

a)   "i"

The short "i" vowel sound heard in "it" may be represented by a single letter "i":

- Followed by two consonants ("**i**mp**i**sh", "b**i**scuit") "")
- Followed by double consonants ("**i**mmigrant", "d**i**nner")
- In closed single-syllable words and final syllables ("b**i**d", "confl**i**ct")

The short "i" vowel sound is heard in a closed syllable.

It may be noted that the "i(r)" spelling pattern often represents the r-influenced schwa vowel sound heard in "after" when followed by a vowel and the stressed r-influenced vowel sound heard in "bird" when followed by a consonant. The final "-ire" spelling pattern usually represents the long "i" vowel sound followed by the r-influenced schwa vowel sound as heard in "fire".

In keeping with the doubling principle, the double "rr" spelling pattern usually follows a regular short vowel sound, as heard in "mirror", and not an r-influenced vowel sound.

With words such as "practice" and "prejudice", the final silent letter "e" signals that the adjacent letter "c" is pronounced with the soft "c/s" consonant sound. With words such as "decisive" and "imaginative", the final silent letter "e" satisfies the convention that words do not end with the letter "v".

Words marked by an asterisk do not follow the doubling principle.

ability*	begin	chemical*	condition*
accomplish	being	chicken	conflict
activity*	bib	children	consider*
admission	biblical*	chimney	consist
admit	bid	chipmunk	constructive
Africa*	big	Christmas	continue*
agriculture*	bilingual	citizen*	contribute*
alphabetical*	bill	city*	convict
ambition*	billion	civil*	council
ambitious*	bin	civilian*	cousin
animal*	biological*	civilize*	credit
Antarctic	bionic*	classification*	cricket
application*	biscuit	clerical*	criminal*
Arctic	bit	cliff	critic*
arithmetic	bitter	clinic*	critical*
article*	brick	clinical*	cylindrical*
artificial*	bridge	clothing	cynical*
assist	bring	coffin	decision*
astonish	British*	collision*	decisive
astronomical*	building	comical*	delicate*
Atlantic	burning	coming	delicious*
atomic*	cabin	commission	deliver*
attic	calling	committee	dentist
atypical*	candlewick	companionship	derrick
basic	carrying	competition*	diabolical*
basin	ceiling	complicate*	dictionary
basis	cervical*	composition*	did

difference	driving	fix	hunting
different	during	flashing	hurricane*
difficult	dynamic*	fling	hurting
dig	eating	flying	hypothetical*
diggings	eccentric	following	hysterical*
dignity	ecclesiastical*	frantic	identical*
diminish*	economic*	frolic*	if
dining	effective	furniture*	igloo
dinner	efficiency*	gift	ignore
dip	efficient*	gigantic	ill
director*	elastic	give*	illegal
disagree*	electric	given*	illness
disappear*	elliptical*	going	imagination*
disappoint*	empirical*	gorilla	imaginative
disapprove*	English	grammatical*	imagine*
disaster*	equipment	graphic	imitate*
discipline*	establish	gratitude*	immediate
discomfort*	ethical*	grip	immense
discontent*	evening	grizzly	immigrant
discover*	excessive	habit	impish
discrimination*	exciting	hanging	important
discuss*	exhibit*	happening	impossible
disease*	exhibition*	heading	in
disgust	exist	hearing	inch
dish	exit	helicopter*	include
dislike	extinct	helping	inclusive
dismiss	falling	hesitate*	income
disregard	familiar*	hid	increase
disrespect	fantastic	hidden	indeed
dissatisfaction	farcical*	hiding	Indian
dissatisfy	feeling	hill	individual*
distance	fellowship	him	industry
distant	fidget	himself	inexpensive
distinct	fifteen	hinder	inflation
distinguish	fifth	hindrance	influence
district	fifty	his	influential
disturb	fighting	historical*	inform
ditch	figure*	history	information
diving	film	hit	injure
division*	finding	holding	inquire
doing	finger	homesick	inquiry
dolphin	finish*	hoping	insect
dreaming	firing	hopping	inside
drink	fish	horizon*	insist
drinking	fishing	horizontal*	instance
drip	fit	hospital*	instant

instead	legislation	Mexico*	original*
instrument	legitimate*	middle	ownership
insult	letting	milk*	Pacific*
insurance	lexical*	mill	packing
insure	liberal*	million	panic*
intelligence	liberty*	mimic*	paradoxical*
intend	lid	mineral*	particle
intention	lift	minimum*	particular*
interest	lighting	mining	patriotism
interfere	lightning	minister*	paying
international	limb	*minute* (Time)	permission
interrupt	limerick*	mirror	permit
into	limit*	mischief	pharmaceutical
introduce	linger	miserable	philosophical*
invent	lip	misery*	physical*
invention	liquid*	miss	pick
invisible*	liquor*	missing	picking
invite	list	mission	picnic
inviting	listen	mistake	picture
involve	listening	misty	pig
irrigate	lit	mitt	pigeon*
issue	literary*	mix	pin
it	literature*	morning	pinch
Italian*	litter	moving	pink
Italy*	little	multiplication*	pit
itself	living	music	pity*
Jupiter*	lizard*	musical*	plastic
keeping	logical*	musician*	poetic*
kick	losing	mystical*	polish
kid	loving	mythical*	political*
kill	lunatic	nautical*	politician*
killing	lying	niche	politics
kin	lyrical*	nickel	position*
king	magic*	noiseless	practical*
kit	magical*	nothing	practice
kitchen	magnetic*	offering	prefix
kitten	making	official*	prejudice
knit	mathematics*	Olympic	president*
lackadaisical*	mechanic*	omission	princess
landing	mechanism	omit	principal
lasting	medical*	opening	principle
laying	meeting	opinion*	print
leadership	membership	opposition*	printing
leading	metaphorical*	optical*	prison
learning	metric	ordinary*	profit
leaving	Mexican*	origin	province

proving	satisfaction	skill	submit
public	satisfy	skin	swim
punish	saying	skinny	swimming
putting	sceptical* (UK, CAN)	skip	swing
qualification*	scientific*	skit	swinging
quick	scientist	sleeping	sympathetic
quit	scissors	slid	sympathetic*
quiz	screaming	sliding	taking
rabbit	seeing	slim	talking
racing	selling	sling	teaching
radical*	sending	slip	technical*
ranking	service	slipping	television
rapid	shaking	sliver*	telling
reading	sheriff	snit	theatrical*
recognition*	shining	Spanish	theoretical*
refit	ship	speaking	thick
reform	shocking	spelling	thin
register	shooting	spherical*	thing
religion*	showing	spill	think
repetition*	sick	spin	thinking
republic	signal	spirit*	this
resist	signature	spit	throwing
responsibility*	silk	spitting	ticket
rhythmical*	silly	splendid	till
ribbon	silver	split	timid*
rich	similar*	splitting	tin
rid	simple	spring	tip
ridiculous*	simplicity*	springing	topical*
riding	sin	squid	topographical*
rigid*	since	standing	traffic
ring	sincere	static*	tragic*
ringing	sing	stealing	trick
rip	singing	stick	trip
ripping	single	stiff	tropical*
rising	sink	still	trucking
risk	sinking	sting	trying
river*	sister	stinging	tulip
roaring	sit	stink	turning
rollick	sitting	stinking	twin
rolling	situation*	stocking	twist
rubbing	six	stopping	twit
rubbish	sixty	strict	typical*
running	skeptical* (USA)	striking	unit
sailing	skiff	string	until
sandwich	skiing	strip	vehicle
satirical*		stupid	vertical*

victim	whimsical*	wind (Noun)	with
victory	whip	winding (Verb)	witness
village	whisper	window	wondering
villain	whistle	windy	working
visit	wicked	wing	worship
vivid*	wicket	winner	wrist
walking	widow*	winning	writing
washing	width	winter	written
watching	wilderness	wisdom	zipper
wearing	will	wish	zit
wedding	willow	wit	
which	win	witch	

b)   "e"

The short "i" vowel sound heard in "it" may be represented by a single letter "e":

- Followed by two consonants ("**Engl**ish", "r**e**flect")
- Followed by double consonants ("pr**e**tty", "actr**ess**")
- In closed single-syllable words and final syllables ("h**e**re", "bull**e**t")

The short "e" vowel sound is heard in a closed syllable. This spelling pattern is seldom found in single-syllable words. The words "here" and "mere" are two exceptions.

It may be noted that the "e(r)" spelling pattern seldom represents a short vowel sound. The word "exp**er**ience" is an exception to the rule. The "e(r)" spelling pattern usually represents the r-influenced schwa vowel sound heard in "after" when followed by a vowel and the stressed r-influenced vowel sound heard in "bird" when followed by a consonant.

With the words "atmospher**e**", "her**e**", "interfer**e**", "mer**e**" and "sincer**e**", the final silent letter "e" signals that the preceding letter "e" is pronounced with a short vowel sound and not the r-influenced schwa vowel sound.

Words marked by an asterisk do not follow the doubling principle. In particular, the doubling principle does not apply when a short vowel prefix is added to a base word as in the words "**de**ceive" and "**re**duce". For this reason, many of the following words do not follow the doubling principle.

actress	bullet	*deceit*	*defence* (UK, CAN)
atmosphere	business	*deceive*	*defend*
basket	careless	*decision*	*defense* (USA)
below*	closet	*decisive*	degree
blanket	college	declare	delicious*
bucket	*decay*	decrease	

delight*	experience*	refer*	require*
demand*	forest	reflect	reserve*
depend*	hatred	reflection	resign*
descend	here	refresh	resist*
descent	hero	refuse*	respect*
describe	honest	regard*	responsible
desert*	interfere	regret	result*
deserve*	interference	rejoice*	retire*
design*	jacket	relate*	retired*
desire*	knowledge	relation*	return*
despair	market	relief*	review*
despite	material*	relieve*	reward*
destroy	mere	religion	rocket
destruction	modest	remain*	secret
destructive	neglect	remark*	series*
detail*	peculiar*	remember*	serious*
detect*	period*	remind*	sincere
determine*	planet	repair*	stewardess
develop*	pocket	repeat*	thesaurus*
disregard*	pretty	replace	ticket
disrespect	privilege	reply	toilet
earnest	receipt*	report*	wilderness
economy*	receive*	represent*	witness
England	reduce*	republic*	women
English	reduction*	request*	

c) "y"

The short "i" vowel sound heard in "it" may be represented by a single letter "y":

- Followed by two consonants ("mystery", "hypnosis")
- Followed by double consonants ("syllable", "symmetry")
- In closed single-syllable words and final syllables ("gym", "analyst")

The short "e" vowel sound is heard in a closed syllable.

This spelling pattern is Greek in origin. It may be noted that the letter "y" represents the same vowel sound as the letter "i" in the same position. Compare the short "i" vowel sounds in "gym" and "bit".

Words marked by an asterisk do not follow the doubling principle.

abyss	crystal	Egypt	hypnosis
analyst	cylinder*	gym	hypnotism
bicycle	cymbal	Gypsy	hypnotize
catalyst	cynic*	hymn	lynch

lynx	Olympic	rhythm	symptom
lyric*	oxygen*	syllable	synthetic
Marilyn	physical*	symbol	syringe*
mysterious	physician*	symmetry	syrup*
mystery	physics*	sympathetic	system
myth	Pygmy	sympathy	typical*
nymph	pyramid*	symphony	tyranny*

d)   "-a_e"

The short "i" vowel sound heard in "it" appears to be represented by the "-a_e" spelling pattern. This is a coincidental spelling pattern found in:

- Closed final syllables ("alternate", "encourage")
- Word to which a suffix has been added ("encouraged", "manager")

In the following words it appears that a final silent letter "e" is helping to represent the preceding short "i" vowel sound. However, the final silent letter "e" is coincidental as it is performing other functions. With words such as "necklace" and "surface", the final silent letter "e" signals that the adjacent letter "c" is pronounced with the soft "c/s" consonant sound. With words such as "average" and "village", the final silent letter "e" signals that the adjacent letter "g" is pronounced with the soft "g/j" consonant sound.

When "alternate", "associate", "certificate", "moderate", and "predicate" are being used as verbs, the final silent letter "e" signals that the preceding letter "a" is pronounced with the long "a" vowel sound. This is an example of morphemic spelling.

With the words "accurate" and "delicate", the final silent letter "e" does not appear to perform a necessary function.

accurate	*carriage*	immediate	percentage
accurately	*certificate*	language	postage
acreage	cottage	manage	*predicate*
advantage	courage	manager	surface
alternate	damage	message	unfortunate
associate	delicate	*moderate*	village
average	encourage	necklace	voyage
baggage	encouraged	orange	
bandage	garbage	package	
cabbage	homage	passage	

e)   "i _ e" and "i_ _e"

The short "i" vowel sound heard in "it" appears to be represented by the "-i_e" and "i_ _e" spelling pattern. This is a coincidental spelling pattern found in:

- Closed final syllables ("examine" and "opposite")
- Words to which a suffix has been added ("actively" and "definitely")

In the following words it appears that a final silent letter "e" is helping to represent the preceding short "i" vowel sound. However, the final silent letter "e" is coincidental as it is performing other functions.

With words such as "office" and "justice", the final silent letter "e" signals that the adjacent letter "c" is pronounced with the soft "c/s" consonant sound. With words such as "bridge" and "hinge", the final silent letter "e" signals that the adjacent letter "g" is pronounced with the soft "g/j" consonant sound. With words such as "eclipse" and "promise", the final silent letter "e" satisfies the convention that base words do not end with the letter "s". In words such as "active" and "expensive", the final silent letter "e" satisfies the convention that words do not end with the letter "v".

In a number of words the final silent letter "e" does not perform a necessary function. This is the case with words ending with "-ine" and "-ite" such as "determine", "medicine", "definite", and "opposite". It is also the case with the word "grille" which is French in origin. Such words would be pronounced the same way without the final silent letter "e".

active	determine	glimpse	office
actively	discipline	grille	opposite
alternative	eclipse	hinge	positive
attentive	examine	imagine	prince
attractive	expensive	inclusive	promise
bridge	explosive	justice	relative
cowardice	extensive	live (Verb)	representative
cringe	favorite (USA)	massive	since
definite	favourite (UK, CAN)	medicine	wince
definitely	forgive	native	
destructive	give	negative	
detective		notice	

C5.2 Minor Spelling Patterns

There are four minor spelling patterns for the short "i" vowel sound heard in "it".

a) "ea(r)"

The short "i" vowel sound heard in "it" may be represented by the "ea(r)" vowel digraph. The doubling principle does not apply to short vowel sounds represented by a vowel digraph. It is found in:

- Closed syllables that end with "r" ("fear", "appear")

appear	dear	fear	near
beard	disappear	gear	year
clear	ear	hear	

b) "ee" and "ee(r)"

The short "i" vowel sound heard in "it" may be represented by the "ee" and "ee(r)" vowel digraphs. The doubling principle does not apply to short vowel sounds represented by a vowel digraph. These spelling pattern are found in:

- Closed syllables ("b<u>ee</u>r", "engin<u>ee</u>r")

been	career	*creek*	engineer
beer	cheer	deer	

c) "ei"

The short "i" vowel sound heard in "it" may be represented by the "ei" vowel digraph. The doubling principle does not apply to short vowel sounds represented by a vowel digraph. It is found in:

- Closed syllables ("w<u>ei</u>rd", "forf<u>ei</u>t")

This spelling pattern is contrary to the "i" before "e" except after "c" rule.

counterfeit	forfeit	surfeit
foreign	sovereign	weird

d) "ui"

The short "i" vowel sound heard in "it" may be represented by the "ui" vowel digraph. It is found in:

- Closed syllables ("g<u>ui</u>lt", "b<u>ui</u>ld-ing")

biscuit	building	guild	guitar
build	built	guilt	

C5.3 Rare Spelling Patterns

There are at least five rare spelling patterns for the short "i" vowel sound heard in "it".

a)   "ai"

The short "i" vowel sound heard in "it" may be represented by the "ai" vowel digraph. The doubling principle does not apply to short vowel sounds represented by a vowel digraph. It is found in:

- Closed syllables ("mount**ai**n")

mountain

b)   "ia"

The short "i" vowel sound heard in "it" may be represented by the "ia" vowel digraph. The doubling principle does not apply to short vowel sounds represented by a vowel digraph. It is found in:

- Closed syllables ("carr**ia**ge", "marr**ia**ge")

In the words "carriage" and "marriage", the final silent letter "e" signals that the adjacent letter "g" is pronounced with the soft "g/j" consonant sound.

carr**ia**ge   marr**ia**ge

c)   "ie"

The short "i" vowel sound heard in "it" may be represented by the "ie" vowel digraph. The doubling principle does not apply to short vowel sounds represented by a vowel digraph. It is found in:

- Closed syllables ("f**ie**rce", "misch**ie**f")

This is an application of the "i" before "e" except after "c" rule.

f**ie**rce   misch**ie**f   s**ie**ve
financ**ie**r   p**ie**rce

d)   "o"

The short "i" vowel sound heard in "it" may be represented by a single letter "o":

- In closed syllables ("w**o**m-en")

The word "woman" does not follow the doubling principle.

w**o**men*

e)   "u"

The short "i" vowel sound heard in "it" may be represented by a single letter "u":

- In closed syllables ("b**us**-iness", "min-**u**te")

In the word "minute", the final silent letter "e" does not appear to perform a necessary function. Words marked by an asterisk do not follow the doubling principle.

b**u**siness*   b**u**sy*   *min**u**te** (Time)

C6   Spelling the Short "O" Vowel Sound

The short "o" vowel sound heard in "l**aw**", "l**o**ng", and "**a**ll" and the broad "a" vowel sound heard in "**a**rt", "b**a**rn", and "sh**a**rk" are very similar. Dictionaries often indicate that words may be pronounced with either vowel sound. The pronunciation given to particular words can change from place to place and not everyone distinguishes between the two sounds.

There are many spelling patterns for the short "o" vowel sound heard in "l**aw**". They have been divided into major, minor, and rare spelling patterns.

C6.1 Major Spelling Patterns

There are four major spelling patterns for the short "o" vowel sound heard in "l**aw**".

a)   "o"

A single letter "o" represents the short "o" vowel sound in the following spelling patterns.

i)   "o"

The short "o" vowel sound heard in "law" may be represented by a single letter "o":

- Followed by two consonants ("l**o**bster", "r**o**cket")
- Followed by double consonants ("c**o**ffee", "c**o**llar")
- In closed single-syllable words and final syllables ("d**o**g", "acr**o**ss")

The short "o" vowel sound is heard in a closed syllable.

Most the following words are also pronounced with the broad "a" vowel sound by some speakers.

In the words "gone", "bygone", and "foregone", the final silent letter "e" does not appear to perform a useful function. The "-o(ne)" spelling pattern, as heard in "done" and "none", also represents the short "u" vowel sound.

Words marked by an asterisk do not follow the doubling principle.

*ab**o**lish**	*d**o**g*	*l**o**ft*	*r**o**ck*
*acr**o**ss*	*d**o**ll*	*l**o**g*	*r**o**cket*
*al**o**ng*	*d**o**lphin*	*l**o**ng*	*sh**o**p*
*auth**o**rities**	*d**o**nkey*	*l**o**ngest*	*sh**o**t*
*bel**o**ng*	*d**o**t*	*l**o**ss*	*s**o**cket*
*b**o**ss*	*ex**o**tic**	*l**o**st*	*s**o**ft*
*b**o**ther*	*f**o**g*	*m**o**nster*	*s**o**ften*
*b**o**x*	*f**o**nd*	*n**o**t*	*s**o**lid**
*br**o**ccoli*	*foreg**o**ne*	*o**ff*	*s**o**lve*
*byg**o**ne*	*fr**o**g*	*o**ffence* (UK, CAN)	*s**o**ng*
*cann**o**t*	*fr**o**st*	*o**ffense* (USA)	*sp**o**t*
*ch**o**colate**	*G**o**d*	*o**ffer*	*st**o**p*
*ch**o**p*	*g**o**lf*	*o**ffice*	*str**o**ng*
*cl**o**g*	*g**o**ne*	*o**ften*	*t**o**nic**
*cl**o**th*	*h**o**mily**	*o**n*	*t**o**p*
*c**o**d*	*h**o**p*	*o**x*	*t**o**pic**
*c**o**ffee*	*h**o**t*	*o**xen**	*tr**o**d*
*c**o**ffin*	*h**o**vel**	*O**z*	*up**o**n*
*c**o**llar*	*inv**o**lve*	*p**o**cket*	*v**o**lcano*
*c**o**st*	*ir**o**nic**	*p**o**p*	*wr**o**ng*
*c**o**t*	*kn**o**b*	*p**o**t*	
*cr**o**p*	*l**o**bster*	*resp**o**nd*	
*cr**o**ss*	*l**o**dger*	*r**o**bot*	

ii) "o(r_)", "o(rr), "-o(re)", and "o(r)"

The short "o" vowel sound heard in "law" may be represented by the "o(r_)", "o(rr), and "-o(re)" spelling patterns in closed syllables. The letter "o" is:

- Followed by "r" and a different consonant letter ("c**or**n", "f**or**get, "f**or**mal")
- Followed by the double "rr" spelling pattern ("b**orr**ow", "s**orr**y")
- Followed by "-re" ("ch**ore**", "carniv**ore**")
- Followed by a single final letter "r" ("f**or**", "'n**or**", and "**or**" only)

This spelling of the short "o" vowel sound is an r-influenced vowel sound.

As a word ending, the letters "-or" are usually pronounced with the r-influenced schwa vowel sound heard in "after". The words "for", "nor", and "or" are exceptions to this rule.

Words such as "chore" and "carnivore" are pronounced with the short "o" vowel sound and not the r-influenced schwa vowel sound. When the "-re" word ending follows vowel letters "a", "e", and "o", as in "dare", "where", and "more", the vowel is usually pronounced with a short vowel sound.

In keeping with the doubling principle, the "o(rr)" spelling pattern usually represents the short "o" vowel sound as heard in "b<u>o</u>rrow" and "s<u>o</u>rry".

Some words, such as "f<u>o</u>rest", are also pronounced with the broad "a" vowel sound. Other words, such as "ch<u>ore</u>" are also pronounced with the long "o" vowel sound.

The "o(r)" spelling also represents the stressed r-influenced vowel sound heard in words such as "attorney", "world" and "worse".

Words marked by an asterisk do not follow the doubling principle.

acc<u>o</u>rd	*fo<u>r</u>eign**	maj<u>or</u>ity*	sc<u>ore</u>
ad<u>o</u>rn	*fo<u>r</u>est**	m<u>o</u>ral	sc<u>o</u>rn
aff<u>o</u>rd	f<u>o</u>rget	m<u>o</u>rale	sc<u>o</u>rpion
auth<u>o</u>rities*	f<u>o</u>rgive	m<u>ore</u>	*sh<u>ore</u>*
bef<u>ore</u>	f<u>o</u>rk	m<u>o</u>rning	*sh<u>o</u>rt*
b<u>o</u>rder	f<u>o</u>rm	n<u>o</u>r	*sn<u>ore</u>*
b<u>ore</u>	f<u>o</u>rmal	n<u>o</u>rmal	s<u>o</u>rdid
b<u>o</u>ring	f<u>o</u>rmer	n<u>o</u>rth	*s<u>ore</u>*
b<u>o</u>redom*	f<u>o</u>rmula	N<u>o</u>rway	*s<u>o</u>rry*
b<u>o</u>rn	*f<u>o</u>rt*	<u>o</u>r	*s<u>o</u>rt*
b<u>o</u>rrow	*f<u>o</u>rth*	<u>o</u>ral*	*sp<u>o</u>rt*
carniv<u>ore</u>	f<u>o</u>rtunate	<u>o</u>range*	*st<u>ore</u>*
ch<u>ore</u>	f<u>o</u>rtune	<u>o</u>rchid	st<u>o</u>rm
cont<u>o</u>rtion	f<u>o</u>rty	<u>o</u>rder	*st<u>o</u>ry*
c<u>o</u>rd	f<u>o</u>rward	<u>o</u>rdinary	supp<u>o</u>rt
c<u>ore</u>	*gl<u>o</u>ry**	<u>ore</u>	sw<u>o</u>rd
c<u>o</u>rk	*h<u>o</u>rizontal**	<u>o</u>rgan	*th<u>o</u>rn*
c<u>o</u>rn	h<u>o</u>rn	<u>o</u>rganization	*tom<u>o</u>rrow*
c<u>o</u>rner	h<u>o</u>rrible	<u>o</u>rganize	t<u>ore</u>
c<u>o</u>rporation	h<u>o</u>rror	<u>o</u>rigin*	t<u>o</u>rtoise
enf<u>o</u>rce	h<u>o</u>rse	<u>o</u>rnament	transp<u>o</u>rtation
en<u>o</u>rmous	*ign<u>ore</u>*	perf<u>o</u>rm	unf<u>o</u>rtunate
expl<u>ore</u>	imp<u>o</u>rtant	p<u>o</u>rt	*w<u>ore</u>*
Fl<u>o</u>rida*	inf<u>o</u>rm	rec<u>o</u>rd	w<u>o</u>rn
f<u>o</u>r	lab<u>o</u>ratory*	ref<u>o</u>rm	
f<u>o</u>rce	l<u>o</u>rd	rep<u>o</u>rt	

b) "a"

A single letter "a" represents the short "o" vowel sound in the following spelling patterns.

i) "a(l)" and "a(ll)"

The short "o" vowel sound heard in "law" may be represented by the "a(l)" and "a(ll) spelling patterns in closed syllables. The letter "a" is:

- Followed by "l" and a different consonant letter ("salt", "also", "balding")
- Followed by the double "ll" spelling pattern ("fall", "caller")
- Followed by a single final letter "l" ("Montreal")

Note that if the "a(l)" spelling pattern is followed by a vowel, the letter "a" is pronounced with the long "a" vowel sound as heard in "whaling".

When "a(l)" spelling pattern is followed by a different consonant letter, the letter "a" is sometimes pronounced with the short "o" vowel sound as in "halt" and sometimes with the short "a" vowel sound as in "alcohol".

In keeping with the doubling principle, the "a(ll)" spelling pattern sometimes represents the short "a" vowel sound as in "gallant" and "shall".

Unfortunately, the "-a(l)" spelling pattern also represents the schwa vowel sound in words such as "equal" and "festival".

alderman	balsam	hallway	smallest
all	call	halt	squall
almanac	called	halter	stall
almond	*caller*	installment	stalling
almost	exalt	mall	tall
already	fall	malt	taller
also	falling	Montreal	wall
alternative	false	pall	walnut
although	falsify	palsy	walrus
altogether	falter	salt	Walter
always	forestall	salty	waltz
bald	gall	scald	
ball	hall	small	

ii) "(qu)a"

The short "o" vowel sound heard in "law" is often heard following the consonant "w" sound. It may be represented by the "(qu)a" spelling pattern in closed syllables:
- Followed by two consonants ("quantity", "squander")
- Followed by double consonants ("quarrel", "squabble")
- Followed by a single letter "l" ("qualify", "quality")
- In closed single-syllable words ("quash", "squad")

The consonant "w" sound is represented by the letter "u".

Most of the following words are also pronounced with the broad "a" vowel sound as heard in "qualify", "quash", and "squash". Note, however, that when "a" is followed by consonant letter "r" the short "o" vowel sound is usually heard as in "quart" and "quarter".

Words marked by an asterisk do not follow the doubling principle.

qualification*	*quarrel*	quarter	*squash*
qualify*	*quarry*	quash	
quality*	quart	squall	

iii)   "(w)a" and "(wh)a"

The short "o" vowel sound heard in "law" is often heard following the consonant "w" sound. It may be represented by the "(w)a" and "(wh)a" spelling patterns in closed syllables:

- Followed by two consonants ("walnut", "wander")
- In closed single-syllable words ("wall", "want", "swan", "wharf")

Many of the following words are also pronounced with the broad "a" vowel sound as heard in "swan", "want", and "wash". Note, however, that when "a" is followed by consonant letter "r", the short "o" vowel sound is usually heard as in "war", "warm", and "wharf".

Words marked by an asterisk do not follow the doubling principle.

reward	walnut	warden	*watch*
swan	walrus	warm	*water**
swap	waltz	warn	*wharf*
swarthy	want	wash	
wall	war	wasp	

c)   "au"

The short "o" vowel sound heard in "law" may be represented by the "au" vowel digraph. The doubling principle does not apply to short vowel sounds represented by a vowel digraph. This spelling pattern found in:

- Closed syllables ("Aug-ust", "aud-io", "applaud", "pause")
- Open syllables occasionally ("cau-tion")

With many words, including "auburn", "audio", and "author", dictionaries show the short "o" vowel sound being pronounced in an open syllable as in "**au**-**b**urn", "**au**-**d**io", and "**au**-thor". However, with such words the short "o" vowel sound may readily be pronounced in a closed syllable as in "au**b**-urn", "au**d**-i-o", and "au**th**-or". For spelling purposes, it is helpful to pronounce short vowel sounds within closed syllables whenever possible.

The "au" spelling pattern is not used as a word ending. It is a convention of English spelling that words do not end with the letter "u". As a word ending, the letter "u" becomes a "w", resulting in the "-aw" spelling pattern. Compare, for example, the words "c**au**tion" and "dr**aw**".

appl**au**d	**au**thor	exh**au**st	n**au**ghty
appl**au**se	**au**thority	f**au**cet	*n**au**tical*
ass**au**lt	**au**thorize	f**au**lt	P**au**l
astron**au**t	**au**to	fr**au**d	p**au**per
auburn	**au**tograph	g**au**nt	p**au**se
auction	**au**tomobile	g**au**ze	s**au**ce
audible	**au**tumn	h**au**l	s**au**cer
audience	**au**xiliary	h**au**nt	s**au**sage
audio	bec**au**se	h**au**nted	sl**au**ghter
audit	c**au**ght	hydr**au**lic	st**au**nch
audition	c**au**liflower	in**au**guration	t**au**ght
auditorium	c**au**se	j**au**ndice	t**au**t
auditory	c**au**tion	j**au**nt	thes**au**rus
August	c**au**tious	j**au**nty	v**au**lt
auk	cl**au**se	l**au**nch	
Australia	d**au**ghter	l**au**ndry	
authentic	dinos**au**r	l**au**rel	

d) "aw" and "awe"

The short "o" vowel sound heard in "law" may be represented by the "aw" and "awe" vowel digraphs. The doubling principle does not apply to short vowel sounds represented by a vowel digraph. The letter "w" is silent. It is found in:

- Closed syllables ("h**aw**k", "l**aw**n", "**aw**k-ward", "**aw**n-ing")
- Open syllables ("**awe**", "dr**aw**", "d**aw**-dle", "colesl**aw**")

Unlike most short vowel digraphs, the "aw" spelling pattern is often found in open syllables and, for this reason, used as a word ending as in "dr**aw**" and "withdr**aw**". That said, the "aw" spelling pattern is also found in closed syllables as in "squ**aw**k", "br**aw**l" and "y**aw**n". However, in closed syllables the "w" often becomes a "u" resulting in the "au" spelling pattern. Compare, for example, the words "dr**aw**" and "j**au**nty". It is a convention of English spelling that words do not end with the letter "u".

With the word "awe", the final silent letter "e" helps to satisfy the three letter rule. The silent "e" is retained in the word "awesome".

aw**e**	**craw**l	**law**	sh**aw**l
awesome	d**aw**dle	**law**n	sp**aw**n
awful	d**aw**n	*lawyer*	spr**aw**l
awkward	dr**aw**	out**law**	squ**aw**
awl	dr**aw**back	p**aw**	squ**aw**k
awning	dr**aw**er	p**aw**n	str**aw**
b**aw**dy	dr**aw**n	pr**aw**n	str**aw**berry
b**aw**l	f**aw**n	r**aw**	th**aw**
br**aw**l	fl**aw**	r**aw**hide	withdr**aw**
br**aw**n	gn**aw**	s**aw**	withdr**aw**al
by**law**	h**aw**k	s**aw**yer	y**aw**n
cl**aw**	jackd**aw**	scr**aw**l	
coles**law**	j**aw**	sees**aw**	

C6.2 Minor Spelling Patterns

There are six minor spelling patterns for the short "o" vowel sound heard in "**law**".

a)   "al(k)"

The short "o" vowel sound heard in "law" may be represented by the "al(k)" vowel digraph. The letter "l" is silent. It is found in:

- Closed syllables that end with the letter "-k" ("w**al**k")

The letter "l", even when silent, can have an influence over the pronunciation of a preceding vowel letter. When vowel letter "a" is followed by the letter "l", it is often pronounced with the short "o" sound.

b**al**k	st**al**k	w**al**k
ch**al**k	t**al**k	

b)   "augh(t)"

The short "o" vowel sound heard in "law" may be represented by the "augh(t)" vowel digraph. The letters "gh" are silent. It is found in:

- Closed syllables that end with the letter "t" ("*caught*", "d**augh**t-er")

aught	d**augh**ter	h**augh**ty	sl**augh**ter
caught	distr**augh**t	*n**augh**ty*	t**augh**t

c) "ho(n)-"

The short "o" vowel sound heard in "law" may be represented by the "ho(n)-" vowel digraph. The letter "h" is silent. The doubling principle does not apply to short vowel digraphs. It is found in:

- Closed syllables that end with the letter "n" ("**ho**n-est", "**ho**n-our")

honest	**ho**nor (USA)	**ho**nour (UK, CAN)	**ho**nourable (UK, CAN)
honesty	**ho**norable (USA)		

d) "oa"

The short "o" vowel sound heard in "law" may be represented by the "oa" vowel digraph. The doubling principle does not apply to short vowel sounds represented by a vowel digraph. It is found in:

- Closed syllables. ("r**oa**r-ing", "abr**oa**d")

abr**oa**d	br**oa**d	**oa**r	r**oa**ring
b**oa**rd	c**oa**rse	r**oa**r	

e) "ou" and "ou(r)"

The short "o" vowel sound heard in "law" may be represented by the "ou" and "ou(r)" vowel digraphs. The doubling principle does not apply to short vowel sounds represented by a vowel digraph. It is found in:

- Closed syllables ("c**ou**rt", "p**ou**r-ing", "res**ou**rce")

c**ou**gh	*f**ou**r*	p**ou**r	*tr**ou**gh*
c**ou**rse	f**ou**rteen	p**ou**ring	*y**ou**r*
c**ou**rt	*f**ou**rth*	res**ou**rce	

f) "ough(t)"

The short "o" vowel sound heard in "law" may be represented by the "ough(t)" vowel digraph. The letters "gh" are silent. The doubling principle does not apply to short vowel digraphs. It is found in:

- Closed syllables that end with the letter "t" ("b**ough**t", "th**ough**t")

b**ough**t	f**ough**t	**ough**t	th**ough**t
br**ough**t	n**ough**t	s**ough**t	wr**ough**t (iron)

C6.3 Rare Spelling Patterns

There are at least ten rare spelling patterns for the short "o" vowel sound heard in "l**aw**".

a) "a"

The short "o" vowel sound heard in "law" may be represented by a single letter "a":

- In closed syllables ("f**a**th-er", "st**a**rr-y")

father *star* *starry*

b) "ach"

The short "o" vowel sound heard in "law" may be represented by the "ach" vowel digraph. The letters "ch" are silent. It is found in:

- Closed syllables ("y**ach**t")

yacht

c) "ah"

The short "o" vowel sound heard in "law" may be represented by the "ah" vowel digraph. The letter "h" is silent. Unlike most short vowel digraphs, It is found in:

- Open syllables ("sh**ah**", "Ut**ah**", "hurr**ah**")

*hurr**ah*** *sh**ah*** *Ut**ah***

d) "e"

The short "o" vowel sound heard in "law" may be represented by a single letter "e":

- Followed by two consonants ("**e**ntrée", "s**e**rgeant")

entrée *sergeant*

e) "ea(r)"

The short "o" vowel sound heard in "law" may be represented by the "ea(r)" vowel digraph. It is found in:

- Closed syllables ("h**ear**t")

heart

f)   "eau"

The short "o" vowel sound heard in "law" may be represented by the "eau" vowel digraph. Unlike most short vowel digraphs, it is found in:

- Open syllables ("bur**eau**-cracy")

*bur**eau**cracy*

g)   "eo"

The short "o" vowel sound heard in "law" may be represented by the "eo" vowel digraph. The doubling principle does not apply to short vowel sounds represented by a vowel digraph. It is found in:

- Closed syllables ("G**eo**r-gian")

G**eo**rgia   G**eo**rgian

h)   "i"

The short "o" vowel sound heard in "law" may be represented by a single letter "i":

- Followed by two consonants ("l**i**ngerie")

*l**i**ngerie*

i)   "oo(r)"

The short "o" vowel sound heard in "law" may be represented by the "oo(r)" vowel digraph. The doubling principle does not apply to short vowel sounds represented by a vowel digraph. It is found in:

- Closed syllables ("d**oo**r", "fl**oo**r-ing")

d**oo**r   fl**oo**r   fl**oo**ring

j)   "ow"

The short "o" vowel sound heard in "law" may be represented by the "ow" vowel digraph. The doubling principle does not apply to short vowel sounds represented by a vowel digraph. The letter "w" is silent. It is found in:

- Single-syllable words ("t**ow**ard")

The word "toward" is pronounced many ways. When the letter "o" represents a long vowel sound, the word is broken into syllables as "to-ward" and the letter "w" may be pronounced.

toward

C7 Spelling the Short "U" Vowel Sound Heard in "Up", "But", and "Run"

There are three distinct short "u" vowel sounds. Listen to the short "u" vowel sounds heard in:

- The words "**u**p", "b**u**t", and "r**u**n"
- The words "p**u**t", "b**u**sh", and "s**u**gar"
- The words "c**u**re", "p**u**re", and "c**u**rious"

Only spelling patterns used to represent the short "u" vowel sound heard in "**u**p", "b**u**t", and "r**u**n" are discussed in this section.

There are many spelling patterns for the short "u" vowel sound heard in "**u**p". They have been divided into major, minor, and rare spelling patterns.

C7.1 Major Spelling Patterns

There are two major spelling patterns for the short "u" vowel sound heard in "**u**p".

a)   The letter "u".

The short "u" vowel sound heard in "up" may be represented by a single letter "u":

- Followed by two consonants ("b**u**cket", "**u**nder")
- Followed by double consonants ("p**u**ppy", "t**u**nnel")
- In closed single-syllable words and final syllables ("n**u**t", "disc**u**ss")

The short "u" vowel sound is heard in a closed syllable.

Words marked by an asterisk do not follow the doubling principle.

abrupt	bucket	butter	construct
abut	budget	button	construction
accustom	bug	buzz	crush
adult	bump	chipmunk	crust
agriculture	bunch	club	cuddle
begun	bundle	clumsy	cultivate
brush	bunny	conduct	cup
bubble	but	conductor	cupboard

custom	hunter	pump	sum
customer	husband	punctual	summer
cut	hut	punish*	sun
deduct	instruct	pup	Sunday
destruction	insult	puppet	sunny
destructive	interrupt	puppy	supper
difficult	introduction	putt (golfing)	supply
discuss	judge	puzzle	support
disgust	jump	reduction	suppose
drug	jungle	reproduction	suspect
drum	junk	republic	thumb
drunk	just	result	thunder
duck	justice	rub	truck
dug	luck	rubbish	trumpet
dull	lump	rug	trunk
dumb	lunch	rugged	trust
dump	lung	run	tunnel
dust	lunge	rush	ugly
fluffy	much	Russia	ultra-
frustrate	mud	Russian	umbrella
fun	mukluk	rust	un-
fund	multiplication	rut	unable*
funny	multiply	shut	uncle
fuss	muscle	skull	unconscious
fussy	must	skunk	under
grumpy	mutt	struck	understand
gum	mutter	struggle	unfortunate
gun	number	study*	unidentified*
gun	nut	stuff	unknown
hug	plumber	sub	unless
hull	plus	subject	until
humble	production	substance	untrue
humdrum	pronunciation	such	up
hunger	public	suck	upper
hungry	publish	sudden	upstairs
hunt	puck	suffer	us

b)   "o"

The short "u" vowel sound heard in "up" may be represented by a single letter "o":

- Followed by two consonants ("m**o**nkey", "br**o**ther")
- In closed single-syllable words and final syllables ("fr**o**nt", "am**o**ng")

The short "u" vowel sound is heard in a closed syllable.

Words marked by an asterisk do not follow the doubling principle.

am**o**ng	disc**o**ver*	m**o**ngrel	s**o**me
am**o**ngst	d**o**es	m**o**nk	s**o**n
an**o**ther	d**o**ne	m**o**nkey	st**o**mach*
br**o**ther	d**o**zen*	m**o**nth	t**o**n
c**o**lor* (USA)	fr**o**m	M**o**ntreal	t**o**ngue
c**o**lour* (UK, CAN)	fr**o**nt	m**o**ther	w**o**n
c**o**me	gentlew**o**man*	n**o**ne	w**o**nder
c**o**mfort	gl**o**ve	n**o**thing	w**o**nderful
c**o**ming*	g**o**vern*	**o**f	w**o**nderland
c**o**mpanies	h**o**ney*	**o**ther	w**o**nderment
c**o**mpany	L**o**ndon	**o**ven*	w**o**ndrous
c**o**mpass	l**o**ve	sh**o**vel*	
c**o**ver*	M**o**nday	sl**o**venly*	
disc**o**mfort	m**o**ney*	sm**o**ther	

C7.2 Minor Spelling Patterns

There are two minor spelling patterns for the short "u" vowel sound heard in "**u**p".

a)   "-o_e"

The short "u" vowel sound heard in "up" may be represented by the "-o_e" spelling pattern. It is found in:

- Closed syllables ("l**o**ve", "s**o**me-**o**ne")

All of the following words end with a final silent letter "e".

With the word "once" the final silent letter "e" signals that the adjacent letter "c" is pronounced with the soft "c/s" consonant sound. With the word "sponge" the final silent letter "e" signals that the adjacent letter "g" is pronounced with the soft "g/j" consonant sound. With words such as "love" and "glove", the final silent letter "e" satisfies the convention that words do not end with the letter "v". With the word "one", the final silent letter "e" helps to satisfy the three letter rule.

With words that end with the letters "-ome" and "-one", such as "come" and "none", the final silent letter "e" helps to signal that the letter "o" is pronounced with a short "u" vowel sound. This is contrary to the general rule that the final "-o_e" spelling pattern represents the long "o" vowel sound. With the word "gone" and derivatives, the letter "o" is pronounced with the short "o" vowel sound.

The words "once" and "one" are pronounced with an initial consonant "w" sound that is not represented in the spelling of the word.

ab**ove**	d**ove**	l**ove**	s**ome**
any**one**	every**one**	n**one**	some**one**
bec**ome**	gl**ove**	**once**	sp**onge**
c**ome**	inc**ome**	**one**	wholes**ome**
d**one**	lones**ome**	overc**ome**	

b) "ou"

The short "u" vowel sound heard in "up" may be represented by the "ou" vowel digraph. The doubling principle does not apply to short vowel sounds represented by a vowel digraph. It is found in:

- Closed syllables ("r**ou**gh", "c**ou**n-try")

c**ou**ntry	d**ou**ble	t**ou**ch	y**ou**ng
c**ou**ple	en**ou**gh	t**ou**gh	
c**ou**sin	r**ou**gh	tr**ou**ble	

C7.3 Rare Spelling Patterns

There are at least three rare spelling patterns for the short "u" vowel sound heard in "**u**p".

a) "a"

The short "u" vowel sound heard in "up" may be represented by a single letter "a":

- In closed syllables. ("w**a**s", "wh**a**t")

was   what

b) "oe"

The short "u" vowel sound heard in "up" may be represented by the "oe" vowel digraph. This spelling results from adding the suffix "-es" to the base word "do". It is found in:

- Closed syllables ("d**oe**s", "d**oe**s-n't")

does   doesn't

c) "oo"

The short "u" vowel sound heard in "up" may be represented by the "oo" vowel digraph. The doubling principle does not apply to short vowel sounds represented by a vowel digraph. It is found in:

- Closed syllables ("bl<u>oo</u>d", "fl<u>oo</u>d-ing")

bl**oo**d   fl**oo**d   fl**oo**ding

C8 Spelling the Short "U" Vowel Sound Heard in "Put", "Bush", and "Sugar"

There are three distinct short "u" vowel sounds. Listen to the short "u" vowel sounds heard in:

- The words "**u**p", "b**u**t", and "r**u**n"
- The words "p**u**t", "b**u**sh", and "s**u**gar"
- The words "c**u**re", "p**u**re", and "c**u**rious"

Only spelling patterns used to represent the short "u" vowel sound heard in "p**u**t", "b**u**sh", and "s**u**gar" are discussed in this section.

There are several spelling patterns for the short "u" vowel sound heard in "p**u**t". They have been divided into major, minor, and rare spelling patterns.

C8.1 Major Spelling Patterns

There are only two major spelling patterns for the short "u" vowel sound heard in "put".

a) "u"

The short "u" vowel sound heard in "put" may be represented by a single letter "u":

- Followed by two consonants ("b**u**tcher", "b**u**shel")
- Followed by double consonants ("p**u**dding", "b**u**llet")
- In closed single-syllable words and final syllables ("b**u**sh", "armf**u**l")

The short "u" vowel sound is heard in a closed syllable.

The suffix "-ful" is usually pronounced with the short "u" vowel sound when it forms nouns such as "armful" and "cupful". It is usually pronounced with the schwa vowel sound when it forms adjectives such as "beautiful" and "painful".

Words marked by an asterisk do not follow the doubling principle.

armful	butcher	insurance*	push
bull	cupful	jury*	put
bullet	cushion	plural*	sugar*
bush	full	pudding	teaspoonful
bushel	input	pull	

b) "oo"

The short "u" vowel sound heard in "put" may be represented by the "oo" vowel digraph. The doubling principle does not apply to short vowel sounds represented by a vowel digraph. It is found in:

- Closed syllables ("b**oo**k", "c**oo**k-ie", "motherh**oo**d")

book	crook	moor	took
brook	fishhook	mooring	wood
childhood	foot	motherhood	woody
cook	good	outlook	woof
cookbook	hood	poor	wool
cookie	hook	shook	
crook	look	stood	

C8.2 Minor Spelling Patterns

There are three minor spelling patterns for the short "u" vowel sound heard in "put".

a) "o"

The short "u" vowel sound heard in "put" may be represented by a single letter "o":

- In closed syllables ("b**o**s-om", "w**o**m-an")
- Followed by two consonants ("w**o**lf", "w**o**lves")

Words marked by an asterisk do not follow the doubling principle.

bosom*	wolves	womanhood*	womanly*
wolf	woman*	womankind*	

b) "ou"

The short "u" vowel sound heard in "put" may be represented by the "ou" vowel digraph. The doubling principle does not apply to short vowel sounds represented by a vowel digraph. It is found in:

- Closed syllables ("t**ou**r-ing", "y**ou**r")

tour	touring	your

c) "oul(d)"

The short "u" vowel sound heard in "put" may be represented by the "oul(d)" vowel digraph. The letter "l" is silent. It is found in:

- Closed syllables that end with the letter "d" ("c<u>oul</u>d", "w<u>oul</u>d")

could   sh**oul**d   w**oul**d

C8.3 Rare Spelling Patterns

There is at least one rare spelling patterns for the short "u" vowel sound heard in "put".

a) "-u(re)"

The short "u" vowel sound heard in "put" may be represented by the "-u(re)" spelling pattern. The final letter "e" is silent. It is found in:

- Closed syllables ("bro-ch<u>u</u>re")

This pronunciation of the "-ure" word ending is rare. Most often, the letter "u" helps to represent an adjacent consonant digraph sound as heard in "in<u>sure</u>", "mea<u>sure</u>", "fea<u>tu</u>re", "rea<u>ssu</u>re", "sei<u>zu</u>re", and "<u>su</u>re". The letters "-re" represent the r-influenced schwa vowel sound pronounced "ur".

brochu<u>re</u>

C9 Spelling the Short "U" Vowel Sound Heard in "Cure", "Pure", and "Curious"

There are three distinct short "u" vowel sounds. Listen to the short "u" vowel sounds heard in:

- The words "**u**p", "b**u**t", and "r**u**n"
- The words "p**u**t", "b**u**sh", and "s**u**gar"
- The words "c**u**re", "p**u**re", and "c**u**rious"

Only spelling patterns used to represent the short "u" vowel sound heard in "cure", "pure", and "curious" are discussed in this section.

What distinguishes the short "u" vowel sound heard in "c**u**re" from the short "u" vowel sound heard in "p**u**t" is that a consonant "y" sound is pronounced before the short "u" vowel sound. The consonant "y" sound is not represented in the spelling of the words. As this vowel sound is always followed by the letter "r", it may be considered to be an r-influenced vowel sound.

There are only four spelling patterns for the short "u" vowel sound heard in "cure". As none of them are particularly common or rare, they will be dealt with together.

a)   "eu(r)"

The short "u" vowel sound heard in "cure" may be represented by the "eu(r)" vowel digraph. The doubling principle does not apply to short vowel sounds represented by a vowel digraph. It is found in:

- Closed syllables ("an<u>eu</u>r-isum", "<u>Eu</u>r-ope")

an<u>eu</u>rism (UK, CAN)	an<u>eu</u>rysm (USA, CAN)	<u>Eu</u>rope
		h<u>eu</u>ristic

b)   "u(r)"

The short "u" vowel sound heard in "cure" may be represented by the "u(r)" spelling pattern. It is found in:

- Closed syllables ("f<u>u</u>r-ious", "<u>ur</u>-ine")

Words marked by an asterisk do not follow the doubling principle.

c<u>u</u>rious*	f<u>u</u>rious*	<u>u</u>rine*

c)   "-u(re)"

The short "u" vowel sound heard in "cure" may be represented by the "-u(re)" spelling pattern. It is found in:

- Closed single-syllable words and final syllables ("c<u>u</u>re", "p<u>u</u>re", "fail<u>u</u>re", "sec<u>u</u>re")

This pronunciation of the "-ure" word ending is rare. Most often, the letter "u" is silent and helps to represent an adjacent consonant digraph sound as heard in "in<u>sure</u>", "mea<u>sure</u>", "fea<u>tu</u>re", "rea<u>ssure</u>", "sei<u>zure</u>", and "<u>sure</u>". The letters "-re" represent the r-influenced schwa vowel sound pronounced "ur".

c<u>ure</u>	fail<u>ure</u>	proc<u>ure</u>	sec<u>ure</u>
end<u>ure</u>	fig<u>ure</u>	p<u>ure</u>	

d)   "you'(re)"

The short "u" vowel sound heard in "cure" may be represented by the "you'(re)" vowel digraph. It is found in:

- Closed syllables ("y<u>ou</u>'re")

The word "you're" is a contraction of the words "you are". While the word "you" is pronounced with a long "u" vowel sound, the contraction "you're" is often pronounced with the short "u" vowel sound.

you're

Part D: Spelling Other Vowel Sounds

D1 Spelling the Vowel Diphthong Heard in "Coin" and "Toy"

There are several vowel sounds that are neither long nor short. One of these is the vowel diphthong heard in the words "coin" and "toy". Unfortunately, there is no simple name for this vowel sound. It is not associated with a particular letter or spelling pattern.

A diphthong is a complex vowel sound that changes in pronunciation during speech. The vowel sound represented by the letters "oi" in the word "coin" is a diphthong. If pronounced carefully, you may note that the vowel sound begins with the long "o" vowel sound and ends with the long "e" vowel sound without a pause or syllabic break. This distinguishes vowel diphthongs from link letter spelling patterns.

While not classified here as a long vowel sound, vowel diphthongs have long vowel properties. It follows that the spelling patterns for vowel diphthongs conform to the spelling conventions that govern long vowel sounds. In particular, diphthongs are always represented by a vowel digraph; a string of two or more letters that represent a unique vowel sound. Occasionally, consonant letters help to represent vowel diphthongs. In the word "lawyer", for example, the letters "aw" represent the diphthong heard in "coin". As well, within words diphthongs are usually heard in open syllables. In final syllables and in single-syllable words, vowel diphthongs are heard in both open and closed syllables.

There are a number of spelling patterns for the vowel diphthong heard in the words "**coi**n" and "**toy**". They have been divided into major and rare spelling patterns.

D1.1 Major Spelling Patterns

There are two major spelling patterns for the vowel diphthong heard in "**coi**n" and "**toy**".

a) "oi"

The vowel diphthong sound heard in "coin" and "toy" may be represented by the "oi" vowel digraph. It is found in:

- Open syllables ("p**oi**-son", "t**oi**-let")
- Closed final syllables ("av**oi**d", "disapp**oi**nt")
- Closed single-syllable words ("c**oi**n", "j**oi**nt")

English spelling does not favour ending words with the letter "i". For this reason, the "oi" spelling pattern is found within words as in "b**oi**l" and "sirl**oi**n" and not as a word ending. As a word ending, the "i" becomes a "y", resulting in the "-oy" spelling pattern. Compare, for example, the words "p**oi**son" and "enj**oy**".

A number of the following words end with a final silent letter "e". With words such as "choice" and "voice" the final silent letter "e" signals that the letter "c" is pronounced with the soft "c/s" consonant sound. With the word "noise" the final silent letter "e" satisfies the convention that base words do not end with the letter "s".

ano**i**nt	disapp**oi**nt	m**oi**sture	sirl**oi**n
app**oi**nt	f**oi**l	n**oi**se	s**oi**l
av**oi**d	f**oi**st	n**oi**sy	sp**oi**l
b**oi**l	h**oi**st	**oi**l	t**oi**l
br**oi**l	j**oi**n	p**oi**gnant	t**oi**let
ch**oi**ce	j**oi**nt	p**oi**nt	v**oi**ce
c**oi**l	l**oi**n	p**oi**son	v**oi**d
c**oi**n	m**oi**st	rej**oi**ce	

b) "-oy"

The vowel diphthong sound heard in "coin" and "toy" may be represented by the "-oy" vowel digraph. It is found in:

- Open first syllables. ("**loy**-al", "**voy**-age")
- Open final syllables. ("con-v**oy**", "en-j**oy**")
- Open single-syllable words. ("b**oy**", "t**oy**")

The "-oy" spelling pattern is used as a word ending. For this reason, it is usually found in open syllables as in "**loy**-al" and "empl**oy**". Within closed syllables, the "y" often becomes an "i", resulting in the "oi" spelling pattern. Compare, for example, the words "enj**oy**" and "p**oi**son". It is a convention of English spelling that words do not end with the letter "i".

all**oy**	destr**oy**	Ll**oy**d	r**oy**alty
ann**oy**	empl**oy**	l**oy**al	s**oy**bean
b**oy**	empl**oy**ee	**oy**ster	t**oy**
conv**oy**	enj**oy**	pl**oy**	T**oy**ota
c**oy**	j**oy**	R**oy**	v**oy**age
depl**oy**	Ll**oy**	r**oy**al	

D1.2 Rare Spelling Patterns

There are at least three rare spelling patterns for the vowel diphthong heard in "c**oi**n" and "t**oy**".

a) "aw"

The vowel diphthong sound heard in "coin" and "toy" may be represented by the "aw" vowel digraph. It is found in:

- Open syllables ("l**aw**-yer")

*l**aw**yer*

b) "eu"

The vowel diphthong sound heard in "coin" and "toy" may be represented by the "eu" vowel digraph. It is found in:

- Open syllables ("Fr**eu**-dian")

Fr**eu**d   Fr**eu**dian

c) "uoy"

The vowel diphthong sound heard in "coin" and "toy" may be represented by the "uoy" vowel digraph. It is found in:

- Open single-syllable words ("b**uoy**")

b**uoy**

D2 Spelling the Vowel Diphthong Heard in "Loud" and "Cow"

There are several vowel sounds that are neither long nor short. One of these is the vowel diphthong heard in the words "loud" and "cow". Unfortunately, there is no simple name for this vowel sound. It is not associated with a particular letter or spelling pattern.

A diphthong is a complex vowel sound that changes in pronunciation during speech. The vowel sound represented by the letters "ou" in the word "loud" is a diphthong. If pronounced carefully, you may note that the vowel sound begins with the short "a" vowel sound and ends with the consonant "w" sound without a pause or syllabic break. This distinguishes vowel diphthongs from link letter spelling patterns.

While not classified here as a long vowel sound, vowel diphthongs have long vowel properties. It follows that the spelling patterns for vowel diphthongs conform to the spelling conventions that govern long vowel sounds discussed. In particular, vowel diphthongs are always represented by a vowel digraph; a string of two or more letters that represent the unique vowel sound. Occasionally, consonant letters function as vowels in representing vowel diphthongs. In the word "brown", for example, the letters "ow" represent the diphthong heard in "loud". As well, within words diphthongs are usually heard in open syllables. In final syllables and in single-syllable words, vowel diphthongs are heard in both open and closed syllables.

Note that if the diphthong heard in the words "loud" and "cow" is followed by the letter "l", as in "fowl" and "owl", it often pronounced with an l-influenced vowel sound.

There are several spelling patterns for the vowel diphthong heard in the words "l**ou**d" and "c**ow**". They have been divided into major and rare spelling patterns.

D2.1 Major Spelling Patterns

There are three major spelling patterns for the vowel diphthong heard in the words "l**ou**d" and "c**ow**".

a) "ou"

The vowel diphthong sound heard in "loud" and "cow" may be represented by the "ou" vowel digraph. It is found in:

- Closed syllables ("c**ou**n-cil", "m**ou**n-tain")
- Open syllables ("th**ou**-sand", "tr**ou**-sers")
- Closed single-syllable words and final syllables ("sh**out**", "surr**ound**")

English spelling does not favour ending words with the letter "u". For this reason, the "ou" spelling pattern is found within words as in "cl**ou**d" and "surr**ou**nd" and not as a word ending. As a word ending, the "u" becomes a "w", resulting in the "-ow" spelling pattern. Compare, for example, the words "th**ou**sand" and "all**ow**".

A number of the following words end with a final silent letter "e". With words such as "announce" and "flounce", the final silent letter "e" signals that the adjacent letter "c" is pronounced with the soft "c/s" consonant sound. With the word "lounge" the final silent letter "e" signals that the adjacent letter "g" is pronounced with the soft "g/j" consonant sound. With words such as "mouse" and "spouse", the final silent letter "e" satisfies the convention that base words do not end with the letter "s".

ab**ou**t	am**ou**nt	ar**ou**se	cl**ou**d
acc**ou**nt	ann**ou**nce	b**ou**nd	c**ou**ch
al**ou**d	ar**ou**nd	b**ou**nty	c**ou**ncil

c**ou**nt	l**ou**nge	**ou**t	s**ou**r
cr**ou**ch	m**ou**ntain	p**ou**nce	s**ou**th
d**ou**bt	m**ou**se	p**ou**nd	sp**ou**se
fl**ou**nce	m**ou**th	p**ou**t	surr**ou**nd
fl**ou**r	n**ou**n	pron**ou**nce	th**ou**
f**ou**l	**ou**ch	pr**ou**d	th**ou**sand
f**ou**nd	**ou**nce	r**ou**nd	tr**ou**sers
gr**ou**nd	**ou**r	sc**ou**t	tr**ou**t
h**ou**se	**ou**rselves	sh**ou**t	w**ou**nd (Verb)
l**ou**d	**ou**st	s**ou**nd	

b) "ough"

The vowel diphthong sound heard in "loud" and "cow" may be represented by the "ough" vowel digraph. The letters "gh" are silent. It is found in:

- Open and closed single-syllable words ("b**ough**", "pl**ough**", "dr**ough**t")

When the word "slough" is used with the meaning "to shed", the consonant letters "gh" are pronounced with the consonant "f" sound.

b**ough**	dr**ough**t	*sl**ough*** (A swamp.)
d**ough**ty	pl**ough**	

c) "ow"

The vowel diphthong sound heard in "loud" and "cow" may be represented by the "ow" vowel digraph. It is found in:

- Open syllables ("fl**ow**-er", "v**ow**-el")
- Open final syllables ("all**ow**")
- Open and closed single-syllable words ("c**ow**", "n**ow**", "cr**ow**d", "**ow**l")

The "-ow" spelling pattern is used as a word ending. For this reason, it is usually found in open syllables as in "p**ow**-der" and "all**ow**". Within closed syllables, the "w" often becomes a "u" resulting in the "ou" spelling pattern. Compare, for example, the words "all**ow**" and "th**ou**sand". It is a convention of English spelling that words do not end with the letter "u".

That said, the "-ow" spelling pattern is often found in closed single-syllable words followed by a consonant letter as in "cr**ow**d", "f**ow**l", and "t**ow**n".

The "ow" spelling pattern also represents the long "o" vowel sound. Depending on the meaning with which they are used, the words "bow" and "row" are pronounced with both vowel sounds.

all**ow**	c**ow**boy	h**ow**	*r**ow***
*b**ow***	cr**ow**d	H**ow**ard	sc**ow**l
br**ow**	cr**ow**n	h**ow**l	sh**ow**er
br**ow**n	d**ow**n	n**ow**	s**ow**
br**ow**se	dr**ow**n	**ow**l	t**ow**el
ch**ow**	fl**ow**er	pl**ow** (USA)	t**ow**er
ch**ow**der	f**ow**l	p**ow**	t**ow**n
cl**ow**n	fr**ow**n	p**ow**der	v**ow**
c**ow**	g**ow**n	p**ow**er	v**ow**el
c**ow**ard	gr**ow**l	pr**ow**	w**ow**

D2.2 Rare Spelling Patterns

There are at least four rare spelling patterns for the vowel diphthong heard in the words "lo**u**d" and "c**ow**".

a)   "aou"

The vowel diphthong sound heard in "loud" and "cow" may be represented by the "aou" vowel digraph. It is found in:

- Open syllables ("c**aou**-tchouc")

c**aou**tchouc

b)   "au"

The vowel diphthong sound heard in "loud" and "cow" may be represented by the "au" vowel digraph. It is found in:

- Open syllables ("s**au**-erkraut")
- Closed final syllables ("sauerkr**au**t")

s**au**erkraut

c)   "eo"

The vowel diphthong sound heard in "loud" and "cow" may be represented by the "eo" vowel digraph. It is found in:

- Closed final syllables ("McL**eo**d")

McL**eo**d

d) "hou"

The vowel diphthong sound heard in "loud" and "cow" may be represented by the "hou" vowel digraph. The letter "h" is silent. It is found in:

- Closed single-syllable words ("**hou**r")

hour   **hou**rly

D3   Spelling the Schwa Vowel Sound

As discussed in A4.4, when pronouncing polysyllabic words, words with two or more syllables, one syllable will be emphasized or stressed more than the other syllables. In stressed syllables vowels are articulated clearly. You can hear a distinctive long, short, or diphthongal vowel sound. Unfortunately, in unstressed syllables vowel sounds are not articulated clearly, and as a result they lose their distinctive qualities. The name "schwa" is given to the weak or neutral vowel sound heard in unstressed syllables. The second vowel sound heard in "circ**us**" and "fam**ous**" is the schwa vowel sound. It is a very common vowel sound and is similar in quality to the short "u" vowel sound heard in "up".

While dictionaries indicate the amount of stress placed on each syllable, our English spelling system does not. However, while there are exceptions, the following generalizations hold true for most words.

1. Single-syllable words, such as "main", "bed", "kind", "pot", and "true" are almost always stressed. Many spelling programs begin with single-syllable words because the spelling-to-sound correspondence for vowel letters is predictable.

2. With two-syllable words, the first syllable is usually stressed, and the second syllable is unstressed as heard in "silent" and "focus". With compound words such as "airplane" and "flashlight", however, both single-syllable words are usually stressed.

3. With longer words, such as "calculus" and "eloquent", the amount of stress placed on each syllable varies. Usually, one syllable is given the most stress (primary accent), and the other syllables are given weaker (secondary accent) or no stress. Often the first syllable is stressed, and the final syllable is unstressed. There may be more than one unstressed syllable.

Not all words follow the above rules. With the word "again", for example, the first syllable is unstressed and the second is stressed. The unstressed first syllable "a-" is pronounced with the schwa vowel sound. The stressed syllable "-gain" is pronounced with the long "a" vowel sound.

The schwa vowel sound is usually represented by a single vowel letter or by the vowel digraph "ou". It is most often found in closed syllables. However, as the schwa vowel sound is heard in unstressed syllables, the doubling principle does not apply. Many word endings including "-al", "-ant", "-ence", "-er", "-our", "-ous", "-tion", and "-ture" are pronounced with the schwa vowel sound.

The schwa vowel sound is not always clearly represented in the spelling of a word. This is heard in words that end with the letters "-le". The word "buckle", for example, is pronounced "buc-k<u>u</u>ll". A schwa vowel sound is pronounced between the hard "c/k" consonant sound and the consonant "l" sound.

A single letter "r" often affects the pronunciation of a preceding vowel letter causing it to be pronounced with an unstressed schwa vowel sound. This is referred to here as an r-influenced schwa vowel sound as heard in "coll<u>a</u>r", "av<u>e</u>rage", "d<u>i</u>rect", "horr<u>o</u>r", and "cent<u>u</u>ry". See D5.1.

For spelling purposes, it is helpful to pronounce unstressed syllables with the most appropriate short vowel sound. With the word "instant", for example, the letter "a" can be pronounced with the short "a" vowel sound rather than the schwa vowel sound.

There are many spelling patterns for the schwa vowel sound. They have been divided into major, minor, and rare spelling patterns.

D3.1 Major Spelling Patterns

There are nineteen major spelling patterns for the schwa vowel sound heard in the second syllable of the words "circ**us**" and "fam**ous**".

a)   An initial letter "a-"

The schwa vowel sound may be represented by an initial letter "a-". The frequent use of the unstressed single-syllable words "a", "an", and "and" makes this a common spelling pattern.

Dictionaries usually indicate that there is a syllabic break following an initial letter "a-". With the words "appear" and "apply", for example, dictionaries show a syllabic break following the schwa vowel sound as in "a-ppear" and "a-pply". However, such words may also be pronounced as "ap-pear" and "ap-ply" with the letter "a" pronounced with the short "a" vowel sound in a closed syllable. This is in keeping with the doubling principle. For spelling purposes, it is helpful to pronounce short vowel sounds, including the schwa vowel sound, in closed syllables.

a	above	abut	across
ability	abroad	accomplish	adopt
about	abundant	accord	affair

afford	amount	applaud	ashamed
afraid	amuse	applause	aside
again	an	appliance	asleep
against	*and*	applied	assist
ago	announce	apply	assistant
agree	annoy	appoint	association
ahead	annoyance	appointment	astonish
alike	another	appraise	attack
alive	apart	approach	attempt
allow	apology	appropriate	attend
allowance	appal (UK, CAN)	approve	attention
alone	appall (USA)	approximate	attentive
along	apparent	arena	attract
aloud	appeal	arise	available
amaze	appear	around	awake
amazing	appearance	arrange	away
among	appease	arrest	awhile
amongst	append	arrive	awoke

b)   "a"

The schwa vowel sound may be represented by the letter "a" in unstressed syllables.

Adam	disagree	madam	salad
avalanche	disappear	magazine	separate (noun)
balloon	disappoint	majority	signature
banana	disapprove	mechanism	stomach
breakfast	especially	organization	suitable
Canada	facility	organize	sympathetic
Canadian	familiar	ornament	sympathy
canal	garage (USA)	Pacific	temperature
canoe	Hawaii	parade	theater (USA)
career	Italy	patrol	theatre (UK, CAN)
character	Japan	penalty	variety
companies	laboratory	permanent	
company	literature	photography	
diamond	machine	purchase	

c)   A final letter "-a":

The schwa vowel sound may be represented by a final letter "-a". This spelling pattern is an exception to the rule that words do not end with a short vowel sound. Short vowel sounds are usually heard in closed syllables that end with a consonant sound. In contrast, long vowel sounds are usually heard in open syllables that end with a vowel sound.

Afric**a**	camer**a**	gorill**a**	tun**a**
Ann**a**	Canad**a**	ide**a**	ultr**a**
are**a**	Cub**a**	llam**a**	umbrell**a**
aren**a**	extr**a**	Russi**a**	vanill**a**
banan**a**	Florid**a**	sod**a**	zebr**a**

d) Word Endings "-able", "-ace", "-ance", "-al", "-an", "-and", "-ant", "-ar", "-ard", "-ary", "-as", "-ass", "-ate", and "-ative"

In polysyllabic words, final syllables are often unstressed. This results in word endings being pronounced with the schwa vowel sound. The letter "a" represents the schwa vowel sound in the following word endings: "-able", "-ace", "-ance", "-al", "-an", "-and", "-ant", "-ar", "-ard", "-ary", "-as", "-ass", "-ate", and "-ative".

With the word ending "-able", the schwa vowel sound is actually pronounced twice. The letter "a" is pronounced with the schwa vowel sound, and a second schwa vowel sound is pronounced following the consonant "b" sound. The word "lovable", for example, is pronounced "love-uh-bull". The second schwa vowel sound is not represented in the spelling.

With the word ending "-ance", the final silent letter "e" signals that the adjacent letter "c" is pronounced with the soft "c/s" consonant sound. With words such as "climate" and "chocolate", the final silent letter "e" does not have a function.

When the word "legitimate" is being used as a verb it is pronounced with the long "a" vowel sound.

accept**able**	avail**able**	centr**al**	doll**ar**
accept**ance**	awkw**ard**	chocol**ate**	domin**ance**
actu**al**	backw**ard**	Christm**as**	domin**ant**
advis**able**	backw**ards**	circul**ar**	electrici**an**
agree**able**	bal**ance**	clim**ate**	eleph**ant**
ali**as**	begg**ar**	coll**ar**	employ**able**
allow**ance**	believ**able**	comic**al**	enforce**able**
alphabetic**al**	bi**as**	comp**ass**	Engl**and**
altern**ative**	biblic**al**	const**ant**	enjoy**able**
ambul**ance**	biologic**al**	contest**ant**	entr**ance**
anim**al**	bound**ary**	cow**ard**	equ**al**
appear**ance**	break**able**	crimin**al**	essenti**al**
appropri**ate**	brilli**ant**	curr**ant**	ethic**al**
arrog**ance**	buoy**ant**	cutl**ass**	expect**ant**
arrog**ant**	burgl**ar**	defi**ant**	extravag**ance**
assail**ant**	Calg**ary**	depend**able**	extravag**ant**
assist**ance**	Canadi**an**	descend**ant**	famili**ar**
assist**ant**	canv**as**	dist**ance**	festiv**al**
attend**ance**	carc**ass**	dist**ant**	fortun**ate**

forw**ard**	internation**al**	observ**ant**	Russi**an**
forw**ard**s	intim**ate**	orch**ard**	sal**ary**
fragr**ant**	intric**ate**	org**an**	schol**ar**
fri**ar**	isl**and**	pal**ace**	serv**ant**
furn**ace**	Itali**an**	particul**ar**	sever**al**
gener**al**	Janu**ary**	peas**ant**	signific**ant**
Germ**an**	leg**al**	peculi**ar**	simil**ar**
gi**ant**	*legitim**ate***	perish**able**	singul**ar**
gramm**ar**	li**ar**	pheas**ant**	sol**ar**
guid**ance**	liz**ard**	physic**al**	speci**al**
hang**ar**	loc**al**	pill**ar**	spectacul**ar**
hesit**ant**	logic**al**	pir**ate**	stand**ard**
hindr**ance**	lov**able**	pleas**ant**	standard
historic**al**	loy**al**	pol**ar**	stew**ard**
Holl**and**	luxuri**ant**	politic**al**	stew**ard**ess
hum**an**	magic**al**	popul**ar**	subordin**ate**
husb**and**	mainten**ance**	postm**an**	subst**ance**
identic**al**	manage**able**	pregn**ant**	sug**ar**
ignor**ance**	materi**al**	priv**ate**	technic**al**
ignor**ant**	medic**al**	prob**able**	ten**ant**
imagin**ative**	memor**able**	radi**ant**	terr**ace**
immigr**ant**	men**ace**	reason**able**	thous**and**
import**ance**	merch**ant**	recharge**able**	toler**ance**
import**ant**	Mexic**an**	regul**ar**	tresp**ass**
Indi**an**	miser**able**	rel**ative**	tru**ant**
indign**ant**	music**al**	relev**ance**	tyr**ant**
inf**ant**	musici**an**	relev**ant**	univers**al**
inform**ant**	must**ard**	reli**able**	veget**able**
inhabit**ant**	mystic**al**	reli**ance**	vulg**ar**
inst**ance**	natur**al**	reli**ant**	wom**an**
inst**ant**	neg**ative**	repent**ant**	workm**an**
insur**ance**	nucle**ar**	represent**ative**	
insur**ance**	nuis**ance**	resist**ance**	

e) "e"

The schwa vowel sound may be represented by the letter "e" in unstressed syllables.

An initial letter "e-" is rarely, if ever, used to represents the schwa vowel sound. Likewise, a final letter "-e" is seldom used to represent the schwa vowel sound. The word "the" is a rare exception.

ag**e**ncy	c**e**ment	**e**levator	gai**e**ty
anxi**e**ty	c**e**remony	**e**mergency	hundr**e**d
av**e**nue	comp**e**tition	**e**nemy	int**e**rrupt
b**e**lieve	**e**lephant	env**e**lope	it**e**m

jew**e**llery (UK, CAN)	m**e**chanic	sci**e**ntific	t**e**legraph
jew**e**lry (USA)	mess**e**nger	sci**e**ntist	t**e**lephone
leg**e**nd	n**e**cessary	sk**e**leton	t**e**levision
l**e**gitimate	po**e**m	soci**e**ty	*the*
lic**e**nse	probl**e**m	sol**e**mn	vari**e**ty
math**e**matics	rep**e**tition	syst**e**m	veg**e**table
	sat**e**llite	tand**e**m	

f) Word endings "-el", "-en", "-ence", "-ent", "-ess", "-est", and "-et"

In polysyllabic words, final syllables are often unstressed. This results in word endings being pronounced with the schwa vowel sound. The letter "e" represents the schwa vowel sound in the following word endings: "-el", "-en", "-ence", "-ent", "-ess", "-est", and "-et".

With the word ending "-ence", the final silent letter "e" signals that the adjacent letter "c" is pronounced with the soft "c/s" consonant sound.

abhorr**ent**	consist**ent**	evid**ent**	jew**el**
abs**ence**	contin**ent**	excell**ence**	kitch**en**
abs**ent**	conveni**ence**	excell**ent**	length**en**
accid**ent**	conveni**ent**	excit**ement**	less**en**
adher**ence**	couns**el**	exist**ence**	lev**el**
ag**ent**	cru**el**	exist**ent**	list**en**
apart**ment**	curr**ent**	experi**ence**	loos**en**
appar**ent**	cypr**ess**	fall**en**	magnific**ent**
audi**ence**	dark**en**	fast**en**	mattr**ess**
awak**en**	deaf**en**	frequ**ent**	mom**ent**
bag**el**	dec**ent**	giv**en**	neglig**ence**
barr**el**	defer**ence**	gold**en**	neglig**ent**
bigg**est**	depart**ment**	gradi**ent**	nick**el**
brok**en**	depend**ence**	happ**en**	nov**el**
cam**el**	depend**ent**	hast**en**	obedi**ence**
carp**et**	deterr**ence**	heav**en**	obedi**ent**
chann**el**	deterr**ent**	helm**et**	occurr**ence**
chick**en**	differ**ence**	impud**ent**	of**ten**
childr**en**	differ**ent**	independ**ent**	op**en**
citiz**en**	doz**en**	influ**ence**	oppon**ent**
cli**ent**	elev**en**	innoc**ence**	Ori**ent**
coher**ent**	eloqu**ent**	innoc**ent**	orna**ment**
compli**ment**	emin**ent**	insist**ence**	parc**el**
confer**ence**	environ**ment**	insist**ent**	par**ent**
confid**ence**	equip**ment**	insol**ent**	parlia**ment**
confid**ent**	ess**ence**	instru**ment**	pati**ence**
congr**ess**	ev**en**	intellig**ence**	pati**ent**
consci**ence**	evid**ence**	intellig**ent**	pay**ment**

perman**ent**	recurr**ent**	soft**en**	treatm**ent**
persist**ence**	refer**ence**	spok**en**	tunn**el**
persist**ent**	resid**ent**	squirr**el**	urg**ent**
po**et**	rever**ent**	stiff**en**	viol**ence**
prefer**ence**	rip**en**	stol**en**	viol**ent**
pres**ence**	sci**ence**	strength**en**	vow**el**
promin**ent**	sent**ence**	subsist**ence**	wak**en**
punishm**ent**	serp**ent**	subsist**ent**	weak**en**
pupp**et**	sev**en**	tak**en**	wool**en** (USA)
quarr**el**	sil**ence**	tal**ent**	wooll**en** (UK, CAN)
qui**et**	sil**ent**	thick**en**	wov**en**
rec**ent**	small**est**	trav**el**	young**est**

g) "e(r)"

The schwa vowel sound may be represented by the "e(r)" spelling pattern in unstressed syllables.

When a vowel letter is followed by a single letter "r", it often represents the schwa vowel sound. This is also referred to as an r-influenced schwa vowel sound. In keeping with the doubling principle, if a vowel letter is followed by a double "rr", as in "merry" and "mirror", the vowel is usually pronounced with a short vowel sound. The word "interrupt" is an exception to this rule.

adv**er**tise	gen**er**al	mod**er**ate	p**er**suade
av**er**age	gen**er**ation	mod**er**n	p**er**suasion
cam**er**a	gen**er**ous	north**er**n	pov**er**ty
comm**er**ce	gov**er**n	num**er**ous	pref**er**ence
conv**er**sation	h**er**self	op**er**ate	prop**er**ty
diff**er**ence	int**er**est	op**er**ation	ref**er**ee
diff**er**ent	int**er**fere	op**er**ator	ref**er**ence
east**er**n	int**er**national	patt**er**n	sev**er**al
eld**er**ly	int**er**rupt	p**er**cent	sheph**er**d
en**er**gy	lib**er**al	p**er**fect	sov**er**eign
ent**er**tain	lib**er**ty	p**er**form	temp**er**ature
ex**er**cise	lit**er**ary	p**er**haps	univ**er**se
exp**er**t	lit**er**ature	p**er**manent	west**er**n
fed**er**al	min**er**al	p**er**mission	wild**er**ness
fun**er**al	mis**er**able	p**er**mit	

h) Word Endings "-er" and "-ery"

In polysyllabic words, final syllables are often unstressed. This results in word endings being pronounced with the schwa vowel sound. The letter "e" represents the schwa vowel sound in the following word endings: "-er" and "-ery".

When a vowel letter is followed by a single letter "r", it often represents the schwa vowel sound. This is also referred to as an r-influenced schwa vowel sound.

after	creamery	hinder	mother
altogether	customer	hunger	murder
anger	cutlery	hunter	mystery
announcer	danger	Jupiter	neither
another	daughter	keeper	never
answer	December	killer	number
bakery	deliver	ladder	nursery
barber	developer	larger	October
batter	dinner	laser	offer
beaver	disaster	later	officer
better	discover	latter	older
bigger	discovery	laughter	order
bitter	diver	lawyer	other
border	doer	layer	over
bother	driver	leader	owner
boulder	eager	leather	paper
bravery	Easter	letter	partner
brewery	either	liter (USA)	passenger
bribery	elder	litter	plaster
brother	employer	lobster	player
bumper	enter	locker	plumber
butter	ever	loser	ponder
caller	farmer	lover	powder
camper	farther	lower	powdery
cancer	father	luster (USA)	power
cannery	feather	machinery	prayer
carpenter	fiber (USA)	maker	prisoner
celery	finger	manager	proper
centimeter (USA)	flasher	maneuver (USA)	pusher
character	flattery	manner	quarter
clever	flower	master	ranger
climber	flowery	matter	rather
closer	foreigner	meager (USA)	register
computer	forgery	member	remember
conquer	former	messenger	rider
consider	further	meter (USA, CAN)	river
consumer	gather	miner	robber
container	grocery	mineral	rocker
cooler	hamburger	minister	rooster
copper	hammer	misery	rubber
corner	hamster	miter (USA)	runner
counter	helicopter	monastery	saber (USA)
cover	hinder	monster	saucer

scatt**er**	soldi**er**	tend**er**	wand**er**
scen**ery**	speak**er**	theat**er** (USA)	wat**er**
scull**ery**	spect**er** (USA)	thund**er**	weath**er**
Septemb**er**	sting**er**	tig**er**	wheth**er**
sepulch**er** (USA)	strang**er**	togeth**er**	whisp**er**
shelt**er**	suff**er**	tow**er**	widow**er**
should**er**	summ**er**	trail**er**	winn**er**
show**er**	sup**er**	transf**er**	wint**er**
silv**er**	supp**er**	trapp**er**	wond**er**
sist**er**	sweat**er**	truck**er**	work**er**
slav**ery**	tann**ery**	und**er**	writ**er**
small**er**	teach**er**	upp**er**	writ**er**
smok**er**	temp**er**	view**er**	young**er**
socc**er**	temperat**ure**	wait**er**	zipp**er**

i) "i"

The schwa vowel sound may be represented by the letter "i" in unstressed syllables.

An initial letter "i-" is rarely, if ever, used to represent the schwa vowel sound. Likewise, a final letter "-i" is rarely, if ever, used to represent the schwa vowel sound.

accident	classification	engin*e*	multiplication
admiral	combination	evidence	multiply
artificial	comparison	exhibition	perspiration
aspirin	competitor	experiment	policy
authorities	confidence	*fertile*	politician
beautiful	confident	Florida	politics
capital	contribution	*fragile*	positive
carnival	criminal	*giraffe*	principal
carnivore	cultivate	holiday	principle
centimeter (USA)	definite	immigrant	qualification
centimetre (UK, CAN)	direct	individual	sacrifice
Chicago	direction	intelligence	similar
citizen	discipline	legitimate	tapir
civilian	divide	maritime	unidentified
civilize	division	medicine	universal
	elixir	*missile*	universe

j) Word Endings "-ible", "-ify", "-il", "-ily", "-in", "-ine", and "-ity"

In polysyllabic words, final syllables are often unstressed. This results in word endings being pronounced with the schwa vowel sound. The letter "i" represents the schwa vowel sound in the following word endings: "-ible", "-ify", "-il", "-ily", "-in", "-ine", and "-ity".

With the word ending "-ible", the schwa vowel sound is actually pronounced twice. The letter "i" is pronounced with the schwa vowel sound and a second schwa vowel sound is pronounced following the consonant "b" sound. The word "possible", for example, is pronounced "poss-uh-bull". The second schwa vowel sound is not represented in the spelling.

With the words "engine" and "medicine", the final silent letter "e" does not have a function.

ability	facility	modify	responsible
activity	family	nostril	reversible
amplify	flexible	opportunity	robin
April	fortify	pencil	ruin
basil	glorify	peril	sensible
civil	horrible	permissible	signify
classify	imperceptible	possible	simplicity
community	impossible	pupil	specify
convertible	indefensible	purify	stencil
corruptible	indigestible	qualify	suggestible
devil	intensify	quality	terrible
dignify	invisible	quantity	terrify
divisible	irresistible	raisin	testify
easily	magnify	ratify	unity
engine	majority	reprehensible	university
evil	medicine	responsibility	

k) Word Endings "-cial", "-cian", "-iard", "-sian", "-tial", and "-tian"

In polysyllabic words, final syllables are often unstressed. This results in word endings being pronounced with the schwa vowel sound.

The letters "ia" appear to represent the schwa vowel sound in the word endings "-cial", "-cian", "-sian", "-tial", and "-tian". However, these spelling patterns are incidental. The silent letter "i" helps to represent the preceding consonant sound. The letter "a" represents the schwa vowel sound.

- With the word ending "-cial", as in "commercial", the letters "ci" represent the consonant "sh" sound.

- With the word ending "-cian", as in "electrician", the letters "ci" represent the consonant "sh" sound.

- With the word ending "-sian", as in "Malaysian", the letters "si" represent the consonant "sh" or "zh" sounds.

- With the word endings "-tial", as in "confidential", the letters "ti" represent the consonant "sh" sound.

- With the word ending "-tian", as in "Egyptian", the letters "ti" represent the consonant "sh" sound.

- With words such as "brilliant" and "Spaniard", which are pronounced "brill-yunt" and "Span-yurd", the letter "i" represent the consonant "y" sound.

In the word "parliament", the "ia" spelling pattern does represent the schwa vowel sound.

academician	electrician	Martian	provincial
aesthetician (UK, CAN)	electrician	mathematician	Prussian
artificial	especially	mortician	racial
Asian	essential	musician	residential
auxiliary	esthetician (USA)	official	Russian
beneficial	facial	optician	social
brilliance	familiar	paediatrician (UK, CAN)	Spaniard
brilliant	financial	Parisian	spatial
Caucasian	genial	parliament	special
Christian	Haitian	partial	speciality (UK, CAN)
circumstantial	Indonesian	partiality	specialty (USA)
civilian	influential	peculiar	statistician
clinician	initial	pediatrician (USA)	substantial
commercial	Italian	physician	superficial
confidential	judicial	politician	technician
credential	Laotian	Polynesian	torrential
Croatian	logician	potential	Tunisian
Dalmatian	magician	presidential	valiant
deferential	Malaysian	providential	Venetian
Egyptian	martial		

l)   Word Endings "-ion", "-gion", "-sion", "-ssion", "-tion", and "-xion"

In polysyllabic words, final syllables are often unstressed. This results in word endings being pronounced with the schwa vowel sound.

The letters "io" appear to represent the schwa vowel sound in the word endings "-ion", "-gion", "-sion", "-ssion", "-tion", and "-xion". However, these spelling patterns are incidental. The silent letter "i" helps to represent the preceding consonant sound. The letter "o" represents the schwa vowel sound.

- With words such "million" and "billion", which are pronounced "mill-yun" and "bill-yun", the letter "i" represent the consonant "y" sound.

- With the word ending "-gion", as in "religion", the letter "i" signals that the preceding letter "g" is pronounced with the soft "g/j" consonant sound.

- With the word endings "-sion" and "-ssion", as in "confusion", the letters "si" and "ssi" represent the consonant "sh" or "zh" sounds.

- With the word ending "-tion", as in "relation", the letters "ti" represent the consonant "ch" or "sh" sounds.

- With the word ending "-xion", as in "complexion", the letters "xi" represent the hard "c/k" consonant sound followed by the consonant "sh" sound.

With the words "cushion" and "fashion", the "sh" consonant sound is clearly represented in the spelling so the "io" spelling pattern does represent the schwa vowel sound.

action	construction	instruction	qualification
addition	conversation	intention	question
admission	corporation	introduction	recognition
adoption	correction	invasion	reduction
ambition	crucifixion	invention	reflection
application	cushion	mansion	region
attraction	decision	million	relation
billion	delusion	moderation	religion
calculation	demonstration	multiplication	repetition
caution	destruction	objection	reputation
classification	digestion	omission	revulsion
collection	discussion	operation	satisfaction
collision	division	opposition	situation
combination	equation	pension	solution
completion	erosion	persuasion	stallion
complexion	evasion	pollution	station
complication	exception	position	suggestion
composition	explosion	possession	television
confession	expression	prevention	tension
confusion	fashion	procession	translation
congratulation	hesitation	production	transportation
connection (USA, CAN)	imagination	profession	vacation
consideration	imitation	pronunciation	vision
	indigestion	protection	

m)   "-le"

The "-le" spelling pattern is syllabic in nature. That is, the letters "-le" form a syllable that is pronounced "ull". The letters "-le" signal that a faint schwa vowel sound is pronounced just before the consonant "l" sound. The schwa vowel sound is not well represented in the spelling.

The word "able", for example, is pronounced "a-bull". Compare the "ull" sound in "able" to the consonant "l" sound heard in "like" or "lucky". The preceding consonant letter attaches to the "-ull" sound to complete the final syllable. This leaves the first vowel in an open, long sounding syllable. Conversely, the word "little" is pronounced "lit-tull". In keeping with the doubling principle, having two consonants between vowel sounds allows one consonant to keep the first vowel in a closed, short sounding syllable.

This is similar to the "-re" spelling pattern. The word "acre", for example, is pronounced "a-cur". The word "lustre" is pronounced "lus-tur".

When the word ending "-le" follows a vowel sound, it often produces an l-influenced vowel sound as heard in "male" and "file". See D4.

able	coddle	kettle	settle
apple	cuddle	little	startle
battle	curdle	middle	table
Bible	double	needle	tattle
bicycle	entitle	noodle	title
bottle	fiddle	paddle	trouble
bubble	gentle	people	turtle
bugle	handle	poodle	valuable
candle	idle	puddle	
cattle	impossible	puzzle	
circle	jungle	saddle	

n)   "o"

The schwa vowel sound may be represented by the letter "o" in unstressed syllables.

As heard in words such as "observe" and "oppose", an initial letter "o" sometimes represents the schwa vowel sound.

With the word "purpose", the final silent letter "e" satisfies the convention that base words do not end with the letter "s".

absolute	automobile	collide	comfort
apology	carrot	collision	command
astronaut	chocolate	colony	commercial
atmosphere	collect	*combine*	commission

committee	content	introduce	pollution
community	contest	mammoth	position
compare	continue	memory	possess
compete	contribute	method	possession
complain	control	mosquito	proposal
complete	convenience	object	propose
compose	convenient	*objection*	purpose
composition	corporation	objective	recognition
computer	correct	observe	recognize
concern	customer	occasion	recommend
condense	develop	octopus	remedy
condition	diamond	offend	reproduce
conductor	dictionary	official	rhinoceros
confess	dinosaur	opinion	satisfactory
confession	discomfort	opportunity	second
confuse	discontent	oppose	society
confusion	effort	opposite	solution
congratulate	economy	opposition	thermos
congratulation	environment	original	*today*
connect	Europe	patriotism	together
connection (USA, CAN)	factory	period	tomorrow
conscience	forgot	photograph	violence
consider	gorilla	photography	violent
construction	history	pilot	welcome
consumer	horizon	police	
contain	improvise	polite	
container	information	political	

o) Word Endings "-ol", "-om", "-on", and "-or"

In polysyllabic words, final syllables are often unstressed. This results in word endings being pronounced with the schwa vowel sound. The letter "o" represents the schwa vowel sound in the following word endings: "-ol", "-om", "-on", and "-or".

There are exceptions to this spelling pattern. In the word "control", for example, the letter "o" is pronounced with the long "o" vowel sound.

With the words "champion" and "scorpion", the letters "io" form a link letter spelling pattern. The letter "i" is pronounced with the long "e" vowel sound and is followed by the schwa vowel sound.

accustom	Alison	ardor (USA)	author
actor	ancestor	armor (USA)	bacon
administrator	anchor	atom	behavior (USA)
advisor	apron	auditor	blossom

boredom	donor	liquor	sculptor
bottom	dragon	major	season
calculator	editor	mayor	senator
cannon	elevator	melon	senior
canyon	endeavor (USA)	meteor	skeleton
carol	error	minor	solicitor
champion	factor	mirror	splendor (USA)
clamor (USA)	favor (USA)	motor	suitor
collector	fervor (USA)	neighbor (USA)	superior
color (USA)	flavor (USA)	odor (USA)	symbol
common	freedom	operator	tailor
comparison	gambol	person	tenor
competitor	governor	pigeon	tractor
conductor	harbor (USA)	pistol	translator
contractor	honor (USA)	poison	tremor
counsellor (UK, CAN)	horizon	prison	tumor (USA)
counselor (USA)	horror	professor	tutor
crayon	humor (USA)	razor	valor (USA)
creditor	inferior	reason	vapor (USA)
cultivator	inventor	ribbon	victory
custom	junior	rigor (USA)	vigor (USA)
demon	kingdom	rumor (USA)	visitor
director	labor (USA)	sailor	wagon
distributor	lemon	savor (USA)	weapon
doctor	lesson	scissors	wisdom
	lion	scorpion	

p) Word Endings "-our" and "-ous"

In polysyllabic words, final syllables are often unstressed. This results in word endings being pronounced with the schwa vowel sound. The letters "ou" represents the schwa vowel sound in the word endings "-our" and "-ous".

Exceptions include the words "our" and "hour" in which the letters "ou" represent the vowel diphthong heard in the words "loud" and "cow".

ambitious	cautious	dangerous	furious
anonymous	clamour (UK, CAN)	delicious	generous
anxious		endeavour (UK, CAN)	glamour
arbour (UK, CAN)	colour (UK, CAN)	enormous	harbour (UK, CAN)
ardour (UK, CAN)	conscious	envious	honour (UK, CAN)
armour (UK, CAN)	conscious	famous	humour (UK, CAN)
atrocious	courageous	favour (UK, CAN)	impetuous
behaviour	courageous	fervour (UK, CAN)	jealous
callous	covetous	flavour (UK, CAN)	joyous
cancerous	curious		labour (UK, CAN)

mischie**vous**	od**our** (UK, CAN)	sav**our** (UK, CAN)	val**our** (UK, CAN)
myster**ious**	poison**ous**	ser**ious**	vap**our** (UK, CAN)
neighb**our** (UK, CAN)	prec**ious**	spac**ious**	var**ious**
ner**vous**	preposter**ous**	splend**our** (UK, CAN)	vig**our** (UK, CAN)
nox**ious**	ridicul**ous**	tempestu**ous**	vorac**ious**
numer**ous**	rig**our** (UK, CAN)	tum**our** (UK, CAN)	
obv**ious**	rum**our** (UK, CAN)	unconsc**ious**	
	sav**iour**		

q) "-re"

The "-re" spelling pattern is syllabic in nature. That is, the letters "-re" form a syllable that is pronounced "ur". The final silent letter "e" signals that a faint schwa vowel sound is pronounced just before the consonant "r" sound. The word "acre", for example, is pronounced "a-cur". Compare the "ur" sound in "acre" to the consonant "r" sound heard in "race" or "ride". This is similar to the "-le" spelling pattern. The word "little", for example, is pronounced "lit-tul". The schwa vowel sound is not represented in the spelling.

For further discussion about the "-re" spelling pattern see D5.2.

r) "u"

The schwa vowel sound may be represented by the letter "u" in unstressed syllables.

In the word "procedure", the letter "u" appears to represent the schwa vowel sound. Actually, the "u" helps to signal that the adjacent letter "d" is pronounced with the soft "g/j" consonant sound. It is the "-re" spelling pattern that signals that the schwa vowel sound. See D5.2. The "-dure" word ending is a rare spelling pattern.

With the word "lettuce", the final silent letter "e" signals that the adjacent letter "c" is pronounced with the soft "c/s" consonant sound.

Aug**u**st	ind**u**stry	Sat**u**rday	s**u**rveyor
a**u**tumn	instr**u**ment	Sat**u**rn	s**u**rvive
cent**u**ry	let**tu**ce	s**u**cceed	s**u**rvivor
congrat**u**late	pean**u**t	s**u**ggest	unfort**u**nate
fort**u**nate	prej**u**dice	s**u**ggestion	**u**pon
fort**un**e	prod**u**ct	s**u**rprise	**u**s**u**al
h**u**rrah	p**u**rsue	s**u**rround	

s) Word Endings "-ful", "-um", "-sure", "-ture", "-us", and "-zure"

In polysyllabic words, final syllables are often unstressed. This results in word endings being pronounced with the schwa vowel sound. The letter "u" represents the schwa vowel sound in the following word endings: "-ful", "-um", and "-us".

The letter "u" appears to represent the schwa vowel sound in the word endings "-sure", "-ture", and "-zure". However, these spelling patterns are incidental. The silent letter "u" helps to represent the preceding consonant sound. It is the "-re" spelling pattern that signals that the schwa vowel sound. See D5.2.

- With the word ending "-sure", as in "mea<u>su</u>re", the letters "su" represent the consonant "zh" sound.

- With the word ending "-ture", as in "fea<u>tu</u>re", the letters "tu" represent the consonant "ch" sound.

- With the word ending "-zure", as in "sei<u>zu</u>re", the letters "zu" represent the consonant "zh" sound.

adven**ture**	fail**ure**	maxim**um**	proced**ure**
agricul**ture**	faith**ful**	mea**sure**	radi**us**
architec**ture**	fea**ture**	medi**um**	sculp**ture**
aw**ful**	foc**us**	minim**um**	sei**zure**
a**zure**	forget**ful**	min**us**	signa**ture**
beauti**ful**	frac**ture**	mois**ture**	sin**us**
bon**us**	fung**us**	muse**um**	stat**us**
calcul**us**	furni**ture**	na**ture**	success**ful**
care**ful**	fu**ture**	nucle**us**	**sure**
cens**us**	geni**us**	octop**us**	syllab**us**
circ**us**	grace**ful**	on**us**	tempera**ture**
clo**sure**	grate**ful**	op**us**	termin**us**
compo**sure**	help**ful**	over**ture**	thesaur**us**
con**jure**	hope**ful**	pain**ful**	thought**ful**
crea**ture**	ignoram**us**	pas**ture**	tor**ture**
croc**us**	in**jure**	peace**ful**	trea**sure**
cul**ture**	in**sure**	pic**ture**	use**ful**
disclo**sure**	joy**ful**	play**ful**	vers**us**
doubt**ful**	lei**sure**	plea**sure**	vir**us**
enclo**sure**	litera**ture**	power**ful**	walr**us**
expo**sure**	litm**us**	pres**sure**	wonder**ful**

D3.2 Minor Spelling Patterns

There are three minor spelling patterns for the schwa vowel sound heard in the second syllable of the words "circus" and "famous".

a) Word ending "-ain"

In polysyllabic words, final syllables are often unstressed. This results in word endings being pronounced with the schwa vowel sound. The letters "ai" represent the schwa vowel sound in the word ending "-ain".

*barg**ai**n*	*capt**ai**n*	*chieft**ai**n*	*mount**ai**n*
*Brit**ai**n*	*cert**ai**n*	*curt**ai**n*	*vill**ai**n*

b) **"ie"**

The "ie" spelling pattern appears to represent the schwa vowel sound in a number of words. However, these spelling patterns are mostly incidental. The silent letter "i" usually helps to represent the preceding consonant sound. The letter "e" represents the schwa vowel sound.

- With the "-cie" spelling pattern, as in "an<u>ci</u>ent" and "effi<u>ci</u>ent", the letters "ci" represent the consonant "ch" and "sh" sounds.

- With the "-scie" spelling pattern, as in "con<u>sci</u>ence", the letters "sci" represent the consonant "sh" sound.

- With the "-tie" spelling pattern, as in "pa<u>ti</u>ent", the letters "ti" represent the consonant "sh" sound.

With the words "mischief" and "mischievous" the consonant "ch" sound is clearly represented in the spelling and so the "ie" spelling pattern does represent the schwa vowel sound.

Words such as "ancient", "efficient", and "sufficient" are exceptions to the "i" before "e" except after "c" rule.

an<u>ci</u>ent	effi<u>ci</u>ency	pa<u>ti</u>ence	quo<u>ti</u>ent
con<u>sci</u>ence	effi<u>ci</u>ent	pa<u>ti</u>ent	suffi<u>ci</u>ency
defi<u>ci</u>ency	mis**chie**f	pre<u>sci</u>ence	suffi<u>ci</u>ent
defi<u>ci</u>ent	mis**chie**vous	profi<u>ci</u>ent	

c) **"y"**

The letter "y" represents the schwa vowel sound in the following words:

eth**y**l	meth**y**l	sat**y**r
mart**y**r	ph**y**sician	synon**y**mous

D3.3 Rare Spelling Patterns

There are at least nine rare spelling patterns for the schwa vowel sound heard in the second syllable of the words "circ**us**" and "fam**ous**".

a) **"au"**

The letters "au" represent the schwa vowel sound in the following words:

authorities	rest**au**rant

**b)	"ea"**

The letters "ea" appear to represent the schwa vowel sound in the following words.

However, in the word "ocean" the letters "ce" represent the consonant "sh" sound. The letter "a" represents the schwa vowel sound. Likewise, in the words "pageant" and "sergeant", the letters "ge" represent the soft "g/j" consonant sound. The letter "a" represents the schwa vowel sound.

o*ce*an	pa*ge*ant	ser*ge*ant

**c)	"eau"**

The letters "eau" represent the schwa vowel sound in the following word.

*bur**eau**crat*

**d)	"eo"**

The letters "eo" represent the schwa vowel sound in the word ending "**-eo**n".

In the words "dungeon" and "pigeon", the letters "ge" actually represent the soft "g/j" consonant sound. The letter "o" represents the schwa vowel sound.

dun*ge*on	lunch**eo**n	pi*ge*on	trunch**eo**n

**e)	"iou"**

The letters "iou" appear to represent the schwa vowel sound in the word ending "**-xious**".

Actually, in the words "anxious" and "noxious" the letters "xi" represent the hard "c/k" consonant sound followed by the consonant "sh" sound. The "ou" vowel digraph represents the schwa vowel sound.

an*xi*ous	no*xi*ous

**f)	"oa"**

The letters "oa" represent the schwa vowel sound in the following word.

cupb**oa**rd

g) "oe"

The letters "oe" represent the schwa vowel sound in the following word.

Ph**oe**nician

h) "oi"

The letters "oi" represent the schwa vowel sound in the following words. The final silent letter "e" satisfies the convention that base words do not end with the letter "s".

porp**oi**se   tort**oi**se

i) "ue"

The letters "ue" appears to represent the schwa vowel sound in the word "**gue**rrilla".

Actually, in the word "guerrilla" the letters "gu" represent the hard "g" consonant sound. The letter "e" represents the schwa vowel sound.

*gu***e**rrilla

D4 Spelling L-Influenced Vowel Sounds

If a long or diphthongal vowel sound is followed by the letter "l", the vowel sound is often affected. This results from our tendency to pronounce a schwa vowel sound between the long or diphthongal sound and the consonant "l" sound. This is sometimes referred to as a syllabic "l" sound. It is referred to here as an "l-influenced" vowel sound. The schwa vowel sound is not represented in the spelling of the words.

Consider the word "seal" which is pronounced "sea-ull. Three sounds may readily be discerned: a soft "c/s" consonant sound, a long "e" vowel sound, and an "ull" sound. The "ull" sound is itself made up of a faint schwa vowel sound followed by a consonant "l" sound. Compare the "ull" sound in "seal" to the consonant "l" sound heard in "like" or "lucky". This is similar to the "-re" spelling pattern. The word "acre", for example, is pronounced "a-cur".

The long or diphthongal vowel sound must be found in the same syllable as the letter "l". Compare the word "dale" with "daily". In the word "dale", a schwa vowel sound is pronounced immediately after the long "a" vowel sound without a syllabic break. In the word "dai-ly", there is a syllabic break between the long "a" vowel sound and the consonant "l" sound, so the letter "l" is not pronounced "ull".

The letter "l" can also have an influence over the pronunciation of short vowel sounds. When a single letter "a" is followed by the letter "l" in a closed syllable, as in "also" and "ball", the "a" is often pronounced with the short "o" sound. In words such "talk" and "walk" the letter "l" is silent.

D4.1 Spelling the L-influenced vowel sound heard in "male"

The l-influenced vowel sound heard in the word "male" occurs when a schwa vowel sound is pronounced between a long "a" vowel sound and a consonant "l" sound. The schwa vowel sound is not represented in the spelling of these words.

a**il**	h**ale**	p**ale**	t**ail**
ale	j**ail** (USA, CAN)	qu**ail**	v**eil**
b**ail**	k**ale**	r**ail**	w**ail**
d**ale**	m**ail**	reg**ale**	W**ale**s
fem**ale**	m**ale**	s**ail**	wh**ale**
g**aol** (UK)	n**ail**	s**ale**	Y**ale**
h**ail**	p**ail**	sc**ale**	

D4.2 Spelling the L-influenced vowel sound heard in "seal"

The l-influenced vowel sound heard in the word "seal" occurs when a schwa vowel sound vowel is pronounced between a long "e" vowel sound and a consonant "l" sound. The schwa sound is not represented in the spelling of these words.

automob**ile**	f**ield**	p**eal**	st**eel**
chen**ille**	h**eal**	r**eal**	t**eal**
cong**eal**	id**eal**	r**eel**	v**eal**
d**eal**	k**eel**	s**eal**	y**ield**
eel	kn**eel**	squ**eal**	z**eal**
f**eel**	m**eal**	st**eal**	

D4.3 Spelling the L-influenced vowel sound heard in "file"

The "l-influenced vowel sound heard in the word "file" occurs when a schwa vowel sound is pronounced between a long "i" vowel sound and a consonant "l" sound. The schwa vowel sound is not represented in the spelling of the words.

a**isle**	gu**ile**	r**ile**	v**ial**
b**ile**	**isle**	sen**ile**	v**ile**
ch**ild**	m**ild**	sm**ile**	wh**ile**
d**ial**	m**ile**	t**ile**	
f**ile**	p**ile**	tr**ial**	

D4.4 Spelling the L-influenced vowel sound heard in "fowl"

The l-influenced vowel sound heard in the word "fowl" occurs when a schwa vowel sound is pronounced between the vowel diphthong sound heard in "loud" and a consonant "l" sound. The schwa vowel sound is not represented in the spelling of these words.

b**owel**	f**owl**	**owl**	t**owel**
d**owel**	h**owl**	P**owell**	tr**owel**
f**oul**	j**owl**	sc**owl**	v**owel**

D4.5 Spelling the L-influenced vowel sound heard in "rule"

The l-influenced vowel sound heard in the word "rule" occurs when a schwa vowel sound is pronounced between a long "u" vowel sound and a consonant "l" sound. As well, with the words marked by an asterisk, a consonant "y" sound may be pronounced before the long "u" sound by some speakers. The consonant "y" sound is heard consistently in the word "mule". The schwa vowel sound and the consonant "y" sound are not represented in the spelling of these words.

c**ool**	f**uel***	n**ewel***	r**ule**
d**ual***	j**ewel**	p**ool**	y**ou'll***
d**uel***	m**ule***	ren**ewal***	

D5 Spelling R-Influenced Vowel Sounds

The consonant "r" sound often affects the pronunciation of preceding vowel sounds. The vowel may no longer be pronounced with the expected long, short, or diphthongal vowel sound. It is referred to here as an "r-influenced" vowel sound.

The influence of the letter "r" can be heard in a number of spelling patterns including:

1. The "a(r)" spelling pattern represents the broad "a" vowel sound heard in words such as "arm" and "card".

2. The "ea(r)" spelling pattern represents the broad "a" vowel sound heard in words such as "heart" and "hearth".

3. The "a(re)", "a(ry)", "a(ri)" and "ai(r) spelling patterns represent the short "e" vowel sound heard in words such as "rare", "librarian", "library", and "air".

4. The "-ere" spelling represents the short "i" vowel sound heard in words such as "here" and "sincere".

5. The "o(r)", "o(rr)", and "o(re)" spelling patterns represent the short "o" vowel sound heard in words such as "born", "borrow", and "more".

6. Unstressed syllables that end with a single letter "r" are usually pronounced with the r-influenced schwa vowel sound heard in "after". See D5.1.

7. The "-re" spelling pattern is often pronounced with the r-influenced schwa vowel sound heard in "after". See D5.2.

8. Stressed syllables that end with a single letter "r" are usually pronounced with the stressed r-influenced vowel sound heard in the word "bird". See D5.3.

Single vowel letters that are followed by the double "rr" spelling pattern are usually pronounced with a regular short vowel sound. See D5.4.

D5.1 Spelling the R-Influenced Schwa Vowel Sound Heard in "After"

As discussed in A4.4, when pronouncing polysyllabic words, one syllable will be emphasized or stressed more than the other syllables. In stressed syllables, vowels are articulated clearly. You can hear a distinctive long, short, or diphthongal vowel sound. Unfortunately, in unstressed syllables vowel sounds are not articulated clearly and, as a result, they lose their distinctive qualities. The name "schwa" is given to the weak or neutral vowel sound heard in unstressed syllables. The second vowel sound heard in "circus" and "famous" is the schwa vowel sound. It is a very common vowel sound.

The schwa vowel sound is very often heard in unstressed syllables that end with a single letter "r" as heard in "after" and "operate". It is a particularly common r-influenced vowel sound. Spelling patterns include "-ar", "-ard", "-ary", "er", "-er", "-ery", "ir", "-or", and "-our".

The schwa vowel sound is similar in quality to short vowel sounds. It is usually represented by a single vowel letter and is most often found in closed syllables. However, as the schwa vowel sound is heard in unstressed syllables, the doubling principle does not apply.

The r-influenced schwa vowel sound is most often found in:

- Closed final syllables that end with the letter "r" as in "aft**er**" and "consum**er**";

- Closed syllables that end with a single letter "r" followed by a vowel letter as in "adm**ir-a**l", "asp**ir-i**n", "bak**er-y**", and "diff**er-e**nt"; and

- Closed final syllables that end with "-re" as in "ac**re**" and "natu**re**".

In a few words, so little stress is placed on the syllable "er" that the vowel sound is lost altogether. The words "interest" and "temperature", for example, are sometimes pronounced "int-rest" and "temp-rature".

Occasionally, a syllable that ends with a single letter "r" followed by a vowel letter is pronounced with a short vowel sound. In "character" and "paragraph", for example, the "a(r)" spelling pattern is pronounced with the short "a" vowel sound.

Occasionally, the r-influenced schwa vowel sound is heard in a closed syllable that ends with a single letter "r" followed by a different consonant letter as heard in "conver-sation" and "ener-gy". However, this spelling pattern usually represents the stressed r-influenced vowel sound as heard in "bur-den", "ear-nest", and "ser-vice".

Occasionally, an r-influenced schwa vowel sound is followed by a double "rr" spelling pattern as in "arrange", "interrupt", and "surround". This spelling pattern is incidental and usually results from adding a prefix. The doubling principle does not apply to unstressed syllables. Single vowels followed by double consonants are usually pronounced with a short vowel sound.

As final syllables are often unstressed, it follows that the r-influenced schwa vowel sound is often heard in final syllables as in "brother" and "sister". In contrast, the stressed r-influenced vowel sound heard in the word "bird" is seldom heard in final syllables.

As single-syllable words are almost always stressed, it follows that there are no single-syllable words listed below. In contrast, the stressed r-influenced vowel sound heard in the word "bird" is often found in single-syllable words.

actor	armour (UK, CAN)	better	camper
administrator	arrange	bigger	cancer
admiral	arrest	bitter	cannery
advertise	arrive	border	carpenter
advisor	aspirin	bother	celery
after	auditor	boulder	centimeter (USA)
altogether	author	boundary	century
ancestor	average	bravery	character
anchor	awkward	brewery	circular
anger	backward	bribery	clamor (USA)
announcer	bakery	brother	clamour (UK, CAN)
another	barber	bumper	clever
answer	batter	burglar	climber
arbor (USA)	beaver	butter	closer
arbour (UK, CAN)	beggar	calculator	collar
ardor (USA)	behavior (USA)	Calgary	collector
ardour (UK, CAN)	behaviour (UK, CAN)	caller	color (USA)
armor (USA)		camera	

colour (UK, CAN)
commerce
competitor
computer
conductor
conquer
consider
consumer
container
contractor
conversation
cooler
copper
corner
correct
counsellor (UK, CAN)
counselor (USA)
counter
cover
coward
creamery
creditor
cultivator
customer
cutlery
danger
daughter
December
deliver
desire
developer
difference
different
dinner
dire
direct
direction
director
disaster
discover
discovery
distributor
diver
doctor
doer

dollar
donor
driver
eager
Easter
eastern
editor
effort
either
elder
elderly
elevator
elixir
empire
employer
endeavor (USA)
endeavour (UK, CAN)
energy
enter
entertain
error
ever
exercise
expert
factor
familiar
farmer
farther
father
favor (USA)
favour (UK, CAN)
feather
federal
fervor (USA)
fervour (UK, CAN)
fiber (USA)
finger
fire
flasher
flattery
flavor (USA)
flavour (UK, CAN)
flower
flowery
foreigner

forgery
former
forward
forwards
friar
funeral
further
garage
gather
general
generation
generous
giraffe
glamour
govern
governor
grammar
grocery
hamburger
hammer
hamster
hangar
harbor (USA)
harbour (UK, CAN)
helicopter
herself
hinder
honor (USA)
honour (UK, CAN)
horror
humor (USA)
humour (UK, CAN)
hunger
hunter
hurrah
inferior
information
interest
interfere
international
interrupt
inventor
January
junior
Jupiter
juror

keeper
killer
labor (USA)
labour (UK, CAN)
ladder
larger
laser
later
latter
laughter
lawyer
layer
leader
leather
letter
liar
liberal
liberty
liquor
liter (USA)
literary
litter
lizard
lobster
locker
loser
lover
lower
luster (USA)
machinery
major
maker
manager
maneuver (USA)
manner
martyr
master
matter
mayor
meager (USA)
member
messenger
meteor
meter (USA, CAN)
miner
mineral

minister	perfect	rubber	splendor (USA)
minor	perform	rumor (USA)	splendour (UK, CAN)
mirror	perhaps	rumour (UK, CAN)	standard
miserable	permanent	runner	steward
misery	permission	saber (USA)	stewardess
miter (USA)	permit	sailor	stinger
moderate	perspiration	salary	stranger
modern	persuade	Saturday	suffer
monastery	persuasion	Saturn	sugar
monster	pillar	satyr	suitor
mother	plaster	saucer	summer
motor	player	savior (USA)	super
mustard	plumber	saviour (UK, CAN)	superior
mystery	polar	savor (USA)	supper
neighbor (USA)	ponder	savour (UK, CAN)	surprise
neighbour (UK, CAN)	popular	scatter	surround
neither	poverty	scenery	surveyor
never	powder	scholar	survive
northern	powdery	scissors	survivor
nuclear	power	scullery	sweater
number	prayer	sculptor	syrup
numerous	preference	senator	tailor
nursery	prisoner	senior	tannery
October	professor	September	tapir
odor (USA)	proper	sepulcher (USA)	teacher
odour (UK, CAN)	property	several	temper
offer	pursue	shelter	tender
officer	pusher	shepherd	tenor
older	quarter	shoulder	theater (USA)
operate	ranger	shower	thunder
operation	rather	silver	tiger
operator	razor	similar	together
opportunity	referee	singular	tower
orchard	reference	sister	tractor
order	register	slavery	trailer
other	regular	smaller	traitor
over	remember	smoker	transfer
owner	retire	soccer	translator
paper	retired	solar	trapper
particular	rider	soldier	tremor
partner	rigor (USA)	solicitor	trucker
passenger	rigour (UK, CAN)	sombre	tumor (USA)
pattern	river	sovereign	tumour (UK, CAN)
peculiar	robber	speaker	tutor
percent	rocker	spectacular	under
	rooster	specter (USA)	

universe	vigor (USA)	western	wonder
upper	vigour (UK, CAN)	whether	worker
valor (USA)	visitor	whisper	writer
valour (UK, CAN)	vulgar	widower	younger
vapor (USA)	waiter	wilderness	zephyr
vapour (UK, CAN)	wander	winner	zipper
victory	water	winter	
viewer	weather	wire	

D5.2 The "-re" Spelling Pattern

The "-re" spelling pattern is syllabic in nature. That is, the letters "-re" form a syllable that is pronounced "ur". The letters "-re" signal that a faint schwa vowel sound is pronounced just before the consonant "r" sound. The schwa vowel sound is not well represented in the spelling.

The word "acre", for example, is pronounced "a-cur". Compare the "ur" sound in "acre" to the consonant "r" sound heard in "race" or "ride". The preceding consonant letter attaches to the "-ur" sound to complete the final syllable. This leaves the first vowel in an open, long sounding syllable. Conversely, the word "lustre" is pronounced "lus-tre". In keeping with the doubling principle, having two consonants between vowel sounds allows one consonant to keep the first vowel in a closed, short sounding syllable.

This is similar to the "-le" spelling pattern. The word "able", for example, is pronounced "a-bull". The word "little" is pronounced "lit-tull".

When the "-re" word ending follows a long "i" vowel sound, a schwa vowel sound is pronounced between the long "i" vowel sound and the consonant "r" sound. Consider the word "tire" which is pronounced "tie-ur". Three sounds may readily be discerned: a consonant "t" sound, a long "i" vowel sound, and an "ur" sound. The "ur" sound is itself made up of a schwa sound followed by a consonant "r" sound. Compare the "ur" sound heard in "tire" to the consonant "r" sound heard in "red" or "rattle". For this reason, "fire" and "tire" may be pronounced as two-syllable words. A similar effect is heard with l-influenced vowel sounds.

When the "-re" word ending follows vowel letter "u", as in "procedure", "measure", "feature", and "seizure", the letter "u" appears to represent the schwa vowel sound. However, these spelling patterns are incidental. The silent letter "u" usually helps to represent the preceding consonant sound. The letters "-re" are pronounced "ur" and represent the r-influenced schwa vowel sound.

- With the word ending "-dure", as in "procedure", the letters "du" represent the soft "g/j" consonant sound.

- With the word ending "-sure", as in "<u>su</u>re" and "in<u>su</u>re", the letters "su" represent the consonant "sh" sound.

- With the word ending "-sure", as in "mea<u>su</u>re", the letters "su" represent the consonant "zh" sound.

- With the word ending "-ture", as in "fea<u>tu</u>re", the letters "tu" represent the consonant "ch" sound.

- With the word ending "-zure", as in "sei<u>zu</u>re", the letters "zu" represent the consonant "zh" sound.

However, in some words the letter "u" is not required to help represent an adjacent consonant sound.

- In the word "inj<u>u</u>re", the letter "u" represents the schwa vowel sound.

- In the word "fail<u>u</u>re", the letter "u" represents the consonant "y" sound. The letters "-re" represent the r-influenced schwa vowel sound.

- In the words "broch<u>u</u>re" the letter "u" represents the short "u" vowel sound heard in "put". The letters "-re" represent the consonant "r" sound.

- In the words "fig<u>u</u>re", "sec<u>u</u>re", and "p<u>u</u>re" the letter "u" represents the short "u" vowel sound heard in "cure". The letters "-re" represent the consonant "r" sound.

When the "-re" word ending follows vowel letters "a", "e" and "o" as in "dare", "there", and "more", the vowel letter is usually pronounced with a short vowel sound, not the schwa vowel sound.

- Words such as "care", "dare", and "scare" are pronounced with the short "e" vowel sound.

- Words such as "there" and "where" are pronounced with the short "e" vowel sound.

- Words such as "bore", "more", and "score" are pronounced with the short "o" vowel sound.

ac**re**	architec<u>tu</u>re	compo<u>su</u>re	di**re**
ac**re**age	a<u>zu</u>re	conj**u**re	disclo<u>su</u>re
admi**re**	centime**tre** (UK, CAN)	crea<u>tu</u>re	empi**re**
adven<u>tu</u>re	clo<u>su</u>re	cul<u>tu</u>re	enclo<u>su</u>re
agricul<u>tu</u>re		desi**re**	enti**re**

expo<u>su</u>re	li<u>tre</u> (UK, CAN)	och<u>re</u>	sepulch<u>re</u> (UK, CAN)
fail<u>ure</u>	luc<u>re</u>	og<u>re</u>	signa<u>ture</u>
fea<u>ture</u>	lus<u>tre</u> (UK, CAN)	over<u>ture</u>	spec<u>tre</u> (UK, CAN)
fib<u>re</u> (UK, CAN)	macab<u>re</u>	pas<u>ture</u>	s<u>ure</u>
fi<u>re</u>	manoeuv<u>re</u> (UK, CAN)	pic<u>ture</u>	tempera<u>ture</u>
frac<u>ture</u>	massac<u>re</u>	plea<u>su</u>re	thea<u>tre</u> (UK, CAN)
furni<u>ture</u>	meag<u>re</u> (UK, CAN)	pre<u>ssu</u>re	timb<u>re</u>
fu<u>ture</u>	mea<u>su</u>re	proced<u>u</u>re	ti<u>re</u>
hi<u>re</u>	medioc<u>re</u>	requi<u>re</u>	tor<u>ture</u>
inj<u>ure</u>	me<u>tre</u> (UK, CAN)	reti<u>re</u>	trea<u>su</u>re
inqui<u>re</u>	mi<u>tre</u> (UK, CAN)	reti<u>re</u>d	wi<u>re</u>
ins<u>ure</u>	mois<u>ture</u>	sab<u>re</u> (UK, CAN)	
lei<u>su</u>re	na<u>ture</u>	sculp<u>ture</u>	
litera<u>ture</u>		sei<u>zu</u>re	

D5.3 Spelling the Stressed R-Influenced Vowel Sound Heard in "Bird"

Stressed syllables that end with the consonant "r" sound are often pronounced with the stressed r-influenced vowel sound heard in the word "bird". This vowel sound is similar in quality to the short "u" vowel sound heard in "put". Spellings patterns include "ear", "er", "err", "eur", "ir", "irr", "or", "our", "ur", "urr", "yr", and "yrrh". A rare spelling pattern is "olo", as heard in the word "c**olo**nel".

The stressed r-influenced vowel sound is similar in quality to short vowel sounds and follows the short vowel spelling conventions. It is usually represented by a single vowel letter and is found in closed syllables. As it is found in stressed syllables, it usually conforms to the doubling principle. The stressed r-influenced vowel sound is found in:

- Closed syllables followed by a different consonant letter as in "b**ur**-**d**en" and "j**our**-**n**al";

- Single-syllable words as in "b**ir**d", "f**ir**", "l**ear**n"; and

- Stressed final syllables as in "chauff**eur**" and "disc**er**n".

If the vowel was followed by a consonant other than "r", it would be pronounced with a regular short vowel sound. Compare, for example, the words "fir" and "fin" or "bird" and "big".

When pronouncing longer words, some syllables are stressed, and some are not stressed. Final syllables are often unstressed. It follows that the stressed r-influenced vowel sound is not often heard in final syllables. In contrast, the unstressed r-influenced vowel sound heard in "after" is often found in final syllables.

Single-syllable words are almost always stressed. It follows that there are many single-syllable words listed below. In contrast, the r-influenced schwa vowel sound heard in "after" is only found in unstressed syllables. For this reason, it is not found in single-syllable words.

Occasionally, a stressed r-influenced vowel sound is followed by the double "rr" spelling pattern as in "cur**r**ent", "hu**rr**y", and "squi**rr**el". However, a single vowel followed by double consonants is usually pronounced with a regular short vowel sound. See D5.4.

Words marked by an asterisk do not follow the doubling principle. The doubling principle does not apply when a short vowel sound is represented by a vowel digraph as in "c**ou**rage" and "n**ou**rish".

abs**ur**d	connoiss**eur**	f**ir**	j**our**nal
adj**our**n	c**ou**rage*	f**ir**m	j**our**ney
al**er**t	c**our**teous	f**ir**st	k**er**b (UK, CAN)
alt**er**native	c**our**tesy	fl**ou**rish*	k**er**nel
att**or**ney	c**ur**	*for*	l**ear**n
b**ir**ch	c**ur**b (USA, CAN)	f**ur**	l**ur**ch
b**ir**d	c**ur**l	f**ur**nace	l**u**stre (UK, CAN)
b**ir**th	c**ur**rent	f**ur**nish	m**er**chant
b**ir**thday	c**ur**se	f**ur**niture	m**er**cy
bl**ur**	c**ur**tain	f**ur**ry	m**er**maid
b**o**rough*	c**ur**ve	f**ur**ther	m**ir**th
b**ur**den	d**ear**th	g**er**m	m**ur**der
b**ur**glar	def**er**	G**er**man	m**ur**k
b**ur**n	des**er**t	g**ir**l	m**ur**mur
b**ur**p	des**er**ve	hamb**ur**ger	m**yrrh**
b**ur**r	det**er**mine	h**ear**d	m**yr**tle
b**ur**sar	d**ir**t	h**ear**se	n**er**ve
b**ur**st	disc**er**n	h**er**	n**er**vous
c**er**tain	dist**ur**b	h**er**b	n**ou**rish*
chauff**eur**	**Ear**l	h**er**d	n**ur**se
ch**ir**p	**ear**ly	h**ur**l	n**ur**sery
ch**ur**ch	**ear**n	h**ur**ricane	obs**er**ve
c**ir**cle	**ear**nest	h**ur**ried	p**ear**l
c**ir**cular	**ear**th	h**ur**ry	p**er**
c**ir**cus	em**er**gency	h**ur**t	p**er**ch
cl**er**k	enc**ou**rage*	in**er**t	p**er**fect
col**o**nel	entrepren**eur**	inf**er**	p**er**pendicular
comm**er**cial	**er**stwhile	ins**er**t	p**er**son
conc**er**n	f**er**n	**ir**ksome	pref**er**
conc**er**t	f**er**vor (USA)	j**er**k	pres**er**ve
conf**ir**m	f**er**vour (UK, CAN)	j**er**sey	p**ur**chase

purple	spur	thirteen	virtue
purpose	spurt	thirty	*were*
purr	squirrel	thorough*	whir (USA)
purse	squirt	Thursday	whirl
quirk	stern	tournament	whirr (UK, CAN)
refer	stir	tourniquet	whorl
rehearse	stirrup	turban	word
research	sturdy	turf	work
reserve	superb	turkey	world
return	surf	turn	worm
scourge	surface	turnip	worry
search	surgeon	turtle	worse
serpent	surname	universal	worship
servant	surplus	university	worst
serve	swerve	urban	worth
service	term	urge	worthy
shirt	third	urgent	
sir	thirst	verb	
skirt	thirsty	verse	

D5.4 The Double "RR" Spelling Pattern

As discussed in C1, double consonants usually signal that the preceding vowel letter is pronounced with a short vowel sound. In keeping with the doubling principle, if a vowel letter is followed by a double "rr", as in "merry", it is usually pronounced with a short vowel sound and not the stressed r-influenced vowel sound heard in "bird" or the unstressed r-influenced schwa vowel sound heard in "after".

In the following words the double "rr" spelling pattern follows a short vowel sound:

arrow	cherry	Kerry	porridge
barrel	corridor	marriage	quarrel
berry	err	married	sorry
borrow	error	marry	starry
carriage	horrible	merry	terrible
carrot	horrid	mirror	terror
carry	horror	narrow	tomorrow

However, there are exceptions. In the following words the double "rr" spelling pattern follows the stressed r-influenced vowel sound heard in "bird":

burr	hurricane	purr	whirr (UK, CAN)
current	hurried	squirrel	worry
furry	hurry	stirrup	

In the following words the double "rr" spelling pattern follows the unstressed r-influenced schwa vowel sound heard in "after":

arrange	arrive	hurrah	surround
arrest	correct	interrupt	

Part E: Spelling Consonant Sounds

E1 Introduction

A consonant is a type of phoneme or word sound. Unlike when we pronounce vowels, with consonant sounds our breath is momentarily restricted from being expelled through our mouth. Our tongue or lips close briefly to block the flow of air. For this reason, it is impossible to recite a series of consonant sounds such as "b - c - d - f - g" without closing our lips or touching the top of our mouth with our tongue. On the other hand, we can recite vowel sounds "a - e -i - o - u" without closing our lips or tongue.

Consonant letters "b", "c", "d", "f", "g", "h", "j", "k", "l", "m", "n", "p", "q", "r", "s", "t", "v", "w", "x", "y", and "z" are all used to represent consonant sounds. It may be noted that the letter "y" is used to represent both vowel sounds and consonant sounds. A few consonant letters, particularly "g", "h", and "w", occasionally help to represent vowel sounds. Conversely, vowel letters are sometimes used to help represent consonant sounds. It appears that only the letter "a" is never used to help represent a consonant sound.

Consonant letters play an important role in forming syllables. As discussed in A7, words are made up of syllables. Syllables, in turn, are made up of "onsets" and "rimes". The onset is that part of a syllable that comes before the vowel sound. Onsets are made up of one or more consonant sounds. The rime includes all of sounds that follow the onset. Rimes always begin with a vowel sound and may end with one or more consonant sounds. The word "rime" is a variation on the spelling of the word "rhyme". A rime, unlike other rhymes, is always spelled the same way.

Consider, for example, the single-syllable words "bet", "bell", "set", and "sell". The words "bet" and "bell" share the same onset which is the letter "b-", and the words "bell" and "sell" share the same rime which is the letters "-ell". Likewise, the words "set" and "sell" share the same onset which is the letter "s-", and the words "bet" and "set" share the same rime which is the letters "-et".

While all syllables have a rime, not all syllables have an onset. The words "art", "in", and "on", for example, are all rimes without onsets. While every rime begins with a vowel sound, not all rimes contain consonant sounds. With words such as "day", "may", and "say", the rime "-ay" does not contain a consonant sound. A single vowel letter syllable, such as the letter "i" in "an-i-mal", may form a rime by itself.

Most consonant sounds are easily named. The first sound heard in "boat", for example, is named the consonant "b" sound. The actual consonant sound, however, is not the same as the letter name. Consonant sounds are best heard pronouncing real words. Several consonant sounds are not associated with a specific consonant letter. These are usually associated with a particular consonant digraph including the consonant "ch" sound heard twice in "church"; the consonant "sh" sound heard in "shell"; and the consonant "th" sounds heard in "this" and "thin". The consonant "zh" sound, heard in the words "beige" and "vision", is not even associated with a particular digraph.

Unfortunately, there is seldom a single, consistent letter or spelling pattern that is used exclusively to represent a particular consonant sound. There are, for example, four spelling patterns for the consonant "b" sound. Also, it may be noted that the soft "c" consonant sound heard in "**c**ity" and "**c**ivil" is the same as the consonant "s" sound heard in "**s**alt" and "**s**illy". Likewise, the hard "c" consonant sound heard in "**c**at" and "**c**ook" is the same as the consonant "k" sound heard in "**k**ey" and "**k**ind". The soft "g" consonant sound heard in "**g**entle" and "**g**ym" is the same as the consonant "j" sound heard in "**j**am" and "**j**elly". The letter "x" does not represent a distinct consonant sound. Rather, "x" usually represents the hard "c/k" consonant sound followed by the soft "c/s" consonant sound as heard in "e**x**tra" and "mi**x**".

In keeping with the doubling principle, short vowel sounds represented by a single vowel letter are usually followed by two consonant letters, often double consonants. Two consonant letters protect the short vowel from the lengthening effect of a following vowel letter. The word "s**upp**er" illustrates the doubling principle. The double "pp" spelling pattern protects the short vowel "u" from being lengthened by the following letter "e". In "s**u**p**e**r", on the other hand, the letter "u" is lengthened by the following letter "e". For spelling purposes, when possible, it is helpful to pronounce both consonants as in "su**p**-**p**er". With single-syllable words, such as "e**bb**" and "i**nn**", it is not possible to pronounce both consonants.

Double consonants are formed with some letters and not others. Common doubled letters include "bb", "cc", "dd", "ff", "gg", "ll", "mm", "nn", "pp", "rr", "ss", "tt", and "zz". Consonant letters "h", "j", "k", "q", "v", "w", and "x" are never or, in the case of the letters "j" and "v", very rarely doubled.

There is less variation in the pronunciation of consonant sounds than in the pronunciation vowel sounds. This helps us to recognize words spoken by someone who speaks with an unfamiliar English accent. Also, consonant letters are of greater assistance than vowel letters in helping us to identify words when reading. It is more difficult, for example, to read "_e _ai_ i_ _ai_ _a__ _ai__ i_ _e _ai_" than it is to read "Th_ r__n _n Sp_n f_lls m_nly _n th_ pl_n". The sentence is entirely unintelligible when the consonants are omitted as opposed to merely difficult to read when the vowels are omitted.

E1.1 Regular Consonant Sounds

There are twenty regular consonant sounds that are commonly associated with a corresponding consonant letter.

1) The consonant "b" sound is heard twice in the word "**b**a**b**y".

2) The first sound heard in "**c**ity" and "**c**ivil" is the same as the first sound heard in "**s**alt" and "**s**illy". In this book it is called the soft "c/s" consonant sound.

3) The first sound heard in "**c**at" and "**c**ook" is the same as the first sound heard in "**k**ey" and "**k**ind". In this book it is called the hard "c/k" consonant sound. The letter "q" also represents the same hard "c/k" consonant sound.

4) The consonant "d" sound is heard twice in the word "**d**ivi**d**e".

5) The consonant "f" sound is the first sound heard in "**f**ather".

6) The first sound heard in "**g**entle" and "**g**ym" is the same as the first sound heard in "**j**am" and "**j**elly". In this book it is called the soft "g/j" consonant sound.

7) The hard "g" consonant sound is the first sound heard in "**g**oat".

8) The consonant "h" sound is the first sound heard in "**h**appy".

9) The consonant "l" sound is the first sound heard in "**l**and".

10) The consonant "m" sound is the first sound heard in "**m**other".

11) The consonant "n" sound is the first sound heard in "**n**ice".

12) There is a second consonant "n" sound which is heard in the words "i**nk**" and "si**ng**". In this book it is called the consonant "ng" sound.

13) The consonant "p" sound is the first sound heard in "**p**et".

14) The consonant "r" sound is the first sound heard in "**r**ice".

15) The consonant "t" sound is the first sound heard in "**t**all".

16) The consonant "v" sound is the first sound heard in "**v**an".

17) The consonant "w" sound is the first sound heard in "**w**in".

18) The letter "x" does not represent a unique consonant sound. Rather, the consonant "x" sound is diphthongal; made up of the hard "c/k" consonant sound followed by the soft "c/s" consonant sound as heard in the words "a**x**e" and "fo**x**".

19) The consonant "y" sound is the first sound heard in "**y**es".

20) The consonant "z" sound is the first sound heard in "**z**oo".

E1.2 Other Consonant Sounds

There are four consonant sounds that are not associated with a particular consonant letter. In this book these sounds are named using the consonant digraph that is most closely associated with the sound.

1) The consonant "ch" sound is heard twice in "**ch**ur**ch**".

2) The consonant "sh" sound is the first sound heard in "**sh**ell".

3) The consonant "th" sound is the first sound heard in "**th**is" and "**th**ink". Actually, there are two different consonant "th" sounds. If you listen carefully, you may note that the "th" sound heard in "**th**is" and "**th**at" is different than the "th" sound heard in "**th**ink" and "**th**in".

4) The consonant sound represented by the letters "-ge" in the word "bei**ge**" and by the letters "si" in the word "vi**si**on" is not associated with a particular letter or consonant digraph and is, therefore, not easily named. In this book it is called the consonant "zh" sound.

E1.3 Silent Consonant Letters

Consonant letters are often silent. This occurs when a consonant letter is part of a digraph that represents a vowel or consonant sound. In the word "stra**w**", for example, a silent letter "w" helps to represent the short "o" vowel sound. In "bri**dge**" a silent letter "d" helps to represent the soft "g/j" consonant sound.

Sometimes, silent letters represent archaic sounds that are no longer pronounced. This makes it uncertain how to best classify silent letters. In the word "flight", for example, the letters "gh" were once pronounced but are now silent. It is uncertain whether the letters "gh" should be considered part of the long "i" vowel spelling pattern or the consonant "t" spelling pattern. Both interpretations are set out in this book.

The Letter B

The letter "b" is silent in consonant digraphs that represent the consonant "b" sound heard in "e**bb**", the consonant "t" sound heard in "dou**bt**", and the consonant "m" sound heard in "bo**mb**".

With the "mb" consonant digraph, the letter "b" is silent in single-syllable words such as "crumb" and "dumb". The letter "b" is also silent in two-syllable words, such as "climb-er" and "plumb-er", that have a syllabic break following the "b". It is difficult to pronounce the consonant "b" sound immediately following the consonant "m" sound. On the other hand, the letter "b" is pronounced in two-syllable words, such as "lum-ber" and "tim-ber", when a syllabic break divides the letter "m" from the letter "b".

Sometimes the letter "b" disappears altogether with the addition of a suffix as in the words "crummy" and "dummy".

The Letter C

The letter "c" is silent in the vowel digraph representing the short "o" vowel sound heard in "y**ach**t".

The letter "c" is also silent in consonant digraphs that represent the hard "c/k" consonant sound heard in "ra**cc**oon", the hard "c/k" consonant sound heard in "zu**cch**ini", the hard "c/k" consonant sound heard in "e**ch**o", the consonant "ch" sound heard in "**ch**urch", the consonant "sh" sound heard in "ma**ch**ine, the consonant "t" sound heard in "y**ach**t", the hard "c/k" consonant sound heard in "bla**ck**", the consonant "z" sound heard in "**cz**ar", the soft "c/s" consonant sound heard in "**sci**ence", the soft "c/s" consonant sound heard in "**sch**ism", the consonant "sh" sound heard in "**sch**edule", the consonant "ch" sound heard in "con**sci**ous", and the consonant "sh" sound heard in "con**sci**ence".

The Letter D

The letter "d" is silent in consonant digraphs that represent the consonant "d" sound heard in "a**dd**", the soft "g/j" consonant sound heard in "ju**dge**", and the soft "g/j" consonant sound heard in "e**du**cate".

The Letter F

The letter "f" is silent in the consonant digraph representing the consonant "f" sound heard in "o**ff**".

The Letter G

The letter "g" is silent in vowel digraphs that represent the long "a" vowel sound heard in "str**aigh**t", the short "o" vowel sound heard in "t**augh**t", the long "a" vowel sound heard in "**eigh**t", the long "i" vowel sound heard in "h**eigh**t", the long "i" vowel sound heard in "h**igh**", the long "o" vowel sound heard in "alth**ough**", the short "o" vowel sound heard in "b**ough**t", and the long "u" vowel sound heard in "thr**ough**".

The letter "g" is also silent in consonant digraphs that represent the soft "g/j" consonant sound heard in "su**gg**est", the hard "g" consonant sound heard in "e**gg**", the hard "c/k" consonant sound heard in "lou**gh**", the consonant "f" sound heard in "lau**gh**", the hard "g" consonant sound heard in "**gh**ost", the consonant "p" sound heard in "hiccou**gh**", the consonant "t" sound heard in "ni**gh**t", the consonant "n" sound heard in "**gn**aw" and "si**gn**", and the consonant sound "ng" sound heard in "ba**ng**".

The Letter H

The letter "h" is always silent after a vowel letter as (not) heard in the words "ah", "eh", "hurrah", "oh", "ohm", "Pharaoh", "shah", and "uh".

The letter "h" is silent in vowel digraphs that represent the short "o" vowel sound heard in "ya**ch**t, the broad "a" or short "o" vowel sound heard in "hurr**ah**", the long "a" vowel sound heard in "str**aigh**t, the long "o" vowel sound heard in "Phar**aoh**", the short "o" vowel sound heard in "t**augh**t", the long "a" vowel sound heard in "**eh**", the long "a" vowel sound heard in "**eigh**t", the long "i" vowel sound heard in "h**eigh**t", the short "e" vowel sound heard in "**hei**r", the broad "a" or short "o" vowel sound heard in "**ho**nest", the vowel diphthong sound heard in "**ho**ur", the long "i" vowel sound heard in "h**igh**", the long "o" vowel sound heard in "**oh**", the long "o" vowel sound heard in "alth**ough**", the short "o" vowel sound heard in "b**ough**t", and the long "u" vowel sound heard in "thr**ough**".

The letter "h" is also silent in consonant digraphs that represent the consonant "b" sound heard in "**bh**ang", the hard "c/k" consonant sound heard in "zu**cch**ini", the hard "c/k" consonant sound heard in "**Ch**ristmas", the consonant "ch" sound heard twice in "**ch**ur**ch**", the consonant "sh" sound heard in "ma**ch**ine", the consonant "t" sound heard in "ya**ch**t", the consonant "d" sound heard in "Gan**dh**i", the hard "c/k" consonant sound heard in "lou**gh**", the consonant "f" sound heard in "lau**gh**", the hard "g" consonant sound heard in "**gh**ost", the consonant "t" sound heard in "ni**gh**t", the hard "c/k" consonant sound heard in "**kh**aki", the consonant "f" sound heard in "telep**h**one", the consonant "r" sound heard in "**rh**ino", the soft "c/s" consonant sound heard in "**sch**ism", the consonant "sh" sound heard in "**sh**ell", the soft "c/s" consonant sound heard in "a**sth**ma", the consonant "t" sound heard in "**Th**omas", the voiced consonant "th" sound heard in "**th**is", the unvoiced consonant "th" sound heard in "**th**in", the consonant "w" sound heard in "**wh**at", and the hard "g" consonant sound followed by the consonant "z" sound heard in "e**xh**aust".

While some people do not pronounce the letter "h" in the word "**h**erb", it is pronounced in related words such as "**h**erbaceous", "**h**erbivore", and "**h**erbal". The letter "h" is also silent in the words "ex**h**ibition", "shep**h**erd" and "sil**h**ouette".

The Letter J

The letter "j" is silent in the consonant digraph representing the consonant "w" sound heard in "mari**ju**ana".

The Letter K

The letter "k" is silent in consonant digraphs that represent the hard "c/k" consonant sound heard in "tre**kk**ed", the consonant "n" sound heard in "**kn**ife", and the consonant "x" sound heard in "ki**cks**".

The Letter L

The letter "l" is silent in vowel digraphs that represent the short "a" or the broad "a" vowel sound heard in "c**al**f", the short "o" vowel sound heard in "w**al**k", the long "o" vowel sound heard in "f**ol**k", and the short "u" vowel sound heard in "sh**oul**d".

The letter "l" is also silent in consonant digraphs that represent the consonant "d" sound heard in "cou**ld**", the consonant "f" sound heard in "ca**lf**", the hard "c/k" consonant sound heard in "wa**lk**", the consonant "l" sound heard in "ba**ll**", the consonant "m" sound heard in "a**lm**ond", and the consonant "v" sound heard in "ha**lve**".

The Letter M

The letter "m" is silent in the consonant digraph representing the consonant "m" sound heard in "sla**mm**ed".

The Letter N

The letter "n" is silent in consonant digraphs that represent the consonant "m" sound heard in "autu**mn**" and the consonant "n" sound heard in "A**nn**".

The Letter P

The letter "p" is silent in consonant digraphs that represent the consonant "b" sound heard in "cu**pb**oard", the consonant "f" sound heard in "tele**ph**one", the consonant "p" sound heard in "sto**pp**ed", the consonant "n" sound heard in "**pn**eumonia", the soft "c/s" consonant sound heard in "**ps**ychology", and the consonant "t" sound heard in "**pt**erodactyl" and "recei**pt**".

The Letter Q

The letter "q" is silent in consonant digraphs that represent the hard "c/k" consonant sound heard in "a**cq**uire" and the hard "c/k" consonant sound heard in "la**cqu**er".

The Letter R

The letter "r" is silent in consonant digraphs that represent the consonant "r" sound heard in "e**rr**" and the consonant "r" sound heard in "my**rrh**".

The Letter S

The letter "s" is silent in vowel digraphs that represent the long "i" vowel sound heard in "ai**s**le", the long "e" vowel sound heard in "debr**is**", and the long "i" vowel sound heard in "**is**land".

The letter "s" is also silent in consonant digraphs that represent the consonant "ch" sound heard in "con**sci**ous", the soft "c/s" consonant sound heard in "dre**ss**", the consonant "z" sound heard in "de**ss**ert", the consonant "sh" sound heard in "mi**ssi**on", and the consonant "sh" sound heard in "i**ss**ue".

The Letter T

The letter "t" is silent in vowel digraphs that represent the long "o" vowel sound heard in "dep**ot**" and the long "u" vowel sound heard in "deb**ut**".

The letter "t" is also silent in consonant digraphs that represent the consonant "f" sound heard in "o**ft**en", the soft "c/s" consonant sound heard in "ca**stl**e", the soft "c/s" consonant sound heard in "a**sth**ma", the consonant "ch" sound heard in "wi**tch**", the voiced consonant "th" sound heard in "**th**is", the unvoiced consonant "th" sound heard in "**th**in", the consonant "z" sound heard in "**ts**ar" and "**tz**ar", the consonant "t" sound heard in "bu**tt**", and the consonant "t" sound heard in "casse**tte**".

The Letter V

The letter "v" is silent in the consonant digraph representing the consonant "v" sound heard in "re**vv**ed".

The Letter W

Following a vowel letter, a silent letter "w" always helps to represent vowel sounds.

The letter "w" is silent in vowel digraphs that represent the short "o" vowel sound heard in "str**aw**", the vowel diphthong sound as heard in "l**aw**yer", the long "o" vowel sound heard in "s**ew**", the long "u" vowel sound heard in "gr**ew**", the long "u" vowel sound heard in "neph**ew**", the long "u" vowel sound heard in "**ew**e", the long "u" vowel sound heard in "rev**iew**", the broad "a" or short "o" vowel sound heard in "kn**ow**ledge", the long "o" vowel sound heard in "gr**ow**", the vowel diphthong sound heard in "c**ow**", and the long "u" vowel sound heard in "t**wo**".

The letter "w" is also silent in consonant digraphs that represent the soft "c/s" consonant sound heard in "**sw**ord", the consonant "h" sound heard in "**wh**o", and the consonant "r" sound heard in "**wr**ite".

The Letter X

The letter "x" is silent in consonant digraphs that represent the hard "g" consonant sound followed by the consonant "z" sound heard in "e**xh**aust" and the hard "c/k" consonant sound followed by the soft "c/s" consonant sound heard in "ta**x**".

The Letter Z

The letter "z" is silent in the consonant digraph representing the consonant "z" sound heard in "bu**zz**".

E2 Spelling the Consonant "B" Sound

There are several spelling patterns for the consonant "b" sound heard twice in the word "**b**a**b**y". They have been divided into major and rare spelling patterns.

E2.1 Major Spelling Patterns

There are two major spelling patterns for the consonant "b" sound heard twice in the word "**baby**".

a)   "b"

The consonant "b" sound heard twice in the word "baby" may be represented by the letter "b".

ability	Barrichello	behave	bit
able	base	behavior (USA)	bite
Ablett	basic	behaviour (UK, CAN)	bitter
aboard	basin	behind	blade
about	basis	being	blood
above	basket	belief	board
absence	bat	believe	boast
absent	bath	bell	boat
absolute	bathe	belong	body
amber	bathing	below	boil
ambition	battle	belt	bold
ambitious	bay	Ben	bomb
ambulance	be	bench	bone
automobile	beach	bend	book
available	beak	beneath	boom
baby	beam	berry	border
back	bean	beside	bore
bad	bear	best	born
bag	beard	bet	borrow
baggage	beast	better	boss
bait	beat	between	both
bake	beautiful	beyond	bother
balance	beauty	Bible	bottle
ball	beaver	bicycle	bottom
balloon	became	bid	bought
banana	because	big	boulder
band	become	bike	bound
bang	bed	bilingual	bow
bank	bee	bill	bowl
bar	beef	billion	box
barber	been	bind	boy
bare	beer	bionic	bribe
bargain	before	bird	bubble
bark	beg	birth	bucket
barn	began	biscuit	bug
barrel	begin		build

built	contribution	library	remember
bullet	cub	lobster	republic
bump	Cuba	lumber	responsible
bunch	December	member	rhombus
bundle	describe	miserable	rob
bunny	disturb	mumble	robin
burglar	double	neighbor (USA)	robot
buried	exhibit	neighbour (UK, CAN)	rub
burn	exhibition	nimble	September
burst	February	noble	sub
bury	garbage	number	subject
bus	grab	obedience	substance
bush	habit	obedient	suitable
business	hamburger	obey	table
busy	harbor (USA)	object	terrible
but	harbour (UK, CAN)	objection	timber
butter	horrible	observe	tribe
button	husband	obvious	trouble
buy	impossible	October	tub
buzz	invisible	possible	tube
by	job	probable	tumble
cabin	laboratory	problem	unable
club	liberal	public	valuable
combine	liberty	reasonable	vegetable
contribute	librarian		verb

b) "bb"

The consonant "b" sound heard twice in the word "baby" may be represented by the "bb" consonant digraph.

Double consonants usually signal that the preceding vowel letter is pronounced with a short vowel sound as in "ebb" and "rubber". For spelling purposes, when double consonants lie between two syllables, it is helpful to pronounce both consonants as in "rab-bit". With single-syllable words, such as "ebb", only one consonant "b" sound can be pronounced.

bubble	rabbit	rubber
ebb	ribbon	rubbing
hobby	robber	rubbish

E2.2 Rare Spelling Patterns

There are at least two rare spelling patterns for the consonant "b" sound heard twice in the word "baby".

a)   "bh"

The consonant "b" sound heard twice in the word "baby" may be represented by the "bh" consonant digraph. The letter "h" is silent.

bhang (Hindi)

b)   "pb"

The consonant "b" sound heard twice in the word "baby" may be represented by the "pb" consonant digraph. The letter "p" is silent.

cu**pb**oard   ras**pb**erry

E3   Spelling the Soft "C/S" Consonant Sound

The first sound heard in "**c**ity" and "**c**ivil" is sometimes called a soft "c" consonant sound. However, it is the same as the consonant "s" sound heard in "**s**alt" and "**s**illy". In this book, therefore, it is called the soft "c/s" consonant sound.

The soft "c/s" consonant sound is phonetically similar to the consonant "z" sound. The difference between the two sounds is that the soft "c/s" consonant sound is unvoiced and the consonant "z" sound is voiced. Our vocal cords do not vibrate when we pronounce the unvoiced soft "c/s" consonant sound heard in "mo**ss**" and "**s**ee". We can feel our vocal cords vibrating when we pronounce the voiced consonant "z" sound heard in "buzz" and "zoo".

There are many spelling patterns for the soft "c/s" consonant sound heard in "**c**ity" and "**s**illy". They have been divided into major, minor, and rare spelling patterns.

E3.1 Major Spelling Patterns

There are five major spelling patterns for the soft "c/s" consonant sound heard in "**c**ity" and "**s**illy".

a)   "c" followed by "e", "i", or "y"

The soft "c/s" consonant sound heard in "city" and "silly" may be represented by the letter "c" when followed by vowel letters "e", "i", or "y". The same three letters also soften the letter "g".

It does not matter what sound the letters "e", "i", or "y" represent or whether they are silent, the letters "c" and "g" are usually soft when immediately followed by "e", "i", or "y".

Conversely, the hard "c/k" consonant sound heard in "cat" and "key" is often represented by the letter "c" when followed by the vowel letters "a", "o", "u" or another consonant letter. These same letters also harden the letter "g".

Words that end with the soft "c/s" consonant sound, such as "race" and "notice", often end with the "-ce" spelling pattern. The final silent letter "e" signals that the adjacent letter "c" is pronounced with the soft "c/s" consonant sound. A final soft "c/s" consonant sound is never represented by the letter "c" alone.

When adding a suffix that begins with a vowel letter to a base word that ends with a final silent letter "e", the letter "e" is usually dropped. However, when adding a suffix that begins with the letters "a", "o", or "u" to a base word that end with a soft "-ce", the final silent letter "e" is retained. It is still required to signal the soft "c" sound. Adding "-able" to "replace", for example, forms "replaceable".

When a double "cc" is followed by the letters "e" or "i", as in "accident" and "success", two spelling patterns come into play. The first letter "c" is pronounced with the hard "c/k" consonant sound because, as discussed above, it is followed by another consonant letter. The second letter "c" is pronounced with the soft "c/s" consonant sound because it is followed by the letters "e" or "i". The word "soccer" is a rare exception to these spelling patterns.

Double consonants usually signal that the preceding vowel letter is pronounced with a short vowel sound as in "accept" and "succeed".

It may be noted that with the word "Celt", referring to a person who speak the Celtic language", the letter "c" is pronounced with the soft "c" or "s" sound in the United States and is pronounced with the hard "c/k" consonant sound in Britain.

absence	cedar	ceremony	conscience
accept	ceiling	certain	consider
accident	celery	chance	convenience
advance	cell	choice	council
advice	Celsius	cicada	cowardice
agency	Celt	cider	cycle
allowance	Celtic	cinder	cygnet
ambulance	cement	circle	cylinder
announce	censorship	circular	cymbal
annoyance	cent	circus	cynic
appearance	center (USA, CAN)	citizen	cypress
association	centimeter (USA)	city	dance
audience	centimetre (UK, CAN)	civil	deceit
avoidance	centre (UK, CAN)	civilize	deceive
balance	century	commerce	December
bicycle	cerebral	concern	decent
cancer		confidence	decide

decision	importance	percent	reference
decisive	influence	performance	rejoice
defence (UK, CAN)	instance	piece	replace
dependence	insurance	place	reproduce
difference	intelligence	police	resistance
distance	interference	policy	resource
efficiency	introduce	practice	rice
emergency	juice	precede	sacrifice
enforce	juicy	preference	sauce
entrance	justice	prejudice	saucer
essence	lettuce	presence	scene
evidence	lice	price	scent
excellence	license	prince	science
excellent	medicine	princess	scientist
except	mercy	principal	sentence
excess	mice	principle	service
excite	necessary	proceed	silence
exercise	nice	process	simplicity
existence	niece	procession	since
experience	notice	produce	sincere
face	nuisance	pronounce	society
facility	obedience	pronunciation	space
fence	office	province	spruce
fierce	once	provincial	substance
force	ounce	race	succeed
France	Pacific	raced	success
frequency	palace	racing	succession
grace	parcel	racy	succinct
grocery	patience	receipt	surface
hindrance	peace	receive	trace
ice	peaceful	recent	twice
icing	pencil	recess	violence
icy	penicillin	reduce	voice

b)   "s"

The soft "c/s" consonant sound heard in "city" and "silly" may be represented by the letter "s". This spelling pattern forms both onsets and rimes.

The letter "s" also represents the consonant "z" sound.

absence	aside	atmosphere	basis
absent	ask	August	basket
absolute	asleep	base	beast
almost	assist	basic	beside
also	astronaut	basin	best

biggest	ourselves	says	silent
biscuit	pastry	scare	silk
comparison	pasture	scary	silly
consumer	person	scatter	silver
conversation	persuade	school	similar
cousin	persuasion	score	simple
custom	plaster	scorpion	simplicity
customer	plastic	scratch	sin
decisive	question	scream	since
deserve	register	sea	sincere
dinosaur	rescue	seal	sing
disagree	research	search	singing
disappear	resource	season	single
disappoint	responsible	seat	sink
disapprove	risk	second	sir
disaster	sacred	secret	sister
discomfort	sacrifice	see	sit
discontent	sad	seed	site
discuss	sadden	seem	situation
disgust	saddle	seen	six
dislike	safe	self	size
dismiss	said	sell	so
disregard	sail	send	soap
disrespect	sailor	senior	soccer
dissatisfaction	sake	sense	social
dissatisfy	salad	sent	society
distance	salary	sentence	sock
distant	sale	separate	socks
expensive	salt	September	soft
explosive	same	sergeant	soften
extensive	sample	series	soil
fantastic	sand	serious	solar
herself	sandal	servant	sold
himself	sandwich	service	soldier
inclusive	sang	set	solemn
insect	sat	settle	solution
inside	satellite	seven	solve
insult	satisfaction	several	some
itself	satisfy	sex	son
loosen	Saturday	sick	song
lots	Saturn	side	soon
mischief	sauce	sight	sore
mistake	saucer	sign	sorry
mosquito	save	signal	sort
nuisance	saw	signature	soul
nursery	say	silence	sound

soup	succeed	sunny	swallow
sour	such	super	sympathetic
south	suck	supper	sympathy
sovereign	sudden	supply	system
square	suffer	support	thesaurus
squeeze	suggest	suppose	thirsty
squid	suggestion	surface	translate
squirrel	suit	surprise	universal
sub	summer	surround	university
subject	sun	survive	whisper
substance	Sunday	suspect	

c) Final "-s"

The soft "c/s" consonant sound heard in "city" and "silly" may be represented by a single final letter "-s".

The final "-s" spelling pattern also represents the consonant "z" sound.

English spelling does not favour base words ending with a single final letter "s". This is because the suffix "-s" is used to create the plural, possessive, and third-person-singular forms of words. To work around this, there are a number of alternative spellings to represent a final soft "c/s" consonant sound including "-se", "-ss", and "-x".

There are exceptions to the rule that only the plural, possessive, and third-person-singular forms of words end with a single final letter "s". The singular form of many Latin nouns, such as "octopus" and "circus", end with the suffix "-us". The plural form is usually created by changing the letters "-us" to "i". The plural of "octopus", for example, is "octopi".

abacus	cactus	nucleus	syllabus
alumnus	circus	octopus	terminus
apparatus	focus	radius	thesaurus
bacillus	fungus	stimulus	

Many adjectives, such as "curious" and "nervous", end with the suffix "-ous".

ambitious	delicious	mysterious	serious
anxious	enormous	nervous	tremendous
cautious	famous	numerous	unconscious
conscious	furious	obvious	various
curious	generous	precious	
dangerous	jealous	ridiculous	

The following words that end with a final letter "s" are French in origin.

corp**s**	chamoi**s**	bourgeoi**s**
chassi**s**	debri**s**	apropo**s**

A number of other words end with a final letter "s".

a**s**	canva**s**	len**s**	thu**s**
basi**s**	Christma**s**	perhap**s**	tonsilliti**s**
bia**s**	cosmo**s**	plu**s**	tricep**s**
bicep**s**	forcep**s**	politic**s**	u**s**
bu**s**	ga**s**	thi**s**	ye**s**

As well, of course, the suffix "-s" forms the plural, possessive, and third-person-singular forms of thousands of words.

1. <u>The Plural Form</u>

Nouns have both singular and plural forms. The singular form of a noun indicates that a single person, place, or thing is being discussed. The plural form of a noun indicates that two or more persons, places, or things are being discussed. With most nouns, the plural form is created by adding the suffixes "-s" or "-es" to the base word. For example, the singular "one dog" becomes the plural "two dog**s**" with the addition of the letter "s". Likewise, the singular "peach" become the plural "peach**es**".

beach**es**	dog**s**	night**s**	peach**es**
card**s**	light**s**	nut**s**	sport**s**
cat**s**	match**es**	park**s**	thank**s**

2. <u>The Possessive Form</u>

The possessive form of a noun or pronoun is used to indicate an ownership relationship between the noun or pronoun and some other thing. The sentence *"That is the boy's coat."* indicates that the boy owns or possesses the coat. The possessive form is most often created using an apostrophe followed by the letter "s".

child'**s**	her**s**	our**s**	women'**s**
David'**s**	his	Sarah'**s**	your**s**
doctor'**s**	it**s**	their**s**	

3. <u>The Third-Person-Singular Form of Verbs</u>

Verbs express action in different tenses such as the past tense, the present tense, and the future tense. The third-person, present-tense, singular form of a verb is created by adding the suffixes "-s" or "-es" to the verb. For example, the third-person, present-tense, singular form of the verb "drive" is "drive**s**".

First-person, present-tense, singular: *"I drive a red truck."*
Third-person, present-tense, singular: *"She drives a blue sedan."*

catch**es**	drive**s**	reach**es**	talk**s**
dream**s**	go**es**	run**s**	walk**s**

d)   Final "-se"

The soft "c/s" consonant sound heard in "city" and "silly" may be represented by a final "-se" spelling pattern forming a consonant digraph. The letter "e" is silent.

English spelling does not favour base words ending with a single final letter "s". This is because the suffix "-s" is used to create the plural, possessive, and third-person-singular forms of words. The "-se" word ending indicates that the "s" is not a suffix, signaling that words such as "house" are not plural, possessive, or third-person-singular.

The "-se" spelling pattern provides a visual distinction between words such as "dens" and "dense"; "divers" and "diverse"; "laps" and "lapse"; and "pleas" and "please".

With words such as "chase" and "vise", the final silent letter "e" also signals that the preceding vowel is pronounced with a long sound.

The final "-se" spelling pattern also represents the consonant "z" sound.

case	expense	*Japanese*	purchase
chase	false	license	purpose
coarse	geese	loose	sense
course	goose	moose	tortoise
curse	grease	mouse	universe
decrease	horse	nurse	verse
defense (USA)	*house* (Noun)	offense (USA)	vise (USA)
dense	immense	pretense (USA)	worse
else	increase	promise	

e)   "ss" and "-ss"

The soft "c/s" consonant sound heard in "city" and "silly" may be represented by the "ss" and final "-ss" consonant digraphs.

English spelling does not favour base words ending with a single final letter "s". This is because the suffix "-s" is used to create the plural, possessive, and third-person-singular forms of words. The final "-ss" word ending indicates that the "s" is not a suffix, signaling that words such as "dress" are not plural, possessive, or third-person-singular.

Double consonants usually signal that the preceding vowel letter is pronounced with a short vowel sound as in "gl**a**ss" and "m**e**ssage". For spelling purposes, when double consonants lie between two syllables, it is helpful to pronounce both consonants as in "blos-som". The words "kiss" and "dressed" are single-syllable words, so only one soft "c/s" consonant sound can be pronounced.

The "-ss" spelling pattern is used in suffixes "-ess", "-less", "-ness", and "-ress" as in "princess", "helpless", "happiness", and "actress".

The "-ss" spelling pattern provides a visual distinction between words such as "his" and "hiss"; "princes" and "princess"; and "needles" and "needless".

The "ss" spelling pattern also represents the consonant "z" sound.

across	cross	kissing	possess
actress	discuss	less	possible
address	dismiss	lesson	press
assist	dress	loss	princess
association	essence	mass	process
bless	excess	mess	professor
blossom	express	message	progress
boss	fussy	messenger	recess
brass	glass	miss	stewardess
business	grass	missing	unless
careless	guess	necessary	vessel
class	impossible	noiseless	wilderness
classification	kindness	pass	witness
confess	kiss	passenger	

E3.2 Minor Spelling Patterns

There are five minor spelling patterns for the soft "c/s" consonant sound heard in "city" and "silly".

a) "ps"

The soft "c/s" consonant sound heard in "city" and "silly" may be represented by the "ps" consonant digraph. The letter "p" is silent. This spelling pattern is Greek in origin.

psalm	**ps**eudonym	**ps**ychiatrist	**ps**ycho
Psalms	**ps**oriasis	**ps**ychiatry	**ps**ychology
pseudo	**ps**yche	**ps**ychic	

b) "sc"

The soft "c/s" consonant sound heard in "city" and "silly" may be represented by the "sc" consonant digraph.

When the letters "sc" are followed by vowel letters "e", "i", or "y" as in "descend", "science", and "scythe", the two letters merge together and are pronounced with the soft "c/s" consonant sound. However, when the letters "sc" are followed by vowel letters "a", "o", or "u", the letter "s" is pronounced with the soft "c/s" consonant sound, and the letter "c" is pronounced with the hard "c/k" consonant sound. This produces the consonant blend heard in the words "scandal", "scone", and "scurry".

With the word "muscle", pronounced "mus-ull", the letters "sc" are followed by a schwa vowel sound that is not represented in the spelling. The schwa vowel sound has the same effect as the letters "e", "i", and "y". "Muscular", on the other hand, is pronounced "mus-cue-lur". The letter "c" followed by the letter "u" signals the hard "c/k" consonant sound.

The letters "sc" stay together in words such as "de-scend" which break into syllables following a long vowel sound. The letters "sc" divide between syllables in words such as "cres-cent" following a short vowel sound.

descend	muscle	scent	scientific
descent	rescind	scepter (USA)	scientist
discipline	scene	sceptre (UK, CAN)	scissors
fascinate	scenery	science	scythe

c) "st"

The soft "c/s" consonant sound heard in "city" and "silly" may be represented by the "st" consonant digraph. The letter "t" is silent.

All of the following words have a root that ends with the letters "st". Some of the root words are free morphemes, such as "Christ", "fast", "moist", and "nest", that can stand on their own. The letter "t" is pronounced in such root words. Other roots are bound morphemes, such as "chast" and "thist", which no longer stand on their own.

Although the letter "t" is silent, in keeping with the doubling principle, the "st" spelling pattern still functions to signal that the preceding single vowel letter is pronounced with a short vowel sound.

apostle	chestnut	forecastle	hustle
bristle	christen	glisten	jostle
bustle	Christmas	gristle	listen
castle	epistle	hasten	mistletoe
chasten	fasten	hostler	moisten

ne**stle**	ru**stle**	thi**stle**	whi**stle**
pe**stle**	thi**stle**down	tre**stle**	wre**stle**

d) "x", "xc(e)", and "xc(i)"

The consonant "x" sound, a hard "c/k" consonant sound followed by a soft "c/s" consonant sound, may be represented by the letters "x", "xc(e)" and "xc(i)". The word "tax", for example, is pronounced "tacks". Neither sound is well represented by the spelling.

In words such as "a**x**e" and "e**x**pert", the letter "x" represents both the hard "c/k" consonant sound and the following soft "c/s" consonant sound. However, if the letter "x" is followed by the letter "c", spelling patterns become complicated:

- In words such as "ex<u>c</u>eed" and "ex<u>c</u>ite", the letter "x" represents the hard "c/k" consonant sound, and the letter "c" (followed by vowel letters "e", "i", or "y") represents the soft "c/s" consonant sound.

- In words such as "ex<u>c</u>use" and "ex<u>c</u>laim", the letter "x" represents both the hard "c/k" consonant sound and the soft "c/s" consonant sound. The letter "c" (followed by vowel letters "a", "o", "u" or a consonant) represents a second hard "c/k" consonant sound.

- In the word "ex<u>ch</u>ange" the letter "x" represents both the hard "c/k" consonant sound and the soft "c/s" consonant sound, and the letters "ch" represent the consonant "ch" sound.

When the letter "x" represents both the hard "c/k" consonant sound and the soft "c/s" consonant sound, there may be a syllabic break between the two sounds. The words "expand" and "explain", for example, are pronounced "ek-spand" and "ek-splain". However, the syllabic break may occur after the soft "c" or "s" sound. The words "expert" and "extra", for example, are usually pronounced "eks-pert" and "eks-tra".

In the words "exhale" and "exhume" the letter "h" is pronounced. The letter "h" is silent in the word "exhibition".

With the word "axe", the final silent letter "e" helps to satisfy the three letter rule.

With the word "exit" the letter "x" is also pronounced with the hard "g" consonant sound followed by the consonant "z" sound by some speakers.

a**x**e	e**x**change	e**x**hale	e**x**pand
bo**x**	e**x**<u>c</u>ite	e**x**hibition	e**x**pend
e**x**<u>c</u>eed	e**x**claim	e**x**hume	e**x**pense
e**x**<u>c</u>ellent	e**x**<u>c</u>use	e**x**it	e**x**pensive
e**x**<u>c</u>ept	e**x**er<u>c</u>ise	e**x**pect	e**x**perience

experiment	express	max	saxophone
expert	extend	maximum	sex
explain	extra	Mexican	six
explode	extreme	Mexico	tax
explore	fax	mix	wax
explosion	fix	next	
explosive	fox	relax	

e)   "z"

The soft "c/s" consonant sound heard in "city" and "silly" may be represented by the letter "z".

It may be noted that in most of the words listed below a pronounced letter "t" precedes the letter "z". With the words "Nazi" and "scherzo", pronounced "Nat-see" and "scher-tso", a consonant "t" sound not represented in the spelling precedes the soft "c/s" consonant sound.

The letter "z", of course, also represents the consonant "z" sound.

chintz	howitzer	quartz	waltz
eczema	klutz	scherzo	
ersatz	Nazi	schmaltz	
hertz	pretzel	seltzer	

E3.3 Rare Spelling Patterns

There are at least five rare spelling patterns for the soft "c/s" consonant sound heard in "**c**ity" and "**s**illy".

a)   "sch"

The soft "c/s" consonant sound heard in "city" and "silly" may be represented by the "sch" consonant digraph. The letters "ch" are silent.

*sch*ism

b)   "sth"

The soft "c/s" consonant sound heard in "city" and "silly" may be represented by the "sth" consonant digraph. The letters "th" are silent.

*asth*ma   isth*mus

c)   "sw"

The soft "c/s" consonant sound heard in "city" and "silly" may be represented by the "sw" consonant digraph. The letter "w" is silent.

sword   an**sw**er

d)   "ts"

The soft "c/s" consonant sound heard in "city" and "silly" may be represented by the "ts" consonant digraph. The letter "t" is silent.

*ts*ar

e)   "tz"

The soft "c/s" consonant sound heard in "city" and "silly" may be represented by the "tz" consonant digraph. The letter "t" is silent.

*tz*ar

E4   Spelling the Hard "C/K" Consonant Sound

The first sound heard in "**c**at" and "**c**ook" is sometimes called a hard "c" consonant sound. However, it is the same as the consonant "k" sound heard in "**k**ey" and "**k**ind". In this book, therefore, it is called the hard "c/k" consonant sound.

There are many spelling patterns for the hard "c/k" consonant sound heard in "**c**at" and "**k**ey". They have been divided into major, minor, and rare spelling patterns.

E4.1 Major Spelling Patterns

There are eleven major spelling patterns for the hard "c/k" consonant sound heard in "**c**at" and "**k**ey".

a)   "c" followed by "a", "o", "u" or another consonant

The hard "c/k" consonant sound heard in the words "cat" and "key" may be represented by the letter "c" when followed by vowel letters "a", "o", "u" or another consonant. The same letters also harden the letter "g".

Conversely, the letter "c" represents the soft "c/s" consonant sound heard in "city" and "silly" when followed by the vowel letters "e", "i", or "y". These same three letters also soften the letter "g".

It follows that soft "c" or "s" words such as "Sam", "sob", and "sue" must be spelled with the letter "s", and not the letter "c", because otherwise the letters "a", "o", and "u" would signal the hard "c/k" consonant sound as in "Cam", "cob", and "cue".

When a double "cc" is followed by the letters "e" or "i", as in "accident" and "success", two spelling patterns come into play. The first letter "c" is pronounced with the hard "c/k" consonant sound because it is followed by another consonant letter. The second letter "c" is pronounced with the soft "c/s" consonant sound because it is followed by the letters "e" or "i". The word "soccer" is a rare exception to this spelling pattern.

The letter "c" is occasionally silent when followed by the letter "t", as in "Connecticut", "indict", and "victuals". This is not a general rule as the letter "c" is pronounced in the word "victim". The letter "c" is also silent in the word "yacht".

accept	camera	cave	come
accident	camp	character	comfort
accidental	Canada	Chicago	coming
acne	Canadian	chocolate	command
acquire	canal	cicada	commerce
acre	cancer	circle	commercial
acreage	candle	circular	commission
across	candy	circus	committee
act	cannon	clap	common
action	cannot	class	community
active	canoe	classification	companies
activity	canyon	claw	companion
actor	cap	clean	company
actress	cape	clear	compare
actual	capital	cliff	compete
Africa	captain	climb	competition
agriculture	car	clip	complain
application	card	coach	complete
article	care	coarse	completion
attract	career	coast	complicate
became	carnival	coat	compose
because	carnivore	cobble	composition
become	carpet	code	computer
bicycle	carriage	coffee	concern
broadcast	carrot	coffin	condition
cabin	carry	coin	conductor
cactus	cart	cold	confess
cage	case	collar	confession
cake	cash	collect	confidence
calculate	cast	college	confident
calculation	castle	collision	confuse
calf	cat	colony	confusion
Calgary	catch	color (USA)	congratulate
call	cattle	colour (UK, CAN)	connect
calm	caught	colt	connect
Cam	cause	Colton	connection (USA, CAN)
came	caution	comb	conquer
camel	cautious	combine	

conquest	cousin	cut	insect
conscience	cover	cute	introduction
consider	cow	cycle	local
constant	coward	decay	medical
construction	crack	declare	Mexican
consumer	crab	decrease	Mexico
contain	craft	deduct	multiplication
container	crash	delicate	neglect
content	crawl	describe	nuclear
contest	crayon	destruction	object
continue	crazy	destructive	objection
contribute	cream	detect	October
contribution	create	dictionary	octopus
control	creature	difficult	particle
convenience	credit	direct	particular
convenient	creek	direction	peculiar
conversation	crew	director	perfect
cook	cried	discomfort	physical
cookie	crime	discontent	picture
cool	criminal	discuss	practical
cooper	crisp	disrespect	practice
cooperate	critic	district	product
cop	crook	doctor	production
copy	cross	economy	project
cord	crowd	eczema	protect
cordial	crown	educate	punctual
cork	cruel	education	qualification
corn	crush	effect	recognition
corner	cry	elect	recognize
corporation	cub	electric	recommend
correct	Cuba	encourage	record
cost	cuddle	exact	reduction
cot	cultivate	exclaim	reflect
cottage	cup	exclaiming	reflection
cotton	cupboard	excuse	reproduction
couch	cure	excused	rescue
cougar	curious	expect	respect
cough	curl	fact	ridiculous
could	current	factory	sacred
council	curse	grammatical	sacrifice
count	curtain	helicopter	satisfaction
country	curve	hurricane	scare
couple	cushion	include	scary
courage	custard	inclusive	scatter
course	custom	income	scold
court	customer	increase	score

sc<u>o</u>rn	sec<u>r</u>et	suc<u>c</u>inct	va<u>c</u>ation
sc<u>o</u>rpion	stri<u>ct</u>	suspe<u>ct</u>	vehi<u>c</u>le
sc<u>r</u>atch	subje<u>ct</u>	theatri<u>c</u>al	vi<u>ct</u>im
sc<u>r</u>eam	suc<u>c</u>eed	tra<u>ct</u>or	vi<u>ct</u>ory
sc<u>r</u>een	suc<u>c</u>ess	un<u>c</u>le	vol<u>c</u>ano
se<u>c</u>ond	suc<u>c</u>ession	un<u>c</u>onscious	wel<u>c</u>ome

b) Final "-c"

The hard "c/k" consonant sound, heard in the words "cat" and "key", may be represented by a final letter "-c".

A final letter "-c" is most often found in words that end with the suffix "-ic" as in the words "atomic" and "music". Very few polysyllabic words end with a final letter "-c" following another vowel or a consonant letter. In "bivouac" a final "c" follows the letter "a". In single-syllable words "arc", "talc", and "zinc", a final "-c" follows another consonant letter.

Most polysyllabic words that end with the "-ic" sound are spelled with the letters "-ic". Only a few, such as "limerick" and "rollick", end with the letters "-ick". On the other hand, many single-syllable words, such as "kick" and "lick", end with the "-ick" spelling pattern.

When adding a suffix that begins with a letter "e", "i", or "y", it is necessary to first add the letter "-k". Adding the suffix "-ing" to "frolic", for example, produces "frolicking". Without the letter "k" the following "e", "i", or "y" would soften the preceding letter "c". The letter "k" preserves the hard "c/k" consonant sound.

Antarct<u>i</u>c	econom<u>i</u>c	magnet<u>i</u>c	poet<u>i</u>c
a<u>r</u>c	elast<u>i</u>c	mathemat<u>i</u>cs	poli<u>t</u>ical
Arct<u>i</u>c	electr<u>i</u>c	mechan<u>i</u>c	poli<u>t</u>ics
arithmet<u>i</u>c	Er<u>i</u>c	med<u>i</u>cal	publ<u>i</u>c
Atlant<u>i</u>c	fantast<u>i</u>c	metr<u>i</u>c	republ<u>i</u>c
atom<u>i</u>c	frant<u>i</u>c	mim<u>i</u>c	scientif<u>i</u>c
att<u>i</u>c	frol<u>i</u>c	mus<u>i</u>c	stat<u>i</u>c
bas<u>i</u>c	gigant<u>i</u>c	Olymp<u>i</u>c	sympathet<u>i</u>c
bion<u>i</u>c	graph<u>i</u>c	Pacif<u>i</u>c	tal<u>c</u>
crit<u>i</u>c	lilac	pan<u>i</u>c	traff<u>i</u>c
dynam<u>i</u>c	lunat<u>i</u>c	picn<u>i</u>c	trag<u>i</u>c
eccentr<u>i</u>c	mag<u>i</u>c	plast<u>i</u>c	zi<u>nc</u>

c) "cc" followed by "a", "o", or "u"

The hard "c/k" consonant sound heard in "cat" and "key" may be represented by the letters "cc" when followed by the vowel letters "a", "o", or "u". The same three letters also harden the letter "g". The "cc" spelling pattern forms a consonant digraph.

In keeping with the doubling principle, short vowel sounds represented by a single vowel letter are often followed by two consonant letters, often double consonants. In the word "tob**a**cco", for example, the letter "a" is pronounced with the short "a" vowel sound. Many of the following words, however, begin with a schwa vowel sound in an open syllable. The word "account", for example, is usually pronounced "uh-count". For spelling purposes, it is helpful to pronounce such words with an initial short vowel sound in a closed syllable as in "**a**c-**c**ount".

acc**o**mplish	acc**u**rate	desicc**a**te	racc**oo**n
acc**o**rd	acc**u**se	occ**a**sion	succ**u**mb
acc**o**unt	acc**u**stom	occ**u**py	tobacc**o**

d)   "ch"

The hard "c/k" consonant sound heard in "cat" and "key" may be represented by the "ch" consonant digraph. The letter "h" is silent. This is sometimes referred to as a "Greek ch".

This is an application of the rule that the hard "c/k" consonant sound may be represented by the letter "c" when followed by another consonant.

The "ch" spelling pattern is a Roman attempt to represent a Greek sound in Latin spelling.[22] The closest the Romans came to pronouncing the Greek sound was with the hard "c/k" consonant sound. This pronunciation of "ch" has been retained, in part, because it is often blended with the consonant "l", "r', and "s" sounds as heard in "chlorine", "chronic", and "school". It is difficult, if not impossible, to pronounce these blends with the consonant "ch" sound heard in "church".

The "ch" spelling pattern is also used to represent other consonant sounds. Most often, the "ch" spelling pattern is used to represent the consonant "ch" sound heard twice in "church". The "ch" spelling pattern is also used to represent the consonant "sh" sound heard in "machine". This is sometimes referred to as a "French ch".

The correct pronunciation cannot be determined from the spelling of a word. However, when the "ch" spelling pattern is followed by a consonant letter, as in "chronic", it usually represents the hard "c/k" consonant sound. A rare exception is the word "fuchsia".

a**ch**e	**ch**arisma	**ch**olera	**Ch**ristian
an**ch**or	**ch**asm	**ch**olesterol	**Ch**ristmas
ar**ch**itect	**ch**emist	**ch**ord	**Ch**ristopher
chameleon	**ch**emistry	**ch**oreography	**ch**rome
chaos	**ch**lorine	**ch**orus	**ch**ronic
character	**ch**oir	**Ch**rist	**ch**ronicle

echo	mechanism	schedule	stomach
loch	orchestra	scheme	technical
mechanic	orchid	*schism*	
mechanical	psychological	school	

e) Initial "k-"

The hard "c/k" consonant sound heard in "cat" and "key" may be represented by an initial letter "k-".

An initial letter "k-" may form the onset of a word or syllable as in "king" and "bas-ket". The letters "sk" also form a consonant blend onset as in "skill" and "skip".

Although more words and syllables begin with the letter "c" than with the letter "k", the letter "k" is usually found when the hard "c/k" consonant sound is followed by the letters "e", "i" or "y". This is because the letters "e", "i", and "y" would soften the sound of a preceding letter "c". It follows that words such as "kept", "kind", and "sky" must be spelled with the letter "k".

basket	kettle	kiss	skill
kangaroo	key	kit	skin
Karen	kick	kitchen	skinny
Kathy	kid	kite	skip
Kaye	kill	kitten	skirt
keep	Kim	Kris	skit
kept	kin	Mackenzie	skull
kerosene	kind	okay	skunk
ketchup	king	ski	sky

f) "-ck" following a single short vowel letter

The hard "c/k" consonant sound heard in "cat" and "key" may be represented by the "-ck" consonant digraph. This is an application of the rule that the hard "c/k" consonant sound may be spelled by the letter "c" when followed by another consonant letter.

In keeping with the doubling principle, the "-ck" spelling pattern is found following a single short vowel letter as in "bla**ck**", "ho**ck**ey", and "du**ck**".

The "-ck" spelling pattern only forms rimes and is, therefore, only found at the end of words and syllables. A final hard "c/k" consonant sound is only rarely represented by a single final letter "-k" following a single vowel letter. The Inuit word "mukluk" is a rare exception to the rule.

Most polysyllabic words that end with the "-ic" sound, such as "atomic" and "music, are spelled with the letters "-ic". Only a few polysyllabic words, such as "limerick" and "rollick", are spelled with the letters "-ick". On the other hand, many single syllable words end with the letters "-ick".

In English spelling, the hard "c/k" consonant sound is often represented by the letter "k" when followed by "e", "i", or "y" which would otherwise soften a preceding letter "c". Words that end with the letter "k" can accept a suffix that begins with "e", "i", or "y" such as "-ed", "-ing", and "-y". It follows that words such as "peeked", "looking", and "leaky" have to be spelled with the letter "k". It also follows that words such as "bucket", "packing", and "picky" have to be spelled with the letter "k". If "picky" was spelled "picy" it would be pronounced "pissy". If "picky" was spelled "piccy" it would be pronounced "pick-sey".

attack	hammock	pack	shucking
attacked	hassock	packed	sick
attacking	haversack	packing	sock
back	heckle	packsack	stick
barrack	hick	paddock	sticker
beckon	hockey	padlock	stock
black	homesick	peck	struck
block	hunchback	pick	suck
bracken	jacket	picky	tackle
bracket	kick	pickle	thick
brick	knapsack	pluck	thicket
bucket	knock	pock	tick
bullock	knocker	pocket	ticket
buttocks	lack	puck	ticking
candlewick	lick	quick	tickle
check	limerick	ransack	track
checker	lock	Rick	trick
chicken	locket	rock	truck
clock	locksmith	rocket	trucker
crack	luck	rollick	wick
derrick	Mick	rucksack	wicked
dock	neck	sack	woodchuck
duck	nick	shack	wreck
hacker	nickel	shock	

g)   "-k" following two vowel letters

The hard "c/k" consonant sound heard in "cat" and "key" may be represented by a letter "-k" following two vowel letters.

A single letter "-k" forms rimes following two vowel letters as in the words "cheek" and "speak". In most of the following words, the two vowel letters represent a long vowel sound. In a few words the two vowel letters represent a short or schwa vowel sound. The doubling principle does not apply when short vowel sounds are represented by two vowel letters. This allows a short vowel syllable to end with a single consonant letter.

In English spelling, the hard "c/k" consonant sound is often represented by the letter "k" when followed by "e", "i", or "y" which would otherwise soften a preceding letter "c". Words that end with the letter "k" can accept a suffix that begins with "e", "i", or "y" such as "-ed", "-ing", and "-y". It follows that words such as "peeked", "looking", and "leaky" have to be spelled with the letter "k". If "leaky" was spelled "leacy" it would be pronounced "lee-see".

The Inuit word "mukluk" is a rare exception to the rule a final hard "c/k" consonant sound is not represented by a single final letter "-k" following a single vowel letter. With the word "awkward", the first letter "w" functions as a second vowel letter.

awkward	creek	looked	speak
beak	crook	looking	spooky
book	Greek	meek	steak
break	hook	oak	took
breakfast	leak	peek	weak
brook	leaking	peeked	week
cheek	leaky	peeking	
cook	leek	sneak	
cookie	look	sneaky	

h)   "-k" following a consonant letter

The hard "c/k" consonant sound heard in "cat" and "key" may be represented by the letter "-k" following a consonant letter.

The letter "-k" forms a consonant blend with the preceding consonant letter as in the words "remark" and "bank".

In keeping with the doubling principle, two consonants usually signal that the preceding single vowel is pronounced with a short vowel sound as in "bark", "milk" and "spank".

In English spelling, the hard "c/k" consonant sound is often represented by the letter "k" when followed by "e", "i", or "y" which would otherwise soften a preceding letter "c". Words that end with the letter "k" can accept a suffix that begins with "e", "i", or "y" such as "-ed", "-ing", and "-y". It follows that words such as "market", "working", and "silky" have to be spelled with the letter "k". If "working" was spelled "worcing" it would be pronounced "wor-sing".

A final letter "-k" following a consonant is more common than a final "-c". A final "-c" following a consonant was only found in three words: "arc", "talc", and "zinc".

ask	drunk	murky	spark
bank	dunk	park	stink
bark	fork	pink	stinking
barking	honk	pork	talk
blanket	irk	rank	tank
chipmunk	jerk	remark	thank
chunk	junk	risk	think
clerk	mark	shark	trunk
cork	marking	silk	walk
dark	market	silky	walking
donkey	milk	sink	work
drank	monk	skunk	working
drink	monkey	spank	yolk

i) "-ke" following a single long vowel letter

The hard "c/k" consonant sound heard in "cat" and "key" may be represented by the letters "-ke" following a single long vowel letter.

The "-ke" spelling pattern forms a rime with the preceding long vowel sound as in the words "brake" and "like". The function of the final silent letter "e" is to lengthen the sound of the preceding vowel letter. The final silent letter "e" is dropped when adding a suffix that begins with a vowel letter. Adding the suffix "-ing" to "brake", for example, produces "braking".

In English spelling, the hard "c/k" consonant sound is often represented by the letter "k" when followed by "e", "i", or "y" which would otherwise soften a preceding letter "c". Words that end with the letter "k" can accept a suffix that begins with "e", "i", or "y" such as "-ed", "-ing", and "-y". It follows that words such as "brake", "making", and "smoky" have to be spelled with the letter "k". If "brake" was spelled "brace" it would be pronounced with the soft "c/s" consonant sound.

alike	cake	making	spoke
awake	dislike	mistake	spoken
awoke	hike	sake	strike
bake	hiked	shake	stroke
bike	hiking	shaking	take
brake	joke	shaky	taken
braking	lake	smoke	wake
broke	like	smoky	woke
broken	make	snake	

j) "qu" and "que"

The hard "c/k" consonant sound heard in "cat" and "key" may be represented by the letters "qu" and "que" forming consonant digraphs.

The letter "q" always represents the hard "c/k" consonant sound and is followed by the letter "u" in English spelling. The letter "u" is usually silent, as (not) heard in "conquer" and "quiche". Sometimes, however, the letter "u" represents the consonant "w" sound as heard in "conquest" and "quick".

The "que" spelling pattern always represents the hard "c/k" consonant sound and is found in words of French origin. The letters "-ue" are usually silent.

The "que" spelling pattern is often found at the end of words. An exception is the word "queue". The initial "que-" spelling pattern represents the hard "c/k" consonant sound and the final "-ue" spelling pattern represents the long "u" vowel sound.

anti**que**	co**qu**ette	mar**qu**ee	pla**que**
Baro**que**	criti**que**	mar**qu**ise	**qu**ay
Bas**que**	cro**qu**ette	mos**que**	**Qu**ebec
bou**qu**et	discothe**que**	mos**qu**ito	**que**ue
brus**que**	eti**qu**ette	obli**que**	**qu**iche
burles**que**	exche**qu**er	opa**que**	statues**que**
che**que** (UK, CAN)	grotes**que**	physi**que**	techni**que**
cli**que**	lac**qu**er	pictures**que**	tor**que**
con**qu**er	li**qu**or	pi**qu**ant	tur**qu**oise
co**qu**etry	manne**qu**in	pi**que**	uni**que**

k)   "x", "xc(e)", and "xc(i)"

The consonant "x" sound, a hard "c/k" consonant sound followed by a soft "c/s" consonant sound, may be represented by the letters "x", "xc(e)" and "xc(i)". The word "tax", for example, is pronounced "tacks". Neither sound is well represented by the spelling.

In words such as "a**x**e" and "e**x**pert", the letter "x" represents both the hard "c/k" consonant sound and the following soft "c/s" consonant sound. However, if the letter "x" is followed by the letter "c", spelling patterns become complicated:

- In words such as "ex**c**eed" and "ex**c**ite", the letter "x" represents the hard "c/k" consonant sound and the letter "c" (followed by vowel letters "e", "i", or "y") represents the soft "c/s" consonant sound.

- In words such as "ex**c**use" and "ex**c**laim", the letter "x" represents both the hard "c/k" consonant sound and the soft "c/s" consonant sound. The letter "c", followed by vowel letters "a", "o", "u" or a consonant, represents a second hard "c/k" consonant sound.

- In the word "ex<u>ch</u>ange" the letter "x" represents both the hard "c/k" consonant sound and the soft "c/s" consonant sound, and the letters "ch" represent the consonant "ch" sound.

When the letter "x" represents both the hard "c/k" consonant sound and the soft "c/s" consonant sound, there may be a syllabic break between the two sounds. The words "expand" and "explain", for example, are pronounced "ek-spand" and "ek-splain". However, the syllabic break may occur after the soft "c" or "s" sound. The words "expert" and "extra", for example, are usually pronounced "eks-pert" and "eks-tra".

In the words "exhale" and "exhume" the letter "h" is pronounced. The letter "h" is silent in the word "exhibition".

With the word "axe", the final silent letter "e" helps to satisfy the three letter rule.

With the word "exit" the letter "x" is also pronounced with the hard "g" consonant sound followed by the consonant "z" sound by some speakers.

axe	exhibition	explain	Mexican
ex<u>c</u>eed	exhume	explode	Mexico
ex<u>c</u>ellent	*exit*	explore	mix
ex<u>c</u>ept	expect	explosion	next
ex<u>c</u>ess	expand	explosive	sex
exchange	expend	express	six
ex<u>c</u>ite	expense	extend	tax
exclaim	expensive	extra	wax
excuse	experience	extreme	
exercise	experiment	fax	
exhale	expert	fix	

E4.2 Minor Spelling Patterns

There are two minor spelling patterns for the hard "c/k" consonant sound heard in "**c**at" and "**k**ey".

a) "kh"

The hard "c/k" consonant sound heard in "cat" and "key" may be represented by the "kh" consonant digraph. The letter "h" is silent.

khaki	**Kh**mer	shei**kh**
khan	**Kh**yber Pass	Si**kh**

b) "lk"

The hard "c/k" consonant sound heard in "cat" and "key" may be represented by the "lk" consonant digraph. The letter "l" is silent.

In keeping with the doubling principle, the single vowel letter preceding the "lk" spelling pattern is usually pronounced with a short vowel sound.

cha**lk**	sta**lk**	wa**lk**
fo**lk**	ta**lk**	

E4.3 Rare Spelling Patterns

There are at least eight rare spelling patterns for the hard "c/k" consonant sound heard in "**c**at" and "**k**ey".

a) "cch"

The hard "c/k" consonant sound heard in "cat" and "key" may be represented by the "cch" consonant digraph. The letters "ch" are silent.

Pino**cch**io   sa**cch**arine   zu**cch**ini

b) "cq"

The hard "c/k" consonant sound heard in "cat" and "key" may be represented by the "cq" consonant digraph. The letter "q" is silent.

In the word "acquire", the letter "u" represents the consonant "w" sound.

a**cq**uire

c) "cqu"

The hard "c/k" consonant sound heard in "cat" and "key" may be represented by the "cqu" consonant digraph. The letters "qu" are silent.

la**cqu**er

d) "cu"

The hard "c/k" consonant sound heard in "cat" and "key" may be represented by the "cu" consonant digraph.

The letter "u", while silent, protects the hard "c/k" consonant sound from the softening effect of the following letter "i".

bis**cu**it

e) "g" and "gh"

The hard "c/k" consonant sound heard in "cat" and "key" may be represented by the letters "g" and "gh". The "gh" spelling pattern forms a consonant digraph.

With some speakers, the letter "g" in "length" and "strength" is silent and helps to represent the consonant "ng" sound.

*len**g**th*
*lou**gh***
*stren**g**th*

f) "kk"

The hard "c/k" consonant sound heard in "cat" and "key" may be represented by the "kk" consonant digraph.

In keeping with the doubling principle, the single vowel letter "e" preceding the "kk" spelling pattern is pronounced with a short vowel sound.

All of the following words are derived from the Afrikaans word "trek" meaning "to travel by ox wagon". The word "trekkie" refers to a fan of the *Star Trek* television and movie series.

The letters "kk" found in compound words such as "bookkeeper" and "knickknack" are incidental. The second letter "k" is pronounced in the word "bookkeeper", but not in the word "knickknack".

| tre**kk**ed | tre**kk**er | tre**kk**ie | tre**kk**ing |

g) "xi"

The hard "c/k" consonant sound heard in "cat" and "key" followed by the consonant "sh" sound may be represented by the "xi" consonant digraph. Neither sound is well represented by the spelling.

| an**xi**ous | comple**xi**on | crucifi**xi**on | no**xi**ous |

h) "x(u)"

The hard "c/k" consonant sound heard in "cat" and "key" followed by the consonant "sh" sound may be represented by the letters "x(u)". Neither sound is well represented by the spelling.

With all of the following words, the letters "x(u)" are also pronounced by some people with the hard "g" consonant sound followed by the consonant "zh" sound heard in "vision".

luxuriant　　　　　*luxuriate*　　　　　*luxurious*　　　　　*luxury*

E5 Spelling the Consonant "KW" Sound

The "kw" sound heard in "quick" and "quiet" is just a consonant blend made up of the hard "c/k" consonant sound followed by the consonant "w" sound. However, it is common enough and unique enough to justify special mention.

The consonant "kw" sound is almost always represented by the letters "qu". Exceptions are generally made-up words or brand names such as "Kwik Cleaners".

The letter "q" always represents the hard "c/k" consonant sound and is almost always followed by the letter "u". Often, the letter "u" is silent as (not) heard in "conquer" and "quiche". In the following words, however, the letter "u" represents the consonant "w" sound. This is a rare example of a vowel letter representing a consonant sound.

This spelling pattern is French in origin.

con**qu**est	**equ**ity	**qu**antity	**qu**ilt
equal	**equ**ivalent	**qu**arrel	**qu**it
equation	fre**qu**ent	**qu**art	**qu**ite
equator	in**qu**ire	**qu**arter	**qu**otation
equidistant	in**qu**iry	**qu**een	re**qu**est
equilateral	li**qu**id	**qu**eer	re**qu**ire
equine	**qu**ake	**qu**estion	s**qu**are
equinox	**qu**alification	**qu**ick	s**qu**eeze
equipment	**qu**alify	**qu**iet	s**qu**id
equitable	**qu**ality	**qu**ill	s**qu**irrel

E6 Spelling the Consonant "D" Sound

There are several spelling patterns for the consonant "d" sound heard twice in the word "**d**ivi**d**e". They have been divided into major and rare spelling patterns.

E6.1 Major Spelling Patterns

There are four major spelling patterns for the consonant "d" sound heard twice in the word "**d**ivi**d**e".

a)　　　"d"

The consonant "d" sound heard twice in the word "divide" may be represented by the letter "d".

aboard	cloud	defeat	dinner
abroad	code	defence (UK, CAN)	dinosaur
accident	command	defend	dip
admire	confidence	defense (USA)	direct
admission	confident	definite	direction
admit	consider	degree	director
adopt	credit	delicate	dirt
adult	cried	delicious	disagree
advance	crowd	delight	disappear
advantage	dad	deliver	disappoint
adventure	daddy	demand	disapprove
advertise	daily	den	disaster
advice	dairy	dentist	discipline
advise	damage	depart	discomfort
afford	damp	depend	discontent
afraid	dance	depth	discover
ahead	danger	descend	discrimination
aloud	Daniel	descent	discuss
already	dare	describe	disease
and	dark	desert	disgust
applaud	Darling	deserve	dish
around	date	design	dislike
aside	daughter	desire	dismiss
attend	Dave	desk	disrespect
audience	David	despair	dissatisfaction
avoid	day	despite	dissatisfy
awkward	dead	destroy	distance
backward	deaf	destruction	distant
bad	deal	destructive	distinguish
band	dear	detail	district
bed	death	detect	disturb
behind	debt	determine	ditch
beside	decay	develop	dive
bid	deceit	devil	divide
bird	deceive	diamond	division
bleed	December	Diane	do
body	decent	dictionary	dock
bodies	decide	did	doctor
border	decision	die	does
bread	decisive	difference	dog
broad	declare	different	doing
Canada	decrease	difficult	doll
Canadian	deduct	dig	dollar
card	deed	digging	dolphin
childhood	deep	dine	done
children	deer	dining	donkey

door	Friday	lord	read
double	garden	loud	ready
doubt	glad	mad	red
Doug	glade	made	reduce
down	God	meadow	reduction
dozen	good	medal	remedy
drag	grad	medical	reproduce
dragon	grade	medicine	reproduction
drank	gratitude	medium	rid
draw	greed	mermaid	ride
dread	guard	method	ridiculous
dreadful	guide	mild	riding
dream	had	model	road
dregs	hand	modem	rod
dress	hard	moderate	rode
drew	hatred	modern	rude
drink	head	modest	sad
drip	hid	Monday	said
drive	hide	mood	salad
droll	hinder	motherhood	Saturday
drop	hindrance	mud	seed
drove	holiday	murder	shadow
drown	hundred	need	shepherd
drug	hundred	needle	side
drum	idea	obedience	slid
drunk	ideal	obedient	slide
dry	idle	order	spade
duck	immediate	ordinary	speed
due	include	pad	splendid
dug	indeed	paid	spread
dull	Indian	parade	squid
dumb	individual	pardon	standard
dump	industry	period	steady
during	inside	persuade	stood
dust	instead	powder	student
duty	introduce	prejudice	study
elder	kid	president	stupid
end	kingdom	pride	succeed
evidence	ladies	produce	Sunday
explode	lady	product	tadpole
federal	laid	production	thread
feed	lead	proud	thunder
flood	leader	provide	Thursday
Florida	led	radar	tide
food	liquid	radio	tidy
freedom	load	rapid	tied

toa**d**	un**d**er	wi**d**ow	won**d**er
to**d**ay	We**d**nes**d**ay	wi**d**th	woo**d**
tra**de**	wee**d**	win**d**ow	wor**d**
Tues**d**ay	wi**de**	wis**d**om	yar**d**

b) "dd"

The consonant "d" sound heard twice in the word "divide" may be represented by the "dd" consonant digraph.

Double consonants usually signal that the preceding vowel letter is pronounced with a short vowel sound as in "a**dd**" and "we**dd**ing". For spelling purposes, when double consonants lie between two syllables, it is helpful to pronounce both consonants as in "hi**d-d**en". With single-syllable words, such as "a**dd**" and "o**dd**", only one consonant "d" sound can be pronounced.

a**dd**	da**dd**y	mi**dd**le	sa**dd**le
a**dd**ition	hi**dd**en	o**dd**	su**dd**en
a**dd**ress	la**dd**er	re**dd**en	we**dd**ing
cu**dd**le	ma**dd**en	sa**dd**en	

c) Suffix "-ed"

The consonant "d" sound heard twice in the word "divide" may be represented by the "-ed" consonant digraph. The letter "e" is silent.

The letters "-ed" form a common suffix that creates the past tense and past participle of regular verbs. Depending on the word to which it is attached, the suffix "-ed" may be pronounced "-id", "t" or "d". With base words that end with the consonant "d" or "t" sound, as in "decide" and "limit", the suffix "-ed" forms a syllable pronounced "id". With base words that end with the hard "c/k" consonant sound or the consonant "p" sound, as in "hook" and "slip", the suffix "-ed" is pronounced "t". With other base words, such as "boil" and "dare", the suffix "-ed" is usually pronounced "d".

In the following words the suffix "-ed" is pronounced "d":

allow**ed**	dar**ed**	learn**ed**	seem**ed**
boil**ed**	dial**ed** (USA)	li**ed**	slamm**ed**
bor**ed**	dialled (UK, CAN)	liv**ed**	snagg**ed**
clos**ed**	dream**ed**	marri**ed**	spell**ed**
color**ed** (USA)	fill**ed**	plan**ed**	*suppos**ed***
colour**ed** (UK, CAN)	frighten**ed**	plann**ed**	tir**ed**
concern**ed**	graz**ed**	receiv**ed**	us**ed**
cover**ed**	hurri**ed**	retir**ed**	weigh**ed**
cri**ed**	identifi**ed**	robb**ed**	worri**ed**
	involv**ed**	sail**ed**	

d) "-ld"

The consonant "d" sound heard twice in the word "divide" may be represented by the "-ld" consonant digraph. The letter "l" is silent.

The letters "-ould" forms a rime pronounced with the short "u" vowel sound heard in "put". While only a few words follow this spelling pattern, they are frequently used.

could	should	would
couldn't	shouldn't	wouldn't

E6.2 Rare Spelling Patterns

There is at least one rare spelling pattern for the consonant "d" sound heard twice in the word "**di**vi**de**".

a) "dh"

The consonant "d" sound heard twice in the word "divide" may be represented by the "dh" consonant digraph. The letter "h" is silent.

dhobi	**dh**ow	jo**dh**pur
dhoti	Gan**dh**i	

E7 Spelling the Consonant "F" Sound

There are several spelling patterns for the consonant "f" sound heard in "**f**ish". They have been divided into major, minor, and rare spelling patterns.

E7.1 Major Spelling Patterns

There are four major spelling patterns for the consonant "f" sound heard in "**f**ish".

a) "f"

The consonant "f" sound heard in "fish" may be represented by the letter "f".

Words and syllables that begin with the consonant "f" sound, but not with the letter "f", always begin with the letters "ph".

Words and syllables that end with the consonant "f" sound may end with the letter "f" as in "che**f**", the letters "-ff" as in "sta**ff**", the letters "gh" as in "rou**gh**", or with the letters "ph" as in "gra**ph**".

afraid	awful	belief	chief
Africa	beautiful	breakfast	classification
after	beef	careful	classify
artificial	before	chef	comfort

confess	fear	for	frontier
confession	feast	force	frost
confidence	feather	force	fruit
confident	February	foreign	frustrate
confuse	fed	forest	fry
confusion	federal	forget	fuel
deaf	fee	forgive	full
defeat	feed	forgot	fun
defence (UK, CAN)	feel	fork	fund
defend	feet	form	funeral
defense (USA)	fell	formal	funny
definite	fellow	former	fur
discomfort	felt	formula	furious
elf	female	fort	furniture
enforce	fence	forth	further
face	few	fortunate	fussy
facility	field	fortune	future
fact	fierce	forty	golf
factory	fifteen	forward	grateful
fail	fifth	fought	herself
faint	fifty	found	himself
fair	fight	four	if
faith	figure	fourteen	inform
faithful	fill	fourth	information
fall	film	fox	interfere
false	final	frame	itself
fame	find	France	knife
familiar	fine	Frank	leaf
family	finger	fraud	life
famous	finish	frazzle	lift
fan	fir	free	loaf
fantastic	fire	freedom	mischief
far	firm	freeze	Pacific
farm	first	freight	peaceful
farther	fish	French	perfect
fashion	fit	frequent	perform
fast	five	fresh	playful
fasten	fix	Friday	powerful
fat	fog	friend	preference
fate	fold	fright	profession
father	folk	frill	professor
fatten	follow	Frisbee	profit
fault	fond	frizzle	proof
favor (USA)	food	frog	qualification
favour (UK, CAN)	fool	from	qualify
fawn	foot	front	refer

referee	roof	self	unidentified
reference	sacrifice	shelf	useful
reform	safe	soft	wharf
refresh	safety	surface	wife
refuse	satisfaction	thief	wolf
relief	satisfy	twelfth	wonderful
rifle	scientific	unfortunate	

b)   "ff"

The consonant "f" sound heard in "fish" may be represented by the "ff" consonant digraph.

Double consonants usually signal that the preceding vowel letter is pronounced with a short vowel sound as in "<u>o</u>ff" and "<u>e</u>ffort". For spelling purposes, when double consonants lie between two syllables, it is helpful to pronounce both consonants as in "traf-fic". With single-syllable words, such as "cliff" and "stiffed", only one consonant "f" sound can be pronounced.

affair	difficult	offence (UK, CAN)	staff
afford	effect	offend	stiff
chauffeur	efficiency	offense (USA)	stiffed
cliff	efficient	offer	stuff
coffee	effort	office	suffer
coffin	fluffy	official	traffic
difference	giraffe	sheriff	
different	off	skiff	

c)   "-gh"

The consonant "f" sound heard in "fish" may be represented by the "-gh" consonant digraph.

The letters "-gh" only represent the consonant "f" sound in rimes at the end of words and syllables and always follow vowel letters "au" or "ou" as heard in "l<u>augh</u>" and "r<u>ough</u>".

The "gh-" spelling pattern also represents the hard "g" consonant sound as an onset at the beginning of words and syllables as in "ghost". The majority of the time, however, the "gh" spelling pattern is silent and helps to represent a wide variety of vowel sounds as (not) heard in the words "high" and "though".

c<u>ough</u>	l<u>augh</u>	r<u>ough</u>	t<u>ough</u>
dr<u>aught</u>	l<u>augh</u>able	r<u>ough</u>en	t<u>ough</u>en
en<u>ough</u>	l<u>augh</u>ter	*sl<u>ough</u>*	tr<u>ough</u>

d) "ph"

The consonant "f" sound heard in "fish" may be represented by the "ph" consonant digraph. This spelling pattern is Greek in origin.

The "ph" spelling pattern is found in both onsets and rimes. Words and syllables that begin with an "f" sound, but not with the letter "f", always begin with the letters "ph".

Fortunately, the "ph" spelling pattern only represents the consonant "f" sound.

al**ph**abet	paragra**ph**	**ph**ilanthropist	**ph**oto
atmos**ph**ere	**ph**alange	**ph**ilharmonic	**ph**otograph
caco**ph**ony	**ph**alanx	**Ph**ilip	**ph**otography
ci**ph**er	**ph**antasm	**Ph**ilippines	**ph**rase
*di**ph**theria*	**ph**antom	**ph**ilodendron	**ph**ysical
*di**ph**thong*	**ph**araoh	**ph**ilosophy	**ph**ysics
dol**ph**in	**Ph**arisee	**ph**legm	**ph**ysiology
ele**ph**ant	**ph**armaceutical	**ph**obia	pro**ph**et
em**ph**asis	**ph**armacist	**Ph**oebe	So**ph**ia
epi**ph**any	**ph**armacy	**Ph**oenix	so**ph**omore
epita**ph**	**ph**arynx	**ph**one	s**ph**ere
geogra**ph**y	**ph**ase	**ph**onetic	telegra**ph**
gra**ph**	**ph**easant	**ph**onics	tele**ph**one
hierogly**ph**ics	**ph**enomenal	**ph**onograph	trium**ph**
hy**ph**en	**ph**enomenon	**ph**oney (UK, CAN)	tro**ph**y
mor**ph**eme	**ph**ial	**ph**ony (USA)	
ne**ph**ew	**Ph**iladel**ph**ia	**ph**osphate	
or**ph**an	**ph**ilander	**ph**osphorous	

E7.2 Minor Spelling Patterns

There are two minor spelling patterns for the consonant "f" sound heard in "fish".

a) "ft"

The consonant "f" sound heard in "fish" may be represented by the "ft" consonant digraph. Some speakers do not pronounce the letter "t".

In keeping with the doubling principle, two consonants usually signal that the preceding single vowel is pronounced with a short vowel sound as in "o**ft**en" and "so**ft**en". For spelling purposes, when two consonants lie between two syllables, it is helpful to pronounce both consonants as in "o**f-t**en".

While only two words that follow this spelling pattern could be found, they are frequently used.

often   soften

b) "lf"

The consonant "f" sound heard in "fish" may be represented by the "lf" consonant digraph. The letter "l" is silent.

In keeping with the doubling principle, two consonants usually signal that the preceding single vowel is pronounced with a short vowel sound as in "calf" and "half".

While only three words that follow this spelling pattern could be found, they are frequently used.

ca**lf**   ha**lf**   ha**lf**way

E7.3 Rare Spelling Patterns

There are at least three rare spelling patterns for the consonant "f" sound heard in "fish".

a) "-ffe

The consonant "f" sound heard in "fish" may be represented by the "-ffe" consonant digraph. The letter "e" is silent and does not appear to have a useful function.

ga**ffe** (Also "gaff")

b) "pph"

The consonant "f" sound heard in "fish" may be represented by the "pph" consonant digraph.

Double consonants usually signal that the preceding vowel letter is pronounced with a short vowel sound as in "sa**pph**ire". Given the pronunciation of the "pph" spelling pattern, it is not helpful to pronounce each consonant.

sa**pph**ire   Sa**pph**ic

c) "ieu"

The word "lieutenant" is pronounced "lef-tenunt" in Britain and Canada. The consonant "f" sound is not well represented in the spelling. In the United States the word "lieutenant" is pronounced "loo–tenunt".

*l**ieu**tenant*

E8 Spelling the Soft "G/J" Consonant Sound

There are many spelling patterns for the soft "g/j" consonant sound heard in "**g**ym" and "**j**am". They have been divided into major, minor, and rare spelling patterns.

E8.1 Major Spelling Patterns

There are two major spelling patterns for the soft "g/j" consonant sound heard in "**g**ym" and "**j**am".

a)   "g" followed by "e", "i", or "y"

The soft "g/j" consonant sound heard in "gym" and "jam" may be represented by the letter "g" when followed by vowel letters "e", "i", or "y". These same three letters also soften the letter "c".

Conversely, the hard "g" consonant sound heard in "goat" is often represented by the letter "g" when followed by the vowel letters "a", "o", "u" or another consonant letter. These same letters also harden the letter "c".

It does not matter what sound the letters "e", "i", or "y" represent or whether they are silent, the letters "c" and "g" are usually soft when followed by "e", "i", or "y".

When vowel letters "e", "i", or "y" follow "g", they are often pronounced in their own right as heard in "**ge**neral" and "**gi**ant". Sometimes, however, they are silent as (not) heard in "conta**gi**ous" and "**Ge**orge". This often occurs when a soft "g/j" consonant sound would otherwise be followed by the vowel letters "a", "o", or "u". Without the silent "e", "i", or "y", the letter "g" would be pronounced with the hard "g" consonant sound.

It may be noted that English words that end with a soft "g/j" consonant sound always end with the letters "-ge" or "-dge" as found in "stran**ge**" and "ju**dge**". A final soft "g/j" consonant sound is never spelled with just a final letter "g" or "j". The final silent letter "e" signals that the adjacent letter "g" is pronounced with the soft "g/j" consonant sound.

With the "-ge" spelling pattern, the final silent letter "e" can also signal that the preceding vowel letter is pronounced with a long vowel sound as heard in "ra<u>ge</u>" and "hu<u>ge</u>". On the other hand, in keeping with the doubling principle, the "d" in "-dge" protects the preceding short vowel letter from being lengthened by the final silent letter "e" as heard in "b<u>adge</u>" and "j<u>udge</u>".

When adding a suffix that begins with a vowel letter to a base word that ends with a final silent letter "e", the letter "e" is usually dropped. The word "bake", for example, becomes "baking". However, when adding a suffix that begins with the letters "a", "o", or "u" to a base word that ends with "-ge" the letter "e" is retained. The silent letter "e" is still required in order to signal the soft "g/j" consonant sound. Adding the suffix

"-able" to the word "change", for example, produces "changeable". Occasionally, the silent "e" is dropped when adding a suffix that begins with a consonant letter as in the word "judgment".

With words of French origin such as "fuselage", "garage", and "rouge", the "-ge" spelling pattern may be pronounced with either the soft "g/j" consonant sound or the consonant "zh" sound heard in "beige" and "vision".

i)   General Rule

In the following words, the soft "g/j" consonant sound heard in "gym" and "jam" is represented by the letter "g" followed by the vowel letters "e", "i", or "y".

In words such as "danger" and "passenger", the letter "g" follows a letter "n" that is pronounced with the consonant "n" sound heard in "nice". This preserves the soft "g/j" consonant sound and allows the rule to apply. However, when the letter "g" follows an "n" that is pronounced with the consonant "ng" sound, as heard in "anger" and "finger", the letter "g" will be pronounced with the hard "g" sound heard in "goat".

Following the doubling principle, words and syllables that end with the letters "-nge" should be pronounced with a short vowel sound as heard in "hinge" and "large". However, words such as "change" and "range" are pronounced with a long vowel sound. English spelling does not have a good solution for this problem given the convention of representing a final soft "g/j" consonant sound with the letters "-ge".

agency	general	gyrate	pages
agent	generation	gyro	paging
angel	generous	hinge	passenger
apology	genie	hinged	plunged
bulging	gentle	hugely	prestigious
change	George	imagination	prodigious
changed	gerbil	imagine	range
changing	geriatrics	intelligence	ranger
contagion	germ	large	Regina
contagious	German	larger	region
courageous	Gerry	legion	register
danger	giant	legislation	religion
dungeon	giblet	legitimate	religious
Egypt	gigantic	magic	sacrilegious
emergency	ginger	mangy	sergeant
energy	giraffe	messenger	stranger
engine	gorgeous	origin	surgeon
forged	gym	original	urgent
gem	gymnast	page	
gender	gypsy	paged	

ii)   Application of the general rule: The "-ge" word ending

In keeping with the general rule, English words that end with a soft "g/j" consonant sound may end with the letters "-ge". The letter "e" is silent.

Following a consonant sound or a long vowel sound only the "-ge" spelling pattern is found. Following a short vowel sound, both the "-dge" and the "-ge" spelling patterns are found.

In the following words, the letters "-ge" follow a consonant sound or a long vowel sound:

age	ginger	outrage	stooge
bulge	hinge	page	strange
cage	huge	plunge	tinge
change	large	rage	urge
charge	lounge	range	wage
exchange	lunge	siege	
forge	merge	stage	
George	orange	Stonehenge	

In the following words, contrary to the doubling principle, the "-ge" spelling pattern follows a short vowel sound:

acreage	damage	marriage	privilege
advantage	encourage	message	privileged
average	fuselage	package	refrigerator
baggage	garage (USA)	pageant	salvage
carriage	garbage	passage	vegetable
college	language	percentage	village
cottage	manage	pigeon	voyage
courage	manager	postage	

iii)   Application of the general rule: The "-dge" word ending

In keeping with the general rule, English words that end with a soft "g/j" consonant sound may end with the letters "-dge". The letters "d" and "e" are silent. The "-dge" spelling pattern is only found following a single short vowel letter.

The "-dge" spelling pattern is an application of the doubling principle. The letter "d" is used because the consonant "d" sound and the soft "g/j" consonant sound are phonetically similar.

Double consonants usually signal that the preceding vowel letter is pronounced with a short vowel sound as in "ba**dge**" and "ri**dge**". For spelling purposes, when double consonants lie between two syllables, it is helpful to pronounce both consonants as in "lod-ging" and "nud-ging". Words such as "fudge" and "nudged" are single-syllable words, so only one consonant "ch" sound can be pronounced.

The "-dge" spelling pattern only forms rimes and is, therefore, only found at the end of words and syllables.

In the following words the "-dge" spelling pattern follows a short vowel sound:

abridge	bridge	fudge	ledge
acknowledge	budget	gadget	lodge
acknowledgement	cadge	grudge	nudge
adjudge	cartridge	judge	nudged
badge	dislodge	judged	partridge
badger	dodge	judgement	porridge
begrudge	edge	(also judgment)	ridge
bludgeon	fridge	knowledge	

iv) Exceptions to the general rule

Unfortunately, there are exceptions to the rule that the letter "g" represents the soft "g" consonant sound when followed by vowel letters "e", "i", "y. In the following words, these spelling patterns represent the hard "g" consonant sound heard in "goat". The hard "g" consonant sound is usually represented by the letter "g" followed by "a", "o", "u" or another consonant.

With words such as "anger" and "longer", the "(n)g" spelling pattern overrides the general rule. See E14.1.

altogether	gear	girl	hunger
anger	geese	girth	longer
begin	get	give	tiger
eager	gift	given	together
finger	giggle	gynaecology	
forget	Gilbert	(UK, CAN)	
forgive	gill (fish gill)	gynecology (USA)	
		hamburger	

b)   "j"

The soft "g/j" consonant sound heard in "gym" and "jam" may be represented by the letter "j".

The letter "j" is always pronounced with the soft "g" or "j" sound even if followed by vowel letters "a", "o", or "u". On the other hand, the letter "g" is pronounced with the hard "g" consonant sound when followed by vowel letters "a", "o", or "u". That is why words such as "jam", "job", and "June" begin with the letter "j", and not the letter "g".

The words "gam", "gob", and "gune" would be pronounced with the hard "g" consonant sound. The letter "j" may also be followed by vowel letters "e" and "i" as in the words "jet" and "jinks".

In English spelling the letter "j" only forms onsets and is, therefore, only found at the beginning of words and syllables. English words and syllables that end with a soft "g/j" consonant sound, such as "judge" and "strange", always end with the letters "-dge" or "-ge". See (a). Only foreign words, such as "raj" and "hajj", end with the letter "j". The words "raj" and "hajj" are, respectively, Hindi and Arabic in origin.

Likewise, in English spelling the letter "j" is never doubled. Only foreign words such as "hajj" are spelled with a double "jj".

enjoy	Jean	joint	Jupiter
injure	jet	joke	just
jacket	jewel	Josh	justice
jail	jewellery (UK, CAN)	journey	major
jam	jewelry (USA)	joy	majority
Jamie	jibe	judge	object
Jan	jiggle	jug	objection
Janet	Jimmy	juice	prejudice
January	jingle	Julie	project
Japan	jinks	July	raj (Hindi)
jar	job	jump	rejoice
jaw	John	June	subject
jay	join	jungle	
jealous		junk	

E8.2 Minor Spelling Patterns

There are two minor spelling patterns for the soft "g/j" consonant sound heard in "**g**ym" and "**j**am".

a)   "d(u)"

The soft "g/j" consonant sound heard in "gym" and "jam" may be represented by the "d(u)" spelling pattern. Most of the following words relate to schooling and are derived from the Latin word "*educare*" meaning to "to bring up, rear, or train".

In most of the following words the letter "u" is pronounced with the long "u" vowel sound. In the words "proce**du**re" and "ver**du**re", the letters "du" form a consonant digraph representing the soft "g/j" consonant sound. The following schwa vowel sound is signaled by the "-re" word ending.

arduous	credulous	educate	educator
assiduous	deciduous	education	fraudulent

glan**du**lar	incre**du**lous	mo**du**late	sche**du**le
gra**du**al	indivi**du**al	pen**du**lum	un**du**late
gra**du**ate	indivi**du**ally	proce**du**re	ver**du**re
gra**du**ation	indivi**du**ality	resi**du**al	

b) "gg"

The soft "g" consonant sound heard in "gym" and "jam" may be represented by the "gg" consonant digraph.

Double consonants usually signal that the preceding vowel letter is pronounced with a short vowel sound as in "exa**gg**erate" and "su**gg**est". With the words "suggest" and "suggestion", some people pronounce the first "g" with a hard "g" consonant sound and the second "g" with a soft "g/j" consonant sound.

exa**gg**erate   su**gg**est   su**gg**estion

E8.3 Rare Spelling Patterns

There are at least three rare spelling patterns for the soft "g/j" consonant sound heard in "**g**ym" and "**j**am".

a) "di"

The soft "g/j" consonant sound heard in "gym" and "jam" may be represented by the "di" consonant digraph.

sol**di**er

b) "dj"

The soft "g/j" consonant sound heard in "gym" and "jam" may be represented by the "dj" consonant digraph. The letter "d" is silent.

Two consonants usually signal that the preceding vowel letter is pronounced with a short vowel sound as in "a**dj**ust" and "a**dj**ective". For spelling purposes, when two consonants lie between two syllables, it is helpful to pronounce both consonants as in "a**d**-just".

a**dj**ust   a**dj**ective

c) "jj"

The soft "g/j" consonant sound heard in "gym" and "jam" may be represented by the "jj" consonant digraph.

The "jj" spelling pattern is rarely, if ever, found in English spelling. The word "hajj" is Arabic in origin. Double consonants usually signal that the preceding single vowel letter is pronounced with a short vowel sound.

ha**jj** (Arabic)

E9   Spelling the Hard "G" Consonant Sound

There are many spelling patterns for the hard "g" consonant sound heard in "**g**oat". They have been divided into major, minor, and rare spelling patterns.

E9.1 Major Spelling Patterns

There are four major spelling patterns for the hard "g" consonant sound heard in "goat".

a)   "g" followed by "a", "o", "u" or another consonant

The hard "g" consonant sound heard in "goat" may be represented by the letter "g" when followed by vowel letters "a", "o", "u" or another consonant. The same letters also harden the letter "c".

Conversely, the letter "g" represents the soft "g/j" consonant sound heard in "gym" and "jam" when followed by vowel letters "e", "i", or "y". These same three letters also soften the letter "c".

Note that the letter "g" is often followed by a silent letter "u" as (not) heard in "**gu**est", "**gu**ide", and "**gu**y". This French spelling pattern occurs when a hard "g" consonant sound would otherwise be followed by vowel letters "e", "i" or "y". The silent letter "u" protects the letter "g" from being pronounced with the soft "g/j" consonant sound. The letter "u" is sometimes pronounced as heard in "an**gu**ish", "dis**gu**st", "distin**gu**ish", and "**Gu**elph".

Likewise, the letter "g" is sometimes followed by a silent letter "h" as (not) heard in "**gh**etto", "spa**gh**etti", and "din**gh**y". This Italian spelling pattern occurs when a hard "g" consonant sound would otherwise be followed by vowel letters "e", "i" or "y". The silent letter "h" protects the letter "g" from being pronounced with the soft "g/j" consonant sound.

Some words, such as "plague" and "rogue", end with the letters "-gue". Both the letter "u" and the letter "e" are silent. The final silent letter "e" is added because it is a convention of English spelling that words do not end with the letter "u". In the word "argue", the letter "u" is pronounced with a long "u" vowel sound.

a**g**ain	a**g**ree	ar**g**ue	be**g**an
a**gh**ast	an**g**le	Au**g**ust	bilin**g**ual
a**g**o	an**g**ry	bar**g**ain	bur**gh**er

burglar	gherkin	grant	guise
Calgary	ghetto	grass	guitar
catalogue	Ghiberti	grateful	gum
Chicago	ghost	gratitude	gun
cougar	ghostly	grave	guppy
degree	ghoul	gray (USA)	guy
dialogue	gigantic	grease	Guyana
dinghy	glad	great	ignore
disguise	glade	greed	illegal
disgust	glass	Greek	immigrant
disregard	glory	green	intrigue
distinguish	glove	greet	league
dragon	glow	grew	legal
England	glue	grey (UK, CAN)	magazine
English	go	grind	Megan
fatigue	goal	grip	negative
figure	goat	gripe	neglect
forgot	God	grizzly	organ
fragment	goes	groan	organization
fugue	going	grocery	organize
gaiety	gold	ground	Pittsburgh
gain	golf	group	plague
gale	gondola	grow	pregnant
gallivant	gone	grown	prologue
gallon	good	growth	recognition
game	goose	guarantee	recognize
gang	gorilla	guard	regard
gap	got	guardian	regret
garage	govern	Guelph	regular
garbage	grab	Guernsey	rogue
garden	grace	guerrilla	signal
gas	grad	guess	signature
gasp	grade	guest	sorghum
gate	gradual	guide	spaghetti
gather	grain	guild	sugar
gave	gram	guile	ugly
gay	grammar	guillotine	vogue
Ghana	grammatical	guilt	wagon
ghastly	grand	guinea	

b)   Exceptions to general rule

As a rule, the letter "g" represents the soft "g" consonant sound when followed by vowel letters "e", "i", "y". Unfortunately, there are exceptions to the rule. In the following words these spelling patterns represent the hard "g" consonant sound heard in "goat".

While the hard "c/k" consonant sound may be represented by consonant letters "c", "k", and "q", English has only the letter "g" to represent the hard "g" consonant sound. This is a problem when the hard "g" consonant sound is followed by a vowel sound represented by letters "e", "i", or "y". The French use the "gu" spelling pattern and the Italians use the "gh" spelling pattern to solve this problem.

altogether	gear	girl	hunger
anger	geese	girth	longer
begin	get	give	tiger
eager	gift	given	together
finger	giggle	gynaecology (UK, CAN)	
forget	Gilbert	gynecology (USA)	
forgive	gill (fish gill)	hamburger	

c) Final "-g"

The hard "g" sound heard in "goat" may be spelled with a final letter "-g".

It may be noted that all of the following are single-syllable short vowel words spelled with a single vowel letter followed by a single final consonant letter. Single-syllable long vowel words do not follow this spelling pattern.

With the addition of a suffix that begins with a vowel letter, however, the short vowel will now be followed by another vowel letter. In keeping with the doubling principle, the letter "g" is doubled. For example, the word "big" becomes "bigger" and "biggest". Double consonants usually signal that the preceding single vowel letter is pronounced with a short vowel sound.

bag	drag	frog	log
beg	drug	gag	pig
big	dug	gig	rug
bug	fig	hag	sag
dig	flag	hug	stag
dog	fog	leg	tag

d) "gg"

The hard "g" sound heard in "goat" may be represented by the "gg" consonant digraph.

Double consonants usually signal that the preceding vowel letter is pronounced with a short vowel sound as in "egg" and "nugget". For spelling purposes, when double consonants lie between two syllables, it is helpful to pronounce both consonants as in "bi**g**-**g**est". The words "e**gg**" and "hu**gg**ed" are single-syllable words, so only one hard "g" consonant sound can be pronounced.

There are three notable exceptions. The words "exaggerate", "suggest", and "suggestion" are pronounced with the soft "g/j" consonant sound.

ba**gg**age	di**gg**er	fla**gg**ing	nu**gg**et
ba**gg**ing	di**gg**ing	fo**gg**ed	pi**gg**y
ba**gg**y	do**gg**ie	fo**gg**ing	ru**gg**ed
be**gg**ed	dra**gg**ed	hu**gg**ed	sa**gg**ed
be**gg**ing	dra**gg**ing	hu**gg**ing	sa**gg**ing
bi**gg**er	dru**gg**ed	le**gg**ings	stru**gg**le
bi**gg**est	e**gg**	lo**gg**ed	ta**gg**ed
bu**gg**y	E**gg**ert	lo**gg**ing	ta**gg**ing

E9.2 Minor Spelling Patterns

There are three minor spelling patterns for the hard "g" consonant sound heard in "**g**oat".

a) "gh"

The hard "g" sound heard in "goat" may be represented by the "gh" consonant digraph. The letter "h" is silent.

This Italian spelling pattern solves the problem of how to represent the hard "g" consonant sound when "g" would otherwise be followed by vowel letters "e", "i" or "y". In words such as "**gh**etto", "**Gh**iberti", and "din**gh**y" the silent "h" protects the letter "g" from being pronounced with the soft "g/j" consonant sound.

The "gh" spelling pattern may also be followed by letters "a", "o", or "u" as in "**gh**astly", "**gh**ostly", and "sor**gh**um".

As an onset, at the beginning of words and syllables, the "gh-" spelling pattern only represents the hard "g" consonant sound as in "**gh**ost". In rimes, at the end of words and syllables, the "-gh" spelling pattern represents both the hard "g" consonant sound as in "Pittsbur**gh**" and the consonant "f" sound as in "lau**gh**".

The majority of the time, however, as heard in the words "high" and "though", the "gh" spelling pattern is silent and helps to represent a variety of vowel sounds.

a**gh**ast	**gh**astly	**gh**ost	sor**gh**um
bur**gh**er	**gh**erkin	**gh**ostly	spa**gh**etti
din**gh**y	**gh**etto	**gh**oul	
Ghana	**Gh**iberti	Pittsbur**gh**	

b) "(n)g"

The hard "g" sound heard in "goat" may be represented by the letters "(n)g" when the letter "n" is pronounced with the consonant "ng" sound heard in "ink".

On the other hand, if the letter "n" represents the consonant "n" sound heard in "nice", as in "passe**n**ger" and "stra**n**ge", then the letter "g" will be pronounced with the soft "g/j" consonant sound.

Most of the following words are consistent with the general rule that "g" followed by "a", "o", "u" or another consonant represents the hard "g" consonant sound. However, in words such as "ang**e**r", "fing**e**r", "hung**e**r", and "long**e**r", the letter "g" is followed by the vowel letter "e". The letter "g" followed by "e", "i", and "y" is usually pronounced with the soft "g/j" consonant sound heard in "gym" and "jam". The "(n)g" spelling pattern appears to override the rule. See E14.1.

anger	bingo	finger	jungle
angle	dingo	flamingo	language
angry	England	hunger	linguist
bilingual	English	hungry	longer

c) "gu"

The hard "g" sound heard in "goat" may be represented by the "gu" consonant digraph. The letter "u" is usually silent.

This French spelling pattern solves the problem of how to represent the hard "g" consonant sound when "g" would otherwise be followed by vowel letters "e", "i" or "y". In words such as "**gu**ess", "**gu**ide", and "**gu**y", the silent "u" protects the letter "g" from being pronounced with the soft "g/j" consonant sound.

However, the "gu" spelling pattern may be followed by letters "a", "o" "u" or a consonant as in "**gu**arantee", "dis**gu**st", and "**gu**ard".

The letter "u" is sometimes pronounced as heard in "ang**u**ish", "dis**gu**st", "distin**gu**ish", and "G**u**elph".

anguish	Guernsey	guild	guise
disguise	guerrilla	guile	guitar
disgust	guess	guillotine	guy
distinguish	guest	guilt	Guyana
Guelph	guide	guinea	

E9.3 Rare Spelling Patterns

There are at least three rare spelling patterns for the hard "g" consonant sound heard in "**g**oat".

a) "x"

The hard "g" consonant sound heard in "goat", followed by the consonant "z" sound, may be represented by the letter "x". Neither sound is well represented by the spelling.

With the word "exit" the letter "x" is also pronounced by some speakers with the hard "c/k" consonant sound followed by the soft "c/s" consonant sound.

e**x**act	e**x**amine	e**x**ecutive	*exit*
e**x**am	e**x**ample	e**x**ist	

b) "xh"

The hard "g" consonant sound heard in "goat", followed by the consonant "z" sound, may be represented by the letters "xh". Neither sound is well represented by the spelling. The letter "h" is silent.

e**xh**aust   e**xh**austion   e**xh**ibit

c) "x(u)"

The hard "g" consonant sound heard in "goat", followed by the consonant "zh" sound heard in "vision", may be represented by the letters "x(u)". Neither sound is well represented by the spelling.

With all of the following words, some people pronounce the letters "x(u)" with the hard "c/k" consonant sound followed by the consonant "sh" sound.

*lu**x**uriant*   *lu**x**uriate*   *lu**x**urious*   *lu**x**ury*

E10 Spelling the Consonant "H" Sound

There are several spelling patterns for the consonant "h" sound heard in "**h**appy". The spelling patterns have been divided into major and rare spelling patterns.

E10.1   Major Spelling Patterns

There are two major spelling patterns for the consonant "h" sound heard in "**h**appy".

a) "h"

The consonant "h" sound heard in "happy" may be represented by the letter "h".

The consonant "h" sound only forms onsets and is, therefore, only heard as the first sound in a word or syllable. The consonant "h" sound is never heard in consonant blends or in rimes at the end of a word or syllable. However, a silent letter "h" helps to form many vowel and consonant digraphs including "ch", "gh", "rh", "sh", "th" and "wh" which may be found in both onsets and rimes.

The letter "h" is never doubled. With compound words such as "ba*th*house", "bea*ch*head", "fi*sh*hook", "hit*ch*hike", and "wi*th*hold" the last letter of the first word and the first letter of the second word are the same creating an incidental "hh" spelling pattern.

ahead	Harry	hen	hold
behave	harvest	her	hole
behavior (USA)	Harvey	herbaceous	holiday
behaviour (UK, CAN)	has	herbal	Holland
behind	haste	herbicide	hollow
childhood	hasten	herbivore	hole
exhale	hat	herd	holy
exhume	hate	here	home
habit	hatred	hero	honey
had	haunted	herself	hook
hair	have	hesitate	hop
hairy	Hawaii	hey	hope
half	hay	hi	hoped
hall	he	hid	hoping
Halloween	head	hidden	hopped
halo	heal	hide	hopping
ham	health	high	horizon
hamburger	heap	hike	horizontal
hammer	hear	hill	horrendous
hamster	heard	him	horrible
hand	heart	himself	horror
handle	heat	hind	horse
handy	heaven	hinder	hose
hang	heavy	hindrance	hospital
happen	height	hire	host
happy	held	his	hot
harbor (USA)	helicopter	history	hotel
harbour (UK, CAN)	hell	hit	house
hard	hello	ho	how
harm	helmet	hobby	hug
	help	hockey	huge

human	hungry	hurricane	husband
humble	hunt	hurried	motherhood
hundred	Hunter	hurry	perhaps
hunger	hurrah	hurt	vehicle

b)   "wh(o)"

The consonant "h" sound heard in "happy" may be represented by the letters "wh" when followed by vowel letter "o". The letter "w" is silent. The "wh(o)" spelling pattern forms a consonant digraph.

The consonant "h" sound only forms onsets and, therefore, is only heard as the first sound in a word or syllable. The consonant "h" sound is never heard in consonant blends or in rimes at the end of a word or syllable. Accordingly, the "wh(o)" spelling pattern is only found at the beginning of words and syllables.

When the "wh" spelling pattern is followed by any other vowel letter, as in "what" and "when", the letter "w" is pronounced and the letter "h" is silent.

who	whole	whomever	whoop
whoever	whom	whomsoever	whose

E10.2   Rare Spelling Patterns

There are at least three rare spelling patterns for the consonant "h" sound heard in "happy".

a)   "ch"

The consonant "h" sound heard in "happy" may be represented by the "ch" consonant digraph. The letter "c" is silent. The word "Chanukah" is Hebrew in origin.

*Ch*anukah (Hebrew)

b)   "g"

The consonant "h" sound heard in "happy" may be represented by the letter "g". The word "Gila" is Spanish in origin.

Gila monster (Spanish)

c)   "j"

The consonant "h" sound heard in "happy" may be represented by the letter "j". The word "jai" is Spanish in origin.

jai alai (Spanish)

E11 Spelling the Consonant "L" Sound

When a long vowel sound is followed by the letter "l", an l-influenced vowel sound is heard. A schwa vowel sound is pronounced between the long vowel sound and the consonant "l" sound as heard in "male", "seal", "file", "fowl", and "rule". See D4.

There are several spelling patterns for the consonant "l" sound heard in "land". The spelling patterns have been divided into major and rare spelling patterns.

E11.1   Major Spelling Patterns

There are three major spelling patterns for the consonant "l" sound heard in "land".

a)   "l"

The consonant "l" sound heard in "land" may be represented by the letter "l".

ability	belief	cool	exactly
absolute	believe	council	facility
absolutely	belong	crawl	fail
accomplish	below	cruel	false
adult	belt	curl	familiar
agriculture	bilingual	daily	family
alive	boil	delicate	feel
almost	bowl	delicious	felt
alone	burglar	delight	film
along	calculate	deliver	fool
aloud	Calgary	detail	formula
already	*calm*	develop	friendly
also	canal	devil	ghostly
alternative	careful	dislike	girl
although	careless	dolphin	goal
altogether	ceiling	early	golf
always	certainly	easily	grizzly
ambulance	children	elastic	halo
apology	chocolate	elder	hardly
applaud	circular	elderly	health
applause	civilize	elect	heavenly
application	class	electric	helicopter
apply	claw	elephant	helmet
asleep	colony	elevator	help
Atlantic	color (USA)	eleven	herself
available	colour (UK, CAN)	elf	himself
avalanche	complain	else	hole
badly	complete	employ	holiday
balance	congratulate	England	holy
beautiful	control	envelope	hotel

hourly	lean	liquor	morale
immediately	leap	list	mostly
include	leapt	listen	motherly
involve	learn	lit	nearly
island	least	liter (USA)	noiseless
Italian	leather	literary	nuclear
Italy	leave	literature	oil
itself	led	litre (UK, CAN)	Olympic
jail	left	litter	only
jealous	leg	little	ourselves
jewel	leggings	live	owl
jewelry (USA)	legal	lizard	palace
July	legislation	load	parliament
knowledge	legitimate	loaf	particular
laboratory	lend	loan	particularly
lack	length	lobster	patrol
ladder	less	local	peaceful
ladies	lesson	lock	pearl
lady	lest	loft	peculiar
laid	let	log	penalty
lake	letter	lonely	pencil
lamp	letting	long	pilot
land	lettuce	look	playful
lane	level	loose	polar
language	Liam	loosen	pole
lap	liar	lord	police
large	liberal	lose	policy
larger	liberty	loss	polish
laser	librarian	lost	polite
last	library	lot	political
lasting	license	loud	politician
late	lie	love	politics
lately	life	lovely	pool
later	lift	low	popular
latter	light	loyal	population
laugh	lighting	luck	possibly
laughter	lightning	lump	powerful
Laura	like	lunch	problem
law	likely	lung	public
lawyer	lily	lunge	pupil
lay	limb	lying	qualification
lazy	limit	Lynda	qualify
lead	line	mainly	quality
leader	lion	mile	quickly
leaf	lip	milk	quietly
league	liquid	Montreal	regular

relate	shelter	splendid	twelfth
relation	silence	split	twelve
relative	silent	spoil	ugly
relief	silk	steal	ultra-
relieve	silver	steel	unfortunately
religion	similar	stole	unless
reply	sincerely	stool	until
republic	skeleton	suddenly	valuable
responsibility	slowly	supply	value
ridiculous	smile	tadpole	violence
role	softly	tail	violent
rule	soil	tailor	volcano
sail	solar	telephone	wealth
sailor	soldier	television	welcome
salad	solemn	toilet	wheel
salary	solution	tool	whole
sale	solve	trail	wolf
school	soul	translate	wolves
self	spelt	truly	wonderful
shelf	splash	tulip	wool

b)   "ll"

The consonant "l" sound heard in "land" may be represented by the "ll" consonant digraph.

Double consonants usually signal that the preceding vowel letter is pronounced with a short vowel sound as in "b<u>e</u>ll" and "ga<u>l</u>lon". For spelling purposes, when double consonants lie between two syllables, it is helpful to pronounce both consonants as in "hol-low". With single-syllable words, such as "hill" and "filled", only one consonant "l" sound can be pronounced.

Words such as "million" and "billion" are pronounced "mill-yun" and "bill-yun". The letter "i" is pronounced with the consonant "y" sound.

The words "belle", "grille", and "vaudeville" are French in origin.

all	bullet	dollar	finally
alley	call	dull	follow
allow	caller	especially	full
ball	carefully	excellent	gall
balloon	collar	fall	gallon
bell	collect	fell	generally
belle	college	fellow	gorilla
bill	collision	fill	grille
billion	doll	filled	hall

Halloween	mall	skull	troll
hell	mill	small	umbrella
hello	million	smell	usually
hill	pall	spell	valley
Holland	pollution	spill	vaudeville
hollow	pull	spill	village
ill	really	stall	villain
illegal	roll	stallion	wall
intelligence	satellite	still	well
jewellery (UK, CAN)	sell	swallow	will
kill	shall	swell	willow
llama	shell	tall	yell
Lloy	silly	tell	yellow
	skill	till	

c) Syllabic "l"

As discussed in A7.4, a syllable always contains a vowel sound. However, a final consonant "l" sound is sometimes syllabic, meaning that it forms a syllable by itself without the assistance of a vowel sound. The word "metal", for example, is usually pronounced "met-'l".

However, what is happening is that a faint schwa vowel sound is pronounced before the consonant "l" sound. The word "metal", for example, is pronounced "met-ull". This pronunciation of the "l" sound is not heard at the beginning of words such as "link" and "luck". Word endings "-al", "-el", "-le", and "-ol" can all represent the syllabic "l" sound. The most common spelling pattern is "-le".

Words such as "noble" and "table" are pronounced "no-bull" and "ta-bull". The final silent letter "e" signals that a schwa vowel sound is pronounced before the consonant "l" sound. The preceding consonant letter attaches to the "-ull" sound completing the final syllable and leaving the first vowel in an open, long sounding syllable. Words such as "battle" and "startle" are pronounced "bat-tull" and "star-tull". In keeping with the doubling principle, having two consonants between vowel sounds allows one consonant to keep the first vowel in a closed, short sounding syllable.

Note that the following words are all spelled with a single letter "l". In keeping with the doubling principle, the double "ll" spelling pattern usually follows a short vowel sound and not the schwa vowel sound. With words that end with "-all", such as "ball" and "small", the letter "a" is usually pronounced with the short "o" vowel sound. With words that end with "-ell", such as "bell" and "shell", the letter "e" is usually pronounced with the short "e" vowel sound.

able	bottle	bugle	channel
battle	bridal	capital	coddle
betel (Portuguese)	buckle	cattle	colonel

cudd**le**	id**le**	need**le**	sett**le**
curd**le**	id**ol**	nob**le**	start**le**
dirnd**l** (German)	kett**le**	nood**le**	strugg**le**
entit**le**	litt**le**	padd**le**	tab**le**
fat**al**	med**al**	ped**al**	tatt**le**
fidd**le**	met**al**	pood**le**	tit**le**
gent**le**	midd**le**	pudd**le**	tot**al**
horizont**al**	mod**el**	sadd**le**	turt**le**

E11.2 Rare Spelling Patterns

There is at least one rare spelling pattern for the consonant "l" sound heard in "land".

a) "lh"

The consonant "l" sound heard in "land" may be represented by the "lh" consonant digraph. The letter "h" is silent.

Lhasa apso (Tibetan)

E12 Spelling the Consonant "M" Sound

There are several spelling patterns for the consonant "m" sound heard in "**m**other". The spelling patterns have been divided into major, minor, and rare spelling patterns.

E12.1 Major Spelling Patterns

There are three major spelling patterns for the consonant "m" sound heard in "mother".

a) "m"

The consonant "m" sound heard in "mother" may be represented by the letter "m".

accomplish	amongst	became	ceremony
accustom	amount	become	charm
admire	amuse	blame	chimney
admission	animal	blossom	chipmunk
admit	apartment	boom	Christmas
aim	arm	bottom	claim
almost	army	broom	clam
am	ashamed	came	come
ambition	atmosphere	camera	comfort
ambitious	attempt	cement	coming
ambulance	automobile	centimeter (USA)	companion
among	beam	centimetre (UK, CAN)	compare

compete	flame	magic	medal
completion	form	mail	medical
complicate	formal	main	medicine
compose	former	major	medium
composition	formula	majority	meet
computer	frame	make	melt
consumer	freedom	male	member
cream	from	man	memory
crime	game	manage	men
criminal	German	manager	mention
custom	gram	manner	merchant
customer	gum	mansion	mercy
damage	gym	manual	mere
December	ham	many	mermaid
demand	hamburger	map	merry
department	hamster	maple	mess
determine	harm	March	message
diamond	helmet	march	messenger
discomfort	him	mare	met
discrimination	himself	mark	metal
dismiss	home	marker	method
dream	human	market	metre (UK)
drum	imagination	marriage	metric
economy	imagine	married	Mexican
emergency	imitate	marry	Mexico
empire	important	Mars	mice
employ	impossible	Martian	middle
employee	improvise	mask	might
enemy	income	mass	mild
enormous	inform	master	mile
environment	information	mat	milk
equipment	instrument	match	milking
examine	instrument	material	mill
excitement	item	mathematics	million
exclaim	itemize	matter	mind
experiment	kingdom	Matthew	mine
extreme	legitimate	may	mineral
fame	limit	May	minimum
familiar	llama	me	minister
family	lumber	meadow	minute
famous	machine	meal	mirror
farm	mad	mean	mischief
farming	madden	measure	miserable
female	made	meat	misery
film	Madison	mechanic	miss
firm	magazine	mechanism	mission

mistake	motor	payment	steam
mix	mountain	perform	stem
model	mouse	permanent	stomach
modem	mouth	permission	storm
moderate	move	permit	stormy
modern	movie	poem	stream
modest	much	problem	streaming
mom	mud	program (USA, CAN)	swam
moment	multiplication	promise	swim
mommy	multiply	punishment	sympathetic
Monday	murder	reform	sympathy
money	muscle	remain	system
monkey	museum	remark	tame
monster	music	remedy	team
month	musician	remember	temper
Montreal	must	remind	them
mood	my	room	time
moon	mysterious	same	tomorrow
moose	mystery	scream	treatment
moral	name	seem	umbrella
morale	normal	September	warm
more	number	similar	welcome
morning	numerous	simplicity	whom
mosquito	Olympic	slam	wisdom
most	omission	slim	woman
motel	omit	slime	women
mother	ornament	some	worm
motion	parliament		zoom

b) "mb"

The consonant "m" sound heard in "mother" may be represented by the "mb" consonant digraph. The letter "b" is silent.

With the "mb" consonant digraph, the letter "b" is silent in single-syllable words such as "crumb" and "dumb". The letter "b" is also silent in two-syllable words, such as "climb-er" and "plumb-er", that have a syllabic break following the "b". It is difficult to pronounce the consonant "b" sound immediately following the consonant "m" sound. On the other hand, the letter "b" is pronounced in two-syllable words, such as "lum-ber" and "tim-ber", when a syllabic break divides the letter "m" from the letter "b".

Sometimes the letter "b" disappears altogether with the addition of a suffix as in the words "crummy" and "dummy".

aplomb	bomber	catacomb	climbed
bomb	bombing	climb	climber

climbing	crumb	numb	thumb
comb	dumb	plumber	tomb
combed	lamb	plumbing	womb
combing	limb	succumb	

c) "mm"

The "m" sound heard in "mother" may be represented by the "mm" consonant digraph.

Double consonants usually signal that the preceding vowel letter is pronounced with a short vowel sound as in "d<u>u</u>mmy" and "gr<u>a</u>mmar". For spelling purposes, when double consonants lie between two syllables, it is helpful to pronounce both consonants as in "sum-mer". With single-syllable words, such as "slammed", only one consonant "m" sound can be pronounced.

command	common	grammatical	mommy
commerce	community	hammer	programme (UK)
commercial	crummy	immediate	slammed
commission	dummy	immense	summer
committee	grammar	immigrant	swimming

E12.2   Minor Spelling Patterns

There are two minor spelling patterns for the consonant "m" sound heard in "mother".

a) "lm"

The consonant "m" sound heard in "mother" may be represented by the "lm" consonant digraph. The letter "l" is usually silent.

Two consonants usually signal that the preceding vowel letter is pronounced with a short vowel sound as in "c<u>a</u>lm" and "ps<u>a</u>lm". For spelling purposes, when two consonants lie between two syllables, it is helpful to pronounce both consonants as in "<u>a</u>l-mond". With single-syllable words, such as "calm" and "palm", only one consonant "m" sound can be pronounced.

almond	*calm*	palm	psalm

b) "mn"

The "m" sound heard in "mother" may be represented by the "mn" consonant digraph. The letter "n" is silent.

The letter "n" is silent because it is difficult to pronounce the consonant "n" sound immediately following the consonant "m" sound. However, the addition of a suffix may create a syllabic break allowing the letter "n" to be pronounced. This is an example of morphemic spelling. The silent letter "n" preserves a common morpheme with words such as "autum-nal", "colum-nar", "colum-nist", "condem-nation", "dam-nation", "hym-nal", and "solem-nity" in which the letter "n" is pronounced.

In keeping with the doubling principle, the single vowel letter preceding the "mn" spelling pattern is usually pronounced with a short vowel sound.

autu**mn**	conde**mn**	hy**mn**
colu**mn**	da**mn**	sole**mn**

E12.3   Rare Spelling Patterns

There are at least two rare spelling patterns for the consonant "m" sound heard in "**m**other".

a)   "-chm"

The consonant "m" sound heard in "mother" may be represented by the "-chm" consonant digraph. The letters "ch" are silent.

In keeping with the doubling principle, the single vowel letter preceding the "chm" spelling pattern is usually pronounced with a short vowel sound.

dra**chm** (Scottish)

b)   "-gm"

The consonant "m" sound heard in "mother" may be represented by the "-gm" consonant digraph. The letter "g" is silent.

In keeping with the doubling principle, the single vowel letter preceding the "gm" spelling pattern is usually pronounced with a short vowel sound.

diaphra**gm**	paradi**gm**	phle**gm**

E13 Spelling the Consonant "N" Sound Heard in "Nice"

There are many spelling patterns for the consonant "n" sound heard in "**n**ice". The spelling patterns have been divided into major, minor, and rare spelling patterns.

E13.1   Major Spelling Patterns

There are five major spelling patterns for the consonant "n" sound heard in "**n**ice":

a) "gn"

The consonant "n" sound heard in "nice" may be represented by the "gn" consonant digraph. The letter "g" is silent.

With the "gn" spelling patterns, the letter "g" is sometimes silent and sometimes pronounced. As an onset, at the beginning of words such as "gnarled" and "gnaw", the letter "g" is always silent. Likewise, in a rime at the end of words such as "foreign" and "sign", the letter "g" is always silent. However, when the letters "gn" are found within words, as in "assignment" and "signal", the letter "g" is sometimes pronounced and sometimes silent. If a third consonant letter follows "gn", as in "assign-ment", there will be a syllabic break between the letters "gn" and the following consonant letter. The letters "gn" will form a consonant digraph, and the letter "g" will be silent.

When the letters "gn" are followed by a vowel letter, as in "signing" and "signal", the letter "g" is sometimes pronounced and sometimes silent. When a native English suffix only changes the inflection of a word, as the suffix "-ing" does in "signing", the letters "gn" will continue to form a rime, and the letter "g" will be silent. Words in which the letter "g" is silent include "aligning", "assigning", "assigned", "campaigned", "campaigning", "designed", "designing", "maligned", "maligning", "resigned", and "resigning". When a Latin suffix changes the meaning of a word, as the suffix "-al" does in "signal", there will be a syllabic break between the letters "g" and "n", and the letter "g" will be pronounced. The word "malignant", for example, is pronounced "mal-ig-nant". Words in which the letter "g" is pronounced include "designate", "ignite", "insignia", "recognize", "resignation", "signal", and "signature".

The letter "g" in the "gn" spelling pattern is visually significant even when silent as it points to a common root which indicates a shared meaning between words. This is an example of morphemic spelling because the letter "g" preserves a common morpheme between words such as:

- malign → malignant
- resign → resignation
- sign → signal, signature, insignia, designate

The "gn" spelling pattern only represents the consonant "n" sound heard in "sign". On the other hand, the "ng" spelling pattern represents both the consonant "n" sound heard in "range" and the consonant "ng" sound heard in "sing".

align	benign	cologne	foreign
aligning	bologna	consign	gnarled
arraign	campaign	consignment	gnash
assign	campaigned	design	gnat
assigned	campaigning	designed	gnaw
assigning	champagne	designing	gnome
assignment	cognac	ensign	Gnostic

gnu	mali**gn**ing	resi**gn**ed	si**gn**ing
impu**gn**	poi**gn**ant	resi**gn**ing	sovere**ign**
mali**gn**	rei**gn**	si**gn**	sovere**ign**ty
mali**gn**ed	resi**gn**	si**gn**ed	

b) "kn-"

The "n" sound heard in "nice" may be represented by the "kn" consonant digraph. The letter "k" is silent. This spelling is German in origin.

The "kn-" spelling pattern only forms onsets and is, therefore, only found at the beginning of words and syllables. In the word "acknowledge", pronounced "ac-knowledge", the letters "kn" represent the consonant "n" sound.

It may be noted that the "kn-" spelling pattern only represents the consonant "n" sound heard in "**kn**ow" and the "n(k)" spelling pattern only represents the consonant "ng" sound heard in "spa**nk**".

ac**kn**owledge	**kn**eel	**kn**ob	**Kn**owles
bow**kn**ot	**kn**ew	**kn**ock	**kn**own
knack	**kn**ickers	**kn**ockwurst	**kn**uckle
knapsack	**kn**ick**kn**ack	**kn**oll	pen**kn**ife
knave	**kn**ife	**kn**ot	un**kn**own
knead	**kn**ight	**kn**ow	
knee	**kn**it	**kn**owledge	

c) "n"

The "n" sound heard in "nice" may be represented by the letter "n".

abse**n**ce	amou**n**t	arou**n**d	ba**n**d
accide**n**t	a**n**	asto**n**ish	bargai**n**
actio**n**	a**n**cient	astro**n**aut	bar**n**
admissio**n**	a**n**d	Atla**n**tic	basi**n**
adoptio**n**	a**n**imal	atte**n**d	bea**n**
adva**n**ce	a**nn**ou**n**ce	atte**n**tio**n**	bee**n**
adva**n**tage	a**nn**oya**n**ce	attractio**n**	bega**n**
adve**n**ture	a**n**other	audie**n**ce	begi**n**
after**n**oo**n**	a**n**swer	au**n**t	behi**n**d
agai**n**	a**n**t	avala**n**che	be**n**ch
age**n**cy	a**n**y	ave**n**ue	be**n**eath
allowa**n**ce	apartme**n**t	awful	betwee**n**
alo**n**e	appare**n**t	awhile	billio**n**
alter**n**ative	appeara**n**ce	bala**n**ce	bio**n**ic
ambitio**n**	applicatio**n**	balloo**n**	blow**n**
ambula**n**ce	are**n**a	bana**n**a	bo**n**e

born	company	cushion	engine
brain	comparison	dance	enjoy
branch	complain	darken	enormous
broken	completion	deafen	enough
brown	complication	decision	entertain
bunch	concern	defence (UK, CAN)	entrance
burn	confess	defense (USA)	envelope
business	confession	definite	environment
cabin	confidence	den	envy
calculation	confident	dentist	equation
can	confidential	dependence	essence
Canada	confuse	destruction	even
Canadian	confusion	determine	evidence
canal	congratulate	dictionary	examine
cancer	congratulation	difference	excellence
cannon	connection (USA, CAN)	dine	existence
canoe	*conquer*	dining	expense
canyon	*conquest*	dinosaur	expensive
captain	conscience	discipline	experience
carnival	conscience	discontent	explain
carnivore	conscious	discrimination	expression
caution	consider	discussion	extension
century	constant	distance	extensive
ceremony	construction	division	fallen
chain	consumer	dolphin	fan
champion	contain	done	fantastic
chance	container	down	fashion
chicken	content	dozen	fasten
children	contest	dragon	fawn
chimney	continue	drown	fence
Chinese	contribute	earn	fifteen
citizen	contribution	earnest	final
classification	control	eastern	fine
clean	convenience	economy	finish
clown	convenient	efficiency	fortunate
coffin	conversation	eighteen	fortune
coin	corn	electrician	fourteen
collection	corner	eleven	France
collision	correction	emergency	French
colony	council	enclose	fun
combine	country	encourage	funeral
command	cousin	end	furniture
common	crayon	enemy	gain
community	criminal	energy	gallon
companies	crown	enforce	general
companion		engine	generation

273

ge**n**erous	i**n**form	librari**an**	**n**arrow
ge**n**ie	i**n**formatio**n**	lice**n**se	**n**atio**n**
Germa**n**	i**n**jure	light**n**i**n**g	**n**atio**n**al
give**n**	i**n**quire	li**n**e	**n**ative
golde**n**	i**n**quiry	lio**n**	**n**atural
go**n**e	i**n**sect	liste**n**	**n**ature
gover**n**	i**n**side	loa**n**	**n**aughty
grai**n**	i**n**sta**n**ce	lo**n**ely	**n**avy
gree**n**	i**n**sta**n**t	loose**n**	**n**ear
groa**n**	i**n**stead	lu**n**ch	**n**eat
grow**n**	i**n**strume**n**t	machi**n**e	**n**ecessary
gu**n**	i**n**sult	magazi**n**e	**n**eck
Hallowee**n**	i**n**sura**n**ce	mai**n**	**n**eed
happe**n**	i**n**sure	ma**n**	**n**eedle
haste**n**	i**n**tellige**n**ce	ma**n**age	**n**egative
heave**n**	i**n**te**n**d	ma**n**ager	**n**eglect
heighte**n**	i**n**te**n**tio**n**	ma**n**sio**n**	**n**eighbor (USA)
he**n**	i**n**terest	ma**n**ual	**n**eighbour (UK, CAN)
hesitatio**n**	i**n**terfere	ma**n**y	**n**either
hi**n**der	i**n**terfere**n**ce	mea**n**	**n**ephew
hi**n**dra**n**ce	i**n**ter**n**atio**n**al	mecha**n**ic	**n**ervous
ho**n**est	i**n**terrupt	mecha**n**ism	**n**est
ho**n**ey	i**n**to	medici**n**e	**n**et
horizo**n**	i**n**troduce	me**n**	**n**ever
huma**n**	i**n**troductio**n**	me**n**tio**n**	**n**ew
hu**n**dred	i**n**ve**n**t	messe**n**ger	**n**ews
hurrica**n**e	i**n**ve**n**tio**n**	Mexica**n**	**n**ext
ig**n**ore	i**n**ve**n**tio**n**	millio**n**	**n**ice
imagi**n**atio**n**	i**n**visible	mi**n**e	**n**ickel
imagi**n**e	i**n**vite	mi**n**eral	**n**iece
imitatio**n**	i**n**volve	mi**n**imum	**n**ight
imme**n**se	Italia**n**	mi**n**ister	**n**i**n**e
i**n**	Ja**n**uary	mi**n**ute	**n**i**n**etee**n**
i**n**ch	Japa**n**	moderatio**n**	**n**i**n**ety
i**n**clude	joi**n**	moder**n**	**n**i**n**th
i**n**clusive	jour**n**ey	Mo**n**day	**n**o
i**n**come	Ju**n**e	mo**n**ey	**n**oble
i**n**crease	kee**n**	mo**n**ster	**n**oise
i**n**deed	kitche**n**	mo**n**th	**n**oisy
I**n**dia**n**	k**n**ow**n**	Mo**n**treal	**N**ola**n**
i**n**dividual	la**n**e	moo**n**	**n**o**n**e
i**n**dustry	lea**n**	mor**n**i**n**g	**n**oo**n**
i**n**expe**n**sive	lear**n**	musicia**n**	**n**or
i**n**flatio**n**	le**n**gthe**n**	**n**ail	**n**ormal
i**n**flue**n**ce	lesse**n**	**n**ame	**n**orth
i**n**flue**n**tial	lesso**n**	**n**ap	

northern	pattern	quantity	shiny
Norway	peanut	queen	shown
nose	pen	Querns	signal
not	penalty	question	signature
note	pencil	raccoon	silence
nothing	pension	rain	sin
notice	performance	ran	since
noun	permanent	reason	sincere
now	person	recognition	situation
nuclear	phone	recognize	sixteen
nuisance	picnic	reduction	skeleton
number	pigeon	reference	skin
numerous	pile	reflection	slain
nurse	pin	relation	soften
nursery	pinch	religion	solution
nut	pine	remain	son
obedience	plain	repetition	soon
objection	plan	reproduction	Spain
ocean	plane	reputation	Spanish
offence (UK, CAN)	planed	resistance	spin
offense (USA)	planet	responsible	spine
often	plenty	return	splendid
omission	poison	ribbon	spoken
on	pony	ripen	spoon
once	possession	robin	stain
one	postpone	ruin	stallion
only	potential	run	standard
onto	preference	Russian	station
open	pregnant	satisfaction	stationary
operation	presence	Saturn	stiffen
opinion	pretense	scene	stolen
opportunity	prevention	scenery	stone
opposition	prince	science	strengthen
ordinary	princess	scientific	substance
organ	principal	scientist	suggestion
organization	principle	scorn	sun
organize	prison	scorpion	Sunday
origin	procession	screen	taken
original	production	season	tan
ornament	profession	seen	telephone
ounce	pronounce	senior	television
own	pronunciation	sense	ten
pain	protection	sentence	tenth
pan	province	seven	term
partner	punish	seventeen	than
patience	qualification	shine	then

thicken	turn	unknown	when
thin	twin	unless	wilderness
thirteen	unable	until	win
thorn	unconscious	untrue	window
thunder	unconscious	upon	wine
tin	under	vacation	winter
tine	unfortunate	vain	witness
tiny	unfortunate	van	woman
ton	unidentified	villain	women
tone	union	violence	won
town	unit	volcano	wonder
train	unite	wagon	woolen (USA)
translate	unity	warn	woollen (UK, CAN)
translation	universal	weaken	worn
transportation	universe	weapon	zone
tune	university	western	

d) "nn"

The "n" sound heard in "nice" may be represented by the "nn" consonant digraph.

Double consonants usually signal that the preceding vowel letter is pronounced with a short vowel sound as in "Ann" and "penny". For spelling purposes, when double consonants lie between two syllables, it is helpful to pronounce both consonants as in "fun-ny". With single-syllable words, such as "inn" and "planned", only one consonant "n" sound can be pronounced.

Ann	cannot	inn	running
announce	channel	Jeanne	skinny
annoy	connect	manner	tunnel
banner	dinner	penny	winner
bunny	Feldmann	planned	winning
cannon	funny	runner	

e) Syllabic "n"

As discussed in A7.4, a syllable always contains a vowel sound. However, a final consonant "n" sound is sometimes syllabic, meaning that it forms a syllable by itself without the assistance of a vowel sound. The word "satin", for example, is usually pronounced "sat-'n".

However, what is happening is that a faint schwa vowel sound is pronounced before the consonant "n" sound. The word "satin", for example, is pronounced "sat-un". This pronunciation of the "n" sound is not heard at the beginning of words such as "noble" and "number". Word endings "-an", "-ain", "-en", "-in", and "-on" can all represent the syllabic "n" sound. The most common spelling pattern is "-en".

With the words printed in italics, the schwa vowel sound may be pronounced more prominently.

avoid**an**ce	eve**n**ing	Lat**in**	sudd**en**
*barg**ain***	fatt**en**	light**en**	sweet**en**
bright**en**	flatt**en**	madd**en**	tart**an**
*Brit**ain***	forgott**en**	*mount**ain***	threat**en**
butt**on**	fright**en**	pard**on**	throw**n**
*capt**ain***	gard**en**	redd**en**	tight**en**
cart**on**	hard**en**	rott**en**	*vill**ain***
*cert**ain***	hidd**en**	sadd**en**	whit**en**
*chieft**ain***	import**an**ce	sat**in**	wid**en**
cott**on**	import**an**t	short**en**	wood**en**
curt**ain**	ir**on**	straight**en**	writt**en**
eat**en**	kitt**en**	stud**en**t	

E13.2   Minor Spelling Patterns

There is one minor spelling patterns for the consonant "n" sound heard in "**n**ice":

a)   "-n(ge)"

The "n" sound heard in "**n**ice" may be represented by the letters "-n(ge)".

With the "-n(ge)" spelling pattern, as in "lu**n**ge", "ra**n**ge", and "si**n**ge", the final silent letter "e" signals that the letter "n" is pronounced with the consonant "n" sound, and the letter "g" is pronounced with the soft "g/j" consonant sound. This is in keeping with the general rule that "g" followed by "e", "i", or "y" represents the soft "g/j" consonant sound. Without the final silent letter "e", as in "lung", "rang", and "sing", the letter "n" is pronounced with the consonant "ng" sound, and the letter "g" is silent. With the addition of a final silent letter "e", "lung" becomes "lunge"; "rang" becomes "range"; and "sing" becomes "singe".

arra**n**ge	fri**n**ge	ra**n**ge	stra**n**ger
cha**n**ge	lu**n**ge	ra**n**ger	
da**n**ger	ora**n**ge	si**n**ge	
excha**n**ge	passe**n**ger	stra**n**ge	

E13.3   Rare Spelling Patterns

There are at least four rare spelling patterns for the consonant "n" sound heard in "**n**ice".

a)   "dne"

The "n" sound heard in "nice" may be represented by the "dne" consonant digraph. The letters "d" and "e" are silent.

In keeping with the doubling principle, the single vowel letter preceding the "dne" spelling pattern is usually pronounced with a short vowel sound.

We**dne**sday

b)   "mn"

The "n" sound heard in "nice" may be represented by the "mn" consonant digraph. The letter "m" is silent.

mnemonic

c)   "mp"

The "n" sound heard in "nice" may be represented by the "mp" consonant digraph.

In keeping with the doubling principle, the single vowel letter preceding the "mp" spelling pattern is usually pronounced with a short vowel sound.

co**mp**troller

d)   "pn"

The "n" sound heard in the word "nice" may be represented by the "pn" consonant digraph. The letter "p" is silent. This is a Greek spelling pattern.

pneumatic   **pn**eumococcus   **pn**eumonia

E14 Spelling the Consonant "NG" Sound

There are many spelling patterns for the consonant "ng" sound heard in "i**n**k" and "si**ng**". The spelling patterns have been divided into major, minor, and rare spelling patterns.

E14.1   Major Spelling Patterns

There are three major spelling patterns for the consonant "ng" sound heard in "i**n**k" and "si**ng**".

a) "-ng"

The consonant "ng" sound heard in "ink" and "sing" may be represented by the "-ng" consonant digraph.

The "ng" spelling pattern represents a number of word sounds. Sometimes the letter "n" represents the consonant "n" sound heard in "nice" and sometimes the consonant "ng" sound heard in "ink" and "sing". Sometimes the letter "g" is pronounced, and sometimes it is silent. If pronounced, sometimes the letter "g" represents the soft "g/j" consonant sound heard in "jam", and sometimes the hard "g" consonant sound heard in "goat".

When the "-ng" spelling pattern forms a consonant digraph at the end of a word or syllable, as in "ha**ng**", "lu**ng**", "picki**ng**", "si**ng**", "stro**ng**", and "you**ng**", it represents the consonant "ng" sound heard, and the letter "g" is silent. As the sample words listed below illustrate, frequent use of the suffix "-ing" makes this is a very common spelling pattern.

With the "-n(ge)" spelling pattern, as in "lu**nge**", "ra**nge**", and "si**nge**", the final silent letter "e" signals that the letter "n" is pronounced with the consonant "n" sound, and the letter "g" is pronounced with the soft "g/j" consonant sound. This is in keeping with the general rule that "g" followed by "e", "i", or "y" represents the soft "g/j" consonant sound. Without the final silent letter "e", as in "lu**ng**", "ra**ng**", and "si**ng**", the letter "n" is pronounced with the consonant "ng" sound, and the letter "g" is silent. With the addition of a final silent letter "e", "lung" becomes "lunge"; "rang" becomes "range"; and "sing" becomes "singe".

When the letters "ng" form a consonant blend with following consonant letters, as in "amo**ngst**" and "le**ngth**", they continue to represent the consonant "ng" sound heard in "ink" and "sing", and the letter "g" is silent.

If there is a syllabic break between the letter "n" and the letter "g", the letter "n" is sometimes pronounced with the consonant "ng" sound and sometimes with the consonant "n" sound . This, in turn, affects how the letter "g" is pronounced.

- When the letter "n" is pronounced with the consonant "n" sound, as in "a**n-ge**l", "co**n-gr**atulate", "e**n-g**ine", "gi**n-ge**r", "ta**n-ge**nt", and "ta**n-ge**rine", the letter "g" will be pronounced with either the soft "g/j" consonant sound or the hard "g" consonant sound in keeping with the general rules discussed in E8 and E9 above.

- However, when the letter "n" is pronounced with the consonant "ng" sound, as in "bi**n-g**o" and "ju**n-g**le", the letter "g" will be pronounced with the hard "g" consonant sound. With words such as "a**n-ge**r", "fi**n-ge**r", "hu**n-ge**r", "lo**n-ge**r", "stro**n-ge**st", and "you**n-ge**st", the letter "g" is pronounced with the hard "g" consonant sound even when followed by "e" contrary to the general rules.

Pronouncing the letter "n" with the consonant "ng" sound trumps the general rules. See (b).

With verbs and words derived from verb roots, the consonant "ng" sound stays together, and the "g" remains silent as (not) heard in "ha**ng**ed", "ha**ng**er", "si**ng**er", "si**ng**ing", and "lo**ng**ing". With adjectives and words derived from non-verb roots, the letters "ng" break apart, and the "g" is pronounced with the hard "g" consonant sound as heard in "fi**n-g**er", "lo**n-g**er", "stro**n-g**er", and "you**n-g**er".

The "ng" spelling pattern can represent both the consonant "n" sound heard in "ra**ng**e" and the consonant "ng" sound heard in "ha**ng**". On the other hand, the "gn" spelling pattern only represents the consonant "n" sound heard in "**gn**aw" and "si**gn**".

advertisi**ng**	fishi**ng**	lighti**ng**	rippi**ng**
alo**ng**	flashi**ng**	lightni**ng**	risi**ng**
amo**ng**	fli**ng**	listeni**ng**	roari**ng**
amo**ng**st	flyi**ng**	livi**ng**	rolli**ng**
ba**ng**	followi**ng**	lo**ng**	rubbi**ng**
bei**ng**	ga**ng**	longi**ng**	running
belo**ng**	goi**ng**	losi**ng**	saili**ng**
bri**ng**	ha**ng**	lovi**ng**	sa**ng**
bri**ng**ing	ha**ng**ed	lu**ng**	sayi**ng**
buildi**ng**	ha**ng**ing	lyi**ng**	screami**ng**
burni**ng**	happeni**ng**	maki**ng**	seei**ng**
calli**ng**	headi**ng**	meeti**ng**	selli**ng**
carryi**ng**	heari**ng**	mini**ng**	sendi**ng**
ceili**ng**	helpi**ng**	missi**ng**	shaki**ng**
clothi**ng**	hidi**ng**	morni**ng**	shini**ng**
comi**ng**	holdi**ng**	movi**ng**	shocki**ng**
diggi**ng**	hopi**ng**	nothi**ng**	shooti**ng**
diggi**ng**s	hoppi**ng**	offeri**ng**	showi**ng**
dini**ng**	hunti**ng**	openi**ng**	si**ng**
divi**ng**	hurti**ng**	ora**ng**utan	si**ng**er
doi**ng**	inviti**ng**	packi**ng**	si**ng**ing
dreami**ng**	keepi**ng**	payi**ng**	sitti**ng**
drinki**ng**	killi**ng**	picki**ng**	skii**ng**
drivi**ng**	ki**ng**	printi**ng**	sleepi**ng**
duri**ng**	landi**ng**	provi**ng**	slidi**ng**
eati**ng**	lasti**ng**	putti**ng**	sli**ng**
eveni**ng**	layi**ng**	raci**ng**	slippi**ng**
exciti**ng**	leadi**ng**	ra**ng**	so**ng**
falli**ng**	learni**ng**	ranki**ng**	speaki**ng**
feeli**ng**	leavi**ng**	readi**ng**	spelli**ng**
fighti**ng**	le**ng**th	ridi**ng**	spitti**ng**
findi**ng**	le**ng**then	ri**ng**	splitti**ng**
firi**ng**	letti**ng**	ri**ng**ing	spri**ng**

spri**ng**ing	stri**ng**	thi**ng**	weddi**ng**
standi**ng**	stri**ng**	thinki**ng**	windi**ng** (Verb)
steali**ng**	stro**ng**	throwi**ng**	wi**ng**
sti**ng**	su**ng**	to**ng**	winni**ng**
sti**ng**ing	swimmi**ng**	trucki**ng**	wonderi**ng**
sti**nk**ing	swi**ng**	tryi**ng**	worki**ng**
stocki**ng**	swi**ng**ing	turni**ng**	writi**ng**
stoppi**ng**	taki**ng**	walki**ng**	wro**ng**
stre**ng**th	talki**ng**	washi**ng**	you**ng**
stre**ng**then	teachi**ng**	watchi**ng**	
striki**ng**	telli**ng**	weari**ng**	

b) "n(g)"

The consonant "ng" sound heard in the words "ink" and "sing" may be represented by the letters "n(g)". The letter "g" is pronounced with the hard "g" consonant sound.

If there is a syllabic break between the letter "n" and the letter "g", the letter "n" is sometimes pronounced with the consonant "ng" sound and sometimes with the consonant "n" sound. This, in turn, affects how the following letter "g" is pronounced.

- When the letter "n" is pronounced with the consonant "n" sound, as in "a**n**-g**e**l", "co**n**-g**r**atulate", "e**n**-g**i**ne", "gi**n**-g**e**r", "ta**n**-g**e**nt", and "ta**n**-g**e**rine", the letter "g" will be pronounced with either the soft "g/j" consonant sound or the hard "g" consonant sound in keeping with the general rules discussed in E8 and E9 above.

- However, when the letter "n" is pronounced with the consonant "ng" sound, as in "bi**n**-**g**o" and "ju**n**-**g**le", the letter "g" will be pronounced with the hard "g" consonant sound. With words such as "a**n**-g**e**r", "fi**n**-g**e**r", "hu**n**-g**e**r", "lo**n**-g**e**r", "stro**n**-g**e**st", and "you**n**-g**e**st", the letter "g" is pronounced with the hard "g" consonant sound even when followed by "e" contrary to the general rules. Pronouncing the letter "n" with the consonant "ng" sound trumps the general rules.

In the following words, there is a syllabic break between the letters "n" and "g":

a**ng**er	di**ng**o	flami**ng**o	li**ng**uist
a**ng**le	disti**ng**uish	hu**ng**er	lo**ng**er
a**ng**ry	E**ng**land	hu**ng**ry	si**ng**le
bili**ng**ual	E**ng**lish	ju**ng**le	
bi**ng**o	fi**ng**er	la**ng**uage	

c) "n(k)"

The consonant "ng" sound heard in "ink" and "sing" may be represented by the letters "n(k)". The letter "k" is pronounced with the hard "c/k" consonant sound.

The "n(k)" spelling pattern forms rimes and is, therefore, often found at the end of words as in "pink". Within words, the letters "n" and "k" may be divided between syllables with the "n" forming the rime of one syllable and the "k" forming the onset of the following syllable. The word "monkey", for example, is pronounced "mon-key". The "n(k)" spelling pattern never forms onsets and is, therefore, never found at the beginning of words or syllables.

In keeping with the doubling principle, the single vowel letter preceding the "n(k)" spelling pattern is usually pronounced with a short vowel sound.

It may be noted that the "n(k)" spelling pattern only represents the consonant "ng" sound heard in "spa**nk**" and the "kn-" spelling pattern only represents the consonant "n" sound heard in "**kn**ow".

ba**nk**	dri**nk**ing	ra**nk**	sti**nk**ing
bla**nk**et	dru**nk**	si**nk**	ta**nk**
chipmu**nk**	i**nk**	si**nk**ing	tha**nk**
do**nk**ey	ju**nk**	sku**nk**	thi**nk**
dra**nk**	mo**nk**ey	spa**nk**	thi**nk**ing
dri**nk**	pi**nk**	sti**nk**	tru**nk**

E14.2   Rare Spelling Patterns

There are at least six rare spelling patterns for the consonant "ng" sound heard in "i**nk**" and "si**ng**".

a)   "n(c)"

The consonant "ng" sound heard in "ink" and "sing" may be represented by the letters "n(c)". The letter "c" is pronounced with the hard "c/k" consonant sound.

This spelling pattern is similar to the "n(k)" spelling pattern discussed above.

With compound words, such as "pancake" and "pincushion", the "nc" spelling pattern occurs incidentally. The letter "n" is pronounced with the consonant "n" sound heard in "nice".

Lin**c**oln	pun**c**tual	un**c**le

b)   "nd(k)"

The consonant "ng" sound heard in "ink" and "sing" may be represented by the letters "nd(k)". The letter "d" is silent. The letters "nd" form a consonant digraph.

ha**nd**kerchief

c) "ngg"

The consonant "ng" sound heard in "ink" and "sing" may be represented by the "ngg" consonant digraph. The letters "gg" are silent.

mah-jo**ngg** (Chinese)

d) "ngue"

The consonant "ng" sound heard in "ink" and "sing" may be represented by the "ngue" consonant digraph. The letters "gue" are silent.

hara**ngue**   meri**ngue**   to**ngue**

e) "n(q)"

The consonant "ng" sound heard in "ink" and "sing" may be represented by the letters "n(q)". The letter "q" is pronounced with the hard "c/k" consonant sound.

ba**nq**uet   *co**nq**uer*   *co**nq**uest*

f) "n(x)"

The consonant "ng" sound heard in "ink" and "sing" may be represented by the letters "n(x)".

In the word "anxiety", the letter "x" is pronounced with the consonant "z" sound. In the word "anxious", the letter "x" is pronounced with the hard "c/k" consonant sound followed by the consonant "sh" sound.

a**nx**iety   a**nx**ious

E15 Spelling the Consonant "P" Sound

There are several spelling patterns for the consonant "p" sound heard in "**p**et". The spelling patterns have been divided into major and rare spelling patterns.

E15.1   Major Spelling Patterns

There are two major spelling patterns for the consonant "p" sound heard in "**p**et".

a) "p"

The consonant "p" sound heard in "pet" may be represented by the letter "p".

acce**p**t   ado**p**t   a**p**e   A**p**ril
accom**p**lish   a**p**art   a**p**ology   aslee**p**

attem**pt**	ex**p**eriment	**p**air	**p**encil
ca**p**	ex**p**ert	**p**alace	**p**enny
ca**p**e	fellowshi**p**	**p**ale	**p**ension
ca**p**ital	ga**p**	**p**an	**p**eo**p**le
ca**p**tain	gri**p**	**p**ants	**p**er
car**p**et	gri**p**e	**p**a**p**er	**p**ercent
chea**p**	grou**p**	**p**arade	**p**erfect
chi**p**munk	hea**p**	**p**arcel	**p**erform
chir**p**	helico**p**ter	**p**ardon	**p**erha**p**s
cho**p**	hel**p**	**p**arent	**p**eriod
com**p**anion	hiccu**p** (USA, CAN)	**p**ark	**p**ermanent
com**p**anionshi**p**	ho**p**	**P**arks	**p**ermission
com**p**are	ho**p**e	**p**arliament	**p**ermit
com**p**ete	ho**p**ed	**p**art	**p**erson
com**p**ose	ho**p**ing	**p**article	**p**ersuade
com**p**osition	im**p**ortant	**p**articular	**p**ersuasion
com**p**uter	im**p**ossible	**p**arties	**p**et
co**p**y	interru**p**t	**p**artner	**p**ick
cor**p**oration	Ja**p**an	**p**arty	**p**icnic
cou**p**le	Ju**p**iter	**p**ass	**p**icture
cree**p**	kee**p**	**p**assenger	**p**ie
cris**p**	ke**p**t	**p**ast	**p**iece
cro**p**	la**p**	**p**aste	**p**ig
cu**p**	leadershi**p**	**p**astry	**p**igeon
dee**p**	lea**p**	**p**asture	**p**ilot
de**p**art	lea**p**t	**p**at	**p**in
de**p**end	li**p**	**p**atch	**p**inch
de**p**ict	ma**p**	**p**ath	**p**ine
de**p**th	ma**p**le	**p**atience	**p**ink
develo**p**	membershi**p**	**p**atient	**p**int
di**p**	na**p**	**p**atriotism	**p**i**p**e
dri**p**	octo**p**us	**p**atrol	**p**irate
dro**p**	Olym**p**ic	**p**attern	**p**it
Egy**p**t	o**p**en	**P**atterson	**p**ity
em**p**ire	o**p**erate	**P**aul	**p**lace
em**p**loy	o**p**eration	**p**ause	**p**lan
envelo**p**e	o**p**erator	**p**aw	**p**lane
equi**p**ment	o**p**inion	**p**ay	**p**ocket
esca**p**e	ownershi**p**	**p**ayment	**p**oem
Euro**p**e	**P**acific	**p**eace	**p**oet
exce**p**t	**p**ack	**p**eaceful	**p**oint
ex**p**ect	**p**ad	**p**eanut	**p**oison
ex**p**end	**p**age	**p**earl	**p**olar
ex**p**ense	**p**aid	**p**eculiar	**p**ole
ex**p**ensive	**p**ain	**p**en	**p**olice
ex**p**erience	**p**aint	**p**enalty	**p**olicy

polish	**p**ower	re**p**etition	stri**p**e
polite	**p**repare	re**p**ly	stu**p**id
political	**p**rice	re**p**ort	su**p**er
politician	**p**rincipal	re**p**ublic	sus**p**ect
politics	**p**rinciple	re**p**utation	swee**p**
pollution	**p**roper	ri**p**	sym**p**athetic
pond	**p**roperty	ri**p**e	sym**p**athy
pony	**p**roposal	ri**p**en	tad**p**ole
pool	**p**ropose	ro**p**e	ta**p**
poor	**p**ublic	scor**p**ion	ta**p**e
pop	**p**uck	se**p**arate	ta**p**ing
popular	**p**ull	Se**p**tember	tar**p**
population	**p**ump	shar**p**	tem**p**er
port	**p**unctual	shee**p**	ti**p**
position	**p**unish	shi**p**	to**p**
positive	**p**up	sho**p**	tra**p**
possess	**p**upil	ski**p**	tri**p**
possession	**p**uppet	slee**p**	tuli**p**
possible	**p**uppy	sle**p**t	ty**p**e
post	**p**urchase	sli**p**	u**p**
postpone	**p**ure	slo**p**e	u**p**on
pot	**p**urple	soa**p**	u**p**stairs
potato	**p**urpose	sou**p**	wea**p**on
potential	**p**ush	s**p**ring	whi**p**
potted	**p**ut	stee**p**	whis**p**er
pound	**p**uzzle	ste**p**	wi**p**e
pour	ra**p**id	sto**p**	worshi**p**
poverty	re**p**air	stra**p**	wra**p**
powder	re**p**eat	stri**p**	

b) "pp"

The consonant "p" sound heard in "pet" may be represented by the "pp" consonant digraph.

Double consonants usually signal that the preceding vowel letter is pronounced with a short vowel sound as in "ha**pp**en" and "p**u**ppet". For spelling purposes, when double consonants lie between two syllables, it is helpful to pronounce both consonants as in "a**p**-**p**ear" and "zi**p**-**p**er". With single-syllable words, such as "sto**pp**ed" and "tri**pp**ed", only one consonant "p" sound can be pronounced.

Many of the following words are pronounced with an initial schwa vowel sound in an open syllable. The words "appear" and "oppose", for example, are pronounced "uh-ppear" and "uh-ppose". For spelling purposes, it is helpful to pronounce such words with short vowel sounds in closed syllables as in "<u>a</u>p-pear" and "<u>o</u>p-pose".

a**pp**arent	disa**pp**oint	o**pp**osition	su**pp**ly
a**pp**ear	disa**pp**rove	po**pp**ed	su**pp**ort
a**pp**laud	ha**pp**en	pu**pp**et	su**pp**ose
a**pp**lause	ha**pp**y	pu**pp**y	ta**pp**ing
a**pp**le	hiccu**pp**ing (USA, CAN)	ri**pp**ed	ti**pp**ed
a**pp**lication	ho**pp**ed	ri**pp**ing	to**pp**ed
a**pp**ly	ho**pp**ing	sli**pp**ed	tra**pp**er
a**pp**oint	o**pp**ortunity	sli**pp**ing	tri**pp**ed
a**pp**rove	o**pp**ose	sto**pp**ed	tri**pp**ing
co**pp**er	o**pp**osite	sto**pp**ing	u**pp**er
disa**pp**ear		su**pp**er	zi**pp**er

E15.2　Rare Spelling Patterns

There are at least two rare spelling patterns for the consonant "p" sound heard in "**p**et".

a)　"gh"

The consonant "p" sound heard in "pet" may be represented by the "gh" consonant digraph.

hiccou**gh** (UK, CAN)
hiccou**gh**ing (UK, CAN)

b)　"ph"

The consonant "p" sound heard in "pet" may be represented by the "ph" consonant digraph. The letter "h" is silent.

In "diphtheria" and "diphthong", the "ph" spelling pattern is also pronounced with the consonant "f" sound. The "ph" spelling pattern usually represents the consonant "f" sound.

With the compound word "shepherd", the "ph" spelling pattern occurs incidentally. As the letter "h" in "herd" is no longer pronounced, only the consonant "p" sound remains.

*di**ph**theria*　　　　*di**ph**thong*　　　　she**ph**erd

E16　Spelling the Consonant "Q" Sound

There is no unique consonant "q" sound. In English spelling, the letter "q" represents the hard "c/k" consonant sound and is always followed by the letter "u". The letter "u" is usually silent, as (not) heard in "conquer" and "quiche".

Sometimes, however, the letter "u" represents the consonant "w" sound heard in "equation", "quick", and "quiet". The "kw" consonant sound heard in "quick" is almost always spelled with the letters "qu". The exceptions are generally made-up words or brand names such as "Kwik Cleaners".

The "que" spelling pattern also represents the hard "c/k" consonant sound and is found in words of French origin. Both the letter "u" and the letter "e" are silent. The "que" spelling pattern almost always occurs at the end of words. An exception is the word "queue". The word "queue" is also unique because the letters "ue" are repeated. The initial "que" spelling pattern represents the hard "c/k" consonant sound, and the final "ue" pattern represents the long "u" vowel sound heard in "feud" and "cute".

It may be noted that very few English words end with the letter "q". The name of the country "Iraq" is a notable exception. Words that sound like they end with a consonant "q" sound usually end with the letters "-c", "-k", or "-que". Also note that very few, if any, English words contain a double "qq" spelling pattern.

E17 Spelling the Consonant "R" Sound

When a vowel sound is followed by a single letter "r", an r-influenced vowel sound is often heard. See D5.

There are several different spelling patterns for the consonant "r" sound heard in "rice". The spelling patterns have been divided into major, minor, and rare spelling patterns.

E17.1 Major Spelling Patterns

There are three major spelling patterns for the consonant "r" sound heard in "rice".

a) "r"

The consonant "r" sound heard in "rice" may be represented by the letter "r".

aboard	alternative	astronaut	bury
across	angry	atmosphere	Calgary
actress	apart	attract	car
address	apparent	authorities	card
admire	appear	bare	care
advertise	approve	bear	career
affair	April	beard	century
afford	arch	beer	ceremony
afraid	area	before	chair
Africa	arena	border	character
agree	argue	born	cheat
air	arise	boundary	cheer
already	around	buried	children

chore	experience	hero	normal
Christmas	experiment	herself	north
clear	explore	history	Norway
coarse	factory	horizon	oar
comfort	fair	horizontal	or
compare	far	horse	orange
construction	fear	hour	order
cork	February	hungry	ordinary
corporation	fierce	hurt	ore
country	figure	ignore	organ
courage	floor	important	organization
course	Florida	increase	organize
court	flour	industry	origin
critic	for	inform	original
crown	force	inquire	ornament
cure	forceful	inquiry	our
curious	forget	insurance	ourselves
customary	forgetful	insure	pair
dairy	forgive	interfere	parade
dare	forgot	January	parcel
dark	fork	jewellery (UK, CAN)	pardon
dear	formal	jewelry (USA)	parent
declare	former	laboratory	perform
deer	formula	large	period
desire	fort	larger	pirate
despair	fortunate	librarian	plural
destroy	fortune	library	poor
dictionary	forty	literary	pour
dinosaur	forward	lord	prairie
direct	four	majority	prepare
direction	fourteen	mare	pure
director	fourth	mark	quart
disappear	furious	material	quarter
disapprove	garage	memory	rabbit
disregard	gear	mere	raccoon
disrespect	giraffe	metric	race
door	glory	momentary	radar
during	gorilla	moral	radio
ear	grace	morale	raft
empire	hair	more	rail
enforce	hairy	morning	rain
engineer	harbor (USA)	mysterious	raise
enormous	harbour (UK, CAN)	near	ran
entrance	harvest	necessary	Randy
environment	hear	nor	rang
Europe	here		range

ranger	relief	ride	rugged
rank	relieve	ridiculous	ruin
rap	religion	rifle	rule
rapid	remain	right	run
rare	remark	ring	rush
rarity	remark	rip	Russia
rat	remedy	ripe	Russian
rate	remember	ripen	rust
rather	remind	rise	Ryan
raw	rent	risk	sacred
ray	repair	rival	sacrifice
razor	repair	rivalry	salary
reach	repeat	river	satisfactory
read	repetition	road	scare
ready	replace	roar	scary
real	reply	roast	scenery
reason	report	rob	score
Rebecca	represent	robber	scorn
receipt	reproduce	robin	scorpion
receive	reproduction	robot	secret
recent	republic	rock	separate
recess	reputation	rocket	series
recognition	request	rod	serious
recognize	require	rode	share
recommend	requirement	role	shark
record	rescue	roll	sharp
red	research	roof	sheriff
redden	reserve	room	shore
reduce	resign	rooster	short
reduction	resist	root	sincere
refer	resource	rope	skirt
referee	respect	rose	smart
reference	responsible	Ross	sore
reflect	rest	rot	sort
reflection	restaurant	rote	sour
reform	result	rotten	spare
refresh	retire	rough	spark
refuse	retired	round	spirit
regard	return	route	sport
register	review	row	square
regret	reward	royal	stair
regular	ribbon	royalty	star
rejoice	rice	rub	stare
relate	rich	rubbish	start
relation	Rick	rude	startle
relative	rid	rug	steer

store	thesaurus	tortoise	wharf
store	thorn	tour	where
stories	thread	unfortunate	wire
storm	threat	upstairs	wore
stormy	three	variety	world
story	threw	various	worn
support	throat	very	year
sure	through	war	your
swear	throw	ware	zero
tear	thrown	warm	
their	tire (USA, CAN)	warn	
there	tired	wear	

b)   "rr"

The consonant "r" sound heard in "rice" may be represented by the "rr" consonant digraph.

In keeping with the doubling principle, the double "rr" spelling pattern usually signals that the preceding vowel letter is pronounced with a short vowel sound as in "err" and "carrot", not an r-influenced vowel sound. See D5. However, there are exceptions. Words marked with an asterisk below are pronounced with an r-influenced vowel sound.

For spelling purposes, when double consonants lie between two syllables, it is helpful to pronounce both consonants as in "ar-row". With single-syllable words, such as "err" and "purr", only one consonant "r" sound can be pronounced.

Some of the following words are pronounced with an initial schwa vowel sound in an open syllable. The words "arrest" and "arrive", for example, are pronounced "uh-rrest" and "uh-rrive". For spelling purposes, it is helpful to pronounce such words with short vowel sounds in closed syllables as in "ar-rest" and "ar-rive".

arrange*	correct*	hurry*	shirr
arrest*	corridor	interrupt*	sorry
arrive*	current*	Kerry	squirrel*
arrow	err	marriage	starry
barrel	error	married	stirrup*
berry	furry*	marry	surround*
borrow	horrible	merry	terrible
burr*	horrid	mirror	terror
carriage	horror	narrow	tomorrow
carrot	hurrah*	porridge	whirr* (UK, CAN)
carry	hurricane*	purr*	worry*
cherry	hurried*	quarrel	

c)   "wr-"

The consonant "r" sound heard in "rice" may be represented by the "wr-" consonant digraph. The letter "w" is silent.

The "wr" spelling pattern only forms onsets and is, therefore, only found at the beginning of words and syllables. The "wr" spelling pattern only represents the consonant "r" sound as heard in "write". Many "wr-" words are related to the idea of twisting.

play**wr**ight	**wr**eck	**Wr**ight	**wr**its
re**wr**ite	**wr**en	**wr**ing	**wr**itten
wraith	**wr**ench	**wr**inkle	**wr**ong
wrangle	**wr**est	**wr**ist	**wr**ote
wrap	**wr**estle	**wr**ite	**wr**ought
wrath	**wr**etch	**wr**ithe	**wr**ung
wreath	**wr**iggle	**wr**iting	**wr**y

E17.2   Minor Spelling Patterns

There are two minor spelling patterns for the consonant "r" sound heard in "rice".

a)   "rh"

The consonant "r" sound heard in "rice" may be represented by the "rh" consonant digraph. The letter "h" is silent. This spelling pattern is Greek in origin.

rhapsody	**rh**eumatism	**rh**izome	**rh**ubarb
rheostat	**Rh**ine	**Rh**ode Island	**rh**yme
rhetoric	**rh**inestone	**Rh**odes	**rh**ythm
rhetorical	**rh**ino	**rh**ododendron	**rh**ythmic
rheumatic	**rh**inoceros	**rh**ombus	**rh**ythmical

b)   "rrh"

The consonant "r" sound heard in "rice" may be represented by the "rrh" consonant digraph. The extra letter "r" and the letter "h" are silent.

cata**rrh**	dia**rrh**ea	hemo**rrh**age
ci**rrh**osis	(USA, CAN)	(USA)
dia**rrh**oea	haemo**rrh**age	my**rrh**
(UK, CAN)	(UK, CAN)	

E17.3   Rare Spelling Patterns

There are at least three rare spelling patterns for the consonant "r" sound heard in "rice".

a) "rps"

The consonant "r" sound heard in "rice" may be represented by the "rps" consonant digraph. The letters "ps" are silent.

co**rps**

b) "rt"

The consonant "r" sound heard in "rice" may be represented by the "rt" consonant digraph. The letter "t" is silent.

mo**rt**gage

c) "lo"

The consonant "r" sound heard in "rice" may be represented by the "lo" consonant digraph.

The word "colonel" is pronounced "kur-nel". The consonant "r" sound is, to say the least, not well represented in the spelling.

co**lo**nel

E18 Spelling the Consonant "S" Sound

The first sound heard in "**s**alt" and "**s**illy" is sometimes called the consonant "s" sound. However, it is the same as the soft "c" consonant sound heard in "**c**ity" and "**c**ivil". In this book it is called the soft "c/s" consonant sound. See E3 for spelling patterns.

E19 Spelling the Consonant "T" Sound

There are many spelling patterns for the consonant "t" sound heard in "**t**all". The spelling patterns have been divided into major, minor, and rare spelling patterns.

E19.1   Major Spelling Patterns

There are four major spelling patterns for the consonant "t" sound heard in "**t**all".

a)   "t"

The consonant "t" sound heard in "tall" may be represented by the letter "t".

ability	accept	active	actress
about	accident	activity	admit
absolute	act	actor	adopt

adult	boat	contest	eat
advantage	bought	continue	educate
advertise	bright	contribute	effect
after	British	convenient	effort
almost	brought	correct	Egypt
alternative	bucket	country	elect
altogether	bullet	court	elevator
amount	but	create	empty
ancient	calculate	credit	entertain
ant	can't	crept	entitle
anxiety	cannot	critic	exact
apart	capital	cultivate	except
apartment	captain	curtain	excite
apparent	carpet	custom	exhibit
art	carrot	customer	exit
article	cart	cut	expect
artificial	cat	cute	extend
assist	caught	date	facility
astronaut	centimeter (USA)	daughter	fact
at	centimetre (UK, CAN)	dealt	factory
ate		deceit	fantastic
Atlantic	certain	deduct	fat
atmosphere	certainty	defeat	fate
attempt	character	definite	favorite (USA)
attract	chocolate	delicate	favourite (UK, CAN)
August	citizen	dentist	
aunt	city	desert	feet
authorities	closet	despite	felt
automobile	coat	destructive	fifteen
autumn	collect	detail	fifty
bait	comfort	detect	fit
basket	community	determine	flat
bat	compete	direct	float
beast	competition	director	foot
beat	competitor	dirt	forgot
beautiful	complaint	disaster	fort
beauty	complete	discontent	fortunate
belt	complicate	disrespect	forty
bent	computer	distance	fought
best	conductor	distant	fourteen
bet	congratulate	district	fruit
between	connect	doctor	frustrate
biggest	constructive	dot	gaiety
bit	contain	dreamt (Also dreamed)	gate
bite	container		get
blanket	content	duty	goat

got
grammatical
grateful
gratitude
great
greet
guitar
habit
habitat
hat
hate
heart
heat
heater
helicopter
helmet
hesitate
hit
hospital
hot
hotel
hurt
imaginative
imitate
immediate
important
insect
intelligence
intend
intention
interest
interfere
international
interrupt
into
invite
it
Italian
Italy
item
itemize
itself
jacket
jet
Jupiter
kept

kit
kitchen
kite
knelt (Also kneeled)
knit
laboratory
late
later
laughter
leapt
learnt (Also learned)
left
legitimate
lent
let
liberty
lift
limit
lit
liter (USA)
literary
literature
litre (UK, CAN)
lost
lot
loyalty
majority
material
mathematics
meant
meat
meet
met
metal
metre (UK, CAN)
metric
mighty
minute
mistake
moderate
mosquito
motel
motor
native
neat

negative
neglect
net
next
nineteen
ninety
not
note
notice
nut
object
October
octopus
omit
onto
operate
operator
opportunity
opposite
out
part
particular
parties
partner
party
pat
patriotism
peanut
penalty
perfect
permit
pet
photograph
photography
pilot
pirate
pit
pity
planet
plaster
plastic
plate
plenty
Pluto
pocket
poet

polite
political
politician
politics
positive
pot
potato
potential
poverty
practical
practice
pretence (UK, CAN)
pretend
pretense (USA)
private
product
profit
project
prompt
property
protect
puppet
put
quality
quantity
quart
quarter
quiet
quit
quite
rabbit
rat
rate
reflect
register
regret
relate
relative
repeat
repetition
report
representative
reputation
respect
responsibility

retire	skit	tank	Timothy
retired	slept	tap	tin
return	smart	tape	tine
robot	society	taste	tiny
rocket	soft	taught	tip
root	sort	tax	tire (USA, CAN)
rot	spat	tea	tired
rote	spelt	teach	title
route	(Also spelled)	team	to
royalty	spent	tear	toad
safety	spilt	teeth	toast
sat	spirit	telegraph	today
satellite	spit	telephone	toe
satellite	spite	television	together
satisfaction	split	tell	toilet
satisfactory	spoilt	temper	told
satisfy	sport	temperature	tomorrow
Saturday	spot	temple	ton
Saturn	start	tempt	tone
scientific	startle	tempting	tongue
scientist	state	ten	too
seat	state	tend	took
secret	street	tender	tool
sent	strict	tent	tooth
separate	student	tenth	top
September	subject	term	tortoise
set	suit	terrible	total
seventeen	support	terror	touch
seventy	suspect	test	tough
sheet	sweat	that	tour
shelter	sweet	theater (USA)	tow
shirt	sympathetic	theatre (UK, CAN)	towel
shoot	system	thirsty	tower
short	tab	thirteen	town
shot	table	thirty	toy
shout	tadpole	thought	tractor
shut	tag	throat	translate
simplicity	tail	ticket	treat
sister	tailor	tide	trout
sit	take	tidy	tube
site	taken	tie	Tuesday
sixteen	talk	tied	tulip
sixty	tall	tiger	Tummers
skate	Tamara	tight	tune
skeleton	tame	till	tunnel
skirt	tan	time	turn

turtle	university	wait	white
two	until	waste	winter
type	variety	water	witness
unfortunate	vegetable	went	write
unit	victory	wet	wrote
unite	visit	what	yet
unity	vote	wheat	

b) "tt"

The consonant "t" sound heard in "tall" may be represented by the "tt" consonant digraph.

Double consonants usually signal that the preceding vowel letter is pronounced with a short vowel sound as in "b**e**tter" and "wr**i**tten". For spelling purposes, when double consonants lie between two syllables, it is helpful to pronounce both consonants as in "ki**t**-**t**en". With single-syllable words, such as "bu**tt**", only one consonant "t" sound can be pronounced.

Many of the following words are pronounced with an initial schwa vowel sound in an open syllable. The words "attack" and "attend", for example, are pronounced "uh-ttack" and "uh-ttend". For spelling purposes, it is helpful to pronounce such words with short vowel sounds in closed syllables as in "**a**t-tack" and "**a**t-tend".

attack	bottle	flatten	pattern
attempt	bottom	forgotten	pretty
attend	butt	kitten	putting
attention	butter	latter	rotten
attentive	button	letter	scatter
attic	cattle	letting	settle
attract	committee	lettuce	spitting
battle	cottage	litter	splitting
better	cotton	little	spotted
bitter	fatten	matter	written

c) "-ght"

The consonant "t" sound heard in "tall" may be represented by the "-ght" consonant digraph. The letters "gh" are silent.

In Old English, the letters "gh" represented a sound that is no longer pronounced.[23] Today, it is uncertain whether the letters "gh" should be considered as part of the consonant "t" sound spelling pattern or as part of the spelling pattern for the preceding vowel sound.

The "-ght" spelling pattern only forms rimes and is, therefore, only found at the end of words and syllables.

It may be noted that the "gh" spelling pattern also represents the consonant "f" sound at the end of words as in "laugh" and the hard "g" consonant sound at the beginning of words as in "ghost. The majority of the time, however, the "gh" spelling pattern is silent and helps to represent a variety of vowel sounds as (not) heard in the words "high" and "though".

bi**ght**	fi**ght**	li**ght**ning	sli**ght**
bli**ght**	fou**ght**	mi**ght**	sou**ght**
bou**ght**	frau**ght**	nau**ght**	strai**ght**
brou**ght**	frei**ght**	nau**gh**ty	tau**ght**
cau**ght**	fri**ght**	ni**ght**	thou**ght**
deli**ght**	hei**ght**	ou**ght**	thou**ght**ful
drou**ght**	kni**ght**	ri**ght**	ti**ght**
ei**ght**	li**ght**	si**ght**	wei**ght**
ei**gh**ty	li**ght**ing	slei**ght**	

d) Suffix "-ed"

The consonant "t" sound heard in "tall" may be represented by the suffix "-ed" forming a consonant digraph. The letter "e" is silent.

The letters "-ed" form a common suffix that creates the past tense and past participle of regular verbs. Depending on the word to which it is attached, the suffix "-ed" may be pronounced "-id", "t" or "d". With base words that end with the consonant "d" or "t" sound, as in "decided" and "limited", the suffix "-ed" forms its own syllable that is pronounced "id". With base words that end with the hard "c/k" consonant sound or the consonant "p" sound, as in "hooked" and "slipped", the suffix "-ed" is pronounced "t". With other base words the suffix "-ed" is usually pronounced "d" as in "boiled" and "robbed".

Regular past-tense verbs that end with the consonant "t" sound are actually spelled with the suffix "-ed". There are, however, a number of irregular past-tense verbs such as "kept", "meant", "spilt", and "spoilt" that are spelled with the letter "t". It may be noted that the past tense of the word "spell" is sometimes spelt "spelled" and is sometimes spelled "spelt".

In the following words the suffix "-ed" is pronounced "t":

accomplish**ed**	deck**ed**	flapp**ed**	lac**ed**
capp**ed**	dock**ed**	forc**ed**	lapp**ed**
check**ed**	duck**ed**	hack**ed**	lik**ed**
*crook**ed***	finish**ed**	hook**ed**	milk**ed**
cupp**ed**	fix**ed**	hopp**ed**	mix**ed**

peck**ed**	ripp**ed**	stopp**ed**	trick**ed**
pick**ed**	slipp**ed**	thank**ed**	tripp**ed**
pluck**ed**	slopp**ed**	topp**ed**	vanish**ed**
press**ed**	smash**ed**	toss**ed**	walk**ed**
rebuff**ed**	stock**ed**	track**ed**	wash**ed**

E19.2   Minor Spelling Patterns

There are three minor spelling patterns for the consonant "t" sound heard in "**t**all".

a)   "bt"

The consonant "t" sound heard in "tall" may be represented by the "bt" consonant digraph. The letter "b" is silent.

In keeping with the doubling principle, the single vowel letter preceding the "bt" spelling pattern is usually pronounced with a short vowel sound.

de**bt**	dou**bt**	su**bt**le
de**bt**or	dou**bt**ful	

b)   "th"

The consonant "t" sound heard in "tall" may be represented by the "th" consonant digraph. The letter "h" is silent.

Es**th**er	**Th**ames	**Th**ompson
Thai	**Th**omas	**th**yme

c)   -te

The consonant "t" sound heard in "tall" may be represented by the "-te" consonant digraph. The letter "e" is silent. This spelling pattern is French in origin.

In French spelling a final letter "t" is silent as (not) heard in "ballet" and "depot". Adding a final silent letter "e" causes the letter "t" to be pronounced.

debutan**te**	fe**te**	garro**te**	rou**te**
eli**te**	for**te**	peti**te**	sui**te**

e)   "-tte"

The consonant "t" sound heard in "tall" may be represented by the "-tte" consonant digraph. The letter "e" is silent. This spelling pattern is French in origin.

In French spelling a final letter "t" is silent as (not) heard in "ballet" and "depot". Adding a final silent letter "e" causes the letter "t" to be pronounced.

Some of the following words have been anglicized by dropping the final "-te". The words "kitchenette" and "cigarette", for example, are also spelled "kitchenet" and "cigaret".

In keeping with the doubling principle, the single vowel letter preceding the "tte" spelling pattern is usually pronounced with a short vowel sound. The word "butte", however, is pronounced with a long "u" vowel sound.

bague**tte**	croque**tte**	laye**tte**	rose**tte**
barre**tte**	etique**tte**	mignone**tte**	roule**tte**
bu**tte**	gavo**tte**	pale**tte**	silhoue**tte**
casse**tte**	gaze**tte**	pipe**tte**	statue**tte**
cigare**tte**	kitchene**tte**	rose**tte**	ushere**tte**

E19.3   Rare Spelling Patterns

There are at least five rare spelling patterns for the consonant "t" sound heard in "tall".

a)   "cht"

The consonant "t" sound heard in "tall" may be represented by the "cht" consonant digraph. The letters "ch" are silent.

ya**cht**

b)   "ct"

The consonant "t" sound heard in "tall" may be represented by the "ct" consonant digraph. The letter "c" is silent.

The letter "c" is not always silent when followed by the letter "t" as the word "victim" illustrates.

Conne**ct**icut	**ct**enoid	indi**ct**	vi**ct**uals

c)   "phth"

The consonant "t" sound heard in "tall" may be represented by the "phth" consonant digraph. The letters "ph" and the second letter "h" are silent.

phthisic	**phth**isis

d) "pt"

The consonant "t" sound heard in "tall" may be represented by the "pt" consonant digraph. The letter "p" is silent. This spelling pattern is Greek in origin.

ptarmigan	**pt**eropod	**pt**omaine
pterodactyl	**Pt**olemy	recei**pt**

e) "z"

The consonant "t" sound heard in "tall" may be represented by the letter "z".

With the words "Nazi" and "scherzo" the letter "z" represents both the consonant "t" sound and the following soft "c/s" consonant sound. Neither sound is well represented in the spelling.

Nazi   scherzo

E20 Spelling the Consonant "V" Sound

There are many spelling patterns for the consonant "v" sound heard in "**v**an". The spelling patterns have been divided into major, minor, and rare spelling patterns.

E20.1   Major Spelling Patterns

There are two major spelling patterns for the consonant "v" sound heard in "**v**an".

a) "v"

The consonant "v" sound heard in "van" may be represented by the letter "v".

The letter "v" is rarely doubled. This is because a double "v v" would be easily confused with the letter "w". The word "never", for example, would look like "newer". Exceptions include the words "re**vv**ed" and "sa**vv**y".

Words that, according the doubling principle, should be spelled with a double "v v" following a short vowel letter are marked with an asterisk.

acti**v**ity*	a**v**enue*	ci**v**il*	de**v**elop*
ad**v**ance	a**v**erage*	ci**v**ilize*	de**v**il*
ad**v**antage	a**v**oid*	cle**v**er*	disco**v**er*
ad**v**enture	bea**v**er	con**v**enience	di**v**ide
ad**v**ertise	beha**v**ior (USA)	con**v**enient	di**v**ision*
ad**v**ice	beha**v**iour (UK, CAN)	con**v**ersation	ele**v**ator*
ad**v**ise	bra**v**ery	co**v**er*	ele**v**en*
a**v**ailable*	carni**v**al*	culti**v**ate*	en**v**elope
a**v**alanche*	carni**v**ore*	deli**v**er*	en**v**ironment

envy	invite	servant	vase
Evelyn	involve	service	vegetable
even	level*	seven*	vehicle
evening	movie	several*	veil
event	navy	silver	verb
ever*	nervous	slavery	verse
every*	never*	sovereign*	very
evidence*	obvious	survive	vessel
evil	over	television*	victory
favor (USA)	poverty*	travel*	view
favour (UK, CAN)	prevent	universal*	village
given*	prevention	universe*	villain
govern*	private	university*	violence
harvest	provide*	vacation	violent
heaven*	province*	vain	virtue
heavy*	rev	valley	visit
improvise*	review	valuable	voice
individual*	revise*	value	volcano
invent	revolve*	van	vote
invention	rival	variety	vowel
invisible	river*	various	voyage

b) Final "-ve"

The consonant "v" sound heard in "van" may be represented by the "-ve" consonant digraph.

The most common function of a final silent letter "e" is to signal that a preceding vowel letter is pronounced with a long vowel sound. In the words "brave" and "save", for example, the final silent letter "e" signals that the preceding letter "a" is pronounced with the long "a" vowel sound.

Many of the following words, however, end with a final silent letter "e" because it is a convention of English spelling that words do not end with the letter "v". The words "give" and "have", for example, are pronounced with a short vowel sound. Two exceptions are the words "rev" and "Slav", which are abbreviations of the words "revolution" and "Slavic" respectively. This convention makes it impossible for English spelling to properly represent the short vowel sounds in words that end with the consonant "v" sound.

above	attentive	cave	destructive
active	attractive	constructive	detective
alive	behave	curve	disapprove
alternative	believe	deceive	dive
approve	brave	decisive	drive
arrive	carve	deserve	drove

effectiv<u>e</u>	hav<u>e</u>	positiv<u>e</u>	solv<u>e</u>
elv<u>e</u>s	imaginativ<u>e</u>	preserv<u>e</u>	starv<u>e</u>
excessiv<u>e</u>	inclusiv<u>e</u>	prov<u>e</u>	stov<u>e</u>
expensiv<u>e</u>	involv<u>e</u>	receiv<u>e</u>	surviv<u>e</u>
explosiv<u>e</u>	leav<u>e</u>	relativ<u>e</u>	swerv<u>e</u>
extensiv<u>e</u>	liv<u>e</u>	reliev<u>e</u>	twelv<u>e</u>
fiv<u>e</u>	lov<u>e</u>	representativ<u>e</u>	wav<u>e</u>
forgiv<u>e</u>	mov<u>e</u>	reserv<u>e</u>	weav<u>e</u>
gav<u>e</u>	nativ<u>e</u>	revolv<u>e</u>	wolv<u>e</u>s
giv<u>e</u>	negativ<u>e</u>	sav<u>e</u>	yourselv<u>e</u>s
glov<u>e</u>	nerv<u>e</u>	serv<u>e</u>	
grav<u>e</u>	observ<u>e</u>	shav<u>e</u>	
griev<u>e</u>	ourselv<u>e</u>s	slav<u>e</u>	

E20.2   Minor Spelling Patterns

There are three minor spelling patterns for the consonant "v" sound heard in "**v**an".

a)   "f"

The consonant "v" sound heard in "van" may be represented by the letter "f".

While the consonant "v" sound is only represented by the letter "f" in the word "of", the word is frequently used.

o**f**

b)   "-lve"

The consonant "v" sound heard in "van" may be represented by the "-lve" consonant digraph. The letters "l" and "e" are silent.

In keeping with the doubling principle, the single vowel letter preceding the "-lve" spelling pattern is usually pronounced with a short vowel sound.

ha**lve**   sa**lve**

c)   "v v"

The consonant "v" sound heard in "van" may be represented by the "vv" consonant digraph.

This is a rare spelling pattern in English. Most words that, according to the doubling principle, should be spelled with a double "v v" following a short vowel letter such as "ever", "never", and "river" are spelled with a single letter "v".

re**vv**ed   re**vv**ing   sa**vv**y

E20.3 Rare Spelling Patterns

There are at least two rare spelling patterns for the consonant "v" sound heard in "**v**an".

a) "ph"

The consonant "v" sound heard in "van" may be represented by the "ph" consonant digraph.

Ste**ph**en

c) "w"

The consonant "v" sound heard in "van" may be represented by the letter "w".

wedeln

E21 Spelling the Consonant "W" Sound

There are many spelling patterns for the consonant "w" sound heard in "**w**in". The spelling patterns have been divided into major, minor, and rare spelling patterns.

E21.1 Major Spelling Patterns

There are four major spelling patterns for the consonant "w" sound heard in "**w**in".

a) "w"

The consonant "w" sound heard in "win" may be represented by the letter "w".

The consonant "w" sound usually forms onsets and is, therefore, most often found at the beginning of words and syllables. An important exception is when the consonant "w" sound is pronounced in the vowel diphthong heard in "loud" and "cow" in words such as "now", "pow", and "wow". See section D2.

The letter "w" only represents the consonant "w" sound when it is followed by a vowel, as in "**w**ay" and "**w**ild", or by a silent letter "h" and a vowel other than "o" as in "**w**hat" and "**w**here". The "wh(o)" spelling pattern, as in "whom" and "whose", represents the consonant "h" sound, not the consonant "w" sound.

Following a vowel letter, a silent letter "w" always forms digraphs representing vowel sounds such as the short "o" vowel sound heard in "str**aw**". As well, a silent letter "w" helps to represent a number of consonant sounds such as the soft "c/s" consonant sound heard in "an**sw**er".

In the following words the letter "w" is followed by a vowel letter:

always	wash	west	witness
awake	waste	wet	woke
away	watch	wicked	wolf
awkward	watching	wide	wolves
awoke	water	widow	woman
backward	wave	width	women
between	wax	wife	won
forward	way	wild	wonder
Hawaii	wayward	wilderness	wood
Norway	we	will	wool
reward	weak	willow	word
sandwich	wealth	win	wore
swallow	weapon	wind	work
wage	wear	window	world
wagon	weather	wine	worm
waist	weave	wing	worn
wait	wedding	winner	worry
wake	Wednesday	winning	worse
walk	weed	winter	worship
wall	week	wipe	worst
wander	weigh	wire	worth
want	weight	wisdom	would
war	weird	wise	wound
ware	welcome	wish	wow
warm	well	witch	
warn	went	with	
was	were	wither	

b)   "wh"

The consonant "w" sound heard in "win" may be represented by the letters "wh" when followed by a vowel other than the letter "o". The "wh" spelling pattern forms a consonant digraph. The letter "h" is silent.

The "wh" spelling pattern only forms onsets and is, therefore, only found at the beginning of words and syllables.

The letter "w" only represents the consonant "w" sound when it is followed by a vowel, as in "way" and "wild", or by a silent letter "h" and a vowel other than "o" as in "what" and "where". The "wh(o)" spelling pattern, as in "whom" and "whose", represents the consonant "h" sound, not the consonant "w" sound.

Many people pronounce the words "wail" and "whale" with the same consonant "w" sound. With the word "whale", however, some people pronounce a consonant "h" sound before the "w" sound. This, of course, is the reverse of how the word "whale" is spelled. This is referred to as an aspirated "h" as it is pronounced with a puff of air.

The aspirated "h" sound is heard in words that begin with "wh" such as "which" and "whether", not in words that begin with "w" such as "witch" and "weather". Also, the aspirated "h" sound may be heard in words such as "marij**u**ana" and "San **Ju**an".

a**wh**ile	**wh**eeze	**wh**iff	**wh**isk
whack	**wh**elp	**wh**ile	**wh**isker
whale	**wh**en	**wh**im	**wh**isper
wham	**wh**ence	**wh**imper	**wh**istle
wharf	**wh**ere	**wh**imsy	**wh**ite
what	**wh**ether	**wh**ine	**Wh**ite
wheat	**wh**ich	**wh**ip	**wh**y
wheel	**wh**ichever	**wh**irl	

c) "(q)u"

The consonant "w" sound heard in "win" may be represented by the letters "(q)u". The letter "q" represents the hard "c/k" consonant sound. The letter "u" represents the consonant "w" sound. This is a rare example of a vowel letter representing a consonant sound.

The "kw" sound heard in "quick" is almost always spelled with the letters "qu". The exceptions are generally made-up words or brand names such as "Kwik Cleaners".

This "(q)u" spelling pattern only forms onsets and is, therefore, only found at the beginning of words and syllables. On the other hand, the "que" spelling pattern, representing the hard "c/k" consonant sound as in "anti**que**", is found at the end of words and syllables. The letters "u" and "e" are silent.

Occasionally, there is a syllabic break between the letter "q" and the letter "u". The word "liquid", for example, is divided into syllables as "liq-uid". The letter "u" still represents the consonant "w" sound. More often, however, the letters "qu" remain together as a consonant blend forming an onset. The word "inquire", for example, is divided into syllables as "in-quire".

con**qu**est	e**qu**ity	**qu**antity	**qu**ilt
e**qu**al	e**qu**ivalent	**qu**arrel	**qu**it
e**qu**ation	fre**qu**ent	**qu**art	**qu**ite
e**qu**ator	in**qu**ire	**qu**arter	**qu**otation
e**qu**idistant	in**qu**iry	**qu**een	re**qu**est
e**qu**ilateral	li**qu**id	**qu**eer	re**qu**ire
e**qu**ine	**qu**ake	**qu**estion	s**qu**are
e**qu**inox	**qu**alification	**qu**ick	s**qu**eeze
e**qu**ipment	**qu**alify	**qu**iet	s**qu**id
e**qu**itable	**qu**ality	**qu**ill	s**qu**irrel

d) "u"

The consonant "w" sound heard in "win" may be represented by the letter "u". This is a rare example of a vowel letter representing a consonant sound.

The letter "u" only represents the consonant "w" sound in onsets and is, therefore, only found at the beginning of words or syllables; never at the end of words or syllables. . In the following words, the letter "u" combines with the preceding consonant letter to form a consonant blend onset. The words "penguin" and "persuade", for example, are broken into syllables as "pen-guin" and "per-suade".

ang**u**ish	disting**u**ish	ling**u**istic	s**u**ave
ass**u**age	g**u**ano	peng**u**in	s**u**ede
biling**u**al	G**u**inevere	pers**u**ade	s**u**ite
consang**u**inity	LaG**u**ardia	pers**u**asion	
c**u**isine	lang**u**age	p**u**eblo	
diss**u**ade	lang**u**id	sang**u**ine	

E21.2   Minor Spelling Patterns

There is one minor spelling patterns for the consonant "w" sound heard in "**w**in".

a) "o"

The consonant "w" sound heard in "win" may be represented by the letter "o". This is a rare example of a vowel letter representing a consonant sound.

With the words "one" and "once", the consonant "w" sound is followed by a short "u" vowel sound. Neither sound is well represented in the spelling.

The letter "o" only represents the consonant "w" sound in onsets and is, therefore, only found at the beginning of words or syllables; never at the end of words or syllables. The consonant blend "cho" forms an onset in the word "choir".

ch**o**ir   **o**nce   **o**ne

E21.3   Rare Spelling Patterns

There are at least two rare spelling patterns for the consonant "w" sound heard in "**w**in".

a) "ju"

The consonant "w" sound heard in "win" may be represented by the "ju" consonant digraph.

The letters "ju" only represent the consonant "w" sound in onsets and is, therefore, only found at the beginning of words and syllables; never at the end of words or syllables. In the following words the letters "ju" form an onset:

mari**ju**ana   San **Ju**an

b)   "ou"

The consonant "w" sound heard in "win" may be represented by the "ou" consonant digraph. This is a rare example of two vowel letters representing a consonant sound.

The letters "ou" only represent the consonant "w" sound in onsets and is, therefore, only found at the beginning of words and syllables; never at the end of words or syllables. In the following words the letters "ou" form an onset:

biv**ou**ac   **ou**abain

E22 Spelling the Consonant "X" Sound

The letter "x" does not represent a unique consonant sound. Rather, the sound associated with the letter "x" is made up of the hard "c/k" consonant sound followed by the soft "c/s" consonant sound heard in "a**x**e" and "fo**x**".

The letter "x" is never followed by the letter "s".

There are several spelling patterns for the consonant "x" sound heard in "a**x**e" and "fo**x**". The spelling patterns have been divided into major and minor spelling patterns.

E22.1   Major Spelling Patterns

There are two major spelling patterns for the consonant "x" sound heard in "fo**x**".

a)   "x"

The consonant "x" sound heard in "fox", (the hard "c/k" consonant sound followed by the soft "c/s" consonant sound), may be represented by the letter "x".

The consonant "x" sound often forms rimes and is, therefore, often found at the end of words and syllables. However, within words, the consonant "x" sound is sometimes divided between two-syllables. In the word "maximum", for example, the hard "c/k" consonant sound forms the rime of one syllable and the soft "c/s" consonant sound forms the onset of the following syllable as in "mack-simum".

The consonant "x" sound never forms onsets and is, therefore, never found at the beginning of words or syllables. When a word begins with the letter "x", such as "Xanadu" and "xylophone", it is usually pronounced with the consonant "z" sound. In the word "x-ray", the letter "x" actually represents a short "e" vowel sound onset followed by a consonant "x" sound rime.

The letter "x" is never followed by the letter "s". The "-x" spelling pattern provides a visual distinction between words such as "tax" and "tacks"; and "wax" and "whacks".

The letter "x" also represents the hard "g" consonant sound followed by the consonant "z" sound as heard in the words "exact" and "exhaust".

The letter "x" is never doubled. The doubling principle does not apply because the letter "x" represents two consonant sounds. A single vowel letter preceding the consonant "x" sound is usually pronounced with a short vowel sound.

axe	expense	extend	next
box	expensive	extra	relax
exchange	experience	extreme	saxophone
exclaim	experiment	fax	sex
excuse	expert	fix	six
exercise	explain	fox	tax
exhale	explode	max	wax
exhume	explore	maximum	x-ray
exit	explosion	Mexican	
expect	explosive	Mexico	
expend	express	mix	

b) "cks"

The consonant "x" sound heard in "fox", (the hard "c/k" consonant sound followed by the soft "c/s" consonant sound), may be represented by the consonant blend "cks".

The letters "cks" only represent the consonant "x" sound in rimes and is, therefore, only found at the end of words and syllables; never at the beginning of words or syllables.

In keeping with the doubling principle, the single vowel letter preceding the "cks" spelling pattern is usually pronounced with a short vowel sound.

ba**cks**	ki**cks**	pa**cks**	ta**cks**
bu**cks**	la**cks**	pi**cks**	tu**cks**
du**cks**	li**cks**	sa**cks**	wha**cks**
ha**cks**	mu**cks**	so**cks**	
ja**cks**	ni**cks**	su**cks**	

E22.2   Minor Spelling Patterns

There are two minor spelling patterns for the consonant "x" sound heard in "fo**x**".

a)   "cc(e)" and "cc(i)"

The consonant "x" sound heard in "fox", (the hard "c/k" consonant sound followed by the soft "c/s" consonant sound), may be represented by the letters "cc(e)" and "cc(i)".

With these spelling patterns, the first letter "c" represents the hard "c/k" consonant sound, and the second letter "c", followed by letters "e" or "i", represents the soft "c/s" consonant sound. This follows the rule that the letter "c" followed by another consonant letter represents the hard "c/k" consonant sound and that the letter "c" followed by vowel letters "e", "i", or "y" represents the soft "c/s" consonant sound. There is a syllabic break between the two consonant sounds. The word "soccer" is an exception to this spelling pattern.

In keeping with the doubling principle, the single vowel letter preceding the "cc" spelling pattern is usually pronounced with a short vowel sound.

a**cc**ent   a**cc**ident   su**cc**ess

b)   "xc(e)" and "xc(i)"

The consonant "x" sound heard in "fox", (the hard "c/k" consonant sound followed by the soft "c/s" consonant sound), may be represented by the letters "xc(e) and "xc(i)".

With these spelling patterns, the letter "x" represents the hard "c/k" consonant sound, and the following "c(e)" or "c(i)" spelling pattern represents the soft "c/s" consonant sound. This follows the rule that the letter "c" followed by vowel letters "e", "i", or "y" represents the soft "c/s" consonant sound. There is a syllabic break between the two consonant sounds. The word "exceed", for example, is pronounced "ek-seed".

In keeping with the doubling principle, the single letter "e" preceding the "xc" spelling pattern is pronounced with a short vowel sound.

exc̲eed   exc̲ellent   exc̲ept   exc̲ite

E22.3   Rare Spelling Patterns

There is at least one rare spelling pattern for the consonant "x" sound heard in "fo**x**".

a)   "xh"

The consonant "x" sound heard in "fox", (the hard "c/k" consonant sound followed by the soft "c/s" consonant sound), may be represented by the letters "xh". The letter "x" represents the consonant "x" sound, and the letter "h" is silent.

In keeping with the doubling principle, the single vowel letter "e" preceding the "xh" spelling pattern is pronounced with a short vowel sound.

e**xh**ibition

E23 Spelling the Consonant "Y" Sound

The letter "y" is unique because it is both a vowel letter and a consonant letter. As a vowel letter it is commonly used to represent the long "e" vowel sound as in "bab**y**" and "embr**y**o", the long "i" vowel sound as in "st**y**le" and "fl**y**", and the short "i" vowel sound as in "m**y**th". As a consonant letter, "y" represents the consonant "y" sound heard in "**y**es".

The consonant "y" sound often forms onsets and, therefore, is often heard at the beginning of words and syllables as in "**y**ear" and "law-**y**er". However, when helping to form the long "u" vowel sound heard "m**u**sic", the short "u" vowel sound heard in "c**u**re", and the schwa vowel sound heard in "reg**u**lar", the consonant "y" sound may be heard in other positions.

There are many spelling patterns for the consonant "y" sound heard in "**y**es". The spelling patterns have been divided into major, minor, and rare spelling patterns.

E23.1   Major Spelling Patterns

There are two major spelling patterns for the consonant "y" sound heard in "**y**es".

a)   "**y**"

The consonant "y" sound heard in "yes" may be represented by the letter "y".

At the beginning of a word or syllable, the letter "y" only represents the consonant "y" sound, never a vowel sound. In any other position, that is in rimes, the letter "y" always represents a vowel sound. The letter "y" represents vowel sounds far more often than it represents the consonant "y" sound.

The consonant "y" sound often forms onsets and, therefore, is often heard at the beginning of words and syllables. The word "beyond", for example, is pronounced "be-**y**ond".

barn**y**ard	**y**acht	**y**earn	**y**ew
be**y**ond	**y**am	**y**east	**y**ield
buo**y**ant	**y**ank	**y**ell	**y**oke
can**y**on	**Y**ankee	**y**ellow	**y**olk
farm**y**ard	**y**ard	**y**elp	**y**onder
law**y**er	**y**arn	**y**es	**y**ore
saw**y**er	**y**ear	**y**esterday	**y**ou
vine**y**ard	**y**earling	**y**et	**y**oung

youngster	yourself	youthful
your	youth	yuck

b) "i"

The consonant "y" sound heard in "yes" may be represented by the letter "i".

The consonant "y" sound often forms onsets and, therefore, is often heard at the beginning of words and syllables. The letter "i" often represents the consonant "y" sound as an onset to the final syllable of a word. The words "brilliant" and "junior", for example, are pronounced "brill-yunt" and "jun-yur".

auxiliary	Christian	Italian	rebellion
battalion	civilian	junior	senior
behavior (USA)	companion	medallion	Spaniard
behaviour (UK, CAN)	convenience	million	spaniel
	convenient	onion	stallion
billion	dominion	opinion	union
brilliance	familiar	pavilion	valiant
brilliant	genial	peculiar	warrior
bullion			

E23.2   Minor Spelling Patterns

An initial consonant "y" sound helps to form the following three vowel sounds. The consonant "y" sound is not well represented in the spelling of the words.

a)   Long "u" vowel sound heard in "music"

With the long "u" vowel sound heard in "music", a consonant "y" sound is pronounced before the long "u" vowel sound. See B7 for spelling patterns.

b)   Short "u" vowel sounds heard in "cure"

With the short "u" vowel sound heard in "cure", a consonant "y" sound is pronounced before the short "u" vowel sound. See C9 for spelling patterns.

c)   Schwa vowel sound heard in "regular"

With the schwa vowel sound heard in "regular", a consonant "y" sound is pronounced before the schwa vowel sound.

The consonant "y" sound often forms onsets and, therefore, is often heard at the beginning of words and syllables. The words "popular" and "regular", for example, are pronounced "pop-**y**uh-lar" and "reg-**y**uh-lar".

circular	population	ridiculous
popular	regular	

E23.3   Rare Spelling Patterns

There are at least two rare spelling patterns for the consonant "y" sound heard in "**y**es".

a)   "e"

The consonant "y" sound heard in "yes" may be represented by the letter "e". The consonant "y" sound only forms onsets, not rimes. The word "azalea" is pronounced "uh-zal-**y**uh".

azal**e**a

b)   "j"

The consonant "y" sound heard in "yes" may be represented by the letter "j". This spelling pattern is German in origin. The consonant "y" sound only forms onsets, not rimes. The word "hallelujah" is pronounced "hal-uh-loo-**y**uh".

halleluj**j**ah   Son**j**a

E24 Spelling the Consonant "Z" Sound

The consonant "z" sound is phonetically similar to the soft "c/s" consonant sound. The difference between the two sounds is that the consonant "z" sound is voiced, and the soft "c/s" consonant sound is unvoiced. We can feel our vocal cords vibrating when we pronounce the voiced consonant "z" sound heard in "buzz" and "zoo". Our vocal cords do not vibrate when we pronounce the unvoiced soft "c/s" consonant sound heard in "moss" and "see".

There are many spelling patterns for the consonant "z" sound heard in "bu**zz**" and "**z**oo". The spelling patterns have been divided into major, minor, and rare spelling patterns.

E24.1   Major Spelling Patterns

There are six major spelling patterns for the consonant "z" sound heard in "bu**zz**" and "**z**oo".

a)   "s"

The consonant "z" sound heard in "buzz" and "zoo" may be represented by the letter "s".

The letter "s" is rarely, if ever, used to represent the consonant "z" sound at the beginning of a word. On the other hand, the letter "z" is often used to represent the consonant "z" sound at the beginning of a word as in "zero" and "zoo".

The letter "s" also represents the soft "c/s" consonant sound.

business	laser	poison	resist
busy	mechanism	position	result
closet	miserable	positive	rising
composition	misery	presence	season
desert	museum	present	thousand
design	music	preserve	Thursday
desire	musician	president	Tuesday
disease	noisy	prison	visit
easily	observe	proposal	Wednesday
easy	opposite	reason	wisdom
hesitate	opposition	represent	
husband	physical	reserve	
invisible	pleasant	resign	

b) Final "-s"

The consonant "z" sound heard in "buzz" and "zoo" may be represented by a single final letter "-s". This spelling pattern, of course, only forms rimes.

The final "-s" spelling pattern also represents the soft "c/s" consonant sound.

English spelling does not favour base words ending with a single final letter "s". This is because the suffix "-s" is used to create the plural, possessive, and third-person-singular forms of words. To work around this, there are a number of alternative spellings to represent a final consonant "z" sound including "-se", "-ze", and "-zz".

There are exceptions to the rule that only the plural, possessive, and third-person-singular forms of words end with a single final letter "s". See the discussion regarding final "-s" representing the soft "c/s" consonant sound in E3.1 (c).

always	goes	Mary's	series
bananas	hers	means	theirs
besides	his	miles	themselves
clothes	hours	needs	Tom's
days	its	news	upstairs
diggings	ladies	ours	ways
does	leaves	ourselves	wolves
dogs	lions	remains	woods
drives	lives	says	yours
friends	Mars	scissors	yourselves

c) Final "-se"

The "z" sound heard in "buzz" and "zoo" may be represented by the "-se" consonant digraph. The final letter "e" is silent.

English spelling does not favour having base words end with a final single letter "s". This is because the suffix "-s" is often added to the end of words to create the plural, possessive, and third-person-singular forms of words. The "-se" word ending indicates that the "s" is not a suffix, signaling that words such as "disease" are not plural, possessive, or third-person-singular.

The "-se" spelling pattern provides a visual distinction between words such as "paws" and "pause", "pleas" and "please", "prays" and "praise", and "who's" and "whose".

With words such as "advise" and "refuse", the final silent letter "e" also signals that the preceding vowel letter is pronounced with a long vowel sound. A final silent letter "e" is not required in words such as "please" and "praise" because the long vowel sound is represented by a vowel digraph. It has only been added because of the convention.

The final "-se" spelling pattern also represents the soft "c/s" consonant sound.

accuse	close	lose	rise
advertise	compose	noise	rose
advise	confuse	nose	suppose
amuse	disease	oppose	surprise
applause	ease	pause	these
arise	enclose	please	those
because	excuse	praise	turquoise
cause	exercise	propose	use
cheese	hose	raise	whose
Chinese	*house* (Verb)	realise (UK, CAN)	wise
choose	improvise	realize (USA, CAN)	
cleanse	*Japanese*	refuse	

d) "z"

The consonant "z" sound heard in "buzz" and "zoo" may be represented by the letter "z". This spelling pattern forms both onsets and rimes.

At the beginning of a word, only the letter "z" is used to represent the consonant "z" sound, as in "zero" and "zoo, never the letter "s".

English words do not end with the letter "z" without it being doubled as in the word "buzz" or followed by a final silent letter "e" as in the word "haze". Abbreviations such as "quiz" and "wiz" and foreign words such as "fez" are exceptions to this rule.

The words "quiz" and "wiz" are abbreviations of the words "quizzical" and "wizard" respectively. Also, the word "Oz" from the Disney movie "The Wizard of Oz" is a made up name.

citizen	lazy	razor	zone
crazy	lizard	wiz	zoo
dozen	magazine	wizard	zoom
fez	organization	zebra	
horizon	Oz	zero	
horizontal	quiz	zipper	

e) Final "-ze"

The consonant "z" sound heard in "buzz" and "zoo" may be represented by the "-ze" consonant digraph.

It is a convention that English words do not end with the letter "z" without it being doubled as in "buzz" or followed by a final silent letter "e" as in "breeze". In words such as "blaze" and "prize", a final silent letter "e" also functions to lengthen the preceding vowel sound. A final silent letter "e" is not required in words such as "braise" and "freeze" because the long vowel sound is represented by a vowel digraph. It has only been added because of the convention.

braze	civilize	maze	size
blaze	freeze	organize	squeeze
breeze	gauze	prize	
bronze	haze	recognize	

f) "zz"

The consonant "z" sound heard in "buzz" and "zoo" may be represented by the "zz" consonant digraph.

The "zz" spelling pattern only forms rimes and is, therefore, only found at the end of words and syllables.

It is a convention that English words do not end with the letter "z" without it being doubled as in "buzz" or followed by a final silent letter "e" as in "breeze".

Double consonants usually signal that the preceding vowel letter is pronounced with a short vowel sound as in "jazz" and "puzzle". In the word "quizzical", the letter "u" represents the consonant "w" sound. Once this is taken into account, the "zz" spelling pattern follows a single short vowel letter. For spelling purposes, when double consonants lie between two syllables, it is helpful to pronounce both consonants as in "daz-zull". With single-syllable words, such as "buzz" and "buzzed", only one consonant "z" sound can be pronounced.

bedazzle	fizz	guzzle	whizz
buzz	fizzed	jazz	
buzzed	fuzz	puzzle	
dazzle	grizzly	quizzical	

E24.2   Minor Spelling Patterns

There are four minor spelling patterns for the consonant "z" sound heard in "buzz" and "zoo".

a)   "ss"

The consonant "z" sound heard in "buzz" and "zoo" may be represented by the "ss" consonant digraph.

Double consonants usually signal that the preceding vowel letter is pronounced with a short vowel sound as in "de**ss**ert" and "sci**ss**ors". For spelling purposes, when double consonants lie between two syllables, it is helpful to pronounce both consonants as in "po**s**-**s**ess".

The "ss" spelling pattern also represents the soft "c" or "s" consonant sound.

de**ss**ert	po**ss**ess	po**ss**ession	sci**ss**ors

b)   "x" (1)

The consonant "z" sound heard in "buzz" and "zoo" may be represented by the letter "x". The word "Xanadu", for example, is pronounced "zanadu".

The letter "x" also represents the hard "g" consonant sound followed by the "z" consonant sound in words such as "exact" and "example". See (c).

anxiety	Xanadu	xenophobia	Xerxes
bateaux	xenon	Xerox	xylophone

c)   "x" (2)

The hard "g" consonant sound followed by the consonant "z" sound may be represented by the letter "x". The word "exact", for example, is pronounced "eg-zact". Neither sound is well represented by the spelling.

In keeping with the doubling principle of English spelling, at least indirectly, the single vowel letter preceding the consonant "x" sound is usually pronounced with a short vowel sound.

The letter "x" also represents the consonant "z" sound in words such as "anxiety" and "xylophone". See (b).

With the word "exit", some speakers pronounced the letter "x" with the hard "c/k" consonant sound followed by the soft "c/s" consonant sound.

exact	example	*exit*
examine	exist	

d)   "xh"

The hard "g" consonant sound followed by the consonant "z" sound, may be represented by the letters "xh". The word "exhaust", for example, is pronounced "eg-zaust". Neither sound is well represented by the spelling. The letter "h" is silent.

Double consonants usually signal that the preceding vowel letter is pronounced with a short vowel sound as in "**exh**aust" and "**exh**ibit".

e**xh**aust	e**xh**austion	e**xh**ibit

E24.3   Rare Spelling Patterns

There are at least five rare spelling patterns for the consonant "z" sound heard in "bu**zz**" and "**z**oo".

a)   "cz"

The consonant "z" sound heard in "bu**zz**" and "**z**oo" may be represented by the "cz" consonant digraph.

With the word "czar", the letter "c" is silent. With the word "eczema", the "cz" spelling pattern is sometimes pronounced with the hard "c/k" consonant sound followed by the soft "c/s" consonant sound. Alternatively, it is pronounced with the hard "g" consonant sound followed by the consonant "z" sound.

With words such as "Czech" and "Czechoslovakia", the "cz" spelling pattern represents the consonant "ch" sound.

czar	e**cz**ema

b)   "sc"

The consonant "z" sound heard in "bu**zz**" and "**z**oo" may be represented by the "sc" consonant digraph. The word "discern" is pronounced "di-zern".

di**sc**ern

c) "sth"

The consonant "z" sound heard in "buzz" and "zoo" may be represented by the "sth" consonant digraph. With the word "asthma", some speakers pronounced the letters "sth" with the soft "c/s" consonant sound.

*a**sth**ma*

d) "ts"

The consonant "z" sound heard in "buzz" and "zoo" may be represented by the "ts" consonant digraph. The letter "t" is silent.

***ts**ar*

e) "tz"

The consonant "z" sound heard in "buzz" and "zoo" may be represented by the "tz" consonant digraph. The letter "t" is silent.

***tz**ar*

E25 Spelling the Consonant "CH" Sound

The consonant "ch" sound heard twice in "**ch**ur**ch**" is most often represented by the letters "ch" forming a consonant digraph. A consonant digraph is a string of two or more letters that join together to represent a single consonant sound. The consonant digraph "ch" functions like an extra letter of the alphabet.

There are many spelling patterns for the consonant "ch" sound heard twice in "**ch**ur**ch**". They have been divided into major, minor, and rare spelling patterns.

E25.1 Major Spelling Patterns

There are three major spelling patterns for the consonant "ch" sound heard twice in "**ch**ur**ch**".

a) "ch"

The consonant "ch" sound heard twice in "church" may be represented by the "ch" consonant digraph.

The "ch" spelling pattern forms both onsets and rimes.

Unfortunately, the "ch" spelling pattern is also used to represent the hard "c/k" consonant sound heard in "chronic" and the consonant "sh" sound heard in "chef". Furthermore, as discussed below, there are many other spelling patterns that represent the consonant "ch" sound.

The "ch" spelling pattern is found i) as an onset at the beginning of words and syllables, ii) following a long vowel sound, and iii) following a consonant sound. The "tch" spelling pattern is usually found following a short vowel sound. See (b).

i) At the beginning of words and syllables.

When the consonant "ch" sound forms an onset at the beginning of a word or syllable, it is almost always spelled "ch". There are rare exceptions to this rule including "**c**ello", "**Cz**ech", and "**Cz**echoslovakia".

In words such as "exchange" and "kitchen", pronounced "ex-**ch**ange" and "kit-**ch**en", the "ch" spelling pattern forms the onset of a syllable.

chain	**ch**arm	**ch**ick	**ch**irp
chair	**ch**ase	**ch**icken	**ch**ocolate
chalk	**ch**eap	**ch**ild	**ch**oice
champion	**ch**eat	**ch**ildren	**ch**oose
Chan	**ch**eck	**ch**ill	**ch**op
chance	**ch**eddar	**ch**imney	**ch**ore
change	**ch**eer	**ch**impanzee	**ch**urch
channel	**ch**eese	**ch**in	ex**ch**ange
chapter	**ch**erry	**ch**inchilla	kit**ch**en
chair	**ch**est	**Ch**inese	mis**ch**ief
charge	**ch**ew	**ch**ipmunk	pur**ch**ase

ii) Following a long vowel sound.

When the consonant "ch" sound follows a long or diphthongal vowel sound, it is usually spelled "ch". The words "couch" and "ouch" are pronounced with the vowel diphthong heard in "cow" and "loud". This spelling pattern forms rimes.

appr<u>oa</u>**ch**	<u>ea</u>**ch**	p<u>oa</u>**ch**	r<u>oa</u>**ch**
b<u>ea</u>**ch**	l<u>ee</u>**ch**	p<u>oo</u>**ch**	sp<u>ee</u>**ch**
c<u>oa</u>**ch**	<u>ou</u>**ch**	pr<u>ea</u>**ch**	t<u>ea</u>**ch**
c<u>ou</u>**ch**	p<u>ea</u>**ch**	r<u>ea</u>**ch**	t<u>ea</u>**ch**er

iii) Following a consonant sound.

When the consonant "ch" sound follows another consonant sound, it is usually spelled "ch". Also see the "tch" spelling pattern in (b).

This spelling pattern forms both onsets and rimes. In the word "lunch", for example, the letters "ch" help to form the rime "-un**ch**". In the word "mer-**ch**ant", the letters "ch" form the onset to the final syllable.

arch	chinchilla	lurch	pinch
avalanche	church	march	poncho
bench	French	March	porch
birch	inch	march	research
branch	launch	merchant	search
bunch	lunch	pilchard	

b) "tch"

When the consonant "ch" sound follows a short vowel sound, it is often spelled "-tch" forming a consonant digraph. The letter "t" is silent.

The "tch" spelling pattern usually forms rimes and is, therefore, most often found at the end of words and syllables.

The "tch" spelling pattern is an application of the doubling principle. The letter "t" is used because the consonant "t" sound and the consonant "ch" sound are phonetically similar.

Double consonants usually signal that the preceding vowel letter is pronounced with a short vowel sound as in "batch" and "ketchup". For spelling purposes, when double consonants lie between two syllables, it is helpful to pronounce both consonants as in "cat-cher" and "pit-cher". Words such as "ditch" and "fetch" are single-syllable words, so only the one consonant "ch" sound can be pronounced.

The letter "t" also helps to signal that the letters "ch" are pronounced with the consonant "ch" sound and not the hard "c/k" consonant sound or the consonant "sh" sound.

The "tch" spelling pattern is rarely used as an onset at the beginning of words and syllables. Exceptions include the Yiddish word "tchotchke" meaning "trinket", and Russians names including "Tchaikovsky" (the great composer) and "Tchekov" (also "Chekhov") the dramatist and author.

In the following words the short vowel sounds are underlined:

batch	Dutch	Mutchmor	sketch
bewitch	etch	notch	snitch
botch	fetch	nuthatch	stretch
butcher	hatchet	patch	**Tchaikovsky**
catch	hopscotch	pitch	**Tchekov**
clutch	itch	pitcher	**tchotchke**
crotch	ketch	satchel	watch
dispatch	ketchup	scotch	witch
ditch	match	scratch	

Unfortunately, there are exceptions to the above spelling pattern. In the following words a short vowel sound is followed by the "ch" spelling pattern, not the "tch" spelling pattern:

atta**ch**	du**ch**ess	ri**ch**	tou**ch**
ba**ch**elor	mu**ch**	sandwi**ch**	whi**ch**
deta**ch**	ostri**ch**	su**ch**	

c) "t(u)"

The consonant "ch" sound heard twice in "church" may be represented by the letters "t(u)". The letter "u" is pronounced in its own right.

The "t(u)" spelling pattern is found in a number of word endings including "-tural", "-tune", and "-ture". This spelling pattern forms both onsets and rimes. The word "nature", for example, is divided into syllables as "na-chure" while the word "natural" is divided into syllables as "nach-ural". The letter "a" in "nature" is pronounced with a long vowel sound in an open syllable. The letter "a" in "natural" is pronounced with a short vowel sound in a closed syllable.

*ac**t**ual*	for**t**unate	na**t**ural	signa**t**ure
agricul**t**ure	for**t**une	na**t**ure	si**t**uation
cen**t**ury	furni**t**ure	pas**t**ure	tempera**t**ure
congra**t**ulate	fu**t**ure	pic**t**ure	unfor**t**unate
crea**t**ure	litera**t**ure	punc**t**ual	vir**t**ue
*fac**t**ual*	mu**t**ual	punc**t**uate	vir**t**uous

E25.2 Minor Spelling Patterns

There are three minor spelling patterns for the consonant "ch" sound heard twice in "**church**".

a) "-sci(ous)"

The consonant "ch" sound heard twice in "church" may be represented by the "-sci(ous)" consonant digraph.

Some speakers pronounce this spelling pattern with the consonant "sh" sound.

*con**sci**ous*	*con**sci**ousness*	*uncon**sci**ous*

b) Final "-te(ous)"

The consonant "ch" sound heard twice in "church" may be represented by the "-te(ous)" consonant digraph.

righ**te**ous	righ**te**ousness

c) Final "-ti(an)" and "-ti(on)"

The consonant "ch" sound heard twice in "church" may be represented by the "-ti(an)" and "-ti(on)" consonant digraphs.

This is a rare pronunciation of the "-ti" spelling pattern. The "-ti" spelling pattern is usually pronounced with the consonant "sh" sound.

Chris**ti**an	indiges**ti**on	sugges**tion**
diges**ti**on	ques**tion**	

E25.3   Rare Spelling Patterns

There are at least three rare spelling patterns for the consonant "ch" sound heard twice in "**ch**ur**ch**".

a)   "c(e)"

The consonant "ch" sound heard twice in "church" may be represented by the letters "c(e)". This spelling pattern is Italian in origin.

cello	con**ce**rto	du**ce**

b)   "ci"

The consonant "ch" sound heard twice in "church" may be represented by the "ci" consonant digraph.

*an**ci**ent*

c)   "cz"

The consonant "ch" sound heard twice in "church" may be represented by the "cz" consonant digraph. This spelling pattern is Slavic in origin.

Czech	**Cz**echoslovakia

E26 Spelling the Consonant "SH" Sound

The first sound heard in "**sh**ell" is most often represented by the letters "sh" forming a consonant digraph. A consonant digraph is a string of two or more letters that join together to represent a single unique consonant sound. The consonant digraph "sh" functions like an extra letter of the alphabet.

There are many spelling patterns for the consonant "sh" sound heard in "**sh**ell". They have been divided into major, minor, and rare spelling patterns.

E26.1   Major Spelling Patterns

There are five major spelling patterns for the consonant "sh" sound heard in "**sh**ell".

a)   "sh"

The consonant "sh" sound heard in "shell" may be represented by the "sh" consonant digraph.

Fortunately, the "sh" spelling pattern is only used to represent the consonant "sh" sound. Unfortunately, many other spelling patterns are also used to represent the consonant "sh" sound.

The "sh" spelling pattern forms onsets at the beginning of words such as "**sh**e" and "**sh**ow". The "sh" spelling pattern also forms rimes at the end of words and syllables as in "wa**sh**" and "fa**sh**-ion". Within words, however, the "sh" spelling pattern rarely forms onsets except in words ending with "-ship" as in "ownership". Other spelling patterns including "ch", "ci", "si", "sci", "ssi", "s(u)", "ti", and "xi" are used to form onsets at the beginning of syllables. This may be heard in the words "ma**ch**ine", "fa**ci**al", "pen**si**on", "con**sci**ous", "admi**ssi**on", "in**su**re", "pa**ti**ent", "no**ti**on", and "comple**xi**on.

Occasionally the letters "sh" occur in a word incidentally, as in the word "mishap", and not as a digraph. In such cases, each letter represents its own regular sound.

accompli**sh**	fellow**sh**ip	refre**sh**	**Sh**eldon
a**sh**	fini**sh**	rubbi**sh**	**sh**elter
a**sh**amed	fi**sh**	ru**sh**	**sh**epherd
astoni**sh**	fla**sh**	**sh**ack	**sh**eriff
blu**sh**	fle**sh**	**sh**adow	**Sh**erlock
Briti**sh**	fooli**sh**	**sh**ake	**sh**ield
bru**sh**	fre**sh**	**sh**aking	**sh**ine
bu**sh**	go**sh**	**sh**all	**sh**iny
ca**sh**	leader**sh**ip	**sh**ape	**sh**ip
child**ish**	lea**sh**	**sh**are	**sh**irt
companion**sh**ip	mar**sh**	**sh**ark	**sh**ock
cra**sh**	ma**sh**	**sh**arp	**sh**oe
cru**sh**	member**sh**ip	**sh**ave	**sh**oot
cu**sh**ion	me**sh**	**sh**e	**sh**op
di**sh**	owner**sh**ip	**sh**ed	**sh**ore
distingui**sh**	poli**sh**	**sh**eep	**sh**ort
Engli**sh**	puni**sh**	**sh**eet	**sh**ot
establi**sh**	pu**sh**	**sh**elf	**sh**ould
fa**sh**ion	ra**sh**	**sh**ell	**sh**oulder

shout	**sh**ut	Spani**sh**	wi**sh**
show	**sh**y	spla**sh**	wor**sh**ip
shower	sma**sh**	wa**sh**	

b) "ch"

The consonant "sh" sound heard in "shell" may be represented by the "ch" consonant digraph.

This is sometimes referred to as a French "ch" as many of the following words are French in origin. The "ch" spelling of the consonant "sh" sound forms onsets as in "**ch**ef" and rimes as in "Mi**ch**-igan".

The "ch" spelling pattern is also used to represent the consonant "ch" sound heard twice in "**ch**ur**ch**" and the hard "c/k" consonant sound heard in "**ch**ronic". When the "ch" spelling pattern is followed by a consonant letter, as in "**ch**ronic", it usually represents the hard "c/k" consonant sound. One exception is the word "fuchsia".

ca**ch**e	**ch**arlatan	**Ch**eyenne	ma**ch**ine
chagrin	**Ch**arlotte	**ch**ic	Mi**ch**elle
chaise lounge	**ch**assis	**Ch**icago	Mi**ch**igan
chalet	**ch**ateau	**ch**iffon	musta**ch**e
chamois	**ch**auffeur	**ch**ivalry	non**ch**alance
champagne	**ch**auvinism	**ch**ute	para**ch**ute
chandelier	**ch**ef	cli**ch**é	pista**ch**io
chaparral	**ch**enille	cro**ch**et	rico**ch**et
chaperon	**Ch**evrolet	e**ch**elon	s**ch**wa
charade	**Ch**evy	gau**ch**e	

c) "ci"

The consonant "sh" sound heard in "shell" may be represented by the "ci" consonant digraph. The letter "i" is usually silent.

The letters "c(i)" often represents the soft "c/s" consonant sound as in "**ci**ty". The consonant "sh" sound is heard when the letter "c" is followed by a Latin suffix that begins with the letter "i" such as "-ial", "-ian", "-ient", "-iency", "-ion", and "-ious. The letters "c" and "i" combine to represent the consonant "sh" sound which is followed by an unstressed schwa vowel sound.

The "ci" spelling of the consonant "sh" sound forms both onsets and rimes. In the word "social", for example, the letters "ci" form an onset as in "so-shal". In "special", the letters "ci" form a rime as in "spesh-al".

academi**cia**n	*an**cie**nt*	atro**ciou**s	benefi**cia**l
aestheti**cia**n	artifi**cia**l	auspi**ciou**s	clini**cia**n

commer**cia**l	judi**cia**l	patri**cia**n	spe**cia**lity (UK, CAN)
cru**cia**l	judi**ciou**s	pediatri**cia**n (USA)	spe**cia**lty (USA, CAN)
defi**ci**ency	logi**cia**n	physi**cia**n	statisti**cia**n
defi**ci**ent	magi**cia**n	politi**cia**n	suffi**ci**ency
deli**ciou**s	mali**ciou**s	pre**ciou**s	suffi**ci**ent
effi**ci**ency	mathemati**cia**n	profi**ci**ency	superfi**cia**l
effi**ci**ent	morti**cia**n	profi**ci**ent	suspi**ciou**s
electri**cia**n	musi**cia**n	provin**cia**l	techni**cia**n
espe**cia**lly	offi**cia**l	ra**cia**l	tena**ciou**s
estheti**cia**n (USA)	offi**ciou**s	so**cia**l	vi**ciou**s
fa**cia**l	opti**cia**n	spa**ciou**s	vora**ciou**s
finan**cia**l	paediatri**cia**n (UK, CAN)	spe**cia**l	
gra**ciou**s			

d) "si" and "ssi"

The consonant "sh" sound heard in "shell" may be represented by the letters "si" and "ssi" forming consonant digraphs. The letter "i" is silent.

The letters "s(i)" often represents the soft "c/s" consonant sound as in "**s**ight". The consonant "sh" sound is heard when the letter "s" is followed by a Latin suffix that begins with the letter "i" such as "-ial", "-ian","-ion", and "-ion". The letters "s" and "i" combine to represent the consonant "sh" sound which is followed by an unstressed schwa vowel sound.

The "si" spelling of the consonant "sh" sound forms both onsets and rimes. In the word "expan**si**on", for example, the letters "si" form an onset as in "eck-span-shun". In "admi**ssi**on" the letters "ssi" form a rime as in "add-mish-un".

i) Latin suffixes "-ial" and "-ian"

The following words end with the Latin suffixes "-ial" and "-ian". Some of the following words are also pronounced with the consonant "zh" sound.

Asian	*Indonesian*	*Polynesian*	Ru**ssi**an
controver**si**al	*Malaysian*	Ru**ssi**a	

ii) Latin suffix "-ion"

The following words end with the Latin suffix "-ion".

The "-sion" word ending is usually pronounced with the consonant "sh" sound when it follows a consonant letter "l", "n", "r", or "s" as in "compul**sion**", "ten**sion**", "aver**sion**", and "impre**ssion**". In keeping with the doubling principle, the vowel letter preceding two consonants is usually pronounced with a short vowel sound. The letter "a" in "pa**ss**ion", for example, is pronounced with the short "a" vowel sound.

Conversely, the "-sion" word ending is usually pronounced with the consonant "zh" sound when it follows a vowel letter as in "ero_sion_". The preceding vowel is usually pronounced with a long vowel sound. The letter "a" in "occasion", for example, is pronounced with the long "a" vowel sound. However, the letter "i" is pronounced with the short "i" vowel sound when followed by "-sion" as in "colli_sion_" and "vi_sion_".

This spelling pattern is often derived from base words, such as "averse" and "tense", that end with "-se"; base words, such as "apprehend" and "convert", that end with "-d" and "-t"; and base words, such as "impress" and "depress", that end with "-ss".

admission	depression	immersion	procession
aggression	dimension	impression	profession
apprehension	discussion	mansion	session
ascension	dissension	mission	submission
aversion	diversion	omission	succession
commission	emulsion	oppression	suspension
comprehension	excursion	passion	tension
compulsion	expansion	pension	transmission
concussion	expression	percussion	version
confession	extension	permission	
conversion	*fission*	possession	

e) "ti"

The consonant "sh" sound heard in "shell" may be represented by the "ti" consonant digraph. The letter "i" is usually silent.

The letter "t" usually represents the consonant "t" sound as in "**t**ime". The consonant "sh" sound is heard when the letter "t" is followed by a Latin suffix that begins with the letter "i" such as "-ial", "-ient", "-ience", "-ion", and "-ious". The letters "t" and "i" combine to represent the consonant "sh" sound which is followed by an unstressed schwa vowel sound.

The "ti" spelling of the consonant "sh" sound forms both onsets and rimes. In "par**ti**al", for example, the letters "ti" form an onset as in "par-shal". In the word "ini**ti**al" the letters "ti" form a rime as in "in-ish-al".

i) Latin suffix "-ial"

The following words end with the Latin suffix "-ial".

circumstantial	essential	partial	presidential
confidential	influential	partiality	providential
credential	initial	potential	residential
deferential	martial	potential	spatial

substantial   torrential

ii) Latin suffixes "-ient" and "-ience"

The following words end with the Latin suffixes "-ient" and "-ience".

patient   quotient   patience

iii) Latin suffix "-ion"

The following words end with the Latin suffix "-ion". This is a very common spelling pattern.

With a few words, such as "question" and "suggestion", the "-tion" word ending is pronounced with the consonant "ch" sound.

action	cultivation	hesitation	position
addition	definition	ignition	prevention
admiration	deletion	imagination	production
adoption	depletion	imitation	prohibition
adoration	description	inflation	promotion
ambition	destruction	information	pronunciation
application	devotion	institution	protection
attention	dictionary	intention	qualification
attraction	digestion	international	ration
calculation	diminution	interruption	recognition
caption	direction	introduction	reduction
caution	discretion	invention	reflection
classification	discrimination	junction	relation
commotion	disposition	legislation	repetition
competition	distinction	mention	reproduction
completion	education	moderation	reputation
complication	election	motion	resolution
composition	examination	multiplication	restitution
concoction	exception	nation	retribution
condition	exclamation	national	satisfaction
congratulation	execution	notion	selection
connection (USA, CAN)	exemption	nutrition	situation
constitution	exhibition	objection	solution
construction	explanation	operation	station
contribution	exploration	opposition	suction
conversation	exposition	organization	translation
corporation	fraction	perfection	transportation
correction	frustration	petition	vacation
corruption	generation	pollution	
	gumption	population	

iv) Latin suffix "-ious"

The following words end with the Latin suffix "-ious".

ambi**tious**	face**tious**	preten**tious**
cau**tious**	ficti**tious**	supersti**tious**
conscien**tious**	infec**tious**	surrepti**tious**

E26.2   Minor Spelling Patterns

There are four minor spelling patterns for the consonant "sh" sound heard in "**sh**ell".

a)   "su", "ssu", "s(u)" and "ss(u)"

The consonant "sh" sound heard in "shell" may be represented by the "su", "ssu", "s(u)", and "ss(u) spelling patterns.

While it appears that the letter "u" represents the schwa vowel sound in words such as "sure", it is the "-re" spelling pattern that signals that a schwa vowel sound is pronounced just before the consonant "r" sound.

With words such as "measure" and "treasure", the "su" spelling pattern represents the consonant "zh" sound heard in "vision".

cen**su**re	in**su**re	**su**gar	ti**ssu**e
era**su**re	i**ssu**e	**su**gary	
fi**ssu**re	pre**ssu**re	**su**re	
in**su**rance	sen**su**ous	**su**rety	

b)   "sch"

The consonant "sh" sound heard in "shell" may be represented by the "sch" consonant digraph.

schedule (UK)	**Sch**indeler	**Sch**jerning
Schep	**sch**ism	**sch**wa

c)   "sci"

The consonant "sh" sound heard in "shell" may be represented by the "sci" consonant digraph.

The consonant "sh" sound is heard when the letters "sc" are followed by a Latin suffix that begins with the letter "i" such as "-ient", "-ience", "-ion", and "-ious". The letters "sc" and "i" combine to represent the consonant "sh" sound which is followed by an unstressed schwa vowel sound.

The words "conscious", "consciousness", and "unconscious" are also pronounced with the "ch" consonant sound.

con**sci**ence con**sci**<u>on</u>able con**sci**<u>ous</u>ness
con**sci**<u>ent</u>ious con**sci**<u>ous</u> uncon**sci**<u>ous</u>

d) "-t(u)"

The consonant "sh" sound heard in "shell" may be represented by the letters "-t(u)" in the word ending "-tual".

ac**tu**al fac**tu**al

E26.3   Rare Spelling Patterns

There are at least nine rare spelling patterns for the consonant "sh" sound heard in "**sh**ell".

a) "-ce"

The consonant "sh" sound heard in "shell" may be represented by the letters "-ce" in the word endings "-cean" and "-ceous". The "-ce" spelling pattern forms a consonant digraph.

crusta**ce**<u>an</u> curva**ce**<u>ous</u> herba**ce**<u>ous</u> o**ce**<u>an</u>

b) "-che" and "chi"

The consonant "sh" sound heard in "shell" may be represented by the letters "-che" and "chi" forming consonant digraphs. These spelling patterns are French in origin.

crè**che** mousta**che** (UK, CAN) musta**che** (USA)
mar**chi**oness

c) "chsi"

The consonant "sh" sound heard in "shell" may be represented by the "chsi" consonant digraph.

The word "fuchsia" is a rare exception to the rule that the "ch" spelling pattern followed by a consonant letter, as in the word "chronic", represents the hard "c/k" consonant sound.

fu**chsi**a

d) "psh"

The consonant "sh" sound heard in "shell" may be represented by the "psh" consonant digraph.

pshaw

e) "sc"

The consonant "sh" sound heard in "shell" may be represented by the "sc" consonant digraph.

The letters "sc" followed by "e", "i", or "y" usually represents the soft "c/s" consonant sound heard in "scene" and "science". The letters "sc" followed by "a", "o", or "u" usually represents the consonant blend heard in the words "scale" and "score".

cre**sc**endo   fa**sc**ism   fa**sc**ist

f) "se"

The consonant "sh" sound heard in "shell" may be represented by the "se" consonant digraph.

*nau*se*ous*   **Se**an

g) "-xi(on)"

The hard "c/k" consonant sound heard in "cat" and "key" followed by consonant "sh" sound heard in "shell" may be represented by the letters "-xi(on)" in the word ending "-xion". Neither sound is well represented by the spelling.

comple**xi**on   crucifi**xi**on

h) "-xi(ous)"

The hard "c/k" consonant sound heard in "cat" and "key" followed by the "sh" consonant sound, may be represented by the letters "-xi" in the word ending "-xious". Neither sound is well represented by the spelling.

an**xi**ous   no**xi**ous

i) "x(u)"

The hard "c/k" consonant sound heard in "cat" and "key" followed by the "sh" consonant sound may be represented by the letters "x(u)". Neither sound is well represented by the spelling.

All of the following words are also pronounced with the hard "g" consonant sound followed by the consonant "zh" sound.

luxuriant   *luxuriate*   *luxurious*   *luxury*

E27 Spelling the Consonant "TH" Sound

The consonant "th" sound heard in "**th**is" and "**th**ank" is only represented by the letters "th" forming a consonant digraph. A consonant digraph is a string of two or more letters that join together to represent a single unique consonant sound. The consonant digraph "th" functions like an extra letter of the alphabet.

Actually, there are two "th" sounds. If you listen carefully, you may notice that the "th" sound heard in "this" and "that" is different than the "th" sound heard in "think" and "thin". The "th" sound heard in "this" and "that" is a voiced phoneme, and the "th" sound heard in "think" and "thin" is an unvoiced phoneme. Our vocal cords vibrate when we pronounce voiced word sounds and do not vibrate when we pronounce unvoiced word sounds.

You can feel and hear the difference between the voiced and unvoiced sound in the following pairs of words.

Voiced	Unvoiced
this	think
than	thank
that	thatch
them	theme
there	theory

A careful consideration of the above table reveals that all of the words pronounced with the voiced "th" sound are structure words. Conversely, all of the words pronounced with the unvoiced "th" sound are content words. Content words, such as nouns, verbs, and adjectives are used in a sentence to express ideas. Structure words, such as prepositions and conjunctives, help to bind content words together into grammatically correct sentences. On their own structure words express very little meaning.

In the following sentence the voiced structure words are in italics and the unvoiced content words are underlined: "She thought *that this* theory expressed *the* theme better *than that other* theory."

There are exceptions to the above rules. The voiced "th" sound is heard in a number of content words. Within words, the voiced "th" sound is heard in content words that rhyme with the words "mother" and "father". A final voiced "th" sound is heard in content words that end with a final silent letter "e" such as "bathe", "breathe", and "clothe". This distinguished them from words such as "bath", "breath", and "cloth" that are pronounced with the unvoiced "th" sound. Also, the voiced "th" sound is heard in the word "smooth" and in the word "mouth" when used as a verb. The word "with" is pronounced with both the voiced and the unvoiced "th" sound.

In the words "asthma" and "isthmus", the "th" spelling pattern is silent. As well, in words such as "Thai", "Thames", and "thyme" the "th" spelling pattern represents the consonant "t" sound.

Dictionaries list more words that begin with the unvoiced "th" sound than with the voiced consonant "th" sound. This is because hundreds of content words such as "earth", "think" and "thread" are pronounced with the unvoiced consonant "th" sound. However, in ordinary use we find more words that begin with the voiced consonant "th" sound. This is because a small number of structure words are frequently used including "than", "that", "the", "their", "them", "then", "there", "these", "they", "this", "those", and "though".

E27.1 Voiced Consonant "th" Sound

The voiced consonant "th" sound heard in the words "this" and "that" is only represented by the letters "th" forming a consonant digraph.

As a general rule, structure words are pronounced with the voiced "th" sound and content words are pronounced with the unvoiced "th" sound.

The voiced "th" sound forms both onsets and rimes. Within words, the voiced "th" sound is heard in words that rhyme with the words "mother" and "father".

At the end of words, a final silent letter "e" usually signals the voiced "th" sound. So, for example, the unvoiced "th" sound heard in "bath", "breath", and "cloth" becomes voiced "th" sound in "bathe", "breathe", and "clothe". There are only a few exceptions to this rule. The voiced "th" sound is also heard in the word "smooth" and in the word "mouth" when used as a verb.

The word "with" is pronounced with the voiced "th" sound when the following word begins with a vowel or a voiced consonant sound.

although	father	mouthing	teething
bathe	feather	other	than
breathe	gather	rather	that
brother	lathe	scythe	the
clothe	leather	sheathe	thee
clothes	loathe	smooth	their
either	mother	soothe	them
farther	mouth (verb)	teethe	themselves

then	this	thy	worthy
thence	those	together	wreathe
there	thou	weather	
these	though	whether	
they	thus	*with*	

E27.2 Unvoiced Consonant "th" Sound

The unvoiced consonant "th" sound heard in the words "think" and "thin" is only represented by the letters "th" forming a consonant digraph.

As a general rule, structure words are pronounced with the voiced "th" sound and content words are pronounced with the unvoiced "th" sound.

The unvoiced "th" sound forms both onsets and rimes. Within words the "th" spelling pattern will usually be pronounced with the unvoiced "th" sound unless the word rhymes with the words "mother" and "father".

At the end of a word, the "th" spelling pattern almost always represents the unvoiced "th" sound heard in "bath", "breath", and "cloth". There are only a few exceptions. The voiced "th" sound is heard in the word "smooth" and in the word "mouth" when used as a verb. Words that end with the voiced "th" sound, such as "bathe", "breathe", and "clothe", usually end with a final silent letter "e".

The word "with" is pronounced with the unvoiced "th" sound when the following word begins with an unvoiced consonant sound.

anthology	method	theft	thought
athlete	moth	theme	thousand
author	mouth (noun)	theory	thread
bath	myth	therapy	three
birth	north	thermometer	thrifty
both	nothing	thesaurus	thrill
breath	oath	thesis	through
cathedral	orthodox	thick	thud
cloth	path	thief	thumb
death	pith	thigh	thump
earth	south	thimble	thunder
eleventh	sympathy	thin	tooth
enthusiasm	teeth	thing	truth
ether	thank	think	*with*
ethics	thatch	thirty	wreath
fifth	thaw	thistle	youth
fourth	theater (USA)	thong	
health	theatre (UK, CAN)	thorax	

E28 Spelling the Consonant "ZH" Sound

The consonant "zh" sound heard in "bei**ge**" and "vi**si**on" is difficult to name because it is not associated with a particular letter or consonant digraph. It is the French equivalent to the soft "g/j" consonant sound heard in English.

The consonant "zh" sound heard in "bei**ge**" and "vi**si**on" is represented by a number of spelling patterns, none of which includes the letters "zh". They have been divided into major, minor, and rare spelling patterns.

E28.1   Major Spelling Patterns

There are three major spelling patterns for the consonant "zh" sound heard in "bei**ge**" and "vi**si**on".

a)   "g(e)", "g(i)" and "-ge"

The consonant "zh" sound heard in "bei**ge**" and "vi**si**on" may be represented by the letter "g" when followed by vowel letters "e" or "i". The "-ge" spelling pattern forms a consonant digraph. These spelling patterns are French in origin.

The "g(e)" and "g(i)" spelling patterns form onsets. The "-ge" spelling pattern usually forms rimes.

barra**ge**	fusela**ge**	massa**ge**	presti**ge**
bei**ge**	gara**ge**	mira**ge**	re**gi**me
bour**ge**oisie	**ge**ndarme	monta**ge**	rou**ge**
camoufla**ge**	lin**ge**rie	negligee	sabota**ge**

b)   "si"

The consonant "zh" sound heard in "bei**ge**" and "vi**si**on" may be represented by the "si" consonant digraph. The letter "i" is silent.

The letters "s(i)" usually represents the soft "c/s" consonant sound as in "**s**ight". The consonant "sh" sound is heard when the letter "s" is followed by a Latin suffix that begins with the letter "i" such as "-ial", "-ian","-ion", and "-ion". The letters "s" and "i" combine to represent the consonant "sh" sound which is followed by an unstressed schwa vowel sound.

The "si" spelling of the consonant "zh" sound forms both onsets and rimes. In the word "A**si**an", for example, the letters "si" form an onset as in "A-**si**an". In "vi**si**on" the letters "si" form a rime as in "vi**zh**-on".

i) Latin suffix "-ian"

The following words end with the Latin suffix "-ian". Some of the following words are also pronounced with the consonant "sh" sound.

Asian	*Indonesian*	Parisian	Tunisian
Caucasian	*Malaysian*	*Polynesian*	

ii) Latin suffix "-ion"

The following words end with the Latin suffix "-ion".

The "-sion" word ending is usually pronounced with the consonant "zh" sound when it follows a vowel letter as in "erosion". The preceding vowel is usually pronounced with a long vowel sound. The letter "a" in "occasion", for example, is pronounced with the long "a" vowel sound. However, the letter "i" is pronounced with the short "i" vowel sound when followed by "-sion" as in "collision" and "vision".

Conversely, the "-sion" word ending is usually pronounced with the consonant "sh" sound when it follows a consonant letter as in "passion" and "mansion". In keeping with the doubling principle, the vowel letter preceding two consonants is usually pronounced with a short vowel sound. The letter "a" in "passion", for example, is pronounced with the short "a" vowel sound.

adhesion	division	inclusion	profusion
cohesion	erosion	intrusion	provision
collision	evasion	invasion	revision
conclusion	explosion	occasion	television
confusion	*fission*	persuasion	transfusion
decision	fusion	precision	vision

c) "-su(re)"

The consonant "zh" sound heard in "beige" and "vision" may be represented by the "su" consonant digraph. The letter "u" is silent.

While it appears that the letter "u" represents the schwa vowel sound, it is the "-re" spelling pattern that signals that a schwa vowel sound is pronounced just before the consonant "r" sound.

The "su" spelling pattern forms both onsets and rimes. The word "closure", for example, is pronounced "clo-zhur". The word "pleasure" is pronounced "pleazh-ur".

In words such as "sure" and "insure", the letters "su" are pronounced with the consonant "sh" sound.

clo**su**re	enclo**su**re	mea**su**re
compo**su**re	expo**su**re	plea**su**re
disclo**su**re	lei**su**re	trea**su**re

E28.2   Minor Spelling Patterns

There are two minor spelling patterns for the consonant "zh" sound heard in "bei**ge**" and "vi**si**on".

a)   "-s(ual)"

The consonant "zh" sound heard in "beige" and "vision" may be represented by the letters "-s(ual)".

ca**su**al   u**su**al

b)   "x(u)"

The hard "g" consonant sound heard in "goat", followed by the consonant "zh" sound heard in "beige" and "vision", may be represented by the letters "x(u)". Neither sound is well represented by the spelling.

All of the following words are also pronounced with the hard "c/k" consonant sound followed by a "sh" consonant sound.

*lux**u**riant*   *lux**u**riate*   *lux**u**rious*   *lux**u**ry*

E28.3   Rare Spelling Patterns

There are at least four rare spelling patterns for the consonant "zh" sound heard in "bei**ge**" and "vi**si**on".

a)   "j"

The consonant "zh" sound heard in "beige" and "vision" may be represented by the letter "j".

Jean (French John)   **j**ongleur

b)   "-ti(on)"

The consonant "zh" sound heard in "beige" and "vision" may be represented by the "-ti" consonant digraph. The letter "i" is silent. This spelling pattern is usually pronounced with the consonant "sh" sound.

equa**ti**on

c) "-zi(er)"

The consonant "zh" sound heard in "beige" and "vision" may be represented by the letters "-zi(er)".

bra**zi**er   gla**zi**er

d) Final "-zu(re)"

The consonant "zh" sound heard in "beige" and "vision" may be represented by the "zu" consonant digraph. The letter "u" is silent.

While it appears that the letter "u" represents the schwa vowel sound, it is the "-re" spelling pattern that signals that a schwa vowel sound is pronounced just before the consonant "r" sound.

a**zu**re   sei**zu**re

Part F: Consonant Blends

F1 Introduction

While syllables have only one vowel sound, they often have a number of consonant sounds. A syllable may begin with one or more consonant sounds and may end with one or more consonant sounds.

A consonant blend occurs when two or more consonant sounds flow together without a syllabic break, and each consonant sound is pronounced. The letters "bl-" in "block", for example, form a consonant blend. Consonant blends may be distinguished from consonant digraphs. A consonant digraph is a string of two or more letters that join together to represent a single consonant sound. The letters "ck" in "block", for example, form a consonant digraph.

As discussed in A7.1, syllables are made up of onsets and rimes. An onset consists of all of the consonant sounds, if any, that are pronounced before the vowel sound in a syllable. A rime consists of all of the sounds that follow the onset. Every rime begins with a vowel sound and may end with one or more consonant sounds. Consonant blends are found in both onsets and rimes. That is, a syllable may begin with a consonant blend and/or end with a consonant blend.

Some consonant blends, such as the letters "cl-" in "clean", only form onsets and are, therefore, only found at the beginning of words and syllables. Other consonant blends, such as the letters "mp" in "stamp", only form rimes and are, therefore, only found at the end of words and syllables. A few consonant blends form both onsets and rimes, and so are found both at the beginning and at the end of words and syllables.

Letters that form a consonant blend at the beginning or end of a word may be divided by a syllabic break in the middle of a word. For example, while the letters "br-" form a consonant blend in "**br**own", they are divided by a syllabic break in the word "Fe**b**-**r**uary". Likewise, while the letters "-mp" form a consonant blend in "sta**mp**", they are divided by a syllabic break in the word "cha**m**-**p**ion".

What then determines where a syllabic break will occur within a word? Three spelling patterns may be noted. First of all, if three consonant letters appear in the middle of a word, a syllabic break will divide one consonant from a remaining consonant blend or consonant digraph. The word "umbrella", for example, is pronounced "**um**-**br**ella". Likewise, the word "e**mpt**y", is pronounced "e**mp**-**t**y". Secondly, a prefix is often followed by a syllabic break allowing a consonant blend to form an onset to the following syllable. This is heard in words such as "a-**br**oad" and "in-**cr**ease".

Thirdly, the doubling principle comes into play. The doubling principle reflects the tendency in English speech for syllables to begin with a consonant sound. If there is only one consonant letter between syllables, it will usually attach as an onset to the following syllable. The result is that the first syllable will be left open and, consequently, pronounced with a long vowel sound. The word "writing", for example, is pronounced "wry-**t**ing". If two consonant letters fall between syllables, one will usually remain attached to the preceding syllable, and the second will attach as an onset to the following syllable. This results in the first syllable being closed and, consequently, pronounced with a short vowel sound. For this reason, consonant blends are often divided between syllables. The words "lasting", "empire", and "window", for example, are pronounced "l**as**-**t**ing", "**em**-**p**ire", and "w**in**-**d**ow". Occasionally, however, a consonant blend will remain intact following a long vowel sound. The word "progress", for example, is pronounced "pr**o**-**gr**ess". Likewise, the word "library" is pronounced "l**ie**-**br**ary".

Note that all of the following consonant blends have at least one of the following consonant letters: "l", "m", "n", "r", "s", "t", or "w".

F2 Common Consonant Blends

"bl-" as in "blue"

The consonant blend "bl-" heard in the word "blue" forms onsets found at the beginning of words and syllables.

Within words, however, the letters "b" and "l" may divide between syllables following a short vowel sound as in "est**ab**-**l**ish" and "pr**ob**-**l**em". The letters "bl-" will usually remain intact following a prefix that ends with a vowel, following another consonant, and following a long vowel sound.

black	**bl**eed	**bl**iss	**bl**oom
blade	**bl**emish	**bl**oated	**bl**ossom
blame	**bl**ess	**bl**ock	**bl**ow
blanket	**bl**imp	**bl**ond	**bl**own
blast	**bl**ind	**bl**ood	**bl**ue

"-bl" as in "table"

The consonant blend "-bl" heard in the word "table" forms rimes found at the end of words and syllables.

This is not a true consonant blend because a schwa vowel sound is pronounced between the letters "b" and "l". The word "table", for example, is pronounced "ta-**b**u**ll**". The final silent letter "e" signals the schwa vowel sound.

a**bl**e	possi**bl**e	sylla**bl**e
bi**bl**e	predicta**bl**e	ta**bl**e
dou**bl**e	suita**bl**e	trou**bl**e

"br-" as in "break"

The consonant blend "br-" heard in the word "break" forms onsets found at the beginning of words and syllables.

Within words, however, the letters "b" and "r" may divide between syllables following a short vowel sound as in "F**eb**-**r**uary". The letters "br-" will usually remain intact following a prefix that ends with a vowel as in "a̱-**br**oad" and "ze̱-**br**a", following another consonant as in "um̱-**br**ella", and following a long vowel sound as in "vi̱-**br**ate".

a̱**br**oad	**br**awny	**br**idge	**br**other
brag	**br**ead	**br**ight	**br**ought
brain	**br**eak	**br**ing	**br**own
brake	**br**eakfast	**Br**itish	**br**uise
branch	**br**eath	**br**oad	**br**ush
brand	**br**eathe	**br**oke	li̱**br**ary
brass	**br**eeze	**br**oken	um̱**br**ella
brave	**br**ibe	**br**ook	vi̱**br**ate
bravery	**br**ick	**br**oom	ze̱**br**a

"chl-" as in "chloride"

The consonant blend "chl-" heard in the word "chloride" forms onsets found at the beginning of words and syllables.

Following a prefix, the letters "chl-" will remain intact as in "tetra-**chl**oride". Occasionally, the letters "chl" appear incidentally as in "sear**chl**ight".

Chlamydia	**chl**oric	**chl**oroform
Chloe	**chl**oride	**chl**orophyll
chloramine	**chl**orine	tetra**chl**oride

"chr-" as in "Christmas"

The consonant blend "chr-" heard in the word "Christmas" forms onsets found at the beginning of words and syllables.

Following a prefix or another consonant letter, the letters "chr-" will remain intact as in "mono-**chr**omatic". In "o**chr**e" and "sepul**chr**e", the letters "chr" do not form a true consonant blend. The letters "ch" and "r" are separated by a schwa vowel sound.

Christ	**Chr**istmas	**chr**onicle	**chr**ysanthemum
christen	**Chr**istopher	**chr**onograph	mono**chr**omatic
Christian	**chr**omatic	**chr**onological	mono**chr**ome
Christianity	**chr**ome	**chr**onology	o**chr**e
Christina	**chr**omium	**chr**onometer	sepul**chr**e
Christine	**chr**onic	**chr**ysalis	syn**chr**onize

"cl-" as in "clear"

The consonant blend "cl-" heard in the word "clear" forms onsets found at the beginning of words and syllables.

Within words, however, the letters "c" and "l" may divide between syllables following a short vowel sound as in "d<u>e</u>c-laration". The letters "cl-" will usually remain intact following a prefix that ends with a vowel, following another consonant as in "i<u>n</u>-clusive" and "e<u>x</u>-claim", and following a long vowel sound as in "d<u>e</u>-clare".

claim	**cl**ean	**cl**oister	**cl**oudy
Claire	**cl**ear	**cl**ose	**cl**own
clam	**Cl**em	**cl**oset	**cl**ub
clap	**cl**erk	**cl**oth	**cl**unk
class	**cl**ever	**cl**othe	de**cl**are
classification	**cl**iff	**cl**othes	en**cl**ose
claw	**cl**imb	**cl**othing	ex**cl**aim
clay	**cl**ock	**cl**oud	in**cl**usive

"cr-" as in "creek"

The consonant blend "cr-" heard in the word "creek" forms onsets found at the beginning of words and syllables.

Within words, however, the letters "c" and "r" may divide between syllables following a short vowel sound as in "s<u>e</u>c-retary". The letters "cr-" will usually remain intact following a prefix that ends with a vowel as in "d<u>e</u>-crease", following another consonant as in "i<u>n</u>-crease", and following a long vowel sound as in "s<u>e</u>-cret".

crack	create	criminal	cruel
cracker	creature	cringe	cruise
craft	credit	critic	crumb
crash	creek	crocodile	crumpet
crawl	creep	crook	crush
crayon	Creole	crop	cry
crazy	crew	cross	decrease
creak	cried	crowd	secret
cream	crime	crown	increase

"-ct" as in "project"

The consonant blend "-ct" heard in the word "project" forms rimes found at the end of words and syllables.

Within words, however, the letters "c" and "t" may divide between syllables, as in "projec-tor", unless they are followed by a third consonant letter as in "respect-ful".

connect	neglect	respect
disrespect	project	respectful
district	reflect	strict

"dr-" as in "drum"

The consonant blend "dr-" heard in the word "drum" forms onsets found at the beginning of words and syllables.

Within words, the letters "d" and "r" rarely divide between syllables. The letters "dr-" will usually remain intact following another consonant as in "hun-dred" and following a long vowel sound as in "hy-draulic".

children	dream	droll	dry
drag	dregs	drop	hindrance
dragon	dress	drove	hundred
drank	drew	drown	hydraulic
draw	drink	drug	Mildred
dread	drip	drum	Sandra
dreadful	drive	drunk	

"dw-" as in "dwell"

The consonant blend "dw-" heard in the word "dwell" forms onsets found at the beginning of words and syllables.

Within words, however, the letters "d" and "w" may divide between syllables following a short vowel sound as in "E<u>d</u>-ward". The letters "dw-" will usually remain intact following a prefix that ends with a vowel, following another consonant, and following a long vowel sound.

dwarf	**dw**ell	**dw**indle
dweeb	**dw**elling	

"fl-" as in "flag"

The consonant blend "fl-" heard in the word "flag" forms onsets found at the beginning of words and syllables.

Within words the letters "f" and "l" rarely divide between syllables. The letters "fl-" will usually remain intact following a prefix that ends with a vowel as in "<u>re</u>-**fl**ect", following another consonant as in "i<u>n</u>-**fl**ation", and following a long vowel sound.

flag	**fl**ew	**fl**oral	**fl**y
flame	**fl**ing	**Fl**orida	in**fl**ation
flash	**fl**ipper	**fl**our	in**fl**uence
flat	**fl**oat	**fl**ow	in**fl**uential
flatten	**fl**ood	**fl**ower	<u>re</u>**fl**ect
flea	**fl**oor	**fl**uff	<u>re</u>**fl**ection
flesh	**fl**op	**fl**uffy	

"fr-" as in "free"

The consonant blend "fr-" heard in the word "free" forms onsets found at the beginning of words and syllables.

Within words, however, the letters "f" and "r" rarely divide between syllables. The letters "fr-" will usually remain intact following a prefix that ends with a vowel as in "<u>re</u>-**fr**esh", following another consonant, and following a long vowel sound.

frame	**fr**eeze	**fr**ight	**fr**ontier
France	**fr**eight	**fr**ill	**fr**ost
Frank	**Fr**ench	**Fr**isbee	**fr**uit
fraud	**fr**equent	**fr**izzle	**fr**ustrate
Fred	**fr**esh	**fr**og	**fr**y
free	**Fr**iday	**fr**om	<u>re</u>**fr**ain
freedom	**fr**iend	**fr**ont	<u>re</u>**fr**esh

"-ft" as in "left"

The consonant blend "-ft" heard in the word "left" forms rimes found at the end of words and syllables.

Within words, however, the letters "f" and "t" may divide between syllables following a short vowel sound as in "raf-ter", unless they are followed by a third consonant letter

aloft	gift	loft	theft
craft	left	raft	tuft
drift	lift	soft	

"gl-" as in "glad"

The consonant blend "gl-" heard in the word "glad" forms onsets found at the beginning of words and syllables.

Within words, however, the letters "g" and "l" may divide between syllables following a short vowel sound. The letters "gl-" will usually remain intact following a prefix that ends with a vowel as in "ne-glect", following another consonant as in "En-gland", and following a long vowel sound.

England	glade	gloat	glue
English	glass	glory	glutton
glacier	glen	glove	neglect
glad	glitter	glow	

"gr-" as in "grass"

The consonant blend "gr-" heard in the word "grass" forms onsets found at the beginning of words and syllables.

Within words, however, the letters "g" and "r" may divide between syllables following a short vowel sound as in "prog-ress". The letters "gr-" will usually remain intact following a prefix that ends with a vowel as in "tele-graph", following another consonant as in "con-gratulate", and following a long vowel sound as in "pro-gram".

agree	Graham	grass	great
congratulate	grain	grateful	greed
grab	gram	gratitude	Greek
grace	grammar	grave	green
grad	grand	gravel	greet
grade	granola	gray (USA)	grew
gradual	grant	grease	grey (UK, CAN)

grind	**gr**ound	**gr**ueling (USA)	**p**hoto**gr**aphy
grip	**gr**oup	**gr**uelling (UK, CAN)	**p**ro**gr**am (USA, CAN)
gripe	**gr**ow	**gr**uesome	**p**ro**gr**amme (UK)
grizzly	**gr**own	im**mi**g**r**ant	**p**ro**gr**ess
groan	**gr**owth	**p**hoto**gr**aph	**t**ele**gr**aph
grocery	**gr**ub		

"gu-" as in "guacamole"

The consonant blend "gu-" heard in the word "guacamole" forms onsets found at the beginning of words and syllables. The letter "u" is pronounced with the consonant "w" sound.

Within words the letters "g" and "u" rarely divide between syllables. The letters "gu-" will usually remain intact following a prefix that ends with a vowel as in "La-Guardia", following another consonant as in "lan-guage", and following a long vowel sound.

an**gu**ish	**gu**acamole	La**Gu**ardia	pen**gu**in
bilin**gu**al	**Gu**am	lan**gu**age	san**gu**ine
consan**gu**inity	**gu**ano	lan**gu**id	
distin**gu**ish	**Gu**inevere	lin**gu**istic	

"-ld" as in "bold"

The consonant blend "-ld" heard in the word "bold" forms rimes found at the end of words and syllables.

Within words, however, the letters "l" and "d" often divide between syllables as in "boul-der", "buil-ding", "el-derly", "shoul-der", "wil-derness", and "chil-dren". In "chil-dren", the letters "dr" form a consonant blend following another consonant.

bo**ld**	gi**ld**	o**ld**	to**ld**
chi**ld**	go**ld**	sca**ld**	wi**ld**
co**ld**	gui**ld**	sco**ld**	wor**ld**
fie**ld**	he**ld**	shie**ld**	yie**ld**
fo**ld**	ho**ld**	so**ld**	

"-lf" as in "wolf"

The consonant blend "-lf" heard in the word "wolf" forms rimes found at the end of words and syllables.

Within words, however, the letters "l" and "f" may divide between syllables, as in "sel-fish", unless they are followed by a third consonant letter.

itself	self	shelf	wolf

"-lk" as in "milk"

The consonant blend "-lk" heard in the word "milk" forms rimes found at the end of words and syllables.

Within words, however, the letters "l" and "k" may divide between syllables, as in "mil-king", unless they are followed by a third consonant letter as in the compound word "milk-shake".

milk	milkshake	silk

"-lt" as in "bolt"

The consonant blend "-lt" heard in the word "bolt" forms rimes found at the end of words and syllables.

Within words, however, the letters "l" and "d" may divide between syllables, as in "cul-tivate", "mel-ting", and "mul-tiply", unless they are followed by a third consonant letter.

bolt	fault	insult	salt
built	gilt	melt	
colt	guilt	pelt	
difficult	halt	result	

"-mbl" as in "gamble"

The consonant blend "-mbl" heard in the word "gamble" forms rimes found at the end of words and syllables.

This is not a true consonant blend because the letters "m" and "b" divide between syllables, and a schwa vowel sound is voiced between the letter "b" and the letter "l". The word "gamble", for example, is pronounced "gam-bull". The final silent letter "e" signals the schwa vowel sound.

amble	gamble	humbling	resemble
disassemble	gambling	humbly	thimble
dissemble	humble	mumble	tremble
fumble	humbled	nimble	

"-mp" as in "stamp"

The consonant blend "-mp" heard in the word "stamp" forms rimes found at the end of words and syllables.

Within words, however, the letters "m" and "p" may divide between syllables, as in "cha**m**-**p**ion", "co**m**-**p**any", "co**m**-**p**etition", and "te**m**-**p**erature", unless they are followed by a third consonant letter as in "e**mp**-ty".

bu**mp**	du**mp**	la**mp**	sta**mp**
ca**mp**	e**mp**t<u>y</u>	li**mp**	
cho**mp**	he**mp**	lu**mp**	
da**mp**	ju**mp**	pu**mp**	

"-mpl" as in "simple"

The consonant blend "-mpl" heard in the word "simple" forms rimes found at the end of words and syllables.

This is not a true consonant blend because the letters "m" and "p" divide between syllables, and a schwa vowel sound is voiced between the letter "p" and the letter "l". The word "sample", for example, is pronounced "sa**m**-**p**<u>u</u>ll". The final silent letter "e" signals the schwa vowel sound.

a**mpl**e	cru**mpl**ing	ru**mpl**e	sa**mpl**ing
cru**mpl**e	di**mpl**e	sa**mpl**e	si**mpl**e
cru**mpl**ed	exa**mpl**e	sa**mpl**ed	te**mpl**e

"-mpt" as in "prompt"

The consonant blend "-mpt" heard in the word "prompt" forms rimes found at the end of words and syllables.

Within words, however, the letters "m", "p" and "t" will likely divide between syllables as in "pro**mp**-**t**er". The letters "-mp" and "-pt" also form consonant blends.

atte**mpt**	pro**mpt**	te**mpt**

"-nch" as in "lunch"

The consonant blend "-nch" heard in the word "lunch" forms rimes found at the end of words and syllables.

Within words, however, the letters "n" and "ch" will likely divide between syllables as in "lau**n**-**ch**ing". The letters "ch" form a consonant digraph.

| branch | brunch | launch | lunch |

"-nd" as in "kind"

The consonant blend "-nd" heard in the word "kind" forms rimes found at the end of words and syllables.

Within words, however, the letters "n" and "d" may divide between syllables, as in "ca**n-d**y", "co**n-d**ition", "co**n-d**uctor", "sa**n-d**al", "te**n-d**er", and "wi**n-d**ow", unless they are followed by a third consonant letter as in "sa**nd-w**ich".

bend	expend	husband	sand
beyond	extend	intend	sandwich
bind	find	island	second
blind	fond	kind	send
blond	found	land	sound
bond	friend	lend	spend
bound	fund	mind	stand
brand	grand	offend	surround
defend	grind	pond	tend
demand	ground	pound	thousand
depend	hand	pretend	wand
descend	handy	recommend	wind
diamond	hind	remind	wind
England	Holland	round	wound

"-ndl" as in "candle"

The consonant blend "-ndl" heard in the word "candle" forms rimes found at the end of words and syllables.

This is not a true consonant blend because the letters "n" and "d" divide between syllables, and a schwa vowel sound is voiced between the letter "d" and the letter "l". The word "candle", for example, is pronounced "ca**n-d**ull". The final silent letter "e" signals the schwa vowel sound.

bundle	fondle	kindle
candle	handle	spindle

"-nk" as in "sank"

The consonant blend "-nk" heard in the word "sank" forms rimes found at the end of words and syllables.

Within words, however, the letters "n" and "k" may divide between syllables, as in "dri**n**-**k**ing" and "Ya**n**-**k**ee", unless they are followed by a third consonant letter as in "tha**nk**-ful".

dru**nk**	oi**nk**	sku**nk**	ya**nk**
fi**nk**	pla**nk**	tha**nk**	
i**nk**	sa**nk**	tha**nk**ful	

"-nt" as in "sent"

The consonant blend "-nt" heard in the word "sent" forms rimes found at the end of words and syllables.

Within words, however, the letters "n" and "t" may divide between syllables, as in "atte**n**-**t**ive", "cou**n**-**t**ing", "e**n**-**t**er", "gra**n**-**t**ed", "hau**n**-**t**ed", "se**n**-**t**ence", and "wi**n**-**t**er", unless they are followed by a third consonant letter as in "eve**nt**-ful" and "joi**nt**-ly".

abse**nt**	disconte**nt**	importa**nt**	pregna**nt**
acce**nt**	dista**nt**	insta**nt**	prese**nt**
accou**nt**	do**n't**	instrume**nt**	preside**nt**
age**nt**	efficie**nt**	inve**nt**	preve**nt**
appoi**nt**	eleph**ant**	joi**nt**	pri**nt**
blu**nt**	environme**nt**	joi**nt**ly	punishme**nt**
ceme**nt**	equipme**nt**	mercha**nt**	ra**nt**
ce**nt**	eve**nt**	mome**nt**	rece**nt**
confide**nt**	eve**nt**ful	mou**nt**ain	re**nt**
consta**nt**	excelle**nt**	obedie**nt**	represe**nt**
conte**nt**	exciteme**nt**	orname**nt**	restaura**nt**
convenie**nt**	experime**nt**	pai**nt**	sce**nt**
cou**nt**	fai**nt**	pa**nt**s	se**nt**
curre**nt**	fli**nt**	pare**nt**	sergea**nt**
dece**nt**	freque**nt**	parliame**nt**	serva**nt**
defenda**nt**	fro**nt**	patie**nt**	sile**nt**
de**nt**	ge**nt**le	payme**nt**	spe**nt**
departme**nt**	gia**nt**	perce**nt**	te**nt**
depende**nt**	gra**nt**	permane**nt**	treatme**nt**
descenda**nt**	hau**nt**	pi**nt**	urge**nt**
desce**nt**	horizo**nt**al	pla**nt**	viole**nt**
differe**nt**	hu**nt**	pleasa**nt**	wa**nt**
disappoi**nt**	immigra**nt**	poi**nt**	we**nt**

"pl-" as in "play"

The consonant blend "pl-" heard in the word "play" forms onsets found at the beginning of words and syllables.

Within words, however, the letters "p" and "l" may divide between syllables following a short vowel sound as in "di<u>p-l</u>omat". The letters "pl" will usually remain intact following a prefix that ends with a vowel as in "<u>re</u>-**pl**ace", following another consonant as in "e<u>m</u>-**pl**oyee", and following a long vowel sound as in "<u>re</u>-**pl**y".

com**pl**etion	**pl**ace	**pl**ate	**pl**ump
com**pl**icate	**pl**aid	**pl**ay	**pl**under
<u>disci**pl**</u>ine	**pl**ain	**pl**easant	**pl**unk
e<u>m**pl**</u>oyee	**pl**an	**pl**ease	**pl**ural
e<u>m**pl**</u>oyer	**pl**ane	**pl**easure	**pl**us
e<u>x**pl**</u>ain	**pl**aned	**pl**enty	**Pl**uto
e<u>x**pl**</u>ode	**pl**anet	**pl**iers	**pl**ywood
e<u>x**pl**</u>ore	**pl**ank	**pl**ink	<u>re</u>**pl**ace
e<u>x**pl**</u>osion	**pl**anned	**pl**ough (UK, CAN)	<u>re</u>**pl**y
e<u>x**pl**</u>osive	**pl**ant	**pl**ow (USA)	si<u>m**pl**</u>icity
<u>multi**pl**</u>ication	**pl**aster	**pl**oy	
<u>multi**pl**</u>y	**pl**astic	**pl**umber	

"pr-" as in "pride"

The consonant blend "pr-" heard in the word "pride" forms onsets found at the beginning of words and syllables.

Within words, however, the letters "p" and "r" may divide between syllables following a short vowel sound as in "re<u>p-r</u>esent". The letters "pr" will usually remain intact following a prefix that ends with a vowel as in "<u>re</u>-**pr**oduce", following another consonant as in "su<u>r</u>-**pr**ise", and following a long vowel sound as in "<u>A</u>-**pr**il".

<u>A**pr**</u>il	**pr**epare	**pr**ide	**pr**oduct
e<u>x**pr**</u>ess	**pr**esence	**pr**iest	**pr**oduction
i<u>m**pr**</u>ovise	**pr**esent	**pr**im	**pr**ofession
practical	**pr**esent	**pr**ince	**pr**ofessor
practicum	**pr**eserve	**pr**incess	**pr**ofit
practice	**pr**esident	**pr**incipal	**pr**ogram (USA, CAN)
pragmatic	**pr**ess	**pr**inciple	**pr**ogramme (UK)
prairie	**pr**essure	**pr**int	**pr**ogress
praise	**pr**etend	**pr**ison	**pr**oject
pray	**pr**etence (UK, CAN)	**pr**ivate	**pr**ominent
preach	**pr**etense (USA)	**pr**ize	**pr**omise
precious	**pr**etty	**pr**obable	**pr**ompt
predator	**pr**event	**pr**oblem	**pr**onounce
preference	**pr**evention	**pr**ocess	**pr**onunciation
pregnant	**pr**ey	**pr**ocession	**pr**oof
prejudice	**pr**ice	**pr**oduce	**pr**oper

property	**pr**otect	**pr**ovide	re**pr**oduce
proposal	**pr**oud	**pr**ovince	re**pr**oduction
propose	**pr**ove	**pr**une	su**pr**ise

"-pt" as in "interrupt"

The consonant blend "-pt" heard in the word "interrupt" forms rimes found at the end of words and syllables.

Within words, however, the letters "p" and "t" may divide between syllables following a short vowel sound, as in "interru**p-t**ing", unless they are followed by a third consonant letter.

interru**pt**   ke**pt**   lea**pt**

"-rd" as in "bird"

The consonant blend "-rd" heard in the word "bird" forms rimes found at the end of words and syllables.

Within words, however, the letters "r" and "d" may divide between syllables, as in "co**r-d**ial", "reco**r-d**ing", and "stewa**r-d**ess", unless they are followed by a third consonant letter as in "cowa**rd**-ly".

acco**rd**	cowa**rd**ly	he**rd**	stewa**rd**
bea**rd**	cupboa**rd**	liza**rd**	swo**rd**
bi**rd**	cu**rd**	reco**rd**	thi**rd**
boa**rd**	disrega**rd**	rega**rd**	wei**rd**
co**rd**	forwa**rd**	rewa**rd**	wo**rd**
cowa**rd**	hea**rd**	standa**rd**	

"-rf" as in "wharf"

The consonant blend "-rf" heard in the word "wharf" forms rimes and is found at the end of words and syllables.

Within words, however, the letters "r" and "f" may divide between syllables, unless they are followed by a third consonant letter.

wha**rf**

"-rk" as in "park"

The consonant blend "-rk" heard in the word "park" forms rimes found at the end of words and syllables.

Within words, however, the letters "r" and "k" may divide between syllables, as in "dar-ken", "mar-ket", and "wor-king", unless they are followed by a third consonant letter as in "spark-ler".

bark	dark	park	spark
clerk	fork	remark	sparkler
cork	mark	shark	work

"-rn" as in "learn"

The consonant blend "-rn" heard in the word "learn" forms rimes found at the end of words and syllables.

Within words, however, the letters "r" and "n" may divide between syllables, as in "bur-ning", "car-nival", "ear-nest", "jour-ney", "lear-ning", "mor-ning", and "tur-ning", unless they are followed by a third consonant letter as in "mourn-ful" and "scorn-ful".

barn	eastern	northern	southern
born	learn	pattern	thorn
burn	modern	return	turn
concern	morn	Saturn	warn
corn	mourn	scorn	western
earn	mournful	scornful	worn

"-rp" as in "sharp"

The consonant blend "-rp" heard in the word "sharp" forms rimes found at the end of words and syllables.

Within words, however, the letters "r" and "p" may divide between syllables, as in "shar-pen", "har-poon" and "tar-paulin", unless they are followed by a third consonant letter as in "sharp-ly".

carp	sharp	tarp
harp	sharply	warp

"-rt" as in "report"

The consonant blend "-rt" heard in the word "report" forms rimes found at the end of words and syllables.

Within words, however, the letters "r" and "t" may divide between syllables, as in "par-ticle", "thir-teen", and "star-ting", unless they are followed by a third consonant letter as in "part-ly".

In words such as "startle", the letters "rt" do not form a consonant blend because there is a syllabic break between the letters "r" and "t". The word "startle" is pronounced "star-tull". The final silent letter "e" signals the schwa vowel sound.

comfort	hurtful	short	start
depart	part	shortly	support
desert	partly	skirt	
discomfort	quart	sort	
hurt	report	sport	

"sc-" as in "scale"

The consonant blend "sc-" heard in the word "scale" forms onsets found at the beginning of words and syllables.

Within words, however, the letters "s" and "c" may divide between syllables following a short vowel sound as in "dis-cover". The letters "sc" will usually remain intact following a prefix that ends with a vowel as in "micro-scope", following another consonant, and following a long vowel sound.

Note that in the following words, the letters "sc" are followed by vowel letters "a", "o", or "u". The letter "c" is pronounced with the hard "c/k" consonant sound when followed by vowel letters "a", "o", or "u". This allows "sc" to form a consonant blend. When the letters "sc" are followed by vowel letters "e", "i", or "y", it forms a consonant digraph pronounced with the soft "c/s" consonant sound as heard in "scene" and "descend".

escape	scapegoat	scone	Scott
microscope	scare	scooter	Scottish
scab	scary	score	scum
scale	scatter	scorn	scuttle
scamp	scold	scorpion	telescope

"sch-" as in "school"

The consonant blend "sch-" heard in the word "school" forms onsets found at the beginning of words and syllables.

schedule	schematic	scheming	schism
schema	scheme	scherzo	schismatic

schizophrenia	**sch**olarly	**sch**olastic	**sch**oolhouse
scholar	**sch**olarship	**sch**ool	**sch**oolmate

"scr-" as in "scream"

The consonant blend "scr-" heard in the word "scream" forms onsets found at the beginning of words and syllables.

Within words, however, the letters "s" and "cr" will divide following a prefix that ends with the letter "s" as in "di**s-cr**imination" and "mi**s-cr**eant". The letters "scr" remain intact following a prefix that ends with a vowel as in "<u>de</u>-**scr**ibe" and "<u>pre</u>-**scr**ibe".

<u>de</u>**scr**ibe	**scr**ape	**scr**een	**scr**um
<u>pre</u>**scr**ibe	**scr**atch	**scr**ibble	**scr**umptious
scram	**scr**eam	**scr**ipt	
scrap	**scr**eech	**scr**oll	

"shr-" as in "shred"

The consonant blend "shr-" heard in the word "shred" forms onsets found at the beginning of words and syllables.

Within words, however, the letters "sh" and "r" may divide between syllables following a short vowel sound as in "m<u>u</u>**sh-r**oom". The letters "sh" form a rime to the first syllable, and the letter "r" forms an onset to the following syllable.

shrank	**shr**ewd	**shr**ine	**shr**ub
shrapnel	**shr**ewdly	**shr**ink	**shr**ug
shred	**shr**iek	**shr**inkage	**shr**unk
shredder	**shr**ill	**shr**ivel	**shr**unken
shrew	**shr**imp	**shr**oud	

"sk-" as in "sky"

The consonant blend "sk-" heard in the word "sky" forms onsets found at the beginning of words and syllables.

Within words, however, the letters "s" and "k" may divide between syllables following a short vowel sound as in "<u>a</u>**s-k**ing", "b<u>a</u>**s-k**et" and "wh<u>i</u>**s-k**ey". The letters "sk will usually remain intact following a prefix that ends with a vowel, following another consonant, and following a long vowel sound.

skate	**sk**etch	**sk**iff	**sk**illet
skeleton	**sk**i	**sk**iing	**sk**im
skeptical	**sk**id	**sk**ill	**sk**in

skinny	**sk**irt	**sk**ull	**sk**y
skip	**sk**it	**sk**unk	

"-sk" as in "risk"

The consonant blend "-sk" heard in the word "risk" also forms rimes found at the end of words and syllables.

Within words, however, the letters "s" and "k" may divide between syllables following a short vowel sound as in "a**s-k**ing", "ba**s-k**et" and "whi**s-k**ey", unless they are followed by a third consonant letter.

a**sk**	kio**sk**	ta**sk**
asteri**sk**	ma**sk**	tu**sk**
de**sk**	ri**sk**	whi**sk**

"sl-" as in "slide"

The consonant blend "sl-" heard in the word "slide" forms onsets found at the beginning of words and syllables.

Within words, however, the letters "s" and "l" may divide between syllables following a short vowel sound as in "legi**s-l**ation". Also, the letters "sl" divide following a prefix that ends with the letter "s" as in "di**s-l**ike" and "tran**s-l**ate", in words such as "notoriou**s-l**y" and "seriou**s-l**y" that end with the suffix "-ly", and in the word "par**s-l**ey". The letters "sl" will remain intact following a prefix that ends with a vowel as in "a-**sl**eep".

a**sl**eep	**sl**avery	**sl**ide	**sl**ippery
slain	**sl**ed	**sl**ight	**sl**op
slam	**sl**eep	**sl**im	**sl**ope
slang	**sl**eigh	**sl**ime	**sl**oping
slap	**sl**ept	**sl**ing	**sl**ow
slave	**sl**id	**sl**ip	**sl**umber

"sm-" as in "smile"

The consonant blend "sm-" heard in the word "smile" forms onsets found at the beginning of words and syllables.

Within words, however, the letters "s" and "m" may divide between syllables following a short vowel sound as in "chari**s-m**a", "co**s-m**os", "di**s-m**ay", "di**s-m**iss", "embarra**ss-m**ent", "sei**s-m**ic", and "sei**s-m**ograph". The letters "sm" will usually remain intact following a prefix that ends with a vowel, following another consonant, and following a long vowel sound.

The letters "sm" may appear incidentally in compound words such as "sale**s**-**m**an".

locksmith	smash	smile	smooth
small	smell	smithereens	smuggle
smart	smelly	smoke	

"-sm" as in "prism"

The consonant blend "-sm" heard in the word "prism" also forms rimes found at the end of words and syllables.

This is not a true consonant blend because a schwa vowel sound is voiced between the letter "s" and the letter "m". The word "prism", for example, is pronounced "pris-**u**m".

baptism	liberalism	optimism	prism
chasm	mechanism	patriotism	socialism
communism	microcosm	pessimism	

"sn-" as in "snap"

The consonant blend "sn-" heard in the word "snap" forms onsets found at the beginning of words and syllables.

Within words, however, the letters "s" and "n" may divide between syllables following a short vowel sound as in "D**i**s-**n**ey" and "m**i**s-**n**omer". Also, the letters "sn" divide in words such as "consciou**s**-**n**ess" and "righteou**s**-**n**ess". The letters "sn" will usually remain intact following a prefix that ends with a vowel, following another consonant as in "ginger-**sn**ap", and following a long vowel sound.

gingersnap	snap	sneeze	snort
rattlesnake	snare	snicker	snow
snail	sneaky	snip	snuggle
snake	sneer	snoop	

"sp-" as in "spell"

The consonant blend "sp-" heard in the word "spell" forms onsets found at the beginning of words and syllables.

Within words, however, the letters "s" and "p" may divide between syllables following a short vowel sound as in "d**e**s-**p**erate". The letters "sp" will usually remain intact following a prefix that ends with a vowel as in "r**e**-**sp**ect", following another consonant, and following a long vowel sound.

despair	spanking	spend	splash
despite	spare	spent	splendid
especially	spark	spider	spoil
respect	spawn	spill	spoke
responsible	speak	spilled	spoken
space	special	spin	spooky
spade	speck	spine	spoon
Spain	speech	spirit	sport
spangle	speed	spit	spot
Spanish	spell	spite	spud
spank	spelt	spitting	spy

"-sp" as in "crisp"

The consonant blend "-sp" heard in the word "crisp" also forms rimes found at the end of words and syllables.

Within words, however, the letters "s" and "p" may divided between syllables, as in "clas-ping" and "whis-per", unless they are followed by a third consonant letter as in "crisp-ly".

clasp	crisply	grasp
crisp	cusp	wisp

"spl-" as in "splash"

The consonant blend "spl-" heard in the word "splash" forms onsets found at the beginning of words and syllables.

Within words, however, the letters "s", "p", and "l" may divide between syllables, unless they follow a prefix as in "re-splendent", or another consonant letter.

resplendent	splashing	splendour (UK, CAN)	split
splash	splendid	splinter	splitting
splashed	splendor (USA)		

"spr-" as in "spring"

The consonant blend "spr-" heard in the word "spring" forms onsets found at the beginning of words and syllables.

Within words, however, the letters "s", "p", and "r" may divide between syllables, unless they follow a prefix as in "off-spring", or another consonant letter.

o**ffspr**ing	**spr**ee	**spr**inkle	**spr**ung
sprain	**spr**ightly	**spr**ocket	**spr**y
spray	**spr**ing	**spr**out	
spread	**spr**inging	**spr**uce	

"squ-" as in "square"

The consonant blend "squ-" heard in the word "square" forms onsets found at the beginning of words and syllables. The letter "u" represents the consonant "w" sound.

Within words, however, the letters "s" and "qu" may divide between syllables, as in "e**s-qu**ire", unless they follow a prefix or another consonant letter.

In words such as "mosquito", "burlesque", and "picturesque" the letter "u" is silent.

squab	**squ**alor	**squ**eak	**squ**irrel
squabble	**squ**are	**squ**eal	**squ**irt
squad	**squ**ash	**squ**eeze	**squ**ish
squall	**squ**aw	**squ**id	

"st-" as in star"

The consonant blend "st-" heard in the word "star" forms onsets found at the beginning of words and syllables.

Within words, however, the letters "s" and "t" may divide between syllables following a short vowel sound as in "di**s-t**urb". The letters "st" will usually remain intact following a prefix that ends with a vowel as in "a**-st**onish" and "e**-st**ablish", following another consonant as in "lo**b-st**er" and "mo**n-st**er", and following a long vowel sound.

a**st**onish	**st**age	**st**ation	**St**ewart
co**n**stant	**st**ain	**st**atute	**St**eve
co**n**struction	**st**air	**st**ay	**st**ick
di**st**inguish	**st**allion	**st**eady	**st**iff
e**st**ablish	**st**amp	**st**eak	**st**ill
ha**m**ster	**st**and	**st**eal	**st**ing
i**n**stance	**st**anding	**st**eam	**st**ink
i**n**stant	**st**andard	**st**eel	**st**inking
i**n**stead	**st**ar	**st**eep	**st**ir
lo**b**ster	**st**are	**st**eer	**st**irrup
mo**n**ster	**st**art	**st**ellar	**st**ock
stab	**st**artle	**st**em	**st**ocking
Stacey	**st**arve	**st**ep	**st**ole
staff	**st**ate	**st**eward	**st**omach
stag	**st**atement	**st**ewardess	**st**one

s**t**ood	s**t**orm	S**t**over	s**t**ump
s**t**ool	s**t**ormy	s**t**ovetop	s**t**upid
s**t**op	s**t**oried	s**t**udent	su<u>bs</u>tance
s**t**ore	s**t**ory	s**t**udy	*up*s**t**airs
s**t**oried	s**t**ove	s**t**uff	

"-st" as in "fast"

The consonant blend "-st" heard in the word "fast" also forms rimes found at the end of words and syllables.

Within words, however, the letters "s" and "t" may divide between syllables, as in "Ea**s**-**t**er", "ea**s**-**t**ern", "ela**s**-**t**ic", "la**s**-**t**ing", "ma**s**-**t**er", and "roo**s**-**t**er", unless they are followed by another consonant letter as in "po**st**-**p**one".

again**st**	du**st**	la**st**	roa**st**
among**st**	earne**st**	late**st**	ru**st**
arre**st**	ea**st**	lea**st**	scienti**st**
arti**st**	exhau**st**	le**st**	smalle**st**
bla**st**	exi**st**	li**st**	sugge**st**
boa**st**	fa**st**	lo**st**	ta**st**e
breakfa**st**	fea**st**	mode**st**	te**st**
broadca**st**	fir**st**	mo**st**	thir**st**
bur**st**	fi**st**	mu**st**	toa**st**
ca**st**	fore**st**	ne**st**	tru**st**
che**st**	gho**st**	pa**st**	wai**st**
coa**st**	harve**st**	pa**st**e	we**st**
conque**st**	ha**st**e	po**st**	wor**st**
conte**st**	hone**st**	po**st***p*one	wri**st**
co**st**	ho**st**	prie**st**	younge**st**
cy**st**	indu<u>**st**</u>ry	reque**st**	
denti**st**	intere**st**	resi**st**	
disgu**st**	ju**st**	re**st**	

"str-" as in "strong"

The consonant blend "str-" heard in the word "strong" forms onsets found at the beginning of words and syllables.

Within words, however, the letters "s", "t", and "r" may divide between syllables as in "illu**s**-**tr**ate" and "indu**s**-**tr**y", unless they follow a prefix as in "<u>de</u>-**str**oy" or another consonant letter as in "co<u>n</u>-**str**ict".

a<u>b</u>**str**act	<u>de</u>**str**oy	<u>de</u>**str**uctive	i<u>n</u>**str**ument
co<u>n</u>**str**ict	<u>de</u>**str**uction	illu**str**ate	<u>re</u>**str**ict

straight	**str**eak	**str**ing	**str**ucture
strait	**str**eam	**str**ip	**str**uggle
strange	**str**eet	**str**ipe	**str**um
stranger	**str**ength	**str**obe	**str**ut
strap	**str**etch	**str**oke	un**str**essed
strategy	**str**ict	**str**ong	
straw	**str**ike	**str**uck	

"sw-" as in "sweet"

The consonant blend "sw-" heard in the word "sweet" forms onsets found at the beginning of words and syllables.

Within words, however, the letters "s" and "w" may divide between syllables following a short vowel sound. The letters "st" will usually remain intact following a prefix that ends with a vowel, following another consonant as in "fo<u>r</u>-**sw**ear", and following a long vowel sound.

In the word "answer" the letter "w" is silent.

fo<u>r</u>**sw**ear	**sw**arm	**sw**eet	**sw**ipe
swagger	**sw**at	**sw**ell	**sw**oop
swam	**sw**ear	**sw**ift	**sw**ung
swamp	**sw**eat	**sw**im	
swap	**sw**eep	**sw**ing	

"su-" as in "suede"

The consonant blend "su-" heard in the word "suede" forms onsets found at the beginning of words and syllables. The letter "u" represents the consonant "w" sound.

With this spelling pattern, the letters "s" and "u" rarely, if ever, divide between syllables.

dis**su**ade	per**su**asion	**su**ede
per**su**ade	**su**ave	**su**ite

"thr-" as in "threat"

The consonant blend "thr-" heard in the word "threat" forms onsets and is found at the beginning of words and syllables.

Within words, however, the letters "th" and "r" may divide between syllables, unless they follow a prefix or another consonant letter as in "a<u>n</u>**thr**opologist" and "phila<u>n</u>**thr**opist".

a<u>nthr</u>opologist	**thr**eaten	**thr**ill	**thr**ong
phila<u>nthr</u>opist	**thr**ee	**thr**iller	**thr**ottle
thrall	**thr**esh	**thr**ive	**thr**ough
thrash	**thr**ew	**thr**oat	**thr**ow
thread	**thr**ift	**thr**ob	**thr**ush
threat	**thr**ifty	**thr**one	**thr**ust

"thw-" as in "thwart"

The consonant blend "thw-" heard in the word "thwart" forms onsets and is found at the beginning of words and syllables.

The letters "thw" are rarely found within words.

thwack   **thw**art

"tr-" as in "tree"

The consonant blend "tr-" heard in the word "tree" forms onsets found at the beginning of words and syllables.

Within words, however, the letters "t" and "r" may divide between syllables following a short vowel sound as in "pa<u>t</u>-rol". The letters "tr" will usually remain intact following a prefix that ends with a vowel as in "<u>re</u>-**tr**act", following another consonant as in "ul-**tr**a", and following a long vowel sound as in "<u>pa</u>-**tr**iot".

The "tr" spelling pattern in "theatre" is not a true consonant blend because a schwa vowel sound is pronounced between the letter "t" and the letter "r". The word "theatre" is pronounced "thee-a- tur". The final silent letter "e" signals the schwa vowel sound.

co<u>nt</u>ribute	<u>re</u>**t**ract	travel	troll
co<u>nt</u>ribution	thea**tr**e	tray	trophy
co<u>nt</u>rol	track	treasure	trouble
ele<u>c</u>tric	tractor	treat	trout
e<u>x</u>tra	trade	tree	truck
e<u>x</u>treme	traffic	tremble	true
ha<u>tr</u>ed	tragedy	trial	truly
indu<u>str</u>y	trail	triangle	trunk
i<u>nt</u>roduce	train	tribe	trust
Mo<u>nt</u>real	translate	trick	truth
pa<u>str</u>y	transportation	trigonometry	try
<u>pa</u>**tr**iot	trap	trip	u<u>l</u>tra
<u>pa</u>**tr**ol	trapper	trivia	u<u>nt</u>rue

"tw-" as in "twist"

The consonant blend "tw-" heard in the word "twist" forms onsets found at the beginning of words and syllables.

Within words, however, the letters "t" and "w" may divide between syllables following a short vowel sound. The letters "st" will usually remain intact following a prefix that ends with a vowel as in "be-tween", following another consonant, and following a long vowel sound.

between	twelfth	twice	twirl
twang	twelve	twilight	twist
tweak	twenty	twin	twister
tweet	twerp	twinkle	twit

"-tz" as in "klutz"

The consonant blend "-tz" heard in the word "klutz" forms rimes and is found at the end of words and syllables.

Within words, however, the letters "t" and "z" may divided between syllables, as in "how-it-zer", "pret-zel", and "selt-zer", unless they are followed by a third consonant letter.

The words "scherzo" and "Nazi" are pronounced with the "tz" consonant blend. The consonant "t" sound is not represented in the spelling. The word "tzar" is sometimes pronounced with the "tz" consonant blend.

chintz	ersatz	klutz	schmaltz
ersatz	hertz	quartz	waltz

Part G: Prefixes

G1 Introduction

Words are made up of component parts called morphemes. A morpheme is the smallest part of a word that conveys meaning. There are three kinds of morphemes: "prefixes", "root words", and "suffixes".

At the core of every word is a root which gives the word its essential meaning. Additional letters, called "affixes", may be added to the beginning or to the end of a root. An affix added to the beginning of a root is called a "prefix". An affix added to the end of a root is called a "suffix". Many words have both a prefix and a suffix, and it is possible to attach more than one prefix or suffix. Prefixes and suffixes create new words by adding to the meaning of the root.

The letters "dict", for example, form a root word that means "to speak" in Latin. Adding the prefix "contra-", meaning "against" or "opposite", to "dict" creates the word "contradict". Adding the suffix "-ate", which forms verbs, to "dict" creates the word "dictate".

A base word is any word to which a prefix or suffix may be added. Some base words are also root words. Most base words are not root words because they already have a prefix or suffix attached.

Morphemes may be divided into "lexical morphemes" and "relational morphemes". A lexical morpheme conveys a particular meaning in and of itself. A relational morpheme only conveys grammatical meaning in relation to the word to which it is attached. Morphemes may also be divided into "free morphemes" and "bound morphemes". Free morphemes can function as free-standing words. Bound morphemes cannot function as free-standing words and are only used attached to other morphemes.

The word "ports", for example, contains two morphemes. The root word "port" is a lexical morpheme that means "to carry". As well, "port" is a free morpheme that can function as a word. The suffix "-s" is a relational morpheme used to create the plural form of words. The suffix "-s" does not convey any meaning on its own. As well, the suffix "-s" is a bound morpheme that cannot stand alone as a word.

Prefixes are lexical morphemes. That is, prefixes have particular meanings and, therefore, add to the meaning of a root in a particular way. Prefixes create distinct new words. For example, adding the prefix "ex-" (meaning "out") to "port" produces "export". Likewise, adding the prefix "im-" (meaning "in") to "port" produces "import". Suffixes, on the other hand, are usually relational and only change the form of a word while preserving the same essential meaning. Both "export" and "import", for example, accept the relational suffix "-ing" to create "exporting" and "importing".

Words that share the same prefix share a degree of common meaning forming word families. Many prefixes were once Old English, Greek, or Latin words. The meaning of a prefix may seem obtuse to modern readers but would have made sense when first used.

As a general rule, a prefix is added to a base word without adding, dropping, or changing any letters. In particular, the doubling principle is not applied. Adding the prefix "dis-" to the base word "appear", for example, produces the word "disappear". The letter "s" is not doubled. On the other hand, the doubling principle is applied when adding a suffix that begins with a vowel letter to a base word that ends with a short vowel syllable. Adding the suffix "-er" to the base word "big", for example, produces the word "bigger". The letter "g" is doubled.

However, adding a prefix to a base word occasionally produces double consonants. So, for example, adding the prefix "mis-" to the base word "step" creates the word "misstep".

The spelling of certain prefixes called "allomorphs" change according to the spelling of the base word to which they are added. Allomorphs conform to the spelling of the base word to ease pronunciation. The final consonant letter of the prefix often changes into the first consonant letter of the base word. For example, the prefix "in-" becomes "il-" when added to base word "legal" to produce "illegal". This often results in double consonants.

G2 Simple Prefixes

"a-" meaning "on"

The prefix "a-", meaning "on", "in", or "engaged in", is Old English in origin.

abed   aboard   asleep
ablaze   afoot

"a-" meaning "motion"

The prefix "a-", meaning "motion", "onward" or "away", is Old English in origin.

arise   awake

"a-/an-"

The prefix "a-/an-", meaning "not" or "without", is Greek in origin.

agnostic	**an**onymous	**a**political
amoral	**an**tinomy	**a**theism
anarchy	**a**pathy	**a**theist

"ambi-"

The prefix "ambi-", meaning "around" or "both", is Latin in origin.

ambidextrous	**ambi**guity	**ambi**valence
ambient	**ambi**guous	

"amphi-"

The prefix "amphi-", meaning "around" or "both", is Greek in origin.

amphibious	**amphi**theater (USA)	**amphi**theatre (UK, CAN)

"an/ante"

The prefix "ante", meaning "before", "prior to", or "preceding", is Latin in origin.

ancestor	**ante**cedent	**ante**diluvian
antebellum	**ante**date	**ante**rior

"anti-"

The prefix "anti-", meaning "against", "opposed to", "preventing", or "destroying", is Greek in origin.

anti-aircraft	**anti**freeze	**anti**personnel	**anti**thesis
antibody	**anti**hero	**anti**perspirant	
anticlimax	**anti**histamine	**anti**septic	
antidote	**anti**pathy	**anti**social	

"aut-/auto-"

The prefix "aut-/auto-", meaning "self" or "self-acting", is Greek in origin.

367

autism	**auto**crat	**auto**matic	**auto**psy
auto	**auto**cratic	**auto**mobile	
autobiography	**auto**graph	**auto**nomous	
autocracy	**auto**harp	**auto**nomy	

"be-"

The prefix "be-", meaning "all around", "all over", "thoroughly", or "excessively", is Old English in origin.

befriend	**be**jewelled (UK, CAN)	**be**loved
begrudge	**be**labor (USA)	**be**moan
behead	**be**labour (UK, CAN)	**be**set
bejeweled (USA)		**be**smear

"bene-/beni-"

The prefix "bene-/beni-", meaning "to do well" or "to do good" is Latin in origin.

benefaction	**bene**ficial	**bene**fit	**beni**gn
benefactor	**bene**ficiary	**bene**volence	

"bi-/bin-"

The prefix "bi-/bin-", meaning "two" or "twice", is Latin in origin.

bicarbonate	**bi**lateral	**bi**noculars	**bi**sect
bicycle	**bi**monthly	**bi**ped	**bi**sexual
biennial	**bi**nary	**bi**plane	**bi**weekly

"cata-"

The prefix "cata-", meaning "down", "downward", "wrongly", or "badly", is Greek in origin.

cataclysm	**cata**strophe

"cent-/centi-"

The prefix "cent-/centi-", meaning "hundred" or "one-hundredth", is Latin in origin.

cent	**cent**enary	**centi**grade	**centi**liter (USA)
centenarian	**cent**ennial	**centi**gram	

centilitre centimeter (USA) centimetre centipede
(UK, CAN)   (UK, CAN)   century

"circu-/circum-"

The prefix "circu-/circum-", meaning "round" or "about", is Latin in origin.

circle	circulate	circumnavigate	circumspect
circuit	circumcise	circumpolar	circus
circular	circumference	circumscribe	

"contra-"

The prefix "contra-", meaning "against" or "opposite", is Latin in origin.

contraband	contradiction	contrarian	contravene
contraception	contradictory	contrary	contravention
contradict	contraindicate	contrast	

"counter-"

The prefix "counter-", meaning "opposite direction", "opposition", or "substitution", is Latin in origin.

counteract	counteroffensive	counterrevolution
counterattack	counterpart	countersign
counterbalance	counterpoint	countersink
counterclaim	counterproductive	
countermand	counterproposal	

"de-"

The prefix "de-", meaning "reversal", "removal", "cessation", or "contraction" is Latin in origin.

deactivate	decode	de-ice	deport
debase	decrease	delouse	depose
decapitate	deduct	demean	deride
decentralize	defect	demonstrate	descend
decide	deflate	demoralize	destroy
declare	degrade	depart	devalue

"dec-/deca-"

The prefix "dec-/deca-", meaning "ten", is Greek in origin.

decade **dec**athlon **dec**agon **dec**ahedron

"dec-/deci-"

The prefix "dec-/deci-", meaning "tenth", is Latin in origin.

December was the tenth month of the year in the ancient Roman calendar which began with the month of March. The months of January and February were added later.

December   **deci**liter (USA)   **deci**mal   **deci**metre (UK, CAN)
decibel   **deci**litre (UK, CAN) **deci**meter (USA)

"di-"

The prefix "di-", meaning "two", "twice", or "double", is Greek in origin.

dichotomy   **di**lemma   **di**oxide
digraph   **di**ode   **di**pole

"dia-"

The prefix "dia-", meaning "through", apart", "across", or "between", is Greek in origin.

diagonal   **dia**meter   **dia**rrhea (USA)
dialectic   **dia**phanous   **dia**rrhoea (UK, CAN)
dialogue   **dia**phragm

"dis-"

The prefix "dis-", meaning "negation", "removal", "separation", or "failure", is Latin in origin.

disable   **dis**bar   **dis**honest   **dis**posal
disadvantage   **dis**belief   **dis**illusion   **dis**pose
disagree   **dis**card   **dis**infectant   **dis**pute
disappear   **dis**comfort   **dis**mantle   **dis**sent
disappoint   **dis**cover   **dis**member   **dis**solve
disapprove   **dis**embowel   **dis**obey   **dis**tinguish
disarm   **dis**entangle   **dis**orderly
disaster   **dis**gruntled   **dis**perse

"e-"

The prefix "e-", meaning "out", or "away", is Latin in origin.

eject	**e**migrate	**e**mit	**e**rupt

"equa-/equi-"

The prefix "equa-/equi-", meaning "equal", is Latin in origin.

equal	**equi**distant	**equi**table
equation	**equi**lateral	**equi**ty
equator	**equi**nox	**equi**valent

"eu-"

The prefix "eu-", meaning "good", "well", or "pleasant", is Greek in origin.

eulogy	**eu**phoria	**eu**rythmics (USA)	**eu**rhythmics (UK, CAN)
euphemism	**eu**reka		

"ex-"

The prefix "ex-", meaning "out of", "thoroughly", "not", "former", or "without", is both Greek and Latin in origin.

When adding the prefix "ex-" to a bound morpheme, a hyphen is not used. For example, when the prefix "ex-" is added to the root word "odus", it is spelled "exodus".

When adding the prefix "ex-" to a free standing word, a hyphen may be used. When the prefix "ex-" is added to "boyfriend", for example, it is spelled "ex-boyfriend".

exacerbate	**ex**-champion	**ex**it	**ex**-president
exact	**ex**clude	**ex**odus	**ex**-spouse
exalt	**ex**-girlfriend	**ex**onerate	**ex**-student
ex-boyfriend	**ex**hale	**ex**-partner	**ex**-wife
excavate	**ex**hibit	**ex**pel	
excel	**ex**-husband	**ex**port	

"extra-"

The prefix "extra-", meaning "beyond" or "outside", is Latin in origin.

extra	**extra**marital	**extra**terrestrial	**extra**vagant
extracurricular	**extra**ordinary	**extra**vagance	

"for-"

The prefix "for-", meaning "prohibit", "abstention", or "to negate", is Old English in origin. It is also used to intensify the meaning of the base word as in "forswear".

forbear	**for**bidden	**for**go	**for**sake
forbid	**for**get	**for**gotten	**for**swear

"fore-

The prefix "fore-", meaning "before in time, place, order, or rank", is Old English in origin.

forearm	**fore**head	**fore**noon
foregone	**fore**man	

"hect-/hecto-"

The prefix "hect-/hecto-", meaning "one hundred", is Greek origin.

hectare	**hecto**liter (USA)	**hecto**meter (USA)
hectogram	**hecto**litre (UK, CAN)	**hecto**metre (UK, CAN)
hectograph		

"hemi-"

The prefix "hemi-", meaning "half", is Greek in origin.

hemiplegia	**hemi**plegic	**hemi**sphere

"hepta-"

The prefix "hepta-", meaning "seven", is Greek in origin.

heptagon	**hepta**hedron	**hepta**meter

"heter-/hetero-"

The prefix "heter-/hetero-", meaning "other" or "different", is Greek in origin.

heterodoxy	**hetero**geneity	**hetero**geneous	**hetero**sexual

"homo-"

The prefix "homo-", meaning "same", "equal", or "alike", is Greek in origin.

homogenize	**homo**graph	**homo**phobia	**homo**sexual
homogenous	**homo**nym	**homo**phone	

"hyper-"

The prefix "hyper-", meaning "more than normal", "excessively", or "beyond", is Greek in origin.

hyperactive	**hyper**critical	**hyper**sonic	**hyper**thermia
hyperbole	**hyper**sensitive	**hyper**tension	

"hypo-"

The prefix "hypo-", meaning "under", "beneath", or "less than normal", is Greek in origin.

hypoallergenic	**hypo**crite	**hypo**tension
hypochondria	**hypo**critical	**hypo**thermia
hypocrisy	**hypo**dermic	**hypo**thesis

"inter-"

The prefix "inter-", meaning "among", "between", or "mutually", is Latin in origin.

interact	**inter**course	**inter**mediate	**inter**rupt
intercede	**inter**dependent	**inter**mission	**inter**section
intercept	**inter**fere	**inter**nal	**inter**vene
intercom	**inter**ior	**inter**national	**inter**view

"intra-"

The prefix "intra-", meaning "on the inside", or "within", is Latin in origin.

intramural	**intra**muscular	**intra**venous

"iso-/isos-"

The prefix "iso-/isos-", meaning "equal", "similar, "alike", or "identical", is Greek in origin.

isometric	**iso**sceles	**iso**tope
isomorphic	**iso**tonic	

"kilo-"

The prefix "kilo-", meaning "one thousand", is Greek in origin.

kilogram	**kilo**joules	**kilo**litre (UK, CAN)	**kilo**metre (UK, CAN)
kilohertz	**kilo**liter (USA)	**kilo**meter (USA)	
			kilowatt

"macr-/macro-"

The prefix "macr-/macro-", meaning "long", "enlarged" or "comprehensive", is Greek in origin.

macrobiotics	**macro**economics
macrocosm	**macro**scopic

"magni-"

The prefix "magni-", meaning "great", "big" or "large", is Latin in origin.

magnification	**magni**fy	**magn**um
magnificent	**magni**tude	

"mal-"

The prefix "mal-", meaning "bad", "evil", "faulty", or "wrongful", is Latin in origin.

maladjusted	**mal**evolent	**mal**ign	**mal**practice
malcontent	**mal**feasance	**mal**ignant	**mal**treat
malefactor	**mal**function	**mal**odorous	**mal**treatment

"mega-"

The prefix "mega-", meaning "large", "powerful", "great", or "one million", is Greek in origin.

megabyte	**mega**lith	**mega**phone
megahertz	**mega**lopolis	**mega**ton

"micro-"

The prefix "micro-", meaning "very small" or "a factor of one-millionth", is Greek in origin.

microanalysis
microbe
microbiology
microchip
microcosm

microeconomics
microelectronics
microfilm
microgram
micromanage

microorganism
(Also **micro**-organism)
microphone
microscope

"mille-/milli-"

The prefix "mille-/milli-", meaning "one thousand" or "a factor of one-thousandth", is Latin in origin.

millennium
milligram
milliliter (USA)

millilitre
(UK, CAN)
millimeter (USA)

millimetre
(UK, CAN)
million
(A thousand thousand.)

millipede
millisecond

"mis-"

The prefix "mis-", meaning "badly", "wrongly", or "unfavorably", is Old English in origin.

misadventure
misalign
misapply
misapprehend
miscalculate
miscarriage

mischief
mischievous
misconstrue
misdemeanor
(USA)

misdemeanour
(UK, CAN)
misinterpret
misjudge
mislead
mismanage

misperception
misplace
misspell
mistake
mistrust

"mono-"

The prefix "mono-", meaning "one", "alone", or "single", is Greek in origin.

monarch
monochromatic
monochrome
monocle
monocular

monoculture
monogamy
monolith
monologue
(Also monolog)
monopoly

monotone
monotonous
monoxide

"multi-"

The prefix "multi-", meaning "many" or "more than one", is Latin in origin.

multicolored (USA)
multicoloured (UK, CAN)
multicultural
multidimensional
multiform
multilateral
multilingual
multimillionaire
multinational
multiple
multiplex
multiplication
multiply
multitude

"neg-"

The prefix "neg-", meaning "nullify", "ineffective", or "non-existent", is Latin in origin.

negate
negation
negative
neglect
negligence
negligible

"neo-"

The prefix "neo-", meaning "new", "modified", or "modern", is Greek in origin.

neoclassical
neoconservative
neoliberal
Neolithic
neologism
neonatal
neophyte
neoplasm

"non-"

The prefix "non-", which creates the opposite sense of the base word to which it is attached, is Latin in origin.

There is virtually no end of words that can be formed using the prefix "non-". Only a few sample words are provided below.

nonabrasive
nonaggression
nonaligned
(Also "non-aligned")
nonathletic
nonbeliever
nonbelligerent
noncancerous
non-Catholic
nonchalant
non-Christian
noncitizen
noncommittal
noncompliance
noncompliant
nonconforming
nonconformist
non-contiguous
noncriminal
nondescript
nondurable
non-English
nonentity
nonessential
nonexistence
(Also "non-existence")
nonfiction
nonlethal
nonpartisan
nonpayment
(Also "non-payment")
nonperforming
non-renewable
nonsense
nonsensical
non-starter
nonstop
(Also "non-stop")
nontoxic
nonviolent

"nona-/nove-"

The prefix "nona-/nove-", meaning "nine" or "ninth", is Latin in origin.

November was the ninth month of the year in the ancient Roman calendar which began with the month of March. The months of January and February were added at a later date.

nonagenarian   **nona**gon   **Nove**mber   **nove**na

"octa-/octo-"

The prefix "octa-/octo-", meaning "eight" or "eighth", is both Greek and Latin in origin.

October was the eighth month of the year in the ancient Roman calendar which began with the month of March. The months of January and February were added at a later date.

octagon   **octa**ve   **Octo**ber   **octo**pus
octane   **oct**et (Also "octette")   **octo**genarian

"omni-"

The prefix "omni-", meaning "all" or "everywhere", is Latin in origin.

omnibus   **omni**present   **omni**vorous
omnidirectional   **omni**scient
omnipotent   **omni**vore

"out-"

The prefix "out-", meaning "to surpass or exceed", "external or separate", or "going away", is Old English in origin.

outback   **out**do   **out**going   **out**number
outboard   **out**doors   **out**house   **out**shine
outcast   **out**er   **out**live   **out**shoot

"over-"

The prefix "over-", meaning "above", "over", "beyond", or "excessively", is Old English in origin.

overactive   **over**cast   **over**come   **over**drive
overbearing   **over**coat   **over**dose   **over**due

overflow	**over**heat	**over**see	**over**whelm
overhang	**over**kill	**over**shadow	
overhead	**over**look	**over**sight	
overhear	**over**run	**over**time	

"para-" as in "parallel"

The prefix "para-", meaning "by the side of", "to one side", or "beyond or distinct from but analogous or parallel to", is Greek in origin.

parable	**para**graph	**para**medic	**para**site
parabola	**para**legal	**para**noia	
paradigm	**para**llel	**para**normal	
paradox	**para**lysis	**para**phrase	

"para-" as in "parachute"

The prefix "para-", meaning "protect" or "ward off", is Latin in origin.

parachute	**para**sol	**para**trooper

"pent-/penta-"

The prefix "pent-/penta-", meaning "five", is Greek in origin.

pentagon	**penta**meter	**Pente**cost
pentahedron	**penta**thlon	

"per-"

The prefix "per-", meaning "through", "all over", or "completely", is Latin in origin.

perceive	**per**emptory	**per**forate	**per**vade
percolate	**per**fection	**per**turb	**per**vert

"peri-"

The prefix "peri-", meaning "about", "round", or "enclosing", is Greek in origin.

perimeter	**peri**pheral	**peri**scope
period	**peri**phery	

"poly-"

The prefix "poly-", meaning "more than one" or "many", is Greek in origin.

polyester	**poly**glot	**poly**syllabic	**poly**urethane
polyethylene	**poly**gon	**poly**technic	
polygamy	**poly**hedron	**poly**unsaturated	

"post-"

The prefix "post-", meaning "after" or "following", is Latin in origin.

postdate	**post**modern (Also "post-modern ")	**post**partum	**post**secondary
posterior		**post**pone	
postgraduate	**post**mortem (Also "post-mortem ")	**post**script	

"pre-"

The prefix "pre-", meaning "before" or "in front of", is Latin in origin.

Sometimes a hyphen is used when the suffix "pre-" is added to a base word that begins with a vowel letter. See N3.9.

preamble	**pre**dominate	**pre**ference	**pre**lude
precede	**pre**eminent	**pre**fix	**pre**pare
precipitate	**pre**-empt (Also "preempt")	**pre**heat	**pre**vent
preclude	**pre**face	**pre**historic	
precondition	**pre**fer	**pre**judge	
prediction		**pre**judice	

"pro-"

The prefix "pro-", meaning "earlier than", "prior to", "in front of", "substituting for", "favouring" or "championing", is both Greek and Latin in origin.

proactive	**pro**fessor	**pro**hibit	**pro**pel
proboscis	**pro**fit	**pro**ject	**pro**phet
procedure	**pro**found	**pro**logue	**pro**pose
proceed	**pro**geny	**pro**long	**pro**secutor
proclaim	**pro**gram (USA, CAN)	**pro**minent	**pro**tect
procreate		**pro**mise	**pro**vide
produce	**pro**gramme (UK)	**pro**mote	
profession	**pro**gress	**pro**noun	

"pseudo-"

The prefix "pseudo-", meaning "false", "pretend", or "not real", is Greek in origin.

pseudo-intellectual **pseudo**science
pseudonym **pseudo**-sophisticated

"quadr-"

The prefix "quadr-", meaning "four" or "fourfold", is Latin in origin.

quadrangle **quadr**aphonic **quadr**uple
quadrant **quadr**uped **qua**rter

"quint-"

The prefix "quint-", meaning "five" or "fifth", is Latin in origin.

quintessence **quint**et **quint**uplet

"re-"

The prefix "re-", meaning "again", "afresh", "back", or "return to a preceding state", is Latin in origin.

There is virtually no end of words that can be formed using the prefix "re-". Only a few sample words are provided below.

Sometimes a hyphen is used when the suffix "re-" is added to a base word that begins with a vowel letter. See N3.9.

reacquaint	**re**cede	**re**cord	**re**enter
react (Also re-act)	**re**ceipt	**re**cover	(Also re-enter)
reactionary	**re**ceive	**re**creation	**re**fer
reaffirm	**re**cession	**re**cuperate	**re**ference
reanimate	**re**charge	**re**cycle	**re**fine
reappear	**re**ciprocate	**re**deem	**re**flect
reapply	**re**cite	**re**do	**re**form
reassure	**re**claim	**re**dress	**re**fuge
rebate	**re**cline	**re**duce	**re**fund
rebel	**re**cognize	**re**duction	**re**gister
rebound	**re**collection	**re**elect	**re**gress
rebuttal	**re**commend	(Also re-elect)	**re**habilitate
recall	**re**concile	**re**enact	**re**hearse
recant	**re**condition	(Also re-enact)	**re**imburse

reincarnation	**re**medy	**re**ply	**re**tract
reinforce	**re**member	**re**port	**re**treat
reject	**re**mind	**re**present	**re**trieve
relate	**re**mit	**re**produce	**re**turn
relation	**re**move	**re**pulsion	**re**veal
relax	**re**nege	**re**side	**re**venge
relegate	**re**novate	**re**sidence	**re**vise
relieve	**re**pair	**re**sidue	**re**vision
relinquish	**re**pay	**re**spond	**re**vive
relocate	**re**peat	**re**stitution	**re**voke
remain	**re**pel	**re**sume	**re**wind
remand	**re**petition	**re**surrection	**re**write
remark	**re**place	**re**taliate	

"retro-"

The prefix "retro-", meaning "backwards" or "in return", is Latin in origin.

retroactive	**retro**grade	**retro**spective
retrofit	**retro**rocket	

"semi-"

The prefix "semi-", meaning "half", "partly", "almost", or "occurring twice in a specific period", is Latin in origin.

semi-annual	**semi**-conscious	**semi**-monthly
semi-arid	**semi**detached	**semi**-permeable
semicircle	**semi**-final	**semi**-professional
semicircular	**semi**-formal	**semi**-sweet

"sex-"

The prefix "sex-", meaning "six", "a sixth part", or "sixth", is Latin in origin.

sextant	**sex**tet	**sex**tuplet

"super-"

The prefix "super-", meaning "greater", "extra", "over", "superior", or "higher in rank", is Latin in origin.

superb	**super**hero	**super**intendent	**super**lative
superfluous	**super**impose	**super**ior	**Super**man

supermarket	**super**power	**super**sede	**super**structure
supernatural	**super**saturate	**super**sonic	**super**vise
supernova	**super**script	**super**star	

"tele-"

The prefix "tele-", meaning "at a distance", "far off", or "remote", is Greek in origin.

telecommunication	**tele**kinesis	**tele**vise
teleconference	**tele**pathy	**tele**vision
telegenic	**tele**phone	
telegraph	**tele**scope	

"tetr-/tetra-"

The prefix "tetr-/tetra-", meaning "four", is Greek in origin.

tetrachloride	**tetra**gon	**tetra**hedron

"tra-/tran-/trans-"

The prefix "tra-/tran-/trans-", meaning "across", "above and beyond", "to change thoroughly", or "into another state or place", is Latin in origin.

transact	**trans**gress	**trans**mute
trans-American	**trans**ient	**trans**parent
trans-Canada	**trans**istor	**trans**pire
transcend	**trans**it	**trans**plant
transcendental	**trans**ition	**trans**port
transcontinental	**trans**itory	**trans**portation
transcribe	**trans**late	**trans**pose
transcript	**trans**lucent	**trans**sexual
transducer	**trans**mission	**trans**vestite
transfer	**trans**mit	
transform	**trans**mitter	

"tri-"

The prefix "tri-", meaning "three", "third", or "every third", is both Latin and Greek in origin.

triad	**tri**athlon	**tri**color (USA)	**tri**dent
triangle	**tri**ceps	**tri**colour (UK, CAN)	**tri**ennial
Triassic	**tri**ceratops	**tri**cycle	**tri**focal

trike
trilateral
trilingual
trillion (A thousand thousand thousand)
trilogy

trimester
Trinity
trio
triode
trioxide

tripartite
triple
triplet
triplex
tripod

triumvirate
triweekly

"ultra-"

The prefix "ultra-", meaning "beyond", "extremely", or "excessively", is Latin in origin.

ultra vires (Latin)
ultraconservative
ultralight

ultramarathon
ultramarine
ultramodern

ultrasonic
ultrasound
ultraviolet

"un-"

The prefix "un-", meaning "not", "opposing", "reversal", "removal" or "release", is Old English in origin.

There is virtually no end of words that can be formed using the prefix "un-". Only a few sample words are provided below.

unabashed
unable
unacceptable
unaccompanied
unaccountable
unachievable
unadvised
unaffordable
un-American
unanswered
unappealing
unappreciative
unarmed
unascertained
unassailable
unassertive
unassuming
unattached
unauthorized
unavailable
unbalanced
unbeatable

unbecoming
unborn
unbroken
un-Canadian
uncanny
unceasing
uncertain
unchallenged
unchaste
uncivilised (UK, CAN)
uncivilized (USA, CAN)
unclear
uncomfortable
uncommitted
unconditional
unconscious
uncouth
uncover
undecided
undemocratic
undeserving

undesirable
undignified
undivided
undo
undoing
undone
undressed
undue
uneasy
uneconomical
uneducated
unemployed
unencumbered
unequal
uneven
unexpected
unfailing
unfair
unfaithful
unfavorable (USA)
unfavourable (UK, CAN)

unfeeling
unfold
unforeseeable
unforgettable
unfortunate
ungraceful
unguarded
unhappy
unhealthy
unheard
unimaginable
unimportant
uninformative
uninhabitable
uninspired
uninterested
unjust
unkind
unknown
unlawful
unlike
unlock

unloved	**un**ravel	**un**scrupulous	**un**tenable
unlucky	**un**realistic	**un**seen	**un**thinkable
unmasked	**un**recognizable	**un**selfish	**un**tie
unmitigated	**un**refined	**un**serviceable	**un**true
unmotivated	**un**related	**un**settled	**un**truthful
unnatural	**un**remarkable	**un**sociable	**un**usable
unnecessary	**un**resolved	**un**sound	**un**usual
unobtrusive	**un**rewarding	**un**stable	**un**willing
unofficial	**un**sanitary	**un**steady	**un**wise
unorthodox	**un**satisfactory	**un**successful	**un**worthy
unpatriotic	**un**savory (USA)	**un**supported	**un**yielding
unpleasant	**un**savoury (UK, CAN)	**un**suspected	
unprofitable	**un**scientific	**un**sustainable	
unqualified		**un**systematic	

"under-"

The prefix "under-", meaning "below", "beneath", "lower in status", "too little", or "insufficiently", is Old English in origin.

under	**under**cut	**under**mine	**under**study
underachieve	**under**dog	**under**neath	**under**take
underarm	**under**estimate	**under**pants	**under**taker
underbrush	**under**foot	**under**pass	**under**water
undercarriage	**under**graduate	**under**pin	**under**way
undercook	**under**ground	**under**shirt	**under**wear
undercover	**under**handed	**under**stand	**under**world
undercurrent	**under**line	**under**stated	**under**writer

"uni-"

The prefix "uni-", meaning "one" or "single", is Latin in origin.

unicellular	**uni**formity	**uni**son	**uni**ty
unicycle	**uni**lateral	**uni**t	**uni**versal
unidimensional	**uni**lingual	**uni**tary	
unification	**uni**que	**uni**te	
uniform	**uni**sex	**uni**ted	

G3 Allomorphs of "ad-": "a-", "ac-", "af-", "ag-", "al-", "an-", "ap-", "ar-", "as-", and "at-"

Allomorphs are prefixes that change in spelling without a related change in meaning. The spelling of the prefix depends upon the spelling of the base word to which it is attached. The prefix is said to "assimilate". The change in spelling makes the derived word easier to pronounce.

"ad-"

The prefix "ad-", meaning "to", "at", "motion toward", "addition to", or "nearness to", is Latin in origin. It has ten allomorphs: "a-", "ac-", "af-", "ag-", "al-", "an-", "ap-", "ar-", "as-", and "at-".

The prefix "ad-" is attached to base words that begin with letters that are not discussed elsewhere in this section. The "ad-" spelling is also found whenever the "nearness to" meaning is intended, even when attached to base words that begin with letters that are discussed elsewhere in this section.

addict	**ad**join	**ad**minister	**ad**renal
adjacent	**ad**journ	**ad**mire	**ad**vocate
adjective	**ad**just	**ad**mit	

"a-"

The prefix "ad-" becomes "a-" with base words that begin with the letters "sc", "sp", and "st".

ascend	**a**spect	**a**stigmatism
ascent	**a**spire	

"ac-"

The prefix "ad-" becomes "ac-" with base words that begin with the letters "c" and "q". Note the double consonant.

accompany	**ac**custom	**ac**quire
accurate	**ac**quaint	

"af-"

The prefix "ad-" becomes "af-" with base words that begin with the letter "f". Note the double consonant.

affirm	**af**fix

"ag-"

The prefix "ad-" becomes "ag-" with base words that begin with the letter "g". Note the double consonant.

aggravate   **ag**grieve

"al-"

The prefix "ad-" becomes "al-" with base words that begin with the letter "l". Note the double consonant.

allot

"an-"

The prefix "ad-" becomes "an-" with base words that begin with the letter "n". Note the double consonant.

annotate   **an**nounce

"ap-"

The prefix "ad-" becomes "ap-" with base words that begin with the letter "p". Note the double consonant.

apparatus   **ap**proach   **ap**propriate   **ap**proximate

"ar-"

The prefix "ad-" becomes "ar-" with base words that begin with the letter "r". Note the double consonant.

arraign   **ar**range   **ar**ray   **ar**rest

"as-"

The prefix "ad-" becomes "as-" with base words that begin with the letter "s". Note the double consonant.

assemble   **as**sert   **as**similate
assent   **as**sign   **as**sort

"at-"

The prefix "ad-" becomes "at-" with base words that begin with the letter "t". Note the double consonant.

attain	**at**tempt	**at**tend	**at**tune

G4 Allomorphs of "com-": "co-", "col-", "con-", and "cor-"

Allomorphs are prefixes that change in spelling without a related change in meaning. The spelling of the prefix depends upon the spelling of the base word to which it is attached. The prefix is said to "assimilate". The change in spelling makes the derived word easier to pronounce.

"com-"

The prefix "com-", meaning "with", "together", "next to", or "jointly", is Latin in origin. It has four allomorphs: "co-", "col-", "con-", and "cor-".

The "com-" spelling is found with base words that begin with the letters "b", "m", and "p". Note the double consonant with base words that begin with the letter "m".

combat	**com**mence	**com**panion	**com**plex
combative	**com**ment	**com**pare	**com**pose
combination	**com**merce	**com**partment	**com**pound
combine	**com**miserate	**com**pel	**com**prehend
combust	**com**mit	**com**pete	**com**promise
commemorate	**com**pact	**com**plain	**com**puter

"co-"

The prefix "com-" shortened to "co-" is associated with a wide variety of spellings. The prefix "co-" also means "to the same degree", "joint effort or action", or "partners". Sometimes a hyphen is used when the suffix "co-" is added to a base word that begins with a vowel letter. See N3.9.

coagulate	**co**efficient	**co**herence	**co**-worker
coalesce	**co**exist	**co**hesion	
coalition	**co**founder	**co**incide	
coauthor	**co**gent	**co**incidence	
(Also co-author)	**co**habit	**co**-pilot	

"col-"

The prefix "com-" becomes "col-" with base words that begin with the letters "l". Note the double consonant.

collaborate	**col**lect	**col**lide
collapse	**col**lection	**col**loquy
collateral	**col**lege	**col**lusion

"con-"

The prefix "com-" becomes "con-" with base words that begin with letters that are not discussed elsewhere in this section.

concave	**con**demn	**con**glomerate	**con**stant
conceal	**con**dense	**con**gratulate	**con**struct
concede	**con**descend	**con**jecture	**con**sume
conceive	**con**dition	**con**jugate	**con**tain
concentrate	**con**federate	**con**nect	**con**template
concern	**con**ference	**con**science	**con**temporary
concert	**con**fess	**con**scious	**con**tingent
concise	**con**fidence	**con**sent	**con**tribute
conclude	**con**firm	**con**sequence	**con**vection
concoct	**con**fiscate	**con**servation	**con**verge
concord	**con**flict	**con**sider	**con**vert
concurrence	**con**form	**con**sistency	
concussion	**con**geal	**con**spicuous	

"cor-"

The prefix "com-" becomes "cor-" with base words that begin with the letters "r". Note the double consonant.

correct	**cor**respond	**cor**rode
correlation	**cor**roborate	**cor**rupt

G5 Allomorphs of "in-" Meaning "Not": "ig-", "il-", "im-", and "ir-"

Allomorphs are prefixes that change in spelling without a related change in meaning. The spelling of the prefix depends upon the spelling of the base word to which it is attached. The prefix is said to "assimilate". The change in spelling makes the derived word easier to pronounce.

"in-"

The prefix "in-", meaning "not", "without", or "lacking", is Latin in origin. It has four allomorphs: "ig-", "il-", "im-", and "ir-".

The prefix "in-" is attached to base words that begin with letters that are not discussed elsewhere in this section.

inaccessible	**in**advisable	**in**convenient	**in**edible
inaccurate	**in**animate	**in**credible	**in**fallible
inaction	**in**appropriate	**in**decent	**in**nocuous
inadequate	**in**capable	**in**decisive	**in**sane
inadmissible	**in**congruous	**in**discretion	**in**transigent

"ig-"

The prefix "in-" becomes "ig-" with base words that begin with the letter "n".

ignoble	**ig**nominy	**ig**norance	**ig**nore

"il-"

The prefix "in-" becomes "il-" with base words that begin with the letter "l". Note the double consonant.

illegal	**il**legitimate	**il**literate	**il**luminate
illegible	**il**licit	**il**logical	**il**lusion

"im-"

The prefix "in-" becomes "im-" with base words that begin with the letter "b", "m", and "p". Note the double consonant with base words that begin with the letter "m".

imbalance	**im**mature	**im**mortal	**im**possible
imbecile	**im**mobile	**im**mutable	
immaterial	**im**moral	**im**penetrable	

"ir-"

The prefix "in-" becomes "ir-" with base words that begin with the letter "r". Note the double consonant.

irrational	**ir**regular	**ir**replaceable	**ir**responsible

G6 Allomorphs of "in-" Meaning "In" or "On": "il-", "im-", and "ir-"

Allomorphs are prefixes that change in spelling without a related change in meaning. The spelling of the prefix depends upon the spelling of the base word to which it is attached. The prefix is said to "assimilate". The change in spelling makes the derived word easier to pronounce.

"in-"

The prefix "in-", meaning "in", "on", "into", "towards", or "within", is Latin in origin. It has three allomorphs: "il-", "im-", and "ir-".

The prefix "in-" is attached to base words that begin with letters that are not discussed elsewhere in this section.

incandescent	**in**duce	**in**flate	**in**ject
incarcerate	**in**duct	**in**flation	**in**sight
incarnation	**in**fatuate	**in**fluence	**in**trude
inception	**in**fer	**in**flux	**in**vade
incident	**in**flame	**in**form	
incline	**in**flammable	**in**habit	

"il-"

The prefix "in-" becomes "il-" with base words that begin with the letter "l". Note the double consonant.

illuminate	**il**lusion	**il**lustrate	**il**lustrious

"im-"

The prefix "in-" becomes "im-" with base words that begin with the letter "m". Note the double consonant.

immediate	**im**mense	**im**migrant	**im**minent
immemorial	**im**merge	**im**migrate	**im**port

"ir-"

The prefix "in-" becomes "ir-" with base words that begin with the letter "r". Note the double consonant.

irradiate	**ir**rigate	**ir**ritate	**ir**rupt

G7   Allomorphs of "ob-": "o-", "oc-", "of-", and "op-"

Allomorphs are prefixes that change in spelling without a related change in meaning. The spelling of the prefix depends upon the spelling of the base word to which it is attached. The prefix is said to "assimilate". The change in spelling makes the derived word easier to pronounce.

"ob-"

The prefix "ob-", meaning "toward", "for", "about", or "before", is Latin in origin. It has four allomorphs: "o-", "oc-", "of-", and "op-".

The prefix "ob-" is attached to base words that begin with letters that are not discussed elsewhere in this section.

obese	**ob**livion	**ob**serve	**ob**struct
obey	**ob**long	**ob**session	**ob**tain
obfuscate	**ob**noxious	**ob**solete	**ob**trude
object	**ob**scure	**ob**stacle	**ob**vious
oblique	**ob**sequious	**ob**stinate	

"o-"

The prefix "ob-" becomes "o-" with base words that begin with the letter "m".

omit   **o**mission

"oc-"

The prefix "ob-" becomes "oc-" with base words that begin with the letter "c". Note the double consonant.

occasion   **oc**cult   **oc**cupy   **oc**cur

"of-"

The prefix "ob-" becomes "of-" with base words that begin with the letter "f". Note the double consonant.

offend   **of**fer

"op-"

The prefix "ob-" becomes "op-" with base words that begin with the letter "p". Note the double consonant.

opportunity   **op**pose   **op**posite   **op**press

G8 Allomorphs of "sub-": "suc-", "suf-", "sug-", "sum-", "sup-", "sur-", and "sus-"

Allomorphs are prefixes that change in spelling without a related change in meaning. The spelling of the prefix depends upon the spelling of the base word to which it is attached. The prefix is said to "assimilate". The change in spelling makes the derived word easier to pronounce.

"sub-"

The prefix "sub-", meaning "under", "beneath", "below", "lower position", "near", "subordinate", "secondary", "inferior", "almost", or "less than perfect or complete", is Latin in origin. It has eight allomorphs: "suc-", "suf-", "sug-", "sum-", "sup-", "sur-", and "sus-"

The prefix "sub-" is attached to base words that begin with letters that are not discussed elsewhere in this section.

subatomic	**sub**due	**sub**mission	**sub**title
subbasement	**sub**human	**sub**mit	**sub**total
subcommittee	**sub**ject	**sub**ordinate	**sub**tract
subcontract	**sub**jugate	**sub**sidiary	**sub**tropical
subcontractor	**sub**let	**sub**sistence	**sub**urb
subculture	**sub**-lieutenant	**sub**standard	**sub**vert
subdivide	**sub**marine	**sub**stitute	**sub**way
subdivision	**sub**merge	**sub**terranean	

"suc-"

The prefix "sub-" becomes "suc-" with base words that begin with the letter "c". Note the double consonant.

succeed   **suc**cess   **suc**cinct   **suc**cumb

"suf-"

The prefix "sub-" becomes "suf-" with base words that begin with the letter "f". Note the double consonant.

suffer   **suf**fice   **suf**fix   **suf**focate

"sug-"

The prefix "sub-" becomes "sug-" with base words that begin with the letter "g". Note the double consonant.

suggest   **sug**gestion

"sum-"

The prefix "sub-" becomes "sum-" with base words that begin with the letter "m". Note the double consonant.

summon

"sup-"

The prefix "sub-" becomes "sup-" with base words that begin with the letter "p". Note the double consonant.

supplant   **sup**plement   **sup**port   **sup**press
supple   **sup**ply   **sup**pose

"sur-"

The prefix "sub-" becomes "sur-" with base words that begin with the letter "r". Note the double consonant.

surreptitious   **sur**rogate

"sus-"

The prefix "sub-" sometimes becomes "sus-" with base words that begin with the letters "c", "p", and "t".

susceptible   **sus**pend   **sus**tain
suspect   **sus**pense

G9   Allomorphs of "syn-": "sy-", "syl-", and "sym-"

Allomorphs are prefixes that change in spelling without a related change in meaning. The spelling of the prefix depends upon the spelling of the base word to which it is attached. The prefix is said to "assimilate". The change in spelling makes the derived word easier to pronounce.

"syn-"

The prefix "syn-" meaning "with", "together", or "at the same time", is Greek in origin. It has three allomorphs: "sy-", "syl-", and "sym-".

The prefix "syn-" is attached to base words that begin with letters that are not discussed elsewhere in this section.

synchronize	**syn**drome	**syn**ergy	**syn**tax

"sy-"

The prefix "syn-" becomes "sy-" with base words that begin with the letters "s" and "z".

system	**sy**stematic	**sy**stemic	**sy**zygy

"syl-"

The prefix "syn-" becomes "syl-" with base words that begin with the letter "l". Note the double consonant.

syllable	**syl**logism

"sym-"

The prefix "syn-" becomes "sym-" with base words that begin with the letters "b", "m", and "p". Note the double consonant with base words that begin with the letter "m".

symbiosis	**sym**bolic	**sym**metrical	**sym**pathy
symbol	**sym**bolize	**sym**metry	**sym**phony

Part H: Root Words

H1 Introduction

Words are made up of component parts called morphemes. A morpheme is the smallest part of a word that conveys meaning. There are three kinds of morphemes: "prefixes", "root words", and "suffixes".

At the core of every word is a root which gives the word its essential meaning. Additional letters, called "affixes", may be added to the beginning or to the end of a root. An affix added to the beginning of a root is called a "prefix". An affix added to the end of a root is called a "suffix". Many words have both a prefix and a suffix, and it is possible to attach more than one prefix or suffix. Prefixes and suffixes create new words by adding to the meaning of the root.

The letters "dict", for example, form a root word that means "to speak" in Latin. Adding the prefix "contra-", meaning "against" or "opposite", to "dict" creates the word "contradict". Adding the suffix "-ate", which forms verbs, to "dict" creates the word "dictate".

A base word is any word to which a prefix or suffix may be added. Some base words are also root words. Most base words are not root words because they already have a prefix or suffix attached.

Morphemes may be divided into "lexical morphemes" and "relational morphemes". A lexical morpheme conveys a particular meaning in and of itself. A relational morpheme only conveys grammatical meaning in relation to the word to which it is attached. Morphemes may also be divided into "free morphemes" and "bound morphemes". Free morphemes can function as free-standing words. Bound morphemes cannot function as free-standing words and are only used attached to other morphemes.

The word "ports", for example, contains two morphemes. The root word "port" is a lexical morpheme that means "to carry". As well, "port" is a free morpheme that can function as a word. The suffix "-s" is a relational morpheme used to create the plural form of words. The suffix "-s" does not convey any meaning on its own. As well, the suffix "-s" is a bound morpheme that cannot stand alone as a word.

Root words are lexical morphemes. That is, root words have particular meanings. The meaning of a root is often augmented by the addition of a prefix or suffix. While many roots are free morphemes that can stand alone as words, others are bound morphemes that are only found attached to a prefix or suffix.

The following list highlights a selection of roots that are most often found bound within longer words with the addition of a prefix or suffix. There are also many roots that can stand alone as English words.

Words that contain the same root share some degree of common meaning forming word families. Most bound morpheme root words are Greek or Latin in origin. The meaning of a root word may seem obtuse to modern readers but would have made sense when first used.

H2 Common Root Words

"act"

The root word "act", meaning "to do" or "doing", is Latin in origin.

act	**act**or	re**act**
action	**act**ress	re**act**or

"aeri/aero"

The root words "aeri/aero", meaning "air", are Greek in origin.

aerial	**aero**dynamics	**aero**plane (UK)
aerobic	**aero**nautics	

"agra/agri/agro"

The root words "agra/agri/agro", meaning "field", are Greek in origin.

agrarian	**agri**culture	**agro**nomist	**agro**nomy

"ama/amo/ami"

The root words "ama/amo/ami", meaning "lover" or "to love", are Latin in origin.

amateur	**ami**cable	**ami**ty
amiable	**ami**go	**amo**rous

"anim"

The root word "anim", meaning "living being", "breath", "air", "spirit", or "life principle", is Latin in origin.

animal	**anim**ated	re**anim**ate
animate	**anim**ation	

"annus/enni"

The root words "annus/enni", meaning "year", are Latin in origin.

anniversary	**annu**ally	cent**enni**al
annual	bi**annu**al	

"aqua/aque"

The root words "aqua/aque", meaning "water", are Latin in origin.

aquamarine	**aqua**tic	**aque**ous
aquarium	**aque**duct	

"arch"

The root word "arch", meaning "main", "chief", "ruler", or "leader", is Greek in origin.

an**arch**y	**arch**bishop	matri**arch**	mon**arch**y
archangel	**arch**enemy	mon**arch**	olig**arch**y

"ast/aster/astron"

The root words "ast/aster/astron", meaning "star" are Greek in origin.

asterisk	**astro**logy	**astron**omical	dis**ast**er
asteroid	**astron**aut	**astron**omy	
astral	**astron**autics	**astron**omy	
astrodome	**astron**omer	**astro**physics	

"aud"

The root word "aud", meaning "hearing" or "listening", is Latin in origin.

audible	**aud**io	**aud**itorium	in**aud**ible
audience	**aud**ition	**aud**itory	

"bio"

The root word "bio", meaning "life" or "to live", is Greek in origin.

biochemist	**bio**graphy	**bio**logy
biochemistry	**bio**logist	**bio**psy

"bene"

The root word "bene", meaning "good" or "well", is Latin in origin.

benefaction	**bene**ficial	**bene**ficiary	**bene**fit

"cap"

The root word "cap", meaning "head", is Latin in origin.

cap	**cap**tain	per **cap**ita
capital	de**cap**itate	

"cap/cip/cept"

The root words "cap/cip/cept", meaning "to take", "to have", or "to hold", are Latin in origin.

ac**cep**t	**cap**acity	con**cept**	prin**cip**al
anti**cip**ate	**cap**tivate	de**cep**tion	
capable	**cap**ture	parti**cip**ate	

"chron"

The root word "chron", meaning "time", is Greek in origin.

chronic	**chron**ograph	**chron**ology	syn**chron**ize
chronicle	**chron**ological	**chron**ometer	

"cracy/crat"

The root words "cracy/crat", meaning "rule", "strength", or "theory of government", are Greek in origin.

aristo**cracy**	auto**cracy**	bureau**cracy**	demo**cracy**
aristo**crat**	auto**crat**	bureau**crat**	demo**crat**

"crit"

The root word "crit", meaning "critical" or "able to discern", is Greek in origin.

critic	**crit**ical	**crit**icize	hyper**crit**ical

"cycl"

The root word "cycl", meaning "circle", is Greek in origin.

bi**cycl**e	**cycl**ical	en**cycl**opedia (USA)
cycle	**cycl**one	tri**cycl**e
cyclic	en**cycl**opaedia (UK, CAN)	uni**cycl**e

"dem"

The root word "dem", meaning "the people", is Greek in origin.

demagogue	**dem**ocratic	epi**dem**ic
democracy	**dem**ographics	

"dent"

The root word "dent", meaning "tooth", is Latin in origin.

dental	**dent**ifrice	**dent**ist	tri**dent**

"dict"

The root word "dict", meaning "to speak", is Latin in origin.

bene**dict**ion	**dict**ate	**dict**ionary	pre**dict**
contra**dict**	**dict**ation	e**dict**	
contra**dict**ion	**dict**ator	in**dict**	

"doc"

The root word "doc", meaning "to teach", is Latin in origin.

docile	**doc**trine	**doc**umentary
doctor	**doc**ument	

"dox"

The root word "dox", meaning "to think" or "opinion", is Greek in origin.

ortho**dox**   para**dox**

"duct/duce"

The root words "duct/duce", meaning "to lead" or "to pull", are Latin in origin.

air **duct**   con**duct**   intro**duct**ion
aque**duct**   intro**duce**

"ethic"

The root word "ethic", meaning "character", "custom", or "moral", is Greek in origin.

ethical   **ethic**s   **eth**os

"ethn"

The root word "ethn", meaning "nation", is Greek in origin.

ethnic   **ethn**icity   **ethn**ology

"fac"

The root word "fac", meaning "do", "that which is done", "deed", "fact", or "make", is Latin in origin.

bene**fac**tor   **fac**t   **fac**tory
facsimile   **fac**tor   manu**fac**ture

"fer"

The root word "fer", meaning "to bring together", "compare", or "confer", is Latin in origin.

con**fer**   de**fer**   re**fer**   trans**fer**

"flex/flect"

The root words "flex/flect", meaning "to bend", are Latin in origin.

deflect flexible reflection
deflection reflect reflex

"form"

The root word "form", meaning "a shape", "figure", or "image", is Latin in origin.

form trans**form** uni**form**
formation trans**form**ation uni**form**ity

"gen"

The root word "gen", meaning "to beget or produce", "race", or "decent", is Greek in origin.

genealogy **gen**eration **gen**ocide
generate **gen**etics pro**gen**y

"geo"

The root word "geo", meaning "the earth", is Greek in origin.

geographer **geo**graphy **geo**metry
geographical **geo**logy **geo**physical

"gnos"

The root word "gnos", meaning "knowledge" or "to know", is Greek in origin.

a**gnos**tic **Gnos**ticism pro**gnos**ticate

"gon"

The root word "gon", meaning "angle" or "corner", is Greek in origin.

dia**gon**al hexa**gon** octa**gon** penta**gon**

"gram"

The root word "gram", meaning "to write" or "written", is Greek in origin.

dia**gram** **gram**mar tele**gram**
epi**gram** **gram**matical

"graph"

The root word "graph", meaning "to write" or "writing", is Latin in origin.

autobio**graph**y	bio**graph**y	photo**graph**
auto**graph**	calli**graph**y	porno**graph**ic
biblio**graph**y	**graph**ic	tele**graph**

"grat"

The root word "grat", meaning "pleasing" or "agreeable" is Latin in origin.

con**grat**ulate   **grat**eful   **grat**ify   **grat**itude

"hydro"

The root word "hydro", meaning "water", is Greek in origin.

de**hydr**ate	**hydro**	**hydro**gen
hydrant	**hydro**electric	

"ject"

The root word "ject", meaning "to throw", is Latin in origin.

e**ject**	ob**ject**ing	pro**ject**	re**ject**
in**ject**	ob**ject**ion	pro**ject**ile	sub**ject**
ob**ject**	ob**ject**ive	pro**ject**ing	sub**ject**ive
ob**ject**ed	ob**ject**s	pro**ject**or	

"jud/jus"

The root words "jud/jus", meaning "law" or "judge", are Latin in origin.

judge	**jus**t	pre**jud**ge
judicial	**jus**tice	pre**jud**ice

"liber"

The root word "liber", meaning "free", is Latin in origin.

liberal	**liber**tarian	**liber**ty
liberate	**liber**tine	

"lingu"

The root word "lingu", meaning "language", is Latin in origin.

linguist   **lingu**istic   multi**lingu**al

"loc"

The root word "loc", meaning "a place", is Latin in origin.

al**loc**ate   **loc**al   **loc**ation
dis**loc**ate   **loc**ate

"log/logue"

The root words "log/logue", meaning "word", "thought", "discourse", or reckoning", are Greek in origin.

ana**log**y   epi**log** (USA)   **log**arithm   pro**logue**
archaeo**log**y   epi**logue**   **log**ic   psycho**log**y
cata**log** (USA)   (UK, CAN)   mono**log**   syl**log**ism
cata**logue**   eu**log**y   (USA, CAN)   theo**log**ical
(UK, CAN)   genea**log**y   mono**logue**   theo**log**y
dia**log**ue   geo**log**y   (UK, CAN)

"luc"

The root word "luc", meaning "filled with light", is Latin in origin.

e**luc**idate   **luc**id   **luc**ent   trans**luc**ent

"lumin"

The root word "lumin", meaning "light", is Latin in origin.

il**lumin**e   **lumin**ary   **lumin**escent   **lumin**ous

"magna/magni"

The root words "magna/magni", meaning "great", "big", or "large", is Latin in origin.

magnanimous   **magni**ficent   **magni**tude
magnate   **magni**fy

"mal"

The root word "mal", meaning "bad", "evil", "wrong", or "ill", is Latin in origin.

maladapted	**mal**function	**mal**odorous
malfeasance	**mal**icious	

"man"

The root word "man", meaning "a hand", is Latin in origin.

manipulate	**man**ual	**man**ufacture	**man**uscript

"mand"

The root word "mand", meaning "to put into one's hand", "to entrust", or "to command", is Latin in origin.

com**mand**	de**mand**	**mand**ate	re**mand**

"mar"

The root word "mar", meaning "the sea", is Latin in origin.

marina	**mar**iner	sub**mar**ine
marine	**mar**itime	

"mech"

The root word "mech", meaning "machine", is Greek in origin.

mechanic	**mech**anical	**mech**anism	**mech**anize

"mega"

The root word "mega", meaning "large", "great", or "powerful", is Greek in origin.

megabucks	**mega**hertz	**mega**lomaniac	**mega**vitamin
megabyte	**mega**lomania	**mega**phone	

"mem"

The root word "mem", meaning "mindful" or "memory", is Latin in origin.

memento	**mem**orabilia	**mem**orandum	**mem**ory
memoir	**mem**orable	**mem**orial	re**mem**ber

"meter"

The root word "meter", meaning "to mark off", "measure", or "a measuring device", is Greek in origin.

baro**meter**	**meter**	thermo**meter**	
hygro**meter**	odo**meter**		

"min"

The root word "min", meaning "small" or "to lessen", is Latin in origin.

Miniature	**min**imize	**min**iscule	**min**us
Mini	**min**imum	**min**or	**min**ute

"mit/miss/mise"

The root words "mit/miss/mise", meaning "to send" or "to throw", are Latin in origin.

de**mise**	**miss**ion	pro**mise**	trans**mit**
dis**miss**	o**miss**ion	sub**miss**ion	
e**miss**ary	o**mit**	sub**mit**	
missile	per**mit**	sur**mise**	

"mob"

The root word "mob", meaning "movable", is Latin in origin.

auto**mob**ile	im**mob**ile	**mob**ile	**mob**ility

"mort"

The root word "mort", meaning "death", is Latin in origin.

mortal	**mort**gage	**mort**uary
mortality	**mort**ician	post-**mort**em

"mot/mov"

The root words "mot/mov", meaning "to move", are Latin in origin.

motion	**mot**ive	**mot**or	**mo**ve

"multi"

The root word "multi", meaning "much" or "many", is Latin in origin.

multiple	**multi**plicity	**multi**ply	**multi**tude

"nat"

The root word "nat", meaning "to be born", is Latin in origin.

in**nate**	**nat**ional	**nat**ive	**nat**ure
natal	**nat**ionality	**nat**ivity	neo**nat**al

"nom/nomos"

The root words "nom/nomos", meaning "law", are Greek in origin.

anti**nom**y	auto**nom**ous	auto**nom**y	Deutero**nom**y

"nov"

The root word "nov", meaning "new" or "to renew", is Latin in origin.

in**nov**ate	**nov**el	**nov**ice	
in**nov**ation	**nov**elty		

"nym"

The root word "nym", meaning "name", is Greek in origin.

acro**nym**	homo**nym**	pseudo**nym**	syno**nym**

"oculus"

The root word "oculus", meaning "of the eyes", is Latin in origin.

bin**ocul**ar	mon**oc**le	**ocul**ar	mon**ocul**ar

"oph/opt"

The root words "oph/opt", meaning "of the eyes", are Greek in origin.

ophthalmology	**opt**ical	**opt**ometrist
optic	**opt**ician	**opt**ometry

"optim"

The root word "optim", meaning "best", is Latin in origin.

optimal	**optim**ist	**optim**ize	**optim**um

"ora"

The root word "ora", meaning "to speak" or "the mouth", is Latin in origin.

oracle	**ora**tion	**ora**tory
oral	**ora**torio	

"ortho"

The root word "ortho", meaning "correct" or "straight", is Latin in origin.

orthodontics	**ortho**paedics	**ortho**pedics
orthodontist	(UK, CAN)	(USA)
orthodox		**ortho**tics

"ped"

The root word "ped", meaning "foot", is Latin in origin.

pedal	**ped**estrian	**ped**igree
pedestal	**ped**icure	**ped**ometer

"path"

The root word "path", meaning "feeling", is Greek in origin.

em**path**y	**path**etic	**path**os	sym**path**y

"pel/puls"

The root words "pel/puls", meaning "to drive", "to beat", or "to thrust", are Latin in origin.

com**pel**	ex**pel**	pro**puls**ion	re**pel**
com**puls**ion	pro**pel**	**puls**e	

"pend"

The root word "pend", meaning "hang", is Latin in origin.

ap**pend**	**pend**ing	sus**pend**	sus**pen**sion
ap**pend**ix	**pend**ulum	sus**pen**se	

"phem"

The root word "phem", meaning "to speak" or "utterance", is Greek in origin.

blas**phem**e   eu**phem**ism

"philo"

The root word "philo", meaning "to love", is Greek in origin.

haemo**phil**ia (UK, CAN)	hemo**phil**ia (USA)	**philo**dendron	**philo**sophy
	philanthropy	**philo**sopher	

"phon"

The root word "phon", meaning "sound", is Greek in origin.

caco**phon**y	micro**phone**	poly**phon**y	tele**phon**e
eu**phon**y	**phon**ics	saxo**phone**	
mega**phone**	**phon**ograph	sym**phon**y	

"photo/phos"

The root words "photo/phos", meaning "light", are Greek in origin.

phosphorescence	**photo**graphy	tele**photo**
photograph	**photo**synthesis	

"physi"

The root word "physi", meaning "nature", is Greek in origin.

physical	**physi**cian	**physi**cist	**physi**que

"pod"

The root word "pod", meaning "foot", is Greek in origin.

podiatrist   **pod**iatry   **pod**ium

"poli/polis"

The root words "poli/polis", meaning "city" or "state", are Greek in origin.

cosmo**poli**tan	metro**poli**tan	**poli**cy	**poli**tician
metro**polis**	**pol**ice	**poli**tical	**poli**tics

"port"

The root word "port", meaning "to carry", is Latin in origin.

ex**port**	**port**	**port**er	trans**port**
im**port**	**port**able	**port**manteau	

"psych"

The root word "psych", meaning "breath", "spirit", "soul", or "mind", is Greek in origin.

psyche	**psych**ologist	**psych**opath
psychiatrist	**psych**ology	

"rect"

The root word "rect", meaning "to make straight" or "to rule", is Latin in origin.

cor**rect**	di**rect**ion	**rect**angle
di**rect**	e**rect**	

"rupt"

The root word "rupt", meaning "to break", is Latin in origin.

ab**rupt**   e**rupt**   inter**rupt**   **rupt**ure

"sci"

The root word "sci", meaning "to know", is Latin in origin.

conscience	omniscient	science	scientist
conscious	prescience	scientific	

"scope"

The root word "scope", meaning "instrument for viewing", is Greek in origin.

microscope	scope	telescope
periscope	stethoscope	

"scribe/script"

The root words "scribe/script", meaning "to write", are Latin in origin.

describe	manuscript	script
description	prescription	transcribe
inscribe	scribe	transcript

"sect"

The root word "sect", meaning "to cut", is Latin in origin.

bisect	dissect	section	sector

"sens"

The root word "sens", meaning "to feel" or "to perceive", is Latin in origin.

sensation	sensible	sensual
sense	sensory	sensuous

"sign"

The root word "sign", meaning "a mark or token", is Latin in origin.

designate	resign	sign	signatory
insignia	resignation	signal	signature

"son"

The root word "son", meaning "a sound", is Latin in origin.

dissonance	sonar	sonnet	unison
resonance	sonic	sonorous	

"soph"

The root word "soph", meaning "wise", is Greek in origin.

philo**soph**er	**soph**ism	**soph**isticated
philo**soph**y	**soph**ist	**soph**omore

"spect"

The root word "spect", meaning "to look at" or "see", is Latin in origin.

circum**spect**	in**spect**ion	**spect**acles	su**spect**
in**spect**	pro**spect**ive	**spect**ator	

"spir"

The root word "spir", meaning "to breathe", is Latin in origin.

con**spir**e	in**spir**e	re**spir**ation	tran**spir**e
in**spir**ation	per**spir**e	**spir**it	

"sta"

The root word "sta", meaning "to stand", is Latin in origin.

stabile	**sta**ble	**sta**nd	**sta**tionary
stability	**sta**gnant	**sta**tion	**sta**tute

"struct"

The root word "struct", meaning "to pile up" or "build", is Latin in origin.

con**struct**	de**struct**ion	in**struct**
con**struct**ion	de**struct**ive	**struct**ure

"temp"

The root word "temp", meaning "to pull or stretch", "time", or "period", is Latin in origin.

con**temp**orary	**temp**erament	**temp**o	**temp**orary
temper	**temp**erature	**temp**oral	

"ten/tent/tin/tain"

The root words "ten/tent/tin/tain", meaning "to hold", are Latin in origin.

abs**tain**	main**tain**	**ten**able	**ten**ure
con**tain**	per**tain**	**ten**acious	
incon**tin**ent	per**tin**ent	**ten**ancy	
lieu**ten**ant	re**tent**ion	**ten**ant	

"terr"

The root word "terr", meaning "land" or "earth", is Latin in origin.

terrace	**terr**estrial	**terr**itory
terrain	**terr**itorial	

"text"

The root word "text", meaning "to weave", is Latin in origin.

con**text**	**text**	**text**ile	**text**ure

"therm"

The root word "therm", meaning "heat", is Greek in origin.

thermal	**therm**ometer	**therm**os	**therm**ostat

"tract"

The root word "tract", meaning "to draw or pull", is Latin in origin.

at**tract**	con**tract**ion	re**tract**or	**tract**ion
con**tract**	re**tract**	sub**tract**	**tract**or

"trud/trus"

The root words "trud/trus", meaning "to thrust or push", are Latin in origin.

ex**trud**e	in**trud**e	ob**trus**ive	pro**trud**e

"turb"

The root word "turb", meaning "disorder" or "confusion", is Latin in origin.

dis**turb**	per**turb**	**turb**ine	**turb**ulent

"urb"

The root word "urb", meaning "city", is Latin in origin.

sub**urb**	sub**urb**an	**urb**an	**urb**ane

"vac"

The root word "vac", meaning "to be empty", is Latin in origin.

vacancy	**vac**ant	**vac**ate	**vac**uum

"val"

The root word "val", meaning "to be strong" or "worthy", is Latin in origin.

valiant	**val**or (USA)	**val**uable
valid	**val**our (UK, CAN)	**val**ue

"var"

The root word "var", meaning "different", "diverse", or "to change", is Latin in origin.

variance	**var**iety	**var**y
variant	**var**ious	

"ver"

The root word "ver", meaning "truth", is Latin in origin.

veracious	**ver**dict	**ver**isimilitude
veracity	**ver**ify	**ver**ity

"verb"

The root word "verb", meaning "a word", is Latin in origin.

ad**verb**	**verb**	**verb**alize
pro**verb**	**verb**al	**verb**atim

"vict/vinc"

The root words "vict/vinc", meaning "to conquer", are Latin in origin.

con**vinc**e	**vict**im	**vict**orious
in**vinc**ible	**vict**or	**vict**ory

"vid/vis"

The root words "vid/vis", meaning "to see", are Latin in origin.

e**vid**ence	re**vis**ion	**vid**eo	**vis**it
in**vis**ible	tele**vis**ion	**vis**ion	

"vit/viv"

The root words "vit/viv", meaning "life" or "to live", are Latin in origin.

re**viv**e	**vit**al	**viv**id
sur**viv**e	**vit**amin	

"voc/vok"

The root words "voc/vok", meaning "to call" or "voice", are Latin in origin.

ad**voc**ate	in**voc**ation	**voc**abulary	**voc**ation
equi**voc**ate	pro**vok**e	**voc**al	**voc**iferous
e**vok**e	re**vok**e	**voc**alist	

"void"

The root word "void", meaning "empty", is Latin in origin.

a**void**	a**void**ance	de**void**	**void**

"vol"

The root word "vol", meaning "to wish" or "to will", is Latin in origin.

bene**vol**ence	male**vol**ence	**vol**ition	**vol**unteer
bene**vol**ent	male**vol**ent	**vol**untary	

"volv"

The root word "volv", meaning "to roll", is Latin in origin.

e**vol**ution in**volv**e re**volv**e
e**volv**e re**vol**ution

"vor"

The root word "vor", meaning "to eat" or "to devour", is Latin in origin.

carni**vor**e herbi**vor**e omni**vor**e **vor**acious

"zoo"

The root word "zoo", meaning "an animal", is Greek in origin.

zoo **zoo**logist **zoo**logy

Part I: Suffixes

I1   Introduction

Words are made up of component parts called morphemes. A morpheme is the smallest part of a word that conveys meaning. There are three kinds of morphemes: "prefixes", "root words", and "suffixes".

At the core of every word is a root which gives the word its essential meaning. Additional letters, called "affixes", may be added to the beginning or to the end of a root. An affix added to the beginning of a root is called a "prefix". An affix added to the end of a root is called a "suffix". Many words have both a prefix and a suffix, and it is possible to attach more than one prefix or suffix. Prefixes and suffixes create new words by adding to the meaning of the root.

The letters "dict", for example, form a root word that means "to speak" in Latin. Adding the prefix "contra-", meaning "against" or "opposite", to "dict" creates the word "contradict". Adding the suffix "-ate", which forms verbs, to "dict" creates the word "dictate".

A base word is any word to which a prefix or suffix may be added. Some base words are also root words. Most base words are not root words because they already have a prefix or suffix attached.

Morphemes may be divided into "lexical morphemes" and "relational morphemes". A lexical morpheme conveys a particular meaning in and of itself. A relational morpheme only conveys grammatical meaning in relation to the word to which it is attached. Morphemes may also be divided into "free morphemes" and "bound morphemes". Free morphemes can function as free-standing words. Bound morphemes cannot function as free-standing words and are only used attached to other morphemes.

The word "ports", for example, contains two morphemes. The root word "port" is a lexical morpheme that means "to carry". As well, "port" is a free morpheme that can function as a word. The suffix "-s" is a relational morpheme used to create the plural form of words. The suffix "-s" does not convey any meaning on its own. As well, the suffix "-s" is a bound morpheme that cannot stand alone as a word.

Many common suffixes, including "-ed", "-ing", and "-s", are relational morphemes. That is, they only communicate meaning in relation to the base word to which they are attached. While prefixes create entirely new words, relational suffixes only change the form of a word while preserving the original meaning. For example, adding the prefix "ex-" to the root word "port" creates "export" which has a very different meaning from "port". Likewise, adding the prefix "im-" to "port" creates "import". Both "export" and "import" accept the relational suffix "-ing", producing "exporting" and "importing", which only changes the form of the words not their essential meaning.

Other suffixes are lexical morphemes that do convey a particular meaning. Compare, for example, the words "mortgag**or**" and "mortgag**ee**". A "mortgag**or**" is someone who borrows money using a mortgage while the "mortgag**ee**" is the person or institution lending the money. A number of lexical morphemes are listed in I12.

The rules governing how a suffix is added to a word depends on the spelling of the base word and on whether the suffix begins with a vowel letter or a consonant letter. These are explored below.

I2 Word Ends with Final Silent Letter "e" Following a Consonant as in "Bake"

I2.1 Suffix begins with a vowel

a) General Rule: Drop the final silent letter "e"

A final silent letter "e" performs many functions. The most common function is to signal that the preceding vowel letter is pronounced with a long vowel sound. In the word "b**a**k**e**", for example, the final silent "e" signals that the preceding letter "a" is pronounced with the long "a" vowel sound.

When adding a suffix that begins with a vowel to a base word that ends with a final silent letter "-e" following a consonant, the general rule is that the final silent letter "e" is dropped before adding the suffix. For example, adding the suffix "-ing" to "bake" creates "baking".

This is because keeping the letter "e" would result in two vowels letters sitting side-by-side forming a vowel digraph which usually represent long vowel sounds. Adding the suffix "-ing" to "bake", for example, without dropping the letter "e" would produce "bak**ei**ng". Following general spelling conventions, the letters "ei" would be pronounced with the long "e" vowel sound, not the short "i" vowel sound.

After dropping the final silent letter "e" and adding a suffix, a different spelling convention often comes into play. The first vowel of the suffix now assumes the function of the final silent letter "e". In the word "ba<u>k</u>ing", for example, the letter "i" now signals that the preceding letter "a" is pronounced with the long "a" vowel sound.

It follows that, after dropping the final silent letter "e", the final consonant of the base word is not doubled. Double consonants would incorrectly signal that the preceding vowel letter is pronounced with a short vowel sound. For example, the word "hop" (pronounced with the short "o" vowel sound) becomes "hopping" while the word "hope" (pronounced with the long "o" vowel sound) becomes "hoping".

- eas<u>e</u> → eas**ed**, eas**y**
- admir<u>e</u> → admir**able**, admir**ed**, admir**ing**, admir**ation**
- amaz<u>e</u> → amaz**ed**, amaz**ing**
- ampl<u>e</u> → ampl**y**
- azur<u>e</u> → azur**ite**
- bak<u>e</u> → bak**ed**, bak**ing**
- bar<u>e</u> → bar**ed**, bar**ing** (While "bar" becomes "barring".)
- bas<u>e</u> → bas**ed**, bas**ing**
- bath<u>e</u> → bath**ed**, bath**ing**
- becom<u>e</u> → becom**ing**
- believ<u>e</u> → believ**able**, believ**ed**, believ**ing**
- blaz<u>e</u> → blaz**ed**, blaz**ing**
- bon<u>e</u> → bon**ed**, bon**ing**, bon**y**
- breath<u>e</u> → breath**ing**
- breez<u>e</u> → breez**ing**, breez**y**
- bubbl<u>e</u> → bubbl**ed**, bubbl**ing**, bubbl**y**
- can<u>e</u> → can**ed**, can**ing** (While "can" becomes "canned", "canning".)
- car<u>e</u> → car**ing**
- cleans<u>e</u> → cleans**ed**, cleans**ing**
- com<u>e</u> → com**ing**
- conceiv<u>e</u> → conceiv**able**, conceiv**ed**, conceiv**ing**
- confin<u>e</u> → confin**able**, confin**ed**, confin**ing**
- confus<u>e</u> → confus**able**, confus**ed**, confus**ing**
- creat<u>e</u> → creat**ed**, creat**ing**
- cuddl<u>e</u> → cuddl**ed**, cuddl**ing**, cuddl**y**
- cultur<u>e</u> → cultur**al**, cultur**ed**, cultur**ing**
- cut<u>e</u> → cut**er**, cut**est** (While "cut" becomes "cutting".)
- debat<u>e</u> → debat**able**, debat**ed**, debat**ing**
- dens<u>e</u> → dens**er**
- desir<u>e</u> → desir**able**, desir**ed**, desir**ing**, desir**ous**
- din<u>e</u> → din**ed**, din**ing**, din**er** (While "din" becomes "dinner".)
- doubl<u>e</u> → doubl**ed**, doubl**ing**, doubl**y**
- ensu<u>e</u> → ensu**ed**, ensu**ing**
- ensur<u>e</u> → ensur**ed**, ensur**ing**
- explod<u>e</u> → explod**ed**, explod**ing**

- fate → fatal
- fine → finery
- freeze → freezing
- gaze → gazed, gazing
- give → givable, giver, giving
- gripe → griped, gripping (While "grip" becomes "gripped", gripping")
- hate → hated, hating (While "hat" becomes "hatter".)
- have → having
- hope → hoped, hoping (While "hop" becomes "hopped", "hopping".)
- horse → horsing
- house → housed, housing
- gaze → gazed, gazing
- imitate → imitation, imitated, imitating
- insure → insurable, insured, insuring
- intimate → intimated, intimating
- leave → leaving
- lobe → lobed
- lope → loped, loping
- love → lovable, loved, lover, loving
- marble → marbled, marbling
- massacre → massacred, massacring
- mate → mated, mating (While "mat" becomes "matted", "matted".)
- mistake → mistakable, mistaken, mistaking
- mope → moped, moping (While "mop" becomes "mopped, "mopping".)
- move → movable, moved, moving
- nerve → nervous
- note → notable, notation, noted, noting
- pipe → piped, piping
- plane → planed, planing (While "plan" becomes "planned", "planning")
- pleasure → pleasurable, pleasuring
- prickle → prickled, prickling, prickly
- procedure → procedural
- propose → proposal, proposed, proposing, proposition
- prune → pruned, pruning
- refine → refined, refining, refinery
- rescue → rescued, rescuing
- ride → rider, riding (While "rid" becomes "ridded", "ridding")
- rise → rising, risen
- sale → salable
- save → saved, saving
- simple → simply
- single → singled, singling, singly
- site → sited, siting (While "sit" becomes "sitting".)

- slope → sloped, sloping
- snipe → sniped, sniping (While "snip" becomes "snipped", "snipping".)
- sponge → sponged, sponging
- subdue → subdued, subduing
- subtle → subtly
- take → taking
- tickle → tickled, tickler, tickling
- time → timing
- treasure → treasurer, treasuring
- trouble → troubled, troubling
- tube → tubing
- use → usable, usage, used, using
- wade → waded, wading
- white → whiten
- wide → wider, widen
- write → writing

b) Exception to the general rule: Base word ends with a soft "-ce" or "-ge" spelling pattern and the suffix begins with vowel letters "a", "o", or "u"

With base words that end with a soft "-ce" or "-ge" spelling pattern, as in "trace" and "change", the final silent letter "e" is kept when adding a suffix that begins with vowel letters "a", "o", or "u" such as "-able" and "-ous".

Vowel letters "a", "o", and "u" all signal that a preceding letter "c" or "g" is pronounced with a hard consonant sound. If the letter "e" was dropped, the letter "a", "o", or "u" of the suffix would incorrectly signal that the preceding letter "c" or "g" is pronounced with a hard consonant sound. The silent letter "e" is still required to signal the soft consonant sound. Adding the suffix "-able" to "enforce", for example, produces "enforceable", not "enforcable". "Enforcable" would be pronounced "enforkable" with the hard "c/k" consonant sound.

- advantage → advantageous
- change → changeable
- charge → chargeable
- courage → courageous
- curvaceous
- damage → damageable
- enforce → enforceable
- exchange → exchangeable
- gorgeous
- knowledge → knowledgeable
- manage → manageable
- marriage → marriageable
- notice → noticeable
- outrage → outrageous
- peace → peaceable
- pronounce → pronounceable
- replace → replaceable
- salvage → salvageable
- service → serviceable
- trace → traceable

c) Application of the general rule: Base word ends with a soft "-ce" or "-ge" spelling pattern and the suffix begins with vowel letters "e", "i", or "y"

In keeping with the general rule, with base words that end with a soft "-ce" or "-ge" spelling pattern, as in "trace" and "change", the final silent letter "e" is dropped when adding a suffix that begins with the letters "e", "i", or "y".

Vowel letters "e", "i", and "y" all signal that a preceding letter "c" or "g" is pronounced with a soft consonant sound. For this reason, the silent letter "e" is no longer needed and, if kept, would only cause confusion. Two vowels sitting side-by-side usually form a digraph representing a long vowel sound. Adding the suffix "-ing" to the word "trace", for example, produces "tracing", not "traceing". The letters "ei" in "traceing" would be pronounced with the long "e" vowel sound, not the short "i" vowel sound.

- advantage → advantaged, advantaging
- age → aging (Also "ageing")
- bounce → bounced, bouncer, bouncy
- cage → cagy (Also "cagey")
- chance → chanced, chancy
- change → changed, changing
- charge → charged, charging
- college → collegial
- damage → damaged, damaging
- edge → edged, edgy
- encourage → encouraged, encouraging
- enforce → enforced, enforcing
- engage → engaged, engaging
- exchange → exchanged, exchanging
- finance → financing, financial
- force → forced, forcible, forcing
- ice → iced, icing, icy
- induce → induced, inducible, inducing
- judge → judged, judging
- large → larger, largest
- manage → managed, managing
- mange → mangy
- notice → noticed, noticing
- outrage → outraged, outraging
- price → pricy (Also "pricey")
- pronounce → pronounced, pronouncing
- rage → raged, raging (While "rag" becomes "ragged".)
- range → ranged, rangy
- reduce → reducible, reduced, reducing
- replace → replaced, replacing
- scarce → scarcity

- service → servi**ced**, servi**cing**
- sin**ge** ("To scorch") → sin**ged** (But not singing, see (d).)
- spon**ge** → spon**ged**, spon**ging**
- tra**ce** → tra**ced**, tra**cing**
- wa**ge** → wa**ged**, wa**ging** (While "wag" becomes "wagged", "wagging".)

d) Exception to the general rule: To avoid confusion with similar words

A final silent letter "e" may be retained when adding the suffix "-ing" to avoid confusion with a similar word that does not end with a final silent letter "e".

- hol**e** → hol**ey** (Avoids confusion with "holy" meaning "sacred".)
- sin**ge** ("To scorch") → sin**geing** (Avoids confusion with "singing".)
- tin**ge** → tin**geing** (Avoids confusion with "tinging".)

e) Other Exceptions

A number of words do not conform with any of the above spelling patterns.

The following words do not conform to the general rule is that a final silent letter "e" is dropped before adding a suffix that begins with a vowel letter.

- acr**e** → acr**eage**
- bla**me** → blam**eable**
- mil**e** → mil**eage**

The following word does not conform to the rule that, with base words that end with a soft "-ce" or "-ge" spelling pattern, a final silent letter is kept when adding a suffix that begins with vowel letters "a", "o", or "u".

- mortga**ge** → mortga**gor**

The following words do not conform to the rule that, with base words that end with a soft "-ce" or "-ge" spelling pattern, a final silent letter "e" is dropped when adding a suffix that begins with vowel letters "e", "i", or "y".

- a**ge** → a**geing** (Also "aging")
- di**ce** → di**cey**
- pri**ce** → pri**cey** (Also "pricy")
- ca**ge** → ca**gey** (Also "cagy")

12.2 Suffix begins with a consonant

a) General Rule

When adding a suffix that begins with a consonant such as "-ly", "-ment", and "-s" to a word that ends with a final silent letter "-e", the general rule is to add the suffix without dropping the silent letter "e". Adding the suffix "-ment" to "base", for example, produces "ba**se**ment".

The final silent letter "e" is still required to signal the preceding long vowel sound. Without the letter "e" there would be two consonant letters sitting side-by-side. In keeping with the doubling principle, "ba**sm**ent", for example, would be pronounced "ba**s-m**ent". The letter "a" would be pronounced with the short "a" vowel sound.

- abridge → abridgement
  (Also abridgment)
- absolute → absolutely
- acknowledge → acknowledgement
  (Also acknowledgment)
- advance → advancement
- advertise → advertisement
- affectionate → affectionately
- amaze → amazement
- apprentice → apprenticeship
- appropriate → appropriately, appropriateness
- arrange → arrangement
- awe → awesome
- base → basely, basement
- breeze → breezeless
- care → careful, careless
- change → changeling
- complete → completely, completeness
- definite → definitely
- dense → densely
- disgrace → disgraceful
- edge → edgewise
- endorse → endorsement
- enforce → enforcement
- engage → engagement
- extreme → extremely
- false → falsehood
- fate → fateful
- flame → flameproof
- force → forceful
- forgive → forgiveness
- game → gamester
- genuine → genuinely, genuineness
- grace → graceful, gracefully
- hope → hopeless, hopeful
- idle → idleness
- involve → involvement
- judge → judgement (Also judgment)
- large → largely
- like → likelihood, likely, likeness
- lone → lonely, loneliness
- loose → loosely
- love → lovely, loveliness
- manage → management
- move → movement
- nice → nicely
- nine → ninety, nineteen
- noise → noiseless
- resource → resourceful
- safe → safety
- scarce → scarcely
- sense → senseless
- shame → shameless
- sincere → sincerely
- state → stately, statement
- strange → strangely, strangeness
- subtle → subtleness, subtlety
  (But "subtly", not "subtlely". See (b).)
- sure → surely
- taste → tasteful, tasteless
- trouble → troublesome

- use → use<u>ful</u>, us<u>eless</u>
- ventur<u>e</u> → ventur<u>esome</u>
- whol<u>e</u> → whol<u>eness</u>
  (But "wholly", not "wholely". See (b).)
- wir<u>e</u> → wir<u>eless</u>
- wis<u>e</u> → wis<u>ely</u>

b) Exceptions to the general rule

There is no apparent pattern to the following exceptions to the general rule that a final silent letter "e" is not dropped when adding a suffix that begins with a consonant.

It may be noted that the general rule applies to base words that end with the soft "-ce" and "-ge" spelling patterns as in "advan**ce**" and "arran**ge**". The silent letter "e" is still required to signal the soft consonant sound. A few words, however, are spelled both with and without the silent letter "e". Keeping the letter "e" is the preferred spelling. When the letters "c" and "g" are followed by another consonant, they are usually pronounced with a hard sound.

- abridg**e** → abrid**gment** (Also abridgement)
- acknowledg**e** → acknowled**gment** (Also "acknowledgement")
- aw**e** → aw**ful**
- judg**e** → jud**gment** (Also "judgement")
- tru**e** → truly
- nin**e** → nin**th** ("Nineth" might be pronounced with two-syllables.)
- subtl**e** → subtly (Not "subtlely".)
- whol**e** → wholl**y** (Drop the "e" and add the suffix "-ly".)
- wis**e** → wisdom (Long "i" becomes a short "i".)

I3 Word Ends with Final Silent Letter "e" Following a Vowel as in "Tie"

I3.1 Suffix begins with a vowel

a) General Rule

The letters "-ae", "-ee", "-ie", "-oe", "-ue", and "-ye" all form long vowel digraphs in open final syllables as in "sundae", "see", "tie", "hoe", "rescue", and "bye". The final silent letter "e" signals that the digraph is pronounced with a long vowel sound. As well, the final silent letter "e" helps to satisfy the three letter rule which is favoured for content words.

When adding a suffix that begins with a vowel letter such as "-able", "-ed" and "-ing" to a base word that ends with "-ae", "-ee", "-ie", "-oe", "-ue", or "-ye", the general rule is to drop the final silent letter "e" before adding the suffix. Adding the suffix "-able" to "argue", for example, produces "arguable".

One reason for this rule is to avoid having three vowel letters in a row which would be confusing to read. A related reason is that the silent letter "e" is no longer required to signal the long vowel sound. The first vowel of the suffix assumes this function.

With base words that end with the letters "-ue", as in "value", the letter "u" does not always form a digraph with the beginning vowel of the suffix. Sometimes the two vowels form a link letter spelling pattern in which both vowels are pronounced. Adding the suffix "-able" to the word "value", for example, produces "valuable". Both the letter "u" and the letter "a" are pronounced.

- agree → agreed (But not "agreable" or "agreing". See (c) and (d).)
- argue → arguable, argued, arguing
- canoe → canoed (But not "canoing". See (c).)
- decree → decreed (But not "decreing". See (c).)
- die → died (But not "diing". See (b).)
- dye → dyed (But not "dying". See (c).)
- ensue → ensued, ensuing
- eye → eyed (But not "eying". See (c).)
- free → freed (But not "freing". See (c).)
- guarantee → guaranteed (But not "guaranteing". See (c).)
- hoe → hoed (But not "hoing". See (c).)
- lie → lied (But not "liing". See (b).)
- pursue → pursuable, pursued, pursuing
- rescue → rescued, rescuing
- shoe → shoed (But not "shoing" See (c).)
- subdue → subdued, subduing
- sue → sued, suing
- tie → tied (But not "tiing". See (b).)
- toe → toed (But not "toing" See (c).)
- value → valuable, valued, valuing

b)   Exception to the general rule: Adding the suffix "-ing" to words ending with "-ie" such as "tie".

When adding the suffix "-ing" to words that end with the letters "-ie", the final silent letter "e" is dropped and the letter "i" is changed to "y". Adding the suffix "-ing" to the word "tie", for example, produces "tying".

These changes avoid spellings such as "tieing" or "tiing" which would be confusing to read. As a general rule, the double "ii" spelling pattern is avoided. This spelling pattern works because both "i" and "y" are able to represent the long "i" vowel sound.

- die → dying
- lie → lying
- tie → tying

c) Exception to the general rule: Adding the suffix "-ing" to words ending with "-ee", "-oe", and "-ye"

With words that end with long vowel digraphs "-ee", "-oe", and "-ye", such as "flee", "hoe", and "dye", the final silent letter "e" is kept when the suffix "-ing" is added. The final silent letter "e" continues to signal the final long vowel sound of the base word and helps to mark the beginning of the suffix. It also helps the reader to more readily identify the base word.

- agree → agreeing
- canoe → canoeing
- decree → decreeing
- dye → dyeing (Avoids confusion with "dying".)
- eye → eyeing
- flee → fleeing
- free → freeing
- guarantee → guaranteeing
- hoe → hoeing
- see → seeing
- shoe → shoeing
- toe → toeing

d) Other Exceptions

The following exceptions to the general rule do not fall under any of the above spelling patterns. Keeping the final silent letter "e" when adding the suffix "-able" to "agree" makes the derived word "agreeable" easier to read.

- agree → agreeable
- disagree → disagreeable

13.2 Suffix begins with a consonant

a) General Rule

When adding a suffix that begins with a consonant letter such as "-less", "-ly", "-ment", and "-s" to a base word that ends with "-ae", "-ee", "-ie", "-oe", "-ue", or "-ye" the general rule is to keep the final silent letter "e". Adding the suffix "-ly" to "free", for example, produces "freely".

The vowel digraph continues to perform the same function and helps the reader to recognize the underlying base word.

- agree → agreement
- die → dies
- free → freedom, freely
- lie → lies
- sundae → sundaes
- tie → ties
- toe → toeless
- vague → vaguely, vagueness

b) Exceptions to general rule: Words ending with "-ue"

With the following words that end with the letters "-ue", the final silent "e" is dropped when adding a suffix that begins with a consonant letter. There does not appear to be a good reason for these exceptions. The words "vaguely" and "vagueness", however, follow the general rule.

- arg**ue** → argu_ment_
- d**ue** → du_ly_
- tr**ue** → tru_ly_, tru_th_

14 Word Ends with "y" Following a Consonant as in "Beauty"

14.1 Suffix begins with a vowel

a) General Rule

With words that end with a final letter "y" following a consonant, as in "beau**ty**", the letter "y" is changed to "i" when adding a suffix that begins with a vowel other than "i". Adding the suffix "-er" to "co**py**", for example, produces "copi_er_".

The reason for this rule is not readily apparent. Fortunately, however, it also applies when adding a suffix that begins with a consonant.

The word "easy" forms a unique exception to this rule. When adding the suffix "-ed" to "easy" the letter "y" is dropped altogether to create the word "eased".

- accompany → accompani_ed_, accompani_es_
- ally → alli_ed_, alli_ance_
- apply → appli_ed_
- army → armi_es_
- authority → authoriti_es_
- baby → babi_es_, babi_ed_
- beauty → beauti_es_
- bunny → bunni_es_
- bury → buri_es_, buri_ed_
- candy → candi_ed_, candi_es_
- carry → carri_ed_, carri_es_, carri_age_, carri_er_
- company → compani_es_
- contrary → contrari_an_
- copy → copi_ed_, copi_er_, copi_es_
- country → countri_es_

- cry → cri_ed_, cri_es_
- curly → curli_er_, curli_est_
- custody → custodi_al_, custodi_an_
- defy → defi_ed_, defi_ant_
- deny → deni_es_, deni_ed_, deni_al_
- dry → dri_er_, dri_est_
- duty → duti_es_
- easy → easi_er_, easi_est_
- envy → envi_able_, envi_ous_
- fallacy → fallaci_ous_
- family → famili_es_
- fluffy → fluffi_er_, fluffi_est_
- fly → fli_er_, fli_es_
- fortify → fortifi_ed_, fortifi_es_
- forty → forti_es_, forti_eth_
- friendly → friendli_er_, friendli_est_
- fry → fri_ed_, fri_es_

- happy → happier, happiest
- heavy → heaviest, heavier
- history → historian
- holy → holies
- hurry → hurried, hurries
- identify → identified, identifies
- Italy → Italian
- justify → justifiable
- lady → ladies
- lively → livelier
- lonely → lonelier
- marry → marriage, married, marries,
- mercy → mercies
- mystery → mysterious
- necessary → necessaries
- party → parties, partier
- pity → pitied
- ply → plies, plied

- puppy → puppies
- rely → reliable, relies, relied
- reply → replies, replied
- salary → salaried, salaries
- satisfy → satisfies, satisfied
- silly → sillier
- sky → skies
- spy → spied, spies
- steady → steadies
- story → stories
- study → studies, studied, studious
- supply → supplies
- terrify → terrified, terrifies
- thirty → thirties, thirtieth
- try → tried, tries
- twenty → twenties, twentieth
- vary → variable, variant, variance, variety
- worry → worried

b) Exception to general rule: Avoid creating a double "ii"

Keep a final letter "y" when adding a suffix that begins with the letter "i" such as "-ing" and "-ish". In other words, avoid creating a word with a double "ii". The word "skiing" is spelled with a double "ii" because the base word "ski" ends with an "i", not "y", so the double "ii" is unavoidable.

- accompany → accompanying
- ally → allying
- apply → applying
- baby → babyish
- bury → burying
- busy → busying
- carry → carrying
- copy → copying
- cry → crying
- defy → defying
- deny → denying
- dry → drying
- fly → flying
- forty → fortyish
- fry → frying
- hurry → hurrying
- identify → identifying

- lobby → lobbyist
- marry → marrying
- occupy → occupying
- pity → pitying
- play → playing
- ply → plying
- rely → relying
- reply → replying
- satisfy → satisfying
- spy → spying
- study → studying
- supply → supplying
- terrify → terrifying
- thirty → thirtyish
- try → trying
- unify → unifying
- vary → varying

c) Exception to general rule: Adding the suffix "-ize"

When adding the suffix "-ize" to a word that ends with a final letter "y" following a consonant, drop the letter "y" and add the suffix.

- agony → agon**ize**
- memory → memor**ize**

d) Words spelled both ways

When adding a suffix that begins with a vowel to a base word that ends with a final "y" following a consonant, some words may be spelled both ways: by changing the "y" to an "i", in accordance with the general rule, or by keeping the final letter "y".

- dry → dry**er** or dr**ier**
- fly → fly**er** or fl**ier**
- fry → fry**er** or fr**ier**
- shy → shy**er** or sh**ier**, shy**est** or sh**iest**
- sly → sly**er** or sl**ier**, sly**est** or sl**iest**

I4.2 Suffix begins with a consonant

a) General Rule

The rule in I4.1 also applies when adding a suffix that begins with a consonant. With words that end with a final letter "y" following a consonant, as in "du**ty**", the letter "y" is changed to "i". Adding the suffix "-ful" to "du**ty**", for example, produces "du**ti**ful".

It may be noted that all of the following base words are polysyllabic, and the letter "y" is usually pronounced with the long "e" vowel sound. In the derived words, the letter "i" is sometimes pronounced with the long "e" vowel sound and sometimes with the short "i" vowel sound. In the word "business", however, the letter "i" is silent.

- accompa**ny** → accompan**i**ment
- app**ly** → appl**i**cable, appl**i**cation
- beau**ty** → beaut**i**ful, beaut**i**fy
- bu**sy** → bus**i**ness, bus**i**ly
  (But "bus**y**ness", "bus**y**work", and "bus**y**body")
- clum**sy** → clums**i**ly
- contra**ry** → contrar**i**ness
- du**ty** → dut**i**ful
- ea**sy** → eas**i**ly
- econo**my** → econom**i**st
  (Drop the "y" and add "-ist".)
- fan**cy** → fanc**i**ful, fanc**i**ly, fanc**i**ness
- friend**ly** → friendl**i**ness
- fun**ny** → funn**i**ly
- hap**py** → happ**i**ly, happ**i**ness
- ho**ly** → hol**i**day
- like**ly** → likel**i**hood
- live**ly** → livel**i**hood
- lone**ly** → lonel**i**ness
- mer**cy** → merc**i**ful, merc**i**less
- mer**ry** → merr**i**ment
- mes**sy** → mess**i**ly
- nas**ty** → nast**i**ly

- necessa**ry** → necessa**ri**ly
- ordina**ry** → ordina**ri**ly
- pi**ty** → pi**ti**ful
- sil**ly** → sil**li**ness
- stea**dy** → stea**di**ly, stea**di**ness
- wea**ry** → wea**ri**ly

b) Exceptions to the general rule.

The following words do not follow the general rule; a final letter "y" following a consonant is kept when adding a suffix that begins with a consonant.

It may be noted that most of the following are single-syllable base words, and the letter "y" is pronounced with the long "i" vowel sound. With the polysyllabic word "busy", the letter "y" is pronounced with the long "e" vowel sound. Retaining the letter "y" in "busyness" helps to distinguish it from "business".

- bu**sy** → bu**sy**ness, bu**sy**work, bu**sy**body (But "business" and "busily".)
- d**ry** → d**ry**ly, d**ry**ness
- s**hy** → s**hy**ness, s**hy**ly
- s**ky** → s**ky**ward
- s**ly** → s**ly**ness, s**ly**ly
- sp**ry** → sp**ry**ly

As well, the general rule does not apply when creating compound words such as "anyhow", "fairyland", and "clergyman".

I5 Word Ends With "y" Following a Vowel as in "Employ"

I5.1 Suffix begins with a vowel

a) General Rule

With words that end with a final letter "y" following a vowel, as in "employ", the letter "y" is kept when adding a suffix that begins with a vowel. Adding the suffix "-er" to "employ", for example, produces "employer".

This is because the letter "y" helps to form a vowel digraph with the preceding vowel letter. In "empl**oy**", for example, the vowel digraph "-oy" represents the vowel diphthong heard in "coin" and "toy". When adding a suffix, the letter "y" is usually kept because it is still required to perform the same function.

As well, the letter "y" helps to clearly identify the base word. Further, if the letter "y" were to be changed to the letter "i", it would often result in a double "ii" spelling pattern which is avoided.

- ann**oy** → ann**oy**ance, ann**oy**ed, ann**oy**ing

- betray → betrayal, betrayed, betraying
- boy → boyish
- buoy → buoyant, buoyancy
- buy → buyer, buying
- clay → clayey
- convey → conveyance, conveyed, conveying, conveyer
- delay → delayed, delaying
- display → displaying, displayed
- employ → employed, employing, employable
- enjoy → enjoyable, enjoyment, enjoying, enjoyed
- gray (USA) → grayed, graying, grayer
- grey (UK, CAN) → greyed, greying, greyer
- journey → journeyed, journeying
- joy → joyous
- key → keyed, keying
- obey → obeyed, obeying
- okay → okayed, okaying
- pay → paying, payee, payer
- play → played, playing, playable
- relay → relayed, relaying
- spray → sprayed, sprayer, spraying
- stay → stayed, staying
- survey → surveyed, surveying, surveyor
- sway → swayed, swaying
- toy → toyed, toying

b) Exceptions to the general rule: Irregular verbs and adjectives

Contrary to the general rule, with certain irregular verbs such as "lay" and "pay" the past tense is not formed by simply by adding the suffix "-ed". Rather, the past tense is formed through other spelling changes.

Similarly, the adjective "gay" becomes the noun "gaiety" through other spelling changes.

- gay → gaiety
- lay → laid
- pay → paid

- say → said
- slay → slain

I5.2 Suffix begins with a consonant

a) General Rule

The rule in I5.1 also applies when adding a suffix that begins with a consonant. With words that end with a final letter "y" following a vowel, as in "employ", the letter "y" is kept. Adding the suffix "-ment" to "empl**oy**", for example, produces "empl**oy**ment". The letter "y" is kept because it is still required to form a vowel digraph with the preceding vowel letter.

- attorn**ey** → attorn**eys**
- b**oy** → b**oy**hood, b**oys**
- chimn**ey** → chimn**eys**
- c**oy** → c**oy**ly, c**oy**ness
- d**ay** → d**ays**
- del**ay** → del**ays**
- empl**oy** → empl**oy**ment, empl**oys**
- enj**oy** → enj**oy**ment, enj**oys**
- journ**ey** → journ**eys**
- j**oy** → j**oys**, j**oy**ful
- k**ey** → k**eys**
- pl**ay** → pl**ays**, pl**ay**ful
- rel**ay** → rel**ays**
- spr**ay** → spr**ays**
- st**ay** → st**ays**
- sw**ay** → sw**ays**
- troll**ey** → troll**eys**
- turk**ey** → turk**eys**
- vall**ey** → vall**eys**

b) Exceptions to general rule

With the following words, the "y" changes to an "i" when adding the suffix "-ly".

- d**ay** → da**ily**
- g**ay** → ga**ily**

I6 Word Ends With a Vowel Other than "y" or Silent "e"

I6.1 Suffix begins with a vowel

Relatively few words end with a vowel letter that is not the letter "y" or a final silent letter "e". Fewer still accept a suffix that begins with a vowel letter.

With words that end with a pronounced vowel letter, such as "radi**o**", the general rule is to simply add a suffix without any other spelling changes. The final vowel of the base word will continue to be pronounced as a linking letter or as the first vowel of a digraph.

The word "skiing" contains a rare instance of a double "ii" spelling pattern. The double "ii" spelling pattern is usually avoided.

- b**e** → be**ing**
- d**o** → do**es**, do**ing**
- extr**a** → extra**o**rdinary
- g**o** → go**es**, go**ing**
- radi**o** → radi**o**ed, radi**o**ing
- sk**i** → ski**ed**, ski**er**, ski**ing**
- tatt**oo** → tatt**oo**ed, tatt**oo**ing
- und**o** → und**o**es, und**o**ing
- vide**o** → vide**o**ed, vide**o**ing

I6.2 Suffix begins with a consonant

The rule in I6.1 also applies when adding a suffix that begins with a consonant. With words that end with a pronounced vowel letter, such as "audio", simply add the suffix without any other spelling changes. Adding the suffix "-visual" to "audio", for example, produces "audiovisual".

- audio → audio<u>visual</u>
- extra → extra<u>bold</u>
- radio → radio<u>s</u>
- ski → ski<u>s</u>
- tattoo → tattoo<u>s</u>

I7 Word Ends With a Single Vowel Followed by a Single, Final, Pronounced Consonant as in "Plan"

I7.1 Suffix begins with a vowel

As discussed in B1.1, long vowel sounds are usually represented by two vowel letters. It follows that very few words end with a single long-sounding vowel followed by a single, final, pronounced consonant. The only examples found are "contr**o**l", "enr**o**l", and "patr**o**l".

On the other hand, short vowel sounds are usually represented by a single vowel letter. Many words end with a single short vowel letter followed by a single, final, pronounced consonant as in "pl**a**n" and "forg**e**t". This is a common short vowel spelling pattern. Double consonants are not required because the short vowel sound does not need protection from the lengthening effect of a following vowel letter.

However, when a suffix that begins with a vowel is added to such words, the short vowel syllable will now be followed by another vowel, and the doubling principle comes into play. As a general rule, when a suffix that begins with a vowel is added to a word that ends with a single vowel followed by a single, final, pronounced consonant, the final consonant letter is doubled. Adding the suffix "-ed" to "pl**a**n", for example, produces "pla**nn**ed". Likewise, adding the suffix "-ing" to "forg**e**t" produces "forge**tt**ing". Double consonants protect the preceding short vowel sound from being lengthened by the following vowel letter.

The general rule applies:

a) To single-syllable words such as "pl**a**n";

b) To polysyllabic words that end with a stressed final syllable that remains stressed after adding the suffix as in "for**mat**";

c) With special considerations to words that end with the "-ic" spelling pattern as in "mag**ic**"; and

d) In British and Canadian spelling to words that end with a single final letter "l", as in "cancel", no matter where syllabic stress falls.

a) Single-syllable short vowel words

The doubling principle applies when adding a suffix that begins with a vowel to a single-syllable short vowel word that ends with a single vowel followed by a single, final, pronounced consonant. Adding the suffix "-ed" to "dro**p**", for example, produces "dro**pp**ed".

Double consonants often distinguish short vowel words from similar looking long vowel words. For example, double consonants distinguish the short vowel words "m**a**tted", "h**o**pped", and "s**u**pper" from the long vowel words "m**a**ted", "h**o**ped", and "s**u**per.

The doubling principle applies even when the derived word remains a single-syllable word after adding the suffix. For example, adding the suffix "-ed" to the word "ro**b**" produces "ro**bb**ed" which is still pronounced as a single-syllable short vowel word.

Note that words such as "quit" and "squat" are included in the following list because the letter "u" functions as a consonant, not a vowel, in representing the consonant "w" sound. Once this is taken into account, the short vowel letter stands alone.

- bag → ba**gg**age
- bar → ba**rr**ing (While "bare" becomes "bared", "baring".)
- bat → ba**tt**ed, ba**tt**ing, ba**tt**y
- beg → be**gg**ing, be**gg**ar
- bet → be**tt**or, be**tt**ing
- big → bi**gg**er → bi**gg**est
- blot → blo**tt**ed, blo**tt**ing
- brag → bra**gg**ing, bra**gg**art, bra**gg**ed
- can → ca**nn**ed, ca**nn**ing (While "cane" becomes "caned", "caning".)
- cap → ca**pp**ed, ca**pp**ing
- clan → cla**nn**ish
- cram → cra**mm**ing, cra**mm**ed
- cut → cu**tt**ing (While "cute" becomes "cuter", "cutest".)
- dig → di**gg**ing
- din → di**nn**ed, di**nn**ing (While "dine" becomes "dined", "dining", "diner".)
- dip → di**pp**ed, di**pp**ing, di**pp**y
- drag → dra**gg**ed, dra**gg**ing
- drop → dro**pp**ing, dro**pp**ed
- fit → fi**tt**ing, fi**tt**ed
- flat → fla**tt**est
- get → ge**tt**ing
- glad → gla**dd**en
- grip → gri**pp**ed, gri**pp**ing (While "gripe" becomes "griped", "griping".)

435

- hit → hitt*ing*, hitt*er*
- hop → ho**pp**ed, ho**pp**ing (While "hope" becomes "hoped", "hoping".)
- hot → hott*er* → hott*est*
- lob → lo**bb**ed, lo**bb**ing
- lop → lo**pp**ed, lo**pp**ing
- lug → lu**gg**ed, lu**gg**ing
- man → ma**nn**ing, ma**nn**ed
- mat → matt*ed*, matt*ing* (While "mate" becomes "mated", "mating".)
- mop → mo**pp**ed, mo**pp**ing (While "mope" becomes "moped", "moping".)
- pet → pett*ing* → pett*ed*
- pin → pi**nn**ed, pi**nn**ing (While "pine" becomes "pined" and "pining".)
- plan → pla**nn**ed, pla**nn**ing, pla**nn**er (While "plane" becomes "planed", "planing", "planer".)
- pot → pott*ed*
- quit → quitt*er*, quitt*ing*
- quiz → qui**zz**ed, qui**zz**ing, qui**zz**ical
- rid → ri**dd**ed, ri**dd**ing (While "ride" becomes "riding", "rider".)
- rob → ro**bb**ing, ro**bb**er, ro**bb**ed (While "robe" becomes "robed", "robing".)
- rub → ru**bb**ing, ru**bb**ed
- run → ru**nn**ing, ru**nn**er
- ship → shi**pp**ing, shi**pp**er, shi**pp**ed
- shop → sho**pp**ed, sho**pp**ing
- sit → sitt*er*, sitt*ing* (While "site" becomes "sited", "siting".)
- skin → ski**nn**er, ski**nn**y
- slam → sla**mm**ed
- slip → sli**pp**age, sli**pp**ed, sli**pp**ing
- slop → slo**pp**ed, slo**pp**ing, slo**pp**y (While "slope" becomes "sloped", "sloping".)
- snip → sni**pp**ed, sni**pp**ing, sni**pp**y (While "snipe" becomes "sniped", "sniping".)
- squat → squatt*ed*, squatt*er*, squatt*ing*
- stab → sta**bb**ing, sta**bb**er, sta**bb**ed
- star → sta**rr**ing, sta**rr**y
- stop → sto**pp**ed, sto**pp**ing, sto**pp**er, sto**pp**age
- sun → su**nn**ier, su**nn**iest, su**nn**y
- sup → su**pp**ed, su**pp**ing, su**pp**er (Not "super".)
- swim → swi**mm**er, swi**mm**ing
- thin → thi**nn**er → thi**nn**ing
- wag → wa**gg**ed, wa**gg**ing (While "wage" becomes "waged", "waging".)
- wet → wett*ed*, wett*ing*
- whip → whi**pp**ing, whi**pp**ed

Note, however, that with words that end with a single letter "-s", the letter "s" is sometimes doubled and sometimes not.

- bus → bus*es*, (Also "busses".) (But "bussed", "bussing".)
- gas → gas*es* (Also "gasses".) (But "gassed", "gassing".)

Also note that consonant letters "w" and "x" are never doubled.

- bow → bow_ed_, bow_ing_
- box → box_ed_, box_es_, box_ing_
- dew → dew_y_
- fix → fix_ed_, fix_es_, fix_ing_
- fox → fox_es_, fox_y_
- tax → tax_ed_, tax_es_, tax_ing_

b) Polysyllabic words

The doubling principle may apply when adding a suffix that begins with a vowel to a polysyllabic word that ends with a single vowel followed by a single, final, pronounced consonant as in "form**at**".

Unfortunately, the application of the doubling principle is not straight forward. The doubling principle only applies to final syllables that remain stressed after adding the suffix. The final short vowel syllable in "for**mat**", for example, remains stressed after adding the suffix "-ing" to produce "for**matt**ing". The double "tt" spelling pattern protects the preceding short "a" vowel sound from the lengthening effect of the following letter "i".

Note that words such as "acquit" and "equip" are included in the following lists because the letter "u" functions as a consonant, not a vowel, in representing the consonant "w" sound. Once this is taken into account, the short vowel letter stands alone.

In the following words the final short vowel syllable of the base word is stressed and remains stressed upon adding a suffix that begins with a vowel letter:

- a**bet** → a**bett**_ing_, a**bett**_ed_
- a**cquit** → a**cquitt**_ing_, a**cquitt**_ed_
- ad**mit** → ad**mitt**_ance_, ad**mitt**_ed_, ad**mitt**_ing_
- a**llot** → a**llott**_ing_, a**llott**_ed_
- be**gin** → be**ginn**_er_, be**ginn**_ing_
- co**mmit** → co**mmitt**_able_, co**mmitt**_ed_, co**mmitt**_ing_,
- com**pel** → com**pell**_ed_, com**pell**_ing_
- con**cur** → con**curr**_ed_, con**curr**_ence_, con**curr**_ent_, con**curr**_ing_
- dis**pel** → dis**pell**_ed_, dis**pell**_ing_
- e**quip** → e**quipp**_ed_, e**quipp**_ing_
- ex**cel** → ex**cell**_ed_, ex**cell**_ing_, ex**cell**_ence_, ex**cell**_ent_
- ex**pel** → ex**pell**_ed_, ex**pell**_ing_
- for**bid** → for**bidd**_en_, for**bidd**_ing_
- for**get** → for**gett**_able_, for**gett**_ing_
- for**mat** → for**matt**_ed_, for**matt**_ing_
- handi**cap** → handi**capp**_ed_, handi**capp**_ing_
- im**pel** → im**pell**_ed_, im**pell**_ing_

- metal → metall__ic__
- occur → occurr__ed__, occurr__ing__, occurr__ence__
- omit → omitt__ed__, omitt__ing__
- permit → permitt__ed__, permitt__ing__
- program → programm__ed__, programm__er__, programm__ing__
- rebel → rebell__ed__, rebell__ing__, rebell__ion__, rebell__ious__
- regret → regrett__able__, regrett__ably__
- remit → remitt__ance__, remitt__ed__, remitt__ing__
- repel → repell__ed__, repell__ent__, repell__ing__
- submit → submitt__al__, submitt__ed__, submitt__ing__
- transmit → transmitt__ed__, transmitt__er__, transmitt__ing__
- unclog → unclogg__ed__, unclogg__ing__
- unzip → unzipp__ed__, unzipp__ing__
- worship → worshipp__ed__, worshipp__ing__ (Also worshiped, worshiping.)

The doubling principle also applies to words that end with a stressed long vowel syllable. This, however, is a rare spelling pattern. Only three examples could be found.

- control → controll__able__, controll__ed__, controll__er__, controll__ing__
- enrol (UK, CAN) → enroll__ed__, enroll__ing__
- patrol → patroll__ed__, patroll__ing__

In the following words the final syllable of the base word is not stressed. Accordingly, the final consonant is not doubled when adding a suffix that begins with a vowel letter. Adding the suffix "-ing" to "**ben**efit", for example, produces "**ben**efiting" with a single letter "t".

- **ben**efit → **ben**efit__ed__, **ben**efit__ing__
- **can**cel → **can**cel__ed__, **can**cel__ing__ (But "cancellation")
- **coun**sel → **coun**sel__ed__, **coun**sel__ing__
- **cov**et → **cov**et__able__, **cov**et__ed__, **cov**et__ing__, **cov**et__ous__
- **cred**it → **cred**it__able__, **cred**it__ed__, **cred**it__ing__, **cred**it__or__
- **deb**it → **deb**it__ed__, **deb**it__ing__
- de**vel**op → de**vel**oped, de**vel**oper, de**vel**oping
- **dif**fer → **dif**fer__ed__, **dif**fer__ence__, **dif**fer__ent__, **dif**fer__ing__
- en**dan**ger → en**dan**ger__ed__, en**dan**ger__ing__
- **en**ter → **en**ter__ed__, **en**ter__ing__
- **e**qual → **e**qual__ed__, **e**qual__ing__
- **fo**cus → **fo**cus__ed__, **fo**cus__ing__ (Also "focussed" and "focussing".)
- **hap**pen → **hap**pen__ed__, **hap**pen__ing__
- **in**dex → **in**dex__ed__, **in**dex__ing__
- in**hib**it → in**hib**it__ing__
- **lab**el → **lab**el__ed__, **lab**el__ing__

- level → lev**el**ed, lev**el**ing
- libel → lib**el**ed, lib**el**ing
- limit → lim**it**ation, lim**it**ed, lim**it**ing
- market → mark**et**able, mark**et**ed, mark**et**er, mark**et**ing
- marvel → marv**el**ed, marv**el**ing, marv**el**ous
- merit → mer**it**ed, mer**it**ing, merit**or**ious (Stress shifts forward.)
- model → mod**el**ed, mod**el**ing
- offer → off**er**ed, off**er**ing
- open → op**en**ed, op**en**ing, op**en**er
- profit → prof**it**able, prof**it**ed, prof**it**ing
- prohibit → pro**hib**ited, pro**hib**iting
- quarrel → quarr**el**ed, quarr**el**ing
- reason → reas**on**able, reas**on**ed, reas**on**ing
- season → seas**on**able, seas**on**al, seas**on**ed, seas**on**ing
- signal → sign**al**ed, sign**al**ing
- solicit → solic**it**ation (Stress shifts forward.), solic**it**ed, solic**it**ing, solic**it**or
- stencil → stenc**il**ed, stenc**il**ing
- total → tot**al**ed, tot**al**ing
- travel → trav**el**ed, trav**el**er, trav**el**ing
- visit → vis**it**ed, vis**it**ing, vis**it**or

With the following words, the stress placed on the final syllable of the base word sometimes shifts away upon adding a suffix. The final consonant of the base word is not doubled if the stress shifts elsewhere. Adding the suffix "-ence" to "con**fer**", for example, produces "**con**ference" with a single letter "r".

- confer → **con**fer**ence**, confer**red**, confer**ring**
- defer → **de**fer**ence**, defer**red**, defer**ring**
- infer → **in**fer**ence**, infer**red** infer**ring**
- prefer → **pre**fer**ence**, prefer**red**, prefer**ring**
- refer → refer**ee**, **ref**er**ence**, refer**endum**, refer**ral**, refer**red**, refer**ring**,
- transfer → **trans**fer**ability**, **trans**fer**rable** (Also transferable), transfer**red**, transfer**ring**

c) Final short vowel syllable ends with the letters "-ic" as in "magic"

The doubling principle applies, with special considerations, to words that end with the letters "-ic" as in "magi**c**".

Polysyllabic words that end with the "-ic" sound usually end with the letters "-ic" and not with the letters "-ick". However, when adding a suffix that begins with a letter "e", "i", or "y", it is necessary to add the letter "-k". Adding the suffix "-ed" to "pan**ic**", for example, produces "pani**ck**ed".

There are two reasons for this. First of all, this is an application of the doubling principle. The two consonant letters "ck" protect the short "i" vowel sound from being lengthened by the following vowel letter. In "pan**i**cked", for example, the letters "ck" protect the letter "i" from being lengthened by the following letter "e". Secondly, in English spelling, the hard "c/k" consonant sound is often represented by the letter "k" when followed by "e", "i", or "y" which would otherwise soften a preceding letter "c". The letter "k" preserves the hard consonant sound when adding a suffix that begins with "e", "i", or "y" such as "-ed", "-ing", and "-y".

- coli**c** → coli**ck**y
- froli**c** → froli**ck**ed, froli**ck**ing
- mimi**c** → mimi**ck**ed, mimi**ck**ing
- pani**c** → pani**ck**ed, pani**ck**ing, pani**ck**y
- picni**c** → picni**ck**ed, picni**ck**er, picni**ck**ing
- shella**c** → shella**ck**ing, shella**ck**ed
- traffi**c** → traffi**ck**ed, traffi**ck**er, traffi**ck**ing

On the other hand, when adding a suffix that begins with the letters "a", "o", or "u" to words that end with "-ic", it is not necessary to add the letter "-k". The letter "c" represents the hard "c/k" consonant sound when followed by vowel letters "a", "o", "u", or another consonant. For this reason, the suffix "-al" may be added to words that end with "-ic" without a letter "k". The word "magic", for example, becomes "magical". Also, "-al" is a Latin suffix, so the doubling principle is not applied.

- magi**c** → magi**ca**l
- musi**c** → musi**ca**l

It may also be noted that when the Latin suffix "-ian" is added to words that end with "-ic", the letter "k" is not added. Adding the suffix "-ian" to "magic", for example, produces "magician". This allows the letters "ci" to form a consonant digraph representing the consonant "sh" sound.

- magi**c** → magi**ci**an
- musi**c** → musi**ci**an

d) British spelling of words that end with "l" as in "cancel"

In British and Canadian spelling, the doubling principle applies to words that end with a single letter "l" as in "cance**l**".

When adding a suffix that begins with a vowel to a base word that ends with a single letter "l", American spelling follows the general rule discussed in (b). The letter "l" is only doubled if the final syllable is stressed and remains stressed after adding the suffix. The British and Canadian practice is to double a final letter "l" no matter where stress falls. One exception is the word "parall**eled**", which already has enough "ls" even for the British.

- **can**cel → **can**cell**ation**, **can**cell**ed**, **can**cell**ing**
- com**pel** → com**pell**ed, com**pell**ing
- con**trol** → con**troll**ing, con**troll**ed, con**troll**able
- **coun**sel → **coun**sell**ed**, **coun**sell**ing**
- en**rol** → en**roll**ed, en**roll**ing
- **eq**ual → **eq**uall**ed**, **eq**uall**ing**
- ex**cel** → ex**cell**ed, ex**cell**ence, ex**cell**ent, ex**cell**ing
- im**pel** → im**pell**ed, im**pell**ing
- **lab**el → **lab**ell**ed**, **lab**ell**ing**
- **lev**el → **lev**ell**ed**, **lev**ell**ing**
- **lib**el → **lib**ell**ed**, **lib**ell**ing**
- **mar**vel → **mar**vell**ed**, **mar**vell**ing**, **mar**vell**ous**
- me**tal** → me**tall**ic
- **mod**el → **mod**ell**ed**, **mod**ell**ing**
- **quarr**el → **quarr**ell**ed**, **quarr**ell**ing**
- re**bel** → re**bell**ed, re**bell**ing, re**bell**ion, re**bell**ious
- re**pel** → re**pell**ed, re**pell**ent, re**pell**ing,
- **sig**nal → **sig**nall**ed**, **sig**nall**ing**
- **sten**cil → **sten**cill**ed**, **sten**cill**ing**
- **tot**al → **tot**all**ed**, **tot**all**ing**
- **trav**el → **trav**ell**ed**, **trav**eller, **trav**ell**ing**
- un**eq**ual → un**eq**uall**ed**

I7.2   Suffix begins with a consonant

The doubling principle does not apply when adding a suffix that begins with a consonant letter to a base word that ends with a single vowel letter followed by a single consonant letter as in "w**et**" and "forg**et**". Simply add the suffix without any other spelling changes. Adding the suffix "-ful" to the word "forg**et**", for example, produces "forgetful".

This spelling pattern applies to both single-syllable short vowel words and to polysyllabic words that end with a short vowel syllable. It results in two consonant letters following a short vowel sound, in keeping with the doubling principle, so there is no need to double the final consonant of the base word. In "forg**e**tful", for example, consonant letters "tf" protect the letter "e" from the lengthening effect of the following letter "u".

As discussed in B1.1, long vowel sounds are usually represented by two vowel letters. It follows that very few single-syllable long vowel words or final long vowel syllables are spelled with a single vowel letter followed by a single consonant letter. This spelling pattern is reserved for single-syllable short vowel words and final short vowel syllables.

- allot → allo**tment**
- ba**d** → ba**d**_ly_
- ba**r** → ba**r**s
- ba**t** → ba**t**s
- be**g** → be**g**s
- bi**g** → bi**g**_ness_
- bra**g** → bra**g**s
- ca**n** → ca**n**s
- ca**p** → ca**p**s, ca**p**_ful_
- ca**t** → ca**t**s
- commi**t** → commi**tment**
- cra**m** → cra**m**s
- cu**t** → cu**t**s
- di**g** → di**g**s
- di**n** → di**n**s
- di**p** → di**p**s
- do**g** → do**g**s
- dra**g** → dra**g**s
- dro**p** → dro**p**s, dro**p**_let_
- equi**p** → equi**pment**
- fi**t** → fi**t**s, fi**t**_ful_, fi**t**_ness_
- fi**x** → fi**x**_ture_
- fla**g** → fla**g**_ship_
- fla**t** → fla**t**s, fla**t**_ly_, fla**t**_ness_
- forge**t** → forge**t**_ful_
- ge**t** → ge**t**s
- gla**d** → gla**d**_ly_, gla**d**_ness_
- gri**p** → gri**p**s, gri**pt**
- hi**t** → hi**t**s
- ho**p** → ho**p**s
- ho**t** → ho**t**_ly_, ho**t**_ness_
- lo**b** → lo**b**s

- lo**p** → lo**p**s
- lu**g** → lu**g**s
- ma**n** → ma**n**s, ma**n**_ly_, ma**n**_fully_
- ma**t** → ma**t**s
- mo**p** → mo**p**s
- pe**t** → pe**t**s
- pi**n** → pi**n**s
- pla**n** → pla**n**s
- qui**t** → qui**t**s
- regre**t** → regre**t**_ful_
- ri**d** → ri**d**s
- ro**b** → ro**b**s
- ru**b** → ru**b**s
- ru**n** → ru**n**s
- shi**p** → shi**p**s, shi**pment**
- sho**p** → sho**p**s
- si**t** → si**t**s
- sla**m** → sla**m**s
- slo**p** → slo**p**s
- sni**p** → sni**p**s
- sta**b** → sta**b**s
- sta**r** → sta**r**s, sta**r**_board_, sta**r**_dom_
- sto**p** → sto**p**s
- su**n** → su**n**s
- su**p** → su**p**s
- swi**m** → swi**m**s
- thi**n** → thi**n**s, thi**n**_ly_, thi**n**_ness_
- wa**g** → wa**g**s
- we**t** → we**t**s, we**t**_ly_, we**t**_ness_
- whi**p** → whi**p**s
- wi**t** → wi**t**_less_, wi**t**_ness_

This spelling pattern applies to a couple of base words that end with a long vowel syllable spelled with a single vowel followed by a single consonant.

- en**rol** (UK, CAN) → en**rol**ment (UK, CAN), en**rol**lment (USA)
- pa**trol** → pa**trol**_man_

Oddly, the British spell certain words such as "skilful" and "instalment" with a single letter "l" when the base words "ski**ll**" and "insta**ll**" end with a double "ll".

18 Word Ends With Two Vowels Followed by a Single, Final, Consonant as in "Boat"

18.1 Suffix begins with a vowel

When adding a suffix that begins with a vowel letter to a word that ends with two vowel letters followed by a single final consonant, as in "b<u>oa</u>t", simply add the suffix without any other spelling changes. Adding the suffix "-ing" to "dr<u>ea</u>m", for example, produces "dr<u>ea</u>ming". In particular, do not double the final consonant of the base word.

This spelling rule applies to short vowel syllables as in "br<u>oa</u>d" and "engin<u>ee</u>r", long vowel syllables as in "b<u>oa</u>t" and "maint<u>ai</u>n", diphthongal vowel syllables as in "sh<u>ou</u>t" and "t<u>oi</u>l", the link letter spelling pattern as in "bi-<u>a</u>s" and "ri-<u>o</u>t", and schwa vowel syllables as in "conq<u>ue</u>r".

The doubling principle does not apply when a short vowel sound is represented by a vowel digraph. In "br<u>oa</u>der", for example, the short vowel sound represented by the "oa" vowel digraph does not require double consonants to protect it from the lengthening effect of the following vowel letter "e".

- appeal → appea<u>led</u>, appea<u>ling</u>
- appear → appea<u>red</u>, appea<u>ring</u>
- bias → bia<u>sed</u>, bia<u>ses</u>, bia<u>sing</u> (Also "biassed", "biassing")
- boat → boa<u>ter</u>, boa<u>ting</u>
- boil → boi<u>led</u>, boi<u>ler</u>, boi<u>ling</u>
- brief → brie<u>fed</u>, brie<u>fer</u>, brie<u>fing</u>
- broad → broa<u>der</u>, broa<u>dest</u>
- chauffeur → chauffeu<u>red</u>, chauffeu<u>ring</u>
- cheer → chee<u>red</u>, chee<u>ring</u>, chee<u>r</u>y
- clamour (UK, CAN) → clamou<u>red</u>, clamou<u>ring</u>
- clear → clea<u>red</u>, clea<u>ring</u>
- colour (UK, CAN) → colou<u>red</u>, colou<u>ring</u>
- complain → complai<u>ned</u>, complai<u>ning</u>
- conquer → conque<u>rable</u>, conque<u>red</u>, conque<u>ring</u>, conque<u>ror</u>
- contain → contai<u>ning</u>
- dread → drea<u>ding</u>
- dream → drea<u>ming</u>, dream<u>y</u>
- endeavour (UK, CAN) → endeavou<u>red</u>, endeavou<u>ring</u>
- engineer → enginee<u>red</u>, enginee<u>ring</u>
- entertain → entertai<u>ning</u>
- fail → fai<u>led</u>, fai<u>ling</u>
- favour (UK, CAN) → favou<u>red</u>, favou<u>ring</u>
- feud → feu<u>dal</u>, feu<u>dalism</u>

- flavour (UK, CAN) → flavou<u>r</u>e<u>d</u>, flavour<u>ing</u>
- forfeit → forfei<u>ted</u>, forfeit<u>ing</u>
- gain → gai<u>ned</u>, gai<u>ner</u>, gain<u>ing</u>
- glamour → glamor<u>ous</u>
- green → gree<u>nery</u>, gree<u>ning</u>
- haul → hau<u>led</u>, haul<u>ing</u>
- hear → hear<u>ing</u>
- honour (UK, CAN) → honou<u>red</u>, honour<u>ing</u>
- humour (UK, CAN) → humou<u>red</u>, humour<u>ing</u>
- labour (UK, CAN) → humou<u>red</u>, humour<u>ing</u>
- loud → lou<u>der</u>, lou<u>dest</u>
- mail → mai<u>led</u>, mail<u>ing</u>
- maintain → maintai<u>ned</u>, maintain<u>ing</u>
- nail → nai<u>led</u>, nail<u>ing</u>
- neighbour (UK, CAN) → neighbour<u>ing</u>
- oil → oi<u>led</u>, oi<u>lier</u>, oil<u>ing</u>, oil<u>y</u>
- poet → poet<u>ic</u>
- rain → rai<u>ned</u>, rain<u>ing</u>, rain<u>y</u>
- remain → remain<u>ing</u>
- rigour (UK, CAN) → rigor<u>ous</u>
- riot → riot<u>er</u>, riot<u>ing</u>, riot<u>ous</u>
- rumour (UK, CAN) → rumou<u>red</u>
- sail → sai<u>led</u>, sail<u>ing</u>
- savour (UK, CAN) → savou<u>red</u>, savour<u>ing</u>
- shout → shou<u>ted</u>, shout<u>ing</u>
- stream → strea<u>med</u>, stream<u>ing</u>
- toil → toi<u>led</u>, toi<u>ler</u>, toi<u>let</u>, toil<u>ing</u>
- vigour (UK, CAN) → vigor<u>ous</u>
- wool → wool<u>en</u> (USA), wooll<u>en</u> (UK, CAN)
- wool → wool<u>y</u> (USA), wooll<u>y</u> (UK, CAN)

I8.2 Suffix begins with a consonant

The rule in I8.1 also applies when adding a suffix that begins with a consonant. With words that end with two vowel letters followed by a single final consonant, as in "cheap", simply add the suffix without any other spelling changes. Adding the suffix "-ly" to the word "ch<u>ea</u>p", for example, produces "ch<u>ea</u>ply".

This spelling rule applies to short vowel syllables as in "br<u>oa</u>d", long vowel syllables as in "ch<u>ea</u>p" and "compl<u>ai</u>n", diphthongal vowel words and syllables as in "l<u>ou</u>d" and "t<u>oi</u>l", and the link letter spelling pattern as in "p<u>o</u>-<u>e</u>t".

Words such as "del<u>igh</u>t" and "r<u>igh</u>t" are listed below because the letters "gh" function as vowels in helping to represent the long "i" vowel sound.

Unfortunately, this spelling pattern often results in two consonant letters following a long vowel sound contrary to the doubling principle.

- brief → briefly, briefness
- broad → broadly
- cheap → cheaply
- cheer → cheerful
- chief → chiefdom, chiefly, chieftain
- complain → complains
- contain → containment
- deceit → deceitful
- delight → delightful
- dread → dreadful, dreadfully, dreadlocks
- dream → dreams
- entertain → entertainment
- fail → fails
- gain → gainful
- hear → hearken
- loud → loudly, loudness
- maintain → maintains
- nail → nails
- poet → poetry
- rain → rains
- remain → remains
- right → rightful, rightly
- sail → sails
- steep → steeply
- sweet → sweetly
- toil → toilsome
- wool → woolly (UK, CAN)

19 Word Ends With a Single Vowel Followed by Two Consonants as in "Child"

19.1 Suffix begins with a vowel

When adding a suffix that begins with a vowel to a word that ends with a single vowel followed by two consonant, as in "child" or "camp", simply add the suffix without any other spelling changes. Adding the suffix "-ing" to the word "camp", for example, produces "camping".

In particular, do not double the final consonant of the base word. The doubling principle is already satisfied because there will be two consonant letters between vowels. In "camping", for example, consonant letters "mp" protect the short "a" vowel sound from the lengthening effect of the following letter "i".

Fortunately, this spelling rule applies to both long vowel syllables as in "child" and "post" and to short vowel syllables as in "accept" and "bend".

- accept → accepted, accepting
- add → added, adding
- ask → asked, asking
- attack → attacked, attacker, attacking
- attend → attended, attending
- back → backed, backer, backing
- bend → bender, bending
- boss → bossed, bossing
- buzz → buzzed, buzzing
- camp → camped, camper, camping
- catch → catching, catcher
- child → childish
- clasp → clasped, clasping

- clock → clocked, clocking
- comb → combed, combing
- construct → constructed, constructer, constructing
- damp → dampen, damper
- discuss → discussed, discussing
- dump → dumped, dumping
- fill → filled, filling
- find → finding
- fuss → fussed, fussing, fussy
- hand → handed, handing, handy
- install → installed, installer, installing
- jump → jumped, jumper, jumping
- kiss → kissed, kisser, kissing
- lend → lender, lending
- mass → massing, massive
- mend → mended, mending
- mess → messed, messing, messy
- mind → minding
- molt (USA) → molted, molting
- pack → packed, packer, packing
- pick → picked, picker, picking
- post → posted, posting
- putt → putted, putter, putting
- remind → reminded, reminding
- rent → rented, renter, renting
- self → selfish
- send → sender, sending
- shell → shelled, shelling
- skill → skilled
- splash → splashed, splashing
- swing → swinging
- talk → talked, talker, talking
- walk → walked, walker, walking
- watch → watched, watcher, watching
- wild → wilder, wildest
- wish → wished, wishing
- young → younger, youngest

I9.2 Suffix begins with a consonant

The rule in I9.2 also applies when adding a suffix that begins with a consonant. With words that ends with a single vowel followed by two consonant, as in "most", simply add the suffix without any other spelling changes. Adding the suffix "-ly" to the word "most", for example, produces "mostly".

Fortunately, this spelling rule applies to both long vowel syllables as in "child" and "post" and to short vowel syllables as in "accept" and "bend".

Note that with words that end with a double "ll", such as "droll", drop one "l" from the base word before adding the suffix "-ly". It is a convention of English spelling that words are not spelled with a triple "lll" spelling pattern. Also, in Canadian and British spelling, one "l" is dropped when adding a suffix that begins with a consonant letter. Adding the suffix "-ment" to "install", for example, produces "instalment".

- accept → accepts
- add → adds
- ask → asks
- attack → attacks
- attend → attends
- back → backwards
- bend → bends
- calm → calmly
- camp → camps
- catch → catchments
- child → childhood, children
- clasp → clasps
- clock → clocks, clockwise
- comb → combs

- construct → constructs
- damp → damps
- droll → drolly
  (Drop one "l" before adding "-ly".)
- dump → dumps
- fill → fills
- find → finds
- foolish → foolishly
- full → fully (Drop one "l" before adding "-ly".)
- install → installment (USA), instalment (UK, CAN)
- jump → jumps
- kind → kindly
- lend → lends
- mend → mends
- mind → mindful, mindless, minds
- most → mostly
- pack → packs
- pick → picks
- post → postman, posts
- putt → putts
- remind → remindful
- rent → rents
- send → sends
- skill → skillful (USA), skilful (UK, CAN)
- talk → talks
- walk → walks
- warm → warmly
- watch → watchful
- wild → wildling, wilds
- wish → wishful
- young → youngster

I10 Word Ends With One or More Silent Consonants as in "Glow"

I10.1 Suffix begins with a vowel

A number of words, such as "high" and "follow", end with an open syllable that is spelled with one or more silent consonants forming a vowel digraph. With such words, a suffix that begins with a vowel is added without any other spelling changes. In particular, the final consonant letter is not doubled. Adding the suffix "-ing" to "debut", for example, produces "debuting".

Most of the following base words end with a long vowel digraph. A few words, such as "claw" and "draw", end with a short vowel digraph.

Many of the following words end with a final consonant letter "w". It may be noted that the letter "w" is never doubled and a final "w" is never pronounced.

- blow → blower, blowing
- borrow → borrowed, borrower, borrowing
- bow → bowing
- chew → chewing
- claw → clawed, clawing
- crew → crewing
- crochet → crocheting
- debut → debuting
- draw → drawing
- few → fewer
- follow → follower, following
- glow → glowing
- gnaw → gnawed, gnawing
- grow → grower, growing
- high → higher
- hollow → hollowing
- know → knowing

- mow → mower, mowing
- narrow → narrower, narrowing
- new → newer, newest
- paw → pawed, pawing
- review → reviewer, reviewing
- ricochet → ricocheting
- row → rower, rowing
- saw → sawed, sawing
- screw → screwing
- sew → sewing
- shadow → shadowing
- show → showing
- sigh → sighing
- skew → skewer, skewing
- sleigh → sleighing
- slow → slower, slowest, slowing
- snow → snowing
- sow → sowing
- stew → stewing
- swallow → swallowing
- through → throughout
- throw → thrower, throwing
- tow → towing
- view → viewer, viewing
- weigh → weighing

I10.2 Suffix begins with a consonant

The rule in I10.1 also applies when adding a suffix that begins with a consonant. With words that end with one or more final silent consonants forming a vowel digraph, such as "blow", simply add the suffix without any other spelling changes. Adding the suffix "-s" to "blow", for example, produces "blows".

Most of the following base words end with a long vowel digraph. A few base words, such as "claw" and "draw", end with a short vowel digraph.

Many of the following words end with a final consonant letter "w". It may be noted that the letter "w" is never doubled and a final consonant letter "w" is never pronounced.

- blow → blows
- borrow → borrows
- chew → chews
- claw → claws
- crew → crews
- crochet → crochets
- debut → debuts
- draw → draws, drawn
- follow → follows
- glow → glows
- gnaw → gnaws, gnawn
- grow → grows
- high → highly
- know → knows
- law → laws
- mow → mows
- narrow → narrowly, narrows
- new → newly, news
- paw → paws, pawn
- review → reviews
- ricochet → ricochets
- row → rows
- saw → saws, sawn
- sew → sews
- show → shows
- sigh → sighs
- skew → skews
- sleigh → sleighs
- slow → slowly, slows
- snow → snowfall, snows
- sow → sows
- stew → stews

- swall**ows** → swall**ows**
- thr**ow** → thr**ows**
- t**ow** → t**ows**
- v**iew** → v**iews**
- w**eigh** → w**eighs**

I11 Word Ends With Two Vowels Followed by Two Pronounced Consonants

Very few, if any, words end with two vowel letters followed by two pronounced consonant letters. No examples of this spelling pattern could be found.

I12 Suffix Word Families

Most of the following suffixes are lexical morphemes that convey particular meanings and create new words. Words that end with the same lexical suffix share a degree of common meaning forming word families. Several of the following suffixes, including "-ing" and "-s", are relational and only change the form of the word. See J2 for further discussion about relational suffixes.

"-age"

The suffix "-age", meaning "act", "condition", or "result of", forms nouns. The suffix "-age" meaning, "amount of", "number of", or "cost of", also forms nouns.

acre**age**	cour**age**	marri**age**	stor**age**
cleav**age**	im**age**	post**age**	us**age**

"-aire"

The suffix "-aire", naming people who are members of a select group, forms nouns.

billion**aire**	legionn**aire**	million**aire**

"-al"

The suffix "-al", meaning "of", "like", or "suitable for", forms adjectives. The suffix "-al", meaning "the act or process of __ing", forms nouns. The suffix "-al" also forms chemical names.

accident**al**	brut**al**	crimin**al**	fin**al**
actu**al**	carniv**al**	critic**al**	form**al**
arriv**al**	centr**al**	detriment**al**	funer**al**
artifici**al**	commerci**al**	essenti**al**	gener**al**
barbit**al**	committ**al**	feder**al**	gradu**al**
bilingu**al**	confidenti**al**	festiv**al**	grammatic**al**

historic**al**	medic**al**	practic**al**	sever**al**
hospit**al**	miner**al**	princip**al**	sign**al**
hysteric**al**	mor**al**	profession**al**	soci**al**
illeg**al**	nation**al**	propos**al**	speci**al**
individu**al**	natur**al**	provinci**al**	spin**al**
influenti**al**	norm**al**	punctu**al**	theatric**al**
internation**al**	occasion**al**	radic**al**	transmitt**al**
leg**al**	offici**al**	rehears**al**	tri**al**
liber**al**	origin**al**	revers**al**	univers**al**
loc**al**	physic**al**	riv**al**	vertic**al**
loy**al**	plur**al**	roy**al**	
manu**al**	politic**al**	roy**al**ty	
materi**al**	potenti**al**	sand**al**	

"-ant/-ent"

The suffix "-ant/-ent", meaning "something that has, shows, or does", forms adjectives. The suffix "-ant", meaning "a person or thing that (verb)s", forms nouns.

assist**ant**	descend**ant**	radi**ant**	superintend**ent**
correspond**ent**	insist**ent**	solv**ent**	
defi**ant**	occup**ant**	stud**ent**	

"-ar"

The suffix "-ar", meaning "of", "relating to", "like", or "of the nature of", forms adjectives. The suffix "-ar", meaning "the agent of a particular action", forms nouns.

cell**ar**	pol**ar**	singul**ar**	vulg**ar**
li**ar**	registr**ar**	sug**ar**	

"-ary"

The suffix "-ary", meaning "relating to" or "connected with", forms adjectives. The suffix "-ary", meaning "a person or thing connected with" or "a place for", forms nouns.

advers**ary**	constabul**ary**	gran**ary**	urin**ary**
annivers**ary**	custom**ary**	legend**ary**	volunt**ary**
arbitr**ary**	di**ary**	mamm**ary**	
bound**ary**	diction**ary**	second**ary**	
can**ary**	document**ary**	summ**ary**	

"-dom"

The suffix "-dom", meaning "rank or position of", "domain or dominion of", or "fact or state of being", forms nouns.

free**dom**	martyr**dom**	sel**dom**
king**dom**	official**dom**	wis**dom**

"-ed"

The suffix "-ed", meaning "provided with" or "characterized by", forms analogous adjectives from nouns and verbs.

The suffix "-ed" also forms the past tense and the past participle of regular verbs. See J4 and J6.

beard**ed**	cultur**ed**	diseas**ed**	measur**ed**

"-ee",

The suffix "-ee", naming a profession, vocation, hobby, or activity that people engage in, forms nouns.

absent**ee**	attend**ee**	mortgag**ee**	refer**ee**
appoint**ee**	employ**ee**	nomin**ee**	

"-eer"

The suffix "-eer", meaning "a person or thing that has to do with (noun)" or "a person who writes or makes something", forms nouns.

auction**eer**	mountain**eer**	profit**eer**
engin**eer**	pamphlet**eer**	

"-el"

The word ending "-el" identifies nouns.

hot**el**	lab**el**	mors**el**	nick**el**

"-en"

The suffix "-en", meaning "of", "belonging to" or "made of", forms adjectives. The suffix "-en", meaning "cause to be" or "come to be", also forms verbs. As well, the suffix "-en" creates the plural form of some nouns such as "children" and "women".

cheap**en**	length**en**	sharp**en**	wom**en**
childr**en**	om**en**	spok**en**	writt**en**
chos**en**	ox**en**	steep**en**	
earth**en**	quick**en**	vix**en**	

"-er"

The suffix "-er", meaning "a person in an occupation or profession", "a person native to or living in a place", "a thing or action connected with (another noun)", or "a person or thing that (verb)s", forms nouns. The suffix "-er" also forms the comparative degree of many adjectives and adverbs. The suffix "-er", meaning "repeated", also forms verbs.

advis**er**	custom**er**	great**er**	patt**er**
bank**er**	danc**er**	lat**er**	report**er**
bigg**er**	driv**er**	London**er**	roll**er**
biograph**er**	farm**er**	manag**er**	small**er**
boat**er**	flick**er**	New York**er**	work**er**
cottag**er**	geograph**er**	paint**er**	

"-ery"

The suffix "-ery", meaning "a place to do something", "a place for something", "the product or goods of some place", or "a practice, act, or occupation", forms nouns.

bak**ery**	cutl**ery**	millin**ery**	scull**ery**
brew**ery**	discov**ery**	monast**ery**	tann**ery**
brib**ery**	flatt**ery**	nunn**ery**	vin**ery**
cann**ery**	flow**ery**	pott**ery**	
cel**ery**	forg**ery**	powd**ery**	
cream**ery**	midwif**ery**	robb**ery**	

"-ful"

The suffix "-ful", meaning "full of", "characterized by", "having the qualities of", or "having the tendency to", forms adjectives. The suffix "-ful" relating to measurement also forms nouns.

arm**ful**	aw**ful**	beauti**ful**	care**ful**

colorful (USA)	faithful	meaningful	respectful
colourful (UK, CAN)	forgetful	merciful	successful
cupful	graceful	mouthful	teaspoonful
deceitful	grateful	painful	thoughtful
disgraceful	handful	peaceful	truthful
doleful	helpful	pitiful	useful
doubtful	hopeful	playful	wonderful
dreadful	joyful	powerful	wrongful
dutiful	lawful	regretful	
	masterful	resourceful	

"-hood"

The suffix "-hood", meaning "a state, quality, or condition" or "the whole of a specified group", forms nouns.

brotherhood	neighborhood (USA)	neighbourhood (UK, CAN)	priesthood
childhood			sisterhood

"-ial"

The suffix "-ial", meaning "of", "like", or "suitable for", forms adjectives. The suffix "-ial", meaning "the act or process of doing something", forms nouns.

artificial	commercial	essential	magisterial
beneficial	confidential	jovial	

"-ics"

The suffix "-ics", meaning "art", "science", "study", "system", or "activities", forms nouns.

acrobatics	electronics	mathematics	politics
aesthetics	ethics	mechanics	statistics
athletics	hydroponics	physics	

"-ide"

The suffix "-ide", meaning "chemical compound", forms nouns that name chemicals.

bromide	fluoride	peroxide

"-in"

The suffix "-in", meaning "chemical compound", forms nouns that name chemicals. The suffix "-in" also forms other nouns.

album**in**	inul**in**	palmit**in**	streptomyc**in**
amygdal**in**	marg**in**	renn**in**	
chagr**in**	orig**in**	sat**in**	

"-ine"

The suffix "-ine", meaning "chemical compound", forms nouns that name chemicals.

chlor**ine**	fluor**ine**	gasol**ine**	iod**ine**

"-ing"

The suffix "-ing" creates the present tense of all verbs, both regular and irregular. See J4 and J5. Only a few sample words are provided below.

accept**ing**	cost**ing**	hav**ing**	offer**ing**
ask**ing**	deal**ing**	help**ing**	plead**ing**
battl**ing**	divid**ing**	ignor**ing**	punish**ing**
beat**ing**	do**ing**	invit**ing**	rac**ing**
blow**ing**	employ**ing**	kiss**ing**	sail**ing**
boil**ing**	explain**ing**	learn**ing**	ski**ing**
burn**ing**	fill**ing**	listen**ing**	stopp**ing**
call**ing**	find**ing**	los**ing**	walk**ing**
chang**ing**	fram**ing**	lov**ing**	wish**ing**
collect**ing**	grow**ing**	notic**ing**	

"-ion"

The suffix "-ion", meaning "the act or condition of" or "the result of", forms nouns.

apprehens**ion**	edit**ion**	omiss**ion**	permiss**ion**
dictat**ion**	fus**ion**	operat**ion**	separat**ion**

"-ious"

The suffix "-ious", meaning "having" or "characterized by", forms adjectives. The suffix "-ious" also forms adjectives from related nouns that end with the letters "-ion".

cur**ious**	fur**ious**	rebell**ious**	ser**ious**
deli**cious**	mali**cious**	reli**gious**	

"-ise/ize"

The suffix "-ise/ize", meaning "to cause to become", "to make something conform with or resemble", "to change into", "to subject to", "to treat with", "to combine with", "to engage in", or "to act in a specified way", forms verbs.

Americanize	compromise	economize	revise
authorize	crystallize	galvanize	
capitalize	democratize	generalize	
comprise	devise	oxidize	

"-ism"

The suffix "-ism", which is used to name a doctrine, ideology, principle, or system of thought, forms nouns.

Catholicism	conservatism	liberalism	socialism
communism	fascism	Protestantism	

"-ist"

The suffix "-ist", meaning "a person who specializes in a certain science", "a person who advocates a particular doctrine", or "a person skilled at something", forms nouns.

anarchist	ecologist	palaeontologist (UK, CAN)	satirist
anthropologist	geologist	paleontologist (USA)	seismologist
archaeologist	ideologist		socialist
biologist	meteorologist	pathologist	technologist
cardiologist	moralist	physiologist	toxicologist
communist	neurologist	pianist	typist
criminologist	novelist	psychologist	violinist
druggist			zoologist

"-ite"

The suffix "-ite", meaning "rock" or "mineral", forms nouns.

anthracite	bauxite	granite

"-itis"

The suffix "-itis", meaning "disease" or "inflammation", forms nouns.

arthr**itis**   laryng**itis**   tonsill**itis**

"-ity"

The suffix "-ity", meaning "a state, character, or condition of being (adjective)", forms nouns.

animos**ity**	familiar**ity**	original**ity**	simplic**ity**
audac**ity**	formal**ity**	possibil**ity**	solemn**ity**
author**ity**	hostil**ity**	qual**ity**	superior**ity**
capac**ity**	infin**ity**	relativ**ity**	tenac**ity**
chast**ity**	legal**ity**	responsibil**ity**	transferabil**ity**
clar**ity**	local**ity**	scarc**ity**	verac**ity**
dispar**ity**	major**ity**	sever**ity**	ver**ity**
facil**ity**	minor**ity**	similar**ity**	

"-le"

The suffix "-le" forms verbs indicating repeated action of a usually small or trivial kind. The suffix "-le" also forms, often diminutive, nouns. As well, the suffix "-le" forms adjectives from verbs.

ab**le**	chuck**le**	ici**cle**	Popsi**cle**
amb**le**	cir**cle**	impossib**le**	possib**le**
ang**le**	clavi**cle**	invisib**le**	prick**le**
ank**le**	coup**le**	jing**le**	princip**le**
app**le**	cuti**cle**	jumb**le**	probab**le**
arti**cle**	cy**cle**	jung**le**	purp**le**
availab**le**	dang**le**	knuck**le**	puzz**le**
babb**le**	dimp**le**	litt**le**	raff**le**
bamboo**zle**	doub**le**	mana**cle**	ramb**le**
bang**le**	eag**le**	map**le**	rif**le**
barna**cle**	examp**le**	marb**le**	ripp**le**
Bib**le**	fab**le**	mira**cle**	rump**le**
bicy**cle**	folli**cle**	miserab**le**	samp**le**
bott**le**	freck**le**	mono**cle**	scuff**le**
britt**le**	fumb**le**	motorcy**cle**	simp**le**
bubb**le**	gagg**le**	mus**cle**	sing**le**
bug**le**	gobb**le**	nob**le**	snugg**le**
bumb**le**	grapp**le**	obsta**cle**	spark**le**
bund**le**	hack**le**	og**le**	specta**cle**
bung**le**	hand**le**	parti**cle**	stap**le**
cab**le**	heck**le**	peop**le**	steep**le**
cand**le**	horrib**le**	pick**le**	stif**le**
cast**le**	humb**le**	pinna**cle**	strugg**le**

suitab**le**	thimb**le**	tricyc**le**	vegetab**le**
tab**le**	this**tle**	troub**le**	vehic**le**
tack**le**	tick**le**	tumb**le**	ventric**le**
tentac**le**	ting**le**	twink**le**	waff**le**
terrib**le**	tit**le**	unc**le**	whis**tle**
testic**le**	tog**gle**	valuab**le**	wres**tle**

"-ment"

The suffix "-ment", meaning "a result or product", "a means, agency, or instrument", "an act, art, or process", or "the state, condition, fact, or degree of being _____ed", forms nouns.

base**ment**	embodi**ment**	judg**ment**
com**ment**	enchant**ment**	state**ment**

"-ness"

The suffix "-ness", meaning "a state, quality, or instance of being", forms nouns.

cleanli**ness**	kind**ness**	sad**ness**	together**ness**
even**ness**	mean**ness**	stubborn**ness**	

"-ol"

The suffix "-ol", meaning "alcohol", forms nouns forms nouns that name chemicals.

ethan**ol**	glyc**ol**	methan**ol**

"-ology"

The suffix "-ology", meaning "theory or science of", forms nouns.

anthrop**ology**	ec**ology**	palaeont**ology** (UK, CAN)	psych**ology**
archae**ology**	ge**ology**	paleont**ology** (USA)	seism**ology**
astr**ology**	geront**ology**	path**ology**	techn**ology**
bi**ology**	ide**ology**	pharmac**ology**	the**ology**
cardi**ology**	meteor**ology**	physi**ology**	toxic**ology**
crimin**ology**	neur**ology**		zo**ology**

"-or/-our"

The suffix "-or/-our", meaning "a person or thing that does a (specified thing)", or "a quality or condition", forms nouns.

act**or**	col**our** (UK, CAN)	fav**our** (UK, CAN)	operat**or**
ard**or** (USA)	competit**or**	hon**or** (USA)	profess**or**
ard**our** (UK, CAN)	debt**or**	hon**our** (UK, CAN)	rum**or** (USA)
arm**or** (USA)	doct**or**	incis**or**	rum**our** (UK, CAN)
arm**our** (UK, CAN)	endeav**or** (USA)	investigat**or**	sail**or**
auth**or**	endeav**our** (UK, CAN)	lab**or** (USA)	sav**ior** (USA)
aviat**or**		lab**our** (UK, CAN)	sav**iour** (UK, CAN)
col**or** (USA)	fav**or** (USA)	mortgag**or**	ten**or**

"-ory"

The suffix "-ory", meaning "having the nature of", forms adjectives. The suffix "-ory", meaning "a place or thing for", forms nouns.

advis**ory**	direct**ory**	sens**ory**	valedict**ory**
cremat**ory**	promiss**ory**	territ**ory**	

"-ose"

The suffix "-ose", which means "carbohydrate" and usually identifies different sugars, forms nouns.

dextr**ose**	gluc**ose**	sucr**ose**
fruct**ose**	lact**ose**	

"-ous"

The suffix "-ous", meaning "having", "full of", or "characterized by", forms adjectives.

beaute**ous**	desir**ous**	homogene**ous**	marvel**ous** (USA)
capaci**ous**	heterogene**ous**	marvell**ous** (UK, CAN)	peril**ous**

"-phobia"

The suffix "-phobia", meaning "fear of", forms nouns.

acro**phobia**	arachno**phobia**	xeno**phobia**
agora**phobia**	claustro**phobia**	

"-s"

The suffix "-s" forms the plural form of many nouns and the third-person, present-tense, singular form of verbs. See K2.1 and K2.2. Only a few sample words are provided below.

apple**s**	cow**s**	judge**s**	ski**s**
arc**s**	crab**s**	lay**s**	sleep**s**
bag**s**	dog**s**	let**s**	spell**s**
boy**s**	face**s**	lose**s**	spit**s**
cage**s**	girl**s**	love**s**	sting**s**
can**s**	grad**s**	mall**s**	swing**s**
car**s**	hedge**s**	pack**s**	thank**s**
cat**s**	home**s**	rib**s**	wage**s**
chair**s**	horse**s**	ride**s**	walk**s**
chop**s**	house**s**	see**s**	win**s**
committee**s**	jam**s**	show**s**	write**s**

"-ual"

The word ending "-ual" forms adjectives.

grad**ual**	punct**ual**	us**ual**
intellect**ual**	unus**ual**	

Part J: Grammatical Considerations

J1 Parts of Speech

The correct spelling of a word is sometimes determined by the word's grammatical function. In order for a collection of words to express a meaningful idea as a sentence, the words must follow accepted grammatical conventions. When we speak or write, each word has a particular grammatical role or function to perform. These grammatical functions are often described as the "parts of speech". There are nine parts of speech: nouns, pronouns, adjectives, verbs, adverbs, prepositions, conjunctions, articles, and interjections.

Parts of Speech	Function	Examples
Nouns	Name a person, place, thing, animal, quality, action, or idea.	Jennifer, Tom, Boston, truck, horse, bravery, sale, think, love
Pronouns	May be substituted for a noun.	It, its, I, me, we, he, she, him, her, his, hers, me, you, they, myself, yourself, himself, herself, itself, ourselves, yourselves, themselves, my, mine, our, ours, your, yours, their, theirs, etc.
Adjectives	Modify, describe, limit, or give more information about a noun or pronoun.	a *lovely* girl, a *green* shirt, the *fastest* horse, *several* people, *that* car
Verbs	Express action, existence, or a state of being.	walk, talk, sit, run, sing, play, be, is, was, being
Adverbs	Modify, describe, or qualify a verb, adjective, or another adverb.	*more* intelligent, talk *softly*, *very* lovely, *extremely* old, *naturally* beautiful
Prepositions	Show the relationship of a noun or pronoun to another word in the sentence.	The money is *on* the table. She drove home *with* John. I like the sound *of* rain. He is going *to* work.

Conjunctions	Join two words or phrases.	and, because, but, for, if, nor, or, since, so, unless, yet Dogs *and* cats. Girls *nor* boys.
Articles	Are used to help define nouns.	a, an, the I want *an* apple and *a* banana. Look at *the* sunset.
Interjections	Are emphatic expressions that display emotion.	My *gosh*! *Wow*! *Oh*! *Alas*, we must part.

Many words can perform several grammatical functions. The function that a word performs primarily depends on how it is being used in a sentence. A word is a noun if it is used as a noun, that is, if it names something. A word is an adjective if it is used to describe a noun. Sometimes a word may be used as a noun, verb, or other part of speech without a change in spelling. Word order alone may indicate the word's grammatical function in a sentence. Often, however, the spelling of a word changes if its grammatical function changes. In such cases, the grammatical function of a word dictates the required spelling.

J2 Use of Suffixes to Indicate Grammatical Function

Many root words are free morphemes that form a part of speech without the help of a suffix. The word "sing", for example, functions as a verb without a verb suffix. Likewise, the word "dog" functions as a noun without a noun suffix.

Often, however, the grammatical function to be performed by a word will require the use of a particular suffix. The noun "navigator", for example, can be changed into a verb by replacing the suffix "-ator" with "-ate" producing "navigate". Likewise, the noun "navigator" can be changed into an adjective by replacing the suffix "-ator" with "-able" to produce "navigable". While some suffixes are lexical morphemes that convey meaning in their own right, see I12, many are relational and only convey meaning in relation to the base word to which they are attached. Prefixes, on the other hand, are lexical morphemes that convey meaning in their own right.

The following chart lists some common suffixes that are used to indicate a word's part of speech. It is important to note that the following are generalizations, not absolute rules. Depending on word order, some words can be used as different parts of speech without changing the suffix.

Noun Suffixes	Verb Suffixes
-ance (entr**ance**)	-age (rav**age**)
-ant (contest**ant**)	-ate (liber**ate**)
-ation (transl**ation**)	-efy (liqu**efy**)
-ator (navig**ator**)	-en (wid**en**)
-dom (king**dom**)	-er (discov**er**)
-ence (ess**ence**)	-ify (myst**ify**)
-ent (presid**ent**)	-ing (hammer**ing**)
-er (carpent**er**)	-ise (advert**ise**)
-hood (brother**hood**)	-ize (harmon**ize**)
-ism (social**ism**)	-yze (anal**yze**)
-ist (alarm**ist**)	
-ition (impos**ition**)	
-ity (lev**ity**)	
-ment (judg**ment**)	
-ness (good**ness**)	
-ology (psych**ology**)	
-or (act**or**)	
-ship (friend**ship**)	
Adjective Suffixes	**Adverb Suffixes**
-able (incur**able**)	-ly (extreme**ly**)
-al (form**al**)	
-ant (hesit**ant**)	
-ar (circul**ar**)	
-ary (sc**ary**)	
-ative (inform**ative**)	
-ent (magnific**ent**)	
-er (brav**er**)	
-ery (pepp**ery**)	
-est (brav**est**)	
-etic (po**etic**)	
-ible (irresist**ible**)	
-ic (histor**ic**)	
-ine (mascul**ine**)	
-ish (child**ish**)	
-less (hope**less**)	
-like (child**like**)	
-ly (love**ly**)	
-ory (transit**ory**)	
-ular (perpendic**ular**)	
-y (funn**y**)	

The following examples show how suffixes may be used to change the grammatical function of a word.

1. Some verbs may be changed into nouns or adjectives by adding an appropriate noun or adjective suffix.

   train + er = trainer (noun)
   train + able = trainable (adjective)

2. Other verbs may be changed into nouns or adjectives by removing the verb suffix and adding an appropriate noun or adjective suffix.

   navigate - ate + ator = navigator (noun)
   navigate - ate + able = navigable (adjective)

3. Some nouns may be changed into verbs or adjectives by adding an appropriate verb or adjective suffix.

   farm + ing = farming (verb)
   artist + ic = artistic (adjective)

4. Other nouns may be changed into verbs or adjectives by removing the noun suffix and adding an appropriate verb or adjective suffix.

   navigator - ator + ate = navigate (verb)
   navigator - ator + able = navigable (adjective)

5. Some adjectives can be changed into nouns and verbs by removing the adjective suffix and adding an appropriate noun or verb suffix.

   resistible - ible + er = resister (noun)
   resistible - ible + ing = resisting (verb)

6. Other adjectives may be changed into adverbs by adding the suffix "-ly" or "-ally".

   efficient + ly = efficiently
   basic + ally = basically

Suffixes also play a grammatical role in inflection. Inflection refers to changes in the form of a word that express grammatical distinctions such as gender, number, tense, person, and voice. The inflection of nouns and pronouns indicates such things as number (singular or plural) and possessive forms. The inflection of verbs, also known as conjugation, indicates whether the sentence expresses an active voice or passive voice, number (singular or plural), person (first person, second person, or third person), and tense. Tense denotes the time in which the action described in the sentence takes place. That is, does the action take place in the past, in the present, or in the future? The inflection of adjectives and adverbs indicates different degrees of comparison.

As mentioned above, suffixes play a role in creating both plural and possessive forms of nouns and verbs. See Part K for a discussion about plurals and Part L for a discussion about possessives.

J3 Verbs

A verb expresses action, existence, or a state of being. Verbs form an essential part of the predicate of the sentence. The predicate of a sentence is what is being said or asserted about the subject of the sentence. Consider the sentence "*Mary kicks the ball*". "Mary" is the subject of the sentence and "kicks the ball" is the predicate. The word "kicks" is the verb.

Every verb has an "infinitive" form. As well, every verb has four other fundamental forms, called the four "principal parts", from which all verb forms and tenses are derived. The four principal parts are the present tense, the past tense, the present participle, and the past participle. Verbs are classified as regular and irregular depending on how the past tense and past participle forms are created.

The **infinitive** form of a verb combines the word "to" with the present tense form as in "to play". Infinitives are used as nouns, adjectives, and adverbs but not as verbs. Infinitives cannot be used as verbs because they do not make assertions about a subject. Consider the following sentences.

- *I like to play*. (Used as a noun. Compare to "*I like ice cream*".)
- *I want someone to play with*. (Used as an adjective to modify the pronoun "someone".)
- *I am ready to play*. (Used as an adverb to modify the adjective "ready".)

The **present tense** form of a verb can make assertions about the subject of a sentence. The present tense may be thought of as the fundamental form of a verb from which the other verb forms are derived. In the sentence "*I walk to school*" the word "walk" is a present tense verb.

The **past tense** form of a verb can also make assertions about the subject of a sentence. With regular verbs the past tense is created by adding the suffix "-ed" to the present tense form. The past tense of "walk", for example, is "walk**ed**" as in "*I walked to school yesterday*." With irregular verbs, the past tense is created through internal spelling changes. The past tense of "drive", for example, is "drove".

The **present participle** is always created by adding the suffix "-ing" to the present tense form of the verb. The present participle of the verb "love", for example, is "lov**ing**". With regular verbs the **past participle** is identical to the past tense. It is created by adding the suffix "-ed" to the present tense form. The past participle of "love", for example, is "lov**ed**". With irregular verbs the past participle is formed through internal spelling changes. Sometimes it is identical to the past tense and sometimes it is not.

The present participle and the past participle verb forms function independently as adjectives, but cannot function independently as verbs. In the phrase "*a loving person*", for example, the present participle "loving" is used as an adjective to describe the noun "person". In the phrase "*a loved doll*", the past participle "loved" is used as an adjective to describe the noun "doll".

The present participle and the past participle can only function as verbs, to make assertions about the subject of a sentence, with the assistance of **auxiliary verbs**. Auxiliary verbs are a small group of words that combine with primary verbs to form verb phrases. Auxiliary verbs include the different forms of "to be" ("be", "am", "is", "are", "was", "were", "being", and "been"), "to do" ("do", "does", "did", and "done"), and "to have" ("have", "had", and "has"). Other auxiliary verbs include "will", "shall", "can", "could", "may", "might", "must", "ought", "should", and "would".

Consider the different forms of the irregular verb "drive":

1. The infinitive "to drive" may be used as a noun, adjective, or adverb.

   - *She likes to drive.* (Used as a noun. The word "likes" is the verb.)
   - *It is time to drive to work.* (Used as an adjective to modify the noun "time".)
   - *We are ready to drive home.* (Used as an adverb to modify the adjective "ready".)

2. The present tense "drive" may be used as a verb.

   - *I drive a truck.* (Used as a verb.)

3. The past tense "drove" may be used as a verb.

   - *I drove to work this morning.* (Used as a verb.)

4. The present participle "driving" may be used as an adjective and as a verb.

   - *Fear is a driving force in business.* (Used as an adjective to modify the noun "force".)
   - *I am driving to work this morning.* (Used as a verb with the assistance of "am".)

5. The past participle "driven" may be used as an adjective and as a verb.

- *He is a <u>driven</u> man.* (Used as an adjective to modify the noun "man".)
- *I <u>am being driven</u> to work this morning.* (Used as a verb with the assistance of "am" and "being".)

A verb must be numerically consistent with the subject noun of the sentence. The third-person present tense form of a verb changes depending upon whether the subject noun is singular or plural. If the subject noun is singular, the verb must also be singular. If the subject noun is plural, the verb must also be plural. However, the spelling of plural nouns and verbs is reversed. Generally, the suffixes "-s" or "-es" are added to make a noun plural. Conversely, the suffixes "-s" or "-es" are added to make a verb singular. The following sentence illustrates this principal. *"One cook (singular noun subject) mixes (singular verb) the cake batter while two cooks (plural noun subject) mix (plural verb) the muffin batter."*

J4   Regular Verbs

The present participle form of all verbs, both regular and irregular, is created by adding the suffix "-ing" to the present tense.

The past tense and past participle forms of regular verbs are always created by adding the suffix "-ed" to the present tense. Unfortunately, the suffix "-ed" is sometimes pronounced with the consonant "d" sound, sometimes with an "id" sound, and sometimes with the consonant "t" sound. See J6.

The following is a sample list of regular verbs set out in their infinitive, present tense, present participle, past tense, and past participle forms.

Infinitive	Present Tense	Present Participle	Past Tense	Past Participle
to accept	accept	accepting	accepted	accepted
to agree	agree	agreeing	agreed	agreed
to allow	allow	allowing	allowed	allowed
to answer	answer	answering	answered	answered
to approve	approve	approving	approved	approved
to arrest	arrest	arresting	arrested	arrested
to ask	ask	asking	asked	asked
to attach	attach	attaching	attached	attached
to attempt	attempt	attempting	attempted	attempted
to bake	bake	baking	baked	baked
to balance	balance	balancing	balanced	balanced
to bat	bat	batting	batted	batted
to battle	battle	battling	battled	battled
to behave	behave	behaving	behaved	behaved
to blink	blink	blinking	blinked	blinked

to boil	boil	boiling	boiled	boiled
to borrow	borrow	borrowing	borrowed	borrowed
to brake	brake	braking	braked	braked
to breathe	breathe	breathing	breathed	breathed
to burn	burn	burning	burned	burned
to calculate	calculate	calculating	calculated	calculated
to call	call	calling	called	called
to camp	camp	camping	camped	camped
to challenge	challenge	challenging	challenged	challenged
to change	change	changing	changed	changed
to check	check	checking	checked	checked
to clean	clean	cleaning	cleaned	cleaned
to collect	collect	collecting	collected	collected
to compete	compete	competing	competed	competed
to consider	consider	considering	considered	considered
to correct	correct	correcting	corrected	corrected
to cover	cover	covering	covered	covered
to damage	damage	damaging	damaged	damaged
to decide	decide	deciding	decided	decided
to deliver	deliver	delivering	delivered	delivered
to develop	develop	developing	developed	developed
to divide	divide	dividing	divided	divided
to dream	dream	dreaming	dreamed	dreamed
to educate	educate	educating	educated	educated
to employ	employ	employing	employed	employed
to enjoy	enjoy	enjoying	enjoyed	enjoyed
to exercise	exercise	exercising	exercised	exercised
to explain	explain	explaining	explained	explained
to fail	fail	failing	failed	failed
to fear	fear	fearing	feared	feared
to fill	fill	filling	filled	filled
to film	film	filming	filmed	filmed
to float	float	floating	floated	floated
to frame	frame	framing	framed	framed
to gather	gather	gathering	gathered	gathered
to greet	greet	greeting	greeted	greeted
to guess	guess	guessing	guessed	guessed
to hammer	hammer	hammering	hammered	hammered
to harm	harm	harming	harmed	harmed
to help	help	helping	helped	helped
to hope	hope	hoping	hoped	hoped
to hunt	hunt	hunting	hunted	hunted
to ignore	ignore	ignoring	ignored	ignored
to inform	inform	informing	informed	informed
to instruct	instruct	instructing	instructed	instructed

to invite	invite	inviting	invited	invited
to jog	jog	jogging	jogged	jogged
to jump	jump	jumping	jumped	jumped
to kick	kick	kicking	kicked	kicked
to kiss	kiss	kissing	kissed	kissed
to learn	learn	learning	learned	learned
to like	like	liking	liked	liked
to listen	listen	listening	listened	listened
to look	look	looking	looked	looked
to love	love	loving	loved	loved
to manage	manage	managing	managed	managed
to melt	melt	melting	melted	melted
to move	move	moving	moved	moved
to multiply	multiply	multiplying	multiplied	multiplied
to name	name	naming	named	named
to notice	notice	noticing	noticed	noticed
to obey	obey	obeying	obeyed	obeyed
to offend	offend	offending	offended	offended
to offer	offer	offering	offered	offered
to pack	pack	packing	packed	packed
to perform	perform	performing	performed	performed
to plant	plant	planting	planted	planted
to present	present	presenting	presented	presented
to print	print	printing	printed	printed
to punish	punish	punishing	punished	punished
to question	question	questioning	questioned	questioned
to race	race	racing	raced	raced
to reach	reach	reaching	reached	reached
to refuse	refuse	refusing	refused	refused
to rescue	rescue	rescuing	rescued	rescued
to rule	rule	ruling	ruled	ruled
to sail	sail	sailing	sailed	sailed
to scratch	scratch	scratching	scratched	scratched
to signal	signal	signaling	signaled	signaled
to ski	ski	skiing	skied	skied
to spray	spray	spraying	sprayed	sprayed
to step	step	stepping	stepped	stepped
to stop	stop	stopping	stopped	stopped
to support	support	supporting	supported	supported
to talk	talk	talking	talked	talked
to unite	unite	uniting	united	united
to use	use	using	used	used
to wait	wait	waiting	waited	waited
to walk	walk	walking	walked	walked
to wash	wash	washing	washed	washed

to watch	watch	watching	watched	watched
to wish	wish	wishing	wished	wished
to wonder	wonder	wondering	wondered	wondered
to work	work	working	worked	worked
to worry	worry	worrying	worried	worried

J5   Irregular Verbs

The present participle form of all verbs, both regular and irregular, is created by adding the suffix "-ing" to the present tense.

The past tense and past participle forms of irregular verbs are created through internal spelling changes. The spelling of the past tense and past participle of irregular verbs is sometimes identical and is sometimes different.

The following is a sample list of irregular verbs set out in their infinitive, present tense, present participle, past tense, and past participle forms.

Infinitive	Present Tense	Present Participle	Past Tense	Past Participle
to arise	arise	arising	arose	arisen
to awake	awake	awaking	awaked, awoke	awaked, awaken
to be	am, are, is	being	was, were	been
to bear	bear	bearing	bore	borne (carried)
				born (given birth)
to beat	beat	beating	beaten	beaten
to become	become	becoming	became	become
to begin	begin	beginning	began	begun
to bend	bend	bending	bent	bent
to bid (offer)	bid (offer)	bidding	bid	bid
to bite	bite	biting	bit	bitten, bit
to blow	blow	blowing	blew	blown
to break	break	breaking	broke	broken
to bring	bring	bringing	brought	brought
to burn	burn	burning	burnt, burned	burnt, burned
to burst	burst	bursting	burst	burst
to buy	buy	buying	bought	bought
to catch	catch	catching	caught	caught
to choose	choose	choosing	chose	chosen
to come	come	coming	came	come
to cost	cost	costing	cost	cost
to creep	creep	creeping	crept	crept
to cut	cut	cutting	cut	cut
to deal	deal	dealing	dealt	dealt
to dig	dig	digging	dug	dug

to dive	dive	diving	dove, dived	dived, dove
to do	do	doing	did	done
to draw	draw	drawing	drew	drawn
to dream	dream	dreaming	dreamed, dreamt	dreamed, dreamt
to drink	drink	drinking	drank	drunk
to drive	drive	driving	drove	driven
to eat	eat	eating	ate	eaten
to fall	fall	falling	fell	fallen
to feel	feel	feeling	felt	felt
to fight	fight	fighting	fought	fought
to find	find	finding	found	found
to flee	flee	fleeing	fled	fled
to fly	fly	flying	flew	flown
to forget	forget	forgetting	forgot	forgotten, forgot
to forsake	forsake	forsaking	forsook	forsaken
to freeze	freeze	freezing	froze	frozen
to get	get	getting	got	got, gotten
to give	give	giving	gave	given
to go	go	going	went	gone
to grow	grow	growing	grew	grown
to hang (suspend)	hang	hanging	hung	hung
to hang (execute)	hang	hanging	hanged	hung
to have	have	having	had	had
to hear	hear	hearing	heard	heard
to hit	hit	hitting	hit	hit
to hurt	hurt	hurting	hurt	hurt
to keep	keep	keeping	kept	kept
to kneel	kneel	kneeling	knelt, kneeled	knelt, kneeled
to know	know	knowing	knew	known
to lay (to place)	lay	laying	laid	laid
to lead	lead	leading	led	led
to learn	learn	learning	learnt, learned	learnt, learned
to leave	leave	leaving	left	left
to lend	lend	lending	lent	lent
to let	let	letting	let	let
to lie (to recline)	lie	lying	lay	lain
to light	light	lighting	lighted, lit	lighted, lit
to lose	lose	losing	lost	lost
to mean	mean	meaning	meant	meant
to pay	pay	paying	paid	paid
to plead	plead	pleading	pleaded	pleaded, pled
to prove	prove	proving	proved	proven, proved
to read	read	reading	read	read
to ride	ride	riding	rode	ridden

to ring	ring	ringing	rang	rung
to rise	rise	rising	rose	risen
to run	run	running	ran	run
to say	say	saying	said	said
to see	see	seeing	saw	seen
to send	send	sending	sent	sent
to set	set	setting	set	set
to shake	shake	shaking	shook	shaken
to shine	shine	shining	shone, shined	shone, shined
to show	show	showing	showed	shown, showed
to shrink	shrink	shrinking	shrank, shrunk	shrunk
to sing	sing	singing	sang, sung	sung
to sink	sink	sinking	sank, sunk	sunk
to sit	sit	sitting	sat	sat
to slay	slay	slaying	slew	slain
to sleep	sleep	sleeping	slept	slept
to slide	slide	sliding	slid	slid
to sow	sow	sowing	sowed	sown, sowed
to speak	speak	speaking	spoke	spoken
to spell	spell	spelling	spelt, spelled	spelt, spelled
to spit	spit	spitting	spat, spit	spit, spat
to spill	spill	spilling	spilt, spilled	spilt, spilled
to split	split	splitting	split	split
to spoil	spoil	spoiling	spoilt, spoiled	spoilt, spoiled
to spring	spring	springing	sprang, sprung	sprung
to stand	stand	standing	stood	stood
to steal	steal	stealing	stole	stolen
to sting	sting	stinging	stung	stung
to stink	stink	stinking	stank, stunk	stunk
to strike	strike	striking	struck	struck
to swear	swear	swearing	swore	sworn
to swim	swim	swimming	swam, swum	swum
to swing	swing	swinging	swung	swung
to take	take	taking	took	taken
to teach	teach	teaching	taught	taught
to tear	tear	tearing	tore	torn
to tell	tell	telling	told	told
to think	think	thinking	thought	thought
to throw	throw	throwing	threw	thrown
to tread	tread	treading	trod	trodden, trod
to wake	wake	waking	waked, woke	waked, woke, woken
to wear	wear	wearing	wore	worn
to weave	weave	weaving	wove, weaved	woven, weaved
to win	win	winning	won	won

to wind	wind	winding	wound	wound
to wring	wring	wringing	wrung	wrung
to write	write	writing	wrote	written

J6 Past Tense Spelled with Suffix "-ed" and "t"

J6.1 Past tense "-ed" pronounced "id"

The past tense and past participle of regular verbs are always formed by adding the suffix "-ed". With the following verbs, the suffix "-ed" is pronounced as a separate syllable as "-id". The word "graded", for example, is pronounced "grad-id".

What the following base words have in common is that they all end with the consonant "d" or consonant "t" sounds. Pronouncing the suffix "-ed" as a separate syllable helps the listener hear it.

accept → accepted
arrest → arrested
bat → batted
collect → collected
complicate → complicated
create → created
crook → crooked
decide → decided
delight → delighted
divide → divided
excite → excited
grade → graded
greet → greeted
haunt → haunted
head → headed
interest → interested
knit → knitted
land → landed

limit → limited
load → loaded
nod → nodded
paste → pasted
point → pointed
pot → potted
rat → ratted
relate → related
report → reported
rugged
sacred
spot → spotted
suppose → *supposed*
trade → traded
unite → united
want → wanted
waste → wasted
wick → wicked

J6.2 Past tense "-ed" pronounced "d"

The past tense and past participle of regular verbs are always formed by adding the suffix "-ed". With the following words, the suffix "-ed" is pronounced with the consonant "d" sound. It is not pronounced as a separate syllable. The letter "e" is silent.

What the following base words have in common is that they all end with a vowel sound or a voiced consonant sound other than "d".

It may be noted that the past tense of the word "spell" is sometimes spelled "spelt" and is sometimes spelt "spelled".

allow → allow**ed**	live → liv**ed**
boil → boil**ed**	love → lov**ed**
bore → bor**ed**	marry → marri**ed**
close → clos**ed**	name → nam**ed**
color → color**ed** (USA)	plan → plann**ed**
colour → colour**ed** (UK, CAN)	plane → plan**ed**
concern → concern**ed**	pull → pull**ed**
cover → cover**ed**	receive → receiv**ed**
cry → cri**ed**	retire → retir**ed**
dare → dar**ed**	rob → robb**ed**
dial → dial**ed** (USA), dill**ed** (UK, CAN)	sail → sail**ed**
dodge → dodg**ed**	seem → seem**ed**
dream → dream**ed** (Also dreamt)	slam → slamm**ed**
fill → fill**ed**	snag → snagg**ed**
frighten → frighten**ed**	spell → spell**ed** (Also spelt)
graze → graz**ed**	suppose → *suppos**ed***
hurry → hurri**ed**	tire → tir**ed**
identify → identifi**ed**	tug → tugg**ed**
involve → involv**ed**	use → us**ed**
learn → learn**ed**	weigh → weigh**ed**
lie → li**ed**	worry → worri**ed**

J6.3 Past tense "-ed" pronounced "t"

The past tense and past participle of regular verbs are always formed by adding the suffix "-ed". With the following words, the suffix "-ed" is pronounced with the consonant "t" sound. It is not pronounced as a separate syllable. The letter "e" is silent.

What the following base words have in common is that they all end with an unvoiced consonant sound other than "t"; in particular, the hard "c" or "k" consonant sound, the soft "c" or "s" consonant sound, the consonant "p" sound, or the consonant "sh" sound.

accomplish → accomplish**ed**	finish → finish**ed**
bake → bak**ed**	fix → fix**ed**
cap → capp**ed**	flap → flapp**ed**
check → check**ed**	force → forc**ed**
crook → *crook**ed***	guess → guess**ed**
cup → cupp**ed**	hack → hack**ed**
deck → deck**ed**	hook → hook**ed**
dock → dock**ed**	hop → hopp**ed**
duck → duck**ed**	lace → lac**ed**

lap → lapped
laugh → laughed
lease → leased
like → liked
mass → massed
milk → milked
miss → missed
mix → mixed
pass → passed
peck → pecked
pick → picked
pluck → plucked
press → pressed
reach → reached
rebuff → rebuffed
rip → ripped

slip → slipped
slop → slopped
smash → smashed
sniff → sniffed
stock → stocked
stop → stopped
thank → thanked
top → topped
toss → tossed
track → tracked
trick → tricked
trip → tripped
vanish → vanished
walk → walked
wash → washed

J6.4 Past tense spelled "t"

A number of past-tense verbs that end with the consonant "t" sound are actually spelled with the suffix "-ed". See J6.3. However, with the following irregular verbs, the past tense and past participle are spelled with a final letter "-t" which, thankfully, is pronounced with the consonant "t" sound.

It may be noted that the past tense of the word "spell" is sometimes spelled "spelt" and is sometimes spelt "spelled".

bend → bent
bring → brought
buy → bought
catch → caught
creep → crept
deal – dealt
dream → dreamt (Also dreamed)
feel → felt
fight → fought
forget → forgot
get → got
keep → kept
kneel → knelt (Also kneeled)
learn → learnt (Also learned)
leave → left

lend → lent
light → lit (Also lighted)
lose → lost
mean → meant
send → sent
sit → sat
sleep → slept
spell → spelt (Also spelled)
spend → spent
spill → spilt
spit → spat
split → split
spoil → spoilt
teach → taught
think → thought

J7 Adjectives

J7.1 Introduction

Adjectives modify, describe, limit, or give more information about a noun or pronoun. In the phrase *"sunny day"*, for example, the adjective *"sunny"* describes the noun *"day"*.

In describing nouns and pronouns, adjectives may also make comparisons. There are three degrees of comparison: absolute, comparative, and superlative.

1. An **absolute adjective** merely describes a singular noun or pronoun and actually makes no comparisons. Example: *"Quartz is a hard mineral.*

2. A **comparative adjective** expresses a relative degree of quality or quantity when describing a noun or pronoun. Example: *Topaz is a harder mineral than quartz.*

3. A **superlative adjective** expresses the greatest degree of a quality or quantity when describing a noun or pronoun. Example: *"Diamond is the hardest mineral of all"*.

Adjectives are also divided into "regular" and "irregular" adjectives. Regular adjectives follow a consistent pattern when transformed from the absolute into the comparative and superlative forms. Some regular absolute adjectives are transformed by adding the suffix, "-er" for the comparative and the suffix "-est" for the superlative. Other regular absolute adjectives are transformed by using the adverbs "more" or "less" for the comparative and the adverbs "most" and "least" for the superlative. The correct method depends on how many syllables are in the absolute form of the adjective.

Irregular adjectives do not follow a regular pattern when transforming from the absolute into the comparative and superlative forms. Instead, entirely different words may be used in the absolute, comparative, and superlative forms. For example, the absolute adjective *"good"* becomes the comparative adjective *"better"* and the superlative adjective *"best"*.

J7.2 Single and two-syllable regular absolute adjectives

Regular single-syllable adjectives, such as the word *"sweet"*, usually transform into the comparative by adding the suffix "-er", as in *"sweeter"*, and the superlative by adding the suffix "-est", as in *"sweetest"*. The adverbs *"more"* and *"most"* are generally not used. However, the adverbs *"less"* and *"least"*, as in *"less sweet"* and *"least sweet"*, are used as there are no equivalent suffixes.

Regular two-syllable adjectives, such as the word *"fancy"*, can usually transform into the comparative and superlative in two ways. The comparative may be created by adding the suffixes "-er", as in "fancier", or by using the adverbs "more" or "less" as in "more fancy" and "less fancy". Likewise, the superlative may be created by adding the suffix "-est", as in "fanciest", or by using the adverbs "most" or "least" as in "most fancy" and "least fancy".

The following is a sample list of regular single and two-syllable adjectives set out in their absolute, comparative, and superlative forms. The two-syllable absolute adjectives marked with an asterisk are also listed in J7.3.

Absolute	Comparative	Superlative
big	bigger	biggest
broad	broader	broadest
cool	cooler	coolest
fancy*	fancier	fanciest
fine	finer	finest
full	fuller	fullest
funny*	funnier	funniest
happy*	happier	happiest
hard	harder	hardest
hot	hotter	hottest
kind	kinder	kindest
large	larger	largest
lazy*	lazier	laziest
long	longer	longest
nice	nicer	nicest
safe	safer	safest
silly*	sillier	silliest
strong	stronger	strongest
sunny*	sunnier	sunniest
sweet	sweeter	sweetest
tall	taller	tallest
young	younger	youngest

J7.3 Regular absolute adjectives with two or more syllables

As discussed in J7.2, regular two-syllable adjectives, such as the word "fancy", can usually transform into the comparative and superlative in two ways: by adding a suffix or by using an adverb. There are exceptions such as the word "careful".

With regular adjectives containing three or more syllables, such as the word "beautiful", the comparative and superlative forms are only created using adverbs. The comparative is created by using the adverbs "more" or "less" as in "more beautiful" and "less beautiful". The superlative is created by using the adverbs "most" and "least" as in "most beautiful" and "least beautiful".

The following is a sample list of regular adjectives containing two or more syllables set out in their absolute, comparative, and superlative forms. The two-syllable absolute adjectives marked with an asterisk are also listed in J7.2.

Absolute	Comparative	Superlative
beautiful	more beautiful less beautiful	most beautiful least beautiful
careful	more careful less careful	most careful least careful
competent	more competent less competent	most competent least competent
descriptive	more descriptive less descriptive	most descriptive least descriptive
fancy*	more fancy less fancy	most fancy least fancy
funny*	more funny less funny	most funny least funny
happy*	more happy less happy	most happy least happy
intelligent	more intelligent less intelligent	most intelligent least intelligent
lazy*	more lazy less lazy	most lazy least lazy
silly*	more silly less silly	most silly least silly
suitable	more suitable less suitable	most suitable least suitable
sunny*	more sunny less sunny	most sunny least sunny

J7.4 Hyphenated adjectives as in "old-fashion"

When two or more words are combined together to form an adjective, the words are hyphenated if they precede the noun that is being modified. They are not hyphenated if they follow the noun. For example:

- Mary is wearing an *old-fashioned* dress.
- Mary's dress is *old fashioned*.

- Tom has written an *up-to-date* report.
- Tom's report is *up to date*.

The use of hyphens helps to clarify, for example, that reference is being made to a "hard-working girl" and not to a "hard working-girl".

J7.5 Irregular adjectives

The following are irregular adjectives that do not conform to the regular pattern when creating the comparative and superlative forms. Entirely different words may be used in the absolute, comparative, and superlative forms.

Absolute	Comparative	Superlative
good	better	best
bad	worse	worst
some	more	most
little	less	least
many	more	most
much	more	most
well	better	best

J8 Adverbs

Adverbs modify, describe, or qualify a verb, adjective, or another adverb. In the phrase "*very funny*", for example, the adverb "very" modifies the adjective "funny". Some adverbs are derived from adjectives.

J8.1 Adverbs that take the suffix "-ly".

The majority of adverbs are created by adding the suffix "-ly" to an adjective. The adjective "happy", for example, becomes the adverb "happily".

- *She sang a happy song.* (The adjective "happy" describes the noun "song".)
- *She happily sang a song.* (The adverb "happily" describes the verb "sang".)

Adjective	Adverb
accidental	accidentally
accurate	accurately
actual	actually
adequate	adequately
appropriate	appropriately
automatic	automatically
basic	basically
careful	carefully
cheerful	cheerfully
conclusive	conclusively
critical	critically
definite	definitely
doubtful	doubtfully
economical	economically
electrical	electrically
exceptional	exceptionally
external	externally
extreme	extremely
final	finally
forceful	forcefully
full	fully
general	generally
happy	happily
hasty	hastily
historical	historically
hopeful	hopefully
immediate	immediately
immense	immensely
initial	initially
intentional	intentionally
mad	madly
meaningful	meaningfully
natural	naturally
occasional	occasionally
partial	partially
periodical	periodically
political	politically
principal	principally
professional	professionally
quick	quickly
real	really
reasonable	reasonably
respective	respectively
scarce	scarcely

separate	separate**ly**
skillful (USA)	skillful**ly** (USA)
skilful (UK, CAN)	skilful**ly** (UK, CAN)
special	special**ly**
strong	strong**ly**
sure	sure**ly**
systematic	systematic**ally**
technical	technical**ly**
total	total**ly**
truthful	truthful**ly**
useful	useful**ly**

J8.2 Adverbs that do not require the suffix "-ly".

The following words are adverbs. They are not created by adding the suffix "-ly" to an adjective. Some of the following adverbs also function as adjectives.

- *He is a <u>fast</u> driver.* (The adjective "fast" describes the noun "driver".)
- *He drives <u>fast</u>.* (The adverb "fast" modifies the verb "drives".)

again	here	most	there
always	least	much	very
everywhere	less	now	well
fast	more	soon	

J8.3 Adverbs that take both forms.

The following words may be used as adverbs both with the suffix "-ly" attached and without. However, in any particular sentence only one form is correct. In most sentences the "-ly" form is correct. As well, without the suffix "-ly" the following words may also be used as adjectives to describe nouns.

- *The train arrived <u>late</u>.* The adverb "*late*" modifies the verb "*arrived*".
- *Have you taken the train <u>lately</u>?* The adverb "*lately*" modifies the verb "*taken*".
- *They took the <u>late</u> train.* The adjective "*late*" describes the noun "*train*".

In the following table, the sample words in the first column function both as adverbs and adjectives. The words in the second column only function as adverbs.

Adverbs/Adjectives Without "-ly"	Adverbs With "-ly"
close	close**ly**
direct	direct**ly**
fair	fair**ly**
hard	hard**ly**

late	late**ly**
loud	loud**ly**
quick	quick**ly**
quiet	quiet**ly**
short	short**ly**
slow	slow**ly**
wide	wide**ly**

J8.4 Adverbs used to make comparisons

Adverbs modify, describe, or qualify a verb, adjective, or another adverb. In doing so, adverbs may also make comparisons. As with adjectives, there are three degrees of comparison: absolute, comparative, and superlative.

1. An **absolute** adverb merely modifies a verb, adjective, or another adverb and actually makes no comparisons. Example: *John runs fast*.

2. A **comparative** adverb expresses a relative degree of quality or quantity when modifying a verb, adjective, or another adverb. Example: *Tom runs faster than John.*

3. A **superlative** adverb expresses the greatest degree of a quality or quantity when modifying a verb, adjective, or another adverb. Example: *Jim runs the fastest*.

J9 Nouns

Nouns name something such as a person, place, thing, animal, quality, action, or idea. The words "Jennifer", "Boston", "truck", "horse", "bravery", "sale", "think", and "love" are all nouns. Some words, such as "love" and "hate", are used both as nouns and as verbs.

There are many suffixes that indicate that a word is a noun. Words that end with the same suffix share a degree of common meaning, forming word families. The suffix "-aire", for example, forms nouns such as "millionaire" and "billionaire" that name people who are members of a select group.

J10 Pronouns

Pronouns are a part of speech that may be substituted for a noun. Pronouns help to make sentences less repetitive and, therefore, less cumbersome and more interesting. For example, the sentence "Jennifer rode Jennifer's bike to school" is more cumbersome to say than "Jennifer rode *her* bike to school.

J10.1 Personal pronouns

Personal pronouns may be substituted for the specific noun that names a person, place, or other thing. The specific noun being replaced is called the "antecedent". In the sentence "Tom forgot *his* lunch", "Tom" is the antecedent for the personal pronoun "his".

A pronoun must reflect a number of grammatical considerations. Is the sentence speaking from the perspective of the first person (the person who is speaking), second person (the person being spoken to), or third person (the person being spoken about)? Does the sentence refer to a singular person, place, or other thing or to two or more persons, places, or other things? Is the pronoun the subject or object of the sentence, or is it making a statement about possessiveness? Is the pronoun referring to a male, female, or neuter subject or object?

Personal pronouns can be used as the subject of a sentence. In the sentence "*She* kicked the ball", the pronoun "she" forms the subject of the sentence. Personal pronouns can also be used as the object of a sentence. In the sentence "The dog growled at *him*", the pronoun "him" forms the object of the sentence. For discussion about possessive forms of pronouns see L5.

The following chart sets out the appropriate personal pronoun to use in each instance.

	Subject	**Object**	**Possessive**
First Person			
Singular	I	me	my, mine
Plural	we	us	our*, ours (not our's)
Second Person			
Singular	you	you	your*, yours (not your's)
Plural	you	you	your*, yours (not your's)
Third Person			
Singular			
Masculine	he	him	his
Feminine	she	her	hers (not her's)
Neuter	it	it	its (not it's)
Any gender	one	one	one's
Plural	they	them	their, theirs (not their's)

* Strictly, a possessive adjective.

Note that "it's" is a contraction of the words "it is" and not the possessive form of the personal pronoun "it". This confuses writers to no end. For further discussion about contractions, such as "you're" and "didn't", see Part O.

J10.2 Reflexive pronouns

Reflexive pronouns "reflect" back to the subject or subjects of the sentence within the same clause. There are two kinds of reflexive pronouns, singular and plural. Singular reflexive pronouns use the suffix "-self" while plural reflexive pronouns use the suffix "-selves".

Singular	Plural
myself	ourselves
yourself	yourselves
himself	themselves
herself	
itself	

- *I did it **myself**, without any help.* (Reflects back to "I".)
- *Jim and Betty did it **themselves**, without any help.* (Reflects back to Jim and Betty.)
- *David helped **himself** to a cookie.* (Reflects back to David.)
- *The **dog** wandered off by **itself**.* (Reflects back to "dog".)

J10.3 Relative pronouns

Relative pronouns act as the subject or object of a dependent clause in a sentence and relate back to a preceding noun that is the subject or object of the independent clause.

	Subject	Object	Possessive
People	who	who, whoever whom, whomever	whose
Inanimate Objects	that, where, which, whichever	that, where, which, whichever	whose

In the sentence "*The bicycle **that he wants to buy** is blue*", the relative pronoun "*that*" is the object of the dependent clause "*that he wants to buy*" and relates back to the noun "*bicycle*" which is the subject of the independent clause "*The bicycle ... is blue.*"

- *This bicycle, **which** is broken, needs to be repaired.*
- *The person **who** called today wants to set up a meeting.*
- *Lynda, **whom** I enjoy working with, is coming to visit.*
- *My brother, **whose** jacket you borrowed, is away today.*
- *One student, **whoever** is finished first, will post his or her work.*
- *Three students, **whomever** volunteer, will present to the class.*
- *We will take one vehicle, **whichever** is in the best repair.*
- *The shirt **that** I bought is too small.*
- *My school, **where** I played in the band, is being renovated.*

Note that "who", "whoever", "whom", "whomever", "which", "whichever", and "whose" are also interrogative pronouns.

J10.4 Demonstrative pronouns

Demonstrative pronouns refer to a particular person, place, or thing. Demonstrative pronouns can be singular or plural and can refer to things that are either near or far in distance or time.

	Singular	Plural
Near in Distance or Time	this	these
Far in Distance or Time	that	those

- *Please deliver <u>this</u> package today.*
- *I want to try on <u>these</u> two pairs of shoes.*
- *You may sit in <u>that</u> chair over there.*
- *We will be camping in <u>those</u> mountains.*

J10.5 Interrogative pronouns

Interrogative pronouns are used to ask questions, as the police do during an "interrogation". They refer to the unidentified subject or object of the question being asked. Note that the word "*who*" is used as the subject of the sentence while the word "*whom*" is used as the object of the sentence.

	Subject	Object
Person	who, whoever, whosever	whom, whomever
Thing	what, whatever	
Person/Thing	which, whichever	
Possessive	whose	

- <u>Who</u> *is going out tonight?* "Who" is the subject of the sentence.
- *With <u>whom</u> are you speaking?* "Whom" is the object of the sentence.
- <u>What</u> *is happening tonight?* "What" is the subject of the sentence.
- <u>What</u> *would you like to do?* "What" is the object of the sentence.
- <u>Which</u> *flavour will you choose?* "Which" is the object of the sentence.
- <u>Whose</u> *keys are on the table?* "Whose" is the subject of the sentence.
- <u>Whoever</u> *wants it can have it?* "Whoever" is the subject of the sentence.
- <u>Whosever</u> *going to attempt that?* "Whosever" is the subject of the sentence.

Note that "who", "whoever", "whom", "whomever", "which", "whichever", and "whose" are also relative pronouns. The interrogative pronouns "whosoever", "whomsoever", and "whatsoever" are seldom used in modern writing.

J10.6 Reciprocal pronouns

Reciprocal pronouns create a relationship between the subjects of a sentence making them objects as well. This helps to prevent confusing repetition within sentences. There are two reciprocal pronouns, "each other" and "one another".

- *The two boys helped <u>each other.</u>*
- *All of the boys helped <u>one another</u>.*
- *The two students blamed <u>each other</u>.*
- *All of the graduates congratulated <u>one another</u>.*

J10.7 Indefinite pronouns

Indefinite pronouns refer to an unknown or unspecified person, place, or thing.

all	both	many	none
another	each	much	one
any	either	neither	several
anybody	enough	no	some
anyone	every	no one	someone
anything	few	nobody	

- *<u>All</u> are welcomed to join in this celebration.*
- *<u>Another</u> customer just walked in.*
- *<u>Anybody</u> want to come with me to the mall?*
- *<u>Both</u> of you are to be congratulated.*
- *<u>Every</u> option is on the table.*
- *<u>Many</u> responded positively to our suggestion.*
- *<u>Several</u> more will be coming later.*
- *<u>Someone</u> must be held responsible.*

Part K: Plurals

K1   Introduction

Both nouns and verbs have singular and plural forms.

The singular form of a noun indicates that a single person, place, thing, animal, action, or idea is being discussed. The plural form of a noun indicates that a quantity of two or more is being discussed. It is necessary to maintain number agreement between a noun and any adjective that modifies or limits the noun. The following sentence illustrates this. *"The boy picked one (adjective) apple (singular noun), and the girl picked two (adjective) apples (plural noun)."*

The third-person present tense form of a verb changes depending upon whether the subject noun is singular or plural. If the subject noun is singular, the verb must also be singular. If the subject noun is plural, the verb must also be plural. However, the spelling of plural nouns and verbs is reversed. Typically, the suffixes "-s" or "-es" are added to make a noun plural. Conversely, the suffixes "-s" or "-es" are added to make a verb singular. The following sentence illustrates this principal. *"One cook (singular noun subject) mixes (singular verb) the cake batter while two cooks (plural noun subject) mix (plural verb) the muffin batter."*

The general rule for creating plural nouns and singular verbs is simple enough. With most words, the suffix "-s" is added to the end of the word. There are, however, a number of exceptions to the general rule. Some words, such as "aircraft" and "deer", do not have different singular and plural forms. With some words the spelling of the base word changes to create the plural. The singular noun "tooth", for example, becomes the plural noun "teeth".

With words that end with the letters "-ch", "-s", "-ss", "-sh", "-x", and "-z", the suffix "-es" is usually added to create the plural form. With such words, it is difficult to pronounce a final letter "s" without an intervening vowel sound. For this reason, the plural form of the word usually requires the speaker to pronounce an extra syllable containing a schwa vowel sound. The plural form of "beach", for example, is pronounced "beach-es". If an extra syllable is heard in the plural form of a word, the "-es" spelling pattern usually applies.

With words that end with the letters "-f", "-fe", and "-ff", the plural is sometimes formed by adding the suffix "-s" and sometimes by changing the letters "f" or "fe" to the letter "v" before adding "-es". Words that end with the letter "o" sometimes take the suffix "-s" and sometimes take the suffix "-es". With words that end with the letter "-y" following a vowel letter, simply add the suffix "-s" to create the plural. With words that end with the letter "-y" following a consonant letter, change the "y" to an "i" and add the suffix "-es" to create the plural. Lastly, special considerations apply to compound words and foreign words.

A final letter "s" is pronounced with either a voiced consonant "z" sound or an unvoiced soft "c/s" consonant sound. With a voiced sound the vocal cords vibrate. With an unvoiced sound the vocal cords do not vibrate. All vowel sounds are **voiced** as are consonant sounds "b", "d", soft "g/j", hard "g", "l", "m", "n", "ng", "r", "v", "w", "y", "z", "zh", and the "th" sound heard in "this". **Unvoiced** sounds include consonant sounds soft "c/s", hard "c/k", "f", "h", "p", "t", "x", "ch", "sh", and the "th" sound heard in "thing". When the letter "s" follows a voiced sound, it is pronounced with the voiced consonant "z" sound as in "plays", "friends", and "hours". When the letter "s" follows an unvoiced sound, it is pronounced with the unvoiced soft "c/s" consonant sound as in "cats", "chops", and "chiefs".

With words that end with "-es" where the "e" is pronounced with a voiced schwa vowel sound, as in "judg**e**s", "hors**e**s", and "bush**e**s", the letter "s" is pronounced with the consonant "z" sound. With words that end with "-es" where the "e" is not pronounced, as in "rides", "athletes", and "tapes", the preceding consonant sound determines how the "-s" is pronounced.

Proper names follow the rules governing the creation of plurals with two general exceptions. One is that the spelling of a proper name is never changed to create the plural form. The second is that the suffix "-es" should not be added to create the plural form of a proper name if the extra syllable would make the name awkward to pronounce.

K2 The General Rule

K2.1 Nouns: Add the suffix "-s"

The general rule is that singular nouns are made plural by adding the letter "-s". For exceptions to the rule, see below.

It may be noted that singular nouns that end with a silent letter "e", as in "horse" and "home", accept the letter "s" to create the plural. This results in a final "-es" spelling pattern. Sometimes, as in the word "hors-es", the letters "es" are pronounced as an extra syllable. Sometimes, as heard in the word "homes", the letter "e" remains silent so an extra syllable is not pronounced.

apple**s**	cat**s**	fac**es**	jam**s**
arc**s**	chair**s**	girl**s**	judg**es**
bag**s**	chop**s**	grad**s**	mall**s**
boy**s**	committee**s**	hedg**es**	pack**s**
cag**es**	cow**s**	home**s**	rib**s**
can**s**	crab**s**	hors**es**	toe**s**
car**s**	dog**s**	hous**es**	wag**es**

K2.2 Third-Person Present Tense Singular Verbs: Add the suffix "-s"

The general rule discussed in K2.1 also applies to verbs. The third-person, present-tense, singular form of a verb is usually formed by adding the suffix "-s".

It may be noted that verbs that end with a silent letter "e", as in "choose" and "give", accept the letter "s" to create the singular. This results in a final "-es" spelling pattern. Sometimes, as in the word "choos-es", the letters "-es" are pronounced as an extra syllable. Sometimes, as in the word "gives", the letter "e" remains silent so an extra syllable is not pronounced.

act**s**	drive**s**	lend**s**	sink**s**
aris**es**	eat**s**	let**s**	sit**s**
awake**s**	fall**s**	lie**s**	ski**s**
beat**s**	feel**s**	light**s**	sleep**s**
become**s**	fight**s**	like**s**	slide**s**
begin**s**	find**s**	listen**s**	sow**s**
bend**s**	flee**s**	los**es**	speak**s**
bit**es**	forget**s**	love**s**	spell**s**
blow**s**	forsake**s**	pay**s**	spit**s**
break**s**	freez**es**	plead**s**	split**s**
bring**s**	get**s**	prove**s**	spring**s**
burn**s**	give**s**	read**s**	stand**s**
burst**s**	grow**s**	ride**s**	steal**s**
buy**s**	hang**s**	ring**s**	sting**s**
call**s**	hear**s**	ris**es**	stink**s**
choos**es**	hit**s**	run**s**	strike**s**
come**s**	hop**es**	say**s**	swear**s**
creep**s**	hurt**s**	see**s**	swim**s**
cut**s**	keep**s**	send**s**	swing**s**
deal**s**	kneel**s**	set**s**	take**s**
dig**s**	know**s**	shake**s**	talk**s**
dive**s**	lay**s**	shin**es**	tear**s**
draw**s**	lead**s**	show**s**	tell**s**
dream**s**	learn**s**	shrink**s**	thank**s**
drink**s**	leave**s**	sing**s**	think**s**

throw**s**	walk**s**	weave**s**	work**s**
tread**s**	want**s**	wind**s**	wring**s**
wake**s**	wear**s**	win**s**	write**s**

K3 Plural Nouns That Do Not Change Form

K3.1 Singular and plural nouns that are the same

The following nouns do not have different singular and plural forms. The same spelling is used to indicate both the singular and the plural forms. It may be noted that the names of some nationalities, tribes, and races such as Iroquois and Chinese do not have singular and plural forms.

aircraft	elk	moose	samurai
chassis	fish	offspring	species
Chinese	grouse	police	sheep
dandruff	humankind	rendezvous	shrimp
deer	Iroquois	salmon	swine

K3.2 Singular form of noun is seldom used

The following nouns either do not have a singular form or the singular form is seldom used.

Sometimes, this is because we are referring to things that come in pairs such as "tongs" and "scissors". We seldom use only one "tong" or one "scissor". Sometimes, with aggregate nouns such as "goods", "remains", and "thanks", it is presumed that more than one item or instance is being referred to.

alm**s**	corp**s**	pajama**s** (USA)	specie**s** (type/class)
amend**s**	forceps	pant**s** (trousers)	stair**s**
annal**s**	eyeglasse**s**	proceed**s**	sweepstake**s**
arm**s** (weapons)	good**s**	pyjama**s** (UK, CAN)	thank**s**
athletic**s**	headquarter**s**	remain**s**	tong**s**
bellow**s**	jean**s**	scissor**s**	trouser**s**
binocular**s**	mean**s**	serie**s**	tweezer**s**
brain**s** (intelligence)	measle**s**	shamble**s**	
clothe**s**	nuptial**s**	short**s**	
content**s**	obsequie**s**	slack**s** (trousers)	

K4 Plurals That Require Other Spelling Changes

With the following irregular plurals, spelling changes beyond adding the suffixes "-s" or "-es" are required to create the plural. Often, the change in spelling reflects a change in a vowel sound.

- brother → brethren (Also brothers)
- child → children
- cow → cattle
- die → dice
- foot → feet
- goose → geese
- louse → lice
- man → men
- mouse → mice
- ox → oxen
- person → people
- tooth → teeth
- woman → women

K5 Words That End With the Letters "-ch"

The plural form of words that end with the letters "ch" is created by adding the suffix "-es" or "-s" depending on how word ending is pronounced.

K5.1 Words that end with the consonant "-ch" sound

With singular nouns that end with the consonant "ch" sound, the suffix "-es" is added to create the plural. The noun "peach", for example, becomes "peaches". The same rule applies when creating the third-person, present-tense, singular form of verbs. The verb "scratch", for example, becomes "scratches".

It is difficult to pronounce a final letter "s" directly following the consonant "ch" sound. For this reason, the plural form of the word prompts the speaker to pronounce "-es" as a schwa vowel syllable. The plural form of "peach", for example, is pronounced "peach-es". As a general rule, if you hear an extra syllable in the plural form of a word, the "-es" spelling pattern applies.

beaches	churches	pitches	scratches
benches	lunches	porches	sketches
birches	matches	reaches	teaches
catches	peaches	sandwiches	watches

K5.2 Words that end with the hard "c/k" consonant sound

With singular nouns that end with the hard "c/k" consonant sound, as in the word "monarch", the suffix "-s" is added to make the plural. The letter "-s" is pronounced without the assistance of a vowel sound and so does not form a distinct syllable.

| epochs | lochs | stomachs |
| eunuchs | monarchs | |

K6 Words That End With the Letters "-f", "-ff", and "-fe"

The plural form of words that end with the letters "-f", "-ff", or "-fe" is usually created by adding the suffix "-s". However, with some words the plural is created by changing the letters "f", "-ff", or "fe" to a "v" and adding the suffix "-es".

K6.1 General rule is to add "-s"

With most singular nouns that end with the letters "-f", "-ff", or "-fe", the suffix "-s" is added to create the plural. The noun "belief", for example, becomes "beliefs". The same rule applies when creating the third-person, present-tense, singular form of verbs. The verb "puff", for example, becomes "puffs". Note that the word "dandruff" does not have a distinct plural form. For exceptions, see K6.2.

- belief → beliefs
- brief → briefs
- café → cafés
- chief → chiefs
- cliff → cliffs
- fife → fifes
- handkerchief → handkerchiefs
- mastiff → mastiffs
- plaintiff → plaintiffs
- proof → proofs
- puff → puffs
- reef → reefs
- safe → safes
- sheriff → sheriffs
- staff → staffs (employees not poles)
- tariff → tariffs

K6.2 Exceptions to Rule K6.1: Plurals spelled "-ves"

With the following words, the plural is created by changing the letters "-f", "-ff", or "-fe" to "v" before adding the suffix "-es". Listen for the consonant "v" sound which is pronounced.

In the following words, the letter "e" is silent so the letters "-es" are not pronounced as a syllable. It may be noted that words that end with the letters "-lf", such as "calf" and "shelf", always form the plural this way.

- calf → calves
- elf → elves
- half → halves
- knife → knives
- leaf → leaves
- life → lives
- loaf → loaves
- self → selves, ourselves, themselves
- sheaf → sheaves
- shelf → shelves
- staff → staves (poles not employees)
- thief → thieves
- wife → wives
- wolf → wolves

K6.3 Plurals that take both forms

With the following words, the plural may be created either by adding the suffix "-s" or by changing the letter "-f" into "v" and adding the suffix "-es".

- dwar**f** → dwar**fs** or dwar**ves**
- hoo**f** → hoo**fs** or hoo**ves**
- roo**f** → roo**fs** or roo**ves**
- scar**f** → scar**fs** or scar**ves**
- whar**f** → whar**fs** or whar**ves**

K7 Words That End With the Letter "-o"

The plural form of words that end with the letter "o" is usually created by adding the suffix "-s". However, with some words the plural is created by adding the suffix "-es".

K7.1 Words that end with the letter "-o" following a vowel

With singular nouns that end with the letter "-o" following a vowel letter, the suffix "-s" is added to create the plural. The noun "patio", for example, becomes "patios". The same rule applies when creating the third-person, present-tense, singular form of verbs. The verb "shampoo", for example, becomes "shampoos".

cameos	portfolios	shampoos	videos
duos	radios	stereos	zoos
folios	ratios	studios	
kangaroos	rodeos	taboos	
patios	scenarios	tattoos	

K7.2 Words that end with the letter "-o" following a consonant

With singular nouns that end with the letter "-o" following a consonant letter, as in "hero", the plural is sometimes created by adding the suffix "-s" and sometimes by adding the suffix "-es". This also applies when creating the third-person, present-tense, singular form of verbs.

i) Words that accept "-es"

The following words accept the suffix "-es". Because vowel letter "o" is pronounced and the letter "e" is silent, the letters "-es" are not pronounced as a syllable. See below for words that take the suffix "-s" and for words that can be spelled both ways.

dingoes	goes	Negroes	vetoes
does	heroes	potatoes	
echoes	innuendoes	tomatoes	
embargoes	lingoes	torpedoes	

ii) Words that accept "-s"

The following words accept the suffix "-s". Note that many of the following words are musical terms that are Italian in origin.

albi**nos**	dit**tos**	me**mos**	sopra**nos**
al**tos**	dyna**mos**	pho**tos**	ta**cos**
burri**tos**	embr**yos**	pia**nos**	tobac**cos**
bur**ros**	ghet**tos**	provi**sos**	t**wos**
cel**los**	lo**gos**	quar**tos**	ty**pos**
concer**tos**	mac**ros**	so**los**	vibra**tos**

iii) Words that accept both "-es" and "-s"

The following words accept both suffixes. The "-s" spelling pattern is recommended over "-es" because it avoids the unnecessary use of a silent letter "e".

- archipela**gos** or archipela**goes**
- ban**jos** or ban**joes**
- buffalo, buffa**los**, or buffa**loes**
- car**gos** or car**goes**
- domi**nos** or domi**noes**
- grot**tos** or grot**toes**
- ha**los** or ha**loes**
- ho**bos** or ho**boes**
- innuen**dos** or innuen**does**
- las**sos** or las**soes**
- man**gos** or man**goes**
- manifes**tos** or manifes**toes**
- memen**tos** or memen**toes**
- mosqui**tos** or mosqui**toes**
- mot**tos** or mot**toes**
- sal**vos** or sal**voes**
- torna**dos** or torna**does**
- volca**nos** or volca**noes**
- ze**ros** or ze**roes**
- fias**cos** or fias**coes**
- tuxe**dos** or tuxe**does**
- place**bos** or place**boes**

K8 Words That End With the Letters "-s" or "-ss"

With singular nouns that end with the letters "-s" or "-ss", add the suffix "-es" to create the plural. The noun "gas", for example, becomes "gases". The same rule applies to creating the third-person, present-tense, singular form of verbs. The verb "kiss", for example, becomes "kisses".

It is difficult to pronounce a final letter "s" directly following a soft "c/s" or "z" consonant sound. For this reason, the plural form of the word prompts the speaker to pronounce "-es" as a schwa vowel syllable. The plural form of "cross", for example, is pronounced "cross-es". As a general rule, if you hear an extra syllable in the plural form of a word, the "-es" spelling pattern applies.

address**es**	bias**es**	class**es**	gas**es**
albatross**es** (Also albatross)	boss**es**	cross**es**	glass**es**
	bus**es**	dress**es**	grass**es**

guesses	messes	octopuses (Also octopi)	summonses
kisses	misses		viruses
losses	mosses	passes	
masses		possesses	

K9 Words That End with the Letters "-sh"

With singular nouns that end with the letters "-sh", the suffix "-es" is added to create the plural. The noun "brush", for example, becomes "brushes". The same rule applies to creating the third-person, present-tense, singular form of verbs. The verb "wash", for example, becomes "washes".

A notable exception to this rule is the noun "fish", which is both singular and plural. A person might catch "one fish" or "two fish" without a change in spelling. However, the third-person, present-tense, singular form of the verb "fish" is "fishes" as in *"he fishes everyday"*.

It is difficult to pronounce a final letter "s" directly following the consonant "sh" sound. For this reason, the plural form of the word prompts the speaker to pronounce "-es" as a schwa vowel syllable. The plural form of "wish", for example, is pronounced "wish-es". As a general rule, if you hear an extra syllable in the plural form of a word, the "-es" spelling pattern applies.

ashes	crashes	flashes	rushes
brushes	dishes	gashes	washes
bushes	fishes (as a verb)	pushes	wishes

K10 Words That End With the Letter "-x"

With singular nouns that end with the letters "-x", the suffix "-es" is added to create the plural. The noun "fox", for example, becomes "foxes". The same rule applies to creating the third-person, present-tense, singular form of verbs. The verb "mix", for example, becomes "mixes".

It is difficult to pronounce a final letter "s" directly following the consonant "x" sound. For this reason, the plural form of the word prompts the speaker to pronounce "-es" as a schwa vowel syllable. The plural form of "box", for example, is pronounced "box-es". As a general rule, if you hear an extra syllable in the plural form of a word, the "-es" spelling pattern applies.

apexes (Also apices)	axes	foxes (Also fox)	lynxes (Also lynx)
appendixes (Also appendices)	boxes	indexes (Also indices)	matrixes (Also matrices)
	faxes		

mixes	vertexes	vortexes
sixes	(Also vertices)	(Also vortices)
taxes		waxes

K11 Words That End With the Letter "-y"

The plural form of words that end with the letter "-y" following a consonant is usually created by changing the "y" to an "i" and adding the suffix "-es". The plural form of words that end with the letter "-y" following a vowel is usually created by adding the suffix "-s".

K11.1 Words that end with the letter "-y" following a consonant

With singular nouns that end with the letter "-y" following a consonant, the plural is created by changing the "y" to an "i" and adding the suffix "-es". The noun "baby", for example, becomes "babies". The same rule applies to creating the third-person, present-tense, singular form of verbs. The verb "fly", for example, becomes "flies". For exceptions, see K11.2.

In the following base words the final letter "y" represents either the long "e" or the long "i" vowel sound. In the plural form of the words, the letter "i" is usually pronounced with the same vowel sound and the following letter "e" is silent. For this reason, the letters "-es" are not pronounced as a syllable.

- army → armies
- authority → authorities
- baby → babies
- beauty → beauties
- bunny → bunnies
- butterfly → butterflies
- canary → canaries
- carry → carries
- city → cities
- company → companies
- copy → copies
- country → countries
- cry → cries
- dictionary → dictionaries
- factory → factories
- fairy → fairies
- family → families
- fly → flies
- fry → fries
- hurry → hurries
- liability → liabilities
- library → libraries
- monopoly → monopolies
- navy → navies
- necessity → necessities
- party → parties
- policy → policies
- pony → ponies
- poppy → poppies
- puppy → puppies
- prophecy → prophecies
- quantity → quantities
- query → queries
- security → securities
- sky → skies
- spy → spies
- story → stories
- theory → theories
- try → tries
- variety → varieties

K11.2   Exceptions to Rule K11.1: Proper nouns

With proper nouns that end with the letter "-y" following a consonant, such as the name "Gary", the suffix "-s" is added to create the plural. As a general rule, the spelling of a proper noun is never changed to create the plural.

- Two Garys
- Three Marys
- Four Larrys
- Five Sallys

K11.3 Words that end with the letter "-y" following a vowel

With singular nouns that end with the letter "-y" following a vowel, the plural is created by keeping the letter "y" and adding the suffix "-s". The noun "boy", for example, becomes "boys". The same rule applies to creating the third-person, present-tense, singular form of verbs. The verb "pay", for example, becomes "pays". The letter "y" is still required to form a vowel digraph with the preceding vowel letter. For exceptions, see K11.4.

assays	donkeys	jays	slays
attorneys	employs	journeys	Sundays
boys	enjoys	keys	surveys
buoys	envoys	moneys	Thursdays
buys	essays	(Also monies)	toys
chimneys	galleys	monkeys	trays
decoys	guys	pays	turkeys
delays	highways	plays	(Also turkey)
displays	holidays	railways	valleys

K11.4 Exceptions to Rule K11.3: Words that end with "-quy"

With words that end with the letters "-quy", change the "y" to an "i" and add the suffix "-es" to create the plural. This is because the letters "qu" represent the "kw" sound with the letter "u" functioning as a consonant letter. The letter "y" is pronounced in its own right and does not form a vowel digraph or diphthong with the preceding letter "u".

- colloquy → colloquies
- soliloquy → soliloquies

K12 Words That End With the Letter "-z"

With singular nouns that end with the letter "-z", the plural is created by adding the suffix "-es". The noun "waltz", for example, becomes "waltzes". The same rule applies to creating the third-person, present-tense, singular form of verbs. The verb "buzz", for example, becomes "buzzes". Note that if the base word ends with a single letter "z" following a vowel, as in the word "quiz", the letter "z" is doubled before adding the "-es".

It is difficult to pronounce a final letter "s" directly following the consonant "z" sound. For this reason, the plural form of the word prompts the speaker to pronounce "-es" as a schwa vowel syllable. The plural form of "fizz", for example, is pronounced "fizz-es". As a general rule, if you hear an extra syllable in the plural form of a word, the "-es" spelling pattern applies.

buzz**es**   fizz**es**   quizz**es**   waltz**es**

K13 Compound and Hyphenated Words

With compound words that contain a primary noun, the spelling changes creating the plural form are made to the primary noun. Sometimes the primary noun is the first word. The plural form of "brother-in-law", for example, is "brothers-in-law". Sometimes the primary noun is the final word. The plural form of "stepchild", for example, is "stepchildren". With compound words that do not contain a primary noun, the spelling changes creating the plural form are made to the final word. The plural form of "show-off", for example, is "show-offs". See N4 for further discussion about the plural form of compound words.

K14 Foreign Plurals

While some foreign words use English plural forms, many retain their original singular and plural forms.

K14.1 French "-eau" and "-ieu" become "-eaux" and "-ieux"

With French nouns the singular forms "-eau" and "-ieu" are changed to "-eaux" and "-ieux" to create the plural.

- ad**ieu** → ad**ieux**
- b**eau** → b**eaux**
- bur**eau** → bur**eaux** (Also "bureaus")
- chat**eau** → chat**eaux**
- mil**ieu** → mil**ieux** (Also "milieus")

- plat**eau** → plat**eaux** (Also "plateaus")
- portmant**eau** → portmant**eaux**
- tabl**eau** → tabl**eaux**
- trouss**eau** → trouss**eaux** (Also trousseaus)

K14.2 Greek "-on" becomes "-a"

With Greek nouns the singular form "-on" is changed to "-a" to create the plural.

- automat**on** → automat**a** (Also "automatons")
- criter**ion** → criter**ia** (Also "criterions")
- phenomen**on** → phenomen**a** (Also "phenomenons")

K14.3 Italian "-o" becomes "-i"

With Italian nouns the singular form "-o" is changed to "-i" to create the plural.

- concert**o** → concert**i** (Also concertos)
- graffit**o** → graffit**i**
- paparazz**o** → paparazz**i**
- temp**o** → temp**i** (Also tempos)
- virtuos**o** → virtuos**i** (Also virtuosos)

K14.4 Latin "-a" becomes "-ae"

With Latin nouns the singular form "-a" is changed to "-ae" to create the plural. There are, however, exceptions. The plural of "agenda" is "agendas", and the plural of "stigma" is either "stigmas" or "stigmata".

Confusingly, singular Latin nouns that end with "-um", such as "datum", change to "-a" to form the plural. See K14.7.

- alg**a** → alg**ae**
- alumn**a** → alumn**ae** (feminine)
- antenn**a** → antenn**ae** (Also antennas)
- formul**a** → formul**ae** (Also formulas)
- larv**a** → larv**ae** (Also larvas)
- vertebr**a** → vertebr**ae** (Also vertebras)

K14.5 Latin "-ex" and "-ix" becomes "-ices"

With Latin nouns the singular forms "-ex" and "-ix" are changed to "-ices" to create the plural.

- ap**ex** → ap**ices** (Also apexes)
- append**ix** → append**ices** (Also appendixes)
- cod**ex** → cod**ices**
- ind**ex** → ind**ices** (Also indexes)
- matr**ix** → matr**ices** (Also matrixes)
- vert**ex** → vert**ices** (Also vertexes)
- vort**ex** → vort**ices** (Also vortexes)

K14.6 Latin "-is" becomes "-es"

With Latin nouns the singular form "-is" is changed to "-es" to create the plural.

- analys**is** → analys**es**
- ax**is** → ax**es**
- bas**is** → bas**es**
- cris**is** → cris**es**
- diagnos**is** → diagnos**es**
- ellips**is** → ellips**es**
- emphas**is** → emphas**es**
- hypothes**is** → hypothes**es**
- parenthes**is** → parenthes**es**
- synops**is** → synops**es**
- synthes**is** → synthes**es**
- thes**is** → thes**es**

K14.7 Latin "-um" becomes "-a"

With Latin nouns the singular form "-um" is changed to "-a" to create the plural.

Confusingly, some singular Latin nouns, such as "larva", end with "-a" and change to "-ae" to form the plural. See K14.4.

- addend**um** → addend**a**
- agend**um** → agend**a** (Also "agendas")
- bacter**ium** → bacter**ia**
- consort**ium** → consort**ia**
- curricul**um** → curricul**a** (Also "curriculums")
- dat**um** → dat**a** (Also "datums")
- errat**um** → errat**a**
- med**ium** → med**ia** (Also "mediums")
- memorand**um** → memorand**a** (Also "memorandums")
- ov**um** → ov**a**
- strat**um** → strat**a**

K14.8 Latin "-us" becomes "-i"

With Latin nouns the singular form "-us" is changed to "-i" to create the plural.

- abac**us** → abac**i**
- alumn**us** → alumn**i** (masculine form)
- cact**us** → cact**i** (Also "cactuses")
- foc**us** → foc**i** (Also "focuses")
- fung**us** → fung**i**
- nucle**us** → nucle**i**
- octop**us** → octop**i** (Also "octopuses")
- rad**ius** → rad**ii**
- stimul**us** → stimul**i**
- syllab**us** → syllab**i** (Also "syllabuses")
- termin**us** → termin**i** (Also "terminuses")

K15 Other Plurals

The following words change from the singular to the plural form in a variety of ways.

- cherub → cherub**im** (Also "cherubs", "cherubims")
- dilettant**e** → dilettant**i** (Also "dilettantes")
- seraph → seraph**im** (Also "seraphs")
- stigma → stigma**ta** (Also "stigmas")

Part L: Possessives

L1 Introduction

The possessive form is used to indicate an ownership relationship, or something analogous to an ownership relationship, between a noun or pronoun and some other thing. The phrase *"the boy's coat"* indicates that the coat belongs to the boy. Likewise, the phrase *"the wolf's howl"* indicates that the howl belongs to or came from the wolf. Possessive phrases can usually be restated using the words "belonging to" or "of the" as in *"the coat belonging to the boy"* and *"the howl of the wolf"*.

Possessive nouns are easily confused with descriptive adjectives that end with the letter "s". Take for example the phrase *"savings account"*. The word "savings" is a descriptive adjective which describes or modifies the noun "account". It is not a possessive form noun because there is no relationship between "account" and "savings". The phrase cannot be rewritten as *"the account belonging to the savings"* or *"the account of the savings"*.

The possessive form is most often created by adding "apostrophe - s" to the end of a word. Sometimes, however, the possessive form is created by adding an apostrophe without the letter "s". It can be difficult to determine whether or not to add the letter "s" following the apostrophe.

Spelling difficulties also arise because possessive pronouns, such as "ours" and "yours", already indicate possession and so do not require the use of apostrophe - s. This is because an apostrophe is also used to form contractions. A contraction is formed when two words are shortened into one word with one or more letters being omitted. The words "do not", for example, may be contracted into "don't". With contractions, an apostrophe substitutes for the missing letter or letters. See Part O.

L2 Singular Nouns

L2.1 Singular nouns that do not end with the soft "c/s" or "z" consonant sounds

With singular nouns that do not end with the soft "c/s" or "z" sounds, such as "girl", the possessive form is created by adding apostrophe - s.

- the auditor's statement
- the boy's coat
- the broker's report
- Canada's lakes
- the cat's meow
- the child's toy
- David's truck
- the girl's bicycle
- the guide's boat
- the postman's route
- Sarah's hat
- Smith's children
- the syndicate's profits
- the wolf's howl

L2.2 Singular nouns that end with the soft "c/s" or "z" consonant sounds

With singular nouns that end with the soft "c/s" consonant sound as heard in "hostess", "Jones", and "fox" or the consonant "z" sound as heard in "Rose", "guards", and "wiz", how the possessive form is created depends upon what effect an apostrophe - s will have on the pronunciation of the word.

Following a soft "c/s" or "z" consonant sound, an added apostrophe - s will be pronounced as an extra syllable. While the word "Jones", for example, is pronounced as a single-syllable, the word "Jones's" is pronounced "Jones-es" with two-syllables.

When an extra syllable is easy to pronounce, the possessive form may be created by adding apostrophe - s. When an extra syllable is awkward to pronounce, the possessive form may be created by adding an apostrophe without the "s". As dictionaries do not set out possessive forms, it is up to each writer to decide whether to add apostrophe - s or just an apostrophe. With single-syllable words, such as "Jones" and "boss", it is generally easy to pronounce the extra syllable. With some polysyllabic words, such as "Moses" and "hostesses", it is clearly awkward to pronounce the extra syllable.

a) Extra syllable is easy to pronounce

With the following words, an extra syllable is easy to pronounce, so the possessive form may be created by adding apostrophe - s.

- the Jones's cottage
- the boss's office
- the fox's den
- Rose's book
- the hostess's secret
- the witness's evidence

b) Extra syllable is awkward to pronounce

With the following words, an extra syllable is awkward to pronounce, so the possessive form may be created by just adding an apostrophe.

- for goodness' sake
- the hostesses' secret
- the witnesses' evidence
- Moses' commandments

L3 Plural Nouns

L3.1 Plural nouns that end with the letters "-s" or "-es"

With regular plural nouns that end with the letters "-s" or "-es", such as the word "boys", the possessive is formed by adding just an apostrophe. Creating an additional syllable by adding apostrophe - s would make the word awkward to pronounce.

- aviators' guide
- boys' game
- chiefs' technique
- churches' purpose
- competitors' challenge
- creditors' collateral
- customers' complaints
- debtors' rights
- doctors' advice
- fathers' responsibilities
- foxes' tails
- girls' toys
- guards' duties
- heroes' welcome
- judges' orders
- manufacturers' convention
- mechanics' tools
- monkeys' tricks
- mothers' delight
- students' textbooks
- teachers' students
- witnesses' testimony
- wolves' den
- writers' conference

L3.2 Plural nouns that do not end with the letter "-s"

With irregular plural nouns that do not end with the letter "-s", such as the word "children", the possessive is formed by adding apostrophe - s.

- children's clothing
- freshmen's classes
- men's team
- oxen's carts
- people's choice
- women's team

L4 Compound Nouns

L4.1 Singular compound nouns

To create the possessive form of singular compound nouns add apostrophe - s to the final word of the compound noun. This applies to combined, spaced, and hyphenated compound nouns.

- babysitter's telephone number
- editor-in-chief's decision
- ex-boyfriend's picture
- father-in-law's cottage
- fireman's truck
- geography teacher's class
- girlfriend's picture
- North Bay's team
- notary public's stamp
- policewoman's uniform

- racehorse's saddle
- schoolgirl's diary
- sister-in-law's car
- taxpayer's file

L4.2 Plural compound nouns that do not end with the letter "-s"

To create the possessive form of plural compound nouns add apostrophe - s to the final word of the compound noun.

- editors-in-chief's policy
- firemen's hose
- humankind's future
- policewomen's committee
- sisters-in-law's party
- stepchildren's toys

While correct, this tends to produce awkward sounding phrases that may be avoided by rewording the sentence. Rather than write "*I am attending my sisters-in-law's party*", one might write "*I am attending a party organized by my sisters-in-law*".

L4.3 Plural compound nouns that end with the letters "-s" or "-es"

To create the possessive form of plural compound nouns that end with the letters "s" or "-es", add an apostrophe to the final word of the compound noun.

- babysitters' course
- classmates' behaviour
- girlfriends' weekend
- roommates' things
- schoolgirls' game
- taxpayers' organization

L5 Pronouns

Nouns name a person, place, thing, animal, quality, action, or concept. Pronouns, such as "me", "her", and "it", may be substituted for a noun. See Part J. There are several types of pronouns, including indefinite pronouns and possessive pronouns.

L5.1 Indefinite pronouns, such as "anybody" or "someone"

Indefinite pronouns, such as the word "anybody", refer to people and things in general rather than to a specific person or thing. With most indefinite pronouns, the possessive form is created by adding apostrophe - s.

- Is this *anybody's* jacket?
- He is *everybody's* friend.
- It is *everyone's* favourite.
- It was *nobody's* fault.
- I hit *someone's* car.
- It is *one's* own decision.
- It has to be *someone's* pet dog.
- Is *anyone else's* light still on?
- We can care for *one another's* children.
- Each child took the *other's* toy.
- It was *no one's* fault.

With indefinite pronouns that do not accept apostrophe - s, such as the indefinite pronoun "each", the possessive form may be created by using the word "of".

- The opinion *of each* person will be considered.
- The skills *of either* applicant will satisfy our requirements.
- The efforts *of both* volunteers will be rewarded.
- The actions *of a few* people spoiled the occasion.
- The dreams *of many* will be fulfilled.

L5.2 Possessive pronouns, such as "mine" and "yours"

Possessive pronouns, such as "mine" and "yours", already indicate possession and so do not require the use of an apostrophe. There are two kinds of possessive pronouns: personal pronouns and relative pronouns.

a) Personal Pronouns

As discussed in J10, personal pronouns may be substituted for the specific noun that names a person, place, or other thing.

A possessive personal pronoun must reflect a number of grammatical considerations. Is the sentence speaking from the perspective of the first person (the person who is speaking), second person (the person being spoken to), or third person (the person being spoken about)? Does the sentence refer to a singular person, place, or other thing or to two or more persons, places, or other things? Is the pronoun the subject or object of the sentence, or is it making a statement about possessiveness? Is the pronoun referring to a male, female, or neuter subject or object?

	Subject	**Object**	**Possessive**
First Person			
Singular	I	me	my, mine
Plural	we	us	our*, ours (not our's)
Second Person			
Singular	you	you	your*, yours (not your's)
Plural	you	you	your*, yours (not your's)
Third Person			
Singular			
Masculine	he	him	his
Feminine	she	her	her, hers (not her's)
Neuter	it	it	its (not it's)
Any gender	one	one	one's
Plural	they	them	their, theirs (not their's)

* Strictly, a possessive adjective.

Note that "it's" is a contraction of the words "it is" and not the possessive form of the personal pronoun "it". This confuses writers to no end. For further discussion about contractions, such as "you're" and "didn't", see Part O.

First Person Singular:

- *That is **my** coat.*
- *The coat is **mine**.*

First Person Plural:

- *That is **our** blue car.*
- *The blue car is **ours**.*

Second Person Singular:

- *John, this is **your** signed copy.*
- ***Yours** is the signed copy John.*

Second Person Plural:

- *Clem and Jamie, **your** canoe is the red one.*
- *Clem and Jamie, the red canoe is **yours**.*

Third Person Singular Masculine:

- *He picked up **his** cell phone.*

Third Person Singular Feminine:

- *She put down **her** book.*

Third Person Singular Neuter:

- *The river overflowed **its** banks.*

Third Person Singular, Any Gender:

- *It is wise to protect **one's** reputation.*

Third Person Plural:

- *They were celebrating **their** victory.*
- *The victory was **theirs** to celebrate.*

b) Relative Pronouns

Relative pronouns relate back to an antecedent noun that is the subject or object of the independent clause. See J10.3.

	Subject	Object	Possessive
People	who	who, whoever whom, whomever	whose
Inanimate Objects	that, where, which, whichever	that, where, which, whichever	whose

There is only one possessive relative pronoun, the word "whose", which can relate back to either a person or an inanimate object.

- *Peter, **whose** watch had stopped working, was late for the meeting.*
- *The watch, **whose** battery had died, stopped working.*

L6 Common and Separate Possession

L6.1 Possession held in common

When possession is held in common between two or more individuals, only the final name is put into the possessive form.

- Mr. and Mrs. Wilson**'s** house
- Peter, Paul, and Mary**'s** album
- Karen and Andy**'s** boat

However, if one of the individuals is identified by a pronoun, then each name and pronoun is put into the possessive form.

- Brian**'s** and my reservation
- Your and Nancy**'s** room

L6.2 Possession held separately

When a number of individuals have separate possession, each name is put into the possessive form.

- John**'s** and Linda**'s** test scores
- the Crawford**'s** and the Reid**'s** cottages
- the vendor**'s** and purchaser**'s** signatures

Possessive pronouns can be used to avoid awkward repetition.

- That is your cup and this is <u>mine</u>. (Not: That is your cup and this is my cup.)
- There is their dog and here is <u>ours</u>. (Not: There is their dog and here is our dog.
- Your house is bigger than <u>mine</u>. (Not: Your house is bigger than my house.)

L7 Inanimate Objects and Abstract Concepts

L7.1 Inanimate objects and abstract concepts

With inanimate objects and abstract concepts, avoid using the possessive form unless the phrase has become a common expression. It is preferable to use the word "of" to create a possessive phrase. For exceptions, see L7.2.

Avoid:	Rephrased using the word "of":
- the wild's call - the meadow's flowers - logic's principles - money's evils	- the call of the wild - the flowers of the meadow - principles of logic - evils of money

L7.2 Exceptions to Rule L7.1: Common Phrases

With certain common phrases, especially in informal writing, it is acceptable to refer to inanimate objects and abstract concepts in the possessive form. This is often found in reference to concepts of time and measurement and for the purpose of personifying inanimate objects.

- a day's journey
- responding to duty's call
- the earth's environment
- a hair's breadth
- a razor's edge
- the ship's crew

- a week's notice
- the sun's warmth
- a penny's worth
- at my wit's end
- today's announcement
- yesterday's news

Part M: Onsets and Rimes

M1 Introduction

Words are made up of syllables. Syllables, in turn, are made up of onsets and rimes. The word "rime" is a variation on the spelling of the word "rhyme". A rime, unlike other rhymes, is always spelled the same way.

An onset consists of all of the consonant sounds, if any, that are pronounced before the vowel sound in a syllable. A rime consists of all of the sounds that follow the onset. Every rime begins with a vowel sound and may end with one or more consonant sounds. Consider, for example, the single-syllable words "day", "dog", "log", and "lay". The words "day" and "dog" share the same onset being the letter "d-", and the words "dog" and "log" share the same rime being the letters "-og". Likewise, the words "log" and "lay" share the same onset being the letter "l-", and the words "day" and "lay" share the same rime being the letters "-ay".

While every syllable has a rime, not all syllables have an onset. The single-syllable word "act", for example, does not have an onset. The whole of the word "act" is a rime. A rime may consist of just a vowel sound. The single letter word "a" only consists of a rime. Likewise, in the words "per-i-od" and "an-i-mal" the single letter syllable "-i-" forms a rime by itself without any consonant sounds.

Onsets and rimes help to mark the beginning and the end of a syllable. An onset may consist of a single consonant letter such as the letter "k-" in "**k**ind", a consonant blend such as the letters "cl-" in "**cl**ock", or a consonant digraph such as the letters "sh-" in "**sh**ow". Similarly, a rime may end without a consonant letter as in the word "go", with a single consonant letter such as the letter "-t" in "se**t**", with a consonant blend such as the letters "-st" in "be**st**", or with a consonant digraph such as the letters "-ck" in "do**ck**".

Onsets and rimes are pronounced with much greater consistency than individual letters. Individual vowel letters, in particular, are given different pronunciations depending on the spelling pattern in which they are found. Consider how the letter "a" is pronounced in the words "fade", "cat", "aisle", "coat", and "beauty". In comparison, the letters making up a rime are consistently pronounced the same way. The rime "-ack", for example, heard in the words "black", "shack", and "track", is consistently pronounced with the short "a" vowel sound followed by the hard "c/k" consonant sound.

Onsets and rimes appear to be a natural component of our spoken language and are, therefore, helpful in developing phonemic awareness. Developmentally, young children are readily able to identify onsets and rimes before they are able to identify individual phonemes. For example, young children can identify that the words "ride" and "rice" begin with the same sound and that the words "rice" and "mice" end with the same sound. However, children of the same age may have trouble identifying that the individual phonemes in "rice" are "r-i-ce". This suggests that learning to distinguish onsets and rimes is a natural stage of phonemic awareness. This, in turn, suggests that focusing on onsets and rimes is a good strategy with beginning readers.

Helping beginning readers learn to recognize common onsets and rimes is particularly helpful because children often learn to read new words by recognizing similarities between familiar printed words and unfamiliar printed words. For example, a reader who knows how to pronounce the onset "bl-" in "blue" can use that knowledge to sound out the same letters in the words "black" and "block". Likewise, a reader who recognizes the rime "-ock" in "rock" will be better prepared to sound out new words such as "clock" and "stock".

Onsets and rimes are also useful for helping students learn to identify individual phonemes. As many onsets consist of individual consonant letters, the use of alliteration to form onset word families such as "sat", "sit", and "sing" helps to isolate particular consonant phonemes. Likewise, the use of rhyming to form rime word families such as "cat", "mat", and "sat" helps to isolate particular vowel phonemes. An advantage to focusing on onsets and rimes, rather than individual letters, is that the phonemes are not pronounced in isolation. That said, children find it easier to read predictable text that is written in a natural style than text that is artificially composed of alliteration and rhyming words. Each form of text has its place.

Only common rimes are listed below, not onsets. As onsets consist of individual consonant letters, consonant digraphs, and consonant blends, see Part E and Part F respectively for numerous examples.

M2   Common Rimes

"-ab"

The following words and syllables end with the rime "-ab". The letter "a" is pronounced with the short "a" vowel sound.

blab	dab	gab	lab
cab	drab	grab	nab
crab	flab	jab	prefab

scab	stab	taxicab	
slab	tab		

"-ack"

The following words and syllables end with the rime "-ack". The letter "a" is pronounced with the short "a" vowel sound.

back	hack	pack	shack
backpack	haystack	paperback	slack
backtrack	icepack	quack	smack
black	jack	quarterback	soundtrack
crack	jacket	racetrack	stack
crackerjack	knack	rack	tack
flack	knapsack	racket	thumbtack
fullback	lack	sack	track

"-ad"

The following words and syllables end with the rime "-ad". The letter "a" is pronounced with the short "a" vowel sound.

ad	doodad	ironclad	pad
bad	fad	keypad	sad
cad	glad	lad	tad
clad	grad	mad	
dad	had	nomad	

"-ag"

The following words and syllables end with the rime "-ag". The letter "a" is pronounced with the short "a" vowel sound.

bag	flag	nag	tag
shag	gag	rag	wag
beanbag	handbag	sag	zigzag
brag	jag	snag	
drag	lag	stag	

"-ail"

The following words and syllables end with the rime "-ail". The letters "ai" form a vowel digraph that is pronounced with the long "a" vowel sound.

a**il**	sn**ail**	j**ail**	pigt**ail**
qu**ail**	fr**ail**	airm**ail**	p**ail**
b**ail**	t**ail**	m**ail**	r**ail**
s**ail**	h**ail**	det**ail**	
f**ail**	tr**ail**	n**ail**	

"-ain"

The following words and syllables end with the rime "-ain". The letters "ai" form a vowel digraph that is pronounced with the long "a" vowel sound.

br**ain**	st**ain**	m**ain**	expl**ain**
Sp**ain**	g**ain**	v**ain**	r**ain**
ch**ain**	str**ain**	p**ain**	sl**ain**
spr**ain**	gr**ain**	compl**ain**	
dr**ain**	tr**ain**	pl**ain**	

"-air"

The following words and syllables end with the rime "-air". The letters "ai" form a vowel digraph that is pronounced with the short "e" vowel sound.

air	f**air**	mid**air**	unf**air**
ch**air**	fl**air**	moh**air**	wheelch**air**
debon**air**	h**air**	p**air**	
desp**air**	imp**air**	rep**air**	
écl**air**	l**air**	st**air**	

"-ake"

The following words and syllables end with the rime "-ake". The letter "a" is pronounced with the long "a" vowel sound. The final letter "e" is silent.

b**ake**	st**ake**	l**ake**	r**ake**
sh**ake**	f**ake**	mist**ake**	s**ake**
br**ake**	t**ake**	m**ake**	
sn**ake**	fl**ake**	rem**ake**	
c**ake**	w**ake**	qu**ake**	

"-ale"

The following words and syllables end with the rime "-ale". The letter "a" is pronounced with an l-controlled long "a" vowel sound. The final letter "e" is silent.

ale	inhale	scale	whale
bale	male	stale	wholesale
exhale	nightingale	tale	
female	pale	tattletale	
gale	sale	upscale	

"-all"

The following words and syllables end with the rime "-all". The letter "a" is pronounced with the short "o" vowel sound.

Double consonants usually signal that the preceding single vowel letter is pronounced with a short vowel sound.

all	appall (USA)	hall	small
tall	fall	Hall	squall
ball	baseball	overall	stall
wall	gall	mall	
call	install	rainfall	

"-am"

The following words and syllables end with the rime "-am". The letter "a" is pronounced with the short "a" vowel sound.

am	exam	scam	tram
camera	gram	scram	yam
clam	ham	sham	
cram	jam	slam	
dam	ram	swam	

"-ame"

The following words and syllables end with the rime "-ame". The letter "a" is pronounced with the long "a" vowel sound. The final letter "e" is silent.

aflame	defame	lame	shame
became	fame	name	surname
blame	flame	nickname	tame
came	game	same	

"-an"

The following words and syllables end with the rime "-an". The letter "a" is pronounced with the short "a" vowel sound.

an	**can**	**man**	**span**
anaconda	**Can**ada	Nor**man**	sun**tan**
ancestor	**can**vas	orangu**tan**	Super**man**
animal	cl**an**	**pan**	**tan**
b**an**	f**an**	pl**an**	th**an**
Bat**man**	h**an**dy	r**an**	v**an**
beg**an**	h**an**dyman	r**an**ch	
br**an**	Jap**an**	sc**an**	

"-and"

The following words and syllables end with the rime "-and". The letter "a" is pronounced with the short "a" vowel sound. The letters "nd" form a consonant blend.

and	dem**and**	h**and**stand	st**and**
b**and**	exp**and**	l**and**	str**and**
bl**and**	gl**and**	quicks**and**	underst**and**
br**and**	gr**and**	s**and**	
comm**and**	h**and**	S**and**s	

"-ank"

The following words and syllables end with the rime "-ank". The letter "a" is pronounced with the short "a" vowel sound. The letter "n" is pronounced with the consonant "ng" sound heard in the words "ink" and "sing". The letters "nk" form a consonant blend.

b**ank**	fl**ank**	pr**ank**	sw**ank**
bl**ank**	fr**ank**	r**ank**	t**ank**
bl**ank**et	Fr**ank**enstein	s**ank**	th**ank**
cl**ank**	gangpl**ank**	shr**ank**	th**ank**ing
cr**ank**	outr**ank**	sp**ank**	y**ank**
dr**ank**	pl**ank**	st**ank**	

"-ap" and "-app"

The following words and syllables end with the rime "-ap" or "-app". The letter "a" is pronounced with the short "a" vowel sound.

cap	cat**nap**	ch**ap**	ch**ap**ter

cl**ap**	h**app**y	n**ap**	sl**ap**
fl**ap**	hubc**ap**	n**ap**kin	sn**ap**
g**ap**	kidn**ap**	overl**ap**	str**ap**
gift-wr**ap**	l**ap**	r**ap**	t**ap**
gingersn**ap**	m**ap**	r**ap**id	tr**ap**
handic**ap**	mish**ap**	s**ap**	unwr**ap**
h**app**en	mousetr**ap**	scr**ap**	wr**ap**

"-ar"

The following words and syllables end with the rime "-ar". The letter "a" is pronounced with the broad "a" vowel sound.

aj**ar**	f**ar**	m**ar**	superst**ar**
b**ar**	guit**ar**	p**ar**	t**ar**
c**ar**	handleb**ar**	sc**ar**	
ch**ar**	jagu**ar**	sp**ar**	
cz**ar**	j**ar**	st**ar**	

"-ark"

The following words and syllables end with the rime "-ark". The letter "a" is pronounced with the broad "a" vowel sound. The letters "rk" form a consonant blend.

ark	d**ark**	l**ark**	p**ark**
aardv**ark**	bookm**ark**	rem**ark**	sh**ark**
b**ark**	h**ark**	m**ark**	sp**ark**
ballp**ark**	postm**ark**	tradem**ark**	st**ark**

"-art"

The following words and syllables end with the rime "-art". The letter "a" is pronounced with the broad "a" vowel sound. The letters "rt" form a consonant blend.

art	ch**art**	k**art**	p**art**
ap**art**	imp**art**	rest**art**	sm**art**
c**art**	d**art**	m**art**	st**art**
dep**art**	outsm**art**	mini-m**art**	t**art**

"-ash"

The following words and syllables end with the rime "-ash". The letter "a" is pronounced with the short "a" vowel sound.

ash	cr**ash**	g**ash**	sl**ash**
ashes	d**ash**	gn**ash**	sm**ash**
ashtray	d**ash**board	h**ash**	spl**ash**
b**ash**	eyel**ash**	l**ash**	spl**ash**ing
b**ash**ful	fl**ash**	m**ash**	st**ash**
c**ash**	fl**ash**er	mishm**ash**	st**ash**ing
c**ash**ew	fl**ash**light	r**ash**	tr**ash**
cl**ash**	fl**ash**y	s**ash**	whipl**ash**

"-at" and "-att"

The following words and syllables end with the rime "-at" or "-att". The letter "a" is pronounced with the short "a" vowel sound.

acrob**at**	chitch**at**	hardh**at**	s**at**
at	cl**att**er	h**at**	sc**at**
Atlantic	comb**at**	m**at**	sc**at**ter
attic	doorm**at**	m**at**ching	scr**at**ching
b**at**	f**at**	m**at**ter	sp**at**
br**at**	fl**at**	muskr**at**	spl**at**
c**at**	form**at**	p**at**	th**at**
ch**at**	gn**at**	P**at**ricia	tomc**at**
ch**at**ter	habit**at**	r**at**	wildc**at**

"-ate"

The following words and syllables end with the rime "-ate". The letter "a" is pronounced with the long "a" vowel sound. The final letter "e" is silent.

ate	deb**ate**	h**ate**	sk**ate**
calcul**ate**	don**ate**	l**ate**	sl**ate**
cr**ate**	f**ate**	m**ate**	st**ate**
cre**ate**	g**ate**	pl**ate**	st**ate**ment
d**ate**	gr**ate**	r**ate**	

"-aw"

The following words and syllables end with the rime "-aw". The letters "aw" form a vowel digraph that is pronounced with the short "o" vowel sound.

cl**aw**	j**aw**	p**aw**	sl**aw**
dr**aw**	jigs**aw**	r**aw**	str**aw**
fl**aw**	l**aw**	s**aw**	th**aw**
gn**aw**	outl**aw**	sees**aw**	withdr**aw**

"-ay"

The following words and syllables end with the rime "-ay". The letters "-ay" form a vowel digraph that is pronounced with the long "a" vowel sound.

alwa**ys**	h**ay**	p**ay**	Sund**ay**
aw**ay**	holid**ay**	p**ay**ment	sw**ay**
b**ay**	j**ay**	pl**ay**	Thursd**ay**
cl**ay**	l**ay**	pr**ay**	tod**ay**
cr**ay**on	m**ay**	r**ay**	tr**ay**
d**ay**	M**ay**	Saturd**ay**	Tuesd**ay**
dec**ay**	*Monday*	s**ay**	w**ay**
Frid**ay**	n**ay**	spr**ay**	Wednesd**ay**
g**ay**	Norw**ay**	st**ay**	
gr**ay** (USA)	ok**ay**	str**ay**	

"-eat"

The following words and syllables end with the rime "-eat". The letters "ea" form a vowel digraph that is pronounced with the long "e" vowel sound.

b**eat**	def**eat**	m**eat**	rep**eat**
bl**eat**	**eat**	n**eat**	s**eat**
ch**eat**	f**eat**	p**eat**	tr**eat**
cl**eat**	h**eat**	pl**eat**	wh**eat**

"-eck"

The following words and syllables end with the rime "-eck". The letter "e" is pronounced with the short "e" vowel sound.

bottlen**eck**	fl**eck**	p**eck**	turtlen**eck**
breakn**eck**	h**eck**	roughn**eck**	wr**eck**
ch**eck**	n**eck**	shipwr**eck**	
d**eck**	paych**eck** (USA)	sp**eck**	

"-ed"

The following words and syllables end with the rime "-ed". The letter "e" is pronounced with the short "e" vowel sound.

b**ed**	f**ed**	pl**ed**	sl**ed**
bl**ed**	fl**ed**	r**ed**	sp**ed**
bobsl**ed**	l**ed**	sh**ed**	T**ed**
br**ed**	mop**ed**	shr**ed**	w**ed**

"-ee"

The following words and syllables end with the rime "-ee". The letters "ee" form a vowel digraph that is pronounced with the long "e" vowel sound.

agr**ee**	fl**ee**	l**ee**	tr**ee**
b**ee**	fr**ee**	s**ee**	
f**ee**	kn**ee**	t**ee**	

"-eek"

The following words and syllables end with the rime "-eek". The letters "ee" form a vowel digraph that is pronounced with the long "e" vowel sound.

ch**eek**	Gr**eek**	p**eek**	sl**eek**
cr**eek**	l**eek**	r**eek**	w**eek**
g**eek**	m**eek**	s**eek**	

"-eep"

The following words and syllables end with the rime "-eep". The letters "ee" form a vowel digraph that is pronounced with the long "e" vowel sound.

asl**eep**	d**eep**	p**eep**	st**eep**
b**eep**	j**eep**	s**eep**	sw**eep**
ch**eep**	k**eep**	sh**eep**	w**eep**
cr**eep**	oversl**eep**	sl**eep**	

"-ell"

The following words and syllables end with the rime "-ell". The letter "e" is pronounced with the short "e" vowel sound.

Double consonants usually signal that the preceding single vowel letter is pronounced with a short vowel sound.

b**ell**	f**ell**	mozzar**ell**a	sw**ell**
c**ell**	f**ell**ow	nutsh**ell**	t**ell**
Cinder**ell**a	foret**ell**	qu**ell**	umbr**ell**a
doorb**ell**	h**ell**o	s**ell**	unw**ell**
dw**ell**	j**ell**	sh**ell**	w**ell**
eggsh**ell**	J**ell**-O	sm**ell**	y**ell**
farew**ell**	j**ell**y	sp**ell**	y**ell**ow

"-en"

The following words and syllables end with the rime "-en". The letter "e" is pronounced with the short "e" vowel sound.

am**en**	h**en**	pigp**en**	th**en**
bullp**en**	m**en**	playp**en**	wh**en**
d**en**	p**en**	t**en**	

"-est"

The following words and syllables end with the rime "-est". The letter "e" is pronounced with the short "e" vowel sound. The letters "st" form a consonant blend.

arr**est**	gu**est**	p**est**	t**est**ing
b**est**	hard**est**	prot**est**	v**est**
bigg**est**	harv**est**	qu**est**	w**est**
ch**est**	inter**est**	requ**est**	wr**est**
cont**est**	inv**est**	r**est**	y**est**erday
cr**est**	inv**est**igate	r**est**ful	z**est**
d**est**ination	j**est**	r**est**ing	
dig**est**	l**est**	sugg**est**	
for**est**	n**est**	t**est**	

"-et"

The following words and syllables end with the rime "-et". The letter "e" is pronounced with the short "e" vowel sound.

alphab**et**	fr**et**	n**et**	w**et**
b**et**	g**et**	p**et**	y**et**
cad**et**	j**et**	regr**et**	
du**et**	l**et**	s**et**	
forg**et**	m**et**	v**et**	

"-ew"

The following words and syllables end with the rime "-ew". The letters "ew" form a vowel digraph that is pronounced with the long "u" vowel sound. A notable exception is the word "sew" which is pronounced with the long "o" vowel sound.

bl**ew**	ch**ew**	d**ew**	f**ew**
br**ew**	cr**ew**	dr**ew**	fl**ew**

gr**ew**	n**ew**	sl**ew**	thr**ew**
kn**ew**	p**ew**	sp**ew**	
m**ew**	scr**ew**	st**ew**	

"-ice"

The following words and syllables end with the rime "-ice". The letter "i" is pronounced with the long "i" vowel sound. The final letter "e" is silent.

adv**ice**	**ice**	pr**ice**	sp**ice**
dev**ice**	l**ice**	r**ice**	suff**ice**
d**ice**	m**ice**	sacrif**ice**	tr**ice**
ent**ice**	n**ice**	sl**ice**	tw**ice**

"-ick"

The following words and syllables end with the rime "-ick". The letter "i" is pronounced with the short "i" vowel sound.

br**ick**	homes**ick**	p**ick**le	th**ick**
candlest**ick**	k**ick**	pinpr**ick**	th**ick**en
ch**ick**	l**ick**	qu**ick**	t**ick**
ch**ick**en	lipst**ick**	seas**ick**	toothp**ick**
chopst**ick**s	M**ick**ey	s**ick**	tr**ick**
cl**ick**	n**ick**	sl**ick**	tr**ick**y
drumst**ick**	n**ick**el	st**ick**	yardst**ick**
fl**ick**	p**ick**	st**ick**y	

"-id"

The following words and syllables end with the rime "-id". The letter "i" is pronounced with the short "i" vowel sound.

am**id**	eyel**id**	k**id**	sk**id**
arachn**id**	forb**id**	l**id**	sl**id**
b**id**	gr**id**	pyram**id**	squ**id**
d**id**	h**id**	r**id**	

"-ide"

The following words and syllables end with the rime "-ide". The letter "i" is pronounced with the long "i" vowel sound. The final letter "e" is silent.

bes**ide**	br**ide**	ch**ide**	coll**ide**

divide	inside	side	tide
glide	outside	slide	wide
guide	pride	snide	
hide	ride	stride	

"-ie"

The following words and syllables end with the rime "-ie". The letters "ie" form a vowel digraph that is pronounced with the long "i" vowel sound. The final letter "e" is silent.

die	lie	necktie	tie
hog-tie	magpie	pie	vie

"-ig"

The following words and syllables end with the rime "-ig". The letter "i" is pronounced with the short "i" vowel sound.

big	fig	rig	twig
bigwig	gig	shindig	wig
brig	jig	sprig	
dig	pig	swig	

"-ight"

The following words and syllables end with the rime "-ight". The letters "igh" form a vowel digraph that is pronounced with the long "i" vowel sound.

blight	fright	might	slight
bright	headlight	night	tight
fight	knight	plight	twilight
flashlight	light	right	
flight	midnight	sight	

"-ike"

The following words and syllables end with the rime "-ike". The letter "i" is pronounced with the long "i" vowel sound. The final letter "e" is silent.

alike	ladylike	pike	unlike
bike	like	spike	
dislike	motorbike	strike	

"-ill"

The following words and syllables end with the rime "-ill". The letter "i" is pronounced with the short "i" vowel sound.

Double consonants usually signal that the preceding single vowel letter is pronounced with a short vowel sound.

anth**ill**	dr**ill**	m**ill**	thr**ill**
armad**illa**	f**ill**	p**ill**	treadm**ill**
b**ill**	fr**ill**	ref**ill**	uph**ill**
caterp**illar**	g**ill**	s**ill**	van**illa**
ch**ill**	gor**illa**	sk**ill**	w**ill**
chinch**illa**	gr**ill**	sk**illed**	windm**ill**
d**ill**	h**ill**	stands**till**	windows**ill**
downh**ill**	**ill**	st**ill**	

"-in" and "-inn"

The following words and syllables end with the rimes "-in" or "-inn". The letter "i" is pronounced with the short "i" vowel sound.

beg**in**	gr**in**	p**in**	th**in**
Berl**in**	gr**inn**ing	sheepsk**in**	t**in**
b**in**	hairp**in**	sh**in**	unp**in**
cab**in**et	**in**	s**in**	w**in**
ch**in**	**inn**	sk**in**	w**in**dow
d**in**	**in**side	sp**in**	w**inn**er
d**inn**er	**in**tend	sp**inn**ing	w**inn**ing
f**in**	**in**vite	spl**in**ter	with**in**
f**in**ish	k**in**	tailsp**in**	

"-ind"

The following words and syllables end with the rime "-ind". The letter "i" is pronounced with the long "i" vowel sound. The letters "nd" form a consonant blend.

beh**ind**	f**ind**	m**ind**	unk**ind**
b**ind**	gr**ind**	rem**ind**	unw**ind**
bl**ind**	k**ind**	r**ind**	w**ind** (verb)

"-ine"

The following words and syllables end with the rime "-ine". The letter "i" is pronounced with the long "i" vowel sound. The final letter "e" is silent.

air**line**	**line**	shr**ine**	tw**ine**
comb**ine**	m**ine**	sp**ine**	v**ine**
def**ine**	n**ine**	sunsh**ine**	wh**ine**
d**ine**	p**ine**	sw**ine**	
f**ine**	sh**ine**	t**ine**	

"-ing"

The following words and syllables end with the rime "-ing". The letter "i" is pronounced with the short "i" vowel sound.

The letters "ng" are usually pronounced with the consonant "ng" sound heard in the word "sing" and "swing". Sometimes, however, the letter "g" is pronounced with the hard "g" consonant sound as heard in "bingo" and "finger". See E14.

anyth**ing**	drawstr**ing**	runn**ing**	st**ing**
awn**ing**	everyth**ing**	shoestr**ing**	st**ing**er
b**ing**o	fi**ng**er	s**ing**	str**ing**
br**ing**	flam**ing**o	s**ing**er	sw**ing**
build**ing**	fl**ing**	s**ing**ing	talk**ing**
burn**ing**	k**ing**	s**ing**le	th**ing**
cl**ing**	play**ing**	sl**ing**	walk**ing**
d**ing**	playth**ing**	someth**ing**	w**ing**
d**ing**o	r**ing**	spr**ing**	wr**ing**

"-ink"

The following words and syllables end with the rime "-ink". The letter "i" is pronounced with the short "i" vowel sound. The letter "n" is pronounced with the consonant "ng" sound heard in the words "ink" and "sing". The letters "nk" form a consonant blend.

bl**ink**	hoodw**ink**	r**ink**	st**ink**
bl**ink**ing	**ink**	shr**ink**	st**ink**y
br**ink**	k**ink**	shr**ink**ing	th**ink**
cl**ink**	l**ink**	s**ink**	th**ink**ing
cr**ink**le	m**ink**	s**ink**ing	tw**ink**le
dr**ink**	p**ink**	sl**ink**	w**ink**
f**ink**	reth**ink**	spr**ink**ler	wr**ink**le

"-ip" and "-ipp"

The following words and syllables end with the rime "-ip" or "-ipp". The letter "i" is pronounced with the short "i" vowel sound.

battleship	drip	ownership	slipping
blip	dripping	quip	snip
catnip	fingertip	rip	spaceship
chip	flip	ripping	strip
chipping	friendship	ship	tip
clip	grip	shipping	tipping
dictatorship	hip	sipping	trip
dip	lip	skip	tripping
dipping	nip	slip	unzip

"-ish"

The following words and syllables end with the rime "-ish". The letter "i" is pronounced with the short "i" vowel sound.

anguish	furnish	publish	squish
dish	goldfish	punish	swish
finish	nourish	radish	varnish
fish	perish	relish	wish

"-it" and "-itt"

The following words and syllables end with the rime "-it" or "-itt". The letter "i" is pronounced with the short "i" vowel sound.

admit	hit	omit	skit
bit	hitting	outwit	spit
bitter	it	permit	split
commit	kit	pit	submit
critic	kitten	pitcher	sunlit
fit	knit	quit	transmit
glitzy	lit	sit	unfit
grit	mitten	sitting	wit

"-oat"

The following words and syllables end with the rime "-oat". The letters "oa" form a vowel digraph that is pronounced with the long "o" vowel sound.

afloat	float	oat	rowboat
bloat	gloat	overcoat	shoat
boat	goat	petticoat	throat
coat	moat	raincoat	

"-ob"

The following words and syllables end with the rime "-ob". The letter "o" is pronounced with the broad "a" vowel sound.

bl**ob**	gl**ob**	l**ob**	s**ob**
b**ob**	g**ob**	m**ob**	thr**ob**
c**ob**	j**ob**	r**ob**	
cornc**ob**	kab**ob**	sl**ob**	
doorkn**ob**	kn**ob**	sn**ob**	

"-ock"

The following words and syllables end with the rime "-ock". The letter "o" is pronounced with the broad "a" vowel sound.

bl**ock**	livest**ock**	p**ock**et	sh**ock**ing
cl**ock**	l**ock**	roadbl**ock**	sm**ock**
cr**ock**	l**ock**er	r**ock**	s**ock**
d**ock**	l**ock**ing	r**ock**er	st**ock**
fl**ock**	m**ock**	r**ock**ing	st**ock**ing
fr**ock**	o'cl**ock**	shamr**ock**	sunbl**ock**
j**ock**	padl**ock**	Sherl**ock**	tick t**ock**
kn**ock**	peac**ock**	sh**ock**	unl**ock**

"-og"

The following words and syllables end with the rime "-og". The letter "o" is pronounced with the broad "a" or short "o" vowel sound depending on the local dialect.

b**og**	d**og**	h**og**	sm**og**
bullfr**og**	eggn**og**	j**og**	watchd**og**
catal**og** (USA)	fl**og**	leapfr**og**	waterl**og**
cl**og**	f**og**	l**og**	
c**og**	fr**og**	polliw**og**	

"-oil"

The following words and syllables end with the rime "-oil". The letters "oi" are pronounced with the vowel diphthong sound heard in "toy" and "coin".

b**oil**	f**oil**	s**oil**	t**oil**
br**oil**	**oil**	sp**oil**	turm**oil**
c**oil**	rec**oil**	tinf**oil**	

"-oke"

The following words and syllables end with the rime "-oke". The letter "o" is pronounced with the long "o" vowel sound. The final letter "e" is silent.

artich**oke**	C**oke**	prov**oke**	st**oke**
aw**oke**	cowp**oke**	slowp**oke**	str**oke**
br**oke**	j**oke**	sm**oke**	w**oke**
ch**oke**	p**oke**	sp**oke**	

"-old"

The following words and syllables end with the rime "-old". The letter "o" is pronounced with the long "o" vowel sound. The letters "ld" form a consonant blend.

beh**old**	f**old**	m**old** (USA)	s**old**
bill**fold**	g**old**	**old**	t**old**
blind**fold**	h**old**	ret**old**	
b**old**	house**hold**	scaff**old**	
c**old**	marig**old**	sc**old**	

"-ole"

The following words and syllables end with the rime "-ole". The letter "o" is pronounced with the long "o" vowel sound. The final letter "e" is silent.

caj**ole**	fishing p**ole**	m**ole**	st**ole**
casser**ole**	flagp**ole**	p**ole**	tadp**ole**
cons**ole**	foxh**ole**	poth**ole**	wh**ole**
Cre**ole**	h**ole**	r**ole**	
d**ole**	keyh**ole**	s**ole**	

"-one"

The following words and syllables end with the rime "-one". The letter "o" is pronounced with the long "o" vowel sound. The final letter "e" is silent.

A few words, such as "one" and "done", do not follow this rime. The word "one" is pronounced "wun" with a consonant "w" sound followed by a short "u" vowel sound.

al**one**	cr**one**	h**one**	ph**one**
b**one**	cycl**one**	l**one**	postp**one**
c**one**	dr**one**	microph**one**	pr**one**

shone	throne	zone
stone	tone	

"-oo"

The following words and syllables end with the rime "-oo". The letters "oo" form a vowel digraph that is pronounced with a long "u" vowel sound.

bamboo	cockatoo	kazoo	too
boo	cuckoo	Koodo	woo
booboo	goo	moo	zoo
boohoo	kangaroo	tattoo	

"-ook"

The following words and syllables end with the rime "-ook". The letters "oo" form a vowel digraph that is pronounced with a short "u" vowel sound.

book	fishhook	mistook	overlook
brook	handbook	nook	rook
cook	hook	notebook	shook
crook	look	outlook	took

"-ool"

The following words and syllables end with the rime "-ool". The letters "oo" form a vowel digraph that is pronounced with a long "u" vowel sound.

cesspool	footstool	preschool	toadstool
cool	Liverpool	school	tomfool
drool	playschool	spool	tool
fool	pool	stool	whirlpool

"-oom"

The following words and syllables end with the rime "-oom". The letters "oo" form a vowel digraph that is pronounced with a long "u" vowel sound.

bathroom	classroom	heirloom	restroom
bloom	doom	homeroom	room
boom	gloom	loom	zoom
broom	groom	mushroom	

"-oon"

The following words and syllables end with the rime "-oon". The letters "oo" form a vowel digraph that is pronounced with a long "u" vowel sound.

bab**oon**	coc**oon**	l**oon**	s**oon**
ball**oon**	cr**oon**	m**oon**	sp**oon**
bass**oon**	g**oon**	n**oon**	sw**oon**
buff**oon**	harp**oon**	pont**oon**	
cart**oon**	lag**oon**	racc**oon**	

"-op"

The following words and syllables end with the rime "-op". The letter "o" is pronounced with the broad "a" vowel sound.

barbersh**op**	eavesdr**op**	non-st**op**	st**op**
bellh**op**	fl**op**	pawnsh**op**	teardr**op**
b**op**	gumdr**op**	pl**op**	tipt**op**
ch**op**	hillt**op**	p**op**	t**op**
cl**op**	h**op**	pr**op**	treet**op**
c**op**	lollip**op**	raindr**op**	worksh**op**
cr**op**	l**op**	rooft**op**	
doorst**op**	m**op**	sh**op**	
dr**op**	mountaint**op**	sl**op**	

"-ope"

The following words and syllables end with the rime "-ope". The letter "o" is pronounced with the long "o" vowel sound. The final letter "e" is silent.

antel**ope**	h**ope**	perisc**ope**	stethosc**ope**
c**ope**	l**ope**	p**ope**	telesc**ope**
d**ope**	microsc**ope**	r**ope**	
envel**ope**	m**ope**	sc**ope**	
gr**ope**	n**ope**	sl**ope**	

"-ore"

The following words and syllables end with the rime "-ore". The letter "o" is pronounced with the long "o" or short "o" vowel sound depending on the local dialect. The final letter "e" is silent.

ad**ore**	b**ore**	c**ore**	g**ore**
bef**ore**	ch**ore**	expl**ore**	ign**ore**

lore	pore	snore	swore
more	score	sore	tore
ore	shore	store	wore

"-orn"

The following words and syllables end with the rime "-orn". The letter "o" is pronounced with the long "o" or short "o" vowel sound depending on the local dialect. The letters "rn" form a consonant blend.

acorn	corn	morn	thorn
adorn	forlorn	popcorn	torn
born	horn	scorn	unicorn
bullhorn	Matterhorn	sworn	worn

"-ort"

The following words and syllables end with the rime "-ort". The letter "o" is pronounced with the long "o" or short "o" vowel sound depending on the local dialect. The letters "rt" form a consonant blend.

airport	export	port	snort
carport	fort	report	sort
distort	import	resort	sport
escort	passport	short	support

"-ose"

The following words and syllables end with the rime "-ose". The letter "o" is pronounced with the long "o" vowel sound. The final letter "e" is silent.

chose	expose	oppose	rose
close	hose	pose	suppose
dispose	impose	propose	those
enclose	nose	prose	

"-ot"

The following words and syllables end with the rime "-ot". The letter "o" is pronounced with the broad "a" or short "o" vowel sound depending on the local dialect.

blot	clot	dot	forgot
cannot	cot	flowerpot	got

h**ot**	pl**ot**	sh**ot**	sp**ot**
jackp**ot**	p**ot**	slingsh**ot**	teap**ot**
kn**ot**	rob**ot**	sl**ot**	t**ot**
l**ot**	r**ot**	snapsh**ot**	tr**ot**

"-ote"

The following words and syllables end with the rime "-ote". The letter "o" is pronounced with the long "o" vowel sound. The final letter "e" is silent.

anecd**ote**	misqu**ote**	qu**ote**	t**ote**
antid**ote**	n**ote**	rem**ote**	v**ote**
d**ote**	outv**ote**	rewr**ote**	
footn**ote**	prom**ote**	r**ote**	

"-ound"

The following words and syllables end with the rime "-ound". The letters "ou" are pronounced with the vowel diphthong sound heard in the words "cow" and "loud". The letters "nd" form a consonant blend.

ar**ound**	gr**ound**	p**ound**
ast**ound**	h**ound**	r**ound**
b**ound**	merry-go-r**ound**	s**ound**
comp**ound**	m**ound**	surr**ound**
f**ound**	playgr**ound**	w**ound** (Verb)

"-out"

The following words and syllables end with the rime "-out". The letters "ou" are pronounced with the vowel diphthong sound heard in the words "cow" and "loud".

ab**out**	fl**out**	sn**out**	tr**out**
b**out**	**out**	sp**out**	try**out**
cl**out**	sc**out**	spr**out**	with**out**
dug**out**	sh**out**	st**out**	

"-ove"

The following words and syllables end with the rime "-ove". The letter "o" is pronounced with the long "o" vowel sound. The final letter "e" is silent.

Notable exceptions to this spelling pattern are the words "love" and "dove" (naming a type of bird) which are pronounced with a short "u" vowel sound.

alcove	cove	drove	stove
clove	dove (Verb)	grove	wove

"-ow" as in "show"

The following words and syllables end with the rime "-ow". The letters "ow" form a vowel digraph that is pronounced with the long "o" vowel sound.

below	glow	rainbow	stow
blow	grow	row	throw
bow (Noun)	know	show	tow
crow	low	slow	
flow	mow	snow	

"-ow" as in "now"

The following words and syllables end with the rime "-ow". The letters "ow" are pronounced with the vowel diphthong sound heard in the words "cow" and "loud".

allow	how	prow	vow
bow (Verb)	now	row (fight)	wow
brow	ow	scow	
chow	plow	somehow	
cow	pow	sow (female pig)	

"-ox"

The following words and syllables end with the rime "-ox". The letter "o" is pronounced with the broad "a" or short "o" vowel sound depending on the local dialect.

box	jack-in-the-box	mailbox	sandbox
chickenpox	lox	ox	sox
fox	lunchbox	pox	

"-ub"

The following words and syllables end with the rime "-ub". The letter "u" is pronounced with a short "u" vowel sound.

bathtub	flub	hubbub	scrub
club	grub	nub	shrub
dub	hub	rub	snub

stub submarine tub
sub subway

"-uck"

The following words and syllables end with the rime "-uck". The letter "u" is pronounced with a short "u" vowel sound.

b**uck**	l**uck**	sn**uck**	tr**uck**ing
b**uck**et	l**uck**y	str**uck**	t**uck**
b**uck**le	m**uck**	st**uck**	unl**uck**y
ch**uck**	m**uck**y	s**uck**	woodch**uck**
ch**uck**le	pl**uck**	s**uck**er	y**uck**
cl**uck**	potl**uck**	thunderstr**uck**	y**uck**y
d**uck**	p**uck**	tr**uck**	
Kent**uck**y	p**uck**er	tr**uck**er	

"-ug" and "-ugg"

The following words and syllables end with the rimes "-ug" and "-ugg". The letter "u" is pronounced with a short "u" vowel sound.

bedb**ug**	h**ugg**ing	m**ug**	sm**ug**
b**ug**	humb**ug**	pl**ug**	sn**ug**
b**ugg**ing	jitterb**ug**	p**ug**	sn**ugg**le
ch**ug**	j**ug**	r**ug**	str**ugg**le
dr**ug**	j**ugg**le	shr**ug**	th**ug**
d**ug**	ladyb**ug**	shr**ugg**ing	t**ug**
earpl**ug**	litterb**ug**	sl**ug**	unpl**ug**
h**ug**	l**ug**	sl**ugg**ing	

"-um"

The following words and syllables end with the rime "-um". The letter "u" is pronounced with a short "u" vowel sound.

b**um**	g**um**	r**um**	sw**um**
ch**um**	h**um**	sc**um**	thr**um**
dr**um**	h**um**dr**um**	sl**um**	y**um**
d**um**d**um**	kettledr**um**	str**um**	
eardr**um**	m**um**	sugarpl**um**	
gl**um**	pl**um**	s**um**	

"-ump"

The following words and syllables end with the rime "-ump". The letter "u" is pronounced with a short "u" vowel sound. The letters "mp" form a consonant blend.

b**ump**	d**ump**ing	j**ump**ing	p**ump**ing
b**ump**ing	fr**ump**y	l**ump**	sl**ump**
b**ump**y	gr**ump**	l**ump**y	st**ump**
ch**ump**	gr**ump**y	pl**ump**	th**ump**
cl**ump**	h**ump**	p**ump**kin	tr**ump**
d**ump**	j**ump**	p**ump**	**ump**ire

"-un"

The following words and syllables end with the rime "-un". The letter "u" is pronounced with a short "u" vowel sound.

beg**un**	home r**un**	outr**un**	sh**un**
b**un**	homesp**un**	p**un**	sp**un**
f**un**	honeyb**un**	rer**un**	st**un**
g**un**	n**un**	r**un**	s**un**

"-unk"

The following words and syllables end with the rime "-unk". The letter "u" is pronounced with a short "u" vowel sound. The letter "n" is pronounced with the consonant "ng" sound heard in the words "ink" and "sing". The letters "nk" form a consonant blend.

b**unk**	d**unk**	j**unk**y	sp**unk**y
b**unk**er	d**unk**ing	pl**unk**	st**unk**
chipm**unk**	fl**unk**	p**unk**	s**unk**
ch**unk**	fl**unk**ing	shr**unk**	s**unk**en
ch**unk**y	f**unk**	sk**unk**	tr**unk**
cl**unk**	h**unk**	sl**unk**	
dr**unk**	j**unk**	sp**unk**	

"-ut"

The following words and syllables end with the rime "-ut". The letter "u" is pronounced with a short "u" vowel sound.

b**ut**	c**ut**	g**ut**	j**ut**
chestn**ut**	don**ut**	hairc**ut**	n**ut**
cocon**ut**	gl**ut**	h**ut**	pean**ut**

rut **shortcut** **shut** **strut**

"-y" as in "baby"

The following words and syllables end with the rime "-y". The letter "y" is pronounced with the long "e" vowel sound.

ability	country	forty	jolly
absolutely	cranny	foxy	juicy
activity	crazy	frequency	laboratory
agency	customary	friendly	lady
already	daddy	funny	lately
angry	daily	fussy	lazy
anxiety	dairy	gaiety	liberty
any	Delany	generally	library
apology	delivery	Germany	likely
army	democracy	ghostly	literary
baby	dictionary	glory	lonely
badly	difficulty	granny	lovely
baggy	dirty	grizzly	loyalty
beauty	discovery	grocery	lucky
berry	duty	grungy	lumpy
body	early	guilty	machinery
boundary	easily	hairy	mainly
bravery	easy	handy	majority
bribery	economy	happy	many
bunny	efficiency	hardly	marry
bury	eighty	Harry	memory
busy	elderly	heavenly	mercy
Calgary	emergency	heavy	merry
candy	empty	history	misery
carefully	enemy	hobby	modesty
carry	energy	holy	momentary
century	envy	honesty	mommy
ceremony	especially	hourly	mostly
certainly	every	hungry	motherly
certainty	exactly	hurry	muddy
cherry	facility	immediately	multiply
city	factory	industry	mystery
classify	fairy	inquiry	naughty
cloudy	family	Italy	navy
colony	February	January	nearly
community	fifty	jealousy	necessary
company	finally	jewellery (UK, CAN)	ninety
copy	fluffy	jewelry (USA)	noisy

nursery	quietly	sixty	tidy
only	rainy	skinny	tiny
opportunity	ready	slavery	treasury
ordinary	really	slowly	trophy
particularly	remedy	smelly	truly
party	responsibility	sneaky	tummy
pastry	rivalry	snowy	twenty
penalty	robbery	society	ugly
penny	rocky	softly	uncanny
photography	royalty	sorry	unfortunately
pity	safety	spooky	unity
plenty	salary	steady	university
policy	sandy	story	usually
pony	sassy	study	variety
possibly	satisfactory	stuffy	very
poverty	scary	suddenly	victory
pretty	scenery	sunny	wavy
property	seventy	supply	wealthy
puppy	shiny	swiftly	windy
qualify	silly	sympathy	witty
quality	simplicity	tacky	worry
quantity	simply	thirsty	
quickly	sincerely	thirty	

"-y" as in "sky"

The following words and syllables end with the rime "-y". The letter "y" is pronounced with the long "i" vowel sound.

apply	fry	pry	spy
by	July	reply	sty
cry	modify	satisfy	try
defy	multiply	shy	why
deny	my	sky	wry
dry	occupy	sly	
fly	ply	spry	

Part N: Compound and Hyphenated Words

N1 Introduction

Compound words are words that are made up of two or more whole words. Writers have long noted that certain words often appear together forming a single distinct concept. To better signal to the reader that the words form a single concept, the words may be joined together with a hyphen. Over time, as the association between the words becomes familiar, the hyphen is sometimes dropped and the words joined together as a single word. There is a lack of consensus as to which compound words should be hyphenated and which should be written as a single word. If in doubt, consult a current dictionary.

Compound words are usually divided into syllables between the words from which they are composed as in the word "cow-boy". These words may be further divided into syllables as in the word "tax-pay-er".

Hyphens are also used occasionally to attach a prefix to a base word as in the words "anti-Semitic" and "ex-boyfriend".

Contractions are a form of compound word. A contraction is formed when two words are shortened into one word with one or more letters being omitted. For example, the words "do not" may be contracted into "don't". With contractions, an apostrophe substitutes for the missing letter or letters. See Part O.

Please note that a full discussion about compound words is beyond the scope of this book. The following is offered as an introduction to the subject. Consult a writing style book for further discussion on this topic.

N2 No Hyphen Required

N2.1 No hyphen Required

The following compound words have become so familiar that they are now joined together without a hyphen.

airplane	downtown	heartbroken	nowadays
airport	dressmaker	highway	nowhere
anybody	drumstick	hilltop	nutshell
anymore	dugout	homecoming	onto
anyone	earthquake	homemade	otherwise
anything	eggshell	homeroom	outdoors
anyway	elsewhere	homesick	outhouse
anywhere	everlasting	homework	outline
babysitter	everybody	horseback	outlive
backpack	everyday	hotplate	outlook
backyard	everyone	household	outnumber
barbershop	everything	however	outrun
baseball	everywhere	humankind	outshine
basketball	fireman	hunchback	outshoot
bathroom	fireplace	indoor	outside
bathtub	fireproof	inward	outsmart
Batman	flagpole	ironclad	outwards
battleship	flashlight	jackpot	outwit
beanbag	flowerpot	keyhole	overactive
bedroom	football	keypad	overall
birthday	forever	landlord	overalls
blackbird	framework	leapfrog	overbearing
boyfriend	gangplank	likewise	overcast
breakfast	gentleman	lipstick	overcoat
businesslike	girlfriend	litterbug	overcome
butterfly	goldfish	livestock	overdose
candlestick	goodbye	lunchbox	overdrive
candlewick	grasshopper	mailbox	overdue
cannot	graveyard	mankind	overflow
checkbook (USA)	gumdrop	maybe	overhang
chequebook (UK, CAN)	haircut	meantime	overhead
chopsticks	hairpin	meanwhile	overhear
classroom	halfway	midnight	overkill
cowboy	handlebar	moonlight	overlap
cowgirl	handshake	moreover	overlook
crackerjack	handstand	motorbike	overrun
cupboard	handwriting	motorcycle	oversee
daylight	handyman	mountaintop	overshadow
doghouse	haystack	mousetrap	oversight
doorbell	headache	myself	overtime
doorknob	headdress	nearby	paperback
doormat	headlight	network	pawnshop
doorstop	headquarters	newspaper	paycheck (USA)
downhill	heartache	nickname	penknife
downstairs	heartbeat	nobody	playground
	heartbreak	notebook	playhouse

playmate	shipwreck	teardrop	underworld
playoff	shoestring	teaspoon	uphill
playpen	shortcut	thanksgiving	uppermost
playschool	shotgun	themselves	upright
plaything	slingshot	therefore	upset
policeman	slowpoke	throughout	upstairs
policewoman	snowman	thumbtack	uptown
popcorn	somebody	thunderstruck	watchdog
postman	someday	toadstool	waterlogged
quarterback	somehow	today	weekday
quicksand	someone	tonight	weekend
racetrack	something	toothpick	whatever
railroad	sometime	trademark	wheelchair
railway	somewhere	treadmill	whenever
rainbow	soundtrack	treetop	wherever
raincoat	spaceship	tryout	whichever
raindrop	splashdown	turtleneck	whirlpool
rattlesnake	standstill	underarm	whoever
redwood	sugarplum	underbrush	wholesale
restroom	summertime	undercover	wholesome
roadblock	sunrise	undercurrent	whomever
rooftop	sunshine	underdog	wildcat
roughneck	suntan	underestimate	withdraw
rowboat	superhero	underground	within
sailboat	superimpose	underline	without
salesman	superintendent	undermine	woodchuck
saleswoman	supermarket	underpants	workingman
schoolboy	supernatural	undershirt	workman
schoolgirl	tablecloth	understand	workshop
searchlight	tailspin	undertaker	yardstick
seasick	taxpayer	underwater	yesterday
sheepskin	teapot	underwear	yourself

N2.2 Double letters

Sometimes with compound words, the last letter of the first word and the first letter of the second word are the same, incidentally resulting in doubled consonant letters. Although the doubled letters may appear to look odd, do not drop the second letter. Both letters are pronounced unless silent for another reason.

bat**hh**ouse	cu**tt**hroat	hea**dd**ress	ove**rr**un
beac**hh**ead	dum**bb**ell	hitc**hh**iker	roo**mm**ate
boo**kk**eeper	fis**hh**ook	knic**kk**nack	wit**hh**old
ca**nn**ot	gran**dd**aughter	ou**tt**ake	

N2.3 Three word compounds

A few compound words join three words together. Some of the words are biblical in origin, and some are found primarily in legal writing.

hereinafter	nevertheless	whatsoever
hereinbefore	notwithstanding	whomsoever
heretofore	thereinafter	whosoever
insofar	theretofore	

N2.4 First word in a compound word ends with the letter "y",

If the first word of a compound word ends with the letter "y", the "y" is kept when forming the compound word as in "handyman".

This is different than when adding a suffix to a base word that ends with the letter "y" following a consonant letter where the letter "y" is changed to an "i". Adding the suffix "-ly" to "clumsy", for example, produces "clumsily". See I4.

hand**y**man
lad**y**like

N3 Hyphens Required

N3.1 Two or more words that are used as a single adjective

When two or more words are combined together to form an adjective, the words are hyphenated if they precede the noun that is being modified. They are not hyphenated if they follow the noun. For example:

- Mary is wearing an *old-fashioned* dress.
- Mary's dress is *old fashioned*.

- Tom wrote an *up-to-date* report.
- Tom's report is *up to date*.

The use of hyphens helps to clarify, for example, that reference is being made to a "hard-working girl" and not to a "hard working-girl". The following is a sample list of hyphenated adjectives.

- dog-tired runner
- first-rate experience
- foreign-born applicants
- foul-smelling sewage
- fun-loving children
- hard-working girl
- interest-bearing account
- iron-clad agreement
- most-favoured nation
- much-needed rest

- never-to-be-forgotten game
- out-of-date clothing
- quiet-spoken student
- ready-made food
- salt-water sailor
- stem-wound watch
- war-torn region
- well-known publication
- well-trained dog
- worm-eaten wood

N3.2 Two or more words that are used as a single part of speech

A hyphen is used to join two or more words that are used as a single part of speech such as a noun or verb.

cross-reference	go-between	hero-worship	ne'er-do-well
editor-in-chief	good-bye	inside-out	upside-down
forget-me-nots	goof-off	life-history	

N3.3 To avoid putting three identical consonants together

A hyphen is used to avoid putting three identical consonant letters together when forming a compound word.

grass-seed	hall-lamp	shell-like

N3.4 Attaching a prefix to a word that begins with a capital letter

A hyphen is used to attach a prefix to a base word that begins with a capital letter. Likewise, a hyphen is used to attach a capital letter to a base word that begins with a lower case letter.

anti-Semitic	pro-British	U-boat
pre-Christian	trans-American	un-Canadian

N3.5 Compound numbers from twenty-one to ninety-nine

A hyphen is used when spelling compound numbers from twenty-one to ninety-nine.

- twenty-one gun salute
- forty-three hundred people
- fifty-five years old
- sixty-four thousand dollar question
- ninety-nine students

N3.6 Fractions that are used as adjectives

A hyphen is used when spelling fractions that are used as adjectives to modify a noun.

- seven-tenths of a mile
- one-half loaf of bread

- three-quarters cup of water
- two-thirds majority

N3.7 Compound adjectives containing cardinal numbers

A hyphen is used when spelling a compound adjective containing a cardinal number, numbers used for counting and specifying quantity, followed by a noun or adjective.

- eight-foot tall monster
- fourteen-hand horse
- ninety-dollar shirt
- one-sided argument
- three-meter wave

N3.8 Compound adjectives containing ordinal numbers

A hyphen is used when spelling a compound adjective that contains an ordinal number, (numbers used to describe place order), followed by a noun or adjective.

- first-class honours
- second-story apartment
- third-class transportation

N3.9 Adding a prefix that ends with a vowel to a word that begins with a vowel

A hyphen may be used when adding a prefix that ends with a vowel to a base word that begins with a vowel to avoid putting two vowel letters together. A hyphen helps to signal that both vowel letters are pronounced. Note, however, that it is often acceptable to spell such words without a hyphen. See G2 ("pre-" and "re-") and G4 ("co-").

co-author (Also coauthor)
co-invent
co-op
co-operate (Also cooperate)
co-operation (Also cooperation)
co-operative (Also cooperative)
co-opt
co-ordinate (Also coordinate)
co-ordination (Also coordination)
co-own
pre-election
pre-eminent (Also preeminent)
pre-empt (Also preempt)
pre-engineer
pre-exist (Also preexist)

re-act (Also react)
re-elect (Also reelect)
re-emerge (Also reemerge)
re-emphasize (Also reemphasize)
re-enact (Also reenact)
re-endow (Also reendow)
re-energize (Also reenergize)
re-enforce (Also reinforce)
re-engage (Also reengage)
re-engineer (Also reengineer)
re-enlist (Also reenlist)
re-enrol (Also reenroll)
re-enter (Also reenter)
re-examination (Also reexamination)

N3.10 Joining the prefixes "ex-" and "self-"

A hyphen is used to join the prefix "ex-", meaning "not" or "former", and the prefix "self-" to a free morpheme base word such as "wife". A hyphen is not required when adding the prefix "ex-" to a bound morpheme root such as "odus". See G2 ("ex-").

ex-boyfriend	**ex**-partner	**ex**-wife	**self**-reliant
ex-champion	**ex**-president	**self**-assured	**self**-satisfied
ex-girlfriend	**ex**-spouse	**self**-hate	
ex-husband	**ex**-student	**self**-made	

N4 Plural Compound Words

N4.1 First word is made plural

With compound words that contain a primary noun, the spelling change creating the plural form is made to the primary noun. Sometimes, the primary noun is the first word. The plural form of "attorney-at-law", for example, is "attorneys-at-law".

- attorney**s**-at-law
- bill**s** of lading
- bill**s** receivable
- brother**s**-in-law
- commander**s**-in-chief
- daughter**s**-in-law
- father**s**-in-law
- m**en**-of-war
- mother**s**-in-law
- notar**ies** public
- passer**s**-by
- runner**s**-up
- son**s**-in-law

N4.2 Final word or syllable is made plural

With compound words that contain a primary noun, the spelling change creating the plural form is made to the primary noun. Sometimes, the primary noun is the final word. The plural form of "stepchild", for example, is "stepchildren".

With compound words that do not contain a primary noun, the spelling change creating the plural form is made to the final word. The plural form of "show-off", for example, is "show-offs".

- bachelor degree**s**
- Brigadier general**s**
- cupful**s**
- drive-in**s**
- handful**s**
- mouthful**s**
- schoolbook**s**
- show-off**s**
- spoonful**s**
- standby**s**
- stepchild**ren**
- teaspoonful**s**
- twelve-year-old**s**

N5 Portmanteau Words

Portmanteau words are a kind of compound word in which two English words have been combined not as whole words, but in bits and pieces. Some of the spelling and meaning of each original word is reflected in the new word, but it has a unique meaning of its own. Author Lewis Carroll is credited with coining the word "portmanteau" in his book *Through the Looking Glass*.

- binary + digit → bit
- breakfast + lunch → brunch
- flame + glare → flare
- glare + shimmer → glimmer
- medical + care → Medicare
- motor + hotel → motel
- transfer + resistor → transistor
- twist + swirl → twirl

Part O: Contractions

O1 Introduction

Contractions are compound words in which one or more letters have been omitted. An apostrophe is substituted for the omitted letter or letters. Contractions more closely reflect how people commonly speak. It is rare for a person to actually say "*I should have been more careful*" or "*we are going to the beach*". It is more likely that a person would say, "*I should've been more careful*", or "*we're going to the beach*".

Spelling difficulties may arise because the apostrophe is also used to create the possessive form. The possessive form is used to indicate an ownership relationship, or something analogous to an ownership relationship, between a noun or pronoun and another thing. See Part L.

O2 Common Contractions

O2.1 Contractions based on the word "am"

The word "am" forms the following contraction.

- I am → I'm

O2.2 Contractions based on the word "are"

The word "are" forms the following contractions.

- they are → they're
- we are → we're
- you are → you're

O2.3 Contractions based on the word "had"

The word "had" forms the following contractions.

- he had → he'd
- I had → I'd

- it had → it'd
- she had → she'd
- they had → they'd
- we had → we'd
- you had → you'd

O2.4 Contractions based on the word "has"

The word "has" forms the following contractions. Note that "its" is the possessive form of "it", not "it's". The contraction "it's" derives from "it has" and "it is".

- he has → he's (Also a contraction of "he is".)
- it has → it's (Also a contraction of "it is".)
- she has → she's (Also a contraction of "she is".)
- that has → that's (Also a contraction of "that is".)
- there has → there's (Also a contraction of "there is".)
- what has → what's (Also a contraction of "what is".)
- who has → who's (Also a contraction of "who is".)

O2.5 Contractions based on the word "have"

The word "have" forms the following contractions.

- could have → could've (Not "could of")
- I have → I've
- should have → should've (Not "should of")
- they have → they've
- we have → we've
- would have → would've (Not "would of")
- you have → you've

O2.6 Contractions based on the word "is"

The word "is" forms the following contractions. Note that "its" is the possessive form of "it", not "it's". The contraction "it's" derives from "it has" and "it is".

- he is → he's (Also a contraction of "he has".)
- here is → here's
- it is → it's (Also a contraction of "it has".)
- she is → she's (Also a contraction of "she has".)
- that is → that's (Also a contraction of "that has".)
- there is → there's (Also a contraction of "there has".)
- what is → what's (Also a contraction of "what has".)
- who is → who's (Also a contraction of "who has".)

O2.7 Contractions based on the word "not"

The word "not" forms the following contractions.

- are not → aren't
- cannot → can't
- could not → couldn't
- did not → didn't
- do not → don't
- does not → doesn't
- had not → hadn't
- has not → hasn't
- have not → haven't
- is not → isn't
- must not → mustn't
- should not → shouldn't
- was not → wasn't
- were not → weren't
- will not → won't
- would not → wouldn't

O2.8 Contractions based on the word "us"

The word "us" forms the following contraction.

- let us → let's

O2.9 Contractions based on the word "will"

The word "will" forms the following contractions.

- he will → he'll
- I will → I'll
- it will → it'll
- she will → she'll
- that will → that'll
- they will → they'll
- we will → we'll
- you will → you'll

O2.10 Contractions based on the word "would"

The word "would" forms the following contractions.

- he would → he'd
- I would → I'd
- it would → it'd
- she would → she'd
- they would → they'd
- we would → we'd
- you would → you'd

O2.11 Other Contractions

The following is a common contraction.

- of the clock → o'clock

Part P: Acronyms

P1 Acronyms

Acronyms are shorthand references that are made up of the initial letter or letters of the words they represent. Acronyms are infamously favoured by large bureaucracies. Most acronyms such as "IRS", which stands for "Internal Revenue Service", never become more than a collection of letters. Other acronyms, such as the ones listed below, have become words in their own right. The following words were originally acronyms.

- Cobol → COmmon Business Oriented Language
- jeep → GEneral Purpose motor vehicle
- laser → Light Amplification by Stimulated Emission of Radiation
- news → North East West South
- radar → RAdio Detection And Ranging
- scuba → Self Contained Underwater Breathing Apparatus
- snafu → Situation Normal All Fouled Up
- sonar → SOund Navigation And Ranging
- swat → Special Weapons And Training

Notes

1. *Beginning to Read: Thinking and Learning about Print*, by Marilyn Jager Adams, A Summary, Center for the Study of Reading, University of Illinois at Urbana-Champaign, 1990, page 5.
2. *Ibid.*, page 6.
3. *A History of English Spelling*, D.G. Scragg, Manchester University Press, 1974, page 1.
4. *Spelling Instruction That Makes Sense*, by Jo Phenix and Doreen Scott-Dunne, Pembroke Publishers Limited, 1991, page 13.
5. *Ibid.*, page 16.
6. *The History of English Spelling*, Christopher Upward & George Davidson, Wiley-Blackwell, 2011, page 5.
7. *Assessment is Instruction: Reading, Writing, Spelling, and Phonics for all Learners*, by Susan Mandel Glazer, Christopher-Gordon Pub., page 221.
8. *Phonics Phacts*, Ken Goodman, Scholastic Canada Ltd., page 41.
9. *Accomodating Brocolli in the Cemetary*, Vivian Cook, Simon & Schuster, New York, 2004, page 7.
10. *Teaching About Phonics*, by Albert J. Mazurkiewicz, St. Martin's Press, 1976, page 3, and *Phonics: Why and How*, Patrick Groff, General Learning Press, 1977, page 70.
11. *Phonics: Why & How*, Patrick Groff, General Learning Press, 1977, page 23.
12. *The American Way of Spelling*, Richard L. Venezky, The Guilford Press, 1999, page 56.
13. *The ABC's and All Their Tricks*, Margaret M. Bishop, Mott Media, 1986, page 49.
14. *Ibid.*, page 24.
15. *Ibid.*, page 24.
16. *Ibid.*, page 308.
17. *Ibid.*, 1986, page 24.
18. *Words: Spelling, Pronunciation, Definition, and Application*, Rupert P. Sorelle and Charles W. Kitt, Gregg Division, McGraw-Hill Company of Canada Ltd., 1926, page 22.
19. *The ABC's and All Their Tricks*, Margaret M. Bishop, Mott Media, 1986, page 31.
20. *Ibid.*, page 31.
21. *Ibid.*, page 24.
22. *Ibid.*, page 51.
23. *Ibid.*, page 139.

www.ingramcontent.com/pod-product-compliance
Lightning Source LLC
Chambersburg PA
CBHW080627170426
43209CB00007B/1528